Anonymous

The Woman's Book

Dealing practically with the modern conditions of home-life, self-support, education, opportunties, and every-day problems. Vol. 1

Anonymous

The Woman's Book
Dealing practically with the modern conditions of home-life, self-support, education, opportunties, and every-day problems. Vol. 1

ISBN/EAN: 9783337290665

Printed in Europe, USA, Canada, Australia, Japan

Cover: Foto ©Lupo / pixelio.de

More available books at **www.hansebooks.com**

THE WOMAN'S BOOK

DEALING PRACTICALLY WITH THE MODERN CONDITIONS OF HOME-LIFE, SELF-SUPPORT, EDUCATION, OPPORTUNITIES, AND EVERY-DAY PROBLEMS

IN TWO VOLUMES

VOLUME I

OCCUPATIONS FOR WOMEN
BY PHILIP G. HUBERT, JR.

WOMEN IN THEIR BUSINESS AFFAIRS
BY W. O. STODDARD

THE PRINCIPLES OF HOUSEKEEPING
BY LILLIAN W. BETTS

SOCIETY AND SOCIAL USAGES
BY CONSTANCE CARY HARRISON

THE ÆSTHETICS OF DRESS
BY EVA WILDER McGLASSON

DRESS FROM A PRACTICAL STANDPOINT
BY SEVERAL WRITERS

HYGIENE IN THE HOME
BY J. WEST ROOSEVELT, M.D.

THE TRAINING OF CHILDREN
BY KATE DOUGLAS WIGGIN

THE EDUCATION OF WOMEN
BY LYMAN ABBOTT, D.D.

BOOKS AND READING
BY THOMAS WENTWORTH HIGGINSON

THE ART OF TRAVEL. BY ELIZABETH BISLAND

WITH FOUR HUNDRED ILLUSTRATIONS

NEW YORK
CHARLES SCRIBNER'S SONS
1894

Contents of Volume I.

                                                          PAGE

I. Occupations for Women *1*

             By P. G. HUBERT, JR.

        × The New Fields of Work Open.—Art Study and Art Workers.—Women Architects.—Teaching.—Typewriting and Stenography.—Women's Exchanges.—Occupations for the Inexperienced.—The Trained Nurse.—Women Physicians and Lawyers.—Newspaper Work and Pay.—Dressmaking and Millinery.—Work Done at Home.—The Stage as a Profession.—Novel Occupations Followed.—Women as Local Photographers.—How Women Workers are Swindled.

II. Women in their Business Affairs 79

             By WILLIAM O. STODDARD.

        Keeping Accounts.—The Rights of Married Women.—The Question of Signatures.—Real Estate and its Care.—Business Papers and Evidences of Ownership.—Personal Property.—Banks and Bank Accounts.—Drafts and Notes.—Building and Loan Associations.—Investments.—Insurance.—Parliamentary Rules.—Wills.

III. The Principles of Housekeeping 107

             By LILLIAN W. BETTS.

        The Science of Housekeeping.—Economy and Expenditure.—" She died of Committee."—The Nutrient Value of Foods.—Cook-books and Food Literature.—The New Cooking Appliances.—Electric Cooking.—Cleaning and Cleanliness.—The Buying and Preparation of Meats.—Good Bread-making.—Marketing and Economy.—The Servant Question.—Entertaining and Hospitality.—System in Housekeeping.

IV. Society and Social Usages 145

             By CONSTANCE CARY HARRISON.

        The Art of Entertaining.—Dinners.—Luncheons.—Teas.—Garden Parties.—Theatre Parties.—Chaperones.—Suppers.—Parties to the Opera.—Dances.—Good Taste in Dress.—Correct Form in Correspondence.—Invitations.—Weddings.—Cards.—Calling.

Contents of Volume I.

V. The Æsthetics of Dress 181

By EVA WILDER McGLASSON.

The Canons of Taste.—Sincerity.—Simplicity.—Unity.—Appropriateness.—Textile Fabrics.—Colors.—Lines.—Hygiene.—Conventionalism.—Individualism.—Originality.—Picturesqueness.—Eccentricity.

VI. Dress from a Practical Standpoint 205

By SEVERAL WRITERS.

Dress for Infants.—Dress for Young Children.—Dresses for School Girls.—Dresses for Adults.—Wraps, Bonnets, and Hats.—Underwear.—Boots, Shoes, and Slippers.—Accessories of Dress.—Wedding Trousseau.—Furs.—Mourning.—The Care of Clothes.—Dressing on an Allowance.—Millinery at Home.—Dressmaking at Home.—Schools for Dressmaking and Millinery.

VII. Hygiene in the Home 263

By J. WEST ROOSEVELT, M.D.

Cleanliness.—Heat.—Light.—Ventilation.—Plumbing.—The Water Supply.—Bathing.—Clothing.—Exercise.—The Nursery.—Education in Hygiene.—Physicians.—Trained Nurses.—The Sick-room.—The Patient.—Medical and Surgical Notes.

VIII. The Training of Children 317

By KATE DOUGLAS WIGGIN.

Early Training—Habits.—The Parental Office.—Froebel.—Evolution in Education.—The Kindergarten.—Rights.—Duties.—Literature for Children.—The Art of Story-telling.—Clothes.—Amusements.—Toys.—Country Life.—Simplicity.—The Relation of Books to Nature.

IX. The Education of Women 339

By LYMAN ABBOTT.

Elementary Education.—The Atmosphere of the Home.—The Kindergarten.—Governesses.—Boarding Schools.—Day Schools.—Public Schools.—Private Schools.—The Higher Education.—Colleges and Universities.—Post-graduate Work.—Advantages of Foreign Study.—Advantages of Study in America.—Study at Home.—Scholarship.—Social Culture.

Contents of Volume I.

	PAGE
X. Books and Reading	358

By THOMAS WENTWORTH HIGGINSON.

American Culture.—Women's Clubs.—Public Libraries.—Systematic Reading. — Greece and Rome. — History.—Biography. — Essays.—Poetry.—Fiction.—Realism.—Romanticism.—The Modern Novel.—Journalism.—Magazine Work.—Personal Equation in Literature

XI. The Art of Travel	370

By ELIZABETH BISLAND.

The Matter of Packing.—Modern Trunks and Dressing-cases.—Clothing and Preparations.—Comfort on the Train.—Seasickness and its Treatment. — Travelling in the Tropics. — Safety in Travelling Alone.—Guides, Money, and Tickets.—Custom Officials and their Treatment.—Living in Lodgings Abroad.—Economical Travelling.—The Value of Coolness.

List of Illustrations to Volume I.

COLORED PLATES

FACING
PAGE

A Summer Gown. From a water color, by Albert Lynch . . . . *Frontispiece*
Book Covers, by *Margaret N. Armstrong* and *Alice Morse* 8
Christ Blessing Little Children. Design for Stained Glass Window, by Miss
    Helen Maitland Armstrong 32
Curtain, decorated by Acid Staining, drawn by Francis Howard, and designed
    for *Tiffany Glass and Decorating Co.* 128
Dinner Table Set for Serving 152
The Living-room. Drawn by Francis Howard 360

Reproductions by Sackett & Wilhelms Co., Fifth Avenue, New York.

TEXT ILLUSTRATIONS

The publishers wish to express their thanks for the assistance of the following firms, who have permitted them to copy objects or drawings for the illustrations in this book: W. & J. Sloane (Rugs), James McCreery & Co. (Laces), A. A. Vantine & Co. (Japanese Goods), Davis Collamore & Co. (Porcelains), Frank Haviland (China), Tiffany Glass and Decorating Co., Fowler & Wells, Jenness Miller Monthly.

PAGE

Headpiece . . . . Designed by Frieda V. Redmond *1*
Initial Letter . . . . Designed by Jessamy Harte *1*
Cooper Union, New York 4
Academy of Design, New York 5
Day Antique Class, Academy of Design 5
Building of the American Fine Arts Society, Fifty-seventh Street, New York . 6
Design for Chandelier for Archer, Pancoast Co. 7
Designs for China made for Maddock & Co. 10
Design drawn in Ink for Woven Silk for Cheney Bros. 10
Same Silk Design when Woven. Photographed from the Goods . . . 11
Pattern of Brussels Carpet made for Bigelow Carpet Co. 12
Design for Oil Cloth. Drawn by Josephine H. Blackfan for D. Powers
  & Sons 13
Design for Wall Paper for Warren Fuller & Co. 14
Design for Silver Piece for Gorham Manufacturing Co. 15
Design for Christmas Card (L. Prang & Co.) Rosina Emmet Sherwood . 16
Calico Design for Printing on the Cloth 16
Wood Carving Design 17

List of Illustrations to Volume I.

PAGE

The Haunt and Home of the Redwing,
             Engraving on Wood by Miss M. J. Whaley,
             from Drawing by William Hamilton Gibson . . 18
Design for a Stained Glass Window . . . Mary E. McDowell 19
House in Germantown, Pa. . . . . . . Mrs. Minerva Parker Nichols, Architect, Philadelphia. 20
Panel for Outline Embroidery . . Drawn by Dora Wheeler Keith . . . 21
Entrance to Armour Institute, Chicago 22
The Nurse . . . . Drawn by A. E. Sterner. 37
In the Children's Ward . . . . Drawn by Francis Day 39
Taking the Morning Temperature and Pulse . C. Broughton 40
The Surgical Ward at Bellevue . . . . . do. do. 42
Elizabeth Blackwell. The first woman M.D. in the United States . . 45
A Millinery Class at Armour Institute, Chicago 60
A View Taken and Published by Mrs. J. C. Kendall, Photographer . . 70
Tail-piece . . . . Designed by Annie G. Prickitt . . 76
Initial . . . . Designed by Herbert Denman . . 107
Kitchen Cupboard with Glass Doors 115
Egg Beater 116
A Set of Skewers 116
Thermometer 116
Stove with Glass Oven Doors 116
Ironing-table Combination 117
The Flat Gas-stove 118
A Modern Gas-stove 118
A Gas Water-heater 118
An Electric Kitchen. (Sketched from one in operation by Wm. Mayer) . 119
A Steam Cooker 120
Silver Chafing-dish (Gorham Mfg. Co.) 121
The Aladdin Oven 122
Plan of the Aladdin Oven, showing distribution of heat 122
Correct Position of the Hands in Bread Making 127
Head-dresses of the Middle Ages 182
Bran Stuffed Sleeves 183
The Hoop Petticoat 183
The Stola 184
A Lissome Girth, 1893 185
Queen Elizabeth in the Costume of her Time 186
Alpine Costume 188
A Greek Girl's Costume, showing the Chiton 189
The Strophion 189
Monument of Hegeso, Daughter of Praxenos—Athens, about 400 B.C. . 190
Short Waist Effects, 1816, 1893 . Drawn by W. L. Metcalf . . 190
The Pannier of 1870 . . . . do. do. . 191
The Hoop-skirt of 1864 . . . . do. do. . 191
The Hoop-skirt and Pannier, 1847 do. do. . 191

List of Illustrations to Volume I.

	PAGE
The Golden Stairs, by Burne-Jones, illustrating the Æsthetic Dress in Art	192
Peplum Effects	193
Study of Drapery. From a drawing by Burne-Jones	194
Street Gown with Train, 1876	196
In the Sixteenth Century	196
In the Year 1806	196
Iron Corset of the Sixteenth Century	197
Corset of the Period of Louis XIV	197
Slashed Corset of the Eighteenth Century	197
The Grotesque in Dress in 1795	198
In the Grecian-bend Period	198
In the Time of Marie Antoinette	198
Perpendicular Lines, 1889	199
Horizontal and Oblique Lines, 1894	199
Decorative Arrangement in 1830 and 1835	200
Fin de Siècle . . . . Drawn by W. L. Taylor	202
House Dress modelled on a Dutch Costume	211
Tea Gown . . . . Designed by Jenness Miller	212
Proposed Business Dress—Front View	214
Rear View	214
Artistic House Gowns	215
Gowns for Stout Women . . . Designed by Helen Ecob	220
Divided Skirt . . . . . Designed by Jenness Miller	222
Modern Russian Fan	230
A Decorative Fancy in a Fan	230
Carved Ivory Guards	231
Modern Lace Fan	231
Fan Painted in the Manner of Watteau	232
Modern Black Lace Fan	233
Escurial Lace	234
Rose Point Lace	234
Duchesse Lace	234
Valenciennes Lace	235
Point de Gênes Lace	235
Cream Chantilly Lace	236
Torchon Lace	236
Point de Gênes—Net Top	237
Venetian Point Lace	237
Gown for Bridesmaid	238
Gown for Bride	239
Making Milliner's Fold	242
Milliner's Fold Finished	242
Half Facing—Plain for Hats	242
Puff Binding for Hats	242
Shirred Facing for Hats	242
Shirred Hat	243

List of Illustrations to Volume I.

	PAGE
Bow for Front of Hat	244
Pretty Striped Bow	244
Small Bow for Bonnet	244
For Side of Hat	245
For Back of Hat	245
Stylish Bow for Front of Hat	245
Alsatian Bow	245
Butterfly Bows	245
Shirring for Rosette	245
Making Rosette	245
Rosette Finished	245
Hemming Velvet	246
Folding Perfect Bias	246
Graduating Gowns	249
Outline of Dress-front	253
Sleeve-board	255
Diagram showing how to fit sleeve to armhole	257
Tailpiece. Designed by E. H. Blashfield	260
Bacteria highly magnified	264
Arrangement of steam-pipes for heating. From "Hygiene" by C. G. Currier, M.D.	268
Radiator with a pipe communicating with the outer air. From "Hygiene" by C. G. Currier, M.D.	270
A Practical Ventilator	272
Diagram showing direction of air-currents when drawn out by a heated chimney through an open fireplace elevation	273
Ground plan of same room	273
Diagram of plumbing with soil-pipe and ventilator running straight to the roof	276
Diagram showing contamination of well-water by cesspool	277
Milk Pasteurizers	290
Making up Sick-beds—Tucking in the sheet	296
Clean sheet folded and overlapping the soiled one	297
Position of hands in drawing the sheet beneath the patient	297
Drawing the sheet under the feet	297
Application of improvised tourniquet to arm	305
Stopping bleeding from a wound in the palm	305
Restoring the breathing by Sylvester's Method—Inspiration	312
Restoring the breathing by Sylvester's Method—Expiration	312
Froeble's House. Card used for Kindergarten Children. From the Milton Bradley Co., Springfield, Mass.	334
Tailpiece. Designed by J. Walker	336
A Bureau Trunk	372
An English Sleeping-car	374
The Porter. Drawn by Victor Pérard	375
A Sleeper on a Vestibuled Train	376
American Dining-car. Drawn by Robert Blum	377

xii *List of Illustrations to Volume I.*

	PAGE
The Deck Steward . . . . . Drawn by Herbert Denman . .	378
More Comfortable on Deck . . . Drawn by R. F. Zogbaum .	379
A Novel Method of Landing Passengers at Natal, South Africa . .	380
Promenade Deck of an Orient Liner. Drawn by Otto H. Bacher . .	381
The Ladies' Saloon of a Hamburg Steamer. Drawn by Harry Fenn .	383
In the Grand Saloon of an Ocean Steamer . Drawn by Otto H. Bacher	385
The Gang-plank—just before sailing . Drawn by Victor Pérard .	386
The End of the Voyage . . . Drawn by C. Broughton .	387
An English Guard	388
An English Dining-car	389
An English Railway Carriage, Midland Road. First and Third Class and Luggage Compartments	390
London Underground Railway Station	391
Café de la Régence, rue St. Honoré. Drawn by Otto H. Bacher . . .	393
Before the Café Riche . . . . . Drawn by G. Jeanniot	396
The Gateway between the East and the West—Entrance to the Suez Canal at Port Said . . . . Drawn by Carlton T. Chapman . . .	398
A House near Tokio occupied by an English Traveller, Drawn by Robert Blum	400

Publisher's Note.

The title of this work accurately describes its purpose. The plan has included the treatment of all the larger subjects which to-day interest and concern women (though many of the topics treated are of equal interest to all readers); and it is hoped that the work will become a thoroughly home book, to be read, consulted, and relied upon in thousands of households.

While it has been the purpose to furnish information, practical and otherwise, the narrative form has been adopted rather than the encyclopedic; but reference to the extremely thorough index, containing more than 5,000 references, makes all subjects readily accessible.

The publishers wish to express their thanks for the generous and enthusiastic help received from the contributors, not only in the preparation of the chapters but in developing and planning the work. Special acknowledgment is due to Miss Celeste Winans Herrick for help in arranging the book, as well as for her valuable editorial work during its passage through the press.

I.

OCCUPATIONS FOR WOMEN.

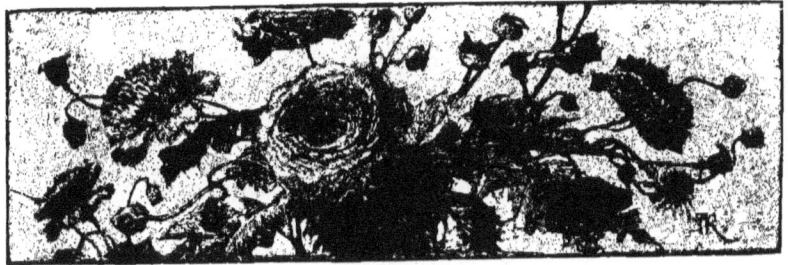

Designed by Frieda V. Redmond.

I.

OCCUPATIONS FOR WOMEN.

By P. G. HUBERT, Jr.

The New Fields of Work Open.
Art Study and Art Workers.
Women Architects.
Teaching.
Typewriting and Stenography.
Women's Exchanges.
Occupations for the Inexperienced.
The Trained Nurse.

Women Physicians and Lawyers.
Newspaper Work and Pay.
Dress-making and Millinery.
Work Done at Home.
The Stage as a Profession.
Novel Occupations Followed.
Women as Local Photographers.
How Women Workers are Swindled.

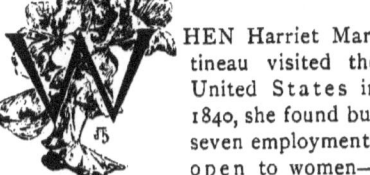

Designed by Jessamy Harte.

I.—WOMEN AS WAGE-EARNERS. HEN Harriet Martineau visited the United States in 1840, she found but seven employments open to women— teaching, needle-work, keeping boarders, work in cotton mills, type-setting, book-binding, and household service.

A brief review of the employments of women to-day, will show how extraordinary, even revolutionary, has been the change that has taken place in the last fifty years. To-day there is scarcely an industry or profession in which women have not made honorable places for themselves. They have virtually monopolized the profession of school-teaching; they do most of the telegraphing, and the office-copying, in large cities; they have displaced men as shop clerks almost everywhere; they turn out hundreds of physicians every year from their own medical colleges; they have raised nursing to the dignity of an art; they have begun to make themselves felt in commercial life. Every day we hear of a woman making her way in some profession or industry until now controlled by men. It is certain that civilized women will never want to be soldiers, and it is improbable that they will enter any employment in which physical endurance and agility are required, such as putting out fires, police duty, the mining of coals and minerals, etc. But aside from these branches, the whole field is open. Farm work is largely done by women in the Old World, but it is to be hoped that labor more adapted to woman's state and power will always be found for her in America. So long as there are any men left behind the counters where ribbons and dry goods are measured out, American women should not be found in the fields, as is still the case in Germany, or in the coal mines, as is the case in England.

Of the 394,584 persons engaged in industrial pursuits in Massachusetts in 1885, the women and girls numbered 112,762, the percentage of women to the whole number of persons employed being as follows in these industries: Federal employments, 12 per cent.; professional service (including teaching), 46.26; personal service (including domestic service), 40.66; trade, 11.09; transportation, 0.29; agriculture, 0.52; fisheries, 0.09; manufactures, 28.58. According to the most trustworthy estimates there were not more than 50,000 wage-earning women in Massachusetts half a century ago, of which number seven-eighths were in domestic service and manufactures.

Women were unknown in professions, except as teachers, and there were almost no means by which they could obtain the education necessary for professional work. To-day there are open to women in this country two hundred and twenty-eight colleges of the liberal arts, and one hundred and ninety-eight institutions for higher instruction than that afforded by the public schools.

In the business colleges, where commercial rules and practice are taught, women have just begun to find their way, and it is reasonable to suppose that, as women constitute nineteen-twentieths of the customers of retail shops, the day is not far off when women shop-keepers will at least share with men the work of supplying the army of women shoppers with what they need. Business training is all that they require in order to utilize their feminine taste and their better knowledge of what women want.

Heretofore the capital necessary for business has been exclusively in the hands of men, but even in the field of money, women have appeared. One of the largest fortunes of the day has been accumulated by the stock and railroad speculations of a woman who is commonly reported to be worth forty millions of dollars.

With the advent of woman as man's competitor in the industrial and professional field, a number of interesting questions arise as to the effects of the change upon woman herself, and upon the social relations between men and women. The old-time fiction to the effect that woman was a tender flower, blooming only when sheltered from the world, and likely either to droop or lose its fragrance when brought into contact with a vulgar, work-a-day, money-grubbing world, has been called into question before now. Some eminent thinkers and essayists, such as Mr. Frederic Harrison, the English writer, dread the effect of political, professional, and business life upon woman. They fear the appearance of the mannish woman upon the scene, the imitation of a man, and they contend that no man wants to discuss politics with his wife, when the day's labors are over. It is possible, however, that if the wife talks politics, the good of the state or village makes it essential that she should do so.

It is, of course, impossible to say that the introduction of women into the professions and industrial life has made any perceptible difference, even upon the women who have become doctors and lawyers and business women. Their numbers are not large enough to affect the whole body of women, and from the nature of things it is not likely that they ever will be, nature having allotted to woman, as a class, the precious duty of bearing and rearing children, and incidentally the care of the home. The great majority of women find by instinct in that sphere their highest happiness. The change now taking place implies, however, that, if for any reason a woman chooses to become a money-earner, she shall have a clear field and a proper equipment. If by way of provision for such a case, possible in every instance, every girl receives a more thorough, broader, and deeper education than is common at present, is it likely that men will object? It is inconceivable that because a girl takes an intelligent interest in science, art, and literature, she should not make a better wife and mother than one to whom all the great intellectual interests of the world are a closed book. Dr. Maudsley, the famous English specialist in nervous disease, traces many cases of hysteria and insanity to the idleness due to brain vacuity. And such vacuity naturally affects more than the woman herself; it reacts upon husband and family.

Mrs. Millicent Fawcett, an English woman who has written much on this subject, contends that many shipwrecks of domestic happiness are due to the fact that the wife really had no vocation for marriage or real affection for the husband. She married because it meant escape from drudgery or dependence. Better education for girls, and a free field in earning money, will certainly decrease the number of such marriages, but marriage will then mean more. When a woman has the opportunity and means of supporting herself, she is more likely to accept only such marriage relations as depend upon the purest and highest companionship. The family, as a resultant of such marriage, will be placed upon a more enduring basis.

The fact that women are paid less than men for apparently the same service seems to disturb a great many people, who find here a conspiracy upon the part of man to keep women out of the wage-earning field so far as this can be done. The maxim, "Business is business," applies here with as much force as anywhere. Both men and women earn, as a rule, just what they are worth. The law of supply and demand comes into play as relentlessly here as elsewhere. If a woman wants more money than a man, she has only to do better and more work in the long run than the man, and she will get more pay as surely as business rules remain in force in the business world. Adelina Patti receives five thousand dollars every time she sings; this is five times as much as the most famous man singer gets, and she receives it simply because it pays her manager to give it. Sentimental forces have no place in the business world, and nothing is more certain than that woman is fairly treated.

There are some reasons for the apparent discrepancy between the pay of men and women, which may serve to clear away some of the false impressions that have grown up about this question. In the first place, women as a class of workers are beginners, comparatively speaking, in the great field of industry; they lack the hereditary instinct for such work, and as beginners their wages are low. Woman's preparation for work is seldom so thorough as with a man, and long technical training for any work is often considered superfluous for a woman because she may marry. Even should she remain a wage-earner, the woman has seldom the strong incentive of others dependent upon her; the man has a wife and children who will suffer, should he relax his efforts; the woman is usually alone.

Another feature of the problem seldom considered is, that women, as a class, are the victims of the enervating influence of the assistance and protection they in most cases receive from family and friends. In the lower ranks of industry, such as factory work and domestic service, the lack of political power and of trade-union influence is also a detriment. Finally, now that women are entering the money-making fields in such vast numbers, the supply is often greater than the demand, and it may take generations before the effect of this big wave disappears.

A curious feature of work by women is that, while in this century and in America work and money-earning have always been considered to be proper in every way for men, there is still some slight social stigma pertaining to money-getting by women. This may be trusted to die out as fast as women show that they can retain all the most attractive attributes of womanhood and yet earn their own living. It may be conceded that, as a class, the most attractive and cultured women have been those whom fortune has placed above the necessity of money-getting. They owe much of their charm to the culture which money has given them. Hence, as money in some degree implies culture, so the absence of it implies lack of culture. To go into any money-getting business or profession is an acknowledgment of poverty, and thus, by inference, of lack of culture. In Europe commercial business was at one time considered beneath a gentleman. No gentleman was " in trade." The prejudice against money-getting by women is just as certain to disappear. The existence of seventy-five Woman's Exchanges in this country, where women may earn money by stealth, so to speak, is proof enough of this absurd prejudice against work by women. It is a pleasure to say, in this connection, that the secrecy surrounding the identity of the thousands of women who earn part or all their living by what they send to such exchanges, is fast being abandoned. The day is not far off when inability to earn money will be considered as much of a disgrace to a woman as to a man ; it will be an acknowledgment of inferior skill, or taste, or energy.

II.—ART AND ART INDUSTRIES.

A CONSERVATIVE estimate of the number of women engaged in America in pursuits either purely artistic in themselves, or in art industries such as designing for manufacturers, photography, decoration, etc., places the number at ten thousand, of which at least two thousand are found in New York City alone. About one-third of this number are teachers of drawing, painting, and modelling in public or private institutions, or make a living by painting; the rest are engaged in designing and in the manufacture of articles requiring some artistic taste or knowledge, such as Christmas cards, bon-bon boxes, crayon portraits, wood carving, etc. The supply of such work-

Cooper Union, New York.

women is unfortunately greater than the demand.

According to the most recent reports,

Academy of Design, New York.

about a thousand young women are engaged in New York every year in the study of art pursuits, with a view to making a living. In one of the most famous of New York's art schools for women, that of the Cooper Union, each applicant for admission to the free classes must furnish proof that she is unable to pay for instruction and is obliged to earn her own living. Of the whole number of women now studying in the various art schools, about half come from other cities. It is not desirable that students should be under sixteen years old, and at the Cooper Union no applicant is admitted who is over thirty-five.

Within the last fifteen years art work has been found so excellent a business for women that, whereas the Cooper Union and the Academy of Design Schools were, a generation ago, the only ones in New York where young women could obtain systematic art instruction, there are now half a dozen such institutions. At the Academy of Design and at the Art Students' League, drawing, painting, and modelling only are taught, while at the Cooper Union, the Artist-Artisans, and the School of Applied Design, designing and various commercial art processes and industries form an important part of the work. Almost every large city now has its art schools, and any person who wishes to study systematically should apply for the circulars, each school having different rules concerning admission.

As a rule, it may be said that no girl is wise in coming to New York to study art unless by the advice of some competent person in her own town or part of the country. At the Cooper Union tuition is free; at most of the other schools the average yearly fees do not exceed one hundred dollars, and exceptional promise on the part of a pupil may win a free scholarship; but aside from tuition, living expenses must be paid for from two to four years, and the chances of earning money while at school are not to be depended upon.

Day Antique Class, Academy of Design.

One of the women most competent to speak of this says that girls who come to any large city expecting to earn enough money to carry them through, are very apt to break down and leave the school permanently injured in health by the strain. It is true that some exceptionally gifted young women do begin almost at once to produce designs or pictures that find a sale; but they are few. The average girl will do better to work at home, doing the best she can with such instruction as her town or village offers, until she is able to command a sum of money—usually about two thousand dollars—sufficient to carry her through four years of work in New York.

Even when a woman is fairly successful in such a career, the gains from art work are by no means large, and the list of failures shows that success is not easily attained. A teacher who has had more than twenty years' experience in one of the largest art schools of New York, says that, so far as she has been able to follow the career of

Building of the American Fine Arts Society, Fifty-seventh Street, New York, where the Art Students' League Classes are held.

the graduates, about one-third of them make a comfortable living, one-third marry and give up work, and one-third retire from the field disheartened. Of the third who succeed, fully one-half become teachers at salaries of from five hundred dollars to eight hundred dollars a year. In many instances they enter boarding-schools, where the salary is from three hundred dollars to four hundred dollars a year, in addition to board. Of the three hundred young women who yearly leave the New York schools to make a living for themselves, not more than a dozen are heard of afterward as earning large sums of money by the sale of pictures or designs. If one succeeds in earning an income of one thousand dollars a year, she is cited as a remarkably successful woman. The rank and file are contented with half that income. One man who has unusual facilities for knowing about the earnings of women in New York City, is confident that stenographers, as a class, are more successful as money-makers than art workers. But while a stenographer never earns an income of more than one thousand five hundred dollars, the woman portrait-painter, if successful, may earn three or four times as much; besides which art work, of whatever character, is in itself more interesting than the office drudgery that falls to the lot of the average stenographer.

The industries in which a competent woman, trained in a good art school, may earn money make a long list. Good designs are always sought after, and this is a field in which women are fast making themselves useful. Every manufacturer of wall-papers needs new designs every year—one large firm having bought from outsiders no less than four hundred designs in 1893, paying an average price of twenty dollars for each design. Every maker of silverware wants designs for plate, or jewelry, even for teaspoons, knives, and forks. Every manufacturer of textile fabrics must have new patterns. One large silk manufacturer pays at least ten thousand dollars a year for designs, the cry being always for novelties. A New York firm manufacturing gas-fixtures spent last year eight thousand dollars in the same way. There is scarcely a manufacturing industry in which designs are not required and paid for. Even a manufacturer of coal-scuttles was glad, some time ago, to pay ten dollars apiece for a dozen good designs. Publishers pay large sums every year for book-cover designs; printers want new and fancy letters and quaint "tail-pieces." Makers of porcelain and potteries are always after new designs; while in the furniture business the demand for new designs is so constant that all large firms keep their own staff of designers. Every manufactured article needs a design, and, as upon appearance will largely depend the sales, it is not surprising that manufacturers are more and more keen in their quest of good designs. It is not sufficient to copy

Design for Chandelier for Archer, Pancoast Co., New York.

old material; the constant demand is for something new.

The very fact that women have made

remarkable headway in the business of designing has brought about a competition that has already proved somewhat disastrous. Prices for good designs in almost every branch of manufacture have fallen in proportion to the supply, and at the same time those who buy designs have become extremely critical. Designs that in 1884 would have found a ready sale are declined in 1894. If the art schools continue to turn out women graduates at the present rate, about three hundred a year, the rank and file of girls who rely upon designing for a living will have a hard time of it. It must also be said, in warning to those who imagine that the art of designing consists solely in the making of pretty pictures, that the technical training in design is something apart from artistic training, and must be learned as a separate art. In fact, it requires such knowledge of weaving, colors, threads, etc., to make a good carpet design, that carpet-designers seldom design anything else. So also with oil-cloths, wall-papers, silks, and cottons. One person seldom designs in more than one material. The chief reason why women designers are at a disadvantage here as compared with men in the regular employ of manufacturers, is that the men are often familiar with the whole process of manufacture, the machinery, the technical part of the art; they live in the factories, watch the actual work, and are therefore familiar with the possibilities as well as the limitations of the material they work in. Sometimes a manufacturer is so impressed with a design offered to him by a woman that, although it cannot be carried out, he will buy it and turn it over to someone who will put its ideas into practical shape. The largest incomes earned by women designers are paid as salaries to regular employees who devote themselves to one branch of design, and, working in the factory, master that one branch in all its details. Such a woman was paid three thousand dollars a year for several years by a prominent manufacturer of printed cotton cloth, and it is not uncommon to hear of salaries of from twelve hundred dollars to fifteen hundred dollars, paid to women who obtain positions of this sort.

The women designers who depend upon the chance sale of their work to this or that manufacturer, can expect no such incomes. Some enterprising young women formerly connected with the school of the Cooper Union, two years ago established a sort of agency under the name of Associated Designers, where designers may send their work, and where manufacturers may go when in need of designs. A small percentage is charged upon the sales made. The designer is thus saved the trouble of personally taking her work around. There are, upon the average, two hundeed women who send their designs to this exchange, and the number is increasing so rapidly that the managers have had to refuse work which did not, in their opinion, reach a certain standard of excellence. An idea of the numbers of designs made in New York may be obtained when it is said that, although the manufacturers buy thousands of designs every year, only about one in ten offered is accepted. The other nine represent time and work wasted. Naturally, the prices paid for designs have fallen. For a fairly elaborate design of a wall-paper, frieze, and ceiling, the three being counted as one design, the average price is twenty-five dollars. For a simple wall-paper alone, it will not be more than fifteen dollars. The price for silk or cotton designs varies from fifteen to twenty-five dollars, according to the amount of work involved. Such designs may have cost a week's work or more. When it is remembered that nine out of every ten

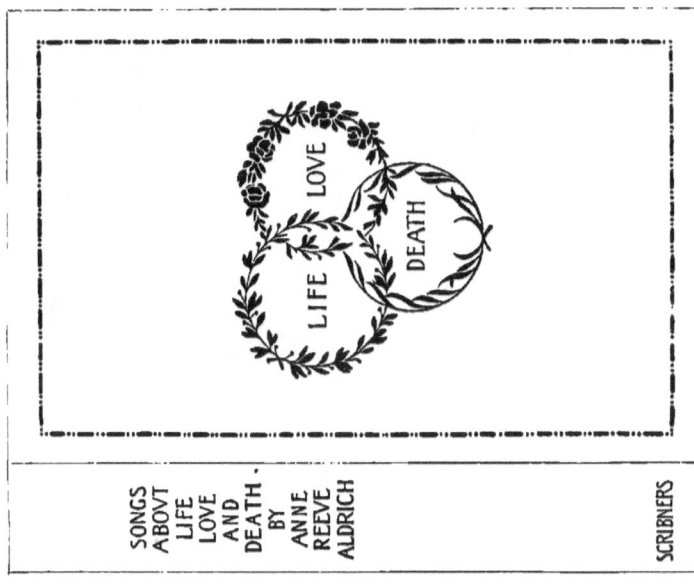

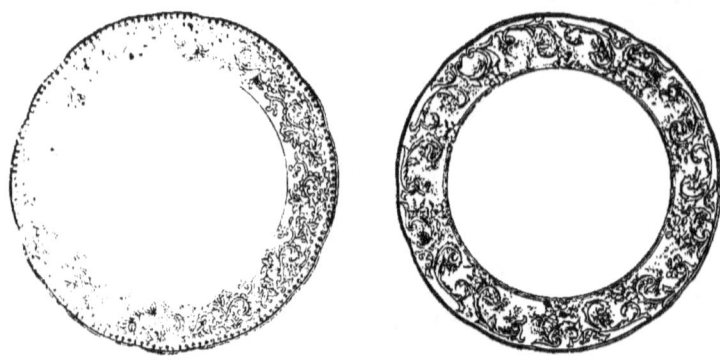

Designs for China made for Maddock & Co., New York.

find no sale, these prices are not exorbitant. The woman designer who earns six hundred dollars a year by the sale of her designs is doing well, but most of the successful designs of silk are made by women.

Besides designing, women make money in art pursuits by painting and illustrating. Some years ago engraving was followed as an occupation by a number of women, but in the present processes the camera has very largely taken the engraver's place. To paint pictures for sale is a luxury which only few artists can afford, and the field is almost closed to women by the fierce competition of cheap work done largely in this country by foreigners. Even the best among the men artists of the day cannot live by the sale of their pictures—they are compelled to teach. The painter who has not pupils, either in some art school or in his studio, must be content with a most meagre income, unless he happens to have private means drawn from other sources than his art. A number of women, graduates of the art schools, do eke out a poor living by painting small pictures, chiefly water-colors, and by the decoration of *menus*, Christmas cards, etc. It is but a poor business, and subject, moreover, to the

Design drawn in Ink for Woven Silk, for Cheney Bros., South Manchester, Conn.

caprice of fashion. The kind of picture or decorative panel that may please one year will find no buyers the next. Illustrating pays far better than painting, as many of the men have already discovered. With trained skill and some felicity of conception, a good woman illustrator is ordinarily sure of a living income from newspaper publishers and magazines. The illustrations and portraits used by the daily newspapers are largely made by a photographic process which requires the original photograph to be redrawn in ink ; the work is comparatively easy, and several women are employed in this manner by the New York newspapers. The sketches of new fashions, household decoration, and generally all the illustrations found upon what is known as the woman's page of the Sunday newspapers, are the work of women employed upon a salary of from twenty to thirty dollars a week. The free use of comic pictures or elaborate designs for advertising purposes in newspapers and magazines has opened a profitable field to women who have ideas as well as artistic skill. Advertisers are always willing to pay well for any design that will attract attention to their wares.

Photography offers an inviting field to women who are content with a small income and have any aptitude for business. Two-thirds of the photographer's customers are women and children ; a quick-witted and obliging woman is far more apt than a man to succeed in getting these customers to "look pleasant" when the critical moment arrives. Good taste in matters of dress, the arrangement of the hair, pose, etc., is so much more common with women than men, that almost

Same Silk Design when Woven—Photographed from the Goods.

every large photographic studio in New York has one or more women in its employ; while in small towns and be mentioned painting on china, the making of miniatures by a process in which a photograph is the basis of the

Pattern of Brussels Carpet, Drawn on Design Paper, the small squares represent loops in the pile of the carpet. Made for Bigelow Carpet Co., New York.

villages, the woman photographer has become an institution. Photography is an art, moreover, that requires but a short apprenticeship as compared with designing. Among the women graduates of several New York schools, more than twenty are known who have made enviable positions for themselves as the leading photographers of their towns. In the photographic galleries managed by men, women are frequently employed at retouching negatives, the salary for such work averaging in New York from ten to fifteen dollars a week.

Among other art industries that employ a small number of women, should work, wood-carving, and metal work. All of these industries employ, however, but a small number of workers, and the pay is low. A good china decorator is fortunate if she earns six hundred dollars a year. In making crayon-portraits and miniatures the demand varies so much with the seasons and the fashions, that it is not to be depended upon. Wood-carving and metal-work are fairly well paid, but there is too little of it to be done to encourage a serious and ambitious woman.

Until the winter of 1893–1894 nearly twenty women designers found work in the designing of stained-glass windows and screens. They were paid from twenty dollars to thirty-five dollars a week. Hard times is an aspect of the business that women should consider; the more closely allied to art, and consequently expensive, the more likely is an industry to suffer from business depression.

thing in the house concerns the mistress more nearly than the master, for most of his life is passed away from it; while according to the taste, the comfort, and equipment of the home, within the limits of her income, the mistress will be judged by visitors and friends.

Design for Oil-cloth, drawn by Josephine H. Blacklan, Philadelphia, for D. Powers & Sons, Lansingburgh, N. Y.

Some of the most notable successes made by women in art industries have been achieved lately in house-decoration. The house is pre-eminently the woman's province, yet it is only within the last ten or twelve years that women have entered the field of house-decoration as original designers. Every-

It is woman's domain, and yet how little has she had to do with the designing of the house, its decorations, coloring, hangings, and furnishings. Men were the architects, men designed the color-schemes of the walls, the carpets, the furniture. Woman has had to do the best she could with what man offered her.

To some extent this has been

changed, and it is highly probable that in this field of house-decoration women will, in the future, find a splendid chance for the exercise of their artistic taste. Already one firm of enterprising women have proved by ten years of admirable work in the designing of textile fabrics, wall-coverings, etc., that as a business it is not beyond their scope, while in a score of small towns the woman decorator has exerted an influence.

Those in the business who have seen much of the work done by women in this field believe that with the success of women architects will come a corresponding success to women decorators. For certain reasons the one is rather dependent upon the other.

The trouble heretofore has been that women have not had the thorough training in design that alone will enable them to make broad schemes and comprehensive combinations. A woman may have exquisite ideas for grouping colors, or she may know how to arrange the draperies of a room with taste and economy; but to decorate and furnish a whole house so that the drawing-room shall harmonize with and accentuate the hall, and the dining-room fulfil the promise of the drawing-room and so on through the whole house—that is an art requiring more training than women have been in the way of getting. It is an art, and as such deserves serious study.

Men devote years to learning first how to design a house, and then decoration comes as a supplementary part of the work. It is a common notion that architects disdain decoration. This may have been true in the past, but to-day most of them take a keen interest in suggesting and superintending, if not in actually designing, the decoration of a house, and the time is evidently coming when decoration will be still more closely associated with the architect's work than it is at present.

Design for Wall Paper for Warren, Fuller & Co., New York.
(*See page 8.*)

When the architect has finished his house so far as walls, floors, doors, and windows go, he feels, if he is a man of artistic conscience, that it is not quite fair to take the work out of his hands at that stage. No matter how admirably proportioned may be the rooms, the effect may be killed. Wrong lines in the paper may defeat his purpose, the colors may "swear at each other," as the French say, and impossible rugs, curtains, and hangings may spoil a house that, under proper treatment, would have been a delight. It is therefore a matter of importance to him to see that the decorations and fitting up of a house are as perfect as circumstances will allow. For this reason almost all architects now expect to be consulted in the painting, papering, and upholstering of a house, if not in the actual selection of the furniture.

Women have so far made but small progress in architecture, the chief reason being that to construct a building needs the preliminary technical training in mathematics and mechanics that girls seldom receive. The working architect is supposed to know how to carry out a design in wood, stone, brick, or iron, as well as to make it; few women have such knowledge, and for this reason they seldom rise above the making of pretty drawings on paper, which may or may not be possible in wood or stone. In New York there are only twelve women employed in architects' offices. There seems to be no reason, however, why women should not attain distinction as architects, and the Woman's Building at the Chicago World's Fair, showed that a woman can design upon a large and effective scale when the opportunity offers. To return to house-decoration; there are several firms of women house-decorators in New York, who do well, artistically and financially. They are always prepared to make designs for a room or a whole house, and to give estimates of the cost. One such firm, which began business in 1882, employs on an average

Design for Silver Piece for Gorham Manufacturing Co., New York.

Occupations for Women.

Copyright, 1891, by L. Prang & Co., Boston.
Design for Card by Rosina Emmet Sherwood, who Won the Prang Prize for $1,000 in Christmas Card Competition, 1880.

sixty women in designing embroidery, and making hangings for houses. In the decade 1884–1894, this firm produced more than five hundred designs in silks and cottons which have been manufactured and sold throughout the country.

Outside of the large cities, women have done exceedingly well as decorators, and a score of instances are cited in which a young woman has created a business in her town, by providing stuffs and hangings more artistic than the local shop-keepers can afford or understand. In a town of a few thousand inhabitants such a business needs no advertising; the fact that some one has good ideas with regard to wall-papers, hangings, rugs, furniture-coverings, as well as samples of artistic goods, is soon known. It is a business which needs no capital beyond taste and tact in dealing with people. One young woman who tried to convert by storm a whole New England village from the wax-flower stage to the most eccentric phases of æstheticism, aroused more antagonism in three months than she could subdue in three years. The honest villagers resented the abuse of their samplers and wax-flowers at the expense of the mediæval lily upon a silk panel, or "something Japanese." This young enthusiast in house-decoration failed to remember that "art is long."

III.—THE TEACHER.

THE noble profession of teaching, in which many thousands of women in America have found a field of usefulness so peculiarly adapted to their powers, that in many branches of teaching women outnumber men twenty to one, is divided into many specialties and grades. In such a paper as this, only the most general outlines can be noted. Whether in the public school, the private school, the kindergarten, the music class, or the gymnasium where girls are taught the art of getting and preserving bodily strength, the principles that underlie

Calico Design for Printing on the Cloth.

good work are about the same—thoroughness and general culture. By the first is meant a complete and practical knowledge of all that pertains to the particular work attempted. If a girl becomes a kindergartner, a profession of great and growing importance, ought to be of interest to her. The ideal teacher never stands still; if she does not advance in her art, gaining new knowledge every year either from her own experiments or the suggestions of experts, she falls back into the ranks of those with whom all work is

Wood Carving Design. (From Leland's "Manual of Wood Carving.")

which now employs four hundred women in New York City alone, she may not need to know the most recent speculations as to the surface of Mars, but she does need to know all that experts in kindergarten teaching have suggested as possible improvements in the system of teaching small children. When she becomes a teacher, she does not cease to be a student, and everything pertaining to kindergartens is or drudgery because it is unintelligent routine.

To a certain extent there is routine in all teaching work. Experience has proved that certain methods of procedure result in teaching a child to read and to write in the quickest and easiest manner. Children are not so different in mental outfit that the task of teaching to read varies much with each child, and the same remark applies to all teaching; every year a number of pupils have to be taught the lessons learned by their predecessors. For this reason it is essential that the teacher should find in general culture an interest outside of her routine work; she will make a better teacher of arithmetic, for instance, because she is an enthusiast in botany or chemistry. General culture, the faculty of finding interest in whatever interests the most intelligent men and women, is the safe-

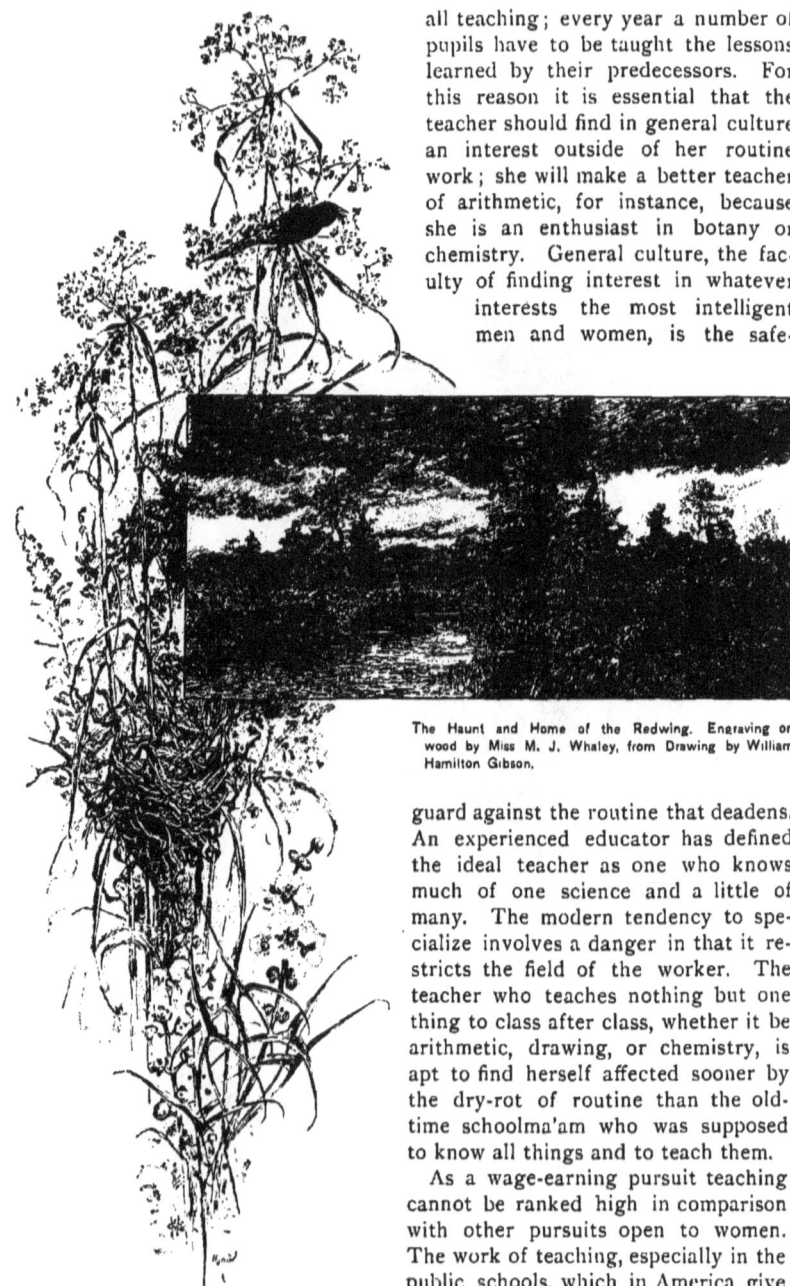

The Haunt and Home of the Redwing. Engraving on wood by Miss M. J. Whaley, from Drawing by William Hamilton Gibson.

guard against the routine that deadens. An experienced educator has defined the ideal teacher as one who knows much of one science and a little of many. The modern tendency to specialize involves a danger in that it restricts the field of the worker. The teacher who teaches nothing but one thing to class after class, whether it be arithmetic, drawing, or chemistry, is apt to find herself affected sooner by the dry-rot of routine than the old-time schoolma'am who was supposed to know all things and to teach them.

As a wage-earning pursuit teaching cannot be ranked high in comparison with other pursuits open to women. The work of teaching, especially in the public schools, which in America give

Advantages and Disadvantages of Teaching. 19

employment to sixty thousand women, of whom three thousand five hundred are in New York, is hard work, wearing upon the nerves, confining, and having nothing of the variety presented by many other occupations. Taking the whole army of teachers employed in New York, the average salary does not exceed eight hundred dollars a year.

The great advantage of the work in public schools is that the salary, if small, is assured, the place is a permanent one, promotion is reasonably certain, and the school is in session but five days a week and ten months a year. The long summer vacation is an attraction that induces many women to become school teachers. The apprentice-

Design for a Stained Glass Window by Mary E. McDowell, for Tiffany Glass Co., New York. (*See page* 13.)

House in Germantown, Pa., Mis. Minerva Parker Nicho's, Architect, Philadelphia. (*See page* 14.)

ship is also commonly looked upon as insignificant in cost of time or money as compared with other professions. The Normal College of New York, from which New York City obtains nine-tenths of its public-school teachers, is a free institution, where graduates of the public schools may obtain the knowledge necessary to become teachers. About four hundred girls are graduated yearly from the Normal College, five-sixths of whom become teachers. The salaries in the private schools of large cities vary from three hundred dollars a year, with board and lodging, to one thousand five hundred dollars for especially competent women in large institutions, but the average is not far from four hundred dollars with board and lodging.

The chief changes brought about in the profession of teaching from 1874 to 1894 may be traced to the introduction of Normal Schools and kindergartens. The manual training, of which so much is heard, seems to be largely an outgrowth of kindergarten methods adapted to older pupils. The normal-school system due to the gradual recognition that teaching is a science, and has to be taught as any other art, dates from 1850–1860; Boston leading the way in establishing a normal school of particular excellence. In 1894 no school system is considered complete without some adequate provision for training teachers; one of the valuable features of most normal schools consisting of a primary department or kindergarten where normal-school graduates may test by actual experience with young children the value of the methods advocated and taught. The large variety of the work done in the kindergarten is a step in the direction of more variety of interest in school work, in contrast with the old-fashioned, cast-iron routine in which the birch-rod furnished the chief variation. The growth of the manual-training system seems to indicate that the endless variation characterizing the work of the kindergarten may prove equally valuable with older pupils. To awaken interest in the pupil, whether a child of five or a girl of fifteen, is the constant aim of the ideal teacher, and this power or faculty implies general intelligence. The immense importance attached to manual training principles in the splendid institutions founded by the late Charles Pratt in Brooklyn, and by Philip D. Armour in Chicago, show the rapid growth of this comparatively new force in education.

In a model school of New York, one of the lessons of the regular course is upon cotton. It takes more than an hour, but it is safe to say that at the end of it the pupils—boys and girls of sixteen—know more about cotton than nine-tenths of intelligent adults.

The lesson in question illustrates the vast change in the system of teaching as compared with that in vogue early in the forties. The teacher began by asking the members of the class to take out their pocket-handkerchiefs, most of which happened to be of cotton. They were asked to examine the strands of the cotton through the pocket-microscopes handed around, and the teacher drew upon the blackboard an exaggerated sketch of a bit of cotton fibre showing its chief characteristics and how it might be easily distinguished from linen, wool, or silk. Then a dried cotton-plant was brought out—not a picture, but an actual plant—with the cotton-boll bursting open. The States and countries producing cotton were spoken of, the culture of cotton, the amount raised on an acre, the total yearly crop, the cost of raw cotton, etc. Then the mode of picking was described, after which a miniature gin was produced and the essential features of Whitney's great invention pointed out ; some of

Panel for Outline Embroidery. (*See page* 16.)

the actual cotton was ginned, then spun into thread, and finally woven with miniature machines, very crude, of course, but sufficient to show the principles of the real ones. Such a lesson required nothing that an intelligent mechanic could not make at small cost, but it taught more than half a book about cotton. Moreover, the teacher, entering into the spirit of the new system, which consists in always interesting the pupil, told the story of cotton so that it was not like a lesson, but like a curious bit of information. The pupils learned without knowing it. In the kindergarten the plays are lessons. Adolphus Trollope says in his autobiography that when he and his brothers were children, his mother taught them to read by throwing on the floor a boxful of letters and offering a little prize to whoever found the right ones for "cat," or any other simple word.

Enough has been said to illustrate the importance, mentioned at the beginning of this paper, placed upon general intelligence in the teacher. Routine methods have had their day. No book lesson will interest the student so thoroughly as an intelligent teacher, mistress of the subject. With regard to the routine work of the teacher, her rewards and hardships, every girl knows enough to decide whether it is the career for her. Unlike a number of other occupations its chief features are familiar to all. But the fact that teaching need not be the tiresome routine sometimes associated with the profession, and that kindergartens, manual-training schools, and normal colleges, have introduced new possibilities for those able to take advantage of them—all this needs to be pointed out.

Entrance to Armour Institute, Chicago. (*See page 21.*)

The chief requisites of the ideal school teacher are, first of all, education; secondly, governing power; thirdly, professional preparation; finally, originality and comprehensiveness of view. By professional preparation is meant the sort of knowledge now given to educators by the several schools of pedagogy, of which that of the University of the City of New York is the oldest. The School of Pedagogy is founded upon the principle that professional preparation and equipment for the work of teaching should be put upon a plane with the preparation and equipment demanded for other professions, such as law, medicine, and theology. In the New York school connected with the University and with Columbia College degrees are granted.

Chairs for giving instruction in the science and art of teaching have for several years been established in many universities and colleges, but the School of Pedagogy is a new departure, having a regular faculty and a course of study covering the whole field. It is not a Normal School, for its work lies beyond this, and begins where the Normal School ends. The last ten years have witnessed marked changes in teaching and in the management of schools, and the next ten will witness still greater changes. The object of schools of pedagogy is to acquaint students with the scientific investigations which will effect these changes and to train them so that they shall be able to take advantage and put into practice a more scientific teaching. Advancement and success await those teachers who thus enlarge the field before them. The work is comparatively young even in New York City, but five women have taken the degree of Doctor of Pedagogy, all of whom are filling important positions, and nearly one hundred pupils are upon the rolls. Applicants for admission to the New York University School must have taught school for three years.

In the teaching of music, perhaps, more than in any other branch of instruction, the compensation, especially in large cities, is apt to vary between a very comfortable income, to just enough to keep body and soul together. Almost every girl in whose home there is a piano picks up some skill in playing. She may know nothing, according to a high musical standard; but this will not prevent her from advertising herself as a teacher of music. She can at least drum out the latest popular song in an easy arrangement, and that is all the teacher to whom she paid fifty cents a lesson for more than a year could do. So, why should she not teach in her turn? And as the field is crowded with girls who can all play one or two popular songs on the piano, she may have to put her prices down to twenty-five cents a lesson. Thus, at one end of the profession we have hundreds of girls, and sometimes even men, giving half-hour lessons upon the piano or melodeon at half a dollar an hour or less; while at the other end of the line are the men and women, musicians of rank and culture, who have all they can do at five dollars a lesson. According to common report, the largest income earned by a piano teacher in this country is that of a lady, a New Yorker, who for the last ten years has averaged eight thousand dollars a year. Her work, however, is incessant. From nine in the morning until evening she is teaching. Pupils pay her five dollars for lessons of an hour's duration. From October till June she gives an average of ten lessons a day—enough to break down any but the strongest constitution.

Taking New York as the city where the highest as well as the lowest prices are paid for music-lessons, there are not more than a dozen women whose incomes from teaching the piano equals four thousand dollars. From time to time a famous concert pianist agrees to give a few private lessons for which she charges twenty dollars apiece, but no regular teacher obtains more than five dollars a lesson. The many conservatories where lessons are given in classes of from five to twelve pupils, have helped to reduce the prices paid to music-teachers, for the tuition terms are small as compared to the cost of private lessons, and all but well-to-do people usually send their children to such classes.

Between the two extremes of twenty-five cents and five dollars for music-lessons, there is to be found a small army, composed chiefly of women, who support themselves fairly well by teaching music. From two dollars to three dollars a lesson is the price demanded by fairly successful women teachers. As a rule, more than half the lessons given by teachers who are able to charge three dollars a lesson are given at the pupils' homes. Most teachers find this no hardship, unless the loss of time is considerable, for they get outdoor exercise between lessons.

Except in the case of exceptional musicians, whose services are in demand by advanced pupils, themselves preparing for the profession, commonsense and business habits, seem to be, according to the views of successful music-teachers, of more value than musical skill. The girl who, with average ability as a musician, makes the greatest success as a music-teacher, is one who treats her profession strictly as a business and conforms to business rules. She is never late at her lessons, no matter how severe her headache may be, or how bad the weather; she never asks favors in the way of changing hours or omitting lessons. Because music is an accomplishment, the pupil is not allowed to look upon the music-lesson as one to be slighted, if a headache makes practice irksome, or a luncheon-party tempts her to omit it altogether. The more music-teaching is regarded as a business, the better for both pupil and teacher. The hardship involved in going from house to house in all sorts of weather is not great when the teacher is properly clothed, and most women who have tried both kinds of work prefer teaching private pupils at their own houses to work in conservatories or in schools, where they are tied down from morning till night.

New York has about a thousand young women studying to become music-teachers, at least half of them coming from smaller towns or cities, to which they will return when competent to begin work on their own account. Some girls of this class study under private teachers, but the majority attend one of the conservatories. Only one institution, the National Conservatory of Music, takes free pupils, and in order to obtain free tuition there, a marked aptitude for music must be shown at the entrance examinations, to which all applicants are subject. If a girl shows sufficient promise to warrant her reception as a free pupil, she agrees to pay to the institution a percentage of whatever income, above a certain amount, she may earn during the first five years after graduation. At several of the conservatories provision is made for boarding pupils in a home attached to the school. The average cost of a two years' course in music, either piano or singing, at a New York conservatory, is, including board, one thousand six hundred dollars, or about eight hundred dollars for each year. A large city is advised by the best judges as the proper place to study music, owing to the facilities for hearing a great deal of good music. Besides the private concerts organized by all the conservatories for the benefit of their pupils, arrangements are often made by which music pupils obtain admission to concerts at reduced rates. A writer upon this matter insists that the privilege of hearing great artists is more important than nine-tenths of the lessons a pupil is apt to receive.

The question of what the six hundred music-teachers of New York and Brooklyn earn upon the average is one that scarcely admits of a definite answer. As already stated, the prices of lessons in singing or in playing the piano range from twenty-five cents to five dollars, with two dollars a lesson as the average price paid by well-to-do people. For a woman to earn more than one thousand five hundred dollars a year by teaching music implies exceptional skill and energy.

A very profitable and popular novelty introduced by music-teachers within the last few years has been the lecture-recital, to which more than a dozen New York women have devoted themselves with much success. The plan is simple enough, consisting in the preparation of a short lecture upon any musical topic, varied by musical illustrations performed by the lecturer. The lectures are usually given in courses of from six to twenty lectures. One whole lecture is usually devoted to a great composer, giving his biography and excerpts from his best known works. The history of music, the origin and growth of the different forms —symphony, sonata, suite—the characteristics and nature of the different instruments of the orchestra, etc., may be made the subject of lectures which a pianist of moderate abilities will make interesting to everyone by appropriate music. Such lectures are not hard to prepare if one has access to any good library. A few good reference books on music, such as Apthorp and Champlin's "Cyclopædia of Music and Musicians," or Grove's "Dictionary of Music," will give most of the biographical facts needed. A few photographs or prints of the great composers and the necessary music from their works will complete the absolute needs of any one of intelligence and musical culture who wishes to prepare such lecture-recitals.

One New York woman has found this work so profitable that for the last two years she has abandoned teaching to give her whole time to lecturing before classes and private schools in New York, Brooklyn, and cities within fifty miles. All her time has been employed, and her income from November, 1892, to June, 1893, was within a few dollars of three thousand.

Most of her lectures were given before classes to which the subscription was ten dollars for a course of twelve lectures, and one class had as many as twenty-eight subscribers. One young woman living in the northern part of New York State, where books were scarce, earned one thousand dollars in two years by such work, and enough money to provide herself with a small library of books upon musical topics.

Still another occupation, upon a lower plane, which a few women music-teachers have found profitable, is piano-tuning. The art requires no great physical strength and may be learned in a few months, the best way being to pay some good tuner for private lessons. In country districts a good woman tuner would find her services in constant demand, the average price for tuning a piano being three dollars, and the work does not require more than two hours. There are several books published upon piano-tuning, but they are of small value in learning the art.

IV.—STENOGRAPHY AND TYPE-WRITING.

IF many women succeed within the next few years in making for themselves fortunes in business, it will probably be thanks to the training received in the counting-rooms into which they first entered as type-writer operators. In fact, considering the number of women who in the last fifteen years have made themselves invaluable in business offices, it is rather surprising that so little is heard of women who launch out for themselves. They have often as much capital as the male clerk or book-keeper who starts out upon his own account, and very often they have a more accurate knowledge of the real resources or dangers of the business, for they have written the confidential letters of some large firm for years. But so few women put this knowledge to practical use as to make the woman in business for herself almost a curiosity. They seem to lack the necessary courage and enterprise.

There are hundreds of businesses which concern women chiefly, and in which a woman's knowledge and taste might be considered essential. Yet they are managed by men. Perhaps it is too early to expect woman to take a leading position where she has only recently managed to get a foothold. It is much for her to have established herself as a part of most mercantile houses and business offices, and only those who can remember the astonishment with which the advent of girls in down-town office buildings was received twenty years ago, can realize the change. To-day young women are found everywhere in business, usually writing letters on the typewriter, but often acting as confidential secretaries, and as such receiving comfortable salaries.

With the appearance of the typewriter came the young woman to operate it, for a woman's fingers do better work, and there are a dozen reasons why a woman finds preference over a man as an operator. The business of stenography and type-writing, which now employs at least fifty thousand women in America, of which eight thousand are in New York, may be divided into three classes. First, letter-writing for commercial houses. This employs four-fifths of all operators. Knowledge of stenography is usually essential, but high speed is not, as the work consists chiefly of short letters, often upon the same subjects and to the same persons, day after day. The operator has often a large number of letters to write, but it is routine work, requiring speed and accuracy only. The salaries for such work vary from eight to sixteen dollars a week. Some firms pay as high as twenty-five dollars to an especially competent woman, but in that case she is often able to answer letters without dictation, merely receiving hints as to the general tenor of the answer, or she supervises the work of several other women. To a woman who likes routine work and small responsibility, such positions are well suited, and require so little in the way of enterprise or intelligence that the business is in some danger of too much competition. Within the last three years the salaries of fair stenographers, able to write out their notes upon the machine with neatness and rapidity, have fallen about one-third, owing to competition.

Second, legal work, in which a woman, although not sufficiently rapid as a stenographer to do court reporting, can take down long legal letters and law briefs with the necessary accuracy. This is far more difficult work than that done in commercial houses and is better paid, many of the good operators in large law firms receiving from twenty to thirty dollars a week, and in some instances even more. A few women have gone into court reporting, but the work is too exhausting as a rule. It requires not only the highest speed but great physical endurance. It is no uncommon thing for male court reporters to work all day in taking short-hand notes, and then all the following night in writing them out or dictating them to a type-writer operator. For the same reason women cannot be much used by newspapers for reporting meetings. Too much of the work is done late at night and under conditions that would soon break any woman down. Few men are able to stand the strain more than ten or fifteen years.

Third, copying and taking dictations from literary workers. This department of stenography and type-writing offers work to both the least and most competent of the army of women typewriters in New York. There are about forty offices, chiefly in the down-town business districts, managed by enterprising women, where papers are copied on the type-writer, or where operators will take down whatever may be dictated to them. The copying part of the work requires no skill or intelligence beyond ability to read manuscript. Much of the work is done by young girls who are learning the business. The charges for copying briefs, architects' specifications, legal papers, etc., average five cents a hundred words; it is more if the manuscript is difficult, and less if simple and in large quantities. Finally, comes the work of taking dictation either in short-hand or directly upon the machine. Thousands of editors, reporters, writers, and clergymen now dictate all they have to say. To them the type-writer is to the pen really what the sewing-machine is to the needle; in the course of a lifetime it does away with years of drudgery. It is evident that a competent amanuensis can do a great deal for a busy literary worker. Take, for instance, an editorial writer whose articles may range from theology to prize-fighting, from musical criticism to dress-reform, and imagine what a saving in time and temper it is for him to be able to dictate in less than an hour articles that would require three hours' hard work with a pen to produce. If the stenographer is a fully competent one, he will find his talk neatly written out within an hour or two and ready for the printer. It is said that some specially competent stenographers do such excellent work in this field that they seldom blunder in proper names, punctuation, or sense.

The writer of this chapter, having had experience with many stenographers, must confess that he has never found one whose notes could be sent off to the printer without reading over. While this is true, there are many women who are accurate, intelligent, and rapid, and without whose services the literary worker of to-day would feel himself lost.

While, unfortunately, the ideal woman stenographer, for literary purposes, has not yet appeared, there are no reasons why she should not find in such work an excellent field. The trouble seems to be that young women of sufficient education to take down understandingly the every-day notes of a literary worker consider the work beneath them and prefer to try teaching. The comic newspapers have had so much to say about "the pretty type-writer," and the idea is so wide-spread that the work is commonplace and mechanical, that the girl of refinement and ambition recoils from it. Nevertheless, intelligent work of the kind indicated is paid for at from one dollar to one dollar and a half an hour, and the more general education a woman has the more in demand her services are likely to be.

The work, as compared with school teaching is not hard, and it is certainly better paid. The girl who is familiar with the ordinary books of the day, who reads the newspapers, who knows something of art, music, and theatrical matters, who does not need to have Chopin's name spelled out to her, or to be told that Matthew Arnold did not write the "Light of Asia," who will punctuate intelligently without directions—such a girl will find her time fully taken up and well paid for.

There are many well-known schools where stenography and type-writing are taught in all the large cities. In New York the Cooper Union classes are free. At the Packard and Paine colleges a tuition fee is charged. In a great many of the large copying offices pupils are taken, sometimes in exchange for their services, sometimes for a fee of from twenty-five to fifty dollars. The course in the regular schools is better because it includes spelling and punctuation. No girl should begin the business before she is seventeen;

until then she ought to be at school. After real work begins she will find it impossible to continue school studies, and she will remain a copyist at ten dollars a week, whereas with a better education she might have earned twice as much money in far pleasanter work.

One of the ladies in charge of the type-writing classes at a large school says that stenographers are now in demand just in proportion to their education and intelligence. The well-bred, intelligent girl is sure to find a place and to make herself worth fifteen or twenty dollars a week, while the girl who is fit for nothing but factory work or serving behind a counter, may never earn more than six dollars a week, and will be dear at that price. Some girls are said to learn type-writing because, in the cheap fiction of the day, the dashing Wall Street broker sometimes marries the type-writer girl who graces his office. And, as already mentioned, the newspapers have much to say about the type-writer girl and her office flirtations. As a matter of fact, the woman stenographer soon finds that business is business ; she will succeed just in proportion to the strictness with which she conforms to business rules. Punctuality, accuracy, industry, are the essentials to success. Business men, as a rule, admit that the general introduction of women into their offices has had an excellent effect upon the manners of the clerks. There is less swearing, loose talk, and drinking where women are employed. Women clerks are often said to be more trustworthy concerning office secrets than men, and if intrusted with money, they never dream of Canada. Upon the other hand, women are apt to demand as a courtesy if not as a right certain indulgences which men do not ask for. If a stress of business necessitates night-work, the men of an office take it as a matter of course, while it is felt that women cannot be depended upon in such emergencies. The average loss of time through sickness or absence is also greater with women than with men. For these reasons it is not likely that women as a class are likely to supplant men in all offices, even as stenographers. But for average work they have the field almost to themselves, and the more they succeed in looking upon business life as a permanent institution for women showing real interest in it and not as a temporary makeshift while waiting for marriage, the more profitable are they sure to find it.

At most of the offices where type-writing is taught, girls are promised a working knowledge of the business within a year. Stenography may require from one to two years, according to the girl, before a speed is acquired that will be useful in office work. As a rule no girl is wise in expecting to earn more than eight dollars a week during the first two years of office work, and she may have to begin at even less. The ranks seem to be always full, but, as in all businesses for women, vacancies are constantly occurring through marriage, and the demand for really competent stenographers is always in excess of the supply. Telegraphy is taught in free classes at the Cooper Institute, but of late years the number of girls who apply for tuition is small. The pay of even good women telegraphers does not equal that of stenographers, and seldom exceeds forty dollars a month.

All young women who, for one reason or another, decide to cut loose from home ties and attempt to earn a living in a large city, will find the Young Women's Christian Associations of the utmost value to them, socially as well as economically. From 1872 to 1894 the Young Women's Christian Association of New York has maintained a number of free classes, which have gradually attained importance. The Y. W. C. A.s of other cities have followed their example in this respect, but none of them to the extent of New York. Brooklyn ranks second in point of the number of students and thoroughness of the instruction offered. The classes of the New York Y. W. C. A. had nineteen hundred and thirty pupils in 1893. There are classes in arithmetic, penmanship, bookkeeping, stenography, typewriting, photography, modelling and designing, choral music, dressmaking, millinery, and machine-sewing and hand-sewing. A fee of five dollars a year is made to cover the rental of type-writers, and a similar fee is asked to pay for material in the dressmaking and millinery classes. All the other classes are free.

V.—WOMAN'S EXCHANGES AS TRAINING SCHOOLS AND MARKETS FOR WORK.

ACCORDING to the most recent estimates, about three thousand women find employment in New York City alone in doing needle-work or embroidery of a character which may come under the class of art work. The Woman's Exchanges which have sprung up all over the country within the last thirty years have helped greatly to educate public taste in this matter of fine needle-work, and have also given invaluable instruction to a whole army of earnest workers.

The Ladies' Depository Association, organized in Philadelphia in 1833, was the first society organized with the end in view of disposing of the handiwork of women of taste who could make pretty and useful things, but who, for one reason or another, failed to make money out of their art. The system upon which this original Woman's Exchange began work was very similar to that followed by the seventy-five Exchanges in operation in 1894. All sorts of work which a woman of refinement is likely to know how to do, or to be able to learn, such as delicate needle-work, fine baby-clothes, embroideries, sofa-cushions, paintings on silk for screens, panels, fans, etc. ; decorated china, *menus*, calendars, embroidered *portières* and curtains, rag-dolls and all kinds of preserves, cakes, and delicacies for the sick—these were the things which were placed upon sale in the Depositories of that day. And they still remain the staple articles to be found in the Exchanges.

In 1878 the New York Exchange for Woman's Work was organized, its object and business being to aid women who are reduced in circumstances to help themselves in any proper manner, and especially by maintaining in New York City a permanent place for the sale of their work. It was at this time that the Exchange idea really took root and became a power for good in the community, and from the impulse given by the society in New York there have sprung up in sixteen years throughout the United States seventy-five Exchanges using its By-laws, Rules, etc.

Some friends of the best of our Exchanges believe that the more completely the idea of charity is eliminated from the system the better it will be for the Exchange and for its workers. Upon the other hand, it is said that not more than two such Exchanges have ever paid expenses, and so far as the large cities are concerned, that in New Orleans is the only Woman's Exchange which has made a profit upon its operations. In their case a fund was given to them. The good done by such Exchanges cannot be measured by the actual sales of the Exchange ; in many instances the women who have succeeded well in disposing of their products through the Exchange have eventually found that they could do even better in regular business, and there are many instances in which a thriving business owed its origin to humble beginnings at some Woman's Exchange.

The Exchange is a benevolent society, and while it cannot as a society be self-supporting, through its educating influences many of its beneficiaries become self-supporting. If the Exchange accepted nothing but the highest grade of work in all its departments, and ran its business as a shop and charging the usual high commissions, etc., it might be made to pay. But the idea of the Exchange is to help just those women to whom the ordinary shop is closed, either because their work is not sufficiently good, or because they do not know how to adapt it to the tastes of the buying public.

The ideal Exchange trains women unaccustomed to work to compete with skilled laborers and those already trained. It accepts whatever work they may do if there is a chance of sale; criticises the work and indicates the vocation for which the applicant is best adapted. If the work is disposed of, present needs are provided for, also the means of continuing work, and if the criticisms and suggestions already given are heeded the new work offered for sale will be an improvement on that first brought. A large part of the time of a clerk at the Woman's Exchange in New York is taken up in writing letters of advice to persons whose work either cannot be accepted and put on exhibition by the Exchange, or when a suggestion as to color, finish, etc., will make it better. For instance, a girl sends in a lot of embroidered pen-wipers which show exquisite workmanship, but so crude a choice of colors as to render them eyesores; the Exchange sends them back with a letter giving advice as to color, and perhaps enclosing a sample of work that has proved successful. And so with the whole list of articles sold by the Exchange. The work is thus largely an educational one, and if the Exchange must be made self-supporting, this feature—perhaps its most valuable feature—must be dropped. The average shop-keeper has no time to give advice to beginners.

One important change for the better that has marked the influence of the Woman's Exchanges, where they have been properly conducted, has been the gradual diminution of false pride concerning work by women. To some extent the Exchange still appeals to women who wish to make money by stealth, so to speak, and as a rule the names of persons who send articles for sale are known only to the officers of the Exchange. So many thousands of refined women have learned to look upon the Exchange as a friend in adversity that this feeling of false pride is to some extent dying out. A woman may confess that she sends her embroideries and fine needle-work to the Exchange, although she might hesitate to have it known that her handiwork went to a regular shop. The Exchange is thus the opening wedge into a useful business life.

Many Exchanges were organized solely with the view of helping people in distress, and one or two stipulated in their circulars that the material they offered for sale came exclusively from women who had been in better circumstances. This stamped the Exchange's work as one of charity, and by so doing lessened its value. The moment it was considered a sign of poverty to make articles for the Exchange there was disinclination on the part of many women to try the Exchange at all. The daughter of a well-to-do family was found fault with by certain friends because she sent some of her own handwork to the New York Society of Decorative Art, and put her own name in the corner of a little water-color picture she exposed for sale. Her explanation was that she did it precisely because it was known that she did not need money. Other young women, who she knew were in sad straits for money, would follow her example, but would not take the lead.

The extent to which Woman's Exchanges have helped people in need may be seen from the following figures: In twelve years the New York Exchange for Woman's Work has paid out $417,435; in eight years the Cincinnati Exchange has paid $175,130; the New Orleans Exchange, in ten years, $173,223; the Boston Exchange, in six years, $148,588; the St. Louis Exchange, in eight years, $55,000; the San Francisco Exchange, in five years, $50,000; the Providence Exchange, in ten years, $48,400; the Richmond Exchange, in seven years, $27,324; the St. Joseph Exchange, in six years, $19,250. A moderate estimate of the amount of money paid to women by the different Exchanges of the country during the last ten years, is one million dollars; and what this represents in comfort and happiness, only those who have had something to do with such institutions have any adequate idea.

In 1893 the New York Exchange for Woman's Work sold $48,966, of which sum $26,316 was for fancy-work, embroideries, and needle-work; $12,199 was for cake; $2,116 for preserves; and $8,334 came from orders for sewing or fancy articles, cakes, preserves, etc. The number of consignors among whom this $48,966 was distributed was about two thousand, so that, upon the average, each woman received nearly $25. This seems a small sum, but, on the other hand, it must be remembered that in many a home a little surplus, even of $20 or $30, at the command of the woman of the family, means comfort, where penury would prevail without it. This sum of twenty dollars may represent the half-penny of Mr. Micawber's famous illustration: that if one's income be eleven pence half-penny, and the expenditure a shilling, the result is abject misery; while, if the income is a shilling, and the expenditure eleven pence half-penny, the result is absolute bliss. Twenty dollars in some country-homes where money is scarce though food may be plenty, may pay off the taxes of the year. It may make the difference of stout shoes for a delicate child; it may furnish school-books to children whose whole after-life may be dwarfed by their need; it might give magazines and weekly papers to people starving for some glimpse of the world beyond their village.

So many thousands of intelligent women would like to know how they may make a few dollars for pressing needs, that some account of the methods and aims of the two institutions in New York, which accept and sell woman's home-work upon commission, may be of interest here. With the older and better known of these institutions, the Exchange for Woman's Work, the fundamental purpose was to help only persons in distress, women and girls in actual need, and this principle is still paramount.

A serious obstacle in carrying out this purpose, has been the dishonesty of women who took advantage of the Exchange to earn money which they really did not need. The Exchange is not designed to furnish women with pin-money, and all consignors are required to state that they need the money for the support of themselves or of those dependent upon them. As the Exchange takes consignments from all parts of the country—the largest proportion of its consignors living out of the city, and some of them so far off as California—it is often difficult to find out the true condition of many of the women who sell a good deal of work through the Exchange. When cases of violation of the rules are proven, the name is crossed off the books. One woman who kept her carriage, sent work to the Exchange until the truth was discovered. This principle of the Woman's Exchange has been the subject of much criticism, as unbusiness-like, and apt to stamp all its consignors as objects of charity. They are not objects of charity, say the managers, inasmuch as they pay a fee to enter their work and a commission of ten per cent. upon all sales. Moreover, after several experiments in the direction of allowing any woman to enter articles for sale, it was decided to follow the original plan, and try to make sure that only women who needed the money for their support should profit by its aid. If no restrictions were insisted upon, the well-to-do woman, often with better taste and better means, would crowd out the work of her poorer sister.

The Woman's Exchange, so far as its means allow, tries to help every poor woman, no matter how little she knows or can do. During the hard times of 1893–1894, when hundreds of women brought up in luxury were thrown upon their own resources through the failure of father or husband, numberless instances have been presented to the officers of the Exchange in which women who needed and asked for work, knew nothing that could be turned to account. To meet such cases a Suggestion Committee was organized and an Information Bureau. Any woman can come before the Suggestion Committee and tell her story; the members listen, put questions, and make suggestions. As an instance of what the Suggestion Committee can do, a young girl came before this body and confessed that she could do nothing, not even sew; she added, in a hopeless tone, that the only thing she knew about was taking care of dogs; she lived in the country, a few miles from New York, and dogs were her pets.

"You can take care of dogs, and know all about them?" said a member of the committee. "Well, perhaps we can send you some dogs." And now this young woman makes quite a little income by the care of pet dogs and birds that patrons of the Exchange leave in her hands when they go to Europe or out of town.

The managers try to make New Yorkers feel that when they need the services of a woman, they may find what they want by applying at the Exchange. Thus a number of women are always registered there as ready to do something for which they are peculiarly fitted. One young girl will read to invalids at fifty cents an hour; another will do shopping, and some do marketing for large families; another will take care of children, or dust valuable bric-à-brac, etc.

A good business has also sprung up in violets, which several of the women connected with the Exchange raise at their country homes and send into the city every day.

Most women know how to cook, or think they do, and so the restaurant and kitchen of the Exchange, where luncheon is served from twelve until three o'clock every day, have become important parts of the institution. Through suggestions given by an accomplished cook scores of women have here learned how to make bread, cake, and fancy dishes that will sell in competition with bakers' products. There is a fine field for such industry in almost every small village. In one village of five hundred inhabitants a young girl, who came to the Exchange knowing nothing, now makes and sells forty loaves of bread daily, besides

Christ Blessing Little Children.
Design for Stained Glass Window, by Helen Maitland Armstrong

cake. Another woman, under similar circumstances, sells one hundred loaves a day.

One woman earned five hundred dollars in one year from the sale of jellies and pickles, and still another does equally well with mince-meat. A woman who had to get credit for a barrel of flour, succeeded in selling ten dollars' worth of bread and rolls every day.

It has been said that the consignors of the Woman's Exchange received, in 1893, an average of nearly twenty-five dollars apiece ; but of course many women who devote most or all of their time to the work, make more important sums. Thus, four hundred and eighteen dollars were paid to one consignor for decorated china ; one woman received for screens and decorated frames, one thousand one hundred and five dollars ; children's wrappers brought five hundred and forty-eight dollars to one consignor ; chicken jelly, pies, and such dainties to the amount of one thousand two hundred and forty-seven dollars was bought from another. These figures do not, however, represent profit, as the cost of the material has to be deducted.

When the managers of the Exchange find one of their former consignors established in a prosperous business of her own, they are proud of the achievement, and they have a right to be. Some consignors have become manufacturers upon a small scale, one woman, who devised and patented a species of perfumed pin-ball made in imitation of an apple, having established a sale for it all over the country.

With the single exception of the Woman's Exchange of New Orleans, it does not appear that such Exchanges have been made self-supporting. Enough has been said of the work in New York to show why this can never be the case there. The education and helping of women to do work for which they may be fit, costs money and brings in nothing to the Exchange. The expenses of the New York Woman's Exchange during 1893 were, in round numbers, twenty thousand dollars, of which only seventy-five hundred dollars came from the commissions upon sales and the profits of the lunch-room ; the remaining twelve thousand five hundred dollars were derived from sources which a business house would not recognize as legitimate — such as donations, subscriptions, readings, concerts, etc.

Some critics of the Woman's Exchange system, as typified in that of New York, the most prosperous of all such institutions, believe that if the idea of charity could be eliminated ; if the word "gentlewoman" could be dropped from the reports ; if the by-law restricting the consignors to self-supporting women could be done away with, together with the idea that the Exchange is to help women only when misfortune comes, the results would be beneficial. They would do away with donations and charity balls as means of raising money, and they would take all articles offered for sale, no matter what the makers' circumstances, provided the articles were sufficiently good. In other words, they would place the Exchange upon a purely business basis, in the belief that it would thus cease to be "a palliative for the ills of the few," and become "a curative for the sufferings of the many."

On the other hand, those who believe in the Exchange idea hold that as the Exchanges have a benevolent and educational, as well as a commercial, end in view, they are warranted in accepting such subsidies as the public may contribute. Why should their beneficiaries be considered objects of charity any more than those who obtain their proficiency through any of our endowed institutions, colleges, etc.? It is true that those who come to the Exchange for training and assistance are handicapped by the necessity of supporting themselves, and are compelled to gain late in life the special training which in early youth seemed unnecessary. That the institution limits its assistance to a special class is as legitimate as it is for others to limit their field of usefulness to helping the blind, or the deaf mutes. From the political economist's view, it is as necessary to help the needy gentlewoman as it is any other member of society, and the problem of how to do it is one of the most difficult. It is not strange, therefore, if the methods adopted to accomplish this result are often the subject of debate. There is little in the way of precedent, because, while many understand and sympathize with the needs of the poor gentlewoman, there are few who have had the courage to initiate any scheme for her help. Many of the criticisms now made of the Exchange system would be heard no more had it its own building or an endowment fund, such as similar institutions have.

The Society of Decorative Art of New York was organized in 1879, virtually upon this latter basis. Its object is to provide a place for the exhibition and sale of art work, the diffusion of a knowledge of such work among women, and their training in artistic industries. Its managers try to induce art workers to master thoroughly the details of some kind of decoration of commercial value; to suggest to those who have worked without success some practical direction for their labor; to enter into business relations with manufacturers and importers, and obtain orders from dealers in decorated pottery and porcelain, cabinet-work, draperies, embroideries, and other articles of household art. The Society receives and sells potteries, china, tiles, plaques, embroideries, hangings and curtains, decorated table and other house linen, articles for infants' wardrobes, painted panels, fans, decorated *menus*, invitations, etc. A charge of ten per cent. is made by the Society upon all sales.

Thus it will be seen that in practice the Society differs but little from the Woman's Exchange. It undertakes to do less, but there are no restrictions regarding the circumstances of the consignor. As with the Exchange, consignors are known by number and not by name.

The Society maintains a large workroom in which orders for sewing and embroidery are executed, the receipts from this source in 1893 being about twenty-five thousand dollars, and most of the money going to women much in need of it. One order made up was for a layette costing two thousand five hundred dollars. In one year, seven thousand and forty-one articles were sent in by consignors, of which number one thousand nine hundred and twenty-four were declined as not up to the standard of the Society. The sum of sixteen thousand five hundred and twenty-eight dollars was paid to consignors. The largest amount paid to one person was five hundred and twenty-one dollars for baby-wrappers; the next largest was four hundred and forty-two dollars for frames and doilies made by a woman seventy years old.

The Society maintains a Committee on Aid to Workers, through which many women utterly destitute receive designs and materials. The advantage of having a specialty has been widely recognized. One young woman has devoted herself for several years to making fancy penwipers. Another organized a regular business in linen sachets, employing assistants, and sending out her work put up in satin-lined boxes. With the

The Rules of the New York Exchange. 35

help of the receipts she was able to pay the expenses of a medical student through the entire course.

With regard to decorative work, needle-work, and embroidery done for the regular shops as a means of getting a livelihood, such work is wretchedly paid and not to be relied upon as permanent. Most of the large houses making a specialty of such material employ their own force of girls, who work under the eye of forewomen, thus insuring a certain uniformity necessary when work is sold in large quantities. When pieces of embroidery are bought from outsiders the price is often at starvation-rates. One woman who receives twenty dollars at the Woman's Exchange for a certain kind of embroidered cushion cannot get more than eight dollars for the same thing in the regular shops. The wages paid by the shops to work-women range from two dollars a week to girls learning the business, to eight dollars a week for experts. Only the forewomen ever receive more than that, and the hours are from 8 A.M. to 6 P.M.

It is a common thing for the New York Woman's Exchange to send detailed information as to methods and results to persons in other cities who may desire to establish similar exchanges, and last winter one of the officers of the Exchange was sent to a Southern city to organize the business of a new exchange. The following rules of the New York Exchange will give further insight into the methods pursued, and may be of interest to those who think of trying this notable help to working-women :

1. We receive work through a subscriber to the funds of the Society to an amount not less than five dollars for the current year.

2. Each subscriber of five dollars may enter the work of three (3) persons for one year.

3. Our commission is ten per cent. on the price received.

4. All work is received subject to the approval of the Managers.

5. Wax and feather flowers, hair, leather, spatter and splinter, and cardboard work, are too perishable and unsalable to be accepted.

6. Articles will not be registered until express and mail charges have been paid on them. Articles are registered between the hours of 11 A.M. and 4 P.M. Packages left at other hours must be marked by consignor, with name, address, and price.

7. Consignors must call or send for their articles at the expiration of one year from the date of their entry. If not sent for within a month after that time, the Society will not hold itself responsible for them. No articles can be withdrawn between December 15th and 27th. Articles cannot be re-entered. Articles sent for by a consignor must be described.

8. The Society does not hold itself responsible for losses, having taken all reasonable precautions against fire and theft.

9. All letters containing information about articles sent to the Exchange should be addressed to the Society, with stamp enclosed for reply.

10. Articles which ladies are obliged to part with are received only upon the recommendation of an officer of the Society, and under the rules which are applied to other consignors.

11. In the cake and preserve department there is a standard, and none can enter cake or preserves without first sending samples of their work. Pickles, preserves, and jellies are sampled every year.

12. No preserves are received before October 1st or after April 1st.

13. No worsted goods are received after June 1st, until October 1st.

14. Prices put upon articles cannot be changed during the year.

15. Consignors desiring articles returned by mail must take all risk, and must give three days' notice for withdrawal of any article.

16. Work is not received from gen-

tlewomen whose circumstances do not make it necessary for them to dispose of their handiwork.

17. Cash payments are made on Saturdays to consignors in the Cake and Preserve Department, and on Wednesdays to all other consignors.

18. Consignors must put their own prices upon the articles they send.

VI.—THE TRAINED NURSE.

THE profession of nursing the sick, according to the advanced ideas now taught in all training-schools for nurses, scarcely dates back more than twenty years, and yet already employs a small army of intelligent, earnest women, whose value the community is learning to appreciate better every year.

England preceded America in this work. When, at the close of the Crimean War the gratitude of England to Florence Nightingale for her remarkable work among the stricken thousands in the hospitals of Scutari, took the shape of a subscription of two hundred and fifty thousand dollars, she refused to receive the money, but requested that it might be used to found the first English training-school for nurses. The institution was opened in 1860, in connection with St. Thomas's Hospital, in London.

It was in 1873 that Miss Richards, the first woman to obtain a diploma as a trained nurse in this country, was graduated from the New England Hospital, in Boston. Bellevue Hospital, in New York, opened its training-school the same year. Since that time physicians and surgeons have been so unanimous and so strong in their commendation of the work done by trained nurses that no hospital staff is considered complete without such assistance; in fact, the importance and absolute necessity of trained nurses are now so widely recognized that no hospital work seems possible without them, and the public has found employment for all the nurses who can be spared from hospital duties.

The condition of affairs in some public institutions before training-schools for nurses were in existence may be inferred from a report concerning the Charity Hospital, on Blackwell's Island, New York City, in 1874, the year before a training-school was organized there. To quote: "In the fever ward (forty beds) the only nurse was a woman from the workhouse, under a six-months' sentence for drunkenness, who told the patients the story of a most shameful life." There were no chairs with backs in the hospital; round wooden benches were the only seats, and the only pillow one of chopped straw. In the fever ward the only bathing conveniences consisted of one tin basin, a piece of soap, and a ragged bit of cloth passed from bed to bed.

A transformation was brought about when the trained nurse appeared, with her neat uniform, her eternal vigilance concerning neatness, order, and cleanliness, and her methodical system of work. Almost every large hospital in this country now maintains a training-school for nurses in connection with its regular wards.

The qualifications needed by the ideal trained nurse are perhaps those of tact, common-sense, and general intelligence rather than physical strength. Of course the last is important, but the occupation is not so exhausting as

The Qualifications of a Good Nurse.

many people imagine. The trained nurse, whether her work is in a hospital or in a private family, usually obtains a sufficient amount of sleep and recreation; if she neglects such precautions her employers as well as herself are likely to suffer.

It is sometimes said that the profession of nursing—and it is really a profession in its ideal condition—is an unpleasant one because of the scenes of suffering and sorrow to which the nurse must become accustomed. The physician has a better chance to recover from the depression he may feel by constant acquaintance with trouble and sorrow; for he, of course, sees a great many cases in which the ailment is but trifling, and when his day's work is over he has his family life and outside distractions. The nurse is tied down more or less to the sick-room, or at least to the companionship of people who are anxious and concerned only for the patient.

Moreover, in most cases the trained nurse is sent for only when there is danger and the case is a serious one, involving work that cannot be done by the members of the family. The trained nurse is often the one upon whom falls the duty of remaining up at night with the patient, and that is the most exhausting part of the task.

Nevertheless, notwithstanding these drawbacks, almost all nurses worthy of the name acquire a certain love and enthusiasm for their work, and by their cheerful bearing bring into the afflicted family just that help which no one personally interested in and anxious about the patient can give. The true nurse takes a scientific interest in every case she is called to, quite as much as the physician in charge, for she sees more of the patient than he, and is thus often a valuable aid to the physician.

Next to general intelligence and sound health the requirements of most of the training-schools include tact and pleasant manners. In a vast number of cases the atmosphere of the sick-

The Nurse.

room requires a calm, pleasant helper more than medicine, and in fully one-third of the women who fail to obtain diplomas as nurses, lack of personal magnetism and tact is the cause. So fully has this been recognized that at all the training-schools in the larger cities no nurse is accepted as a pupil until she has passed through a term of probation, usually of from two to three months. This is also the reason why few schools accept students who are under twenty-five years of age; they have not the settled character needed for the work.

The course of training in the New York schools is two years, during which the nurse serves in the hospital to which the school is attached. No charge is made for tuition or board, the nurse practically giving her services as assistant nurse, and, during the last year, taking her share of the regular work of the hospital. Classes are held daily in every duty which a nurse may expect to be called upon to do. In the best schools, such as those attached to the New York Hospital, Bellevue, St. Luke's, and Mount Sinai, the school life of nurses is a pleasant one, and hospital positions are much sought after by graduates. About two hundred nurses a year are graduated from the training-schools of New York. There are in all nearly two hundred schools for trained nurses now in this country, of which the largest are in Philadelphia and Chicago. So many schools have been organized within the last two years that it is difficult to give statistics regarding the number of trained nurses graduated yearly, but it is safe to say that it does not fall far short of two thousand. As yet the supply of trained nurses is not equal to the demand, and, if anything, the demand seems to be growing faster than the ability of the schools to turn out graduates.

Until within the last year the average pay of trained nurses who are graduates of well-known schools was twenty-one dollars a week. Such is the demand for their services, however, that this rate of pay has been recently increased, and it is now twenty-five dollars a week. This seems a liberal salary, considering the comparatively short apprenticeship needed and the fact that the training costs nothing. But it must be remembered that no nurse can work steadily through the year. Most physicians do not believe that a nurse ought to work more than seven or eight months out of the year, taking a rest in proportion to the length of time she has served a patient.

The disadvantages and drawbacks to this profession are not sufficient to prevent far more applicants presenting themselves than the best schools can accommodate—five apply where one is taken—but they are very real, notwithstanding. In the first place, a trained nurse, unless she has family connections and a home with relatives, can have very little home-life. She may be away upon duty for a night, a week, a month or a year. Usually she has a room somewhere in which she stores her belongings, and to which she goes for rest when her patients recover. Naturally, this room cannot be in an expensive boarding-house, and is usually in some building given up to cheap lodgings, so that the nurse is compelled to take her meals outside.

Another very serious drawback is that although a nurse does not obtain her diploma until she is twenty-three years old, her efficiency begins to wane soon after she is forty. At one of the large training-schools in New York, where many well-to-do people go for nurses, three-fourths of the requests are for young women; a woman past forty frequently lacks the physical vitality required for long night vigils or other hard work connected with nursing. It might be supposed that the experienced nurse would find occupation in hospital-wards, where her experience would be of value; but the practice in surgery changes so rapidly from year to year that it is necessary for her to go through another course of training in order to do hospital work.

Thus it is frequently the case that a nurse who has served fifteen years finds herself put aside in favor of a younger woman. The business is still so recent that there may be said to be as yet few veterans in the ranks, but the problem of how to dispose of or provide for nurses past fifty is a serious one, which has already engaged the attention of those interested in the profession. Fortunately, the experience gained by most trained nurses during their fifteen years of activity is such as to make them often invaluable as matrons of charitable institutions or superintendents of homes, and fits them for any other position in which they may have a number of children or women to look after. It should also be said that many nurses obtain permanent positions in families of wealth, where they have no more arduous duty than to superintend the nurses under them. An instance is cited in which a trained nurse who was sent from this country to Europe, found that her sole work was to make sure that the petted daughter of a millionnaire never went out in damp weather without overshoes.

The chief reasons why many intelligent women, fully competent to begin the study of medicine, enter a school for nurses instead, are, in the first place, that the training costs nothing, many of the best schools paying a salary of from ten dollars to sixteen dollars a month to the pupils, in addition to free board and tuition; and, secondly, the trained nurse is almost certain to find employment as soon as she graduates. It is notorious that competent women physicians are often years before they attain an income sufficient for their support; and the college course of four years costs from two to three thousand dollars. On the other hand, the woman physician has the more interesting life of the two, and when the nurse has outlived her greatest usefulness, the woman physician is just beginning to reap her harvest. In this connection it should be said that while some trained nurses do enter a medical college and graduate—many medical students acting as nurses, in order to obtain money for their college expenses—the best authorities do not recommend women medical students to begin in the nurses' schools, their chief reason being that

In the Children's Ward.

whereas the nurse is trained to carry out the physician's directions, always subordinating her own opinion, the physician must take an independent view of the case. The two modes of looking at a case are radically different, and experience has shown that the woman guests, owing to the fact that they have sometimes to attend cases of contagious disease. Their social acquaintances, even in a large city, are not likely to be many, because the training-schools insist that a pupil must give up all idea of social recreation ; pupils are

Taking the Morning Temperature and Pulse.

who has been graduated as a trained nurse often lacks independence as a physician and willingness to assume responsibility.

One of the great needs of the trained nurses in every large city is a home club where the nurse, released from duty, may find comfort and pleasant acquaintances. In the best boarding-houses nurses are not received as allowed one afternoon a week away from the hospital, and a two weeks' vacation. A nurses' co-operative club-house is one of the great needs of the profession, and after that a pension fund for the support of nurses disabled by age, or perhaps by disease contracted while upon duty.

Those who imagine that the chief duties of the trained nurse, whether in private or hospital practice, are to take the temperature of patients and make delicacies in the way of jellies, broths, and eggnog have but small knowledge of the real duties devolving upon the competent nurse. Even the use of the familiar thermometer, when the morning and evening temperature of a ward full of patients has to be taken, requires patience and time. The importance attached to a clinical thermometer by those in ignorance of its office approaches a superstition. Patients will close their lips tightly upon it. Their eyes roll wildly around the room. They believe that the tube contains some mighty gas or a metal of mysterious power. "There ain't much taste to it, docther," said one of these credulous fellows, "but I s'pose it's *turrible sthrong*."

An excellent idea of the routine work done by the trained nurse may be obtained from the following extract from the journal of a head nurse at the Charity Hospital, New York, quoted by Mrs. Frederic Rhinelander Jones in an excellent article entitled "The Training of a Nurse," which appeared in *Scribner's Magazine* for November, 1890:

"Time: 7.30 A.M.

"Scene: Ward 3, Medical. Beds all unmade, a few patients up—these have faces washed and hair combed—the majority in bed with this duty still to be performed for them. A part of the floor at the front of the ward has been scrubbed. Mary, one of my prison helpers, is washing dishes at the table, and Bridget, the other, is taking soiled clothes from a large can and sorting them for the wash.

"The atmosphere contains none too much oxygen; this can be explained by saying that the night-nurse is finishing her work in one of the other wards, and the patients in her absence have taken the precaution to close all of the windows for fear of taking cold. After giving an order for the windows to be let down, I take up the night notes and read:

"'Murphy—Died at 3 A.M.

"'Ryan—Temperature, 108°; pulse, 120; respiration, 30. Antifebrine, grains iij., and other medicines given as ordered. Poultice applied last at 6 A.M.

"'Patient passed a very restless night.'

"And so on, through the other cases in the ward. These notes are signed by the night nurse, who now comes in with the keys, looking pretty well fagged.

"'Good-morning · I am sorry I have kept you waiting for the keys, but I have been so busy I could not get down sooner. Had a death in Ward 4, as well as the one here, and a patient in Ward 6 suffering from delirium tremens, besides the ordinary work.'

"I now go over to where my assistants are putting on their caps and aprons and getting together the things necessary for work. Miss W. and Miss A. are here, but where is Miss H.? Miss W. answers:

"'She was called up last night to go on the maternity service. The superintendent missed you, and asked me to tell you that another nurse could not be spared to-day.'

"Oh, dear, thirty-two patients in the ward, and five of them so helpless that they have to be fed and cared for like babies, two pneumonia cases, and the usual number of phthisical and rheumatic subjects. Well, well, grumbling won't do the work, so we'll have to make the best of it.

"Each of my assistants, armed with a pile of clean sheets and pillow-cases, proceeds to the lower end of the ward and commences the task of getting beds made, while I go to write the list of clothes for the laundry. Bridget counts the clothes while I stand by and take down the number of each of the different articles. This done, they are tied in large bundles and sent to the washhouse.

"Now the medicines are to be given out. I measure and prepare them, while a convalescent patient carries them round to those in bed. My list is a long one, and it takes fully thirty-five minutes before they are all distributed, the bottles wiped off, and the medicine closet put in order. My next move is to take a list of medicines which need to be renewed, and leave it ready for the doctor's signature. It is now twenty-five minutes past eight, and Miss A. and Miss W. are making as good progress as possible at their respective sides ; for it must be remembered that a nurse has often to stop what she is doing to attend to the wants of some particular patient, or to carry out an order if the time is due.

"The 'railroad beds' * are still unmade. Occasionally we have a convalescent patient who can do this part of

The Surgical Ward at Bellevue.

the work very well. We had one in this ward last week, but alas, for the frailty of human nature, she showed a disposition to quarrel with the other patients on very small pretexts, so she was dismissed. With a rueful thought of what might have been, I go to work at the beds. A patient goes ahead and strips them for me. We work with all our might, and they are finished at ten

* A " railroad-bed " is one that is unoccupied during the day, and therefore, as it were, "shunted" and only rolled out at night. They stand close together in the middle of the ward.

minutes past nine. The side beds, too, are nearly finished. This part of the work necessarily takes much longer, as sick patients have to be placed in chairs and wrapped up in blankets, or, if they are too weak, lifted into other beds, so that their own can be made.

"My next work is to take morning temperatures; when I have finished this I see a large tin can standing near my table. It contains crackers, butter, eggs, and sugar. These have to be put away in their proper place, and the quantity noted. Now, I must write my diet-sheet, and order the supplies necessary for to-morrow. It is twenty-five minutes past nine, the beds are all made, the stands in order, the floor swept, and the table scrubbed. The junior nurses are about through with washing faces and combing heads, and it is now high time that I should make a round of the ward and find out if there is any change in the patients' condition to which the doctor's attention should be called.

"While this has been going on the gruel and milk have been standing on the table, and the distribution of this falls to my share to-day also, as I have no senior nurse. Each bed-patient who cares for it is served with a portion on a tray; afterward the walking patients seat themselves at the table and take theirs. Now the doctors come in to make their morning visit, the house-doctor is told of any special complaints; he examines these patients, also any new ones who may not yet be under treatment, and leaves the new orders on my book.

"While doing this work all the morning I have been trying to keep an eye on what my helpers are doing, and now take this time to make a thorough inspection of all parts of the ward, bath-room included. In the meantime the special diet has been divided among the patients needing it most. At eleven o'clock tonics are given out, afterward eggnogs and milk-punches are made and distributed.

"We now begin to breathe freely—the worst pressure is over if we get no new patients. Our hopes along that line are doomed to disappointment, for the helpers from the women's bath-room now announce the arrival of two new patients, and Miss W. disappears to superintend their bathing.

"I am congratulating myself on not having a 'stretcher case' at any rate, when two men come in with one. Miss A. quickly places screens round a bed, and a rubber sheet over the clean bed-clothes. The woman is lifted on the bed, and her temperature, pulse, etc., taken. Her own clothes are soon removed, and a warm sponge-bath given and hair combed. These operations have effected a wonderful change in her appearance, and she now looks a little more like a Caucasian, whereas, before the bath, she might have belonged to one of the darker races of mankind.

"The doctor is notified that there are three new patients in the ward. It is twelve o'clock; Miss A. and I go to dinner, and leave Miss W. to superintend the patients' noonday meal, and give out medicines afterward. We return at one o'clock, and Miss W. goes, with the right to remain off duty till four o'clock.

"The ward is now to be swept again and put in order for the afternoon. This is hardly accomplished when two huge bundles of clothes are carried in, and in ten minutes' time two more. These have to be sorted and counted. Before we proceed to the folding of them the afternoon milk and other extras are given out. That done and the table cleared, we fold the clothes as quickly as we can. In due time this is finished, Miss A. is making a poultice in the bath room, and I am putting the clothes in the closet, when someone calls 'Nurse, nurse!' I turn to see where the sound comes from, and notice several patients pointing to a bed in the far corner of the ward. I hurry down and find the patient's clothes saturated with blood—a hemorrhage from the lungs. Screens are immediately placed around the bed, cracked ice given, and the doctor summoned. He comes at once, the flow of blood seems to have ceased, medicine is ordered, and the doctor goes. The patient's clothes are now changed very carefully, and she is made as comfortable as possible. The screens are just put away when another stretcher is brought in, and Miss W., who has now returned, gives the usual treatment.

"It is time for the afternoon tonics, and eggnogs and punches are again distributed; after this I take advantage of a few spare minutes to enter the names and addresses of patients in a book kept for the purpose. Discharged patients are also marked off.

"The patients have supper between half-past four and five. At half-past five Miss A. retires from the ward, the remaining time till half-past seven being hers to rest. In the meantime the doctor has been in and left a few orders.

"The giving out of the evening medicines falls to me, while Miss W. attends to the patients' needs in other ways. If I had a fourth nurse I might be relieved from duty; but it cannot be thought of now. This is the evening for carbolizing the side beds; the helpers do this, while we follow and restore things to order. The rest of the time till half-past seven is spent in making patients comfortable for the night, and writing down new orders and notes on the patients' condition for the night nurse. We are quite willing to deliver her the keys when she comes in, and bid her good-night, while we go home tired enough to sleep soundly."

VII.—WOMEN AS PHYSICIANS.

THE profession of medicine as a vocation for women has lost many of the disadvantages which, thirty or forty years ago, rendered it more than unpleasant for a woman.

When Dr. Elizabeth Blackwell applied for a medical diploma, in 1848, and was refused by a dozen colleges, it was thought highly improper, not to say indecent, for a woman to study medicine. The fact that there are now no less than a thousand women engaged in medical practice in America, shows that there is a demand for women's services in this field.

What the women medical students of to-day owe to the pioneers in this field, only those familiar with the events of forty years ago have any idea. Medicine was not an absolutely new field for women, even before those days, but women doctors practised without a diploma. During the first half of the century Harriet K. Hunt, of Boston, who had studied with a private physician, supported herself for many years as a practising physician in Boston. When laws were passed making medical practice without a diploma a misdemeanor, such practitioners were debarred.

The entrance of women into the medical profession must, therefore, be reckoned from the time when a woman first obtained admission to a regular college, to pursue the course of study required by law as a preparation for the degree which carried with it legal authority to practise, and the professional recognition as a physician which the degree confers. This dates from the admission of Elizabeth Blackwell to the Geneva Medical College.

This pioneer M.D. among the women of this country, was born in England and came to the United States as a child in 1838. Her father failed soon afterward. Thrown upon her own resources, and with younger brothers and sisters to look after, Elizabeth determined to study medicine.

She had happened to take a position as governess in the family of a South Carolina physician, Dr. John Dixon, and became absorbed in the medical books of his library. She needed money, and the salary paid to governesses was pitifully small. Dr. Dixon offered no encouragement to the extraordinary plans of the young girl, but advised her what to read. Her earnings went for books, which she read to such purpose that, when she finally obtained a position as governess in the family of Dr. S. H. Dixon, of Charleston, S. C., he admitted her among his students and helped her to begin regular medical studies.

In 1844, Elizabeth Blackwell considered that she knew enough to enter some regular medical school, and, moreover, her aim being a diploma and practice, it was necessary that she should pass through a school to obtain it. She soon found that all doors were closed to her. Her request was commonly declined upon the ground that it was "without precedent." One of the physicians under whom she had studied, advised her to adopt male attire, but the idea was repulsive. She was not laboring for herself alone. Her next step was to apply to medical colleges in different parts of the country, accompanying her request with a certificate from several physicians, her teachers. Twelve colleges sent refusals. One of these was based upon "the dependent position assigned to women, as much by nature as by society;" another upon the fact "that it would be unbecoming and immoral to see a woman instructed in the nature and laws of her organism."

Elizabeth Blackwell. The first woman practising physician.

From one only, the Geneva, N. Y., Medical College, was a favorable answer received; and it was afterward learned that the Geneva Faculty were averse to granting the request, but referred the matter to the students, who, out of a spirit half-mischievous, half-chivalrous, voted in the affirmative. Elizabeth Blackwell followed the class that term, and never was better order observed. Such annoyances as she met with came from outside the college. Many of the Geneva boarding-houses refused to receive her. The epithet of "she-doctor" greeted her from all sides. But perseverance carried the day, and the "she-doctor" received her hard-earned diploma. That, however, was by no means the end of her troubles.

In order further to fit herself for active work, Dr. Blackwell went to Europe and passed six months in the Paris hospitals, and an equal time in London. In 1851 she returned to America and established herself in New York. At first physicians refused to receive her in consultation. House-owners either refused to lease apartments to her, or asked an exorbitant price, upon the ground that a woman doctor would be an injury to their property.

The young doctor's first years were passed in cruel isolation. Again her indomitable perseverance conquered. A few physicians of repute, chief among them Dr. Willard Parker, learning her worth and the extent of her medical attainments, met her in consultation. In 1852 she delivered a series of lectures to women upon hygiene and gymnastics, that were published in book form and did much for her reputation. The following year, thanks to a public subscription, a dispensary for women and children was founded, and in 1854 a charter was obtained for the New York Infirmary and Dispensary in Second Avenue, at the head of which Dr. Elizabeth Blackwell continued until her departure to England in 1878.

The experiment made by Dr. Elizabeth Blackwell in venturing to practise medicine, was repeated by her younger sister, Emily, four years afterward, and a few medical colleges opened their doors to women. But invariably, such pressure was put by the medical societies upon these colleges that they were soon closed again. Exclusion of women from all medical institutions became the settled policy. Separate colleges were, therefore, promptly established, Boston taking the lead in 1850, and Philadelphia following the same year.

Now began, however, the period of the greatest depression for the new movement. The first few women students had, to a certain extent, the advantages of the system organized for the instruction of men; they could find male physicians to give them private lessons, and a few small colleges might be induced to award them diplomas. The students who came immediately after them found the road harder. Reputable physicians were virtually forbidden by their associates, either to teach girls medicine in private, or at the colleges organized by women for women. The unfriendly tone of the profession merely reflected that of the public. Social and professional ostracism was the rule in regard to both students and teachers, and a movement so unpopular could not hope to attract the best class of women-students. While there was always a fair sprinkling among the early students of young women of character and intelligence, a large part of the classes were made up of unpromising material—women who had failed as nurses or teachers, and eccentric persons of all sorts. The colleges themselves were hampered, not only by poverty and the difficulty of obtaining teachers, but by this poor quality of the material offered. For years, while a degree could be obtained with great ease at such schools, a woman desiring anything deserving the name of a medical education had to supplement her college course by European study.

The woman who thinks of studying medicine to-day need fear neither the social ostracism of forty years ago, nor lack of competent instruction. There are seven medical colleges for women in the United States and two in Canada. The most important are the Woman's College of the New York Infirmary, the Woman's Medical College of New York (Homœopathic), and those of Philadelphia and Chicago. In the last ten years the New York Infirmary College has graduated ninety-three students, the Philadelphia College, two hundred and eighty-nine students, and the Chicago College, two hundred and ten students. The number of women now practising medicine in the United States has been recently estimated at about one thousand.

A far higher class of women now enter the medical colleges, and perhaps to this more than to anything else is due the greater favor with which women doctors have been received by the community within the last few years. The many literary colleges for women—Harvard Annex, Vassar, Smith, Mount Holyoke, Bryn Mawr, Wellesley—have called into existence a class of educated young women such as did not exist even twenty-five years ago.

The social influence of college training for women cannot be measured by the number of their graduates alone. It has raised the whole standard of education given in girls' schools, and has familiarized the community with the possibility and legitimacy of intellectual life for women. The instruction offered by the women's medical colleges and their requirements have been raised accordingly. It is but fair to add, however, that women do not yet enjoy the educational advantages of men in this field, and that there are still some social disadvantages attached to medicine as a profession for women.

There are two sides to medical education : the theoretical, given by the college, and the practical, given by the hospital. In the United States the colleges are independent institutions relying upon their own resources. The hospitals and dispensaries, on the other hand, are supported by the public. The colleges would be unable to support so immense a number of institutions, but they virtually have the entire use and control of them for purposes of medical study and instruction. Every ambitious graduate seeks a hospital post as a supplement to his college training. Every ambitious physician seeks a permanent connection with the hospitals. It is not too much to say that, almost without exception, eminence in any department of medicine—in practice, surgery, medical teaching, or writing—is founded on the wide experience due to such connections. The leaders of the profession everywhere are hospital workers. From this great field of post-graduate study, so essential to supreme excellence, women physicians are still practically excluded. There are a few instances where women have been admitted to subordinate positions as a matter of convenience, but as a rule women physicians are not eligible, either as resident or attending physicians, in any of our public hospitals and dispensaries. For actual experience they are still dependent on their private practice, and on the few and small institutions which they have built up for themselves. It seems but just that the graduates of colleges chartered by the State should be eligible to medical positions in State charities, and the active part taken by women in the support and management of our immense body of private charities should also entitle them to a share in the medical work.

In regard to the social aspect of medicine as a woman's profession, it may be said by some people that, even if women are competent to become good doctors, they will lose more than they gain. People will ask concerning the woman doctor, not, Is she capable? but, Is this fearfully capable person nice? Will she not upset our ideals of womanhood and the relations between the sexes? Can a woman-doctor be a womanly, lovable person? Can she marry? Can she have children? and, if so, will she take care of them? If not, what is she? "God," once declared a certain Boston physician, "never intended women to practise medicine;" and hence the inference that piety, if nothing else, demanded the exclusion of women from the Massachusetts Medical Society.

Absurd as all this may appear, social opinion is of importance here, for success in a professional career depends largely upon the taste of the community. There must be a readiness to consult women physicians, a willingness to educate them, and a sufficiently widespread desire on their part to be educated. If the social prejudice be too strong, no young woman will dare to study medicine, for should the fancy arise, it will be frowned upon as highly improper, like going upon the stage, or riding bareback. The fact, however, that many women do practise medicine and support themselves by it, shows that such prejudice is not prohibitory. Yet, the discussion is by no means closed, and any review of the field should take this factor into consideration. In the field of medicine, as in many others, the question of capacity is often outranked by the question of taste. It may be conceded that certain women make good doctors, to whom large numbers of their own sex are glad to go for advice and treatment. While this is freely admitted, the average man and woman are still apt to regard the woman doctor as a social anomaly. This feeling will be lived down in time, but that it now exists cannot be questioned.

Thousands of women earn their living by trades and professions. Teaching is almost monopolized by women, and no one contends that the foundations of society are liable to be upset. What is it, then, in the profession of medicine, which excites even to-day such bitter prejudice?

In the first place, the science of medicine has always been regarded as more or less of a mystery, involving things more or less secret and improper, and doubly so for a woman. In the next place, by a social fiction, it is assumed that the money-making employments of women are to be filled only while waiting for marriage, or as a resource in widowhood or desertion. Even such professional work as teaching is expected to be laid aside after a few years. Medicine differs from teaching and all other work for women in that it must be chosen deliberately and not as a makeshift or from temporary economic necessity. It requires serious and prolonged preparation, and must be entered upon at the age at which most women marry; it does not yield its best returns until middle-age is well reached, and must be adopted, if at all, for life. Hence it requires either celibacy for the sake of medicine, or such a readjustment of the usual domestic arrangements as shall make practice possible for married women. On the theory that work is a mere personal hardship, to be evaded whenever possible, and always implying for women a faint social disgrace, such objections to medicine are likely to prevail. But whatever real difficulties may lie in the way, that one at least should certainly disappear which is created by the half-avowed dictum : " No woman has any right to work who can get a man to support her."

To the question : " Is it possible for married women to practise medicine?" it may be answered that many women now practising have either married after entering upon medical practice, or were already married when they began. To what extent either their household or their practice may have suffered by the combination it is impossible to say. It is not even certain that the combination has influenced the size of their families. So far as statistics show, this remains at the average found in the families of professional men. The rearrangement of domestic work in the direction of simplifying the preparation of food and clothing, may eventually allow a woman to do something more valuable than sewing and cooking.

As to the wide-spread assumption that a woman physician must be inferior to other women in refinement and social culture, some excuse may be found in the conditions under which women were formerly obliged to study medicine. The obloquy heaped upon women students of medicine has been so great as to deter many women of refinement from a pursuit to which their natural bent inclined them. Conversely, many women have entered upon it without aptitude or understanding, attracted by the flavor of notoriety. Not these ignorant women, but society is to blame for the refusal to admit to a disciplined education and to subject to suitable tests the women who were really fitted ; this has resulted in the superficial education of the unfit.

The serious study of any scientific subject cannot be injurious to anyone. It has also been said that if the study of medicine did not injure a woman, its practice would develop an unfeminine amount of self-reliance; that society would have a feeble imitation of a man in place of its ideal woman. Certainly the woman doctor does acquire self-reliance and firmness ; vacillation would be as fatal to her reputation as to a man's. Her patients must know that beneath gentleness of manner there is no self-distrust or shrinking from responsibility. But all women who manage their own property and households, whether engaged in a profession or not, soon find out that they cannot afford to exercise the sweet womanly grace of helplessness.

Concerning what a woman who thinks of taking up medicine ought to know, the wider the culture the better. The course of four years is not an easy one, and should be supplemented by hospital practice if possible. If the conditions of graduation were made easier, a larger number of women might come forward to study, but the graduates would be unfit for work. The best of the women's colleges recognize that there is nothing to be gained by making the degree easy.

The isolated qualities essential to medical study are not hard to find ; the difficulty consists in uniting them in the same person. Thus the requisite energy and native intelligence is far from rare among American women. But the average grade of female education is still low and unfit as a preliminary training for medical study. Women from remote country places, from district schools, whose ideas of scientific medicine are of the vaguest, and who have been led to think of it only as an extension of the daily work of nursing sick relatives—these are the women who most frequently come forward.

They are often quite susceptible of being effectively educated, but they lack the facility born of inherited culture. Again, the practice of medicine involves the incessant adjustment of delicate social relations. These are more easily managed by people born into some kind of social position than by others. It too often happens that women coming forward to study medicine have the requisite energy and tenacity of purpose, but are lacking in the necessary refinement; while those who have inherited refinement are too much accustomed to soft living to brave the hardships of the profession. As the medical education of women rises in efficiency, dignity, and recognized importance, this difficulty, as already remarked, tends to disappear.

The pecuniary questions involved in the study and practice of medicine are not without importance. No one can study medicine without some resources to pay for instruction and support during the years of study. Some time ago a French journal estimated that the sum thus required would be, in France, about four thousand dollars. But, continued the writer, any girl possessed of 20,000 francs would have no difficulty in finding a husband, and therefore she would have no excuse for studying medicine.

In America, far more than in Europe, is the idea prevalent that a woman is always warranted in looking for support to some man—either father, brother, or husband—without equivalent in dowry or household labor. Partly for this reason, perhaps, women are inclined to choose occupations that are considered as temporary, and that may be dropped at any moment.

One consequence of the general admission of women to medicine might be a radical change now held concerning the relations of women to work. Women may honorably claim support upon one of three grounds—weakness, maternity, or useful work. But a subsistence accorded for either of the latter reasons is not bestowed gratuitously; it is very well earned. To assume that a woman who does all the work of the house, besides bearing and bringing up children, is being supported by her husband, is a singular injustice. She is earning her living quite as much as he is, and it will be seen, when this is once clearly understood, that she has a right to choose her method of work.

Many women have, of late years, studied medicine for the purpose of becoming missionaries in China and India. The fact that in these countries women are not allowed to be treated by men physicians at all, offers an obvious field. One graduate of a New York college has been established for some years in China, where she directs a large hospital, and has a large practice. She is a surgeon as well as physician, and has performed many important operations.

Of the recent New York graduates, many have returned to the country towns whence they came, and share the best patronage with the local physicians.

Several students who have made names for themselves have supported their families when business disaster overtook the husband.

It is said that among the present list of students are some whose fathers are physicians, who have decided to give their daughters a professional education, whether they may need it for self-support or not.

The heroism shown by many quite young girls in fighting for a medical education through extreme poverty, is often remarkable. Frequently they are obliged not only to support themselves, but also an invalid mother or other relative, by work accomplished in addition to studies quite sufficient to occupy all their time. Sometimes they teach; sometimes they keep boarding-houses for other students; sometimes they employ their vacations in nursing.

Good health is, of course, an essential for so arduous a life, but a physician need not be so strong physically as a nurse, a washerwoman, or a charwoman. She does not need the endurance of the woman who sews or stands behind a counter for fourteen hours a day. Medical practice is an active life, and therefore a healthy one. It is notorious how many women there are whose physical and mental health is injured by the dreary vacuity of the lives they lead, by enforced idleness, a life void of any keen interest, of invigorating intellectual discipline. Mere idleness is demoralizing. It is, as Dr. Maudsley says, the immediate parent of hysteria, insanity, and vice. The statistics gathered by the secretaries of New York's colleges for women, do not show that the average of graduates who give up practice from ill-health is any greater than among men.

What women doctors earn depends wholly, as in the case of men, upon their own capacity and energy. Taking the average earnings of the women graduates for the first ten years of practice, as estimated by a woman physician in a position to know the truth, it is said that their incomes do not fall below those of men. The great prizes of the medical world, the incomes of from $25,000 to $100,000 a year, are in the hands of men and are likely to remain so, for it must be remembered that a man's practice includes men, women, and children, whereas the woman-physician is almost always restricted to women and children.

Whether women will ever do as much, or as remarkable, work in this field as men, has but little to do with the question. The law of supply and demand may be trusted here as elsewhere, and if women doctors do not meet a real need they will die out. At present it is certain that a definite demand for their services does exist. And as an injustice is not small because it concerns a small number, if a single woman desires to consult a doctor of her own sex, and if one other woman desires to qualify herself to be that doctor, no obstacles ought to be placed in the way. No one has the right to decide what is or is not another person's proper sphere. The proper sphere for all human beings is the largest and the highest they are able to attain to, and what this is cannot be ascertained without complete liberty of choice.

VIII.—WOMEN AS LAWYERS.

THE law may be called the earliest and the latest profession open to women. The first woman lawyer of whom we have any knowledge is that Deborah of Israel, who judged under a palm-tree, and was not only the law-giver but the warrior and poet of her people. In Grecian history there was the brilliant Aspasia, who pleaded causes in Athens. Coming down to a later time, we have a number of Roman women who not only appeared in court, but argued cases in the Forum. Valerius Maximus, the historian, devotes a chapter to the Roman women who argued in the Forum.

The exclusion of women from the Roman bar came about in a singular manner. It appears that a certain woman lawyer, named Calphurnia, was very litigious and so annoyed the judges by her persistency and wrangling, that she was forbidden to practise at all. The law which excluded her was later construed as excluding all women, and at the beginning of the Christian era it was set forth in the Roman law that "it is not permitted that women and slaves should hold office." The only reason alleged for women's exclusion was the shrewishness of this Calphurnia.

During the Middle Ages and in modern times women have not appeared in the courts as lawyers. Until the year 1833 the question of allowing them to appear at the bar was not even raised in Europe. In that year Signorina Lidia Poët, having taken a course of study in the office of her brother, an advocate in Turin, applied for admission to the bar of that city. In a lengthy opinion the court denied her petition, alleging as a reason the old argument that it was not fitting or becoming to have a woman take part in the animated discussions of the Forum.

In 1886 Madame M. Emilie Kempin, who took a course of law in the University of Zurich and received a degree, made application to the Legislature, and, meeting with no success, decided to come to the United States. Two years afterward the question of admitting women to the bar came up in Belgium, when Marie Popelin was graduated in Brussels and applied for admission to the bar. The courts decided uniformly against her.

The only well-known woman who has attempted to make her way before the French bar is Mlle. Bilesco, who was graduated in Paris three years ago.

In England the question has not yet been raised, no woman having applied for admission to the bar, although there are several women who do work as attorneys and solicitors. The English custom of separating the pleading in court from the preparatory work of the lawyer makes it possible for women to carry on the latter part of the profession without formal admission to the bar. Woman has thus been excluded in modern Europe, and has not yet asked for admission to the bar in England.

There remains but one country outside of the United States where a woman practices law. This is Hawaii. Miss Almeda Hitchcock, the daughter of a lawyer in the Sandwich Islands, went through the Law School of Michigan University and was graduated in 1888. She went home to the Sandwich Islands, and upon presenting her license from the Michigan court was admitted to the bar and became her father's law partner. Soon after her admission to the bar, in March, 1889, she was temporarily appointed sheriff of Hilo. She discharged the duties of the office for three months, and was successful in keeping order and bringing a number of criminals to justice.

The history of the woman lawyer in the United States may be said to begin with the application of Mrs. Arabella ·A. Mansfield to the Supreme Court of Iowa, in 1869, for admission to the bar. The statute specified that persons applying for admission to the bar must be "white male citizens;" the Judge remarked that as to a certain extent words upon the statute-books implying the masculine gender might be construed to include women, he admitted her. Although Mrs. Mansfield was the first woman to be admitted to the bar of the country, there were other women who began the study of law about the same time or a little earlier.

The first law school to admit women was that of Washington University, in St. Louis. Miss Phœbe Couzins was the first applicant for admission to the school; but a Miss Barkaloo, who had tried unsuccessfully to obtain admission to the Columbia College Law School, was admitted at the same time, and was the first woman to be admitted to the bar in Missouri. This was in 1870.

The first college of the country to graduate a woman lawyer, for Miss Barkaloo was not graduated, was Union College of Law, in Chicago. Mrs. Ada H. Kepney was the first woman to graduate from a law school and obtain the degree of Bachelor of Laws. Although this was in 1870, she was not admitted to the bar until two years afterward, when an act was passed which made her admission possible.

There are now more than a dozen law schools that admit women, and probably many others would admit them if they were to apply.

The greatest number of women graduates from law schools hail from Michigan University, which has awarded diplomas to more than thirty. The Boston University Law School has also graduated a number of women. The three leading universities of the country—Harvard, Yale, and Columbia—have so far refused to admit women. The alleged reasons at Harvard was that if women were admitted to the Law School they must use the Law Library in connection with the men students, the force of which excuse is not very clear.

At Yale a certain Miss Jordan was admitted, and after going through the course obtained a degree in 1887. The next catalogue of Yale contained this significant clause: "It is to be understood that courses offered in this University are only open to the male sex, unless otherwise specifically stated." And the Dean of the Law School is said to have remarked that the clause was intended to prevent a repetition of the Jordan incident.

Mrs. Myra Bradwell, the wife of Judge James B. Bradwell, of Chicago, was the first woman to ask admission to the bar of Illinois. She passed the examination, but was refused upon the ground that she was a married woman. The matter was carried to the Supreme Court of Illinois, again rejected, and then taken to the United States Supreme Court, where the case was argued by Senator Carpenter, of Wisconsin. In 1873 another adverse decision was rendered.

Twenty-three States now admit women to the bar. In 1879 an Act of Congress was passed whereby women were admitted to the Supreme Court of the United States, and many women lawyers have already availed themselves of the privilege, several of them being married women. Some of the States, among them Massachusetts, New York, and Illinois, found it necessary to send women to the Legislature for an enabling act. Various reasons were assigned for this. Some of the States had statutes similar to that of Iowa, where the word " male " was used in describing the qualifications, and it was thought necessary that an act should be passed dropping the word " male " from the statute. Other statutes had the word " voters " in them. It was generally held that the act did not exclude people who were not voters, and that women might be admitted. The disabilities of married women were invoked as an obstacle. It was said, for instance, that as a married woman could not make a contract, it was not possible to admit her to the bar, because the practice of law requires the making of binding contracts.

At present there are no less than one hundred and twenty women lawyers in America, but the number of those who practise in the courts does not exceed two score. Many women do not practise at the bar, just as many men who are graduated as lawyers go into other professions or business, finding their legal knowledge of value elsewhere. There seems to be no particular kind of work especially adopted by women lawyers, but naturally they prefer office work. As a rule, women have succeeded fairly well, and they have been treated with much kindness by the male members of the bar and the judges.

Two women lawyers have published books in America. Mrs. Shay published the "Students' Guide to Common Law Pleading," and Mrs. Sawtelle published "Law Made Easy," and "The Law of Husband and Wife."

Women have also delivered many lectures upon law and some of them have given regular instruction. Miss Waugh, an Illinois lawyer, was for a time professor of Commercial Law in a business college in Rockford, Ill. Lassel's Seminary, at Auburndale, Mass., was the first school in the country to give a regular course of law to girl students. Miss Mary A. Greene delivered a course of lectures there on "Business Law for Women." Mrs. Bradwell, already mentioned, edited for a long time the *Legal News* of Chicago, and Mrs. Waite edits the *Chicago Law Times*. Mrs. Bradwell's daughter, herself a lawyer and the wife of a lawyer, as well as the daughter of two lawyers, has edited the last twelve volumes of the reports of the Appellate Court of Illinois. Her father, Judge Bradwell, says that while the reports bear his name, they are really the work of his daughter, Mrs. Bessie Bradwell Helmer.

Four years ago a regular law course for women was begun under the auspices of the University of the City of New York, the only Eastern college which has taken such a step. Last year three women were graduated from the University, and one of them has been admitted to the bar of New York.

The law does not, however, seem to attract a large number of women; for, notwithstanding the facilities offered, there are not now more than a dozen women law students at the University, counting all four classes. But these are serious students who expect to take degrees, and probably to practise law.

There are at the University nearly seventy young women who follow a series of law lectures given twice a week to women who wish to make themselves acquainted with legal matters. These lectures are given under the auspices of the Woman's Legal Educational Society.

In other States women seem to be more eager to accept the privilege. In Pennsylvania there is a law firm composed of a mother and four daughters, all actively engaged. San Francisco has a law club known as the "Portia," composed wholly of women, which meets once a week in the law-office of the Dean of the club, Mrs. Clara S. Foltz, owing to whose efforts women are now entitled to the privilege of attending the Hastings College of Law. The members of the club do not intend to become lawyers, but wish to obtain legal lore enough to make them intelligent guardians of their legal rights. From time to time eminent lawyers address the club, and women lawyers who visit the city are invited to lecture upon the rights of women before the courts.

Of course the same old objections made in the case of women doctors and women clergymen are used with regard to women lawyers. It is said that they have not sufficient strength for the hard work involved, that as married women they may not be able to give all their time to it, and that their work will be subject to interruptions; also that the scandalous causes frequently tried at the bar will prevent many women from doing the work of a man. There is, however, enough legal work free from exhaustive strain or from scandal, and requiring chiefly knowledge and accuracy.

Although women are welcomed by several religious denominations as pastors, and have preached for large congregations, the theological colleges do not as yet encourage women to enter the profession. It is nearly fifteen years since a woman was first settled over a congregation in New York State, but the growth of the movement is slow.

IX.—NEWSPAPER WORK AND PAY.

JOURNALISM is one business in which women beginners are paid equal rates with men, for almost all newspapers pay so much a column for the articles they accept, and it makes no difference whether a man or a woman is the writer.

Another reason why women sometimes plunge into reporting rather than into teaching or art work, is that it requires virtually no apprenticeship. Any clever girl with an aptitude for the profession can report a lecture, a meeting, or an interview, after a few months' practice, and she will be well paid for it if the style is smooth and the ideas brightly set forth. The teacher must have years of preparation, and even stenography and typewriting require months of practice before a bare living can be made.

Whether the chronicling of gossip and what is known as the Woman's Page in the Sunday newspaper was the cause or the effect of the appearance of women in newspaper offices, no one seems to know. At all events, women began to do regular reporting upon the great daily newspapers about twenty years ago, and now there are on the regular newspaper staffs at least fifty women in New York City alone who make a living by writing for the press. They go about their work as systematically as men, they have a club of their own, and if there are any branches of reporting that woman cannot do, they are not ready to admit it. In some departments women are naturally at home. So long as the newspapers give elaborate accounts of social events, such as weddings, receptions, etc., a woman will be needed.

All articles concerning fashions and household matters fall naturally into the province of the woman writer, and when noted women have to be interviewed the woman reporter will often succeed where the man fails.

It is frequently the trifling incidents in life which, well told, obtain for a girl a favorable introduction to newspaper life. One day some years ago a young woman who had come to New York to try literature, meaning by that poetry, magazine essays, and stories, happened to witness an exciting encounter between a lady and a ruffian who had stolen her dog. The girl was on her way to mail a letter to her friends in the country, confessing failure and asking for money to return home. Six months of New York had convinced her that literature was a delusion. As she joined the group around the dog-thief and his victim, and listened to the lady's graphic story of the loss of the dog, which she now recognized, it occurred to this girl that here was an incident that might at least furnish matter for a story half a column long. She walked home with the woman and her dog, got all the particulars of the loss and recovery of Fido, and two hours later, with fear and trembling, she carried her tale to the city editor of a big newspaper.

"Is this a fancy story or something that happened?" he asked, glancing at the manuscript.

"It happened two hours ago, at Fourth Avenue and Sixteenth Street, and all the names are correctly given," answered the girl.

"We'll try to use it to-morrow."

Instead of mailing her piteous confession of failure the girl waited till the next day, and at dawn bought a copy of the paper. Her dog story made nearly a column. She had told it in as amusing a way as she knew how, and the dreaded blue-pencil, which sub-editors use to "cut down" articles, had scarcely been used. Much elated, she called on her friend the city editor and told him she should like more work of the kind. For the next year she earned on that one paper alone nearly five hundred dollars—enough to pay her board—and enough more from other sources to dress herself and put a little by.

Thus began a connection with daily journalism that lasted ten years. During the first years the work was often hard and frequently discouraging. After a whole day's tramping, and perhaps another day's hard writing, the result in print was not sufficient to pay for the car-fares expended. This, however, was only so long as the young reporter wrote as an outsider. When she became recognized as a regular member of the staff, the city editor gave her regular assignments, recognizing her ability to find out the interesting feature of any event and tell the story effectively. When an assignment or regular order is given to a reporter, the newspaper pays for the time occupied in the work, should the results in type not be sufficient. The rate of pay for ordinary reporting on the New York papers is from six to eight dollars a column, or if time is charged, half a dollar an hour.

When a girl begins to earn more than thirty dollars a week "on space," as payment by length of article is called, she is usually put on the salary list at from twenty dollars to twenty-five dollars, and upon the whole a salary is preferred, because the regular day's assignment finished, she has often time to write for magazines or for other papers, in this way increasing her income.

The work is often unpleasant for a woman, but it is not dangerous, as some people imagine. Women reporters have written hundreds of articles within the last ten years describing the painful and criminal sides of New York life, and, judging from their experience, it may be said that if a woman meets with insult, even in such newspaper work as that, it is usually due to her own want of sense or tact.

The danger from cold and exposure is greater than from insult. It is not uncommon for a woman reporter to return to her newspaper office with soaked feet and damp clothes to write for hours before she can think of home or food. And, unlike a man, she cannot take refuge in hot whiskey. The more important and arduous the work, the sooner must it be done, and women as well as men, in newspaper life, must learn to ignore regular hours by day or night.

The disappointments are many. The woman reporter may sometimes wait in cold reception-rooms for hours and then have the information she seeks curtly refused. She may work for a week to get a "yes" or a "no" to an important question, and then not get it. She must be prepared for the slights and slurs of ill-bred people. When she has done her best it is discouraging to find that the city editor discards her work for reasons which she is unable to fathom; and it is almost equally disturbing to be praised for work which she knows is bad and careless.

What newspaper men term the "news instinct" is something that some women find hard to acquire, and many never acquire at all. It consists simply in distinguishing rapidly from among the events or happenings that may come to a reporter's knowledge such as may have value and interest as news. The "news" quality is always paramount in the city editor's eyes.

One day a woman, Miss A——, was sent to give an account of a small exhibition of pictures at a club-house. There was some delay in getting into the gallery, owing, as she was incidentally told, to the absence of a well-known citizen who had been taken seriously ill while arranging the pictures that morning. Our young woman reporter thought no more of the matter, but went on making up her little account of the pictures. After an hour's work another woman reporter, Miss B——, arrived, and to her Miss A—— mentioned the illness of the club member in excuse for her slow work. The new woman said nothing, but in half an hour she was on the way to that man's house; she found that it was a case of apoplexy; she interviewed the doctors; she hunted up some members of the club and obtained accounts of the illness and materials for a good obituary. The next day her paper had a column account of the dangerous illness of the well-known man, and it was the only paper that contained the news. As to the picture show, no paper printed more than ten lines about it. When Miss A—— saw the paper she learned one more lesson as to the value of news.

All newspapers are willing to pay well for exclusive news, or "beats," as they are called in the slang of the business, and no reporter's work is such that he may not at any moment hear news that has not reached the newspapers. The trained reporter "smells" news, and often a casual word or a hint leads him to important discoveries. This is a faculty which few women in the business seem to possess; they are apt to waste time on comparatively unimportant matters. Another instance will suffice. A woman reporter was sent to see a leader of the fashionable world to get an account of the gowns to be worn at a big ball.

"I don't know anything about Mrs. A——'s costume," said the lady, "because since her husband lost one hundred thousand dollars last month in a railroad speculation with my husband we do not speak."

The ball lost all interest for the reporter, who hurried down to the office with news that gave a clew to some strange happenings in the Stock Market that had been puzzling Wall Street for a fortnight. Half a dozen reporters were despatched on the trail, and the result was a whole page of Wall Street news of absorbing interest to financial men. No one outside of that office knew for months how the reporters got track of the matter. The woman reporter received three dollars for her account of the gowns at the Patriarchs' Ball, and a check for one hundred dollars for her Wall Street "tip."

According to one woman who has seen newspaper reporting in all its phases, a woman, in order to succeed, must never, as she expresses it, "take refuge behind her petticoats." If the editor wants certain work done, and believes that a certain woman can do it, no excuses should be offered upon the ground of sex.

One day news came to a great New York daily that Sarah Bernhardt would arrive that afternoon in Philadelphia and perform at a certain theatre. The famous actress had just returned from a tour in South America and was supposed to have an interesting story to tell. It happened that no man in the newspaper office could speak French, and Bernhardt speaks no English. But there was a woman on the staff, a young girl of twenty-two, who knew French, and the order went to her: "Go to Philadelphia, find Sarah Bernhardt, and write four columns about her South-American trip."

A girl who lacked the newspaper instinct would have been dismayed. To go alone to a strange city one hundred miles away, to hunt around theatres until she found an actress she had never seen, and then get out of her an interview four columns long — that was a good job for a man, but queer work for a refined girl of twenty-two. But the reporter in question simply said, "Yes."

She reached Philadelphia at seven

o'clock, found Bernhardt at the theatre, talked to her between the acts, was invited to sup with her after the play, and did so, taking copious notes during the meal, took a train at three o'clock in the morning back to New York, began to write her interview at eight o'clock, and had it done at four o'clock that afternoon — in less than twenty-four hours after the assignment had been given to her.

The article happened to take the public's fancy. It was copied from one end of the country to the other and brought the young woman reporter fame, and, what was better, work from all sides. In the same line of readiness to accept any duty asked of a man may be cited Miss Bisland's start on her famous trip around the world. She was asked at eleven o'clock in the morning to take a trip around the world, and she started at six that evening.

One of the foremost women journalists of the last ten years has frequently insisted that the chief essentials to a newspaper woman are good health and strong nerves. Newspaper life is commonly conceded to be one of the most exhausting a man can go into. Its tax upon a woman is evident. The chief part of the work is done at night, until nightwork becomes a bad sort of second nature, and the old man is rather a curiosity upon the active staff of a daily newspaper. Women are spared some of the hardships of the life, but certain evils remain.

One woman journalist says that it makes her nervous to know that every day she is expected to produce a better article than the one she wrote yesterday. There is no such thing as routine in the highest and best class of the work—there must be a constant effort to do something not only better than you have done before, but better than any other newspaper has done.

The mere physical exertion of long hours when some important piece of work has to be done soon tells upon a woman's strength, and the list of breakdowns among newspaper women is almost as long as the list of workers.

Too many girls come to New York expecting to make a living at once, and are starved out. One woman of wide acquaintance among newspaper workers says that no girl should go to any large city, expecting to get into journalism, unless she has money enough to live for six months at least. And she must not expect to attain a salaried position until she has had at least four years' experience in the work.

Women in newspaper work are paid as much as men for the same sort of material, if measured by quantity, but when it comes to salaries, men receive more because they can do some things physically beyond a woman's power. Another reason why the managing editors of newspapers look with less favor upon women as assistants is that after an apprenticeship of years they are likely to get married just when most valuable.

The most successful women reporters are those who do not consider any part of the newspaper field as out of their sphere by reason of sex. The woman who because she is a woman confines herself to fashions, and weddings, and woman's doings never gets very far. The broader the field the better for her. The salaries given to most women reporters are small—seldom more than twenty dollars a week—because too often they are not equipped for work outside of a narrow range. It is not desirable that women should do nightwork as a regular thing, and for that reason they are at a disadvantage in morning journalism. Aside from that, they can do anything that men can do. The best cattle and stock reporter in New York for many years was Miss

Morgan, who tramped around the stockyards in men's boots.

It must be said also that journalism offers a steady income as compared with any other literary employment. The business of magazine-writing and book-writing furnishes a good living to but one woman in a thousand who tries it. The magazine field is especially limited. The Sunday newspapers of New York alone publish more articles of a miscellaneous character in one issue than all the magazines of the country in a month. The demand for newspaper material is thus constant, and the quantity needed is such that editors cannot be over-particular as to quality.

A few newspaper women have become quite well known as magazine contributors, but their real income has been drawn from the newspapers. One woman, who for several years before she married and left the business, earned five thousand dollars a year, received four thousand of this sum from newspapers and one thousand from magazines. The women editors of a few periodicals devoted to women are said to be paid even more than five thousand a year, but as there are not half a dozen such posts in the country, it is not worth while talking about them.

The rank and file of the newspaper women may consider themselves fortunate if they earn fifteen hundred dollars a year by work which, though hard, is not unpleasant. Should a woman have especial literary talents, the newspaper training and the varied views of life she is sure to get as a reporter will be of inestimable value to her after she has been graduated to more dignified work.

X.—DRESS-MAKING, MILLINERY, AND PLAIN SEWING.

THE business of dress-making and millinery seems to be one in which a comparatively few persons make all the money, while the rank and file do most of the work. At least such is the case with regard to this industry in large cities.

In small towns and villages it is different, and the village dress-maker is an institution in herself, and frequently a person who has attained to no little importance in the community. The familiar type of the village dress-maker, who carries the gossip of the place from house to house, portioning out her time between the different well-to-do villagers in need of her services, and acting as the arbiter of taste and fashion in the community, has by no means disappeared; and perhaps it is just as well to say that in the smaller villages and towns the person who devotes herself to dress-making will probably find the best field for her activity. The expenses of business in a large city, and the constant risk of bad debts, make the life of most fashionable dress-makers far from a bed of roses.

There is a common impression to the effect that all fashionable dress-makers and milliners accumulate fortunes, but as a matter of fact it is said by those in the business that the fortunes made in dress-making in New York City in the last twenty years may be counted on the fingers of one hand. It is true that some women have succeeded exceedingly well, one fashionable dress-maker having invested a large amount of money in real estate in New York City and Long Branch, and thereby more than tripled her earnings; the fortune of this dress-maker was recently estimated at nearly a million dollars, but probably not more than a quarter of this sum was due to the dress-making business she carried on for nearly twenty-five years.

Very much the same may be said as to the business of millinery shops. It is notorious that the cost of the raw material which enters into a bonnet or hat is absurdly out of proportion to the price asked for the finished article in fashionable shops; and yet very few milliners grow rich, or even succeed in acquiring enough money to withdraw from the business.

The chief troubles of the trade, according to one of the best milliners of New York, are bad debts and the impossibility of disposing of materials which have become a trifle out of fashion. The business, like that of fashionable tailors, is one largely run upon long credits; some of the best customers of the leading milliners of New York allow their bills to run from two to three years, and, of course, in some instances such bills are never paid. Yet, from the peculiarities of the business, fashionable milliners and dress-makers, as well as tailors, cannot afford to press their customers too hard for money, or to take the debt into the courts, unless the sum is exceedingly large. They are afraid of having, or acquiring, the reputation of harsh dealing, and prefer to lose the money rather than appear in court.

The rank and file of the workers for milliners and dress-makers do not have an over-easy or over-pleasant life, according to the stories told by themselves.

A Millinery Class at Armour Institute, Chicago.

In most of the shops work begins at eight o'clock, or even earlier, and lasts until six, with extra hours until eleven or twelve at night in the height of the busy season. The wages vary from three dollars a week, paid to girls who are of some use, but are not yet competent workers, to twelve and fifteen dollars a week for expert workwomen, who must, however, be competent to take charge of a number of hands.

Estimating by the returns made from a number of shops, it is safe to say that the average working dressmaker, who has a place in a good shop, does not earn more than eight dollars a week. Moreover, there are slack seasons when the force of the shop is cut down sometimes to one-quarter of the number usually employed, and then the dress-maker has to look for still cheaper grades of sewing, such as shirt-making and sewing upon clothing for the wholesale houses. Many women who have the necessary knowledge and taste for dress-making say that they are driven to this cheaper grade of work every summer for several months, and are glad to get it.

As a rule, the provision made by the best dress-makers in large cities, such as New York, for the comfort of their employees and sewing-women is ample, and no such fault is to be found as in the case of factory work upon shirts or clothes. Very few dress-makers in New York employ more than sixty hands upon the average, and the rooms are usually well ventilated and well lighted.

One woman, who has been sewing for such a firm for ten years, states that were it not for the annual lack of work, when three-quarters of the hands are discharged, dress-makers and milliners have a pleasanter time of it in New York City than shop girls. But there is the constant fear present to many such workers that they may be displaced by younger women, with better eyesight, who can do finer work. Much of the best work is still hand-work, and the workwoman whose eyesight fails her has to take to the machine.

When we come to rough sewing and machine work, very few women succeed in making more than six or seven dollars a week, all of the work being piece-work and much of it being done in the homes of the workers. The large wholesale manufacturers of men's clothing, shirts, and women's underclothing find it more profitable to have the work done outside of their own buildings, as they are thus able to employ five times as many people as they could accommodate.

Year after year the price paid to women for such sewing has been constantly upon the decrease. The fact that all underwear can be bought more cheaply than it is possible to make it at home, shows how little the women who do the work are paid for it. It is not worth while going into the prices paid for different garments, or to give the figures received for piece-work at the different shops; the story has been told over and over again in the newspapers, and it is unfortunately too true that New York has about twenty-two thousand women whose life is one long echo of Hood's "Song of the Shirt."

Improved methods of manufacture and cheap sewing-machines seem to have brought no relief to this army of workers—rather the contrary. It is seldom that one can find among this class a woman who makes more than three hundred dollars the year through, even by the hardest and most persistent toil. She probably works from seven in the morning until nine at night, with two hours taken out for meals, or twelve hours' steady labor; she has to pay for her machine and for her thread, and the net profit of the labor at the end of the week is considered satisfactory if she receives from five to six dollars. Thousands of instances are cited in which the results are even less satisfactory, but in such cases it is often the fault of the workwoman, and there would be suffering for the same person in any line of industry.

The greatest cause of the depression of wages among the sewing-women of large cities is, of course, the fierce competition encouraged by manufacturers. If such competition came only from city workers in the tenements, it would be bad enough; but the women who make clothing and underclothes are subject to the competition of the country districts, and this is what forces prices down so near to the starvation point. Hundreds of large wholesale firms send out every week wagon-loads of clothing, cut out and basted, to be distributed throughout the farming districts of New York and New England. The farmers' wives and daughters get very little for the work, the average payment, according to one estimate, being at the rate of four cents an hour. But the work is done at odd moments, or in the evenings; it is brought to the farm-house by the manufacturer's wagon, and every few weeks the man comes around to collect the finished garments and leave more material. Even at four cents an hour, the farmer's daughters can afford to sew for the city manufacturer, and count themselves fortunate if their winter's work brings them in from thirty to fifty dollars. In many districts where food and fuel are plenty and the people live comfortably, there is an extreme scarcity of money, and this is one means by which the farmer's women-folk get the few dollars which they absolutely need for things not produced in the neighborhood. There are thousands and thousands of farm-houses where such work is done in the winter in competition with the wretched people of the city tenements, and so long as the system continues, there is small hope of larger earnings for those who do rough sewing.

The ambition of most women who enter the workshops of fashionable dress-makers and milliners is naturally to establish a business of their own, and there are nearly four hundred dress-makers in New York City who do work in their own flats and employ from two to ten assistants. Such dressmakers do not make fortunes, but they appear to make a comfortable living; they are not haunted, as a rule, by bad debts, for their customers are among the people who pay as they go, and they are not brought into competition with the army of women, both city and country, who sew for the wholesale houses.

In the same way there are many small milliners, chiefly upon the cheaper avenues, who appear to make a very modest but sufficient income, so that if a woman has some business capacity as well as taste, the field of dress-making and millinery is not necessarily one of drudgery or starvation. The apprenticeship is, however, a hard one, and most girls who have homes in the country will do well to make their business where they are, rather than risk the troubles and possible dangers of life in a large city.

The shops naturally attract an army of women from the country to large cities every year, and New York is said to give employment to sixty thousand shop-girls and women. The life is, at best, one of long hours and small pay, very few saleswomen, even in the best New York shops, receiving more than six dollars a week.

A number of influential men and women have worked for years to better the condition of the New York shopgirls, in the way of seats behind the counters, easier hours, improved ventilation and sanitary arrangements. The *White List* is a publication widely circulated by one such association, which contains the names of shops where employees are humanely treated. The members of the association agree, so far as it is convenient, to deal only with the shops found in this list.

The law compelling shop-keepers to provide at least one seat for every six shop-girls, was due to the efforts of such a society, and now that some laws exist for the protection of shop-girls an attempt is made to see that they are enforced. Violations are frequently discovered. In one large shop where the law has been obeyed to the extent of putting in the one seat required for every six girls, a fine was imposed upon any girl found sitting on it!

The scope of these papers does not include a detailed account of all the industries in which women are employed, but only of such employments as may attract women of some intelligence and education. Nevertheless it may be well to repeat, concerning the hundreds of trades and industries in which thousands of untrained women enter —from domestic service and factory work to shop service—that nine-tenths of those who come from country homes to get work in New York or any other large city, would have done far better in every way, even financially, to have remained in their homes. The loss of home comforts and influence is not to be made up by a few more dollars a month, and in countless cases even this return for a dreary homeless life fails.

The life of the work-woman who comes from the country to a great city, and is driven to cheap boarding-houses or lodging-houses, is one of the most forlorn that can be imagined. She is within sight of all the luxury and amusements of the rich, and yet unable to share in them; as compared to the simple, plentiful fare of the farm-house, she starves upon tea and rolls in order to compete in finery with the work-girl who lives at home and can put all her earnings upon her back. The country girl who goes to a great city to work, has not only to compete with the country workers at four cents an hour, if her trade is sewing, as already described, but no matter what her occupation, she must compete with the city girls who have homes and can often afford to work for less than it takes to keep body and soul together.

XI.—THE STAGE. THE ACTRESS—STAGE-WORK.

IN talking about the stage as a profession for women, a well-known actress once said that her advice to young people who wanted to act, was that of *Punch* to those about to marry—"Don't." But the fact that more girls turn to the stage every year as a means of earning a living, makes it important to give trustworthy information as to the exact requirements of this profession, about which there seems to be a glamour as deceptive as it is dangerous. The fact, also, that some two thousand women in the United States now find a living upon the stage, entitles the question to consideration in these pages. Information will therefore be given as to what kind of a woman is warranted in trying stage-work, what she must know, what money rewards she may reasonably expect, what she should avoid, and what pitfalls to manners and morals lie in the way of the girl who wants to act.

By some experts health is placed first on the list of essentials for a successful stage career. Others declare that an artistic temperament—in other words, extraordinary sensibility, imagination, glow—is even more important, because sometimes a woman by no means robust, may carry through a long season by sheer nervous force and strength of will. Good health, however, means nervous force or magnetism, a species of animal enthusiasm sufficiently pronounced to become contagious. Nevertheless, a weakly girl should be discouraged from the stage. At best the life is a wearing one, and must remain so as long as the system of one-night stands (stopping at towns where the company gives but one performance) remains in force. It means constant travel, life in poor hotels, and exposure to dangerous changes of temperature, from the over-heated railroad-car to the under-heated theatre or hotel bedroom.

It often happens that a theatrical company must travel all day in order to reach a town in time for the next performance. For weeks the life will consist of railroad, hotel, theatre; railroad, hotel, theatre, and so on. On Sunday, the record will probably read simply, railroad. It is hard even upon a man. What must it be upon a woman? No matter what her fatigue, she will be expected to play her best. She may have to wear a low-cut gown with arctic blasts blowing across the stage, or she may have to stifle in heavy dresses with the thermometer above 100° F.

One well known actress said that she

once played in Fresno, California, when the mercury marked 115° F. ; and as the play was Bartley Campbell's "Siberia," she had to wear furs all the evening.

It requires unflagging spirits, otherwise no end of health, to stand the hardships of the travelling player. One who has seen much of this life upon the "road," says that she has often tramped from her hotel to the railway-station at four o'clock in the morning, with the snow three inches deep. Sometimes the cars would be as cold as an ice-box, at others too hot for breathing. Once this woman travelled from five in the morning until seven o'clock at night, with no more nourishment than crackers and water; at half-past seven she had to play a light-hearted daughter of a millionnaire. Here was irony of fate, indeed ! Apple-pie and doughnuts constitute many a breakfast in this life.

If a girl decides that her vocation is the stage, here is a list of the qualifications for success compiled by an expert :

A strong physique.
An unimpaired digestion.
A slender figure.
A marked face.
Strong features.
A carrying voice.
A lack of real feeling.
An abundance of pretended feeling.
Much magnetism.
Great fascination of manner.
Purity of speech.
Elocution to a degree.
A general knowledge of history.
A good general education.
A general knowledge of costuming.
A practical knowledge of economy in dress.
An artistic knowledge of the effects of distance.
Considerable business faculty.
Unflagging industry.
Undaunted ambition.
An utter lack of sensitiveness.
A capacity for taking pains.
An absolute and undisputed devotion to the theatre.
An unwedded life.
An ability to distinguish criticism from abuse or fulsome gush.
A readiness to profit thereby.
Some genius at advertising.
A quickness at seizing opportunities.
An adeptness at making herself necessary.
A well-defined specialty.
A good memory.
Good luck.
Quick study.
Talent.

Should the aspirant for stage honors go through this list and not be dismayed, it may be said that something else is yet needed if she expects to get from the stage more than she loses— namely, the power of preserving her own identity and self-respect. There are many reasons why a woman may lose mental and moral fibre in this profession. Its associations are often not of the best. Many of the girls who go upon the stage begin young, often without much education, and at a time when their character is still unformed, and they are most easily led by flattery, love of ease, and display ; they are removed from family influence to be thrown into the company of men and women to whom nothing is sacred.

There are excellent people upon the stage, but, as in every business, there are also black sheep, and, under the peculiar exactions of stage-work the girl who goes into a theatrical company must see more or less of every person in it. It may be her fate to be made love to every night before the footlights by a man whom she abhors and detests. Night after night she may have to mimic the holiest and most sacred emotions before a crowd of perhaps vulgar and coarse-minded people, making sport of her own acts and words when the curtain is down, but doing her best to make them seem real while it is up.

It is not possible that this constant playing with the emotions does no harm. A girl may keep her self-respect in any reputable company. It will depend upon herself. But it requires tact and wisdom. She need not be called by her first name by every Tom, Dick, and Harry in the company; she need not share in the petty scandals and squabbles of the organization. But she must be called by her first name for the moment, and treated with familiarity on the stage, by every actor who plays with her.

So far as morals go, a woman may, of course, remain untainted upon the stage. It depends upon herself. When it comes to manners, the best authorities have confessed that the girls who can resist the Bohemian influence of stage-life are so few as to be scarcely worth mentioning. No matter how refined and quiet a girl may be when she enters this feverish life, the stage will leave its marks upon her. Insensibly she will contract some of the free and easy manners of the life. A famous Frenchman once said that there were three sexes — men, women, and players, meaning that people lost their individuality in this profession. The constant intimate association of men and women on the stage, the constant playing of the emotions, the mockery of love that goes on, end by dulling even the most sensitive nature.

There is probably no profession in which the woman of refinement and sensibility meets with greater disappointment than in stage-life. She will so often find that notoriety counts for more than merit. Theatrical stars, especially women, are so frequently the creatures of circumstance. Notoriety of one kind or another, even scandal, makes them profitable to their managers; sometimes they may have personal beauty of so rare a quality that it suffices; again, there may be peculiar fitness for a particular line of character. One instance is cited in which a young woman of very modest equipment was sent to the front because of an infectious laugh which seemed to please the public.

Suppose a girl succeeds in getting a small place upon the stage. What is she warranted in expecting at the close of a year or two of hard work? Taking the average of the girls who a.e graduated every year from our dramatic schools, their pay for the first two years upon the stage is not likely to exceed thirty-five dollars a week, and unless a woman shows a peculiar aptitude it is not likely to rise above that figure in later years. There are hundreds of hard-working women of some ambition and intelligence who never receive more than twenty-five dollars.

Stage salaries are deceptive. Do not imagine that an engagement of thirty dollars a week means one thousand five hundred dollars a year. The theatrical season is supposed to last about forty weeks, but as a fact it is more apt to be thirty, and there is also the possibility of a closing at any time, when it is hard to find anything else to do before the next season begins. The expenses to which an actress is subject are larger than in other businesses for women. It will cost her at least fifteen dollars a week to live decently when travelling. Then she will be expected to spend from one hundred dollars to one hundred and fifty dollars upon her costumes, so that in the end the income dwindles down to what a clever girl may make in almost any other business.

The great attraction is that there are possibilities of far greater gain than in ordinary business life. The soubrette who makes a hit may jump from thirty dollars to one hundred and fifty dollars a week. This is the will o'-the-wisp that leads so many on. It must also be remembered that the effective years of a woman's life upon the stage are between twenty and thirty-five. If she is to make fame and fortune, she must do it before she is thirty, or never.

A common misapprehension under which young women labor as to the stage, is that its life is one of ease and pleasure. On the contrary, it means hard work, and not only that, it means extraordinary deprivations in many respects. The play-goer can scarcely realize what the actress loses in this way. In the popular mind she is always a creature of bright surroundings, wearing the same gay smile and the same fine clothes. But behind this brightness is the machinery, the constant rehearsal, and the unremitting study, study, study, if she expects to rise. Do young women consider what it means to act in sickness as well as in health, to smile and caper, or storm and struggle, when every nerve is throbbing with pain? Yet every pang must be hidden. Audiences are hard taskmasters—they pay not to pity but to applaud.

The actress belongs to a class apart. It is one of the penalties she has to pay for such success as may be won in this profession. More serious than the hard work, the long hours, and the excitement, is this deprivation of social life. An actress constantly employed can really have no social life; she can never dine with other people, can never spend an evening with friends, can never see a play or hear a concert. At the end of several years of hard work the actress may find that her time has been wholly thrown away, and that this irregular, Bohemian life has unfitted her for anything else.

Education and intelligence are not sufficient to enable one to rise in this business. It is even held by some competent critics that acting and intelligence have but little in common. The power to picture emotion may exist without the appreciation of that emotion or the power to analyze it. Nevertheless, success on the stage is—putting aside the question of great fame or fortune —usually won by the same qualities that make success elsewhere, namely, industry, patience, and sincerity. There are exceptional temptations to a girl to fritter away her time. That is one of the dangers of the profession. A woman who wants to keep above the petty atmosphere of the green-room, its gossip and jealousies, can do so only by the exercise of eternal vigilance.

If, after reading these pages, a girl is convinced that stage life is the vocation for her, the best thing she can do is to enter some dramatic school of good repute. In two years at such a school she can learn more of the rudiments of dramatic art than she can pick up in five years on the stage. The faculty in dramatic schools of good repute is made up of professional actors. The pupils have daily lessons in pantomime, elocution, fencing, singing, dancing, take part in plays, hear lectures upon the history and traditions of theatrical art, and upon the literature of the stage—all under the direction of men and women who have made the stage their life study. The course of such schools is usually two years, the pupil being engaged from morning until night, from October to June. The average cost of tuition is two hundred dollars for the first year and three hundred for the second. No reputable dramatic school guarantees to find positions for its graduates.

XII.—MISCELLANEOUS OCCUPATIONS.

ASIDE from the familiar professions and industries in which women find a living there are many occupations, growing more and more numerous every year, not familiar to the public, and yet by which thousands of women are enabled to support themselves.

In many industries of this kind a certain degree of technical knowledge and originality are often necessary, but it is just these requisites which make the business worth pursuing, for they keep out disastrous competition.

DELICACIES.

For instance, one woman in New York has made a business for several years of supplying delicacies for the sick which cannot be obtained in ordinary houses or restaurants. She rented two little rooms where she began work, sending out circulars to all the persons she knew, and from the very first the enterprise grew and succeeded. It is a lady's occupation, inasmuch as it implies good taste and delicacy. The institution is known as the *Home Bureau*, and beyond the prettily furnished office, with its desks, easy-chairs, rugs, and hangings, may be seen a model kitchen and some pantries and packing-rooms full of goods ready for delivery. In the kitchen are two large gas-ranges, each suitable for cooking anything, from a batch of bread to a pint of soup.

In the morning certain things, like beef, mutton, and chicken broths, are prepared in quantities sufficient to last through the day, after which the ranges are used for the preparation of special dishes made to order, including nearly a score of other broths and beverages, ranging from oatmeal caudle with wine to flax-seed lemonade, jellies, and anything else an imaginative physician or capricious invalid may suggest. Orders are filled for places as far off as Lakewood and Newport.

The persons who patronize this establishment get the very best and are prepared to pay for it at the rate of sixty-five cents a pint for broths, seventy-five cents a pint for soups, from fifty cents to sixty-five cents per half-pint for jellies, and from fifty cents to four dollars a quart for beverages. There is a good demand for home-made bread at twenty-five cents a loaf, and for chicken sandwiches at twenty-five cents each. The jars and bottles in which broths, jellies, and beverages are sent out are first scoured and then kept in a dust-proof glass case.

The owner of the business found last year that many people who came to her for invalids' food also inquired for experienced nurses, and she added a sort of nurses' club to her business, the members doing some of the work of the *Home Bureau* while waiting for calls to sick people.

LECTURE RECITALS.

The fact that many music teachers in New York City have in recent years made money by giving what are known as lecture recitals—lectures upon any musical subject, varied by illustrations upon the piano by the lecturer, has already been noted, and many of the best schools for girls now employ women lecturers upon other subjects than music.

LECTURES ON HISTORY.

A young college woman, who was known a few years ago as an especially clever student of history, has become quite a well-known and popular lecturer upon historical subjects, giving recently a course of lectures to a class of more than two hundred women. As no single tickets were sold for this course, the receipts were at least one thousand dollars, and this was but one course of several lectures delivered by the same woman, who was invited to deliver many single lectures upon special topics before girls' schools and women's clubs.

LECTURES ON BOTANY.

Lectures upon botany have also proved to be popular among schools, and two New York women have made large incomes by preparing such lectures with elaborate stereopticon illustrations.

SEA-WEEDS.

A still more unusual way of making a living has been tested by a woman, who, not many years ago, went to the Pacific coast, exhausted by the labors of school-teaching. She knew that her next occupation, if she ever had one, must be out of doors. She became interested in sea-weeds, and found at Monterey Bay a splendid field for collecting marine *algæ* (sea-weeds). Her first collection, to which she devoted several years, is valued at five thousand dollars ; and when it is disposed of, the woman in question proposes to make another for the Paris Exhibition of 1900. Several young women interested in the subject are working under her direction, preparing a collection of sea-weeds for the Leland Stanford University. Miss Westfall is an enthusiast on the subject, and has often spent an entire day in mounting a single specimen ; she has gone many a morning at four o'clock to study the growth of these lowly plants, when first uncovered by the tide.

DRIED FLOWERS AND CRYPTOGAMS.

In the same field may be mentioned the collections of sea-weeds, dried flowers and mosses, gathered into albums and sold by several young women living on Long Island to a number of schools in New York City and elsewhere. Such albums give the scientific information about the plants they contain, and prove to be far more interesting to the students than any pictures. There seems to be no reason why such work should not be done upon a large scale and become of great value in the study of botany.

FLOWERS, FRUIT, AND POULTRY.

Another occupation which women living in the country may find it profitable to consider is the cultivation of flowers and fruit, and although this is already done by women everywhere, there seems to be room for improvement, especially in devising means for marketing the product.

Poultry-keeping is commonly recommended to women in need of an income, and most farmers' wives owe what little pin-money they may get to their chickens. In this department, also, the greatest rewards go to the women who study best the mercantile side of the business, making sure not only that they raise all the eggs and chickens that can reasonably be expected, but that they get the best prices for them. That women can make large sums of money out of poultry has been proved over and over again on Long Island, where many of the famous duck-farms, from which New York City is supplied with a thousand ducks a day, in the season, are entirely managed by women, mostly Germans. It is not uncommon to find a duck-farm of from three to five thousand ducks upon which all the work is done by women.

BEES.

Many of the books which profess to teach women how to make money recommend bee-keeping as an infallible means of getting an income. It is a delightful and profitable occupation on paper, and shares this characteristic with many others recommended. As a matter of fact, while bees may be made profitable to a small extent, they require care and knowledge of the business. The woman who expects to live in luxury upon the produce of the fifty bee-hives which are spoken of in some books as sufficient to produce a comfortable income may be much disappointed when she finds that bees sometimes die from starvation and cold, and sometimes refuse to work even when honey is plenty. There seems to be no reason, however, why farmers' wives and daughters should not engage in bee-keeping far more than they do, especially if they are able to market the honey in an intelligent fashion. The fact that an ordinary hive of bees will produce upon the average from thirty to fifty pounds of box-honey a season, and that such honey sells in the New York groceries at twenty cents a pound, shows that there is here a profit for some one. The management of bee-hives has been so simplified and perfected of recent years by the invention of the wax "foundation," which insures regular comb, and by the invention of hives that may be taken apart, that there is much more certainty in the industry than used to be the case in the days of straw hives.

TYPE-SETTING AND PROOF-READING.

Nearly five hundred women are employed in New York City as compositors and proof-readers, the first-named receiving from twelve to eighteen dollars a week, and the proof-readers as high as twenty-five dollars. For a long time the Typographical Unions refused to admit women to their ranks, upon the ground that the change would tend to reduce wages, but this opposition has died out. Intelligent women find proof-reading a comparatively profitable field, and in the case of some publishing houses where scientific and technical books are made, the women proof-readers are very well paid, one woman in particular receiving a salary of two thousand dollars a year. Among the rank and file of compositors women are at a disadvantage, for the reason that most of the work upon the daily newspapers is done late at night or in the early morning, and under exhausting conditions.

LIBRARIES.

Within the last fifteen years women have entered the chief libraries of the country as librarians, and there are now several schools where they are taught the profession, for it really is a profession, under the best conditions. While a librarian was formerly simply the custodian of a number of books, he is now expected not only to care for them intelligently and to see that they are scientifically arranged, but to know something about them all in order to be of help to others. Columbia College has maintained a Library School for the last eight years, three-fourths of the pupils being women, and its graduates are to be found in responsible positions all over the country. The course is two years, and includes practically everything that the ideal librarian ought to know, including the modern systems of indexing and cataloguing. To any one fond of omnivorous reading, such a position offers a particularly good field, and it is exceedingly well paid, several of the graduates of the Columbia College school receiving salaries of more than two thousand dollars a year.

BRIC-A-BRAC.

Among the uncommon industries to which women have devoted themselves in several large cities in America in recent years has been the collection and sale of artistic bric-a-brac. For years

London has had many women employed in such shops, as proprietors or saleswomen, and there is no reason why women should not do the same work in the United States. It requires chiefly taste, artistic knowledge, and business instinct.

ANTIQUE FURNITURE.

Two Boston girls, both graduates of a college, are said to have earned four thousand dollars last year by the sale of the old-fashioned furniture, andirons, candlesticks, clocks, and china that they picked up in a six months' tour through some parts of New England not overrun with collectors. They fitted out a shop with the proceeds of their trip. Bureaux and sideboards for which they paid ten dollars apiece in villages not two hundred miles from Boston, sold for ten times that amount when polished up and put in the window of a Boston bric-a-brac shop.

WATCH-MAKING.

An industry in which it seems that women ought to succeed particularly well, for it requires delicacy of touch and patience, is watch-making, and many women are employed in watch factories. For some reason or other very few of them find positions in the jewelry and clock stores of large cities, probably for the reason, as suggested by one watch-maker, that women do not often obtain a thorough knowledge of watch-making, and that as the work in the repair departments maintained by the different large shops consists largely in treating watches of a hundred makes,

A View Taken and Published by Mrs. J. C. Kendall, Photographer, Norfolk, Conn.

foreign and domestic, only an experienced workman will suffice.

In the big factories, where women find employment, they do but one thing month after month—some detail in making up the finished watch, and many of them never get beyond this or see more than one kind of watch during the years they remain in the factory. Yet their accuracy and delicacy of touch in handling the minute parts of watches is generally commented upon, and women with intelligence and industry enough to enable them to master the trade as a man does might find it a profitable one in hundreds of small towns and villages, where, in connection with watch-repairing and clock-repairing, they might maintain a jewelry store.

THE LOCAL PHOTOGRAPHER.

Another business in which hundreds of intelligent women might do far more than at present, is photography. The fact that many have already succeeded well in it, shows that the business side of the industry is not too difficult for a woman to manage, while in artistic taste the woman photographer of the country village is usually superior to the man.

In its earlier stages photography required for its best results a certain knowledge of chemistry, and was rather an untidy sort of work, necessitating blackened hands and soiled clothes. With the new processes all this has been done away with, and it is now as simple as it is cleanly. Almost every large photographer in New York has one or more women in his employ to help in posing people, especially children, and in retouching and finishing the pictures.

The salaries paid are very fair, averaging from ten to twenty dollars a week for competent women. It is also to be noted that in many villages the woman photographer can live where her male competitor fails.

THEATRICAL MANAGEMENT.

Women theatrical managers have succeeded in doing well in several large cities, and one woman in New York is said to derive an income of ten thousand dollars a year as the American agent of a number of French and English playwrights, who intrust her with the sale of their plays. She finds managers to perform them and collects the royalties due. The work involves, however, much travelling and a technical knowledge of the theatrical business.

THE SALE OF MANUSCRIPTS.

A business in which many women find profit is the revision and sale of manuscripts of stories and articles to publishers and magazines. One woman in Boston is said to earn five thousand dollars a year in this work, which requires literary skill and patience. Thousands of persons write stories without any technical knowledge of the art, and are without any knowledge or facilities for disposing of them. This lady and her assistants first read the story and make a criticism upon it, for which a fixed price is charged. If the author desires it, the story will be revised, typewritten, and sent to such publications as in the judgment of the firm may be likely to accept and pay for it. For such work the firm receives the actual cost of doing the typewriting, and a percentage on the sum received for the article should it be accepted. The number of persons who scribble stories, especially women, is growing so rapidly that there appears to be an important future for a well-conducted business of this type.

It is to be noted that most of the occupations for women just mentioned may be carried on in the country, as well as in large cities, and a last word should be said as to women's folly in attempting to earn a living in large cities without exceptional preparation, resources, or influential friends. Some time ago a young girl—a stenographer—intent upon exchanging the humdrum life of her country town for the fancied advantages of New York, took the trouble to write to a number of well-known women whose names she had seen in the newspapers, asking their advice. Some of the advice received from women of large experience, called upon every few days for help by young girls and struggling women, is well worth quoting. The wife of Dr. C. H.

Parkhurst, the well-known clergyman, wrote:—

"You do not realize how many of the unemployed crowd New York. It is said that a competent worker can always find employment. They may, but sometimes the struggle is enough to crush them, and for a young girl without family or friends it would prove too severe. I have a friend connected with the Margaret Louisa Home for Working Women and she tells me sad tales of the struggles of the workers. Board is very high. Boarding-houses are not homes in any sense, and the forlornness of a girl's life without a home in a big city is appalling. . . . Take whatever comes first to hand. Do not consider anything too small for careful doing, and if it is really proved that the place is not large enough, another will open for you. *I do not believe in girls going out from home and into the turmoil of life and struggle in a big city unless it is unavoidable.* The tales of distress and defeat that so often come to me make me want to protest against the cityward tendency. There are opportunities in New York, opportunities for everything and everybody, but don't try it. It is too hard."

Mrs. Ballington Booth, the leader of the woman's work in the Salvation Army, to whom more appeals of the kind come, perhaps, than to any other woman in the country, wrote:—

"If your home influence has been good, and you can have good companionship here, I see no reason why you should not come, but do not be too hasty about leaving home and friends for something you know not what. The business road of New York over which we travel in pursuit of wealth is not often a pleasant one. On the contrary, it is rough and rugged at the best, beset with disappointments and pitfalls—snares for the young, sorrow and discontent for the old. You will miss the warm greetings of loved ones; your heart will grow sad and hardened, unless you have interested friends or relatives to look after you and see that your disappointments do not crush you. Be sure you're right, then go ahead. Don't try to do something you know nothing about, and do well what you undertake. Remember the importance of little things. If you are a good stenographer, we can doubtless help you along until you see a better opening, but my advice would be, if you see your way clear to come, to connect yourself with some church—become acquainted and enlist the sympathy and interest of the members, when they will at once recognize your true merit and extend a helping hand. But it would be far better for you to enlarge your opportunities throughout the West, as there is more chance of hasty promotion there."

XIII.—How Women Workers are Cheated.

Women in need of money appear to be the special victims of the swindlers, or semi-swindlers, who use the country newspapers for their purposes. Almost everyone must have noticed the peculiar advertisements, the gist of which is that anyone who wants to make an assured income has only to write to the advertiser, and that thereafter such things as poverty and debts will be unknown. Sometimes these cards are headed: "A sure fortune for every one." At one time they were apt to lead off with the number of dollars which the reader might make every week if she went into the business offered by the advertiser. Forty dollars a week was a favorite sum; again it was twenty-five dollars a week, or five dollars a day, or any other income which might impress the impecunious person as much to be desired. All such cards began with cheering words as: "If you are in debt and out of work, write to us and fortune will be yours."

Within the last few years there have been so many pitiful stories from women who were cheated out of hard-earned dollars, which they could not spare, by devices baited in this fashion, that several experts have investigated the matter.

Most persons who answer such advertisements find themselves invited simply to canvass for this or that worthless book or article manufactured by the advertiser. This method became so widely known that the advertisers who were anxious to enable every one to make a handsome income tried a new bait. People, and especially women, were informed through cards in countless newspapers that the work which they were invited to do called for no canvassing; moreover, it could be done at home in odd moments if necessary; it was suitable for ladies or invalids, etc. "No canvassing" became one of the features of most of these cards.

The number of such advertisements is amazing. An expert in such matters says that their victims are to be found all over the country.

Some time ago the police of Brooklyn received information that many complaints were coming from country people as to a certain business firm that advertised a gorgeous prize and an income of thirty dollars a week to whoever would send money for a bottle of Doctor Somebody's "Unrivalled Consumption Cure." The Post-Office authorities reported to the police that the business firm in question received from three to six hundred letters a day; and as nothing to the credit of the establishment could be found, a descent upon it was made. Some detectives went to the house or office of the "Doctor," and broke into a back room where eighteen girls were engaged in wrapping up and preparing for the mail a little bottle of some compound, supposed to be whiskey and water. The prize aforesaid consisted of a rolled-gold breast-pin, worth perhaps five cents, and the work to be done in order to earn the thirty dollars a week promised consisted in selling fifty bottles of the medicine at a dollar a bottle. The canvasser was offered the "Consumption Cure" at twenty cents a bottle. At the same time that the raid was made the mail for that day was stopped, and was found to consist of three hundred and forty-two one-dollar bills sent in answer to the advertisement, sixty-eight letters of abuse from victims who wanted their money back, and, strangest of all, twenty or more letters from persons who had found themselves greatly benefited by the Consumption Cure and wanted more.

This out-and-out swindle, in which money is received for practically nothing, is worse than the hoaxes which are occasionally played upon people who bite at attractive advertisements. The man who sent a dollar for a prescription that would enable him to do without eating, and got in reply a slip of paper upon which was printed, "Take a dose of poison," ought to have known better. Also the man who sent a quarter of a dollar for a fine steel engraving of Queen Victoria, and got a three-cent Canada postage-stamp. Also the man who in return for his half-dollar, sent for a sure method of killing the potato-bug, got by mail two little pieces of wood with the directions, "Place the bug between these two pieces of wood and squeeze hard." The victims of such hoaxes lose but little money, while in most other cases the sums lost are important ones to very poor people.

The offers of employment to women out of work that are likely to be found in country newspapers may be divided into three classes: 1. That in which you are invited to canvass for some object which you buy from the advertiser. 2. That in which you buy a process for making some compound which you must afterward dispose of either by peddling it yourself or getting others to peddle it for you. 3. That in which you are invited to do some kind of work at starvation prices, or work which cannot be done at all. In the first of these two classes the business may, of course, be a perfectly proper and legitimate one.

The typical advertisement of the third class reads: "If a lady wishes to make a comfortable income at home, varying from fifteen to fifty dollars a week, write to the International Art Company, Post-Office box ——. No previous knowledge of the business required." The person who answers this advertisement will receive a letter couched somewhat as follows:

"DEAR MADAM:—The business we advertise and in which we need the services of many ladies and gentlemen, is the making of a beautiful picture which we call the Artograph. We send you a certain kind of picture on a delicate, specially prepared china paper. We require you to put it on card-board and apply the colors as directed. You can do it after a very few days' practice. We send you, when you decide to undertake the work, a book of instructions, for which we charge you nothing, being desirous to have you in our employ, and a box of paints and brushes, for which you pay less than cost price—namely, $1.50. No natural taste or artistic training is needed for this work; bear in mind that any one can do it. For every picture you send to us satisfactorily finished we pay you forty-five cents. We send you at first five, which when finished will net you $2.25, and after a little practice you can easily finish them in one day's work. We sell these pictures to canvassers, and have never been able to get enough of them to supply the demand. As a matter of form, before sending you the first five pictures we require you to make a deposit of one dollar as a guarantee of good faith, and we cannot undertake to start any one in the business who is not willing to make this deposit.

"We feel sure that you will be able to do this work well and that the money earned will surprise you. State how you prefer to be paid—by the week or by the month, or whenever you send us the finished pictures."

Together with this printed circular comes a paper, supposed to be a contract, in which the victim states her willingness to do the work required, and agrees to devote so many hours a day to it and to do her best. She is supposed to sign this and enclose it with two dollars and a half to the Artograph Company. In return will come five little pictures on tissue-paper, some card-board on which to mount the pictures, and a little box of cheap paints and brushes, the whole outfit worth perhaps half a dollar at retail figures. This is the comedy part of the performance. The tragedy part begins when the unfortunate victim attempts to do the simple work which requires "no artistic skill or previous knowledge of the business." It is suspected the work is made purposely impossible; when the attempt is made to paste or mount the tissue-paper picture upon the card-board it seems to dissolve. No matter how much care is given or how delicately it is done—and even experts have tried their hand at it—the result is a wretched botch, which the Artograph Company will be perfectly justified in refusing as "not up to the high standard required by our patrons." Of course the upshot of the business is that the victim loses her faith in human nature, her two dollars and a half, and a good many hours' annoying work. This is exactly what the Artograph Company expected, and the profits on the transaction are probably sufficient to pay a handsome income to the rascals who thus prey upon unsuspecting women.

There are a few concerns who do pay for mounting and coloring cheap photographs, but the work is paid for at such a rate as to make the earnings a mere bagatelle. As it can be done by little girls, who are paid two dollars a week for coloring such prints from morning till night, it pays the outsider still less to do it. Where the scheme is a swindling one, pure and simple, the police may interfere if complaints are made; but as the victims are mostly at a long distance and are people of very small means and intelligence, there is little chance of punishment. No answer is made to the indignant protests of the victims of the Artograph Company beyond a printed circular, regretting that the victim is not sufficiently expert to do the work required. In the original circular it is stated that the victim will be surprised at the money she earns, and the amount does surprise her.

Not a week passes that the Post-Office authorities in New York do not receive complaints from persons in the country who have been swindled by mail; they have sent money and have received no adequate return. In one of the types of this swindling game which no amount of interference upon the part of the police seems to break up, attractive advertisements in the country newspapers offer profitable work to women. The applicant is told that the "Artistic Needle-work Company" does a large wholesale business in disposing of work performed by ladies at their own homes, and that upon receipt of one dollar samples of the work to be done will be forwarded. The one dollar is "simply to protect ourselves;" in return for the money are sent by mail a piece of cotton velvet with a small flower stamped upon it, a piece of felt of the same size, and a small amount of silk, the whole having cost not more than twenty cents. When the pattern has been worked out and returned for inspection the applicant for work receives word that it is satisfactory, but that before regular employment is secured it will be necessary to forward five dollars "in accordance with long-standing commercial usage."

When the five dollars, which may be the scanty savings of some poor woman, have been forwarded she receives a piece of goods, such as a mantel-cover to be embroidered, for which, when finished, she is to receive five dollars and regular employment.

In due time the work is done and sent to the company, and that is the last the victim hears of her work or her money, no matter how many indignant letters she may send. The concern is thus six dollars and some fine needle-work in hand, and the sum is so small that there is little likelihood of trouble with the police, especially as the victims are poor and the advertising is done in newspapers hundreds and even thousands of miles away from New York. This particular swindle is perennial. If the victim becomes really troublesome, she is told that her work was not good enough to pass muster, and that the company has a counter-claim against her for spoiling its material, but that it will charitably stand the loss.

A species of work that women and girls do in all large cities, but at starvation prices, consists in coloring cheap lithographs with an opaque color-wash laid on to imitate oil. For months before Christmas hundreds of women find work in the houses which make a specialty of these cards. The average price paid is two cents for each card, and it is an expert worker who can do more than twenty-five a day. It is really no more difficult than the coloring a bright child does with paints in a picture-book, but it requires time, no matter how simple. Many of these cards afterward appear in the shop-windows as "Hand-painted cards by artists of high repute." They are sold at about twenty-five cents each.

There is no swindling about the other classes of advertisements, and it is possible that the advice given in some instances and the methods explained for making money by peddling are of value to people out of work. Of course there may be men and women who will make fifty dollars a week, but they will be in proportion to the whole number of peddlers as one in a hundred. Between the scheme of the advertiser who sells outright the article to be peddled and that in which the peddler is expected to make his own stock in trade, there does not appear to be much preference. To begin with the first, the circulars assure the correspondent that the scheme offers her the chance of a lifetime. She is told that if she undertakes the canvass of her neighborhood for the photograph-album, the silver-plated spoons, the gold-plated watch-chains, the patent hair-crimper, or button-fastener, the fifty-cent diamond ring, the one-dollar Cremona violin, etc., fortune will smile upon her. In all cases the correspondent is invited to sign a contract by which she becomes the agent for the said firm over a certain territory. Most women peddlers are invited to invest in cosmetics or perfumery, or patent kitchen utensils. The prospective canvasser is assured that taking subscriptions for this or that perfume or hair-dye is easier than luxurious idleness. The circulars say nothing about walking from house to house for days at a time, getting nothing but angry words instead of dollars.

Certain manufacturers, who hope to make money by inducing people to believe that fortune is theirs if they will sell the goods of this or that concern, content themselves with offering some particular process or secret for making a variety of articles to be peddled at a tremendous advance over the original cost. For instance, you are told how to make a bottle of hair-restorative for eight cents which you can sell for a dollar, a bottle of hair-oil for four cents that you can sell for a quarter, a ten-cent package of stove-polish for three cents, a fifty-cent rubber hand-stamp for five cents, etc. Starch enamel, indelible ink, washing powder, shoe-blacking, cough-syrup, fly-paper, silver-plating fluid, rubber stamps, artificial honey, freckle-lotion, perfumery, court-plaster, etc., are some of the things that poor people are invited to make and spread through their neighborhoods, the profit to the advertiser being in the shape of whatever money he may get in return for the secret, or that he may derive from the sale of boxes, bottles, and labels with which to put up the goods.

Tailpiece designed by Annie G. Prickitt.

[*For further information see section on* OCCUPATIONS FOR WOMEN *in the chapter of* SUPPLEMENTARY INFORMATION.]

II.

WOMEN IN THEIR BUSINESS AFFAIRS.

II.

WOMEN IN THEIR BUSINESS AFFAIRS.

By WILLIAM O. STODDARD.

Keeping Accounts.
The Rights of Married Women.
The Question of Signatures.
Real Estate and Its Care.
Business Papers and
Evidences of Ownership.
Personal Property.

Banks and Bank Accounts.
Drafts and Notes.
Building and Loan Associations.
Investments.
Insurance.
Parliamentary Rules.
Wills.

IT has been said, and it has been repeated until many thoughtless persons have tried to accept it as a rule of conduct, that in transacting business affairs a woman should forget that she is a woman and proceed altogether as if she were a man.

This is an exceedingly stupid, pernicious, and false teaching.

In the first place, it proposes to ignore or set aside an immutable fact, and that can never be done. Beyond that fact, and naturally growing out of it, are laws, usages, social and personal forces.

With reference to all these, a woman may have, doubtless has, sundry disadvantages, of more or less importance, varying here and there, in various places, and under various circumstances. She has also her correlated advantages, of which she has a perfect right to avail herself.

In approaching any question relating to the conduct of affairs or the care of property, a woman should remember that she is a woman and not a man. All the laws, and all the decisions of the Courts, and all the relationships of trade, finance, politics, and manners, retain distinct traces, however minute or subtle, of the sexual distinction. Should they ever cease to do so, it will be time then, but is not time now, for any one to disregard the first principle.

A woman proposing to conduct her own affairs with propriety, security, and success, will do well to begin by studying herself. It is of importance to her to ascertain her own position with reference to all her external circumstances, and to consider what it will probably be with reference to such as may come, or to such as she may create. Some of her existing circumstances may be of her own making; so may be those which are to come; but more must be resultants of causes with which she can have little to do and which she cannot change.

She may ask, for example, whether she is under age, or of full age; or maid, or wife, or widow; whether she is rich or poor, or neither; dependent or independent; with or without children or others to care for or support; in debt or out of debt; capable or incapable of earning her own living; and she will do well to sift, vigorously, all her stock of knowledges concerning business affairs in general and her own affairs in particular.

Every woman would do well to acquire a knowledge of the rules of simple book-keeping. The care of her own pocket-money, be it more or less, should not be left to that curious pocket-with-holes-in-it, her memory. She may, if she chooses, keep a pen and ink account with her own name, as with that of a business customer, charging herself with every

Keeping accounts.

penny received, and crediting herself with every item paid out. She will soon learn how to keep a separate account, debit and credit, with every several department of her receipts and expenditures, and also how to make the several totals balance.

Her first general settlement with herself may remind her of a Chinese puzzle, where the pieces refuse to come together, but in due season it will become a very simple and very interesting matter. It is found that women make the very best of book-keepers.

After making a thorough and comprehensive study of herself and of her circumstances, a woman's next inquiry will be, in nine cases out of ten, as to the manner in which she will meet, not the next affair, but the person or persons in charge of the next affair. If they are women, she may not think of it at all, and this is sure to be a mistake, since forethought is also preparation and gives an advantage. If she is to deal with men, a first blunder would be that she can leave it all to them ; a second might be that she can meet them as if she were a man, which is impossible ; a third, and sometimes the worst blunder of all, would be the semi-sentimental, ill-balanced idea that she can take spec'al advantage of the fact that she is a woman, expecting attentions, concessions, or facilities of any kind which do not belong to her. This is all wrong. In her business relations a woman's manner should be affable, dignified, and business-like.

Manners in business.

The number of women who are complete business successes increases rapidly. In the city of New York, for instance, as in all other business centres, there are scores of trained and capable business women, whose manner of meeting whomsoever they are called upon to meet, is simply beyond criticism.

A great deal is to be gained when something of a man who is to be met can be known beforehand. What are his character and reputation? Is he of kith or kin or of any established relationship, and, if so, what is its nature ? Is he a man of work or a man of leisure ? Is he professional or otherwise? What is he supposed to know ? The answer to the last inquiry is apt to be more or less misleading, if made carelessly by a clever woman, conscious of her faculties or too well aware of her position. She may too readily forget, if a man whom she is to meet is a specialist, for instance, a very wooden lawyer, that, within his province and training, he must know a great deal more than she can possibly know, and that her ignorance cannot be substituted for his knowledge. Not at all a bad rule for a first conversation was the one adopted by an eminent English barrister and man of affairs, who said that he always began upon the basis of supposing the other fellow to know more than he did ; he was so sure to discover what the fellow really did know and to beat him if he did not know enough.

Knowledge of men.

The woman who has first established good and entirely confidential relations with herself and with the fact that she is a woman, of whatever kind of woman, may turn from the consideration of persons, or may not need to consider them at all, and may direct her mind entirely to the affair, great or small, which next requires to be dealt with. It might seem that general rules can hardly be made, considering how almost infinitely multifarious affairs must be, but there are general rules, almost as plain as are so many streets and avenues. The numbers and characters of the houses on the streets and avenues are not always so plain.

With reference to some of these rules and their applications, many a woman might be surprised to find how wide is already her acquaintance with the statutory laws of the commonwealth of which she is a citizen. Like the man who stumbled upon a grammatical definition and was astonished to find that he had all his life been talking "prose," she has been obeying, with a very clear knowledge of the meaning and effect of, many a dry legal precept.

It is true that every effort, printed or otherwise, to constitute "every man his own lawyer" has at least pointed out the boundary line beyond which every such man has a fool for a client, but within that barrier there is a continual opportunity for so acting as to render professional help unnecessary. The maxim that "whoever will obey the Ten Commandments will never run against the Revised Statutes," may belong to the "tissues of glittering generalities" of which the Declaration of Independence was said to consist, but clear perceptions of right and wrong, with simple common sense, are indeed the best basis for a fund of legal information.

The legal aspects of business.

With reference to Statutes or Court decisions presenting or defining any of the distinctions between men and women in the management of affairs, those of the State of New York will be taken as a guide in whatever may be said here. The reason for this is not only the excellence of the New York Code, but the fact that so many of the States recently created have either adopted it as a whole or accepted it as a model. Besides this are the efforts made and making by many of the older States to attain greater uniformity of precept and practice. The original Thirteen States and those which were earliest admitted to the Union, were all under the old English common law, at first, and some were slower than others in pruning away its excrescences. These were of many kinds, and some were absurd and barbarous enough, including the whipping-post of Delaware and the antediluvian law of Maryland, by means of which a woman not only may throw away herself, but her property also, upon the man she marries. No perceptible change is effected by marriage in the property rights of a woman living under any of the codes modelled upon that of New York. Her control of all that was her own remains the same during her life, and any right passing to her husband at her death is limited by the questions of children or no children, as well as by any last will and testament which she may leave behind her.

Married women's rights.

She, on the other hand, acquires no right in his personal property beyond her right to be supported, sometimes pretty widely interpreted with reference to debts of her contracting, but capable of strict, if not even of vexatious, limitation. In his real estate she acquires a "right of dower," the only visible effect of which, during his life, she will discover to be the necessity he is under of obtaining her signature, jointly with his own, to any deed or other instrument affecting the ownership of his landed estate. She cannot be compelled by him to sign any such paper. It must be done with her free will and consent, and she must say that it is so in a written affidavit, or the paper is defective and the title does not pass away, so far as her rights are concerned, whatever may become of his own.

The laws of the several States relating to divorce, unfortunately, vary too much for useful generalization. The decisions of the Courts, from time to time, under these laws, set forth the complicated nature and kaleidoscopic variety of the cases presented for action. It should be said, however, in view of the solemnity of marriage and the importance of forethought concerning it, that no possible decree of divorce can annul a marriage contract, either as to its social or legal consequences.

In accepting what is sometimes called a "partner for life" a woman does not *Partnerships.* of necessity become his business partner. He may become bankrupt without harm to her estate. It is easy, however, for her imprudently to entangle her affairs with his. If, for instance, she has advanced him sums of money, it is often difficult to place her debt in the same position with that of another creditor. The money should have been loaned through a third party, or under special methods provided for her protection, and these vary widely in different States. She had better not let her signature appear at all among the papers of the firm.

It might be supposed, indeed, that any educated woman knows how and when *Signatures.* and where to write her own name, but either it is not so, or very few women write as well as they know how. Every man in the habit of receiving extended correspondence can record a continuous series of perplexities and vexations along this line of his experience.

For instance, the morning mail has brought him a neatly written epistle, square envelope, and the best of stationery, from a person of whom he has never heard before, but who signs herself—he is sure it is she and not he,

WILHELMINA S. GIBBS.

He wishes to reply. He must do so, for her inquiry is pertinent and he is an exceedingly prompt and courteous business man ; but how shall he address her ? It will not do to make a blunder. He knows a man from her place of residence and he goes to him for the needed information. The response is :

"Wilhelmina ? Oh, yes, I know all the Stebbins girls. Wilhelmina married old John R. Gibbs. He buys his goods of our house. Her oldest daughter is named after her. Resembles her, too."

"Heavens ! Is it the girl or her mother ? I will try the old lady first. There ought to be a rule for such matters. Isn't there ? If there is, she ought to know it."

So the puzzled man writes, to the best of his knowledge and belief, and almost by return mail he is informed :

"However taken by surprise, I handed your letter to my daughter. Young as she is, she should have known better. I entirely disapprove of her opening such a correspondence with a stranger. That you should have addressed your reply to myself is a further astonishment, and Mr. Gibbs will call upon you when he visits your city next week.

"WILHELMINA S. GIBBS."

By the same mail comes another dainty envelope, containing no actual reproaches, but, with other matter, the expostulatory termination :

"How could you have mistaken ma for me ? Our names, indeed, are alike. Oh, dear ! Ought I not to have signed myself,

"Very sincerely yours,

"(MISS) WILHELMINA S. GIBBS ?"

Also there came another epistle, in a mercantile house advertising envelope of the firm of Gibbs, Crushington, Holmead & Co., and it was opened almost with trepidation. There was not much in it, and yet there was, for it was in part somewhat in the nature of an inquiry concerning forms, and it asked :

"Ought not a married woman to sign her husband's name, so that folks won't get an idea that he is dead and that she is a widow?

"(Mr.) John R. Gibbs."

The replies to Mr. Gibbs and to his estimable wife and to his charming daughter contained, in varying forms, the same information. This was that, "in writing to a stranger or to any man or woman with whom she is imperfectly acquainted, every married woman should let her signature tell him how to address his reply. He has no more right to know by letter the first name of a matron than he would have if he were presented to her at an evening party." A wife should use her husband's name with Mrs. attached, in all such cases, for more reasons than one. If, however, she is writing officially—for instance, as a member of a committee or officer of a society—she may tell the world her first name if the prefixed, parenthetical (Mrs.) also separates her from the great mob of the unmarried. Even then, however, (Mrs.) Birdie Violet DeVere does not look as well as would Mrs. Peter DeVere, and the latter would not leave half so many people still in ignorance as to whom she might be. Peter being dead, nevertheless the use of his name would be admissible, although optional. Its discontinuance might not always be a compliment to him. The rule, of course, only holds good up to a certain point, for there are women of both social and literary distinction whose very rank provides its own rule. In fact, they cannot be actual strangers to the recipients of their epistles, and no rule is needed. The unmarried woman who omits the Miss in parenthesis from before her signature, thereby simply asserts her understanding that she is addressing an acquaintance. She may so give a man credit for more information than he really possesses. There is, therefore, but one absolute rule for any woman to follow, and that is, to leave her correspondent in no doubt whatever as to how he may correctly address his reply.

At the correspondence line, this rule dies out, for in any signature to a business document, bank-check, deed for land, lease, note, draft, or affidavit, another rule comes in. The woman signing such a paper must take it for granted that the question of her personal identity is settled. Her married or unmarried state has nothing to do with the matter. She cannot use the first name of her husband if she is married. She must use her own, written in every case as if she were a spinster. Should it be an instrument in which her name is mentioned, written out in full, she should write as fully, even if it compels her to sign herself as:

"Wilhelmina Stebbins Gibbs."

Upon a check or draft, or other every-day piece of paper, her husband, or father, might pen his accustomed brief business signature, and men would see the well-known

"J. R. Gibbs."

The woman's signature is legally entitled to the same brevity, and in constant practice would lose its calligraphic beauty.

The women cashiers of our business houses present good illustrations of this result, but, for the great multitude of women who merely attend to the incidental business attaching to other modes of life and do not scrawl so much, a better practice, giving more information concerning the maker of the signature, is to write the first name in full, as

"Wilhelmina S. Gibbs."

Returning to the woman who has been making a primary study of her own position, financially, before going out into business affairs, one of her inquiries should relate to the general subject of real estate.

Has she any? Or, if not, does she intend or expect to own any? and if so, *Real estate.* by what means, or from what source?

If she has an expectation through probable inheritance, it would surely be well for her to obtain, as best she can, every possible information relating to the property indicated; but beyond that point she cannot go.

If she has as yet no real estate, but has her eye upon a piece which she may see fit to purchase, she cannot know too much of its history and condition. Prudence requires her to know all there is to know, with the certain advantage that no important fact can be concealed from her, even by a dishonest seller, if she is on the alert.

So complete is the public record required by law, and obtained in practice, of the origin of all real estate titles and of their subsequent transfers, that a full history of any town-lot or farm may be readily found. Any fact not on the record at the hour of purchase may be disregarded by the buyer with a fair degree of safety, but with one vitally important provision. The hour of accepting a deed for real estate should also be the hour for its presentation for record at the office of the County Clerk. That official should give a written assurance that the paper is duly accepted and filed for record. This done, any other paper than the one in question, even if ten years older, if not recorded, and if it belongs to the same chain of titles, is deprived of almost all of its effect as against the recorded deed, provided that the latter was given and accepted without actual notice of the prior deed. If any adverse paper, however, had obtained a first record, whatever force was in it would thereby be preserved.

It is probable that a woman buying real estate would do so under the direction of a man-of-law, but his assistance does not excuse her from knowing, at the time, the nature of whatever he does or directs her to do, and the reasons for every act. She should know that what is called a deed in fee simple, a Warranty Deed, on its face declares that there is no flaw in the title conveyed. [*See Appendix.*] This declaration may be trusted if sustained by the official record, but not otherwise. She should know and commit to memory, if she can, the exact description of the property, as it is written out in the deed. She should go and compare the description with the thing described, and be sure that they agree in every particular. She should also compare the same description with any that preceded it, written in the title-deeds upon which her deed is based, lest an error or omission should bring trouble upon her. Illustrations are only too abundant, but one will do. A woman in New York owned a lot and built upon it a house, after having carelessly read her description. She had the house put up close to the one next to it, and nobody said a word until all was done. That next house, however, did not stand within a foot and a half of the edge of its lot, and therefore the whole side of her new building stood on land not belonging to its builder. The owners took advantage of the situation, and it cost many times the value of that foot-and-a-half of land to correct the effect of her carelessness. No property ought to be accepted and paid for without an official survey, establishing its map or diagram.

Another form of instrument transferring real estate is called the Quit-claim Deed. Its very name suggests the idea that its maker cannot give, and that it does not convey, a perfect title. It insinuates a possible flaw, somewhere, sufficient to warn the seller against making himself liable, by an absolute Warranty. Just how great the defect may be in his right and power to convey title, is a question so wide that no more need here be said about it. Many a Quitclaim is as good as any man's Warranty, so far as perpetual possession by the buyer is concerned, but the offer of such an instrument is a plain demand for an exceedingly rigid investigation. [*See Appendix.*]

The buyer of land may not be ready or willing to pay for it at once and in full. More frequently, she will wish to pay part down, and the rest at some time or times in the future. She will obtain and record a deed, but she will give in return, as security for the remainder due, what is known as a Mortgage. She will be given a printed form, neatly filled up, ready for signature, and she may be even over-ready to sign—for the seller, and his lawyer, and other very good men, may tell her it is all right. But she should read the Mortgage thoroughly before signing, and know what it contains, for there are several kinds of mortgages, and some have sharper teeth than others. She should demand and keep a copy of the instrument she has signed, that she may study it a little afterwards however clear may seem to be her first understanding of its generally pretty severe provisions. It will surely provide for the return of the property to the seller, with or without the aid of a formal "foreclosure" suit and public auction, but it may also give away at the outset, any or all of the common law and statutory protections provided for unfortunate mortgagors. If the provisions of the proposed instrument are too severe, a woman can refuse to sign it as quickly as could a man. She may have visited a law stationer's beforehand, and invested a few cents in a set of printed forms of the several kinds of mortgages, leases, and deeds, and then, having read them at home, she may be competent to say which of them she prefers, if a town-lot or farm of her own is to be encumbered by one or the other of their "dead hands." [*See Appendix.*]

Time may pass, after such a purchase, and the buyer may be making payments on the mortgage, according to its requirements. If about to do so, she may well consider how and where. Of one thing she may be assured—she has nothing to do with the man of whom she purchased, the mortgagee. Her only interest is in the mortgage, the piece of paper itself, that she signed. She will make her payment to that piece of paper, and to that only, wherever she may find it, but she will look for it at the place, the house, or bank, or County Clerk's office named in the paper, and in the copy she kept. She has a right to find it there, and if it is not there for her to pay, she has a right, to be asserted carefully, to offer her payments then and there, before witnesses. As a rule it will be there, even if the original mortgagee has sold it to a second party, and so on; but she must see the paper to which she pays her money, and she must see that her partial payment is fully indorsed and acknowledged upon it, in writing, and witnessed. In some places a notary's seal is called for as witness of such a payment. It will never do any harm. But if the payment be final and in full, then she will receive, under notarial seal, a " satisfaction piece " acknowledging payment, and with it the original mortgage itself, which she must not leave behind her. Both must go at once to the Record Office at the County Court House, and there the clerk must record, before she leaves him, that the mortgage is off forever. The paper itself must be cancelled, her own signature "marked out" of it, and it may then be filed away. With reference to any duty of this kind, it is well never to forget the maxim that "delays are dangerous."

Much more frequently acquired than any other real estate interest is that which is to be obtained by means of a lease. There are many varieties of this kind of paper, for longer or shorter terms, for residences, for business uses, or for farm property.

Leases.

Of course, the first consideration is as to whether or not the person proposing the lease has a legal right to make it. If he has one at the time of making, he may next day sell the property, or become bankrupt, but the rights of the lessee will not be affected if she has taken proper care of them. [*See Appendix.*]

Her first care is that of taking possession. If she has received the key of the outer door and has used it, she is reasonably safe, but if she has actually landed anything of her own within the premises she is more so. All the better if, in the city, she has lighted a fire in the range, or if, in the country, she has put a cow in the barn.

Any lease for longer than one year, or of any considerable importance, should also be recorded. It is not always easy to tell, in these days of rapid changes and property improvement, how great may be the value of a leasehold. There are large numbers of people whose finances have been unexpectedly improved by the sums they have received for the surrender of long-time leases. Probably not one of them, when asked to surrender, failed to inquire why, of other parties than the one asking. No such favor should be granted in a hurry. What is much wanted can be paid well for, and it is honestly the property of the lessee, and not of her landlord, to the last dollar.

The covenants contained in any lease should be read with care before accepting or signing, and it is quite likely a prudent woman may insist upon having some of the too strict provisions marked out with pen and ink, not with a pencil, both on the copy kept by her landlord and on her own copy, in order that they may perfectly agree. Both papers are related records, and her own must also become part of her bookkeeping. The dates for payments to the lessor will of course be found plainly stated. She knows who he is, and she can safely go on paying directly to him, or to his agent, if he has one, who has already acted as such in regard to that lease. His cashier, or bookkeeper at his office—not outside of it—is such a known agent. If he has discharged his first agent and has not notified her, she is still safe. If he has sold the property, she is not supposed to know it, unless notified. But if by accident she does know it, or that he is publicly declared a bankrupt, she must inquire to whom, instead of him, her payment must be made. She will not do this, full of nervous uncertainty, on the last day in the afternoon, but she will do her best to make her regular payments at least one day before the day specified in the lease. Three days is a safer allowance. For every payment she will insist upon a receipt, duly signed, and she will attach each receipt, in series, to her lease, with a memorandum of the payment also written upon the lease. If she has paid with a check on a bank, she will attach that check also, with the receipt, as soon as it returns from the bank. The entire paper, neatly folded away in an envelope, the superscription of which tells what is in it, will be part of the treasures of her strong-box, and this may very wisely be in a Safe Deposit

Company's little crypt. Her lease, with its gummed-at-the-edge attachments, and its written memoranda, added to the entry made in her cash-book and journal, will be her perfect protection in case of any dispute with her landlord.

Every paper of any importance should be folded lengthwise, and filed away for examination. Letters upon business subjects should not be left among other letters. Nobody can say what may become the value of a letter relating to business. A promise made in a letter is a contract in writing, under some circumstances, or it may be made an explanatory part of some other contract, greatly increasing its force. It is not so needful as some suppose to retain copies of business letters. It is well for purposes of reference, but the letter itself, with its envelope and postmarks, or in the hands of the recipient, is the best evidence a court can have of the fact that it was ever sent. A person might, indeed, write letters all day, and copy them, and that might be the end of it. If, however, a letter is to be sent, concerning the character and delivery of which the sender is especially interested, a copy—best of all a letter-press copy—should be taken, and value may be given to this copy by having the letter sent duly registered. Thus it may almost be proved that it went and was received, for the return receipt from the post-office will be kept with care.

Business papers and letters.

Speaking of receipts, there is one curious point concerning consecutive payments. It may be illustrated by an ordinary grocer's running account, with regular Saturday payments. For each week's purchases a receipt is given upon payment, and each is duly filed away. There may be fifty of them when the house burns down and all go up in smoke.

Receipts.

How, then, if a dispute should arise concerning some of those old payments? What if they are denied by the grocer, and if his carelessly kept books contain no record of the money handed in? Is the payer at the mercy of that accident? By no means. If she but have her last Saturday's receipt, it is regarded as obviously in full of all demands to that date. All that were given before it were of no account. But this rule applies only to consecutive payments.

The suggested inspections of affairs already existing or proposing, may assume another aspect, even with reference to real estate. There may be none to purchase or to lease, but there may be some person already in possession. For instance, a woman may be the owner of a farm or a residence. She may or may not be occupying either, and this point is important. If she is occupying, she is in possession. If not, she still may be, for the actual occupant may be her agent, holding for her, acknowledging her ownership, and thereby giving or continuing her legal, possessory right. If the occupant is such by reason of a written lease from her, or pays rent, in any way or form, that is enough. If merely by verbal permission, that may or may not be enough, and requires consideration, unless the owner's right has previously been fixed beyond dispute.

Evidence of ownership.

In any event, next to the fact of possession, an important question is whether or not there is any other known or possible claimant to the property. Each separate piece of property presents its own distinct set of inquiries, and in each case the first answers must come from the deed or other instrument in writing, and that should also be of record, by means of which the ownership is supposed to exist.

There are several ways of acquiring

a property in real estate. One is by inheritance, and closely allied to this is that by testamentary devise. In each of these the recipient, now the apparent owner, must have been given the papers required by the laws of her State. These are by no means everywhere the same, but they everywhere carefully guard all rights and all limitations to all rights. An immediate duty is a thorough reading and understanding of those papers. They may have conveyed sole ownership, like a Warranty Deed; or a defective, incomplete title, like a Quitclaim Deed; or a life estate, terminable with life; or some kind of joint estate, more or less perfectly defined; or even an estate prospective, not yet ready for actual enjoyment. A very good test of the matter is the inquiry, "What can I do with this property? Can I merely use it, in whole or in part? Can I sell it, and if so, what kind of title can I give?"

Inheritance and testamentary devise.

The last inquiry calls for a history of the title in other hands, and here begins another sort of study, relating to property not derived in any of these ways. An instrument commonly described as a "deed for land" can be understood readily, and a woman of common intelligence can discover how much and in what way it conveys to her. She can understand, therefore, what kind of title she could give to another person, for she cannot sell any more than she really has, and a deed from her must express no more than did the deed to her.

Behind her title, however, there is a field that goes back to some historic boundary line. This paper should be accompanied by another, known as a "search of title," by some competent lawyer. It may go back directly, in an unbroken line, to some old colonial grant or Indian

Search of title.

transfer, or to the Land Office patents of the United States, which should be good titles, but are not always so. Such a deed, with such an ancestry on paper, contains no very difficult problem other than the questions of its due delivery, its record, and the act of possession consequent.

The "search," however, may have led back to and through old-time lawsuits and decisions of courts, and these are always interesting. They become less and less so as the years go by, for the length of time during which an undisputed possession has been held of any piece of land is an important factor in the validity of its possessory title. The disputed point grows into the main point in some cases. For instance, in the heart of the city of New York there were once large tracts of rocky ground, seemingly worthless in the earlier days of Manhattan Island. They were not distinctly included in any of the earlier recorded grants or titles. They were a kind of "no man's land," until, as the city grew, they were occupied by squatters. These were of the very poor, and their rude, squalid shanties were perched picturesquely enough on the rocks and in the hollows. It seemed as if some of them could be more easily reached by goats than by human beings. As time went on, however, all that land or rock became of value. Streets and avenues were to be laid out through it, and it was to be built upon. But by whom? Who owned it? The public interests, and those of enterprising speculators required the creation of an ownership. This was done in many cases merely by obtaining quitclaim deeds from the miscellaneous squatters actually holding the rocks in possession.

The goats were but driven away, and wherever a rock had no occupant one was duly obtained for it. Then began the regular process of improvement, and as soon as assessments and taxes were levied and paid, the original titles were also greatly improved. The main feature requiring note at this day is, however, that these titles are among the best in the city, because they are not, and cannot be, disputed. The "search," or history of any woman's title to her real estate, may or may not assure her that she is secure from controversy. It is her duty to settle her mind on that point, even if she has to pay for a search among the records in the office of the county clerk, or exercise her right to go and make one herself. If she elects the latter course, she will no doubt learn a great deal and severely try the courtesy and patience of one or more important officials.

If, now, by thoughtful investigation, a woman has ascertained exactly the source and present nature of her title to any real estate under her control, by inheritance, purchase, or otherwise, her following business duty, disconnected at first from any thought about a possible sale, relates to "What can I do with it?"

As a rule the best reply is, "I can keep it," and that may lead on to matters of taxes, assessments, *Disposition of real estate.* and the advisability and cost of feasible improvements. Whatever may be the nature or amount of operations designed to make a given property of greater comfort, use, or profit, questions of finance will at once arise which will attach themselves and their conduct to an entirely different branch of her primary investigation. She will step forward at once into the wide domain of personal property, its perils, and its management.

If her thoughts of improvement tend toward any kind of building or construction, she will be met by the general question of "contracts." The first rule, to be kept also for strict application elsewhere, is that every contract for making any part of her improvements must be in writing. If the contract involves a large amount, it should be signed by one or more witnesses. She must know what she intends to have done, and be sure that the terms of the contract describe clearly her purpose. The contractor is not bound to do anything that is not expressed in the contract, including the qualities and kinds of work and materials, and the time set for part and full performance. If he is not pecuniarily responsible, he should give security. The property itself is his security, as a general rule.

Real estate itself has its many difficulties, variations, and uncertainties, but there is nothing else excepting snow, perhaps, that is so evanescent as is the magical entity so vaguely described as "personal property." Part of the uncertainties of its being, or rather of its definition, belong to the fact that at one of its edges it blends more or less with real estate, since the paper evidence of a debt for which real estate is pledged as security may be so shaped that the unpractised eye can hardly tell whether it be land or water.

Every woman is a holder of personal property of some kind, and almost every woman is quite willing *Personal property.* to have more. She will best prepare for obtaining more by putting what she has in perfect order and forming a clear idea of her right to it, of its value, and of what can best be done with it.

Whatever she has may be classified for future reference. One class readily may be scheduled, for it is made up only of such things as she has actually in possession under her own hand. Another class is made up of such things as she owns without dispute, but which, at the time of noting them, are held for her in other hands whatsoever. Yet another class may consist of claims which she has, or believes she has, upon property in the hands of others, and to which her claim is not defined or acknowledged. Yet a fourth class, not to be lost sight of nor despised, consists of her own business capacity, her ability to earn, win, or create property, for this is often the largest part of the capital of a successful merchant. Illustrative of this is the case, not by any means standing alone, of a well-known New York merchant whose entire assets were swept away by a financial panic. He could pay his creditors but in part with what was left him of visible resources, but they all recognized the true nature of his personal property in his ability and integrity; they "set him up again," to go right on, and the penniless bankrupt soon regained his old position as a millionaire.

The several classes of personal property indicated, however, require different treatments, even in their first analysis, since they hold varying relations to business usages and to the provisions of the statute books.

It is the part of a woman to be neat and orderly, but the moment a woman steps out from among her wardrobe matters, her home concerns, her heirlooms, and the like, she finds the need of a kind of order and arrangement, to the rules of which she may be but imperfectly accustomed. Much of it, at first sight, does not look very orderly, for it is in various kinds of motion, here and there, and is more or less affected by the pell-mell rush of business life.

She may leave behind now part of the first class of her personal property, all of it which must remain at home; but it is business-like for her to have in mind a clear idea of its value and of its bearing upon her social position, her means of support, and her probable outlays. It is a distinct item in what is called her "fixed capital," the "plant" of her general activities. It must be kept up; it may be increased; it must be guarded.

There are good reasons why it should be insured against loss by fire, *Insurance.* and in the selection of a fire insurance company she will prudently avoid companies with a small capital and a narrow surplus. She will prefer well-established companies, and, among them such as make a specialty of household risks. In all of them the rates are low enough for safety at the present day. She will not attempt to insure for a larger sum than will cover the present value of her goods, and she will carefully read her "policy," noting what it covers. As a rule, she will need to insure her piano or her pictures, and some other matters, separately; anything, in fact, which is not properly described as household furniture or by other of the express terms printed or written in the policy.

Once taken out, an insurance policy must be kept up by renewed payments at the required dates, for it will not renew itself, but dies by its own limitation, without mercy, and with no especial courtesy to women. If among the personal property on hand there are such matters as are produced upon a farm under her management, advice as to its treatment and sale would be a work of supererogation, for our women-farmers, married or single, are already noted for their superiority as bargaining sellers of all manner of farm products. Other women, however, who have some property and resources, may not have received the same life-long training of their original faculties.

Nearly all that can be said concerning the treatment of other items, of personal property owned and under hand, may be summed up in directions for treating the whole as cash, and considering what is to be done with the money.

It should not require argument that money ought not to be kept in the house or on the person, beyond the sum required for immediate outlays of a minor kind. The risk of loss is too great, and to this may often be added the temptation to spend. It is much better in the box of a Safe Deposit *Safe Deposit* Company, along with all the *Companies.* papers representing money or other kinds of value.

The consideration of a place for the safe keeping of money, in the form of *Banks and* cash for immediate use, sug-*banking.* gests the subject of banks and banking, and with it the question of how to select a bank.

In small country places there may often seem to be no choice, for there is but one banking institution within the town limits. The kind of prudence required in such a case, however, is precisely the same as if there were a dozen within convenient reach.

The character of a bank should not be taken for granted, any more than if it were an individual, and its reputation, or that of its managers, can always be ascertained by reasonably careful inquiry. This means a consultation with perhaps more than one competent man of business. Any such man will generally be found willing to advise. There should never be any hesitation about seeking needed information. No business man ever fails in this respect, for obtaining, weighing, and using information is the sum and substance of his every-day transactions. *The difference between successful and unsuccessful men turns mainly upon their capacity for estimating the value of what is told them.* As a rule they obtain more than one testimonial, and their example is good to follow, in this or in any other important matter of business, remembering that the best proof of capacity is often evinced in the rejection of doubtful advice.

As savings banks are at the present day managed, restricted, and inspected, under the sharp eyes of State officials, jealous of their own reputations, these institutions are very good safe-deposit boxes, with the additional advantage that they pay interest on deposits. The rate of interest is low, but they cannot safely pay more, for they are different from other banks in a very important particular. They are strictly "investment agencies," provided for the safe investment of aggregates of funds made up of all their small deposits.

They are limited by law to a certain range of manifestly sound securities, such as selected mortgages upon real estate, United States Government bonds, State bonds, and, in some cases, specified municipal bonds, like those of the City of New York. The list of those permitted investments varies in the several States, but is everywhere carefully guarded. Nearly all of the money in the care of a savings bank must be continually so invested or it could not pay its expenses and its interest.

It keeps on hand merely enough to meet ordinary drawing out, and its cash-box would soon be emptied by anything like a "run." In that case it may borrow, if its directors see fit to do so, but otherwise it must shut off further demands by applying its reserved right to thirty or sixty days' notice. This is for the protection of all concerned, but it may at any time lock up, temporarily, all the savings deposited with the bank as a general agent for their safe investment. If, therefore, a woman's money is to be deposited with reference to any payment which she must make at a given date, as a note, her rent, or a payment on mortgage or other interest account, she will hardly permit herself to take that risk. It might involve her in serious loss, and of this there are numberless instances. She will probably turn, therefore, to National or State banks, for the deposit of any funds which she wishes to use from day to day, or on a given day.

She will be met at the threshold by striking differences in the manner of her reception. At the savings bank she required no introduction. Her own statements as to her name, residence, and one or two other small matters, were accepted. She was given a book in which her deposits were entered, but she was told that the book itself was her evidence of identity, and she must bring it with her when she came to draw out money. If she could neither read nor write, could not sign her own name, the book would act as her signature, with her "mark" upon her order for money. This is actually the method in many thousands of cases. The savings bank book also contained a blank form, adopted by that bank in particular, according to which any order must be drawn, but no other blank forms were given her to carry away. The deposits at this bank were also required to be in the form of currency, paper, or metal, for the teller would not accept the best bank check that could be brought him. His institution had no exchange dealings with any other.

National and State banks accept checks on deposit. Persons desiring to do business with these institutions must be properly introduced, that is, by some one whose identity and financial standing are known at the bank in question.

National banks, organized and existing under the laws of the United States, are under the inspection of capable officers of the National Treasury, and their capital is invested in United States bonds, in order that, for the greater part of them, they may obtain return currency in the shape of national bank notes. Once obtained, these notes are ordinary capital, subject to the ordinary rules of profit and loss, while the bonds deposited in the Treasury, for the security of the currency issued for them, form no part of the security of the bank's depositors.

At the present time State banks do not issue currency. They are under the inspection of State officers, upon a system very like that adopted by the Treasury.

Is there any choice for a depositor between the two classes of banks? So far as the best financiers can see, not any. The record of bank failures during the critical year of 1893 does not indicate any preference either way. Reckless or dishonest bank officers can wreck any kind of institution, and sound-minded, honest managers are likely to steer their ship through the cyclone of a great financial panic.

Another question relates to the personal character of the managing officers and directors of the bank. The mere fact that a woman knows them, or some of them, should not send her there. She may know that which ought to send her somewhere else.

Have the president, cashier, leading directors of this bank been very keen and successful speculators? Have they, or any of them, accumulated much money by brilliant gambling? If so, a woman may admire them at a distance, but let her put her money into a bank managed by merchants or others who have climbed the regulation stairway of legitimate business. The whole coast of finance is littered with the wrecks of dashing millionaires and of the banks they ornamented, and whose capital and deposits they obliterated.

Actually bad character will forbid a

woman from dealing with any man, and no caution is needed in such a case, but she should not object if her proposed president or cashier, and the rest, are a "wooden-faced lot," who go through their business, to all outward seeming, as if they were so many banking-machines. The receiving teller, in particular, has no time either to speak or smile, for he is a perpetual example in simple arithmetic.

A bank of deposit is but to a limited extent an investment agency, for its leading character is that of a collector and disburser. Out of this grows its entire usefulness as an agent for making exchanges for the mercantile people in different localities. Out of this grows also its great function of credit-merchant, for it must deal with all manner of evidences of debt as any other merchant deals with any other wares.

It is the duty of the officers of a bank, the cashier generally performing it, to know something about any person asking the privilege of making deposits in, and collections or payments through, their institution. They are polite enough, always, and it is not often that they reject an applicant of ordinary respectability, but there is one especial reason for the introduction and assurance of personal identity. That is, they must become certain in their own minds that the person opening this account with them is entitled to write the signature which must be entered at once upon the book of signatures. To the paying teller, more than to any other officer, this book is as a photograph gallery, and from it he thenceforth knows you, whether or not he ever sees your face. Your written name is much more, in this place, than was the pass-book at the Savings Bank, and you should write it at first in your most accustomed way. To that, whatever practice you have had, has given character and ease. Always, afterward, on any piece of paper, for that bank or any other, write your name precisely in the same way, that it may be promptly and surely recognized. Too great a variation might lead even to the rejection of a check.

Identity and respectability being settled to the satisfaction of the cashier, you will once more receive a pass-book and with it some printed deposit-tickets. One of these you will fill up with the items—check, draft, currency, coin—which make up your present deposit. Book and ticket and money you will hand in at the receiving teller's window, and his concern with your signature belongs to its use upon the back of any other person's check which you are depositing. He will enter the amount upon your book and return it to you, and, at the same time, you will receive, probably, another small book of blank checks upon that bank.

It is for convenience only, however, since you are not at all restricted to it, and the bank will as readily pay any other proper form of check or draft with your signature at the bottom. How great a convenience it is you will learn, nevertheless, when you examine the stub, the system of numbering consecutively, and see what a perfect record it can be made to keep of all your disbursements made by checks on the bank. At any subsequent time, if you are ordinarily careful in filling up both check and stub, the latter will preserve proof of the amount, the date, the number, and the person for whose benefit each of your payments was made. The cash-book, which should be kept at home, must tally with this and be ready to show, at any hour, just how much money remains in the bank. The one must prove the other.

The mere form of a check explains itself. Those in use by large mercantile concerns are of similar form, but are often of more ornate character, finely engraved or lithographed, printed on better paper, and there are special punches and other devices for the prevention of forgery, particularly the kind of forgery performed by raising the amount of the check. One ordinary safeguard against this is the rule that figures are of small consequence, but that the amount called for is the one written out. For additional security, begin to write at the extreme left of the space provided on the face of the check, write plainly, blackly, and then draw a deep black line through the remaining space.

Checks.

You can draw a check "to bearer," but it is not well to do so, for that check is thenceforth somewhat like a greenback, affording no better security against loss. If you are paying it to another person or firm, near or far, draw the check to the order of that person or firm. If you wish to use it in shopping, where you are known, draw it to your own order and put your name on the back of it, near the middle, when you pay it out. If you wish to use it where you are not known, have the paying teller "certify," and it is then charged to your account, but cannot be drawn without your "order" signature on the back. Even if you are taking out currency with a check, follow the rule, draw to your own order and endorse on the back. Turn the check over facing toward you. Write your name straight across, beginning on the left side, nearly half way down. It is a safe and orderly habit to form.

Knowing what to do with your own checks, you will know how to handle a check paid you by another person. Suppose it to be your first experience. If, unwisely, it was made payable to bearer, still follow your own rule and endorse it before depositing it, for it is itself a kind of memorandum record of that transaction. If drawn to the order of another person, it is worth nothing to you until that person has endorsed it. If it is so endorsed, it is again unsafe against loss unless the endorser has written above the signature on the back that it is now payable to you. This transfers it, and it becomes as if it had originally been drawn to your order, that is, your signature written under the other on the back.

A check drawn in one city to pay a debt in another, may often pass through several hands, and all the space on its back may be written full of transfer endorsements. If not paid by the bank on which it is drawn, it must then go back through the several accounts in which it has been handled, charged, or credited, until it is presented for redemption to the first person depositing it for collection. Specific variations from this practice do not require elucidation here.

If the check in your hand is drawn to your own order, endorse it, deposit it at once, noting its source and amount first in your cash-book, then on the deposit-ticket. Deposit at once, because if you delay (as the law provides "use reasonable diligence") and the bank should fail, the loss is your own and not that of the person who gave you the check. When deposited, it is in the collection agency on its way for collection, but you cannot check out money on account of it until after it is collected. Even if the bank, knowing your solvency, should courteously permit you to consider it already collected, do not do so unless you are sure of other funds coming in at once, to make good the deficit in your bank balance in case that check should fail of collection. If it is on a bank near by, you can indeed prevent all difficulty, by first taking the check to that bank and having it certified before deposit. There are a great many people, in and out of business, whose checks should

New York, *May 1st, 1896* No. *27*

NINETY-THIRD WARD BANK
OF THE CITY OF NEW YORK

Pay to the order of *Wilhelmina S. Gibbs* ————————

Forty-eight ⁰⁰/₁₀₀ ———————————— **Dollars**

$48.00

Wilhelmina S. Gibbs

Wilhelmina S. Gibbs

No. 27
DATE *May 1st 1896*
NAME *Wilhelmina S. Gibbs*
AMOUNT $48.
——

Form of Check and Stub Filled Out and Endorsed.

be certified at once, for they may be good to-day and not good to-morrow. Never be careless or sentimental about a check certification.

Confidence in the solvency of the bank one deals with is pretty sure to grow with continuous dealing until any depositor may find herself quoting the proverb "safe as the bank," but a day may come when her confidence is shaken. It is not well heedlessly to join in a "run" upon a bank of deposit or of savings, but it is well to listen even to rumors concerning its solvency, to investigate them if possible, and to let one's account run very low in a bank concerning which rumors are beginning to circulate. These may themselves create a pernicious "run," and your money may be locked up, out of your reach for a time, by the difficulties into which even a solvent institution may be thrown. Look out for your own interests, but do not be scared into hasty action by a shadow or a whisper.

Drafts. A draft is simply an order or request for the payment of money, and on its face it implies, first that there are funds ready to meet it, or, second, that such funds can and will be provided on or before the expiration of the time named in the draft. To that apparent time, three days, commonly called "days of grace," must be added, unless they are in set terms disallowed upon the face of the paper. Every draft also bears legal interest, days of grace included, unless this also is in like manner disallowed, for the draft, as soon as it is accepted, becomes a time-promise to pay money, as if it were a promissory note. It is "accepted" when the bank messenger or other collector places it before the person or firm on whom it is drawn, and obtains his or their signature written across its face. [*See Appendix.*]

Intermediate collecting agents writing on the back of a draft do not become responsible for anything but the safe transmission of any money finally paid on it, plus interest account and minus collection charges.

If, therefore, you have a draft instead of a check to deposit, deal with it as if it were a check, and the bank will attend to all the remaining operations. With either form of collection, check or draft, the bank's work may include a formal "protest" in case of failure to collect. But the very word "protest" brings up the consideration of a third kind of paper, which is not so simple. It is well for a business woman to familiarize herself with all the peculiar features of that dangerous piece of paper, the promissory note, before she accepts one or gives one, and particularly before she brings one to her own bank for collection.

Promissory notes. Any, the very simplest form of written acknowledgment of a sum of money due, is, in its legal effect, a promissory note. The most perfectly engraved and worded form of note is nothing more, for it declares the existence of a debt or obligation at the date of signature. In law, a person who in writing acknowledges a debt, by the same act promises to pay it, with legal interest from date, unless the form used in the paper expressly says "without interest." The note, in whatever form, may name a future day of payment. The debt or obligation at present existing, does not in that case become due and payable until the date set forth, but it exists all the same, and there is no getting away from it. Even a church subscription, with a signature attached, is a promissory note. If not paid when it should be, a time can be ascertained and fixed beyond which it is an over-due obligation, drawing interest. [*See Appendix.*]

This being true, the first, most obvious deduction is that a woman should always consider well before signing her name to anything. She should help herself to see clearly how much of her personal property she is parting with, or endangering, and what she is doing it for.

In the first place, if she is merely borrowing money needed for some immediate exigency, or for some business use, like the purchase of real estate, or its improvement, or to help a friend, she may not go to a bank but to a person. No matter who may be the money-lender, however, all the points of the transaction may best be dealt with if she gives a note, precisely as if she were dealing directly with a bank. Not only is the bank the best and most usual form of money-lender; not only is it, to that extent, a "person;" but any note given is pretty sure to be payable at some bank or other, or will be sent to one for collection. If it should not be, all the laws and methods are the same, and if she learns how to deal with a bank, she will know how to deal with anybody else.

Wishing to borrow money, therefore, she will obtain one of the ordinary printed forms of promissory notes. There is little variation in these forms, and she will readily see how one is to be filled up. She will see that she writes a promise to pay, for instance, "to John Jones or order." It would make small difference if she should strike out the words "or order." Nothing in the body of a note can prevent it from being transferable, and she may in the end pay it to somebody else. The note is but proof of the debt to John Jones, and if he were to die the next hour it would be collected by his "heirs, administrators, or assignees." He made no contract to live for thirty days, and his death does not wipe out that debt.

She will notice also, that the form specifies "for value received," and that is a point of great importance, for, primarily speaking, the note is void without it. In making a note and parting with it, she must be careful to obtain "value" to the full extent of her contract, but will do well to remember that if she has not done so there is a weak spot in that merely formal claim against her. She can protect herself against being made to pay it, by giving due notice to certain persons, particularly to the bank at which it makes itself payable. "Due notice" is instantaneous notice, as soon as she discovers that she is in danger of a fraud or imposition.

The date of making, the date of payment, the name of the bank, the amount covered, having been entered upon her account-book, pretty fully, the note is ready and she may go to the bank. It is the one where she makes her deposits, and where she and her business character or "credit" are already well known. If it is to another bank or person, she will need to become well known, as to her character and resources, before she will obtain any money.

In any event, with her promise to pay, the bank will demand ample security. It is a collecting and disbursing agent, anxious to lend in a safe way, the entire mass of its capital and of the current amount on hand of its collections, made and making, over and above its current disbursements. That is its character as a money-merchant. So it must make the most of its profits. It does not wish to keep on hand a dollar of its loanable funds, and these are carefully estimated by its officers. As a rule it has money to lend, but it is forbidden to take any risk whatever. That is the theory, whatever may be the practice, and the borrower is required to protect the bank from all loss. There are three kinds of such security, generally speaking. One is given by

Mrs. Commodore Crœsus, when she offers merely her note. It is "single-name, gilt-edged paper," and is secured by her known millions. Even then, for form's sake, her note may be endorsed by Mr. Straw, who adds nothing to the certainty of its payment.

Another kind of security is given by means of what are known as "collaterals," and the sooner a woman has a pile of these, the better. The pile may not grow so fast if she signs her name frequently or carelessly. It may consist either of several kinds of personal property, as bank stock or other stocks; or railway bonds or other bonds; or of a mortgage on land; or of a warehouse receipt for produce delivered; or of salable goods and chattels. Anything offered to a bank as collateral security, however, must be of such a kind and in such a shape that the bank can sell it on a sure market, if need be, for more than money enough to pay the note. How much more is a matter for the bank to decide. The note made and the proposed collaterals must be submitted to the officers of the bank. Often these will include the board of directors on a day of the week called "discount day," when they meet to pass judgment on paper offering. Quite as frequently, nevertheless, the president and cashier act upon minor notes, and the directors permit and accept their action. If the loan is approved, the person making the note will be presented with and required to execute a paper which is in the nature of both a transfer and a power of attorney, for, whatever form it is in, it becomes a part of the contract contained in the note, and it gives the bank power to sell the collateral security and pay itself the amount of the note, with interest and expenses, out of the proceeds thereof. During the time following the date of the loan, to the date of actual payment, the bank holds the security, and the owner cannot do anything with it, except to sell it, for instance, subject to the lien on it held by the bank.

It seems hardly necessary to point out that no woman in her senses will borrow money in this way, unless she feels absolutely sure of paying her note at maturity. She had better sell her collateral, unless, and this may be often the case, the market for its sale is at present bad, but promises to become better before the note will be due. This, indeed, may be a very good reason for borrowing, but its existence should be plainly settled in the mind of the would-be borrower.

The third kind of security, altogether the most in use in commercial transactions outside of imports, exports, and the movement of instantly salable produce, like wheat or tobacco, is that to be given by an acceptable "endorser."

Endorsement is not always easily to be had, and should never be accepted without serious consideration. One of the considerations, even if the note-maker feels absolutely sure of paying the note, is that the acceptance of endorsement places her under a strong sense of obligation to her endorser. She almost agrees, without saying it, that under similar circumstances she will return the favor. She borrows the credit of another person, because she gets that person to sign, on the back of her note, an agreement to pay it in case she does not. That person practically makes a second note, inside of the other, just like it, just as binding in case the first note breaks down. So does the second and third endorser, in turn, if the bank calls for more than one before lending the money named in the note. If any other person is in any way interested in the use of the money borrowed, the bank will prefer that person, if financially solvent, for the first endorser, because of the question of "value received." At all events, the person endorsing should be made perfectly aware of the nature and circumstances of the transaction.

Something more will be said about endorsements further on, but there is also what is described as "discounting" a note. The rules of discount and the laws governing it are not the same in the several States, nor is the practice relating to it the same in banks under State or National laws, and with private banking-houses and individual money-lenders. Any woman, however, already acquainted with the nature of a note, and who will take the trouble, as she ought, to read the "usury statute" of her own State, will be prepared to perceive just what the word "discount" means when a bank officer or other person tries to explain what he means by it in her case.

Discounting a note.

A note once made and given, the date of its maturity must be kept in mind. It will pretty surely have the proverbial effect of hastening the flight of time, but the end ought not to be permitted to come as a surprise. Perfect provision must be made for payment; probably by successive deposits in bank; and the final payment is to be made by a check on the bank, drawn to your own order, but specifying that it is for the principal and interest of such and such a note. If there is to be any doubt of means of payment, do not leave all to the last, but call at the bank and say so.

Except there is a stringency in the money-market, or a doubt of the security, the bank would much prefer to renew the note, rather than to protest, sue, and collect it, or sell the collaterals. If all is right with the note, it is the interest of the bank to have it renewed, and they will at no time wish to harm a respectable depositor.

Renewal of notes.

If not the whole, they may renew a part. If there are collaterals, and if these must be sold, go and see about their sale at once, for you may find a better purchaser, at a higher price, than the bank can or will do. If it is an endorsed note, consult with your endorser or endorsers, as it is not for the interest of an endorser to have a note protested with his name on it, and he should not be taken unawares by your failure. He should have time to make provisions. If you do not pay, the bank will see to it that he is notified, in due form, under the seal of a notary public, because if this is not done his liability under that note ceases and it cannot afterward be collected of him. He will also probably receive a prior notification that a note with his endorsement is about to fail due, and may come to inquire of you about it. Do not neglect any part of your own duty, and by all means do not worry about it. Getting ready beforehand is a prevention of worry.

The subject of banks and banking, as related to any woman's personal property, stands by itself, and next to it is that of investment of any surplus funds that she may have, without immediate need for their expenditure. Studying this subject may often throw light upon the reality of any seeming need for that very expenditure, for investment is the father and mother of economy. A deposit in a savings bank is a genuine form of investment, made through that agency; but a deposit in National and State Banks is not so; it is only a placing of funds in a convenient and reasonably secure shape for paying them out again.

Investment of capital.

Having money on hand, or nearly come to hand, the question of its investment should come with it, for money is a capable workman and ought not to be allowed to remain idle. Hoarding is a bad practice and does not, after all, provide the safety which is its only attractive feature. Concerning any proposed investment, however, the first and vital consideration is that of safety. There is no such thing as absolute safety "where moth and rust doth corrupt and thieves break through and steal;" but something closely resembling it may be obtained by the exercise of proper care. The secondary object to be sought for is "revenue," the dividend to be paid for the use of the money. Many real estate investments pay this, and pay it well, eventually, by the rise in the value of property. This is a wide and fascinating field, always partaking somewhat of speculative adventure, and it has its possible crop of disappointments as well as of prizes. Here, too, the question of sound titles comes in, with those of taxes, assessments, the ability to meet them, and also the general subject of improvements to be made in the neighborhood by others, or on the premises by the owner.

All real estate investments are not speculative, and all are not strictly individual. The purchase of a house, already built, to live in, or of a lot to build a house on, ought not to be at all speculative, excepting that any such property may rise in value. Neither is an investment through any well organized and managed local "building association."

Building and Loan Associations are numerous and have been found exceedingly good means for putting money where it will be secure and will yield a fair return, with or without actual building on one's own account. Each scheme of each of these associations is a separate study, to be considered mainly with reference to the character of its management.

Building and Loan Associations.

Now and then schemes are offered, so brilliant, promising so much, that they openly invite the employment of the ordinary rules of arithmetic and an inquiry as to the real nature of the magic which puts one dollar into a hat and takes out two without injury to the hat or to any of the other dollars said to be in it. For the greater part, however, careful investigation compels the admission that our local building associations, on the whole, offer admirable investments to the classes of small capitalists likely to make use of them. [*See Appendix.*]

Another form of investment in real estate is the "bond and mortgage." In this, again, the question of title comes in and with it an inspection as to whether the property itself, without any help from its owner, the mortgagor, can pay the interest regularly, by rental or otherwise, and then the principal, at auction sale, in case of foreclosure.

Owning bond and mortgage.

The best investors, the savings banks, will lend only one-half of the apparent productive value of a house and lot. The rule they follow is a good one for any individual. The rate of interest to be obtained cannot be higher than the legal rate and may be lower, but the borrower must pay for search of title and all other expenditures relating to the loan.

Where the property is within the range of operation of a respectable "Title Guarantee Association," such as are everywhere becoming more and more common, a trustworthy search can be had without great cost and with the gain of additional security. The searches of these companies have unearthed a great many titles which they did not care to insure.

Title Guarantee Association.

One more desirable feature of any real estate investment, by purchase, mortgage, or otherwise, is that it should be near at hand, within reach of per-

The Various Forms of Investment.

sonal observation, and, if need should ever be, of personal supervision and management. A resident of New York is a very defective owner of even good landed property as near as Pennsylvania, much more so if it is anywhere in the Mississippi Valley or at the foot of the Rocky Mountains.

Beyond the comparatively solid and tangible realm of real-estate investments, is the vast and almost infinitely varied region where the money paid by the investor does but give her a measured interest in some business operation and its plant or property, under the direction of other people. That her interest, so acquired, shall be strictly measured, defined, and limited, should be her first care in making any such investment. Certain classes of purchasable interests are invariably so limited; as all railway stocks, all bonds, all promissory notes, and here no such care is needed; but the stocks of many corporations not organized under "limited liability" acts, ordinary business enterprises, partnerships, improvement undertakings, and the like, require watching and the adoption of protective measures provided for by existing laws.

Limited liability.

A woman known to have money in her pocket is very likely to find herself asked for it much more directly than by the advertisements to be read in the newspapers. There are both relatives and friends who are either needy or enterprising beyond their present resources, and they are generally capable of presenting their cases in the most plausible form. A good and searching question to propound, with reference to each application, may be formulated: "Is this a loan, a business investment, or is it a gift?" The merely needy person may not be actually insolvent, but the question of the gift, and of one's ability or willingness to make the gift, eventually, must be clearly settled before that of solvency.

Thus the lender should mentally and practically resolve herself into a bank cashier and protect herself as he would protect the capital under his care. Take such a note as he would take, with all the securities, collaterals, endorsements, that he would require, and the loan becomes an investment. If these are in part to be dispensed with, by reason of good will, or the known integrity of the borrower, it is still an insecure investment.

If the money is for use in a business enterprise, the special reason for notes and formalities is the danger of becoming a "partner" in the eye of the law, with an interest in the success of the business, other than that of a money-lender, and so liable for its general debts of every kind. A stock-holder in an old time joint-stock bank was so liable, and so, to the full face value of the stock held, is the owner of corporative stock not under the "limited liability" act, unless such stock was duly paid for, in full, in cash, in the first place.

It is, however, possible to become a "silent partner" in any business concern, with a liability limited to the cash put in, by having the partnership contract express that fact, first, and second, by having the fact of limitation advertized in the newspaper named for that purpose by the laws of one's own State and municipality. The latter provision is vitally important. A copy of that paper, with the notice in it, should be kept.

Any loan expressed in a promissory note must be made for a given time and payable at the bank named, selecting very positively the bank in which you make your own deposits. You may wish to use the money expressed in that note, some day, before it is due, and so may take it to your bank for "discount;" you will surely deposit it there for collection days before it is due, in order that the processes of demand and collection, if paid, of "protest," if not paid, and of formal renewal, if the loan is renewed, may be in the regular channels of business. On no account allow an endorsed note to fail of formal "protest for non-payment," lest you release the endorser.

Municipal loans, or those of cities, towns, and counties, are a favorite investment with many. The rule is to take none that come from too far away. If they are good, they should have friends nearer home. Take none without knowing the population, tax-list, and existing debt of that public borrower, for even rich and prosperous communities have now and then been so liberal in spending borrowed money that they broke down under the burden of payment. Precisely the same rule applies to State loans and to railway loans guaranteed by States.

Municipal loans.

The loans of the United States are always safe, but that is their main feature, for at current market rates they are practically "three per cent." loans or a little better.

United States, State, and Railway Loans.

Railway bonds are like a flight of stairs, somewhat crowded on the lower and middle steps, but not so much so near the upper landing. The price list of the Stock Exchange will at any time inform an investor what opinion prevails among the keen-eyed operators who are studying the prospects of all this kind of securities. The same is true of railway and bank stocks, of all the kinds not at the moment most largely dealt in. Never buy a security over which the "bulls and bears" are fighting, for its nominal value may be too largely fictitious and a small investor does not need to ask how or why. If any "bond" is purchased for merely temporary investment, so that the money need not be idle, buy a "coupon bond," but if it is to be permanent, get a "registered bond," if possible, diminishing risk of loss and with easier collections. Any bank will accept bond coupons on deposit and collect them as it collects checks.

With reference to each and every class of personal property investment, one evil to be prepared for, mentally, is a "panic," or anything like it. When there has been a sudden decline in the stock and bond market, nervous investors are too apt to help it by a rush to sell. It is probably their best time to stay at home until the storm is over, unless they have more money and the courage and judgment to go in and pick up good things that other people are dropping.

The prudent woman, studying her financial position, before going out to her business, may find among her personal property certain items which may be generally classed as "claims and contingencies."

If any of these are in written or recorded form, she ought to have small difficulty in ascertaining what they are worth at present, but may have more in making up her mind what to do with them. There are claims which might have a value if dealt with at once, yet which would vanish into thin air, if left to take care of themselves.

If there are any on hand not yet in visible, concrete forms, but which can be made so, the business woman will not wait or hesitate. She will obtain a settlement if there is one to be had, and she will decide what to do with the written form of that settlement. A verbal promise cannot be deposited for collection at her bank.

One thought is pretty sure to come to a person considering property in ownership, and it takes the form of: "Whose shall this be if I should die to-night?" Whatever the answer is, in the will of the thinker, that answer should at once be written out in clear memoranda, and taken to a lawyer, who shall put it into form for execution, and then it can be filed away in the safest place attainable, safe-deposit box or the like. Even a small estate should not be left to costly processes of uncertain direction and division; but the fewer the bequests, the simpler the form of will, the better, without providing for too many contingencies. Each expressed uncertainty is a possible gap, through which a wasteful dispute may enter.

Wills.

There are hardly any more interesting duties, outside of her household and her finances, upon which all her other activities depend, than are such as come to a woman in connection with "societies," organizations for all manner of purposes, social, literary, charitable, or religious. In any such society, her value largely depends upon her business ability. For the performance of any duty outside of the assembled membership, hardly any suggestion ought to be needed, but when once she and her friends have met, as a society, they have become a kind of legislature, and must govern themselves accordingly. For this purpose they do not require the full and elaborate instructions of "Cushing's Manual" nor the Rules of the House of Representatives, but something like a brief and condensed digest of the principles set forth in the received authorities.

Societies, Clubs, etc.

Every such association should adopt something equivalent to a "constitution," tersely setting forth its purpose and its plan for accomplishing that purpose. It should so limit the objects of the society, that incongruous subjects can be the more readily shut out. It should designate, as nearly as may be, who may or may not become members. It should name the officers and standing committees, state that these are to be chosen by ballot, and for how long, and how vacancies are to be filled. It should provide for its own amendment, by a two-thirds vote, specified notice of the vote being given beforehand. It should state what number of members are to constitute a quorum for transacting business at any meeting of the society.

The president of such a society should be an *ex-officio* member of the executive committee, but the treasurer and secretary should not be members of it without regular election as such.

The vice-president, or if more than one, in the order of their election, should perform the duty of president in the absence of that officer, including service on the executive committee.

The secretary is the scribe, custodian of documents, official correspondent, jointly with the president, and is the proper "reader" at any meeting. The correspondence may be transferred to a corresponding secretary, if need be, and a secretary *pro tempore* may be chosen, by vote, at any meeting.

The treasurer is the keeper of funds and accounts, but need not also be burdened with the duties of collector. All disbursements must be made on authority of a recorded vote at a regular meeting. No other payments are legal. It is well if they are ordered to be made on orders signed by the president, that the treasurer may have vouchers equivalent to bank-checks, for her own protection.

The order of business at a meeting should be adhered to, with scrupulous care. The society being called to order, a quorum being found present, with or without the calling of a roll, there are sometimes what are called "opening exercises," with which business has nothing to do, excepting to expect brevity.

The first business in order is the

reading, correction, and approval, by vote, of the minutes of the preceding meeting. The next indispensable thing is the report of the treasurer, and any action thereon, other than simple approval or disapproval, must be postponed until "new business" is reached. The next in order are the reports of the executive and other standing committees. These may be accepted and approved, or accepted without approval, but any further action or debate must also be postponed to the "new business" department, where it belongs. Next in order is unfinished business, and there is much freedom here, for any obnoxious item of it, in the way of current affairs, may be laid on the table or referred to a committee, to keep it still for the time being.

When new business is now reached, and not before, is the time for announcements and communications to be made through the presiding officer, other than those made by the secretary, on her own behalf or that of the corresponding secretary.

Many "motions" can as well be merely verbal, but any motion calling for a payment of money ought to be written, to avoid misunderstandings and to secure the treasurer. No motion is before the society for debate or amendment until duly seconded and announced by the chair.

An amendment is simply another motion requiring action before the first can be acted on. A second amendment cannot crowd out of place the first, nor can there be an amendment to an amendment.

A motion to adjourn is always in order, but cannot be debated. A motion fixing a given hour for adjournment is under the same rule.

The various duties falling upon the officers of such a society require small comment. Those of the treasurer surely require her to keep accurate accounts; to pay out nothing without due authority, nor without receiving and keeping a voucher. She is a kind of bank, but must remember that her private capital is liable for the repayment of the society's deposits.

In these days of cheap printing every such association should provide good stationery of its own, including printed letter-heads. The corresponding secretary will also make a specialty of punctuality and of carefully filing away all communications.

When once a woman of ordinary capacity has put her house and her external affairs, her business of every name, in perfect order, knowing it well and watching it from day to day, she will probably be astonished to find how easy its management has become and how much better are its varied proceeds.

It was said by one of America's greatest merchants that he worked harder, with greater and more numerous perplexities, when he was running a small "country store," than when, a perfected man of business, he was directing commercial transactions of seventy millions of dollars per annum. The secret of his later ease was in the success of his persistent demand for, and attainment of, perfect system and perfect punctuality.

[*For legal forms and other specific information see section on* WOMEN IN THEIR BUSINESS AFFAIRS *in the* APPENDIX—SUPPLEMENTARY INFORMATION.]

III.
THE PRINCIPLES OF HOUSEKEEPING.

III.
THE PRINCIPLES OF HOUSEKEEPING.

By LILLIAN W. BETTS.

The Science of Housekeeping.
Economy and Expenditure.
"She Died of Committee."
The Nutrient Value of Foods.
Cook-books and Food Literature.
The New Cooking Appliances.
Electric Cooking.

Cleaning and Cleanliness.
The Buying and Preparation of Meats.
Good Bread-making.
Marketing and Economy.
The Servant Question.
Entertaining and Hospitality.
System in Housekeeping.

GOOD housekeeping involves a knowledge of art and science. A knowledge of the first is essential, if the element of beauty is to be in the home; a knowledge of the second is essential to the health of the home.

A good housekeeper is an executive officer, an accountant, a chemist, a sanitary officer. She *The attributes of a good housekeeper.* possesses more than an elementary knowledge of hygiene. She is a household physician, and possesses, either as a gift or as the result of training, or both, the elementary knowledge, at least, of a trained nurse. On her diplomatic abilities depends the harmony of the home. Her social graces determine, to a large degree, the social opportunities of the family at home and abroad. In short, woman, as a home-maker, is responsible for the health and the happiness of her family, whether that numbers two or more. Never in the history of the family has it been so possible for a woman to gain the knowledge which fits her to meet the demands of her position as chief officer of the household as to-day. Science is her handmaiden; invention a servant following her, often preceding her, to light the path where she had not yet discovered the need of light. Science and invention have revolutionized housekeeping. They have made it possible for a woman to fill the office of a housekeeper and yet have leisure to enjoy the graces of life. Woman is the power she is to-day, in the church, in charity, and in the philanthropic world, because science and invention have freed her from labor that women of preceding generations were compelled to do with their own hands, for the preservation of the home and the comfort of the family.

Whether woman will abuse the freedom, and in the first flush of liberty that should mean leisure enchain herself to outside responsibilities, until home becomes the secondary, not the primary object of her life, future years will determine. To-day the home-maker has at her feet the genius of the world to equip her for her field of pleasure and opportunity—the home. The first essential to filling her position is an appreciation of the opportunity it offers. If considered wholly from the standpoint of responsibilities, home-making is a burden, not an opportunity. If it is considered from the material point of view, the house and its furnishings become a fetich, an altar on which are sacrificed husband and children; the perfection of its furnishings and preservation standing before the custodian's mind as the paramount duty of life.

The first essential of the perfect home is its adaptation to the family. It is this adaptation to the financial or social standing of the family that makes its harmony. If its cost exceeds the financial freedom of the family; if it is a house that expresses what the family are reaching after, not what they are, there can be no harmony, for there is no rest. Rest, repose is the foundation of peace, and peace is the angel that guards every true home. It is not the amount of money spent in a week, a month, or a year in maintaining the home that determines its character. It is the results obtained by the expenditure, whether the amount be large or small. If the home-maker has placed at her disposal the sum of twelve thousand dollars a year, and through ignorance or indifference is not able to secure the best possible results from this amount, she is as culpable, as much to be condemned as the home-maker who fails to produce the best possible results from the expenditure of three hundred and sixty-five dollars per year. The happiness of the family depends on the purchasing power of the money expended by the home-maker. If her ignorance reduces its purchasing power, the family must suffer.

The adaptation of the home to the family.

No law can be laid down for the expending of a family income. The needs, the tastes, the conditions of no two families are the same, while the incomes of thousands of families are identical. We cannot proceed upon the principle that, the division of expenditures being identical, the results would be equally good for all. It were easy to make a law, were this true. It is this diversity of life that is at once its beauty and its difficulty. Each family must be a law unto itself. The wisdom of the controller is shown in the adapting of income and expenses, whether for necessities or luxuries. The home-maker equals her opportunity as she is able to use the income placed in her hands so that it secures the greatest freedom for each member of the family to grow in health, morals, and spiritual grace. The foundation, then, of the family life is the income, plus the intelligence of the heads of the family. The social position of the family is the accident, the result of this combination in addition to antecedent conditions. The income of the average American family is estimated at about five hundred dollars a year. The incomes above and below this average represent the upward and downward scale of social opportunities. The problem of living is hardest to solve in the United States for families of refinement who have the natural ambitions of intelligence—how to live that they may secure at the same time the greatest freedom and the greatest privacy.

Expenditure.

Rent is the first item. What proportion of the income can be expended for rent? We are told that no man should spend more than one-fourth of his income for rent. But we cannot accept this as an unchangeable law, for one-fourth of the income of some families will not secure space enough for privacy, and a greater proportion than one-fourth must be spent for rent. This extra allowance, then, must be secured by economy in other expenditures. The social life, the wardrobe, or the food-supply must pay their tribute to this absolute expense, that cannot be brought below a certain point without affecting not only the comfort but the health and morals of the family.

Having settled the proportion of the family income that must be expended in rent, the balance of the income then must be divided to meet all the other demands of the family life. Now the problem becomes intricate and tests the wisdom and intelligence of the determining power. Each family differs in the standards of the necessities imperative for the maintenance of family life. Opportunity for education is the uppermost need of one family. Establishing the semblance of social prominence is the one universal want of another family. Clothes that attract the eye of the passer-by is the one desire of another family. What we term "a good table" satisfies the wants of another family. It is the gratification of the special taste of each family that secures for that family the greatest happiness. We may admire or condemn, but if we are discerning we shall know that we, in turn, are being criticised for the arrangement of our own lives; that in the judgment of many we are sacrificing the best things of life; we are not securing the best results for the amount of money at our disposal. Accepting this fact, then, it behooves us to concentrate our attention on our own affairs, being careful to secure the results in our own family life that minister best to the life of that family, without regard to outside standards.

Strength, time, and practical knowledge are the servants that increase the family income threefold. The first should be administered as one administers the income of the family. If it is abused, used recklessly, it brings physical bankruptcy as surely as the reckless use of money brings financial failure. Many women are old at middle life, and become burdens carried with loving patience, or even endurance, by their families, when they could have gone down to old age helping to carry the burdens and pleasures of life with ease and grace, had they used intelligence in expending their strength. It is this danger that threatens the women of to-day. They dissipate their physical powers, not in the home, but in meeting outside demands. If tombstones recorded truth always, in many a graveyard in this country would appear this legend: "She died of Committee." It has become, within the past year, the proper thing to justify this outside work of women on the ground that women are the leisure class. It would appear that this must be sarcasm, were it not for the deeply earnest quarter from which this justification comes. A woman of leisure to-day would either be a curiosity or an object of veneration or envy, according to the standpoint from which we view her. Women of the past did abuse their strength in the labor they performed in their homes and for their families. This is not possible to-day, where woman has the intelligence to use the labor-saving machines that science and invention have placed at her disposal. To-day her physical bankruptcy is due to concessions made to the world outside her home; to her own ignorance or false economy. Hundreds of husbands in our day stand patient, willing, loving attendants on wives who are invalids because of the service they rendered outside their homes, and this often without the assurance that the victim of her own temperament or mistaken zeal has rendered true service. Wise is the woman who knows the measure of her strength and uses it to enrich the home life, making it increase the family income by saving the money, economizing the strength when the expending of money means greater happiness for the family; giving of her abundance where it tells for the world's good; making that service to the world a part of the intellectual life of her own

Economy.

home. This it is that marks the woman of character. The centre of her life is her home. All that she does tends to its happiness, to the growth, morally and spiritually, of the family circle.

Time is the second factor that increases the family income. The way in which time is used by the homemaker increases or diminishes the family income. We live in what might be termed "ready-made days." We no longer make our own clothing because we can buy it so cheaply ready-made. No one disputes that the materials made up at home without expense produce a better and a cheaper garment. The truth of the matter is that sewing is a lost art with the majority of American women. Decorative art has now stepped in with its dainty suggestions, and supplies even the quiet, stay-at-home woman with occupation and entertainment for her leisure. To make a garment, when the making saves so little money, seems foolish to many women who acknowledge that it is the penny saved that counts in the close of the yearly account. There are married women to-day who are intelligent and thoughtful, living on limited incomes, with no possibility of an increase except by the investment of capital secured by the saving of the family income, who have never made a garment worn by themselves or their families. They have grown up with the idea that it is a waste of time — that is, that time and knowledge can be better used. There are men and women who have come from homes where the burden of life was a limited income, who have never worn a garment fashioned by a mother's brain and hand. The picture of the young mother fashioning, in love and fear, the garments for the baby whose coming is the promise of her womanhood, the bond and pledge of her love, is fast becoming only a picture, to give sentiment to a story of days departing, if not already gone. It is not considered a mark of wisdom to save small amounts in the use of time, there are so many things to do. Are they worth the doing? Will they count in making and preserving the family life, the financial freedom of the family? These are the important questions.

There is another influence potent in family life in America to-day — the tendency of the American woman, though married and a mother, to become a wage-earner. Among the so-called poor people this is made necessary, often because the wife is so ignorant that she cannot make her time count as a money factor in the domestic economy. She does not know how to cook or sew. She even does not know how to keep her house clean; and so she uses the time for which she has no use, and she earns money, not because her husband's earnings could not be made to support the family, but because she does not know how to make her time count for dollars and cents by using it. There are thousands of intelligent married women to-day in America who are wage-earners because they cannot endure the monotony of home-making; because they are ambitious; because they, no more than the ignorant woman whose husband earns a dollar a day, can make their time count dollars and cents by the application of knowledge and skill in the home. There comes to mind now a school-teacher in a village school, the mother of nine children and the wife of a trained mechanic, who, in reply to the query of why and how it was possible for her to leave her family to fill her position, replied that her husband's wages would not supply the needs of the family. Further conversation revealed that she paid a relative two hundred dollars a year to do the housework, that she paid a char-woman about one hundred dollars a year, and she paid about one hundred and fifty dollars for sewing done by another relative. She earned four hundred dollars a year. What was the actual gain to this family for the loss of a mother's time and brooding? The secret of the matter, which she did not appreciate herself, was that she disliked housework and the detailed care of young children. She exchanged labor ; but to herself, her husband her neighbors, she was to be pitied because she had to earn money to support her family. All were deceived. There is too much of this deception for the real growth of American character. If a woman chooses to earn money that she may buy that labor which she cannot, for lack of strength or knowledge, perform, let her be careful to be candid to herself, her husband, and her friends, and not set herself on a pedestal and belittle her husband in his own eyes, or those of the world, by putting necessity in the foreground as the reason for her activity, and not choice, which is the true reason. Let her examine carefully that, in choosing her position, she may not interfere with the rights of others, or the duties of her own position as a wife or mother. For a wife and mother to become a wage-earner to gratify pride or social desires is contemptible, and the world soon gives to that woman her true position. The use of time is a positive factor in the increasing of the family income.

Practical knowledge of the various departments of home-making is the *The value of practical knowledge.* third and most important factor in the increase of the family income. If the home-maker has little or no knowledge of the problems that housekeeping involves, she necessarily increases the expenses of the family, lessening the purchasing power of the income she commands or administers. She may be ignorant when she is first placed in her position, but if she remains ignorant the fault is her own. Art, literature, science, invention, mechanics, are the servants of every intelligent housekeeper. If she buys an ugly tea-cup, it is because she chooses to be ignorant of the laws of beauty ; she does not seek to know the elements of beauty. The paper-maker, the textile-manufacturer, the thread-manufacturer, the potter help to maintain schools of art that our homes may be beautiful. The art schools, by lectures and exhibitions as well as training, seek to enlighten the seeker after the knowledge of how to discern the beautiful. Artists and architects and decorators create free schools for the education of the tastes of the people by their exhibitions ; while magazines and newspapers seek to educate the critical faculty. The home devoid of beauty to-day is the home of ignorance.

The laboratories of the world are at the service of the home-maker who *Science in the home.* chooses to profit by the results of scientific discovery and investigation. Not only are these investigations carried on to discover food values, but the principles of cooking are considered worthy of the attention of the scientist, who frequently gives his knowledge to the world in the most elementary form possible, for the education of the housekeeper, that she may purchase and cook her food, securing the best results with the least expenditure of time and money.

To many women, even women of intelligence, there is a sense of security if a cook-book is owned. *Cook-books.* With all due respect to makers of recipes, the housekeeper who depends for her catering on the cook-book cannot obtain, by closest following, the best results in nutrition or palatableness. As an illustration, there is a book issued by the American Public Health Association, entitled " Practical Sanitary and Economic Cooking," published by that Association at Rochester, N. Y. The title-page tells us that the book is "adapted to people of moderate and small means." This book is the Lomb prize essay for 1888, and was written by Mary Hinman Abel, of Ann Arbor, Mich. In this book, beef and calves' hearts are spoken of as being cheap and nutritious articles of food not appreciated by the American people. Explicit directions are given for cooking these articles of food by Mrs. Abel. She says: "Soak the heart overnight; beef heart to boil all day, calves' heart to boil two hours." Seven other standard books were consulted. One stated, in italics: "Do not soak. Boil two hours." Another said nothing of preparation, and said: "Boil six hours hard." Two agree on four hours' cooking, one says hard boiling, and the other simmering. To take another illustration of the difficulty that besets the housekeeper who knows nothing of the chemistry of food or the principles of cooking. Crullers are not hygienic, but they are enjoyed by many people. A recipe for crullers was given to the writer by an old housekeeper: "One quart and one-half pint of flour, three teaspoonfuls of baking powder, one tablespoonful of butter melted, two small eggs, one cup of milk, one of sugar, one even teaspoonful of salt, one-half nutmeg. Cook in three pounds of lard." With a view to saving gray matter and time, it was decided to consult all the cook-books in the kitchen library, and dispense with another written recipe, if possible. The first cook-book consulted said: "Four tablespoonfuls of sugar, five of melted butter, three eggs, one teaspoonful of cinnamon." No proportion for flour was given, yet the whole success of frying crullers depends on the consistence of the dough and the temperature of the lard. Another: "One and one-half cup of sugar to a teaspoonful of butter, three teaspoonfuls of baking-powder, one and one-half nutmeg;" no proportion of flour. The differences were as great in all the others consulted. One book indexed crullers as doughnuts, which, as we all ought to know, are an entirely different kind of cake. The resemblance is only in the method of cooking. These illustrations are given to prove that the writers are not infallible, because they are not scientific. As a rule, they do not understand the chemistry of food nor the principles of cooking well enough to make them rank with the scientist. The books are good servants, but bad mistresses. The housekeeper must fit herself to separate the chaff from the wheat when reading them, and if she is wise she will cull the best into a book of her own, after experiment and investigation. There is no better field for the display of art and originality than is offered three hundred and sixty-five days in the year, three times each day, to the mistress of the household; and the wife who meets this opportunity, not as a servant, but as a mistress, is the one of whom the prophets foretold, "Whose husband praises her in the gates, and whose children rise up and call her blessed."

The catering for a family involves more than the tickling of the palate or the pleasing of the artistic sense. It means securing the family health, increasing the working force. This cannot be done unless there is knowledge *The value of foods.* of the value of foods, their strength and heat-giving qualities. A physician of standing not long since said that women and children starved to death in this country because they did not know the kind of food to eat, or would not take food enough to meet the demands made upon their vitality. It is quite common to hear the busy women of our large cities, especially, say : " Oh, if we only had some form of concentrated food ! I feel faint, famished, but I don't want to eat." This condition of mind or stomach, or both, has been recognized, and we have columns in our newspapers advertising concentrated food, nervines, and tonics. A knowledge of the chemical values of the several kinds of food would save doctors' bills, prolong life, and increase the working powers of the whole people. Many times the habit formed in childhood, of eating but little and eating food unsuited to the physical condition, is the cause of the habit of eating, in adults, that leads to disease, impaired vitality, depleted nerve-force. It is a fact that working-girls, when at the vacation houses, prefer bread and tea to the nourishing food furnished. They do not care for meat and vegetables, being unused to them. Their stomachs seemingly reject such strong food. Children who are not taught to eat nourishing breakfasts, when they cannot have a supply of nourishing food until late afternoon or evening dinner, pay, through all their lives, the penalty. The habit is formed and is never broken. Each day's labor is undertaken without, to use a figure, sufficient fuel to maintain steam enough properly to run the engine. This almost national habit cannot be remedied until proper feeding becomes a moral responsibility. Ignorance cannot be pleaded in our days. The laboratories of the world are at the service of the housekeeper ; governments think it a part of their duty to discover how the people may be well fed at the least cost ; how the best physical conditions can be supported. The health of the people is protected, as far as governments can protect the individual, from the adulterations of food, or the use of deleterious substances in food preparations. How many housekeepers avail themselves of this avenue of useful knowledge, which costs nothing but time to write a note to the Government at Washington for the pamphlets that are being constantly issued by the Department of Agriculture ?

There are standard books on the adulterations of food, but their sales *The adulteration of foods.* never make the fortunes of the scientists who write them. Publishers do not clamor for the privilege of putting their imprint on the title-pages, while not a few are put in printed form by the efforts of the philanthropist. " The American public is to be congratulated upon this useful and valuable contribution to the needs of its great army of working-people, made possible through the humanitarian benevolence of a private citizen. This was the fifth prize offered by the same citizen through the same channel, for the noble purpose of ameliorating, in some degree, the hardships which baffle mankind in the tireless struggle for existence." *

Yet no intelligent woman ought to feel that her household furnishings are complete unless her kitchen library contains the standard books, not only on recipes, but the scientific books on the basis of foods and their preparation in the manner that secures the preservation of their values.

Simple tests are possible to detect adulterations in food, yet few housekeepers know how to make these tests. It is not possible, in the limits of this chapter, to give chemical tests. Mrs. Ellen H. Richards has published two books, one on " Food Materials and their Adulteration," and one on " The Chemistry of Cooking and Feeding," both published by Estes & Lauriat, of

---

* Report of the Secretary of the American Public Health Association—referring to the prizes offered by Mr. Henry Lomb, of Rochester, N. Y., through the American Public Health Association.

Boston, Mass. These books are necessary in every house where its mistress has a care for the best results for money expended, and the desire to secure these results with the least waste.

We are beginning to understand the importance of a pure water-supply. We are also beginning to understand that there are certain chemical properties of water that are detrimental, if not harmful, to certain physical conditions. How many housekeepers submit the water that must be used by the family to a chemical test? Yet a note, the paying expressage of a bottle of water to a chemist, and the expenditure of a few dollars might save many dollars, and even life. There are a few simple tests that any housekeeper may try, such as the dissolving of a few grains of white sugar in a pint of water and exposing the bottle to the light in a warm room for ten days; if the water is turbid there is danger from sewer contamination. But there are other perils, other dangers that threaten the life of the family through the water-supply, and a chemist should be employed to test the water-supply, as we employ a sanitary engineer to determine questions of plumbing and sewage.

Pure water.

The waste through adulteration of food is not as great as some would have us believe. The development of machinery, the discovery of valuable food in materials considered of no value, has increased the world's food-supply and cheapened production of food so much that it does not pay to adulterate. The articles of food that are most adulterated are condiments. The staple articles of food are, on the whole, pure. Science has forced this. By her laboratories, microscopes, and spirit of research, she compels pure food. The manufacturer of food dare not defy her, for he knows that she is searching always to prove her value to the world. She cannot be bought, for her disciples are ready to defend her, should one be weak enough to yield to the touch of gold. Public sentiment is the best safeguard, and that is possible only when the intelligence of the community is active and compels purity and cleanliness in the sources of food-supply. If the food-supplies are bought without due care as to the sources, then the community must suffer in health and pocket.

The food-supplies.

The president of the American Institute of Mining Engineers in 1882 said: "Scientific housekeeping is neither beneath the attention of the refined, nor beyond the reach of the uncultured. It is the duty of the rich; it is the salvation of the poor." This truth is becoming popular.

Ellen H. Richards, in "Food Materials and their Adulteration," says: "It is only in the undeveloped stages of a mechanical invention that it is complicated and runs with friction. The perfected machine is noiseless in its action and simple in construction. The machinery of daily life should respond to the slightest touch of the household engineer, one who knows all about it." Again she says: "Cooking has become an art worthy the attention of intelligent and learned women. The laws of chemical action are founded upon the laws of definite proportion, and whatever is added more than enough is in the way." That sums up the whole principle of housekeeping. Not the proper way to dress the maid, serve a dinner, nor the proper furnishings of a table is the sum of knowledge that constitutes housekeeping, but the knowledge of every department in theory, if not in practice. This it is to "know it all."

The kitchen is a most important part of every house. On it depends the physical life and, we now know, to a

The Kitchen and Cooking Utensils.

The kitchen. large degree, the spiritual life of the family. Realizing this importance, we give to it the time and thought necessary to secure its perfection in furnishing and management. In furnishing, the prevention of friction is the most important thing. We now paint our kitchen walls, because it makes cleanliness possible without making great demands on strength, and without causing the disarrangement of the days of whitewashing and kalsomining. A cupboard with glass doors not only ornaments the kitchen, but is an incentive to have bright cooking-ware in orderly arrangement. The perfect kitchen will have glass doors to all closets, that the mistress, on entering the room, may at a glance discover disorder.

Within a year aluminum has been produced so cheaply that it is now made into kitchen utensils, and sold at a price that is not beyond the purchasing power of the housekeeper of even limited means. The utensils are as beautiful as silver, and so light in weight as to startle one on first handling. They can be kept as bright as silver with very little effort, and are indestructible. The agate ware, which is deservedly so popular because of the ease with which it can be cleaned and its lightness, is probably the next best ware for cooking-utensils to-day. The number and variety of pots, pans, and boilers depend on the size of the family and scale of living maintained. One large pot for boiling meats and soups, with one medium and two small pots, or the reverse, according to the size of the family; a soapstone griddle is essential, if pancakes are to gladden the hearts and stir the imaginations of the family on winter mornings; a waffle-iron, gridiron, cullender, steamer, two sizes of pudding-boilers, large and small, are among the first essentials.

Decorative pie-plates are the most attractive, but the white porcelain and the pottery with white glaze are much better than plates of any other material.

Kitchen Cupboard with Glass Doors.

The decorated plates add to the appearance of the dessert when it is placed on the table. Care should be taken in selecting all pie-dishes, no matter what the material, to select those that do not rise in the centre. That makes the pie thin in the middle. A good pie is always thick, no matter what the filling. A covered bread-raiser is an absolute necessity, if one wishes good bread. This should never be used for anything but the raising of bread. Earthen bowls must be many and of all sizes, if the mistress expects to keep her table dishes out of the refrigerator and wire-closet. If she wishes to save her table silver, she must provide at least one half-dozen of large and small spoons, with steel knives and forks of good quality, besides cake and cooking spoons for the kitchen. A Dover egg-beater, a whip-churn, cake-board, glass or porcelain rolling-pin, measuring-cups, thermometer, scales, all are absolute necessities of a well-appointed kitchen. Tin boxes for sugar and cereals. Tin closets, with shelves, are the best kind of cake-boxes. Flour-closets or boxes, with sifters in the bottom, are convenient, as they can stand on a shelf in the kitchen. The flour is sifted into a drawer at the bottom, and the quantity, large or small, can be measured out of the drawer. In addition, the flour-scoop and flour-sifter should be kept conveniently near, as cake is better if the flour is sifted into the measuring-cup; the flour packs when lifted in the spoon. Wire straining-sieves, a double-boiler, and a frying-basket are among the conveniences. A set of skewers, salt-box, pepper-boxes and flour-dredgers, spice-box, and knife-box are the possessions of every mistress who values a place for everything and everything in its place. Glass or porcelain jars for coffee, glass jars for rice, barley, tapioca, sago, tea, and the like, save time and temper. Tin boxes should have the names of the contents on the outside. Provision for the care of every article of dry groceries should be made, so that there would be no excuse for paper parcels on pantry shelves or in closets. It should be possible for every housekeeper to take an account of stock, dressed for the street, if necessary. Papers are a bid always for carelessness and disorder. When the groceries are delivered, they should be put in their appointed place at once. This rule is economical. If the proper vessel is empty, supplies are needed. If groceries are left in paper bags, there is always the possibility of a double supply, or no material, at the moment it is wanted for cooking. In these days of enamelled paint, the walls and shelves of all kitchen closets should be painted. Painted shelves can be wiped off with a damp cloth every day, if need be. Paper in kitchen closets is always a bid for dust and vermin; a painted shelf permits no hiding-places. Zinc-covered tables are the best kitchen tables, if one cannot have marble. Every house-keeper knows that the condition of the wooden-topped kitchen table offers the possibility of discussion every day. A zinc-covered table cannot be burned, and can be kept bright at so little expense of strength that even an indifferent maid is ashamed to have it warrant rebuke.

The range or stove is a most important article of furniture, and is always selected for its reputation for economizing heat. The beautiful tiled ranges exhibited at the Columbian Fair were works of art, and are the fitting outcome of this age when art is the handmaiden of the home. The perfect range has glass doors, a recent invention, and a hook on the inside for a

Stove with Glass Oven Doors.

A Set of Skewers.

thermometer. The range should be so placed as to command the best light.

Hard-wood floors are the best kind of floors in a kitchen. Linoleum or oilcloth, according to the purse of the buyer, are the second and third choices. Intelligence does not countenance carpet on kitchen floors in these days.

Soapstone or earthen tubs are now the rule, not the exception, where there are set tubs in laundry or kitchen. For the portable tubs, those of paper are lighter and more durable than the wooden tubs. Paper pails are more durable than wooden, as they do not shrink. A wringer is an economy for laundress and clothes. Galvanized iron clothes-lines are better than rope. No patent clothes-pin surpasses the old-fashioned pin cut from one piece of wood. Zinc wash-boards are better than wooden ones. There are patent boilers in the market for boiling clothes, but the use of them adds to the labor of washing, and the results gained do not equal the results obtained by the old-fashioned method of boiling. Washing-machines are a very great help in laundry work, if the cook-laundress can be persuaded to use them. For the smaller articles — napkins, handkerchiefs, fine aprons, and such articles as are more rumpled than soiled, the washing-machine performs all the labor of rubbing. For sheets and tablecloths they are a great labor-saver. Servants refuse to use them because they must be carried from the cellar and back again. It is intelligence that is able to appreciate the difference in expending strength, not ignorance. Ignorance fights innovation. The combination ironing-table and seat and closet is a most convenient article of furniture. This, with a skirtboard, four irons, holders, and wax-rubbers, completes the laundry department of the kitchen.

Fuel is a constant, and therefore important, item of expense. Probably there is as much friction between the mistress and the maid on this one item as on all other subjects combined. Every housekeeper must experiment if she is to produce the best results with the least cost. Having discovered the best, it is her business to see that the maid is informed on this subject, and then insist on obedience to the law discovered. We keep too hot fires in our ranges. One reason is, we do not make ourselves familiar with the various kinds of fuel. Charcoal is not used in the United States except by chefs. An American family will keep up a coal fire large enough to roast a large piece of meat to broil two pounds of steaks or chops. A few pieces of charcoal, burning in what we might call a slitted pan, or in one of the larger iron baskets sold for frying crullers, and set down on a coal fire which only half fills the grate, broils far better than a large coal fire, and costs but a trifle. For all quick cooking two handfuls of charcoal are much better than a full grate of coal.

Fuel.

Gas, in most cities, is a cheaper fuel than coal, for it burns only while required for cooking. There is no waste

Ironing Table Combination.

The Flat Gas-stove.

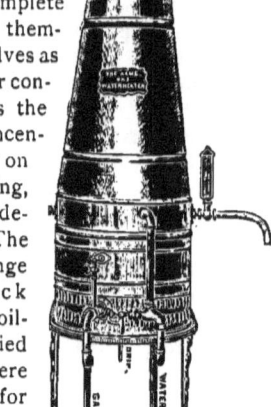

A Gas Water-heater.

and no dirt. If but one pot is needed for cooking, but one burner is needed, and gas-stoves are perfect in equipment to-day. The cheapest gas-stove is the flat gas-stove, to be used on a zinc-covered table. Its first cost is less, and the consumption of gas in running it is less than with any other gas-stove. The oven bought with this stove should always be the one of Russian wrought iron. These ovens are double and the heat circulates around the entire oven. The lower shelf of this oven has a V-shaped piece of iron attached to the under part of the lower shelf to deflect the heat. Even then, a pan of water should be placed in the bottom of the oven. Tin ovens should never be bought to use on these gas-stoves. The cast-iron gas ranges are as complete in themselves as a coal range. Their construction equalizes the heat, instead of concentrating it directly on one point for baking, as must be in a detachable oven. The large-sized gas-range has a water-back which heats the boiler, keeping it supplied with hot water. There is also a gas-heater for water which can be attached to any boiler; but the cost of a cheap gas-stove and the heater equals the cost of the gas-

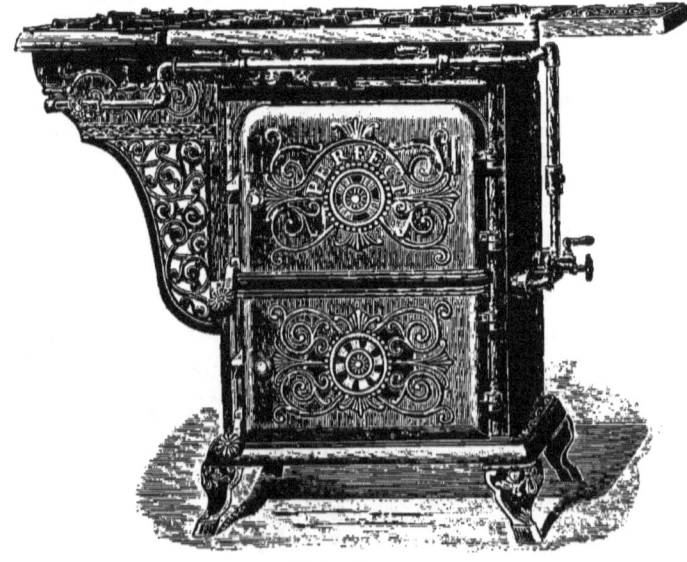

A Modern Gas-stove.

range with water-back, which is the more economical to run.

Oil has the element of danger, and requires care and labor in its use, but it is far preferable to coal in summer, both for cheapness and comfort.

There are patent fuels—that is, they will always be found a great convenience.

The perfect house has the kitchen heated through radiators; water is supplied for kitchen, laundry, and bath purposes from boilers in the cellar.

Electricity is the household servant

An Electric Kitchen. (Sketched from one in operation.)

are patented in America, but have long been in common use in France—that are made of coal-dust, tar, and saw-dust, and by pressure are reduced to different sizes. This fuel is very useful where space is limited and gas unavailable. Stoves are made that are adapted to the use of these fuels, and for the woman without a servant they of the near future. At present it is only possible where there is a current running through the streets, or where there is wealth enough to maintain dynamos and a competent engineer. Cooking by electricity costs very much more than by gas. It is somewhat cleaner, and the heat can be controlled better. An oven designed for roasting and heated by electricity will do half the cooking after the electricity is turned off. Meters are now made which will

A Steam Cooker.

admit the regulating of the current that enters the house. This puts the control of the supply in the hands of the servant. There has recently been invented and brought into general use, especially for the tenement-house people, a gas meter in which, by mechanical arrangement, a twenty-five cent piece can be dropped, and only twenty-five cents' worth of gas can be consumed. The attachment of this meter to the kitchen supply of gas would reduce the cost very greatly, for servants would then see the immediate expenditure of money, which they could not realize unless a forcible illustration were brought to them in this way. This is one reason why it is well to accustom a servant to do the marketing once in a while, giving her the money. She realizes, as in no other way, the cost of things, and particularly the cost of waste. The convenience of electricity and its healthfulness are well understood. There comes to mind now a parlor where electricity supplies the heat, where it boils the water for the five o'clock cup of tea, where it furnishes light at every conceivable point of convenience, where it does part of the work of cooking. But the head of the house is a noted electrician. Electricity will yet be the quiet, obedient servant of the housekeeper of limited purse. But its application to the service of the family has hardly even reached the stage of well-developed infancy, because of its cost and ignorance of how to control it. It will only be the useful servant of the housekeeper when it is as fully under her control as coal, wood, and steam.

Cooking with steam is not as common a practice as it should be with us. *Steam cooking.* The Arnold steamer is one of the best on the market. The entire dinner can be prepared for cooking and placed in the compartments of the steamer, without fear of scorching. The lower pan must be kept supplied with water, and for this reason, even for a small family, the largest-sized cooker is the best; the water-pan of a small cooker is too little, the water evaporates too rapidly. The several pans are lighter to wash than the ordinary cooking utensils. The woman who owns a steam-cooker and knows how to use it does not fear the discomfort of being without a cook. For the woman with no servant the steam-cooker is essential, because it lightens labor. It has also the quality of preserving food flavors.

The chafing-dish is another essential of the kitchen—or more truly, of the *The chafing-dish.* dining-room. Someone has said that a woman never looks better than when preparing a salad. But the man who said it certainly never saw her cooking breakfast or lunch on a chafing-dish. A fine table-cloth, pretty dishes, a vigorous fern in the centre of the table, a brass kettle for boiling water for the coffee, a chafing-dish, a bowl of eggs, a silver fork, a daintily-clad woman, leisurely preparing the attractive dish for the breakfast, is a background that lends poetry to the hardest and most vexatious day. With its aid cold meat can be made delicious, and many dainties too delicate for the clumsy brain and hand of the maid-of-all-work can be easily supplied by the mistress, even in her dinner toilet. For the Sunday night tea it becomes a pan of magic, the contents of which are mixed with grace and home love. (See Appendix.)

A sudden transition to the Aladdin Oven, which stands for nutrition and the first year. Professor Atkinson, who speaks with authority, says:

"All the modern cooking stoves and ranges are wasteful and more or less unsuitable for use. All the ordinary methods of *quick* baking, roasting, and boiling are bad; and, finally, almost the whole of the coal or oil used in cooking is wasted.

"The smell of cooking in the ordinary way gives evidence of waste of flavor as well as a waste of nutritious

Silver Chafing-dish.

economy, must be made. The Aladdin Oven has its place in every kitchen. *The Aladdin Oven.* For the house without a servant, it is indispensable. Professor Edward Atkinson says: "The true science of cooking consists in the regulated and controlled application of heat, by which flavors are developed and the work of converting raw, indigestible materials into nutritive food is accomplished." This the Aladdin Oven does.

The Aladdin Oven costs twenty-seven dollars. The first outlay is more than met in the economy of fuels and foods properties; in most cases the unpleasant smell also gives evidence that the food is being converted into an unwholesome condition, conducive to indigestion and dyspepsia.

"Nine-tenths of the time devoted to watching the process of cooking is wasted; the heat and discomfort of the room in which the cooking is done are evidence of worse than waste.

"The warming of the room or house with the apparatus used for cooking is inconsistent with the best method of cooking and might be compassed at much less cost if the process of cook-

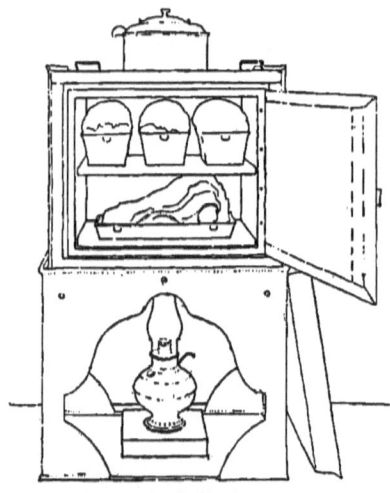

The Aladdin Oven.

ing were separated from the process of warming the room or dwelling.

"No fuel which cannot be wholly consumed is really fit to use in the process of cooking."

And again:

"If the common range or stove now in position in your dwellings were used only for heating the kitchen, boiling water, boiling potatoes, and heating water for circulation through the house, the saving of the mere *excess* of coal which is now burned in order to force the oven to a heat suitable for quick cooking would weigh more than the food to which that heat is applied. I think, but I am not sure on this point, that one-half or more of the coal which is now used to do the cooking, as well as to warm the kitchen and heat water, may be saved by the adoption of my apparatus for the cooking, while only depending on the ordinary range or stove for the rest of the service."

Women are conservative. They do not welcome innovation. The beaten track, the pitfalls and snares of which are familiar, is preferred to the untried road, which has a new set of dangers.

Then in economics women see the first outlay rather than future savings. To spend money to-day with a hope that it will be an investment that will yield returns in profits, and finally become a sinking fund, requires a wider knowledge of the laws of investment than the majority of women possess. The mistake is constantly made of looking upon household expenses as wholly matters of outlay that do not make returns. That is a mistake. No money invested yields the returns that wisely expended house-money returns. There is as great an opportunity for investing money that means profits in the management of a home as in the management of any business. It has been said with great truth that the destruction of the poor is their poverty, which is saying they never have the money to use that would save money. This makes their condition more pathetic. When

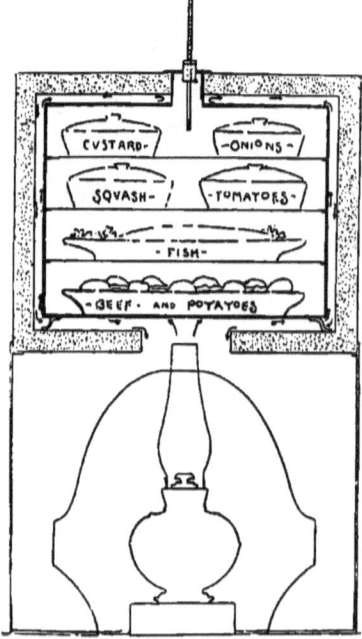

Plan of the Aladdin Oven, showing distribution of heat.

intelligence refuses to take advantage of present outlay to secure future returns in comfort, as well as dollars and cents, the revelation of this mental condition adds contempt to pity.

The Aladdin Oven suffers, in common with the gas-stove, in that it does not keep water hot, during the cooking process, for the purposes of household use. No method of cooking arrangements which does not keep hot water available for the many purposes necessary in every kitchen can meet the need of the woman who depends on the fuel used in cooking for her hot-water supply. Until hot water is supplied from mains in the streets, as cold water now is, or from boilers in the basement, as it is now in the best apartment-houses, no method of cooking can meet the demands of the family life as well as our present method of range and boiler heated by coal, though it is by far the most wasteful. The Aladdin Oven has proved its value. Where the question is how to secure the greatest amount of nutrition at the least expense of money, time, and strength, this wonderful invention of Professor Atkinson has answered it. A great bar to its acceptance has been removed since the "Mode of Cooking in the Aladdin Oven," by Helen H. Richards and Mary Hinman Abel, has been published by Clark W. Bryan, Springfield, Mass. No cook-book met the difficulties of the principles of slow cooking, and the Aladdin Oven suffered because time could not be given in each household for the experiment that each meal became when the oven was used by a novice. Now we have a scientific cook-book adapted to a scientific method of cooking. To the housekeeper who never expects to use the Aladdin Oven, this book is invaluable, because in language that is intelligible to the lay mind the money value of foods is clearly shown. The chief advantages of the Aladdin Oven are economy of foods, saving of fuel, the preservation of food flavors, so that the materials left over from one meal to the next are found as nutritious and appetizing, cooked a second or even a third time; the great economy of labor. A dinner of materials that require about the same amount of cooking can be placed in the oven, and if the lamp has been properly regulated and the directions carefully followed, at the expiration of the specified time the dinner can be served properly cooked. There is no possibility of its being underdone or overdone. It has been cooked without any sense of responsibility after it has once been placed in the oven. Cooking is not a mystery, a gift limited to a certain few; it is based on scientific principles that, once understood, insure success if always heeded. Professor Atkinson says that good material, in this country, is converted into bad feeding. "In other words, for lack of science in the economy of the kitchen, one billion dollars' worth a year of potential energy is wasted." Producing the best results in cooking is a subject worthy of every housekeeper's attention and investigation. Learning recipes will not make a cook; it is the learning of principles. There comes to mind now the graduate of a cooking-school who filled an order for gingerbread, using syrup instead of molasses, producing a sticky and coffee-colored cake. The first pan should have shown her that she had made a mistake, but apparently it did not. She filled her order to serve one hundred and twenty-five people with this stuff. Professor Atkinson says: "A good cook must put forth a little gumption." This cook lacked gumption. No amount of training would make her a cook. The basis of cooking, as of everything else, is the degree of intelligence given to the subject. If the interest is superficial, the attention subdivided, the result must always be uncertain, a matter of chance.

Cleanliness. Cleanliness in housekeeping is of the first importance. Time-savers are as plenteous in this field of housekeeping as in any other, and the market is flooded with materials that are said to lighten labor and save time. Blank walls and fences are decorated with the worn-out woman still washing, with the hands of the kitchen clock pointing to the hour of five, while the companion picture represents another kitchen all in order, with the hour not yet mid-day, the washing all done, and the worker in afternoon neatness of apparel, resting, because she has used some advantageous powder or soap to do her work. Professor Atkinson tells us that kerosene oil is one of the greatest labor-savers. A teaspoonful put in tepid dish-water removes the grease from the dishes; and clothes, it is said, are made far whiter by its use than by the use of soap. It is right here that the housekeeper shows her wisdom. She does not let doubt stand in the way of conviction. She experiments and is convinced by the results of her own experiments carefully conducted.

It has been said that the quantity of soap consumed by a nation would be a fairly accurate measure of its degree of civilization. Cleanliness is one of the first essentials of health, and how to secure its perfection with the least expenditure of strength is a subject of study and experiment. In "The Chemistry of Cooking and Cleaning," by Ellen H. Richards, the use of ammonia is recommended for cleaning, both for scrubbing and for laundry purposes, especially for the washing of woollens. The properties of ammonia, Mrs. Richards tells us, afford a safeguard against careless rinsing, and that imperfect rinsing is at the bottom of most of the trouble in washing woollens with soap or caustic alkalies. Mrs. Richards cautions against the use of impure ammonium, which cannot be used with safety in the laundrying of woollens. The best ammonia costs about thirty cents a quart, and should be diluted with cold water before being put in warm water, never too hot to put the hand in. The solid ammonium carbonate costs twenty-five or thirty cents a pound, and it has the alkaline value of two pounds of *sal sodæ*. The cheapest form of alkalines is *sal sodæ*, and the knowledge of this fact will guard many housekeepers in buying the new washing fluids and powders that are offered.

Nature has provided valuable aids to the housekeeper. Science gives her generous service to the discovery of these agents and the application of them to household purposes. The result to the homes of the world is the saving of strength, time, and money. The intelligent housekeeper uses the discoveries of science and increases the happiness of herself and of her household. Mrs. Richards has discovered one compound offered to the public for washing purposes that contains one pound of washing-soda. It costs as much as ten pounds of washing-soda, and if used as directed it would allow two ounces of washing-soda in solution to a large tubful of water. Borax is a safe substance to use for delicate fabrics. Soft soap leaves a pure lye, to be held in mass. This it is that makes soft soap a favorite with many laundresses. Javelle water, a preparation of *sal sodæ*, lime, and alcohol, if used with great caution, is an aid in the laundry. The removal of stains from fabrics that cannot be washed requires care and judgment, and a certain knowledge of chemistry. Chloroform is a valuable agent, but must be carefully used. A piece of clean white blotting-paper must be held underneath the place to be cleaned, and the chloroform applied with a sponge, and rubbed until the spot is dry. Other agents are ether, benzine, turpentine, and alcohol. Water will often remove a spot, when it is used with judgment. A clean sponge, wrung almost dry through clean water, and rubbed on the spot until the dampness has entirely disappeared will sometimes remove the spot as effectively as any chemical. The ring that often appears after the use of chloroform, ether, benzine, or turpentine will gradually disappear, unless the material has been rubbed violently enough to disturb the color. Buckwheat flour, Indian meal, magnesia, and French chalk are all valuable dry cleansing agents. Laces and white flannel garments, if not too soiled, may be cleaned by Indian meal. Roll the laces in a fine towel, after they have been sprinkled plentifully with meal. After a week or more, gentle rubbing will remove the dirt and leave the laces soft. White wool garments can be kept fresh all the season by rolling the garment, covered with Indian meal, in a cloth for a day or two, and then rubbing with a small cloth or between the hands if the hands are dry.

Hot water is an agent convenient and valuable for the removal of fruit stains. It must be used at once. Iron rust yields to muriatic acid, which must be rinsed in hot water immediately after using. Oxalic acid is another agent that acts effectively on ink stains. Unless removed by washing thoroughly, using ammonia water for final rinsing, fabrics may be injured by its use.

Bluing is one of the laundry perplexities — so great a perplexity that we quote Mrs. Richards as an authority again. She tells us that the clothes must be rinsed free from soap before they can be put in bluing. Often mysterious spots of iron rust appear, caused by the decomposition of the bluing, which to-day usually consists of a preparation of Prussian blue. Indigo, enclosed in a bag, is the best kind of bluing in solution. Indigo gives a tint which is suggestive of absolute cleanliness. Mrs. Richards tested fifteen of the bluings on the market, and found that all were Prussian blue of greater or less strength ; and Prussian blue contains iron.

Acetic acid will restore some shades of blue, if added to the second rinsing water. Try a piece of the goods before washing the whole garment. Muriatic acid has been known to remove iron-rust stains from blue cambric. A drop of the acid was applied to the stain, while held over a bowl of hot water, and plunged at once in the water. The garment was finally rinsed in several waters, the last one being ammonia water. This acid is a powerful agent, and its use must always be followed by a plentiful use of water. It will remove stains from porcelain. It cannot be used on marble, as it destroys the polish.

In catering for a family there are three things to be considered : Nutrition, palatableness, and attractiveness. The last has much to do with the appetite. The most nutritive food, carelessly served, cannot tempt the appetite. It is useless to talk of its strength-giving qualities, if the imagination has been offended. Food has moral and artistic values, and the wise housekeeper pays due regard to them. We may consider food as the element of life upon which the power of man to sustain himself wholly depends. Almost anything can be spared except food. "Again, if the measure or quantity of food is not sufficient, and is not rightly adjusted to the conditions of complete nutrition, both the manual and mental efficiency of the man will

Moral and artistic values of food.

be impaired," says Professor Atkinson in his "Science of Nutrition." A recognition of this fact makes the food eaten as important to the millionaire as to the man working for a dollar a day. Nutrition, then, becomes the science of life. The smaller the income, the greater the importance of the question of waste. But health is as important to the rich man as to the poor, as life can be but a burden to a man who is suffering. A clear brain is of as great importance to the capitalist, the thinker, as a vigorous, flexible muscle is to the laboring man; and to know the kind of food that will supply each with the force or energy that he most needs is the duty and should be the privilege of the one who buys the food for the family. This involves a knowledge of the food-principles, the values of food; and there are books that put this knowledge within the possession of every housekeeper.

The first result of careful study of scientific cook-books is the demolition *Scientific cook-books.* of many practices and beliefs. Take soup-making. We have been taught by standard cook-books to skim soup; on no account to omit this important act from soup-making. Mrs. Mary Hinman Abel, in her prize essay published by the American Public Health Association, says: "We have seen that hot water coagulates proteid, and once coagulated it will not dissolve in water, and for this reason the soup contains of this valuable principle only the soluble albumen which rises as scum. If the cook has skimmed this off the soup, the soup she calls strong is strong with flavors rather than with nutritive principles. Proteid is one of of the five important food-principles. They are the flesh foods."

In buying meat we should remember that about sixty per cent. is water, and that fat takes the place of water. This *Meat.* is a scientific fact based on investigation. It is for the housekeeper to decide what her money shall buy. For making soup bones are as valuable as meat. The bones and meat, the scientists tell us, must be put in cold water and soaked two hours, if possible, and then the meat should be allowed only to simmer. No flavor should be added until an hour before serving. If the fat is to be removed it is better to make the soup the day before using, removing the fat when the soup is cold. Meat, to be boiled, should be immersed in boiling water and brought quickly to a boil again, then complete the cooking at a temperature of 170° F. Mrs. Abel suggests a thermometer made by inserting a tube registering 300° Celsius, through a cork, with the bulb below, and encased in a cylinder of wood. This thermometer can be floated on water. It can also be used by placing in a wire frame to test the heat of an oven. Baking meats is not understood. The outside should be browned rapidly in a broad kettle or pan. This done, it is ready for the oven, standing on a rack in the pan. Baste with the hot fat, do not use hot water, are Mrs. Abel's directions for baking meats. Allow twelve to fifteen minutes to the pound. Mrs. Rorer says, eight to twelve. Broiling is one of the fine arts, and is to be acquired only by experience. Coal is not the proper fuel for broiling; charcoal should be used, and it should be so placed as to admit of keeping the meat at a distance from the coals after the outside is browned. Broiling, Professor Atkinson tells us, is the most extravagant form of cooking meat.

Bread is a most important article of food, and for that reason its preparation *Bread.* is of the greatest importance. In America, baker's bread is neither nutritive nor healthful. Mrs.

Able believes that the time is not far distant when baker's bread in this country will have so improved that it will not be necessary to consider bread-making a part of the housekeeper's responsibility.

The best flour for bread-making is the rich, yellow-looking flour. The best flour is always the cheapest. It produces better bread, and more of it, than a poor grade. Professor Atkinson, Mrs. Ewing, and Mrs. Abel agree that the best bread is made in the least time. There is little difference in the recipes given. The writer, since attending Mrs. Ewing's lecture, has used her recipe. One pint of wetting, equal parts of milk and water, brought to the degree of heat known as lukewarm; one compressed yeast-cake, dissolved in two tablespoonfuls of cold water. The yeast-cake dissolved is added to the wetting, and then the sifted flour stirred in with a flat wooden spoon until the dough can be handled with ease, when it is placed on the bread-board and kneaded with the back of the hand, by a movement that would more properly be called stretching. The back of the hand is used, not the fists or fingers. Salt is sifted into the dry flour—about one tablespoonful. When the dough has been kneaded ten or fifteen minutes, it is placed in the bread-raiser, and in one hour is ready for moulding.

Correct Position of the Hands.

The best bread-pans used must be ordered. They are of sheet iron like a scoop without ends, about eight inches long and four inches wide. When in the pans, the top of the dough is brushed lightly with melted butter and allowed to rise until the loaf is twice the bulk of dough that was put in the pan. The oven is brought to 370 degrees, and the bread is baked from twenty to fifty minutes, according to the size of the loaf. It comes out of the oven a light crisp brown, with a tender crust all around the bread. Any housekeeper who once tries this process of making bread will never go back to the old process of having the bread rise overnight. The quick-raising process admits of the control of the temperature from the beginning of making the bread. Bread cannot sour, neither can it lose its sweetness by being chilled, and so delayed in rising. Mrs. Abel, who is an authority on bread-making, gives the proportions of two and one-half quarts of flour to one quart of water, one yeast-cake or one-half cup of liquid yeast, one tablespoonful of salt. The flour and salt are put in the pan, and the wetting gradually poured into a hole made in the middle of the flour. Very little flour is used in kneading, which Mrs. Abel says should be gentle, and should be done in from fifteen to twenty minutes. The bread should rise in a temperature of about 72 degrees. Dough made according to these directions should be raised in one to two hours. For the second moulding, Mrs. Abel advises the use of milk, warm water, or milk on the hands, never flour. The dough should about half fill the pan, and rise to nearly twice that quantity. The oven should be hot enough to brown the bread in ten minutes.

There are many kinds of bread the process of making which is neither difficult nor mysterious. Mrs. Abel's book gives eleven recipes for the making of eleven kinds of dough, and for five kinds of bread, made from thin batter, the basis of which is flour, yeast, and salt. When the housekeeper has learned the principles of bread-making, she is mistress of the situation, for it becomes then only a matter of proportion and materials as to what kind of bread she makes. The basis is always the same. The same law holds good in cake-making. Once understand the principles, certain proportions of flour, eggs, butter, sugar, wetting—milk, molasses, or water—and all kinds of cake other than the plain are in reality differences of flavor. Any careful comparisons of recipes will prove this.

The cooking of meats and vegetables is not a matter of a mysterious witch's *Cooking meats and vegetables.* cauldron; it is the application of dry heat, steam heat, or water, used to produce certain results on material, or rather materials, that undergo certain chemical changes when subjected to certain treatment. That the result is not the same always is because the conditions are not always the same. Ignorance, not realizing that cooking is a science, does not compel the same conditions each time certain foods are cooked, and the results vary because the process varies. The seeming contradiction in the unvarying success that attends certain cooks who have no rules is that they have trained their eye and touch so that they produce the same effects. Watch them closely, and you find their uniform success is only in the cooking of certain things. They have failures, and frequently in the making of the simplest things. You can no more produce uniformly good results in cooking without clear and definite ideas of how to produce those results, than you can produce moral reform in your own nature without knowing its weakness and its strength. Certain lines of conduct, produced by certain methods of thought, result in a certain kind of character.

Marketing is the foundation of a good table. Poor raw materials can *Marketing.* never be made into good foods. Careless marketing is extravagant marketing. In these days, when committee work consumes so large a portion of the time of most women, there is a tendency to slur over this part of the housekeeper's responsibility. Women of even limited incomes frequently give orders through a servant to a boy at the door. And these orders are frequently given without any investigation of the larder, just on the word of a servant who has proved again and again her incompetency. The second evil is the book-account. The handling of money each day is a check on extravagance in housekeeping.

Putting aside a given sum each week for the table expenses of a family, and keeping the exepnses within that limit, is the only sure control of that proportion of the income set aside for table expenses. The possibility of exceeding the fair proportion of the living expenses of a family is greater here than anywhere else. A fixed sum means a fixed average sum. Some weeks certain large quantities must be bought and the average will be exceeded, but it will not be reached the next week. The supplies having been purchased in advance, it is only business-like to set aside the difference between the apportioned amount and the actual sum expended, to meet the next large outlay. There comes to mind now a housekeeper who produces wonderful results with a very small expenditure. She begins with the first beginning of small fruits, for instance, to can, preserve, or sweet-pickle. When she begins using a special fruit, she knows what each can, glass, or jar has cost, and that sum is put into a bank on the mantel, from her self-allowed weekly allowance. That fund is her fruit fund, and each year is called upon to meet the outlay that preserving fruit compels. This is only applying business methods to housekeeping expenses. It is turning over capital, and it is the more economical way. The money is always at hand to meet the best conditions of the market. That brings up the question of buying in large amounts, an ever open and disputed question that must be settled by each housekeeper. If there is a good store-room, and the housekeeper is careful and systematic, buying in quantities is wise, not because it saves money, but because it is a great convenience. In sickness, in stormy weather, under the pressure of outside things, it is a convenience to have a store-room supplied to meet an emergency. Canned goods are valuable, but they should not be a dependence; they should be only the occasional market-supply, and should always be used with care. A can once opened, its contents should be immediately put into porcelain or glass. They should never be left in the tin can. In our Northern markets fresh vegetables are a possibility even to the poor man all the year, and of late this has been usually true of fruits. A few years ago this was not so, and canned goods were the dependence of a family of limited income. Canned soups are palatable, but it is only necessary to compare the price of one can of soup, and the quantity and quality that can be prepared, with little outlay of strength, time, or fuel, with fresh meat, to realize how extravagant canned soups are. Yet it would not be good housekeeping not to keep them in the house to meet an emergency. Plum-puddings are staple articles of prepared food for sale at all high-class groceries, but puddings that will keep for two months can be made at home for at least one-third less cost.

The following is the recipe: One cup of molasses, one of sweet milk, one of raisins, one of currants, three of flour, one-half cup of suet chopped fine, one teaspoonful of ginger, one of cinnamon, one of soda, and a little nutmeg. Pour the batter into a well-buttered mould, and steam three hours.

To keep the house-stores so replenished as to meet the emergencies of weather, illness, company, or the sudden pressure of outside affairs is but to conduct the affairs of a household on a business basis. A large percentage of the friction of the housekeeping comes from running out of supplies when needed, compelling the whole household machinery to stop. The purchasing of supplies in large quantities is not a matter of dollars and cents, so much as a matter of convenience.

The buying of meats and vegetables is important. The first thing to secure is a trustworthy market-man. No housekeeper should trade with a man whose honesty and cleanliness she doubts. It is wisest, if possible, to trade at a market where there are three or four grades of customers. This secures better service. The butcher who knows that he can sell what you do not want will give you far more liberty in selection. The selection of meats, except where the housekeeper has made a special study of this subject, must be far more a matter of honest butcher than of intelligent housekeeper. Vegetables show their condition much more than meat. Stale vegetables can be detected on sight, and no intelligent woman buys them. This is one of the first advantages of marketing by the housekeeper. She sees what she buys. The cook sees the supplies first when they are delivered, when the order goes through the cook to the boy at the door, with the order-book. The going to market implies, perhaps, the sacrifice of slippers and house-dress, but it means greater variety for the table. No woman can market as well through a cook as she can by going to market each day and supplying her table from sight. Suggestions are constant while marketing. Market prices vary, and often an unusual luxury will be within the reach of a limited purse. The price of fruits, vegetables, and game are controlled by the law of supply and demand, and there are variations in price from day to day. If "eternal vigilance is the price of liberty," eternal alertness is the price of good housekeeping.

All housekeepers must market either in person or by proxy, but not all housekeepers must be employers. The woman who employs servants must first consider her relation to her servants from the commercial standpoint. If the subject is considered from the housekeeping standpoint alone, future peace and stability is sacrificed to present emergency. It becomes a question of "anybody" to meet the present conditions of pressure. It is this that brings the constant procession of "anybodys" through our homes, and is responsible, to a large degree, for the present unnatural condition of the servant question. It has lowered the standard of intelligence among the household servants.

Housekeepers do not make the demand for character that they should, in *The servant question.* the servants they employ. The servant comes into the closest relations to the family. Her character is as important to the family well-being as her skill. Yet the first question of the housekeeper-employer is on the coming servant's—we cannot say applicant's, for we have the sad picture of the employer always being the applicant—ability *to do*, and not *to be*, which is by far the most important question. Every woman who knows how to run a house knows that a servant who has character and intelligence can be trained, while the servant who is skilful and lacks character is always a disturbing element; there is constant friction because of lack of confidence, or untrustworthiness. There can be no stability in the family life if there is always the element of uncertainty as to how long the relation between mistress and maid will continue at its present status. The employer who sees only present conditions when making a contract or business connection is short-sighted, and never makes a success. It is far better to meet emergencies by transitory arrangements from day to day than to go through the farce of making a seemingly permanent arrangement, when there is no solid foundation of confidence based on investigation.

The best servants any housekeeper can employ are the labor-saving de- *Labor-saving devices.* vices which will enable her to meet an interregnum in the kitchen with dignity. The woman who owns an Aladdin Oven and a chafing-dish, a gas-stove and a steam-cooker, and knows how to use them, is the true mistress of her home. She can meet the servant question, fortified ; the family are living comfortably, and the housework is reduced to a minimum.

Of course, if the housekeeper is inefficient, or lacks either health or executive skill, she must pay the penalty of her limitations, and the family must suffer with her. She can never be the mistress, if she is a creature of inexorable conditions. A housekeeper who can meet the emergency in any department of her household-staff by readjustment, or by doing the labor with her own hands, can always choose whom she shall employ. Having come to that decision, the next subject is a clear and full understanding of the service required, the rights conceded on both sides. Those whom we employ to do our household labor are human beings, not machines. Rules must be firm, and if the contract is to be satisfactory, they must be flexible at times. There are sure to be faults and weaknesses on both sides, and the need of patience. The old lady's declaration that there were two "bears" in every marriage, "bear and forbear," may be startling, but it is true; and it is equally true of a mistress and maid. The sense of justice that realizes this is the one that prevents friction.

The woman who employs one maid-of-all-work, and then demands that she shall be a superior cook, laundress, waitress, parlormaid, and chambermaid, is an impossible mistress to suit. The housekeeper who, on being interviewed in the character of a reference as to the abilities of a maidservant who had been in her employ some time, was asked the question, "Is she a first-class waitress?" and responded: "No, she does chamber-work. You didn't expect a first-class waitress to do chamber-work," was the reply of the mistress, who knew what to demand and what to expect. It is just this lack of worldly experience that is responsible for the constant friction and resulting change in domestic service. Servants are untrained, because of the varying standards of employers, and ignorance of what are the duties pertaining to certain domestic positions. The lessons to be learned in order to adjust the domestic problem are as much a duty of the mistress as of the maid. What we want is character for both, a clear comprehension of the duties of both, a recognition of the purely commercial relation under the most complex conditions—conditions that involve intimacies that are only second to those of relatives—interdependence that is as close, if harmony is to be preserved, as family life can make it. Yet the bond, in all but rare instances, is that of dollars and cents. There are evils in the situation that only the mistress, by creating public sentiment, can remedy. Take the first evil, the sleeping-room of the servant. It is usually the hottest and coldest room in the house, too often uncomfortably furnished. The bathing facilities are usually a two-quart basin, and yet cleanliness is exacted. The kitchen and servants' rooms, in even first-class apartment-houses, are tangible evidence of the consideration given to the comforts of servants. One apartment-house recently erected in New York, costing three hundred and fifty thousand dollars, has every kitchen and servant's room so arranged as to require gas-light all day long on even bright days, below the sixth story. One would not expect one's horse to live under such conditions and preserve health and temper.

Comparatively few of the houses in America are arranged to give bathing facilities to servants. It is often the case that one bath-tub must serve the whole family, and the conditions must be met, and rules developed, to meet the unfortunate standards of architects and builders. The woman who commands comfortable working conditions for her servants is the one who secures the best working-force. She does not pay the highest market price for unskilled labor; she does not excuse or ignore carelessness with indifference or laxity; she does not demand special skill for general service. Her servants appreciate the humanity of her arrangements, and respect the business ability which holds them up to their best standards for every service rendered. It is only necessary to enter an intelligence office, and see the unnatural attitude of the employer and employed, to realize how fully the untrained mistress is responsible for the impudent, arbitrary demands, and general indifference of servants. In engaging a servant, be exact in explaining duties, wages, days out, requirements of skill, the possible emergencies that may make sudden demands, and then live up to the mistress's standards. Laxity in the mistress begets laxity in the maid; extra demands from mistresses beget extra demands from servants. You cannot get away from the law of interchange. Where there are continued extra demands made on servants because of visitors or illness, there should be extra compensation. Every man doing business expects to give extra compensation when he makes extra demands on his workmen. He expects to employ people who have character. The relation of mistress and maid is a business relation, not a complimentary one, or one of neighborly or friendly service on one side.

Outside laundry service is appreciated by the wise housekeeper. Every woman who can afford it should send the family washing to the laundry. It will raise the grade of service more quickly than any other one influence, to remove from the kitchen this disturbing and laborious work. It is a source of discomfort to the whole family. It is usually the cause of discussions weekly between the mistress and maid. Take the washing of flannels. The waste of money through the shrinkage of flannel garments would pay a two months' laundry bill in most families. Yet it is possible to find trained laundry-men and women who make a specialty of washing flannels without shrinkage. It is next to impossible to wash blankets or curtains at home. Few houses have the facilities for washing or drying these heavy or delicate articles. Blankets should always be sent to a trustworthy laundry or cleaner's. There is no economy in washing them at home. Even with all the technical knowledge necessary, space and machinery are also necessary to accomplish successfully the washing of blankets.

True economy. True economy is not always the saving of dollars and cents. It often means the spending of money. For *true economy means the preservation of life at its best for each one.* Sometimes it is the wisest economy to spend money. Take the matter of entertaining. To suggest to some housekeepers that outside skill should be employed is to make them feel at once that a suggestion of the wildest extravagance is being made. Yet it is a wise economy if the home skill is deficient. The housekeepers of to-day are fortunate, for the intelligence of the country has developed until cooking has become an art worthy of special study and training by intelligent, refined women. There is no dainty for the table, nor any substantial, that cannot be supplied by trained cooks without any anxiety to the hostess, and with but little extra expense. Every city, almost, has a Woman's Exchange, and in addition to that, caterers, women, who have been trained and who fill orders for the things that require time, care, and daintiness that are usually the bugbears of the housekeeper who entertains on a limited income.

To buy this outside skill and keep nerve-force and mental quiet is the wisest economy.

Entertaining. This brings up the subject of hospitality. The family of limited means in America too often laments that the grace of hospitality is denied it. There is no greater mistake made than to deny one's self the privilege of entertaining friends. It is a privilege only as it is a pleasure. If it is a burden, then it is done as a duty. If the manner of entertaining is to be according to the standards of other people whose income represents dimes or dollars where ours does cents, then both for entertainer and entertained the occasion is a burden. No guest feels comfortable who knows that the entertainment provided has used more than its share of the limited income. When the vulgarity of entertaining out of proportion to the family income is fully understood, hospitality will be one of the familiar graces of every home, not the spasmodic, herculean efforts of strength and finance that mean an after-state of collapse. One of the first anxieties of easy entertaining is to train the servants, one or many, to nicety of service for the family, no matter how small. No servant can be trained to serve nicely for guests if she is not trained to exactness for the ordinary family life.

The matter of carving is a very important one for the ease and comfort of all at the board. Rarely is the host found who does not show how great a burden this duty is. Where the host cannot train himself to carve easily, it is far wiser to have the carving done in the kitchen. With even one or two servants this is easily managed, if the mistress is competent. With steam or hot-water platters, a mistress can do the carving herself, and have the meat placed on the course platters by the cook. For lunches, it is an easy matter to have all the carving and cutting done in the kitchen. Carving must take the attention of the one who does it. If he is competent the duty is simple and easily performed, but if incompetent it becomes oppressive, and often causes a bad quarter of an hour for the guests. Having the carving done in the kitchen and the meat or game served in the dining-room by the servants, from course platters, permits the host and hostess to give their entire attention to the guests, and prevents those awkward, solemn silences when the carver is hunting for a joint. The art of carving is a lost art, almost, and when we discuss the subject it is always grandfathers and uncles who were marvels of the art. There is no way to acquire it but by study and practice. There is something homelike in the appearance of the generous roast, but all enjoyment is destroyed if the host gazes upon it with anxious frown and calls to mind the suggestive "no talking to the man at the veal." The hostess who has taken a course of cooking lessons learns in theory how to carve, and she can train her cook, if the right relations exist, to bear this burden of carving, and so reduce the sense of responsibility, and give freedom to all. That carving is not considered the duty of host or hostess is proven in that not one of the modern cook-books gives any instructions. A text-book can only suggest. Practice is the only surety of success in carving.

The arranging of the table should always bear the mark of the mistress, whether the pleasure of the family alone or of guests is considered. The wares may be cheap, but in these days they may always be pretty. To avoid confusion, it is best to train servants to recognize certain dishes to be used invariably with certain courses. When guests are to be entertained, it is best to see that this rule is understood, and that all the necessary appurtenances are arranged in proper place for immediate serving before leaving the dining-room. To have to wait for spoons or forks for the serving of a course is as much an evidence of neglect on the part of the mistress as of the servant. The carefulness with which details are attended to in the home is the degree of the perfection of the housekeeping. Neglect at any point means that much loss, with the possibility of friction, annoyance, impatience. It is this carefulness of arrangement of details by the mistress of the family that makes entertaining a pleasant incident, not a burdensome occasion. It is attention to details that insures quiet and smoothness in the daily home life.

No amount of economy in buying will counterbalance carelessness in using the materials bought.

Housekeeping is analogous to business. It is the expending of money to produce certain results. A man would not be considered a good business man who did not watch his expense account and make it bear its proper relation to the income from his business. A good housekeeper does this. She knows, or should know, what she receives from every dollar expended, whether it is expended in wages or material. If she secures an honest return in services, in health, nutrition, enjoyment for herself and her family, she is meeting fully what the highest standards demand.

The house once furnished and in order, the maintenance of a condition of cleanliness and order is the next step. The perplexities are determined largely by the way in which a house is furnished, and the sum of money that can be expended for service. If economy of money is not of importance, the family can take a spring or a fall vacation, and the professional cleaner and her assistants can be put in charge. The annual or semi-annual house-cleaning, under such conditions, becomes a pleasure. The family who must live at home during the house-cleaning seasons must be considered and considerate.

House-cleaning.

If the floors of the house are covered with carpets nailed to the floor, the period of discomfort and disorganization must be one that depends on the will of those who cannot be controlled, the carpet renovators. The mistress is helpless. She cannot rearrange the rooms until the floors are covered. Carpets that are in rooms occupied and used constantly ought to come up at least once a year. Where the rooms are not in constant use, such as parlors and guest-rooms, the carpets can remain on the rooms two years at a time, or even longer, without injury. They must, however,

Floors.

be carefully watched for moths. The carpet sweeper is a much greater protection than a broom, because it parts the pile. The edges and corners of the carpets must be ironed with irons, not heated to the scorching point, two or three times a year. This destroys all moth eggs. When the house is to be closed for any length of time, tobacco or camphor must be sprinkled freely about on the floor, especially in the corners. Hard-wood floors and matting-covered floors relieve the housekeeper greatly. The house can be kept much cleaner during the entire year, and the house-cleaning period becomes one of comparative comfort—absolute ease in comparison with the house-cleaning days of our mothers and grandmothers. House-cleaning with hard-wood floors or matting becomes a simple matter. It is then but to dust walls and ceilings, wash paints, and oil the wood-work, after a thorough sweeping.

To the systematic housekeeper the house-cleaning time comes when the wardrobe requires changing to meet the conditions of temperature. Then closets, drawers, and trunks are thoroughly overhauled to take account of stock, to renovate, to mend, to take out and put away. The house must then, in all its parts, receive the same attention. The housekeeper who works systematically puts every box, every shelf, every drawer and trunk, above or outside of the kitchen and dining-room, in order, before she disturbs or disarranges any room. Having had the inside of the closet thoroughly cleaned and put in order, close and lock the door. If there is a space between the door and the frame, crowd in some soft paper, and the closet is thoroughly protected from dust during the period of cleaning of the room with which it is connected.

Closets, etc.

The Care of Beds, Bedrooms, and Furniture.

Bedrooms. After the closets and store-rooms are in order the bedrooms should receive the first attention. The mattresses are dusted and brushed on the roof or piazza; for as long a time as possible, mattresses and pillows, if not of feathers, are exposed to outside air and sunshine. Feathers should never be exposed to direct sun rays, as they melt or soften the oil in the feathers and frequently cause an odor. Feather pillows may be beaten with a light cane or rattan duster, and the dust removed. When new pillow-ticks are needed, make them of the required size; leave an opening in one end of from four to six inches, rip a corresponding opening in the old ticks, baste, with close stitches, the old and the new edges together, and shake the feathers down in the new ticks, being careful to shake out all the feathers. This work should be done in a room with all the windows closed, that the feathers, on turning the old ticks inside out for the down that may cling, may not be blown about. A bare floor is better than a carpeted one for this work, and whoever does it should fold over the mouth and nostrils a thin handkerchief, as the fine particles of down are apt to cause great discomfort. When as much furniture as can be moved readily from the room has been moved, thoroughly wipe, with a cloth wrung from hot suds in which there is soap and ammonia, every crack and crevice in the bedsteads and wire mattresses. With a fine brush apply corrosive sublimate to the ends of slats, to all knot-holes in the slats, and to the slat-rests on the inside of the sides of the bedstead. If the bed is not to be used daily, as a precaution sprinkle insect powder freely in all cracks and in the slat-rests. Slats should be thoroughly scrubbed, and it is a good idea to paint them lightly on both sides with corrosive sublimate. *This is a deadly poison, and should be used with great care.* It causes the skin on the hands to dry, and for that reason it is best to use a long-handled brush and gloves. Beds should be cleaned in March thoroughly, in order to secure absolute freedom from vermin.

Servant's room. The greatest care is needed in the servant's room. Beds should be cleaned thoroughly three or four times a year, and no dust should be allowed to accumulate on slats or wire mattresses of any kind. A servant's room should be cleaned once a month, at least, until the mistress is sure that the servant is perfectly cleanly in all her habits. Walls, ceilings, and floors in a servant's room should always be painted. The walls should be kept absolutely free from nail-holes, and all cracks should be closed with plaster as soon as they appear. The paint used in a servant's room should always be light. No boxes should be tolerated under the bed, nor bundles, and it is wise to insist that all clothing in the room should be exposed to the outside air at least three times after the outside temperature demands closed windows.

Frequency of house-cleaning. If a house is to be occupied during the whole year, it should be thoroughly cleaned twice a year. If the house is not occupied during the summer, the fall is the best time of the year to clean.

Furniture. The family occupying a house the whole year will enjoy it much better if a change is made in the furnishing. If after the spring house-cleaning, rugs and heavy curtains, bric-à-brac, and books in handsome bindings are all carefully put away; thin curtains, linen-embroidered table-covers and cushion-covers taken out to supply the places of heavy and elaborate ones, the whole family will feel as if they are having a change—an outing. If the floors are carpeted, a linen drugget covering the floor will pay for itself in the sense of cleanliness and coolness it conveys. The living-room, where the family must spend their evenings in warm weather, should be furnished as airily and simply as possible. This is not difficult if the furniture is willow or cane. If the furniture is upholstered, linen covers are possible. The first cost is apparently not economical, but these covers last for years and save the permanent furniture cover.

To the woman furnishing a house, and who does not expect to keep more than one or two servants, upholstered furniture is a great care, and unless carefully selected, rarely beautiful. It is always a source of anxiety, and seems to have the disposition of total depravity that is the innate tendency of all furniture, to need repairing at the moment when other and more imperative demands are made on the income. Tufted furniture should not be bought by people of limited incomes. It is difficult to keep it free from dust and moth. A painter's camel's-hair brush should be kept for brushing upholstered furniture. All tufted furniture and carved wood needs the special attention of the mistress, if it is not to be a mortification and a reproach.

Willow furniture is beautiful and well made. With cushions, it can be made warm, cosey, and attractive for winter, and solid and fancy chairs are now made that are within the limits of a narrow purse. A parlor or living-room can be made beautiful without the aid of the "parlor set" of a few years ago.

One thing to avoid in furnishing any room is the bringing together of furniture which belongs to several periods. There should be an equality of age and cost, and at least a relationship of color.

Kerosene oil will clean all polished surfaces. It should be applied lightly, with a cloth, and rubbed hard with a clean dry cloth. The final polishing should be done with the palm of the hand. This requires strength, and a man trained to the work should be hired by the day to do this work after the whole house has been put in order.

If the maid in charge of the kitchen has been well trained, the cleaning of *Cleaning the kitchen.* the kitchen is a comparatively easy matter, unless walls and woodwork are to be painted. If the kitchen has received the attention it should, pots and pans are in good condition, the painted shelves have been wiped off at least weekly, and it is a simple matter to remove the shelves and wipe the painted walls and ceilings and floors of the closets. If pots and pans show that they have not been thoroughly cleaned after each using, put them in the wash-boiler, cover with cold water in which a good handful of washing soda has been thrown, put the boiler over the fire, where it will heat slowly until it boils, lift out the cooking utensils one by one and wash in ammonia water, with soap. Every particle of black will have disappeared, unless they have been greatly neglected, in which case fine ashes or sapolio will be necessary for rubbing. If ammonia is put in the dish-water, it will keep both the glass and silver in better condition. Silver washed in hot, soapy water, to which ammonia, diluted by cold water, has been added at about the proportion of a tablespoonful to a gallon and a half of hot water, will be kept in order much better than silver washed in ordinary dish-water. After the silver has been washed in the ammonia-water, put it in a pan and pour boiling water over it, and wipe while the silver is hot. If treated in this way, it will not be necessary to polish the silver used every day oftener than once in two weeks. All silver not in daily use should be cleaned and wrapped in tissue-paper and put away.

Curtain Decorated by Acid Staining.
From a Water Color Drawing by Francis Howard.

The Care of Walls and Woodwork.

Silver. Plated silver should be used in every family where there is no safe or strong-box. Silver should not be a temptation to a poor man's servants, nor a burden of responsibility to the poor man's wife. Whiting, dusted through a fine cloth, polishes silver as well as any of the much-advertised polishes on the market, and costs very much less.

The dining-room. The cleaning of the dining-room should hardly be more than half a day's work, for the linen and china closets have presumably been put in order at least once every month during the entire year while the house is occupied. The cleaning of the dining-room then becomes merely a matter of washing of paints, thorough dusting of walls, and in case of a nailed carpet, the taking up of the carpet, cleaning, and putting down again.

Walls. A long-handled feather duster,—the feathers of which, in order not to scatter dust, should be enveloped in a piece of soft cotton cloth—is an absolute necessity for the care of walls and ceilings. This should be used at the weekly cleaning. For cleaning papered walls and ceilings, a piece of old soft flannel, tied on a broom or used carefully in the hand, is the best method. French chalk, finely powdered, will remove marks from some kinds of papers, but it is best not to make the experiment on exposed places. The attempt to remove a mark on papered walls should be made as soon as the defect is discovered. The longer the dirt or disfigurement remains, the more difficult it is to remove it. One should as quickly remove the marks or dirt from a painted wall as one would from a painted door.

To repair papered walls, never put on the patch with a straight edge. If possible, in cutting it out, follow the run of the pattern of the paper. If this cannot be done, cut the edge in uneven scollops and points, and match the figures perfectly. Sometimes it will be almost impossible to discover the patch on the walls. Painted walls or wood-work should never be scrubbed with a brush. Warm water, in which a very little ammonia has been put after diluting in cold water and a little of the best soap dissolved, will clean better than any amount of scrubbing, provided the paint is not covered with greasy smoke-stains. Use a flannel cloth wrung out of the warm water and rub carefully over the painted surface, and another cloth wrung out of clean warm water, then rub the surface with a dry woollen cloth; this treatment will leave the paint unharmed and perfectly clean.

Kalsomined walls can only be cleaned by the application of a new coat of that covering.

Wood-work. Linseed oil, applied to a polished surface of wood, after it is cleaned with kerosene oil, is the only treatment for unvarnished wood surfaces. A damp cloth should be passed rapidly over varnished surfaces, which should then be polished dry with the palm of the hand. Wood should be rubbed with the grain. All varnished surfaces, to be kept in perfect condition, should be subjected to treatment only by a trained polisher. Care to prevent spots and blemishes on highly polished surfaces is the only way to prevent their becoming a constant source of annoyance and expense. Hard-wood floors should be put in order twice a year by a trained workman. If the floor is constantly used, it may require treatment every two months. In the interval it is only necessary to use clean warm water and a woollen cloth, and dry thoroughly, to keep hard-wood floors in perfect condition, if the polish is of the right kind. No amount of work will keep a floor, finished with a poor polish, in good order, and an oily surface holds dust; it cannot be kept clean. Painted floors should be treated as any painted surface is treated, washed with a cloth wrung from hot, soapy ammonia suds, and wiped dry. All corners of windows, base-board, and floors and doors, should be cleaned with a cloth held over a finely pointed stick. This stick will be found very valuable for stair-corners, and should have its regular place in the broom-closet. Brushes, whisk-brooms, and dusters should be kept on every floor; it is an economy in money and time. The broom-closet should be furnished with all kinds of brushes and dusters, and cloths and oils for the rubbing of furniture. It is the constant and equal care of the house that insures its cleanliness and order, and reduces the misery of the house-cleaning season. It is better to rub the scratch off of the polished surface as soon as it is seen, than to have it stand, an annoyance, until the semi-annual cleaning day.

The bath-room is an important room, and one that requires constant care. *The bath-room.* The basins must be cleaned every day with sapolio. If the faucets are wiped dry each morning with a dry woollen cloth, they will need polishing but once a week. The bath-tub, if of zinc, will always be an annoyance. It is only pretty if it is kept as brightly polished as silver. This can be done with very fine brick dust and kerosene oil. The polishing process is most laborious, as any mistress may discover by a little practical experimenting. Having once tried, she will be patient with defects in the polishing process. In a house where the services of only one or two maids are commanded, each person using the tub should rinse it out after using. It is then a comparatively easy matter to avoid the forming of the disagreeable water-line which is sure to form on a zinc bath-tub if the stopple is drawn and the water allowed to run out of the bath. Porcelain or stone tubs are easily kept in order. Oxalic acid will remove all stains from porcelain. The lamp-chimney cleaners, of lamp-wick, are useful for applying the acid, the long handle making it impossible for the acid to touch the hands.

The only safe disinfectant is plumbing in a perfect sanitary condition. To *Disinfectants.* secure this, *an examination of the house should be made once a year by a sanitary engineer.* If the householder has doubts of the condition of traps and pipes, it is wise to buy ten cents' worth of oil of peppermint, close every basin connected with the plumbing of the house, pour the oil in the pipes at the highest point of connection with the plumbing, with the door of the room where the oil is poured tightly closed, that there may be no communication with the hall. The odor of peppermint through the house will show that there is a leak in traps or pipes, that needs attention by a skilled workman.

Every morning, every pipe in the house should be flushed, and it is a good idea to pour a pail of hot water, in which half a pound of washing soda has been dissolved, into the basin of each closet and into the kitchen-sink, at least once a week.

Painted walls, or varnished paper, is the only tolerable finish for bath-room walls and ceiling. There should never be a house-cleaning season for the bath-room, for it should always be in a spotless condition. Great care should be taken not to throw any kind of fuzz or burnt matches or hair into any passage leading to the sewer pipes, unless one is ambitious to pay heavy bills for plumbing.

The cellar of a house is properly the test of a housekeeper's standards. A disorderly, dirty cellar shows that her

The Care of the Cellar and Disposition of Garbage.

The cellar. standards are for the outside world, not for her own comfort and that of her family. The walls and ceiling of the cellar should be whitewashed twice every year. The perfect cellar has a cement floor. A pantry with slatted sides is a convenience for storage. Hanging shelves—that is, shelves supported from the ceiling—are an absolute necessity. Shelves against the walls will also be found useful. No barrel or box should rest on the cellar bottom, but on broad shelves raised about four to six inches above it. This makes it possible to sweep the whole cellar bottom. Potatoes, turnips, beets, etc., keep much better when raised above the cellar floor. No good housekeeper keeps garbage receptacles in the cellar. It is kept pure and clean, and is always ventilated. Wood piled in the cellar should not be piled on the floor, but on boards raised above the floor.

The coal-bin should be thoroughly swept and allowed to dry before each supply of coal is deposited in it. Nails and hooks, strong and well driven, should be in liberal numbers in the beams of the cellar ceiling, and everything possible to hang should be hung on these hooks. The cellar floor should be so free from obstruction that sweeping it should be an easy operation. Do not allow an accumulation of old tins, pots, papers, etc., for the semi-annual clearing out. See to it that the barrels for rubbish are emptied every two weeks. Tie all papers in bundles before sending down cellar. Avoid causes for disorder and general upheavals.

A stupid, inefficient servant can be trained to take care of a cellar as she can of a refrigerator, through a fear of sickness. Make her understand that it is her personal health that suffers, if she does not take care to prevent causes for disease. A refrigerator should be wiped out every day with a cloth wrung out of hot water in which soda has been dissolved. Once a week every part of the box should be scalded out with hot water. The pipe connected with the ice-chamber should be washed out with the hair-brush that comes with the refrigerator, and the hot water poured down the pipe. It is wise to have nothing kept in the ice-box that is not going to be used. Little scraps of doubtful importance would better be thrown away at once.

The care of garbage is another test of a housekeeper's standards. If it is *Garbage.* to be burned it should always be dried first. One of the plate ovens of the range should be devoted to this purpose. A pan made to fit it can be bought. All moisture should be drained from the parings, and they should be dried out until they will burn like paper. This is the only method that prevents the burning of garbage being a nuisance to the whole neighborhood. Wet garbage, burned in a range, makes the cleaning of the range and of the chimney a necessity at least twice a year, and it is impossible to burn wet garbage in a range and not have the whole air of the house polluted.

In a city where many of the residents do burn their garbage, the atmosphere at sundown, in that city, is tainted with the odor that results from the practice. Where a receptacle for garbage is kept, a supply of chloride of lime, or some tested disinfectant, should be kept, and each deposit of garbage should be sprinkled with the disinfectant.

The daily care of a house, if reduced to a system and accepted as a pleasant *System in housekeeping.* and imperative duty, never burdens a rightly balanced woman. The woman who frets at the necessary detail care of a house, because she feels that she is neglecting things of greater importance, does find the care of a home burdensome, wearisome, and she leads a life of constant friction. Her investigations and care are not systematic, but spasmodic, and are generally attended with unpleasant revelations that make a change of servants seem imperative, when what is imperative is a change in the attitude and method of the mistress. A busy woman, who had had in her home a thoroughly trustworthy, competent cook, was compelled to make a change because of her cook's marriage. She was not an experienced housekeeper, and her experience with servants had always been of so pleasant a character that it had never been necessary for her to introduce the habit of daily inspection. One day, wishing to experiment somewhat, she went into the kitchen and opened the closet door, when, to her surprise, she found there were several layers of paper on the shelves. The maid was engaged cleaning windows in another part of the house, and the mistress began removing the things from the kitchen closet, to find that the washing of pans was evidently a promise of the future and not a feature of the past. When the kitchen closet had been thoroughly emptied, and the innumerable papers pulled out on the floor, she called the new maid into the kitchen; and said, "Annie, I don't know what excuse you can give for this;" whereat the girl looked at her in a perfectly calm manner and said, "Well, if you hadn't been snoopin', you wouldn't have to hunt up a new girl."

Bedrooms. The bedrooms, if crowded with furniture, bric-à brac, and the misplaced decorations of bad taste, cannot receive the attention they should receive daily. The bedroom should only have drapery enough at the windows to secure privacy. The walls, as far as possible, should be free from any decoration. If pictures are on the walls, they should be in simple frames, easily dusted. The dressing-table should hold only necessary articles. These, if well chosen and clean, will serve the purpose of ornament. All heavy furniture should be kept on rollers that move easily in any direction. Perfect cleanliness is possible in any home, only when it is furnished with due regard to the amount of labor involved in keeping each part clean and wholesome. It is for this reason that bedroom furniture should present plain surfaces.

Sweeping days. Sweeping days may mean every day in the week, or one or more days of the week. Some mistresses prefer having one room swept each day. Others prefer a floor each day. Others, one general sweeping-day. The method is always the same.

Every movable article should be carefully dusted, and placed where it can be covered up, if not removed from the room. The walls having been dusted with a long feather duster, the room should then be carefully swept, every heavy piece of furniture moved from its place. When the dust is settled, the wood-work can be dusted. Upholstered furniture should have been thoroughly cleaned before sweeping has been begun, and covered. Windows should be wiped with a damp cloth, as should all mirrors in the room, and then rubbed dry. By this time the air is pure in the room, and is fresh. The porcelain vessels, if the room is a sleeping-room, should be washed each day with hot water in which soap and ammonia have been dissolved, and thoroughly dried. The washstand should be washed thoroughly and the closet scrubbed, if the wood of this piece of furniture is pine. For hard wood, careful washing and airing each day is necessary, but the closet should be varnished at house-cleaning time. The bottom of every closet should be wiped out each sweeping-day, and the shelves once a month. Constant watchfulness, until daintiness becomes a habit to the maid, is the price that must be paid for clean chamber-work. The time to accomplish this depends on the character of the maid. If she cannot be trained in a month, she should not be tolerated. The test is the condition of her own room.

Beds. The beds in every room should be uncovered and exposed to the outer air, if possible, when the occupant goes down to breakfast. This makes it possible for the rooms to air and to be put in order immediately after breakfast. This is comparatively easy when two maids are kept, and can be accomplished where one maid is kept, with careful planning and uniform system. No room should be considered in order until the maid has picked up any threads or brushed up any fuzz that may be on the floor; and, of course, a well-kept room is dusted every day.

Dining-room. The dining-room should be put in order before the family come to breakfast. That is, it should be dusted and present a fresh and attractive appearance. Breakfasts, in America, are becoming more and more the continental breakfast, and even for the family with one servant it is possible to have an immaculate dining-room for the family to meet in the morning.

The front door. When possible, the street doors and front doors should be kept in order by a man. A servant's clothing is hardly in fit condition for the dining-room, or even the house, when she has swept the street and walk. There is usually a man or a boy who can be hired to do this work, who would otherwise be an object of charity. It is far better for the morals of the community that services should be rendered and wages paid, rather than that beggars should be supplied. Outside doors finished with wax must be kept in order by rubbing. Varnished doors require dusting only. The wise man is the one who has plain doors. Every moulding, every corner, every ornament presents one more resting-place for dust.

Ammonia and sapolio are the housekeeper's friends, if used in connection with intelligence and strength. Paint, glass, silver, china, all yield the accumulations on their surfaces to ammonia, while tins and cooking utensils return smooth, clean surfaces, without blemish, when subjected to sapolio.

Furnaces and chimneys, every fall, should be examined by an expert. This is cheaper than a fire from a defective flue.

Income and expense. In the management of the income is the secret of financial freedom, or distress, in every family. When possible a bank account should be kept in the wife's name. This bank account should represent the allowance for all household and family expenses, and should be paid weekly, monthly, or quarterly, as is most convenient to the husband. If his salary is paid weekly it becomes a simple matter. Each week the amount that is allowed for the table expenses should be set aside. The balance of the allowance should be deposited in the bank. This system makes the keeping of weekly accounts unnecessary. The sum set aside for the table expenses and car-fare is known. The purchases made both for house and wardrobe of the family are recorded on the stubs of the check-book and at the end of the month can be added and set down under special heads. This system must be maintained on the strictest business principles to succeed. A wife must learn to live within her allowance; she must prevent deficiencies by learning to gauge her expenses. It is not uncommon for a wife to find herself the owner of capital the result of economies, when her income is settled. Where it is impossible to have a bank account for the family expenses, there must be more or less confusion, and opportunity for friction and anxiety. There must be some determined sum for the table expenses, and should be proportionate sums for clothing, school, and other imperative expenses. The haphazard money arrangements of many families is the cause of much unhappiness and distress. There must be a clear understanding as to the amount of the income, and there should be a unity of standards as to its application. Constant discussion of the money question leads to unhappiness, and often to distrust. The income should be disbursed according to mutual arrangement and agreement between husband and wife, and this agreement should be maintained with the strictest integrity. Honor is the safeguard of love and happiness.

Housekeeping, as a profession, requires what success in any profession requires—knowledge, a mind open to experiment, common sense, and a desire—an ambition, would be the better word—to succeed. If it receives grudging attention, the natural results follow—failure, defeat, unhappiness.

[*For further and specific information see section on* THE PRINCIPLES OF HOUSE KEEPING *in* APPENDIX—SUPPLEMENTARY INFORMATION.]

IV.

SOCIETY AND SOCIAL USAGES.

IV.

SOCIETY AND SOCIAL USAGES.

By CONSTANCE CARY HARRISON.

The Art of Entertaining.
Dinners.
Luncheons.
Teas.
Garden Parties.
Theatre Parties.
Chaperones.
Suppers.

Parties to the Opera.
Dances.
Good Taste in Dress.
Correct Form in Correspondence.
Invitations.
Weddings.
Cards.
Calling.

Entertaining.

DISRAELI once said, "the conduct of men depends upon the temperament, not upon a bunch of musty maxims"—a statement in which I so thoroughly agree, that it "gives me pause" on the threshold of this sketch. Often, in glancing over the flat and stale and confusing dicta of books on etiquette, I have wondered what they accomplish; whether people can behave by them any better than they can carve fowls by a diagram; whether, bearing them in mind, the disciple enters upon the society of his fellows with the "papa, potato, poultry, prunes and prism" expression recommended by Dickens' chaperone; whether before he or she has half done with the manual, the author be not objurgated as tiresome or ridiculous!

And yet suggestions as to the manners and customs that prevail in an impermanent society like ours in America, are sometimes interesting and may be helpful. It is in that hope, and protesting against any desire to dogmatize, that I am nerved to write what here follows.

Entertaining in large cities has unfortunately come to mean, in many cases, a struggle to make moderate resources accomplish what is done by a mere wave of the hand among rich people. Plutocracy has many sins to answer for, but none worse than having snuffed out the old spirit of kindly hospitality that in some mysterious way one always associates with shining mahogany, with Canton china dishes, with delicious "sweet" pickles, with being asked by the host whether one prefers white meat or dark.

It would be foolish, in our generation, to say we do not remember the houses where such artless forms prevailed. We all remember them, and, I venture to assert, with pleasure. And that feature of country entertaining, the "tea," with its rich variety of cakes and preserves, the chipped beef in cream, the cup of tea beside one's overcrowded plate—one rose from it, perhaps, with a vague sense of to-morrow and a consciousness of the organs of digestion; but one came away in an agreeable frame of mind! In an assemblage of founders of a now most fashionable summer resort in the hill country of Massachusetts, last autumn, talk turned reminiscently to the days when every one of the cottage folk gave teas; "sit-down" teas at seven o'clock with the best china and silver and flowers; with sweetbreads and croquettes, and salads, and waffles to follow, with cinnamon and sugar sprinkled o'er! When they played "twenty questions" afterward, or had chat and music, before the carriages, or maids with lanterns, arrived to break up the sport!

"And now, we drive over the same roads, to summer palaces erected on our hills, to dinners at eight o'clock, with half a dozen flunkeys in livery and a bewildering *menu*. We wear low-cut gowns and all the jewels we can rake and scrape together. We talk of the party the day before, the party to come to-morrow. We are dull and formal, and as soon as the carriage is announced are glad to hurry away in it!"

So said a lively lady who had been leader in the early movement, and had not been suffered to lose her place in the later one. And what she said was echoed by every woman in the group.

It is true. In the evolution of modern American society we have lost the savor of the past. And while none of us would perhaps care to rejoin our idols (which gain charm, no doubt, by remoteness), we can at least aim to see clearly the mistakes of some of our present methods.

Straining is the death-blow to any entertainment. It shows everywhere in the result. There is not one among one's guests who is not perfectly conscious of it; who would not be better pleased with things in a more normal state. A domestic duck is far more toothsome cooked as one's plain cook knows how to serve him, than a redhead disguised as canvas-back. Terrapin should only be offered when a butler and silver dishes accompany him to his last home. How infinitely more welcome to the habitual diner-out is a glass of good claret than indifferent champagne!

In the matter of wines, the dinner-goers of America have learnt a lesson which reacts to the advantage of their entertainers. In a stimulating climate wines are not needed; their quantity *Wines.* and variety have undergone a visible diminution on American tables within the last few years. Champagne, always the American favorite, is served early in the fray—some offer it as the fish is taken off and continue it throughout the dinner, with no other adjunct save bottled table-waters. It is a common thing to see all the glasses, put to the places, left unfilled at the guests' request. Women, especially, drink very little wine. It is not worth the discomfort that follows to a person going night after night into the world. Sauterne and sherry, served with oysters and with soup, are still found in their old places; but, as I said, they are apt to have the cold shoulder turned on them.

Apropos of declining wines, it has been a subject of discussion how this mighty matter is to be accomplished at a dinner *à la mode*. I have seen recommendations to ladies to put their gloves—removed in sitting down and rolled into a ball—into the largest glass, in token of intended abstinence! An Englishman asked if it were possible American women could do this thing, adding, "Why not overshoes, or a handkerchief?"

A hint, by motion, to well-trained servants ought to be all that is needful. No butler who respects himself or his office will waste his employer's wines by pouring them out into the glasses, merely to lose their aroma!

As in the matter of fewer wines, there has been of late a movement toward shorter dinners, fewer dishes, *Dinners.* less elaborate table service. The guests, arriving at half-past seven or at eight o'clock, according to the convenience of the hostess, no longer go always upstairs to seek dressing-rooms. Although such rooms are ready, and are offered by the servant admitting the arrivals, it is quite common, at a little dinner, for both men and women to throw off their wraps in the hall and allow them to be carried into places of safety upstairs, whence they are returned when it is time to leave.

The wife and husband go into the drawing-room apart, he straggling after her, with the usual melancholy expression of the unfed man at the anteprandial hour. When all are assembled, ensues the agreeable stir of marshalling in to dinner. This, in America, is commonly manœuvred beforehand by a card bearing the lady's name, offered in an envelope in the hall, to the gentleman who is to take her in. It is a question whether the old commotion caused by the host telling Jones that he is to take Mrs. Robinson, and Jones expressing his delight, is not, at this juncture, a loss. As they proceed to the dining-room, the host goes first with the lady who is to sit at his right; the hostess goes in last, with her escort; each of the gentlemen offers his right arm to the lady he conducts for convenience in assuming their places at table.

On coming away from table it is the present (but not invariable) mode in America for the couples to return arm-in-arm to the drawing-room, as they went out. Of course, the gentlemen do not offer their arms to the ladies, unless the host himself sets the example and leads the way. This —the French fashion—is not half so pleasant as the flight of the women past a line of men (of whom the youngest generally reaches the door first, to hold it open) one is accustomed to see in England. Women enjoy getting away from their partners of the last hour and three-quarters, as much as their partners like to see them go. In both cases the parting is tempered by the prospect of reunion after coffee and *crême de menthe !*

In the matter of decorations of the dinner-table a marked change has been noticed. A few years ago it was common to see the board loaded with dainty objects in porcelain or silver; and the side-dishes, of fruit and bonbons and cakes and crystallized fruits, were a mighty matter to the intending dinner-giver who had pricks of economy conflicting with the desire to "do the thing in proper style !" Now we have fine napery, a super-cloth of antique embroidery in silks or thread; a few dishes or silver baskets of hot-house grapes and other fruit in season; a centre-piece of flowers or ferns; candles or candle-lamps; other little dishes of bonbons and olives and salted almonds—suggesting an effort, manifest through all, that the eye shall be rested, not confused !

Green and white, so much seen of late, is a charming color-scheme for a dinner. In this, the usual centre-piece of ferns of the home-table (provided it has not reached that exasperating stage of turning brown and curling at the edges, and demanding to be sent back to the florist, despite all one's fondest care !) may be made to do duty, with a few yards of those floating, fragile, exquisite vines that trail in the florists' windows. The candle-shades—little monsters of annoyance to the housekeeper and servants, from their incessant habit of catching fire—may be of pale green; and the vacant spaces on the table that need filling may be supplied with fascinating bits of Bohemian or Venetian glass of the same vernal hue, reappearing in finger-bowl and ice-plate.

The chief exhibitor of the Salviati glass factory in Venice displayed to me last summer, with great pride, some new designs in the last-named articles.

They were made to represent doilies of fine white lace lying across plates of blue or green or amber. A marvel of workmanship, but false in artistic conception ; and so, with polite phrases, I ventured to suggest. .

"Oh ! but, madame, they were made expressly for the American market," I was told ; and I ventured no more.

Flowers are pre-eminently the choicest decoration for the dinner-table, be the dinner great or small. In this matter, one is inclined to apply the homely adage, "Enough is as good as a feast," since a vase with two or three royal roses opening their hearts to the softened glow of candles may convey as much refreshment to the observer as a mound of the same beauties crowded and wired and doomed to an early death. Loose roses, scattered on the table-cloth, are sometimes charming in effect. Jonquils, daffodils, and tulips are a boon to the hostess in the time of declining winter. They are so crisp and spring-like, they flower in such tender tints, and the price of them is so comforting !

Decorations for the table.

There is one modern fashion I should like to inveigh against in decoration of the dinner-table ; that of introducing large bows of ribbon on baskets or groups of flowers. Ribbon has no place among articles for food. Everything served on the table should be washable, or clearly perishable and evanescent.

Of all dinners, great or small, whence in coming away one bears a distinct and pleasant impression of the individuality of the hostess, one is inclined to think gratefully. The cold hostess ; the distracted hostess, who sits with one eye on the screen before the butler's pantry, the other on her interlocutor ; the indifferent hostess, who, having spread her feast and set her people down to it, abandons them to their fate ; the fussy hostess, interfering with talks happily begun ; the affected hostess, apologizing for her banquet, or for the failure of certain guests, in order that she may be contradicted by assurances that she has left nothing to be desired—do we not know them all ? Do we not turn from them with satisfaction to her who is quiet, watchful, gracious, tactful, clever enough to make her guests feel it is *they*, rather than *she*, who stamp the affair as a success ?

The hostess.

Of entertaining at dinner—deemed *the* entertainment of all others in the world of conventionality—I have spoken first. A luncheon, usually given by a woman to women, is regarded abroad as a purely American outgrowth. In London and Paris, one is asked informally to the mid-day meal, which is extremely simple according to our ideas, usually what one has for one's own household, and nothing added. The "pink," "yellow," "violet," and "blue" luncheons of the United States, as described in newspapers, are a source of astonishment to our transatlantic neighbors. They never weary in asking questions about our habit of shutting out daylight, and turning on gas or electricity or lamp-light upon our lunch-tables. They, who are satisfied with a growing fern in an "art-pot" and a handful of cut flowers in specimen glasses, cannot believe in the "pounds and pounds' worth" of costly roses or orchids ordered by us for a woman's luncheon. Stories of those entertainments from which have been carried away presents of expensive knick-knacks set by the plates of guests, are listened to as to a new tale of a thousand-and-one nights.

Luncheons.

The giving of gifts has, however, declined. A single rose, or a cluster of roses and other blossoms, is alone permissible as a souvenir to-day. The name-card once painted and illuminated, has come down to be a simple bit of pasteboard, sold in the shops for the purpose (with perhaps a gilded edge), on which the hostess writes her guest's name, and which is swept away by the servant with the crumbs. One wine, or two, at most—sauterne and claret, or sherry and claret—are now seen at a woman's lunch. The use of champagne —having been pronounced as inappropriate as a low-cut gown in daylight— has gone out entirely. Table-waters are offered from the bottle; though any good natural water is deemed all-sufficient.

Chocolate or tea is not expected to be present on these occasions. Coffee, served without cream after luncheon, in the prettiest little cups the hostess can muster, is generally at hand.

Bouillon, an *entrée* of fish or lobster or crabs, chops (let them be broiled skilfully, for the sake of rarity!) with green peas; some dainty, like mushrooms on toast; game and salad; with ices and bonbons, are enough and more than enough for a luncheon, of no matter how many guests. More is a burden to the habitual partaker of choice hospitalities, who is generally the one her hostess desires to please. Compelled to sit through the lengthening ordeal of an elaborate *menu*, she thinks of her dinner out that evening, of her many engagements during the afternoon, of her wearied digestion; at length she asks herself, impatiently: "Did this woman bring me here to be *fed*, or to be entertained?"

Of all meals spread for guests the luncheon is the one that should have least of the "defacing finger" of the caterer. If he must, let that functionary appear in warmed-over *entrées* at dinner. (Yet could we wish him far from there!) Welcome his ices, his little cakes, his pastry shells for patties or *vol-au-vent*, his rolls, his salted almonds, his *gâteau St. Honoré*, his brandied cherries in their concealing vestments of white icing, his cut paper for the dishes, his bonbons and crystallized fruits! These are not to be easily supplied at home—I speak of moderate homes—and they relieve the cook and housekeeper alike. But do we not all agree that at luncheon one likes home-made dishes, dishes without mystery or paper frills—dishes, in fine, to be compassed by an ordinarily good cook? One has been to luncheons where, if the caterer were not indisputably revealed by the made dishes, one saw him in the plated candelabra twisted with smilax and fitted out with *un*lighted candles under many little shades. That is the finishing touch of unreality, hired silver candlesticks with unlit candles!

For a luncheon—to be imitated if wealth, high social place, and an establishment perfect in details may set a fashion—half a dozen congenial women once met in the library of a friend, whom they found with her two youngest children at her knee.

"If I didn't have them at odd moments, where should I be?" she asked, laughing, as the nurse arrived to carry her treasures off. The women, left alone, chatted together, which must not be misinterpreted to mean all at once! In a short time, they were led by their hostess across a hall dim with stained glass and tapestries and ancient iron-work, into a stately dining-room, where they sat around a small, circular table that seemed a mere dot in the vast apartment. The table of old oak, polished, was bare but for a square of linen drawn-work in the centre, on which was set a silver vase of white orchids with purple centres. The salt-cellars, claret-jugs in silver coasters, silver dishes with radishes, curled shreds of celery, olives, chocolates and cream peppermints, were the only other ornaments. The china used was all fine white porcelain with gilt edges and monograms. The napkins were large affairs meant to cover one's skirt like an apron, of rough-grained linen trimmed with coarse thread lace. The repast, beginning with eggs served in individual platters, and cooked to disguise skilfully the fact that eggs they were, progressed through a few simple, deliciously flavored courses, to, not an ice, but an *omelette soufflée*. Two servants only were in waiting, and although the *chef* who had sent it up was known to be an artist in receipt of an income of proportions that might be envied by many a college-bred man delving in offices down-town, the meal made no impression upon the guests beyond that of general nicety. It was, in short, in perfectly good taste; and, surely, to reach that pinnacle, one need not be possessed of a *chef* and a palace on Fifth Avenue!

The luncheons introduced at a place of summer resort, a few years ago, to include a larger number of guests of both sexes than can be easily accommodated at ordinary tables, were a distinct success. The hostess who gave the first one of these unconventional and jolly parties, had tables of various sizes spread in her dining-room, hall, and veranda. Upon each table were placed napkins, rolls, plates, knives, forks, glasses, bottles of Apollinaris, and jugs of claret-cup and lemonade. On the main table and buffets were found galantines, jellied *filets*, cold chickens, croquettes, a ham, salads, and other dishes hot and cold. Gentlemen who had seats of their own, left them to assist in serving their ladies, and returned carrying plates-full for both. Servants, from time to time, passed around dishes, and removed plates, etc., without confusion. The picnic quality of the affair gave it a relish. Forty guests were in this way accommodated as easily as ten under the usual conditions. Ices, cake, and black coffee completed the little feast, from which the guests arose, protesting themselves well provided. The hostess on this occasion had no especial seat, but moved from table to table, looking after the comfort of her friends, and indulging in a taste of the society of all in turn.

At a luncheon in London, last spring, I saw what most American housekeepers would deem a homely array of food, presided over by an aristocratic hostess in a dining-room of high æsthetic beauty. As it tends to support my plea in behalf of a greater simplicity than we consider admissible for invited guests, I may mention the *menu* of this household. At one end of the table were seen two fowls with the inevitably accompanying bread-sauce. These were carved and served by the host, while, opposite him, the hostess carved and dispensed a joint of lamb with mint-sauce, after asking her guests which dish they would choose! Two men-servants, who withdrew when the sweets came on, handed peas and potatoes. I seem to recall a dish of tarts, another of strawberries, upon the table; and, of drinkables, we had beer, claret, and lemonade. One can safely aver there were cheese, biscuits, and a salad. But of elaborate made dishes, courses, making of the luncheon an earlier dinner, there were none. The talk flowed freely, and everybody was at ease!

The universal, the all-embracing "tea," from four until seven—that is to

Teas. serve as an opportunity to present the daughter of the house to her parents' friends, or else to wipe off the obligations of a family to society at large—seems to flourish like a bay-tree. Every season sees it crop up, renewed in strength, its features hardly altered. It is, to the accustomed, a dreary function, with its crowds of indifferent folk who come, one knows not why, protesting they "never go to teas." But it is cheap and respectable; the only known method of including all one's acquaintance in one invitation list; and, as a fashion, it is not likely, in our time, to go out.

The season for large general "teas" is naturally in the late autumn, when the housewife, having set her affairs in order for the winter, lets her fancy lightly turn to thoughts of entertainment. In New York, where the so-called visiting list (of people there is no time to visit) is continually elongated by brides and grooms, it is a formidable matter to send out the cards one's self. There are, indeed, expert professors of this art of regulating lists, of checking off the departed, of adding the new-comers, the returned from foreign sojourn, the married daughters and married sons now entitled to a showing on their own account. And there is a little black book with red lettering seen on every writing-table and carriage-cushion, wherein puzzled mater-familias finds her bearings annually among her cherished acquaintances, many of whom the little black book alone keeps in her recollection!

With such aids the list is made, the invitations scattered, and if the house be large and attractive, or the hostess a social favorite, the *débutante* reputed pretty, the "tea" is sure to be crowded to excess with the guests desired.

"I have come out of respect to the family," is a commonly heard excuse on the lips of those who attend "teas" under protest, lest they be suspected of having no invitations to more exclusive parties. Be it as it may, every one turns out for the early season teas.

In the great houses, there is an orchestra provided for the upper landing of the stairs; there are flowers in lavish numbers, and greenery to make a tropic forest of retreats. But the service of the table is always the same—tea, bouillon, chocolate, little cakes, big cakes, bonbons, ices, lemonade on a side-table, *pâté de foie gras* sandwiches, and buttered "finger" rolls—no more! Here are always the same young ladies who allow the kettle to boil out, or the alcohol to become exhausted in the lamp; who serve tea lukewarm to indignant leaders of society, while they turn aside to gossip with their chums, or receive attention from young men. In this connection, one might suggest that the young lady tea-maker has had her day. Why should she not be relegated to a side-table to preside over lady-fingers and macaroons, and let her substitute be an elderly aunt or cousin—a maiden, perchance, whose heart is in her work—who knows to a nicety when the water has reached the culminating point; when the tea is steeped; when the leaves should be thrown away and fresh ones substituted; those things that come by experience, and through true love for the subject?

This might result in a falling off of a few long-tailed, black body-coats with white buttonhole bouquets, from around the tea-board; but oh! the gain to the suffering tea-lovers who come in out of the wintry air eager for their stimulating cup.

I confess to a weakness for the American young girl. With all the shortcomings attributed to her by foreign critics, she is a charmer not to be surpassed by her kind in any society I have seen. She is vivid, original, clever, adaptable. But I don't know that she has ever learned to make tea. Of course, I allude to the variety of her generally on exhibition in pursuance of this art at fashionable gatherings. It may be that she is confused by too much observation. The men who in white paper-caps and aprons make bonbons in confectioners' windows, and the Orientals who in native dress ply their looms at rug-making, in similarly exposed positions, may have become used to it. But the girl of society fortunately is not called on to pour tea under scrutiny every day of the week. Perhaps, hidden away in many households, there are girls who, conscious of excellence in this detail, are entitled to resent this slur of mine, and their pardons I ask in advance. I should like to meet them.

Another wrong to the tea-lover, perpetrated by society at large, is the setting forth upon its tea-trays of the tiny cups meant for after-dinner coffee, and expecting *them* to consort with ordinary-sized lumps of sugar. At a tea-drinking which I had the honor to attend, given in the harem of a Moorish Bashaw, the pot was stuffed with aromatic herbs and as many lumps of sugar as it would contain, after the tea and hot water had been first put into it. This mixture, served in little porcelain cups in settings of filigree gold, made one rejoice at the diminutive size of the vessels in which it was transmitted to the drinker!

At an ordinary Christian tea-drinking, the cups should be of respectable dimensions, and of thin, translucent porcelain. The cups for breakfast *café au lait* may belong to the habitually used " set " of English or American faïence; but not those that convey the nectar of five o'clock!

For days " at home," the tea-table may be spread either in the dining-room, or, as is more fashionable, at the elbow of the hostess in her drawing-room.

In the latter case, it is a low, wide-spreading affair. On another little table at hand are the thinnest of sandwiches, and cakelets, mere mouthfuls for Titania. But it is a bold mortal who accepts, under these circumstances, with people coming and going and the hostess continually rising and sitting again, her offer of refreshment. The would-be tea-drinker has not the courage to break the uninvaded cleanliness of that circle of cups, for which those who preceded have apparently had the same consideration. Better the black tea-pot of Sairey Gamp and the science of tea-making, than silver and porcelain and indifference therewith!

In England, where the stimulus of tea is generally demanded by all classes of the population, the beverage is, as a rule, good wherever found. In drawing-rooms, in lodgings, at railway-stations —who that has ever been pulled together after crossing the Channel, by a cup of tea served in the railway carriage at Dover while waiting the departure of the train, can forget its sovereign excellence? Ask for tea in one of our stations, and consider the result!

With us, tea-drinking is a fashion adopted of late years—a vehicle for the transmission of æsthetic ideas in grouping people and furniture—and, except in isolated cases, not yet a genuine cult. But the habit is as likely to spread as the thistle-seeds carried on the brake-rods of railway-trains into the Western country—as the fashion-plates that have done most to abolish plural marriages among the Mormons. If we are to take to it, let us do so in good form! And the first principle to lay to heart is "see that the kettle boiling be."

The garden party, that agreeable annual transplanted from English soil,
Garden parties. flourishes better in America than in England. One is filled with admiration of the pluck that supports British hostesses in their efforts to defy the continually dropping skies of spring and summer. Their lawns—deep-green, of even, fine grass, to which a " wee modest crimson-tipped " daisy is a reproach—are a standing invitation to " come out and

A Dining Table Set for Serving.

walk on me." Their groups of glorious great-armed trees, with dense, lustrous foliage, are apparently meant to shelter damsels and swains in gala-dress. Their rose gardens, with vines trained on the walls and arched trellises overgrown with masses of bloom and fragrance, offer enchanting harborage for a *tête-à-tête*. Their clumps of rhododendrons, spreading in pink-purple splotches on the velvet lawns, present an artistic background to ambulating guests. The tent for refreshments, sometimes pitched on the edge of a pond or river, is a delightful resort, keeping people in motion in the open. Under these conditions, their houses, delightful as English country-houses are, are deserted. People go from them, do not seek to cling to them and fill the rooms with chatter, as at some American garden parties fallen short of the mark! But, alas! the reverse of the English medal shows, eight times out of ten, a shower, arriving unexpectedly, coming from skies erstwhile blue! That they are lovely showers, leaving the earth dewy, not wet; that they serve to retain the delicate tints of the flowers and deepen the emerald of the grass, does not comfort the hostess, who sees her guests flying pellmell into rooms too small to contain their numbers.

At Newport, Lenox, Bar Harbor, and other such places known to pleasure-seekers in summer-time, garden parties are a safer enterprise to the giver. They are popular, as they deserve to be, and may be infinitely varied. Dazzling skies, the abundant watering of the lawns, the beautiful, picturesque, or stately (or all three combined) backgrounds of the modern summer homes, make these out-door *fêtes* something to be remembered. There is more gayety and sparkle in a mass of people broken up in groups, wandering upon a wide stretch of turf to the music of a band in some kiosk or summer-house, than in the same people herded between walls. And where there is a dance upon the grass, how charming the effect of the gay colors, the moving figures—a canvas of Watteau come to life!

A suburban hostess in the neighborhood of a large city, or one accessible by comfortable trains, may score a success with a simple party out-of-doors, that will outrank, in pleasant memory, many a costly dinner or musicale or dance, given in town.

But there is always the weather to be considered, and even in our favored clime the weather sometimes plays pranks with our best-laid plans. There is, too, the trouble and expense of conveying guests from the station to the house and back again. Surmount these two, and the other difficulties are practically *nil*. A band, an orchestra, while they lend animation, are not indispensable. People who have danced and pranced all winter to the same old tunes, are not longing to see the face of a well-known leader peer from behind an improvised bower, and to be recalled to town by the lifting of his *bâton*.

What such guests ask is change—a breath of country air, a flavor of the unaccustomed, a pretty out-door scene, if possible. Something original in the way of diversion to eye and ear. But it is hard to be original.

A famous Frenchwoman, author and journalist, entertained a party of Parisians and others at her country-seat in the environs of Paris, by a rustic party. The hostess received in calico; great lights of the literary horizon, artists and musicians, were in bucolic costumes; the feast spread was as for peasants; the drink, cider and cheap wines of the country.

This affair, a "*succès fou*" as it was termed, brought out much wit and sentiment impromptu. No one withheld contribution to the fun. There was a rustic dance in which grave academicians took a turn.

We might introduce something of this kind in the suburbs of New York, Boston, or Philadelphia, but I question the assistance of the guests. There are one or two luminaries of our world of art and letters I cannot fancy as skipping in the costume of Colin Clout through the mazes of a contra-dance. And their impromptus—these would, I fear, be saved for copy or for the little dinners at the club where women are not admitted!

For the material element of a garden party—or *lawn* party, as, with us who have no real gardens, it might better be styled—the refreshment offered—there is no great addition made to the tea at five o'clock indoors. If the guests come from a distance, a substantial dish or two, strawberries and cream, and salads may be added; and, in that case, a punch upon a side-table is not always passed by. The table, spread under a marquee on the lawn, is always pretty; but most hostesses find it simpler and more satisfactory to the household staff to set the refreshments, as usual, in the dining-room; allowing the guests to come in as they like, to fortify themselves.

Hired entertainers—Tyrolean singers in national costume, recitationists, and the like—are sometimes introduced upon the lawn, but they present a direful suggestion of the breakfast of Mrs. Pott, whereat Mrs. Leo Hunter favored the company with her poem on the Expiring Frog. There is always, in the fantastical habit worn in the broad light of day, a power to depress, quite unconquerable. Shepherds and shepherdesses, Chloes and Strephons, fitted out by the costumer at so much per head, may be less provocative of mirth to lookers-on, because more in keeping with rural surroundings. But even then, poor Strephon, wearing his "lendings" shyly, generally comes in for comments containing more satire than unmixed admiration. Unless meant for a performance apart, the assumption of fancy dress is hardly to be recommended in entertainments out of doors. Modern costumes of women are so charmingly picturesque—the wash-stuffs that, made up, cost a little fortune; the infinite variety of summer silks; the rivers of soft lace; the tags of flying ribbon; the big hats and the veils that make plain women pretty—it is easy, with these alone, to "dress" the scene of a lawn party!

Games of chess with living figures manœuvred on a square of velvet verdure, have been made to produce results beautiful to the eye, if puzzling to the brain, of the ordinary observer. A pastoral play in miniature, or a comedy in verse adapted to outdoor surroundings, has won its laurels in the hands of clever amateurs. But all these things are risky; and unless the intending hostess be gifted with great executive ability and much patience, and be willing to renounce all enjoyment of her own party, she had better steer clear of them. People who go much into the society of each other in the world, are quite satisfied to meet and talk; they, as a rule, regard all "shows" as an interruption. They keep silent with an effort till the performance is over, then burst again into discussion of their own affairs.

I have been asked to say a word about the *formulæ* in use in giving parties to the play. The most easy and *Theatre parties.* convenient method of assembling guests on time, is to ask them to dinner; but this would serve for a small number only; and an accepted fashion is for the guests to meet in the drawing-room of the hostess, and thence to repair with her to the theatre selected, in a large omnibus of the sort kept for such purposes.

It should be the first care of the hostess or chaperone to see that the party do not arrive late at the play, and do not go in bustling with their own petty importance, to disturb people already seated and interested in the stage. This is an offence against good manners so common one despairs of reforming it. To denounce it is crying in the wilderness and being hearkened to by none. I have seen—as who has not—absorbed auditors turn with glances of positive hatred upon the selfish and silly invaders who have rustled into their seats, whispering and laughing audibly long after they have had time to settle down in quiet.

A party in a box may be less annoying to the general public, but it is more conspicuous. Talking, posturing, change of seats, the misuse of the opera-glass, tittering, eating bonbons for the benefit of an audience, are social crimes that rightly stamp the offender as half-bred. With some people the mere possession of a box seems to tempt them to believe themselves entitled to take liberties with the people in the parquet and balconies. One is inclined to think their cheap pre-eminence an affair of exceeding rarity !

A trifle to be considered—the eccentricity of wearing lace veils over the face at the play ! If ever in fashion, it was the caprice of a moment, and was discarded when its absurdity became manifest. In the year of Our Lord 1894 it is distinctly out of vogue.

Theatre bonnets — mere delightful apologies for a head-covering—a band, *Bonnets at* a couple of roses, or a but-*the theatre.* terfly bow—are now, blessedly, in the forefront of fashion. The women who belong to the second stratum of American civilization — those who are on their way to, not up with, the knowledge of customs of good society — are easily detected at the play. Waving over *their* heads may still be seen Hamlet's " forest of feathers," and sky-scraping bows of ribbon, that conceal the stage from the hapless soul behind. Consideration of others is the first indication of the civilization which expresses itself in politeness ; people who wear things of that kind in a theatre are not to be classed among the considerate.

The use of strong perfumes at the play or elsewhere cannot be too much *Perfumes.* decried. To many people, the presence of any foreign essence in the air is insupportable. Sachets, scent-bags, and their congeners, worn about the person in an over-heated atmosphere, are far from alluring admiration to their wearers' charms !

Costumes worn at the theatre have of late undergone a change for the prettier. The sober street dress, the tailor-made gown with its jacket thrown aside, have been superseded by the blouse or bodice of light-tinted silk, profusely trimmed with lace, which may be worn so conveniently with a dark skirt. The parquets of our best theatres are now parterres of many-colored blossoms. If the day ever dawns when we adopt the cheap cab system, and the mass of our play-goers are able to indulge in driving to the theatre, then we may see the unbonnetted head, the low-cut or half-low gown which make gay the auditoriums of similar pretension abroad. But as long as huddling into a crowded cable-car is the chief method of arriving at our goal and getting away from it in freezing winter nights, it is not likely the reform yearned for by managers and insisted upon by critics—evening dress for a drawing-room—will be successfully achieved for theatres.

A supper—at home or elsewhere—after the play, is a matter to be decided *Suppers.* by the length of the host's purse and the judgment of the hostess as to whether or not her guests have had enough of one another's company. Generally, the omnibus which brought them is in waiting to return the party to the house of the giver of the treat. A light supper, merry talk, perhaps a dance to the piano, may conclude the evening. If it is a party for young people, maids and carriages are sent from their homes to fetch the girls. The duty of the hostess has ended in returning them to her own residence. If there is to be no supper, the hostess drives from the theatre to the different houses, to set down each of her maidens at the parental threshold.

Chaperones. The vexed question of chaperones does not assail the conscience of young women in the large Eastern cities of the United States. There, they know too well what would be thought of their going alone to the play or opera in company with young men, to want to risk doing it. A party of three, however uncomfortable in the sense of companionship, is safer, even if two unmarried girls are escorted by an unmarried man. But even this would be objected to, unless the man was either old enough to be safe, beyond peradventure, from thoughts of love-making, or a relative, or engaged to one of them! Elsewhere in America, notably in the South and Southwest, the same standards are not yet followed, the liberty is far greater. A young man wishing to pay attention to his fair, takes tickets for her, calls for her, brings her home, and no one gives the matter a second thought. In a southern town recently illuminated by the matchless genius of Coquelin, the young men of society—as a rule more backward in French than the young women—made rueful complaint that it was all very well to pay double prices for tickets to the French plays—but what fun was it to sit up through the whole evening, mumchance, when their partners were laughing or thrilling under the spell of Coquelin? No doubt the same sufferers took comfort in the thought that, in the course of time, they might have "Charley's Aunt" to divert them, instead of "that dull Tartuffe!"

Chaperones at a party given in a town-house of limited proportions, are now often merged into the persons of the hostess and a few friends of her own age and standing, whom she has invited to assist. The young girls, arriving in custody of their maids, are awaited by those functionaries in the dressing-room. (One often wonders what family secrets, what social mysteries are not divulged among these weary, nodding abigails, who *must* find something to talk about as the "small hours" wear on!)

A party to the opera is an affair of more weight than one to the play. *Parties to the opera.* When a guest is bidden to sit in the box of a subscriber, or stockholder, it goes without saying that full evening toilet is indispensable. Nowhere in New York does one see the dress-parade of society to such advantage as behind the glittering horse-shoe curve of the Metropolitan Opera-house. As in the world of fashion people generally resort there to pass the hours intervening between a dinner and a ball, the freshest gowns, the most lavish jewels are in evidence. Flowers, long banished from the ball-room, are rarely carried to the opera. Whatever is seen in decoration is of the solidest, richest. The toilet, down to extremest flounce of lace petticoat or pointed satin slipper, is complete in elegance. The cloak left in the ante-chamber on entering the box, is oftentimes more costly than the dress it has covered. One occasionally wonders that, in these socialistic times, kings and queens and princesses of commerce in New York have the courage to flaunt (as some of them do) their extraordinary splendor of "increment," even though not "unearned," before the eyes of a mixed public.

Until quite recently it has been said by foreigners visiting America that the women dressed better, but wore fewer jewels, than those of any other nation *en grande toilette*. This can no longer be remarked; for the glow and glitter of tiaras, sun-bursts, collars, and necklaces of gems on gala occasions at the opera, now dazzle all observers. A girl's dress, however, even when her mother or matron is able to assume such splendor, is still noticeably simple. She wears few, if any, jewels, and is in better form without them altogether. For her, a charming old-time fashion of coiffure, which recalls pictures in "Books of Beauty," and is still universally in use among the fair Andalusians, is a rose-bud or some other flower worn nestled in the hair. How long since one's eyes have been gladdened by this pretty sight among the decorations of beauty in American society! But the fashion has returned, has been much in vogue among young girls latterly, and we must hope it will not be displaced.

The use of ornaments.

It would seem a superfluity, indeed, when setting forth the habits of good society, to suggest that a girl appearing at opera or theatre (or anywhere!) is judged by her misuse of cosmetics. A young woman of distinctly high social position in the great centres of American civilization would no more think of showing there a face painted or powdered than she would her nose with a ring in it.

The use of cosmetics.

When such a face presents itself, it is at once written down a stranger to the canons of good form. It is smiled at and pitied behind the wearer's back. The fresco of the feminine countenance is, by tacit consent, left to dowagers, who, it must be, employ it frankly and without hope of imposition on the most credulous. No paint can deceive, no blackening of the eyes seems natural, no reddening of the lips attracts to them! Pearl powder can never evade a side-light. In sum, the practice of any such art is wholly reprehensible, and is justly made awful by its revelation in electric light.

After a ball given as a house-warming in a New York establishment, from which everything had been expected by the fashionable world—an "universal" party, where all met—loud and long were the complainings against the hostess.

Her ball-room, lit from the dome by electricity, had, through some mistake, been permitted to shed an unshaded glare upon the guests. As a direct consequence, the place was soon almost depopulated, except by girls in their first season, and young matrons secure in unimpaired bloom. Women of a certain age—women conscious of the "applied arts" upon their countenances — met together in halls, supper-room, and ante-chambers, exchanging condemnation of the affair, while secretly examining each other, to see "if it is as bad, out here." For the remainder of that season, everyone fought shy of new houses, with new systems of electric lights as yet untried!

In connection with ornaments and cosmetics, I must touch on the subject of dress, with no wish to dictate in a matter that must necessarily be governed by time, and place, and means, and possibilities. It may be a comfort to some women who do me the honor to peruse these pages, to know that among the "leaders" they perchance read of in the bewildering columns of "society" description, there are many who appear time after time in the same gown, without giving

Dress and overdress.

a thought to it after they come into the room. These women are constantly amused and surprised by reading details of their own costumes, reported to have been worn on such and such occasions — accounts so varied from the fact, they can be only put down to the good nature of the reporter, who desires, perhaps, to supply the variety they would like to see. Life is too full, for a woman of good sense and means and assured position in a large community, to permit her, if there were no higher reason, to be forever turning over stuffs, and planning different outfits for herself. By the time the necessary provision for her own and her daughters' wardrobes is complete, in spring and autumn, she is aweary in spirit and body, and ready never to hear of finery again. She puts on her evening frock, and goes out, night after night, to dinner, and to sit against the wall while her daughter dances, longing, most often, to exchange it for something loose and light and easy—for a comfortable chair and a pleasant book at home! Far from her thoughts is the consideration of the attire of her neighbor (similarly employed). The younger women, who are dancing and passing back and forth in the promenade, are too busy and self-absorbed to take in the details of each other's gowns. In the ceaseless whirl of a large society these matters are far less discussed than in a village or country neighborhood. One generally hears the dress question disposed of as "such a bore, and it takes so much good time that might be spent enjoying one's self!"

But while such a woman of society does not make dress her chief object, *Good taste in dress.* she is ordinarily anxious it should be well chosen, harmonious, striking in refinement and in style, and above all not overdone. She looks with disapproval on the modes likely to become too popular and vulgarized before the garments illustrating them shall have gone the way of all garments. She eschews "loud" patterns, conspicuous sleeves and capes and hats, such as one sees by the million in the thoroughfares of a great city, made up in cheap materials. She would no more be seen in these, than in hair made artificially blond and pierced behind with an arrow set with artificial gems.

For her carriage, she reserves the French gown sent out from a great *Parisian gowns.* maker, which may be so much in advance of prevalent fashion as to be conspicuous. She would not walk abroad in it any more than she would wear over muddy crossings a white petticoat frilled and trimmed with lace. For the street, she sets aside a dark, trig, stylish gown and coat and hat, which may reveal its artificer and value to the initiated eye, but will never invite attention from the crowd.

The young girl of the same class is easily recognized by distinguishing simplicity in dress. The costliness of her apparelling appears in stuff, cut, and the indefinable appurtenance of style. The linings and unseen parts of her costumes are oftentimes of better material than that used for the exterior. Her trimmings are few, and those put only where trimmings have a natural right to be. She wears no jewelry other than a necessary clasp or pin, omitting bracelets and bangles, long since relegated to the *habituées* of cheap shops and remote avenues. In damp weather, one sees this girl of society walking in a skirt that clears the ground, thick boots, a petticoat of dark silk or stuff, a jacket or coat or cape that suggests utility, and carrying a sensible umbrella.

Whatever the women of the world (so-called) have to be reproached with in the matter of bringing up their children, they do not, nowadays, neglect considerations of health, either in exercise or in appropriate dress to meet the varieties of the American climate. It may be that this habit of compact simplicity in outdoor dress, is one of the benefits we derive from our supposed cult of English ways.

Hygiene in dress.

One is struck, in visiting in English country-houses, with the custom universal among the women, of wearing all day the plain tailor-made tweeds they appear in at breakfast, ready to walk about the grounds afterward. In the evening, at a dinner later than is usual with us, they emerge, resplendent in jewels and low-cut gowns, even when the house-party is a small one. In contrast, we see, in America, women and girls wearing at breakfast confections of pink or blue, covered with lace, in which it would be impossible, with the necessary equipment of slippers and lace-edged skirts, to do more than step off a veranda upon a gravel-walk. If they go out, it is generally after eleven o'clock and after a second elaborate toilet, to make calls or to drive.

A woman of the world calling recently upon the mother of a certain charmingly pretty girl at their country home, was received, after a delay—palpably to dress—by the daughter of her friend. This delay, in itself annoying, was not atoned for by the appearance of the girl in a morning-gown of Parisian stamp and elaboration, that might have served appropriately for the "young widow" in a curtain-raiser at a French play. The gown was exquisitely refined in tint and fashioning; in it the wearer resembled a bit of "fine-paste" porcelain fit to be set in a cabinet and locked in behind plate-glass. But suitableness, harmony, good-taste were all lacking, in her assumption of this costly belonging of one twice her age as a home-dress on a bright summer's morning. The visitor went away, wishing she had the courage to tell the child's mother what a mistake had been made!

Low-cut gowns—now so universally in use in evening dress that they have ceased to be a vexed question—should be worn neither by light of day, nor by people they do not become. It is lamentable to see women whose anatomy rebels against exposure, equip themselves, for fashion's sake, in such wise. Not only is attention called to the want of beauty in the neck; but the face suffers. A thin face and throat are generally much improved by the fluffiness of lace or feathers rising almost to the chin. And there is a wide latitude permitted in this matter among us, who have not a queen to lay down the law of exclusion from her presence on state occasions of those who are not fortified by a physician's certificate to excuse a dress worn high in the throat! A low-cut gown should not be allowed to show itself at any function of the afternoon, even in an artificial light intended to suggest the evening. The simple fact that her invited guests must appear in street costume with bonnets, should indicate to the hostess the propriety of a house-dress high in the throat. And although afternoon receptions may be still given, where the gas is turned on and the daylight shut out, and a number of women, convened to aid in receiving, assemble in full evening dress to claim the admiration of their friends, it is not in the best houses they are seen.

Low-cut gowns.

Thus, at weddings in a church. No longer do we see arriving members of the family and especially invited guests, bonnetless, wearing semi-evening dresses, to take their places in the reserved pews. What is called a reception toilet for weddings, as light in tint and as elaborate as

Reception gowns.

may be desired, but always accompanied with a bonnet (retained or not, afterward, at the house) is in vogue. Bridesmaids generally prefer becoming hats, though they sometimes wear short veils. The bride, if in travelling costume, wears a bonnet or hat; if in the regulation bridal gown, a long tulle or point lace veil.

Another point, on which there seems much confusion of ideas, is as to the exact definition of the words "evening dress," now often added to cards for public entertainments of the musical or literary sort. By women, this should be read as "Come in whatever gown you possess, a little better than that worn in the morning, but come without your bonnet!" Those who have dined out, or are going on to dances, often appear in full evening toilet, retaining cloaks or some covering for bare necks and arms. But it is the bonnet that is the especial foe to the gala appearance desired by managers in an auditorium at night! It has proved hard to dislodge; but it now does really seem to grow less year by year, in size, and to be less frequent.

Evening dress.

Pass we now to the question of correspondence, its forms and substance. One who is in receipt of letters from strangers living in sundry parts of the North American continent, has a fair opportunity to judge the fashion of our country in these particulars. It is rare to find an American woman's letter lacking in ease, liveliness, graceful expression; but in the form—there is often much left to be desired.

Correspondence.

The commonest fault is the eccentric course followed by their chirography to arrive at a fourth page. The first page finished and turned, the reader is distracted by searching for the sequence to what has preceded. The letter is turned in and out several times before its recipient is lucky enough to discover that a third page, written upon lengthwise, is intended to precede a second page written crosswise — this, again, followed by a fourth page inscribed from end to end. There is no meaning in this, and the fashion, if ever it was one among people of good form, has utterly gone out. The present note or letter of good society goes from beginning to end in regular sequence over pages one, two, three, and four. If there is material only to fill two pages, or to lap over from the first page, it should be written on pages one and two, not on pages one and three, as is most often seen, leaving an intermediate blank page.

The letter should be preceded by the house address and date, the note by the house address alone—and at its lower left-hand corner the day of the week is to be added. A young lady of vague if charming habits as a correspondent was recently rallied by a friend upon her method of prefacing letters with a simple "Wednesday, 1894."

Date and address.

A point here occurs to me to note a habit of certain amiable precisians of always writing in full the year of grace —as "eighteen hundred and ninety-four." No doubt through lack of time, a *fin-de-siècle* excuse for many derelictions, this has begun to fall into disuse; "1894" appears boldly below invitations to weddings, and at the heads of letters; though the day of the month is still written wherever it is summoned to give evidence in fashionable correspondence.

There seems to have arisen no new law as to style in engraving the house address. It should be in legible text, in gold, bronze, silver, or color; but a little touch of recent fashion, borrowed from the English, is a comma after the number, as in "12, Berkeley Square." Monograms or crests are added according to the taste of the owner; but a woman's right to use a crest on her *Arms, crests, own paper, or elsewhere and mono- grams.* on anything distinctively her own, is not allowed by the authorities. If it be understood that she is using her husband's paper, provided by him for his household, and having about it no individual mark of herself, his crest may appear at the head of her letters and notes. She may, however, use the arms of her family. If a spinster or widow, her arms should be placed upon a lozenge; if married, they should be impaled with those of her husband—though never, in any case, surmounted by a crest. But a monogram containing the letters of her name, or those letters simply, or the signature of her Christian name reproduced in fac-simile, are all more graceful and appropriate to a woman than a coat of arms, the use of which emblem in this country has indeed been so much derided that one hesitates to recommend it at all.

In some English country-houses, remote enough from a telegraph-station *Telegraphic* to make horse-flesh and the *addresses.* time of messengers in delivering telegrams a consideration, they have a convenient fashion of engraving across the left-hand upper corner of the letter-paper, opposite the name of their place and post-office, an announcement like this—

"STATION, CLUMBER,
TELEGRAPH, LYNTON, 6 MILES."

With such a provision of information, the guest or correspondent can hardly go astray as to what method he should employ in endeavoring to put himself in communication with his friend. The fashion has merit enough to warrant its adoption among us.

Paper of the "Scotch granite" va*Paper.* riety, octavo size, is so much used for ordinary house-correspondence abroad, it has come into general vogue here, having the double attraction of cheapness and a pleasant green-gray tint.

For answering invitations, for writing the dainty missives that fly back and forth between a woman and her numerous friends, in a period when half the civilities of society are executed under the ægis of a two-cent postal stamp, there is no limit to the variety of paper and envelopes to choose from. Here feminine fancy may have full sway, and to femininity many caprices are forgiven that would elsewhere be challenged. The tints of mignonette, pale lavender, pale blue, pearl, or white, are, however, most seen in use upon writing-tables of refined women, who hold back from extremes in everything. The use of sealing-wax, for *Sealing-wax.* years deemed indispensable, has gradually drifted out of our busy end of the century's life, although it is surely, of all minor additions to the form of correspondence, the most elegant.

Colored inks, save for business purposes, are never used. Anything that *Inks.* savors of eccentricity—dark-hued paper, an odd shape in envelopes, etc.—creates distrust of the polite information of the writer. In all such matters there is a golden mean of simplicity and good taste, hard to define, but felt to the finger-tips by those who are accustomed to pass judgment upon form, and most earnestly recommended to the seeker for information in such channels.

Scented paper is, except perhaps for that faintest fragrance of violet that *Perfumes.* comes from orris-root, apt to be an offence to the recipient. But the tastes of no two people agree as to good perfumes, and, on safety's side, it is better to avoid them altogether. Strong, vivid odors intended for the masses, so frankly vulgarize everything they touch, it seems hardly worth while to urge that the sachets containing them be thrown into the fire, rather than among one's boxes of letter-paper.

Handwriting. Handwriting of the fine slanting "Italian" kind, taught to our mothers and handed down to be a scourge to the friends of their descendants, has not entirely passed from among us, although modern taste is doing its best to eliminate it. No letter, no matter what its intrinsic charm or pathetic appeal, will be read nowadays with patience to the end, if written in this style of chirography. Better a thousand times the type-writer, that foe to sentiment and finer phraseology—better anything—than MS. made illegible on account of pallid ink and hair-strokes from a minikin pen!

One feels like appealing in tears to the school-mistresses of our land, to bring up our coming women to write legibly, fearlessly; leaving spaces before their lines and between their lines; with pens broad enough of nib to make the words stand out in full relief to the reader's eye. Would not the universal adoption of such practices gild anew the waste of ordinary correspondence, rob charity-work and work for philanthropy's sake of their terrors, and put all men who have to deal with women on business subjects in an attitude of greater resignation toward their fate? What student of the genealogy of America since the beginning of the century—and in the new waves of enthusiasm about our ancestors, the country is full of such—has not heaved a sigh at finding himself, upon the threshold of desired information from old family letters, face to face with numerous thin, crackling sheets written in faded ink, in which, say, a great-grandmamma has poured out to her first married daughter all the delightful gossip and *Coteriesprache* of the household since she left it? How one longs to be possessed of the contents of these and many like them from "the same to the same!". And yet, how the overtaxed eyes shrink from the task! How reluctantly one puts away a crisp bundle of such precious old documents, tied with ribbons of a forgotten pattern, determining that—"when the time comes"—one will read every word.

Then the "foreign" letters — the "travels" abroad of our fathers and mothers when travel meant something, and "impressions" were eagerly received by home-admirers. How deplorably thin their paper, how evasive to the touch, how trying the sheen of its surface to the eye! They, too, must be laid aside and relegated to the happy times cherished in all imaginations, "when we have nothing else to do." If postage had not been so high, and the education of polite society had not then entailed a "flowing" hand, we might enjoy them as did the generation ahead of us.

There is a small, but distinct "literary" hand-writing familiar to the correspondents of one or two great publishing houses, that is a charm to the recipient. It is compact, neither round nor pointed, generally seen upon fair white linen paper in good black ink. It sets forth dates and signatures with absolute precision—a first glance reveals every shade of meaning it is intended to convey. A few men and women of literary bent have this chirography; but it is never enough seen among us, and its possession is one distinctly to be envied.

Substance. Having said this much about outward form in correspondence, I feel less confident in touching the matter of substance. The pen, in these days, is a little instrument fraught with danger to the community, for its success in private experiment is no sooner ascertained than there is the risk that its achievements may immediately seek print! The letter-writer renowned in her private circle, is so sure to find herself "urged to publish." The schoolgirl, the travelled spinster, the busy mother of a family, the girl of society who has written a lucky essay for her literary club—all yearn to secure for their productions a baptism of printer's ink. It really is not safe to urge women to be more clever than they are, or the publishers will yearn for them, and then there will be none left to write those delightful chatty letters about domestic life *our* descendants will expect to find in *our* old trunks and desks!

No woman—so far as one can judge from printed collections—ever wrote more pleasant letters than do the American women. They have in their style English simplicity joined to French grace and spirit; when they are natural, they are best. They dress up little nothings with infinite drollery, they possess a keen apprehension of character, and they are, as a rule, good-tempered. I have no doubt the great Atlantic liners bring home in those leathern post-bags, thrown aboard just as the ship is ready to leave her dock, more wit in description from travelling American women, than could be found in the mails of any other nation. The perpetual brightness of feminine American comment upon foreign ways must have been at the bottom of the ill-nature of an English man of letters, who remarked to an American in London, "I don't doubt they are charming, your countrywomen, but they see too much, and they write home too much, and give one no rest as to what they will next disclose."

Of the small coin of correspondence, all invitations are couched much in the same form, and give little opportunity for the fair author to show her originality. If Mrs. Murray-Hill, for instance, desires to include Mrs. Washington Park in her list of guests for a dinner three weeks distant, she makes use, generally, of an engraved card, running as form shown on page 164, its blanks filled in with names and date.

Invitations.

But if the dinner is one of the less formal banquets, to which friends are bidden, Mrs. Murray-Hill sits down to her davenport, and dashes off a few lines like these:

— Fifth Avenue.

My dear Mrs. Park:

I hope you and Mr. Park will give us the pleasure of your company at dinner, very informally, on Thursday, March eighth, at a quarter before eight o'clock. Trusting this may not find you engaged elsewhere, believe me,

Yours faithfully,

Josephine Murray-Hill.

Tuesday.

> Mr. & Mrs. Murray Hill
>
> request the pleasure of
>
> Mr. & Mrs. Washington Park's
>
> company at dinner
>
> on Thursday, March the Fifteenth
>
> at eight o'clock.
>
> Fifth Avenue.
>
> February, twenty-ninth.

The polite fiction, "very informally," be it understood, is meant to cover the failure to notify her friend a longer time ahead; otherwise, there would seem to be little difference in the service of the small dinner of eight or ten, given on the eighth, and the banquet of eighteen or twenty on the fifteenth.

People have, indeed, ceased speculating as to the exact definition of "informally" in notes of invitation. Although beloved of hostesses, it would be a rash person who would presume on it to dress "informally," or act "informally;" *i.e.*, otherwise than according to accepted tenets laid down for dinners great or small.

A Congressman newly arrived in Washington, acting on this delusive word in his note of invitation, repaired to a dinner at the house of his acquaintance dressed in a frock coat, a light-blue satin scarf, and pearl trousers; just what, with propriety, he would have worn out to "tea" at the same hour in his native town. His wife, attired in a high black silk, and wearing a shawl of white point d'Alençon fastened with cameo brooches upon the shoulders, was more chagrined than he, to find a large dinner in prospect, the other women, assembled in the drawing-room, dressed for it in all the bravery of low gowns and many jewels. But she said nothing, kept her eyes and ears open, like a sensible woman as she was; and a year afterward, might have been found in the act of giving just such "informal" dinners, at which everything was done according to the most exacting "form"—on her own account.

In case one desires to decline a formal invitation—to dinner for instance —one may write in this wise: Mr. and Mrs. Murray-Hill regret very much that they are prevented by an engagement elsewhere from accepting Mr. and Mrs. ——'s kind invitation to dinner, on Thursday, the twenty-fifth.

Invitations for luncheons follow exactly the same lines as those given above for dinners. If the luncheon is fixed for a fortnight or three weeks later—this applying, of course, only to the crowded life of a large city—an engraved card bears the message. If Mrs. Murray-Hill desires to bring together a few congenial spirits around her board at mid-day, she addresses to each a friendly note as many days in advance as she thinks needful to secure the presence of those she particularly wants.

To convene friends on the occasion of a cup of tea to be given in behalf of some recently arrived stranger, some lion great or small, or some old acquaintance returned to the haunts of her youth, it is enough to send a small envelope containing one's visiting card. Over the engraved name of the sender is written in ink in her own hand—not too carefully—" To meet Mrs. Blank," while below are similarly inscribed the date and hour. To such invitations answers are not usually expected, and those who fail to go generally call on the hostess extending the summons a few days later. If it is desired to pay this attention to the guest of the occasion, the people invited may also call upon that guest; but it is hardly obligatory in the numerous demands of a busy social life.

In New York, little informal—for here the word fits in—gatherings so assembled are often among the most pleasant of the season. A much invited person cares little for what is set before her in the way of refreshment. Liberty to go or not, as she may find herself able to do, often induces her to drop in upon what, to an invitation requiring response, she would have refused off-hand. She can appear in the crowd—speak to her hostess—speak a word to the guest of the hour—fall away in a corner, into a comfortable chair, and talk with some agreeable man or woman she has not recently met—and then, if she likes, glide out without saying good afternoon. This latter fashion, at first sight a little cavalier, has grown out of two things—the crowds in modern houses, and the wish not to appear in the eyes of others to terminate a festivity. It is no longer necessary for husband and wife, or mother and daughter, to walk up in the manner of the procession into Noah's ark, two and two, to seek out the hostess to take formal leave after a ball, or reception, or tea, or any crowded function. On the other hand, a guest escaping after a dinner or luncheon without saying good-by to the entertainer and giving light compliments for her entertainment, would be adjudged outside the pale, and never again deemed worthy to be asked within it!

For a large "tea" or reception given for a *débutante* by her mother, it is customary to send cards about 3½ by 4½ inches, engraved as follows:

In England, the custom of amassing names upon one visiting-card is carried to a greater extent than here. I note one, to be remembered as almost covered with engraving; and away down in the lower left-hand corner was the announcement of the day when it would be possible to expect to find this numerous family at home.

For the benefit of those curious, I would say that Miss Edith Gresham, (whose name like the others, is imaginary), was a ward of the family living in their house, and had been, by Mrs. Cholmondeley, recently presented at court.

In New York, it is quite common to see the names of the mother and eldest daughter supplemented by that of the next sister in society, but I am not

> *Mrs. Washington Park.*
> *Miss Park.*
> *At Home*
> *Saturday, January tenth,*
> *from four until seven o'clock.*
>   *Washington Square.*

Or, when it is desired to make the affair less formal—again our word, without which, after all, it seems impossible to deal with society's code of minor laws!—the visiting card of mother and daughter is used.

aware that we have yet had the official presentment of the resident niece or cousin thus included.

For a cotillon given elsewhere than in one's own home, the invitation form would be on a square card, as opposite.

> Mrs. Cholmondeley.
> Miss Cholmondeley.
> Miss Gwendoline Cholmondeley.
> Miss Edith Gresham.
>
> Tuesdays.   Cadogan Square.

The same formula would be used if music were to be the entertainment of the evening, substituting that word for cotillon; but in such case, is wisely added, after the hour specified, the word "*punctually*."

> Mr. & Mrs. Murray Hill
> request the pleasure of
> <u>Mr. & Mrs. Park's</u> company
> at Sherry's,
> on Monday evening December fourth,
> at nine o'clock.
>
> R.s.v.p.   Cotillon.

Nine o'clock, the hour named in general upon a card for a ball, must never be taken literally. In New York it is usually eleven o'clock and after, before the fashionable folk make their appearance, and a ball is not really under way till midnight. Decry as we may, and should, these hours in communities whereof most of the men are working-folk, due at offices and places of business by ten o'clock the next day, the reform so ardently desired by sensible people has not yet been brought about. A step in the right direction was a series of dances instituted this past season, by some well-bred and kindly women of society, to begin strictly at nine and terminate at twelve; to these were bidden a number of young men engaged in business and in professional pursuits. But I am not sure the young men who attended and enjoyed them acquired from them sufficient strength of mind to refuse subsequent invitations to the great cotillons and assemblies, or balls, given by the Patriarchs.

When cards are sent out by a number of patronesses for a subscription dance at some semi-public hall engaged for the occasion, the best form is as below:

Here follows a list of names of patronesses, and in the invitation (engraved upon a sheet of octavo size of fair white paper) is enclosed a card of admission, meant to be presented by the bearer at the door. Another form is an oblong double card of thick pasteboard, on the outer face of which is read:

The pleasure of
Mrs. Helm Veuy's
company is requested at the
Second Assembly,
Thursday evening, February the first,
at nine o'clock.

Inside are found engraved names of the subscribers and patronesses, filling several columns, and perhaps on the last page is read:

RECEPTION COMMITTEE.

Mrs.——   Mrs.——
Mrs.——   Mrs.——

The Committee consists of the ladies selected from the rest to do the hon-

> *The pleasure of Mrs. Helm Vesey's company is requested at the Cotillon at Delmonico's, on Monday evening, January fourth, from nine until one o'clock.*
>
> *Cotillon at half after ten.*
>
> *R.s.v.p.*

ors of the evening. They stand (in some eyes, a sufficiently formidable battery) in an ante-chamber, or near the door of the ball-room, to receive the guests as their names are announced. A bow, a courtesy—for the pretty old-fashioned "reverence" of young maidenhood is now quite in vogue among her elders—a word with an acquaintance or friend among the quartette, and you are expected to pass on. Nothing is more tiresome than people who settle down for an evening's conversation with a committee on reception at a large affair like this. They block the way for others, and there is no time to attend to them.

A hostess who wishes to assemble a number of strictly "dancing" people for a party, to be by none confounded with her large and general affairs, sends out a card of this kind:

are most commonly engraved on a sheet of about 4¼ by 6½ inches, of finely grained white paper, in reasonably large round script, omitting all flourishes (see page 172); they are sent most often through the mail—as indeed are most invitations of the day, including many to dinners of ceremony three weeks in advance—in two envelopes; the inner one to match the paper and without gum, the outer envelope of a thinner and cheaper sort, to receive the stamp and post-mark.

These notifications of a wedding are

Mr & Mrs Richard Hunter

At Home

on Thursday, December fourteenth,

at ten o'clock.

Fifth Avenue.

Small Dance.
R. s. v. p.

Again, when the hostess whose acquaintance passes in numbers the limits of her house, desires to bring out her daughter, a late fashion has been to engage, for the purpose, rooms *à la mode*, and to inscribe the invitation on her cards.

Elsewhere, I have seen "*Thé dansant,*" used instead of the franker English word—not, we will agree, to the advantage of the card.

The invitations in use for weddings

generally sent two or three weeks in advance of the intended ceremony. If there is to be a breakfast or reception following the ceremony, to which a limited number of intimate friends are to be invited, the favored ones are notified either by a separate card included, or by especial note (see page 171). For a large church wedding, cards of admission, to be presented at the door, may be enclosed.

> Mrs. Alfred Hamilton
> requests the pleasure of your company
> At Tea,
> on Wednesday, January fourth,
> from four until seven o'clock.
> Sherry's Rooms, 1 West Street.
> Dancing.

When it is desired that the wedding shall be witnessed by a few only, and be followed by a general reception, a separate card to the friends expected at the ceremony is enclosed in the invitations sown broadcast for the reception (see page 173). In this case, meaning a large general reception, invitations to the wedding at four o'clock would be extended, orally or by note, to particular friends and members of the family.

> At Home
> from one until three o'clock.
> West 37th Street.

> Mr. & Mrs. James Cartwright
>
> request the honour of your presence
>
> at the marriage of their daughter
>
> Louise
>
> to
>
> Mr. George Henry Hamilton,
>
> on Tuesday, November eighteenth,
>
> at twelve o'clock,
>
> Saint Mary's Church,
>
> Fifth Avenue and Eighty-ninth Street.

For many reasons — chief among which is that a wedding in a large city is heralded by the daily newspapers until the church is likely to be packed with pushing, scrambling, self-invited guests — the house-wedding has of late been more frequently adopted. To Church people, and to many others, this practice divests the ceremony of the solemnity and dignity it demands by right. But, remembering the chatter and comment of vulgar-minded outsiders, and the chatter and comment of insiders who take the whole affair as a function of their "set," is such a ceremony in church likely to seem more

> Mr. & Mrs. John Cameron
>
> request the honour of your presence
>
> at the wedding reception of their daughter
>
> Mary
> and
> Mr. Julian Pierepont,
>
> on Tuesday, January seventeenth,
>
> from half after four until six o'clock.
>
> Gramercy Square

sacred? The size of modern houses in proportion to the extent of visiting lists, has next to be considered. One cannot send cards for a wedding, of all things, without consideration of a hundred people passed over in making ordinary lists. Offence given at this juncture often remains for a lifetime to confront the young couple. In many cases, therefore, to avoid all misunderstanding, friends clearly entitled to be present are asked privately to the ceremony, immediately after which are sent out, to everyone possibly concerned, a card of announcement (see page 175).

If the ceremony has been performed in church, the name of the church is given. If at home, the house address is not mentioned.

Should one be unable to attend a wedding or wedding-reception, it is customary to call and leave cards for those in whose name invitations are issued, and also for the bridal pair—or, if at a distance, to send a double set of cards, and, for cards of announcement, to return cards—two for a man and one for a woman.

In the event of such a marriage, the mother of the bride will most often *Cards.* wish to give for her a general "tea" or "at home" on her return from the wedding journey. In this case, the united names of the young couple—what Dickens used to laugh at as the "connubial copper-plate"—"Mr. and Mrs. Louis Francis Childs," appear on a card enclosed with that sent by Mrs. Douglas to invite her friends to tea, or to an evening party.

The "connubial copper-plate" has not its old vogue in society. Except *Of married people.* when they come together for bridal announcement or for invitations, "Mr." and "Mrs." keep each an individual card for general use. When Mrs. Douglas—for, to invent new names for each set of dummies has begun to tax the imagination of the scribe!—goes on her rounds of visits, she leaves at each door where there is a married couple, one of her own cards, and two of her husband's. If there is an unmarried Miss Douglas, and a Miss Winifred Douglas, they will be found on their mother's card. If there are grown sons still under her roof, Mrs. Douglas leaves also one card for each of them—and drives away, feeling a sense of virtue which is to be derived only from this indiscriminate waste of pasteboard.

A young man, making calls in his own person, leaves two cards, of course, *Of a bachelor.* —one for the master, one for the mistress of the house; and should the object of his attention be the young lady of a house, the card left for her mother will also suffice for her.

A young girl, calling on her own friends, leaves her own card. But, in a *Of a girl.* large community, she is apt to be more quickly recognized and placed, if her name, following her mother's as has been suggested, be left in the hall with the crowd of other cards.

It seems hardly worth while to say here that a girl's name upon her card should always be preceded by "Miss;" that a man's name upon his card, in good society, must bear the prefix "Mr.;" and that nicknames, pet names, and the like, are outlawed from appearance upon cards.

Cards should be firm, substantial, purely white, engraved in round script, *Forms of cards.* and printed legibly. A woman's is of good size, a man's not so large—even diminutive. A woman's, for ordinary use, contains her name, her address in the lower right-hand corner, and her day at home (if she have one) in the left-hand lower corner. An unmarried man sometimes puts upon his card both his house ad-

> *Mr. & Mrs. Alexander Douglas*
>
> *have the honour to announce*
>
> *the marriage of their daughter*
>
> *Florence*
>
> *to*
>
> *Mr. Louis Francis Childs,*
>
> *on Wednesday, April twenty-fifth,*
>
> *eighteen hundred and ninety-four.*
>
> *New York.*

dress in the lower right-hand ⟨ incumbent as that of trousers rolled up and the address of his accustomed ⟨ in New York when it rains in London ! in the lower left-hand corner. As th⟨ married man has his house address, an English fashion, it may come to be ⟨ his wife's, in the lower right-hand corner of his card, or sometimes none at all. A fashion quite often seen, is that of dispensing with the Christian name upon cards. In America it has

A mother having two daughters to take into society, inscribes herself and them upon her card, not infrequently, thus :

> *Mrs. Carlton.*
> *Miss Carlton.*
> *Miss Agnes Carlton.*
>
> *Tuesdays.*   *Washington Square.*

no doubt been spread by the appearance upon cardboard, in this guise, of certain officials of government, who, on returning to private life, cannot entirely divest themselves of all the panoply of Jove. "Mr. Jupiter" has undoubtedly a more imposing effect than "Mr. John T. Jupiter," as he used to style himself before going into office. Not to be outdone, " Mrs. Jupiter" follows her husband's lead. All it is necessary for her friends to know is thus conveyed to them ; with the general public she has really so little to do !

This idea is a good one when there are two or three married sons known in a community, from whom and their families it is right that the father and mother should be set, in dignity, apart. The fashion is generally assumed by the head of an important family ; and it is always accorded to those who have borne really distinguished public offi

In England, the husband's Christian name is much less used in addressing *Christian and* married women than here. *middle names.* Their letters and notes are directed to "Mrs. Devon" simply, rarely to "Mrs. Henry Devon" and very rarely "Mrs. Henry A. Devon," as with us. The America͏̈ ͏an's habit of retaining her pa͏ ͏ic to precede her married n ͏ ͏a her signature, and then lea ͏ ͏er cards with her husband's f ͏ ͏mes or all his initials, is the ͏ ͏e of great confusion in Engl͏ ͏inds. It leads our British cous͏ ͏ to commit various eccentricitie͏ ͏ nomenclature upon the backs of ͏ ͏s and notes they send to us ; to ͏ ͏ess one now in this way, now ͏ ͏t, then finally to hyphenate our ͏ ͏ral names in a row ! After r ͏ ͏d experiences of this kind, the ͏ ͏tage of the English custom be ͏ ͏es patent. A month of note-writ ͏g and receiving of notes in London in the season, will drive even a stanch American to signing herself as does her English correspondent, "M. Jones" or "I. Plantagenet;" *i.e.*, with a single initial preceding the family name.

Since Thackeray's "General Jedediah B. Bung," the middle initial of an American has been set as a stigma, by foreign writers, upon the typical Brother Jonathan they delight to introduce into their pages. It is not that the English have no middle names; they frequently have several; but they are not apt to employ a middle name or its initial for every-day use, or to repeat it, as we do, with every utterance of the family name, until it becomes grotesque. Nor do they think it necessary to put initials of middle names always upon a card. The time lost in trying to recall people's middle initials is worthy of higher achievement. I believe that when the common conveniences of life come to be rounded into a perfect whole, men and women will be known by not more than two names apiece to the public.

In the same bright period, somebody will have devised a method of paying *Calls.* the small debts of society without the empty ceremony of a call, which means simply to ring a bell —to leave a card—to escape, rejoicing that one more name is crossed off the list of dues.

It is not heartlessness that inspires this common frame of mind, it is disgust of one's self that one is not able to rise out of the necessity for this conventional interchange of civilities, with people who would regret nothing more than to be caught at home. And, yet, the same people meeting each other on shipboard, in a foreign hotel, or in summer leisure by the sea, in the mountains, would often be sincerely interested each in the other, and glad of an opportunity to make closer acquaintance.

But calls remain, calls must be made, and the burden of them is our old man *Times for* of the sea. For the sake of *calling.* simplifying the matter, many women remain at home on certain afternoons during the season, and are quite satisfied with the appearance once a year, in their drawing-rooms, of the "friends" with whom they regularly exchange cards. It is not considered necessary to call, after a single large "tea." But after an evening party, a dinner, a luncheon, an invitation to theatre or opera, or any distinct personal civility, a call is incumbent upon well-bred people.

Men's calls are, like most of men's privileges in the nineteenth century, very much at their own pleasure. For the busy ones, calls in the late afternoon, over the tea-table at five o'clock, when one may always safely presume upon finding a lady willing to receive, are almost impossible. Calls in the evening, unless at a house where the visitor is sure of being made one of the family, are not expected in New York. In other less over-hurried cities, the evening is the time for pleasant rendezvous of familiar friends. In the South, the practice of visiting at this hour is the inalienable privilege of the youths who devote themselves to repeated attentions to "the ladies." But in New York it is hardly worth the young fellow's trouble to equip himself in evening dress, to compass by street-car or on foot the magnificent distances of the town, for the pleasure of consigning his card to a surprised or somnolent flunkey, who murmurs reproachfully, "The ladies are not at home, sir!"

Therefore the habit has arisen for men to call on their friends on Sunday afternoons, between four and half-past six. Whatever objection may be urged to it by people living at a distance, this way of spending the afternoon is better for the average young man than the dreariness of a boarding-house or the idle gossip of a club.

To sum up what I have written, if a certain degree of artificiality, of uncertainty, makes itself apparent to the observer of the customs of conventional society with us Americans, we must not complain. Evolution, like electricity, has us in her grip. Our great-grandchildren will no doubt laugh at our poor dear innocent old ways! A moment since, I read a passage in a letter from Horace Walpole—the fine flower of the best English society in his time—wherein he lamented the necessity of having to dine as late as nearly six o'clock, and complained that they would be soon beginning their balls at ten!

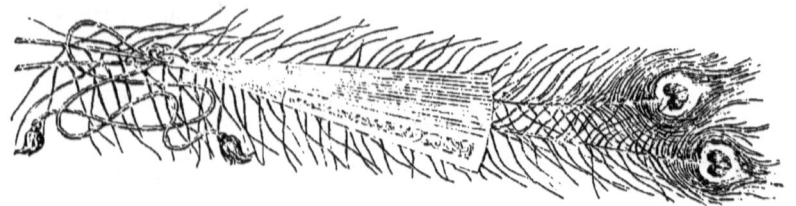

V.

THE ÆSTHETICS OF DRESS.

V.

THE ÆSTHETICS OF DRESS.

By EVA WILDER McGLASSON.

The Canons of Taste.	Lines.
Sincerity.	Hygiene.
Simplicity.	Conventionalism.
Unity.	Individualism.
Appropriateness.	Originality.
Textile Fabrics.	Picturesqueness.
Colors.	Eccentricity.

IT is said that whenever any art, whatever its origin, attains such excellence as to regard beauty as a main object, it becomes thereby of the æsthetic class. It need not be demonstrated that the art of dress has reached this point. Whatever strange whims the motley goddess of Fashion has compelled her votaries to endure, beauty has even from very early times been in some sort an end toward which she struggled.

In view of some of the monstrous effects which she has produced this statement might seem to be of a paradoxical nature; but it must be remembered that ideas of beauty have always varied greatly. It has been shown that almost the only objects which have seemed beautiful alike to all peoples, barbaric and civilized, ancient and modern, have been certain natural aspects, such as flawless skies or foam-streaked waters, or fresh hills and grassy glades. Beauty has depended entirely on the point of view of its age. It is a most illusive thing to pin down to analysis; and the recognition of its essentially subtle nature has entered into all such statements of results as philosophy has been able to make. It has been profoundly considered as a quality of things, as a mental endowment, and as a relation between these. But each of these modes of viewing it is confessedly not demonstrable; so that we violate no canon if we choose to consider beauty, in respect to the subject of apparel, as residing not in apparel solely, nor yet solely in the wearer, but in the establishment of a perfect accord between them.

This is, in fine, the actual stand-point of every woman who has thought at all upon the weighty subject of what is becoming to her. Those who think upon it most deeply are not always successful, it must be admitted, in their achievements; for while the sex at large is gifted with an instinct in this direction which is as incomprehensible as an actual impulse of genius, women are greatly misled by their traditions, their sentiments, their friends, and their ideals. The eye of criticism seldom levels itself accurately upon its own counterfeit in the looking-glass. The woman who observes herself sees not merely the actual physical proportions she has in view. She sees, it may be instanced, a member of the Van Broeck family, noted always, as her childish recollections affirm, for their dignity of port and aristocratic profiles. She sees a woman who wears a violet gown, not because it suits her, but because she has a fondness for it, as the color of romance, beloved of poet and painter—tender, pensive, semi-religious; she sees, further, a person whose hair is worn painfully smooth, perhaps because some acquaintance has remarked in a moment of unjudged good-will, ent development, a knowledge of these plainly ought to control all those hallucinations to which the most sensible people are liable when under the lens of self-examination—though self-examination is most necessary not only is respect to colors, textures, carriage,

Head-dresses of the Middle Ages.

that with such features one can afford to forswear crimps; and finally, if she has a vestige of imagination she is likely to behold a woman whose differentiation from the real one is such as might lie in a description written by herself and one written by a dispassionate observer.

Imagination does not always clothe its possessor with unreal charms. Not infrequently the arch-deceiver paints things much blacker than they are, exaggerating defects until the owner of them is forever clothed in a wretched and hopeless self-consciousness. Women are usually very adept at discovering their bad points, but even with a full consciousness of these, there exists a wide-spread tendency to dress, as someone once said, "by the way it sounds."

If there are any radical principles of art which regulate apparel in its pres- height, and weight, but in regard to the whole effect, spiritually as well as physically.

Art has been defined somewhere as personality, and especially is it so in the æsthetics of apparel. Taste must be the final criterion, and it is a comfortable circumstance that taste is not the arbitrary choice of the individual, but must rest upon acknowledged principles. Being a union of judgment and sensibility, good taste is, to some extent, a natural endowment, in its fullest expression, perhaps entirely so—as all principles of all art revert to the undisciplined expressions of genius. But these being formulated, are for the use of such as are not geniuses, and a knowledge of structural facts is obviously necessary to those who wish to make correct decisions in the science of apparel, or in any science.

The most cursory glance into the history of raiment discloses the apparently curious fact that men have been even more passionately devoted to national peculiarities of costume than to established religions. Legislation has now and again been able to direct, even to obliterate, prevalent forms of worship, but fashion is a rebel against whom kings and parliaments have in vain hurled threats and issued proscriptions. The hearts of the great masses have been with the impenitent offender always, and as the human heart in its natural aspect is generally a kindly thing, it would seem clearly that in herself the arbiter of vogues must have something which appeals to human nature in a deeper sort of way than through mere caprice.

Mrs. Oliphant has justly pointed out that fashion, so far from being an incarnation of cruelty and whim, has always been rather of a considerate turn of

The Hoop-Petticoat. 1840.

Bran-stuffed Sleeves. 1828.

mind, with a favoring impulse toward age and defects, and even deformities. Fashion, this minx who sways princes and potentates, has been used to bend a very compassionate eye upon the unhappy possessors of wens and club-feet and bent spines and other miseries of the sort. She has seemed to proceed upon a reasonable supposition that youth needs her less than those whose bloom is waning. Ruffs to hide the flaccid throat, wimples and coifs to shade the insidious crow's-foot, wigs for thinning hair, bran-stuffed sleeves for bony elbows, hoop-petticoats to take from weak knees the burden of heavy skirts, stays to control the lavish contours of over-ripe loveliness, these things fashion has wrought; and though she has sometimes wrought upon a basis of error, those for whom she worked have seemed to feel her purpose, and have stood by her and made her strong to resist the law that menaced and the prophets that foretold awful woes to all them that countenanced her.

The English houses of legislature spent much time in gravely debating upon the size of "verdingales." They severely condemned face painting and patching, and by their sumptuary ordinances again and again they have striven to control extravagances in apparel. But the instinct that demanded clothes, it has been said, preceded even the need for them. It arose from a desire of decoration, that first ideal of the savage heart. Being grafted thus in a soil anterior to that which produced religious or civil notions, man's "habilatory endeavors" are too deep and strong to be swayed by the passing regulations of legislative bodies.

The instinct for "vestural tissues," rooted in an unchanging soil, has been prolific in the variability of its blossoming. From a decorative design of tattooing, even from a thorn-pinned goat-skin to the carefully fabricated creations of a Parisian master of modes, is a range of progression in which every conceivable arrangement of fabrics has perhaps prevailed. The first æsthetic movement on the part of the early Britons, queerly enough, was toward a habit of attire which our own dress reformers in some measure advocate at present. With Roman rule came in Roman dress, which the women wore as three tunics; the stola was its distinctive feature—a long, loose garment, girded up about the waist and decorated for folk of exclusive pretensions with a border of rich purple. This raiment, however appropriate to Italian climates, could scarcely have been remarkable for its comfort in the chill atmosphere of the northern isles.

An account of Boadicea driving her chariot to war in flowing white stola, with long sleeves that swept back in the breeze and mingled their airy tissues with her flowing hair, furnishes a delightful picture of feminine incongruity. She went to battle fired with righteous indignation, a wronged mother, an affronted queen, but she went with all the impediment and vanity of long skirts and clinging draperies and unbound hair. Women in our age do not go about their household tasks, scarcely about their pleasures, in this way. Perhaps we are farther than we think from barbarism.

It is odd to reflect that Fashion's most atrocious conceptions have been in periods of great intellectual achievement—notably in the Elizabethan era. Wise men who wielded the pen of the writer, forerunners of the literary gentlemen of our own day who dip their instruments in gall to inveigh against the irrationality and general foolishness of woman's attire, had begun to utter unpleasant remarks upon the follies of the sex in regard to dress. Women were affirmed "to love strange habits." They were scored for wear-

The Stola.

ing "tails that trail in the mud." And in the heroic time of chivalry and tournament arose the never-to-be-exhausted tirade upon over-small waists. This bane of modernity came to pass long before the invention of stays. A slim and lissome girth has always been the desire of womanhood, and despite their noble scorn of it as produced by artifice, it has generally been also the admiration of the other sex. Belts, stomachers, girdles, have always prevailed in feminine attire. They have a meaning, just as long skirts have a meaning. The one defines the soft rise of the bosom, and furnishes a firm support for the radiation of skirt folds. The other lends height and grace. It is, therefore, most unlikely, however detrimental to health they are asserted to be, that either of these features will ever be wholly banished. They have certainly, during past centuries, had time to work their worst upon the well-being of women.

That Shakespeare and Bacon and Johnson and Marlowe and Sidney and Raleigh should have had their being in a time when Fashion was most intolerable in her dictates, and that these noble gentlemen seemed not to have wasted time and energy in beating the air with vain maledictions against the mode, but the rather to have conformed quietly to the pressure of the time, is matter for consideration. If ever papal edicts were needed, it was then. If ever dress reformers had cause for being, it was surely when men's attire was both absurd and inconvenient, and when women were clad in iron-ribbed petticoats and heavy stomachers, steel-edged ruffs and unbearably weighty fabrics, additionally loaded with jewels and woven with gold. Elizabeth herself, that person of appalling masculine intelligence and genius for sovereignty, appears in a portrait of the period encased to the ears in a ruff of the solidity of marble. Her brocaded skirt has a metallic set, the projection of her fardingale is most violent. The waist line is prodigiously low, and its falsity maintained with an inflexible mass of gems. Behind her shoulders rises a great heart-shaped arrangement of stiffened muslin. The only modest and comparatively unnoticeable thing about the woman who is noted as being the paragon of queens, is the crown upon her head—an amusing symbol of the meek and lowly position which the divine right of kings is forced to assume at the behest of Fashion.

Having reached the uttermost extreme of sumptuousness, inconvenience, and ugliness, and having bent to her dictates some of the greatest minds humanity has knowledge of, Fashion seems to have relaxed her ingenuity for a time. Certainly the vanities of Elizabeth's day took no impetus from James, a gentleman whose principal anxiety about his raiment was that it should be stuffed heavily enough to withstand dagger thrusts. Nor did modes begin to display renewed activity of invention until ascended that Charles whose image still suggests ribbons

A Lissome Girth.

and ruffles and lovelocks and general light-heartedness. This inconsequent spirit, upon whose frivolous impulses so heavy a penalty fell, was succeeded by a rule which made much of fustian, and set buff and brown as its colors. Then Fashion pursed her lips, wore her hair trimly or cut it round, and donned straight skirts and Puritan capes and neatly laced bodices, and perhaps carried a housewifely little bag. It was the most modest and womanly garb she had ever attained. But these effects passed also, and royalty rose again, and Pepys speaks feelingly upon "the fine and handsome attire of the king." It is Pepys who, out of the dead past, declares an inveterate masculine prejudice for those forerunners of the tailor-made girl—"ladies dressed in coats and doublets, so that only for a long pettycoat under their men's coats, nobody could take them for women." It is this ingenuous spirit also who guilelessly declares the "long trayne to be mighty graceful." His opinion of hoops, which about this time began to draw forth loud public protest, is unhappily not known. With his easy good-nature he would doubtless have recognized in crinoline those elements of utility, that effect of aggran-

Queen Elizabeth in the Costume of her Time.

dizement, which however hideous its actual appearance, projected it clean into the nineteenth century.

It was on the edge of Pepys's time that those French methods and French notions which have ruled the dress of the civilized world down to our own enlightened times began to have marked influence upon fashions.

The question of apparel which of late years has most interested and most confused women is the question of hygiene. It is a subject whose real importance would apparently need no demonstration; yet books are written conclusively to prove that health is the very last thing which women care for, or provide for in their attire. This may indeed be true, for however unreasonable it may sound, health is not the main object of dress. It has never been a primary object at all. Fashion has coolly refused oblation to Hygeia, and if this last mistreated goddess secures the least scantling of sacrifice she may rejoice.

It is not to be maintained that this is just to the race. It is simply stated as fact that only by rare chance and at long intervals have styles of apparel been simple, noble, useful, and in accordance with the laws of health. That the human species, especially the frailer half, should have struggled through ages of inconvenient and distressing fashions without any sensible diminution of strength or intelligence, is indeed odd enough. That there has been a very sensible loss of physical vigor in women is frequently stated. But the alteration of habits of life, the mere progress of civilization may perhaps account largely for this. The rude woman of the field, hardened by sun and storm and labor, and exempt from the enervating effects springing from the institutions of hearth and cloister, is no figure with which to compare the woman of a highly organized society. If against this standard the latter appears frail and debilitated, it must be remembered that a like difference exists between the men of the two social poles.

Men's garb, it is true, is usually admitted to be anything but prejudicial to their physical well-being; but some of the very worst phases of fashion have been peculiar to the sex which has engagingly described woman as "an animal fond of finery." The peruke, stuffed trunk-hose, lace-trimmed boots, and other enormities have ruled the sterner half of the world; and if of late years men have dropped meekly into a uniform, which, however unbeautiful, chances to be at least comfortable, the general levelling of things will not show that in the course of the ages women have been the greater sufferers.

Dress reform, we may vaunt ourselves, is the offspring of our own free land and of no other. There have been many attempts at revolutionizing established modes of feminine apparel, since long ago Bloomers, the first "dual garment," was advocated as an initiatory measure of the system that was to give to woman, long impeded with skirts and stays and false educations and legal nullity and the effects of hereditary helplessness, and the rest of it, her health and her rights. It was supposed that woman would grasp eagerly at the ideas thus provided for her advancement. But woman in the abstract, that noble, rational creature, ought never to be relied on to furnish even a theory of what woman in the concrete will do in a given case. The abstract woman desires more than her own good, the good of posterity. She decries the small human vanities that make her specific sisters cheerfully blind to the future of the race. The balance of power, however, lies always with the ordinary woman, and this very sane person refused to be emancipated from skirts. She scorned the dual garment that was to replace her draperies. More than this, she added her own light laugh to the heavy masculine guffaw which greeted the new idea; for naturally enough man, the very person who, since the thirteenth century or thereabouts, has been calling high Heaven to witness the wild vagaries and general unwholesomeness of woman's attire, now turned on himself with shameless versatility and pointed jibes at an attire which could neither be arraigned on the grounds of vanity, extravagance, or health. Nothing survives ridicule. No variation of Bloomers or other bisected garment, has ever, in a number of attempts to foist them on the feminine public, made much, if any, headway.

In late years trousers, as a feature of feminine garb, have had a recognized place in the gymnasium, in the surf, in bicycle riding, and in equestrianism. They are usually accompanied with short skirts, but quite recently there has been a movement to do without even the abbreviated outer garment which was once thought necessary. It is not uncommon to see women bicyclers in Turkish trousers. English, French, and German women have within the last year or so worn, for mountain climbing in Switzerland, these same gathered trousers without the skirt. In London there has begun a movement among certain women of standing for the adoption of long-tailed coats and trousers in equestrianism. It is a proceeding important enough to have won attention from leading English fashion periodicals; but its eventual success must, of course, depend largely on time. For special occasions trousers have their use in woman's garb. Draperies, whatever hindrances to movement and health may lie in them, are sanctified by too many ages of use, too many traditions of beauty, too many sentiments, to be done wholly away without a complete revolution of feeling.

Alpine Costume.

Latterly it has been recognized that any change in woman's garb must paramountly consider beauty. In spite of their love of novelty, women in large things are radically conservative. To whatever is usual and accepted they adhere, and wisely. Therefore any system which does not provide also for conventional results will never take strong hold upon women's imaginations. There is, of course, the sort of unusualness of effect in dress which proceeds from the wearer's individuality. This, controlled with judgment, is altogether desirable; but to look oddly different from everybody else is not an ideal which commends itself.

A number of prominent advocates of reformation in woman's dress gave lately, in a periodical, their views as to what would constitute a correct and comfortable garb for women attending the World's Fair. Each of the costumes described manifestly secured to the wearer freedom of motion, the least possible weight, and such ease of mind as may be supposed to result from a body which is not bound with ligatures, nor trammelled with long skirts, nor made to sustain undue weight from the hips. Some of these had elements of beauty. The circling Figaro fronts, so becoming to the figure; kilted skirts, always composed and susceptible of graceful action; soft blouse fronts; adaptations of Turkish costumes; and many variations of modern vogues were developed in these gowns. Had they been a prevalent, or even an occasional feature of costumes at the Fair, it might have been judged that women were willing, for the sake of their health and comfort, to disregard conventionality, at least a little. The fact is that women refused to make themselves objects of marked notice by appearing in a street dress which so differed from ordinary garb as to leave the leg partly in evidence. The costumes described had short skirts, and short skirts are indeed defensible in garments designed for such a purpose as were these garments. But, as has been shown, rationality is no argument by which to protect that which is not a mode. Shorts skirts were "not worn." Therefore they were not to be considered.

There are " reform " garments which seem to conform sufficiently to the ordinary to make them popular. The system of union underwear, with the divided petticoat, and a gown fashioned in flowing lines, with the weight suspended from the shoulder, and having no suspicion of belt or ligature, is certainly to be commended on all hygienic grounds. But, unhappily, though the Venus de Medici might doubtless present a charming appearance in one of these semi-æsthetic, semi-hygienic arrangements, the average woman finds that with the loss of stays definite trimness has forever departed from her. Whether it was or was not an actually graceful, actually defensible trimness, does not matter. Something has gone, and she regrets it. At this point of the reformatory progress it is encouragingly suggested that the weak waist-muscles, limp from long ages of " lacing," demand exercise and development. There is no doubt that the body may be made at least to approach correct proportions. But women have not always time, opportunity, and patience for that physical culture which is unquestionably desirable, however little it can be depended upon to make a fat person of forty or so take on classic modelling.

A Greek Girl's Costume, showing the Chiton.

Greek fantasies of costume are absolutely not for our time, nor for our habits of life. Greek dress is constantly suggested by artists and reformers as the most beautiful and healthful apparel possible. In point of fact it is said by Professor Blümner that the greatest misconception exists as to what the ancient Greeks really wore. He states that the draperies of the female figures in the Parthenon are by no means typical of the actual costume of Hellas. According to his account Greek women wore, first, a short undergarment, then a close band called strophion, which corresponded to the modern corset, and was used to check excessive development of the breasts or to hold them up. Over this was worn the chiton, a fitted garment, reaching to the feet and bound with a girdle about the hips. The chiton was fastened down the front with hooks and eyes, and the long sleeves were secured by the same means. Instead of white, which one is accustomed to think usual in Greek dress, the ancients were fond

The Strophion.

waist-line itself be lifted. A shortening of the waist is both graceful and youthful. It also lends the figure height. In the modes of the Second Empire this lengthening of the skirt prevailed; but, oddly enough, when Second-Empire modes were reproduced some little time since, it was noticed that modistes preferred, while retaining the short-waisted effect, to do so without changing the actual waist-line as it exists in a well-corseted figure.

Natural structure ought at least not to be forsworn and forgotten, however curious the conceits of fashion which has hoop-skirted and pannièred and bunched and otherwise distorted the human figure to suit herself. It is always easy to preserve essential lines. Garb may follow ordinary conventions and yet be individual, and not in any way detrimental to health.

Monument of Hegeso, Daughter of Praxenos—Athens, about 400 B.C.
(Showing a lady in drapery attended by a slave in a shaped garment. From a bas-relief in the Boston Museum of Fine Arts.)

The question of textures must largely be a question of climate, of the variations of which man, by reason of of very bright colors and gay decoration, though in the classic period the tendency to gaudiness and display was somewhat checked.

That conventional dress should be close fitting does not necessarily imply that it should be agonizingly tight or painfully heavy. It generally does demand, it may be admitted, stays or some substitute for stays. A bodice wrinkling with every turn of the body is not beautiful. No lines can be trimly preserved unless there be some support, or unless the

1816.   Short Waist Effects.   1893.

clothing, is measurably independent. It is generally understood that heat is not produced by clothing, but only retained by it. The power of thus holding bodily heat depends less upon the substances of which stuffs are woven than upon the amount of air entangled in their meshes. To prevent the escape of heat a non-conducting medium is necessary; and air, like gaseous bodies in general, is a bad conductor. Woollen fabrics are warmer than cotton or linen because they are bad conductors of reasonable restraint of the waist-muscles need not be considered injurious,

The Pannier of 1870.

and weight is an inconsiderable matter in this age of fabrics woven with an express view of combining beauty, utility, and lightness.

The Hoop-skirt of 1864.

heat. From this same principle it is evident that two garments are warmer than one of the same material but double the thickness. The additional warmth is due to the intermediate layer of air, and it is said that the Chinese and Japanese have long since applied this knowledge in the use of many strata of garments made of the same material.

Whatever impedes circulation or wearies the muscles with unnecessary weight is, of course, distinctly undesirable in women's apparel, or in any one's apparel; but both of these injurious conditions are easily avoidable. A

The Hoop-skirt and Pannier, 1847.

The matter of Art in dress, it will be remembered, was violently agitated

192   *The Æsthetics of Dress.*

The Golden Stairs, by Burne-Jones, illustrating the Æsthetic Dress in Art.

some years ago when a number of enthusiastic young Englishmen, oppressed with the almost hopeless vulgarity of the decorative notions of their neighbors, banded themselves together with a design of doing something to ameliorate the lack of beauty in modern life. They believed that even in the face of conservatism and prejudice, English homes and English dress might be made more attractive. They regarded the gilt paper of the conventional drawing-room, its white marble mantel, glaring velvet carpet, tufted satin chairs, alabaster ornaments, and bulky pictureframes; they observed the baglike appearance of the gowns which the prevailing mode then dictated for women; and they told each other with just confidence that no revolution of decorative sentiment could possibly make these things any worse.

That they might be made, if only in a small way, somewhat better, they pledged themselves personally to eschew the use of articles which did not conform to the dictates of art; and upon this meagre foundation the edifice of modern æsthetism rose to the view of a wondering world. Instead of admiring, or at least respecting the efforts of the fervent devotees who were thus vowed to the regeneration of beauty, the world, after its first amazement, smiled broadly. Such directors of its dread laugh as Mr. Punch, assisted in making sport of the reformers.

Long-haired youths posed in attitudes after Fra Angelico, dishevelled ladies swaying fans of peacock feathers, were depicted with all the resources of caricature. Much was said in these times of the darkly sage-green drawing-rooms girt with blue delft and dados of water-fowls and strange things generally, in which the sad-visaged votaries of the new gospel took their melancholy pleasure. Intent on high designs, the band pursued its way bravely. But sooner or later ridicule kills; and the transitory flower of æsthetism soon gave its petals to the wind.

The movement lapsed from such overt manifestations as had brought attention upon it; but its effects were much more cogent than is commonly thought. For whatever absurdities in the way of decoration were perpetrated by the pre-Raphaelites, there was nevertheless in them that which also sanctified the vagaries of the Spanish gentleman who tilted at windmills—an idea, however misty, of ideals.

It was their special ignorance which gave the general impetus to Art knowledge. When so much was being said with every indication of authority about old Japanese ware, and Indian tissues and antique arms and illuminated parchment, people became ashamed not to know the difference between a pillow-cover done in Berlin wool and a piece of veritable Rhodian work. When Boticelli and Rossetti were confidently discussed, even the Philistines who sat by preparing to laugh when they should understand what it was all about, found themselves in need of at least cursorily examining the subtle figures which pervade the canvases of the one, and the rhythmic mysticism which glooms and shines upon the pages of the other.

The new art-league struck its strongest blow at conventionalism in apparel. It was indeed its abhorrence of the costume ideas then ruling English dress which aroused so much vituperative merriment on the part of the masses. The masses, it has been shown, will stand by national articles of attire at risk of life. No number of hare-brained reformers could persuade John Bull that his apparel was unbeautiful. The women of his large family are not notably independent, and though their feminine instinct for beauty had to acknowledge something fascinating in the soft fabrics, neutral tones, and flowing lines of the æsthetic costumes, they too, for the most part, left themselves, with a sense of virtuous irresponsibility, in the hands of the dress-makers, who went on mapping out side-forms and boning waists as if peplum effects had never been heard of.

Those few elect ladies who were in actual range of the inner circle took up, however, with passionate zeal, whatever novelties or resurrected antiquities of costume the masters of the movement advocated. For the first time in English history absolute individualism in dress was encouraged. By a really concerted action the bonds of fashion were broken and cast aside, and it remained to the Æsthetes to prove, if possible, that Art is a wiser and kinder mistress than the Mode. The pre-Raphaelites ardently took up the study of personality—a study which, virtually originating with them, has not

Peplum Effects.

been without effect even upon the arbiters of our present vogues.

Félix has recently stated that it is his invariable rule in composing a costume to ask himself not only how it would appear to the eyes of the next century, but if the harmony between garb and wearer is maintained. The principle of individualism in dress was one which naturally enough appealed more forcibly to women who were plain than to those who were beautiful. It has long been an established dictum of the average mind that pretty women may wear what they will, and this dictum contains also the tacit reservation that ugly women have less liberty of choice. There are women, however, of art and story, who rise almost above the plane even of beauty by the magical force of a perfectly expressed personality. This sense of material and spiritual correspondences even the poets have caught at. Vivien in her robe of priceless samite, so clinging that it half expressed that sinuous shape of hers; Guinevere riding through the summer sunshine clad in grass-green silk and bearing a tuft of like-colored plumes; the Princess Ida, robed to the feet in her silken-hooded academy gown of serious lilac zoned with gold; these women are marvellously developed by their apparel.

In even a subtler way those priests of art to whom the Æsthetes vowed special faith expressed by dress the spiritual quality of their subjects. This is notable in a certain Madonna of Botticelli's—a sweet, mysterious creature whose childlike head is bowed with the weight of an incomprehensible blessing and burden. There is no maternal feeling in that forlorn, fair face. She does not pretend to know why this great awe has come upon her. She does not know anything except that an hour ago she was young, filled with the common happiness of life, musing upon a future that should lie among the blossoms and thorns of ordinary things. And now an angel has spoken. She will never be young any more forever, or glad—except, indeed, when this first terrible strangeness is past, it were with that marvellous blessedness the Voice promised. But whether it come or not, there is still a knotted heaviness of hair upon her neck. The coif of finely wrought lawn rests daintily, almost coquettishly, upon her bowed head. A length of soft silk falls against the bosom. That little struggling human effort for beauty which speaks in her attire, helps to unravel the secret

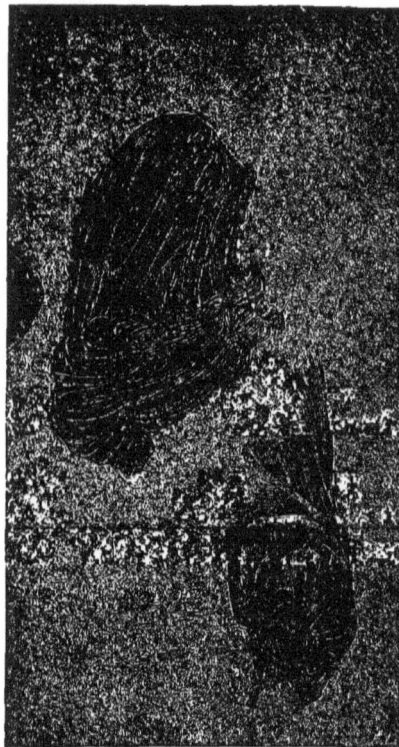

Study of Drapery. From a drawing by Burne-Jones.

in her face—the mystery written there of a nature oppressed with a benediction beyond its understanding or desire.

The wisest of those who were swayed by pre-Raphaelitism distrusted very often and very judiciously their own powers of personal analysis. They preferred rather than their own judgment the judgment of the high-priests of Art, and rather than design raiment for themselves they sought out, in galleries of paintings, types which they more or less resembled and whose garbs they studied. Many were the old canvases which yielded up suggestions for modern costumes. Angels and ministers of grace, saints, martyrs, madonnas, contributed their share of costume-suggestion to the time. The madness for art clothes rose to an unparalleled height, and having reached the zenith it discovered in itself that germ of decay which the newest systems must always contain. After a number of years of adherence to the lowest of tones, the most flowing of lines, and the most unconventional of effects, it dawned slowly but surely upon the followers—especially the less beautiful followers of the new creed—that Fashion, however exacting, is really a more merciful ruler than Art.

Fashion is charitable to human failings. She never presents a mode which is restricted to one expression. She balances one effect with its extreme, so that the biggest of big hats never appears to the delight of tall women but that the tiny capote accompanies it for women who do not in respect to height resemble the daughters of the gods. On the other hand, Art cares only for beauty or for those peculiar and suggestive types which are more valuable to her than beauty itself. It is obvious that the slender, the youthful, the uncommon woman will look particularly well in clinging garb of Pompeiian red, dull blue, or faded green, girdled with dull silver below the bosom and furnished out with sweeping lengths of sleeve draperies; but any similar arrangement upon the comfortably built matron, the elderly woman, or the small, plump girl, is as obviously impracticable. Besides the more important question of art effect, it became gradually clear enough that art gowns lacked the essential element of utility. They were well enough for occasions of leisure and *fête*, but not for practical life. Whatever her whims, practicality is usually a consideration of Fashion. She has, indeed, designed street gowns with trains, and in her time commanded the use of winter garments of thin muslin; but in her commoner and later manifestations she remembers daily uses and makes it possible for the business woman to be clad according to the modes which convention directs and still be able to attend to her affairs without the consciousness of being unfittingly or inconveniently dressed. Vogue seldom considers the few, but more commonly the many. The lithe young figure may go stayless, girdleless, swathed from head to foot in loose vestments of strange cut. This is Art's province. But Fashion, smiling a little amiable disdain upon the fresh face and *svelte* shape, asks herself what this lady needs whose cheeks are sinking, whose muscles need sustainment, whose angles demand concealment. An idea of the greatest good to the greatest number is admitted to be just, and as to the pretty women!—the frame is not important when the picture has in it that which rivets the eye.

It may be judged, therefore, that "gowns which would paint" did not prevail over gowns which were prescribed by the modes simply because they were undeserving such a victory. Their vogue was for a day and for a clique. They had their part in awakening women to a better idea of colors and textures, and to a sense of personal characteristics. These important features of æsthetic movement in apparel have remained with us to modify the proceedings of Fashion, for she is always ready to take new ideas. The contrasts of an autumn woodland, the shimmer of a green sea, the changing green of wind-smitten grass, all appeal to her and impress her. And in winnowing out of the great heap of pre-Raphaelite chaff such grain as had actual value and substance, Fashion showed her willingness to be taught and her intelligence in selection.

Fabrics became infinitely more beautiful, designs, instead of being mere meaningless repetitions of spots and dashes and lines and flower-conceits, began to develop some sense of motive in their patterns. It would be difficult in these times to come upon a really ugly textile from any celebrated loom. Color combinations are rare, exquisite, and various; and being really beautiful, instead of only temporarily interesting, the fabrics of the last dozen years, especially in the softer silks and woollens, have a value which the change of styles cannot greatly affect.

We are constantly told that the fashions into which we shape these textiles for our own adornment are alone ugly enough to spoil the most exquisite stuff ever produced. It may not be beyond our province to give a little unprejudiced thought to the subject of recent

Street Gown with Train, 1876.   In Sixteenth Century.   In 1806.

modes, with a view to their positive qualities, whether ill or good.

Women are constantly confronted by statements concerning the radical badness and foolishness of the fashions to which they surrender themselves. These statements are variously humorous, persuasive, or contemptuous, according as the point of view is that of men, reformers, or painters. No one listens seriously to the first. Men have been having their fling at women's costume ever since the twelfth century or thereabouts. They have been equally ready to double with disdainful laughter, whether the "animal fond of finery" has swept the streets with long petticoats, has worn Bloomers, or followed the masculine vogue so closely that only the undivided skirt differentiates a tailor-made gown from a man's habit. It is manifest that such facility of light sarcasm is not to be trusted to point the way of truth.

Iron Corset of the Sixteenth Century.

It must rest with every woman to decide if the appealing or imperative voice of those who, in a wilderness of stays and bones and biases and ligatures, cry out upon these evils as detrimental to the physical welfare of born and unborn generations, is any worthier of consideration. So wise and just a critic as Mrs. Oliphant has spoken with her usual moderation of the impracticable character of almost all projects of clothes reform. She has much to say of the "learned folly of classicism" as applied to those who would have us wear Greek draperies, the Indian ayah's garb, or the wrapper-like dress of the Japanese woman. In commenting upon these various clothes suggestions she adds the succinct statement that "Fashion herself is not so wild as the critics and reformers of Fashion."

Waist-belt and stays are radically the point of divergence between those who walk after the flesh and those who would fain snatch the flesh from the bondage of the world. It is most insulting to women to argue against stays upon the germinal idea that the survival of these baleful articles is solely a matter of vanity. Women must indeed be irrational and worthy the disdain of the most merciless misogynist if, since the early ages of creation, she has wilfully clung, from motives of pure vanity, to an arrangement which is said to be calculated to defeat the very ends toward which vanity strives. There can be no beauty without health. If it is also true that there can be no health with stays, it is a matter of simple deduction, since stays or waist-belts or girdles have always been a feature of feminine costume, that therefore there is not, nor has ever been, any beauty among women. That stays have been misused by ignorant women is past doubt. That their use has actually a hygienic basis, has lately been set forth in an English periodical, by two English scientists of sufficient note to make their opinions worth considering.

These men call attention to the fact that abdominal pressure, or any constriction of the waist, increases the amount of blood placed at the disposal of muscles, skin, and brain. They state, too, that this increased supply of blood, on which the activity of the tissues so greatly depends, may be obtained without serious interference with the nutrition of the organs that fill the abdominal cavity. The muscles about the abdomen having no bone framework, contract involuntarily

Corset of the Period of Louis XIV.

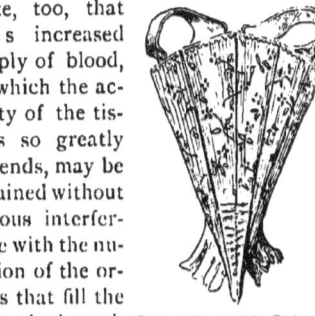
Slashed Corset of the Eighteenth Century.

The Grotesque in Dress in 1795.

during physical exertion. The action of these, even in the healthiest savage, is assisted rather than opposed by a belt. That all peoples have recognized this principle of the girdle their records show. The tombs and temples of ancient Egypt disclose figures clasped about with close, broad belts. We know that the Jews and Phœnicians recognized the office of the girdle. With Arab tribes children are belted in from earliest infancy. Professor Robertson Smith relates that among Bedouins a loosening of the girdle is regarded as a

In the Time of Marie Antoinette.

sign of dissolute character. And the fashion of binding themselves tightly with bandages is known to have prevailed among Greek and Roman women. The efficacy of waist constriction in promoting physical and mental endurance is apparently regarded even by the peasants of our own day; since we are told that the women of this class, in France, Switzerland, and Hungary, wear stays during hours of labor and remove them in time of leisure.

In the Grecian-bend Period.

If these statements are accurate the modern crusade against stays would appear not to be justified. The much-vexed question of wearing them, since it seems to be hygienically defensible, would perhaps better be left entirely to individual taste. Some women look better without them. Individualism in dress must decide the problem. If a trim effect is desirable, stays or some substitute for stays must aid in producing it. If slimness and sinuosity are characteristics of the figure, the girdle should not be an affair of bones, but slim and sinuous also, a mere drooping line about the hips or below the bosom.

The last class given by nature to the aspersion of fashion's notions is the class which looks in humanity for models. Art gowns have their vogue, and still have their place. Their specific success for afternoon and evening wear in this year of grace is the result of their general failure a dozen or more years since.

In the face of criticism both witty and hostile, conventionality has gone on arranging and varying women's garb from season to season. That there have been styles deserving both laughter and contempt, no one who has cast an eye over old fashion plates will attempt to deny. That the modes of late years have lacked beauty, artistic proportion, and comfort when rationally followed, would be hard to prove. The Parisian designers by whom modes are made, or at least directed, are not whimsical imbeciles as likely to produce effects which shall deform as those which shall beautify. Though usually supposed to be despots, these men and women know better than to use tyrannous power to their own undoing. Their office is decorative. Like all great law-makers, they know how to make the laws themselves pliant. The woman is not required to conform to the mode, but the mode to the woman.

For a number of years there has been in the costume ideas coming from these departments of art, a distinct and ever distincter regard for the principles of sincerity, simplicity, and unity. Fashion is based upon geometry; and the value of lines is considered and must be considered by those who design clothes. That perpendicular lines give height, and horizontal lines breadth, are facts generally recognized by the humblest seamstress who makes children's cotton frocks. That a straight line is the shortest distance between two points is the simple fact which was perhaps negatively considered in the conception of the gracefully flaring skirts of recent modes. Whatever clings to the figure produces an effect of meagreness and a reduction of height. Whatever flows out from the waist, producing oblique lines by elongating the range over which the eye travels, invariably increases the illusion of height. All divisions in way of skirt trimmings, if placed across this range, assist in taking away from the general effect of height. On the contrary, all longitudinal arrangements of trimming which carry the vision in sweeping curves

Perpendicular Lines. 1889.

Horizontal and Oblique Lines. 1894.

from shoulder to hip, give both slenderness and height.

Breadth of decorative arrangement at the bosom lends slimness to the waist; and width of sleeve also conduces to this result. In like manner, whatever combines to give the throat

Breadth of Decorative Arrangement in 1830.

slightness and length, enhances the curves of the bust and the correct carriage of the head. Such effects as these have for a number of years been specially and notably provided for in established fashions; nor have these fashions been so unbending and rigorous but that they have readily lent themselves to every personal variance of æsthetic need.

The human form is intensely expressive. It is clear enough that garments which are left altogether to the judgment of the town dress-maker, who provides herself with a dozen late fashion-plates and religiously adheres to the authoritative trimmings and cuts displayed in these, cannot possibly fulfil the conditions of that beauty which depends, as we have agreed, on harmony between wearer and garb. Only the masters of the craft of dress, with perhaps here and there a disciple

having a natural genius for this perception of relations, can tell at a glance what are the essential traits, mental and temperamental, of the woman to be gowned, and what therefore the dress must be. It is a more delicate thing, indeed, this perception of relations, than a mere knowledge that certain lines and certain colors mean certain effects. For the woman in those numerous walks of life which do not lead with pleasing annual sameness to the doors of the great ones who sit sublime above the fashions, there is no rule so commendable as that which impresses the need of self-comprehension. "Know thyself;" for otherwise it is impossible to know what to wear. The secret of individualism once unravelled, remains a definite guide through all the mists and clouds and uncertainties of changing modes. It is the spell which makes the medley of sleeves and collars and skirts and

In 1835.

draperies cohere as if they were integral parts of the whole, and not scattered elements which have been arbitrarily put together in a certain way because there was custom for it, or what is worse, a lack of custom. For individuality in dress is by no means the same thing as that which is usually meant by the term originality.

Originality is indeed a very indefinite term. It commonly carries an idea of some newness of system whose originator has been indifferent or defiant toward existing laws, and has wilfully produced a result of singularity and oddity. Singularity and oddity may perhaps be defended in dress upon the ground of announcing the existence of these traits in the wearer, but eccentricity in its ordinary acceptance of meaning is not an effect to be desired.

The style of dress which is described as picturesque is generally better adapted to use after it has passed through the alembic of the conventional mode. Picturesqueness implies something lawless. Wildness and irregularity have come to be attached to the implications of this word. To leap the rotten pales of prejudice may be a noble and heroic enterprise. It is believed, however, that in matters of dress, what is correct and therefore not calculated to startle observation, will generally be adhered to by women of good taste. Simplicity, one of the primary regulations of all æsthetics, is not incompatible with extreme elegance; but the commendable tendency of the times and the advice of the best modistes is toward concealment rather than ostentation. So that we have simple wool frocks lined with fine silk, a bit of rare lace rather than yards of a cheaper quality; one priceless clasp of plainly set jewels instead of a predominating glitter of wealth.

So with sincerity. If anything in æsthetics can be said to be demonstrable is that cause must always be adequate to effect. The futility of trying to produce results which are utterly inconsistent with the nature of the material employed, can hardly be too strongly insisted upon. Stuffs which seem to be what they are not, fringes of different color and texture from the stuffs they trim, ribbon bows which are set without obvious purpose upon a garment, thin materials made up over heavy linings, heavy materials made up with an airy disregard of weight—whatever, in short, is inherently false is openly bad.

Unity in costume is also most important, resting the eye as it does with an effect of order in design. There is dignity and composure in a gown which is the expression of one idea faithfully considered and consistently carried out.

In view of any fashion it is well always to remember that its first representation or embodiment had a meaning. Sometimes, through a lack of intelligence in applying the modes which are presented, the costumer produces results altogether ugly and frivolous. For the sentiment of the thing must be understood, or the result will be simply vulgarity and foolishness.

To understand one's looks, to accept the hints of the mode and wisely to adapt the fashions to personal uses, would seem to comprise all such regulations for attire as can be compiled in little for the intelligent woman. Not hygiene, art, or convention is all; but each is to be considered. When these elements are in judicious proportion, and all so subordinated to the whole personal effect that, as clothes they shall seem merely to array the wearer "in modesty and honor," then indeed apparel may be said to have attained its best development.

In face of all arguments against the fashions of our day it may be said that, honestly viewing their worst features in comparison with details of the vogues which have swayed other ages, the most pessimistic of those spirits which periodically, and often unjudgedly, utter their lamentations against modern women's folly and perversity of attire, must certainly own that we have reached a state of raiment as nearly ideal as the nature of things permits.

Fin de Siècle.

VI.

DRESS FROM A PRACTICAL STANDPOINT.

VI.

DRESS FROM A PRACTICAL STANDPOINT.

By SEVERAL WRITERS.

Dress for Infants.
Dress for Young Children.
Dresses for School Girls.
Dresses for Adults.
Wraps, Bonnets, and Hats.
Underwear.
Boots, Shoes, and Slippers.
Accessories of Dress.

Wedding Trousseau.
Furs.
Mourning.
The Care of Clothes.
Dressing on an Allowance.
Millinery at Home.
Dressmaking at Home.
Schools for Dressmaking and Millinery.

WHETHER the human race was intended by nature to be naked or clothed; whether civilization, in putting man into garments, has not merely shifted the chains of his bondage; whether the male sex in sloughing off that instinct for personal decoration which a few centuries ago characterized men as well as women, and which is still distinctive of the lower orders of male creation, has not proven itself the superior of woman; just how much the progress of woman, with a capital W, has been impeded by petticoats — all these are interesting matters for discussion—in another place. In this place the topic must be dress, considered not from the standpoint of the sociologist or the artist, but from the practical standpoint of the utilitarian, of the woman who either makes her own clothes or who directs responsibly the often incompetent seamstress, whose periodical appearance in the home marks the procession of the equinoxes as unerringly as does the almanac.

If I were asked to define a heroine I should be tempted to say, "An educated American woman who wears gowns that she has made herself." This is not because the educated American woman could not achieve gowns lacking nothing of the *cachet* of the French atelier if she gave her whole mind to it. It is only because the mind of the educated American woman is so split up by a diversity of interests, from political equality to to-day's luncheon, that, while she loves good clothes with an integral enthusiasm, she finds an exceedingly small share of her working force available for their construction. And when to this problem must be added those special problems that come with limited means, when the work of creation must be carried on within the circumference of a dollar, why, then the situation is one worthy of all the brains and all the resources of the American woman. It is for this woman, the woman whose practised eye must survey the entire feminine family wardrobe from boots to bonnets, and through whose fingers, whether practised or not, must pass all the money and much of the material that goes into the family garments, that these pages are prepared. If this heroine finds herein aught of direct suggestion or indirect helpfulness, "I shall," in the humble words of The - Person - Who - Writes - a - Preface, "have had my reward."

It may be well to say at the outset that it is clearly impossible in an article of this kind to state prices with absolute exactness, as these vary from season to season, and yet, since there is but little difference from time to time in the price of such staples as muslin and flannel and silk, the prices given may be safely taken as approaching closely enough to the current ones not to impair the value of the estimates.

DRESS FOR INFANTS.

To begin the practical discussion of dress in the order in which nature makes it necessary to us, these general principles are first to be laid down in regard to the layette. Next to the right of being well born, a baby has the right to be rationally dressed, and no baby is rationally dressed whose garments in any way impede the involuntary muscular activity, which is the first instinct of a healthy child. The old-fashioned wardrobe for children, consisting of flannel bands, tiny cold linen shirts, pinning blanket, skirts, and slips, all fastened with innumerable pins, has very properly, in these days of hygienic enlightenment, been laid aside in favor of simple unified garments that provide a maximum of protection at a minimum of discomfort, and in no way interfere with the vital action of the body. Almost any mother with a proper instinct for comfort and a pair of scissors can herself devise little garments entirely suited to the needs of any baby by bearing in mind the first two laws of baby rights—that all parts of the baby's body must be equally clothed, and that all garments must hang from the shoulders. But it is always helpful to know where others have trod in the same way, and so it will be of undoubted service to give here the main principles of the two best-known reform costumes for babies —the Gertrude and the Dorothy suits. The Gertrude suit is the device of the united intellects of a mother and a physician-father, trying to give their own little one a fair chance at life from the start. This suit at the time of its invention offered many innovations. To begin with, there is no band compressing the abdomen and chest. The navel is dressed only "with a pad of absorbent cotton and a light band held by two pins, just enough to retain the navel dressing to be used only so long as the navel dressing needs to be applied." This is the advice of Dr. Grosvenor, the originator of the suit. As to the danger of rupture and shapelessness in discarding the band, "Nonsense!" says the author. "Nature does not do her work in any such careless way. . . . It is bandaged babies who rupture." Next the skin is worn a single garment made either of the choicest Canton flannel or of Jaeger all-wool stockinget, exquisitely fine and soft, "cut princess, reaching from the neck to ten inches (twenty-five inches long) below the feet, with sleeves to the wrist, and having all the seams smooth and the hems at neck, wrist, and bottom on the outside, the latter turned over once and felled or cat-stitched with silk, the garment fastened by a tie and one button behind. Here you have a complete fleece-lined garment, comfortable and healthful, and one that can be washed without shrinking. The next garment is made of baby flannel, also cut princess, in the same pattern, only one-half inch larger, reaching from the neck to twelve or fourteen inches below the feet, so as to cover the other, with generous arm-holes pinked or scalloped, and with two buttons behind at the neck." There is no objection to the ordinary baby dress, except that the originator of this suit recommends that it be only thirty inches to a yard in length. He, however, prefers the baby dress in princess cut to match the other garments. These three garments are put together before dressing, sleeve within sleeve, and then put over the little one's head at once, buttoned behind and the baby is dressed, there being but one pin—the diaper-pin—in the entire costume. The night dressing consists simply of a gown like the undergarment of the suit, only a little longer, made of Canton flannel or of Jaeger wool, and the ordinary diaper. As to the diaper, Dr. Grosvenor by no means recommends the old-fashioned linen, or even cotton diaper, but prefers Canton flannel as being softer, warmer, and more absorbent than anything else. These diapers are of two sizes, 18 by 18 and 10 by 10 inches, the larger to be folded across diagonally to an even-edged triangle.

The insertion of the smaller one where most needed saves the heat and discomfort of unnecessary thickness over the hips and kidneys, and has the advantage of reducing the size of pieces for washing.

Three changes of Dorothy suits are usually sufficient.

The Dorothy garments are made of the Jaros hygienic wool in very much the same pattern as the other, particular attention being paid by the manufacturer of these to the beauty as well as to the healthfulness of the wardrobe. Mrs. Jenness Miller's baby daughter, Vivian, wore from her birth the Dorothy garments, and the following explanation of them, given by Mrs. Miller, will be of interest: "For the first two weeks of my baby's life she wore the band until the navel healed, but no longer. After that her wardrobe consisted of one little princess slip of silk flannel, high-necked and long-sleeved, thirty inches in length. Another garment in silk flannel, without sleeves, was thirty-two inches in length, and her little dimity and nainsook dresses were thirty-six inches long. Her diapers were absorbing Jersey cloth, which I find far better and warmer than linen. For very cold days I add to the above a very fine-ribbed wool undervest, in preference to outside jacket and pinning blankets. Everything is of flannel and perfectly loose. The result of this kind of clothing is absolute health; a more vital and muscular child of three months could not be found in the United States."

The advantages of this method of dressing babies ought to be instantly clear to every mother, providing, as it does—

(1) Perfect freedom to all thoracic, abdominal, and pelvic organs.

(2) That all the clothing shall hang from the shoulders.

(3) The greatest saving of the time and strength of the mother in caring for the child.

(4) The evenness of the covering of the body, there being the same covering over the shoulders as elsewhere.

For those mothers, however, who prefer the older method there are knitted shirts, in silk and wool, with high necks and long sleeves, and buttoning down the front. These are of very moderate cost and well suited to their purpose. The conventional wardrobe for a baby is also to be found in the shops, lacking a little, perhaps, in the extreme daintiness which only the love of the mother can give to a garment, but so cheap as to make the mother feel that nothing but the delight she gets from it justifies her in making the tiny wardrobe herself. Outside dresses are made of cambric or linen, very simply, and can be bought for from sixty-five cents upward. Nainsook and batiste are pretty for finer wear. Simply trimmed slips, in these finer materials, can be bought ready made for one dollar and upward. Either cotton or linen diaper can be used, the linen being preferable to the cotton. A good supply is two pieces of linen diaper, eighteen inches wide, costing one dollar and seventy-five cents a piece; two pieces, twenty inches wide, at a shilling more a piece; and one piece, twenty-two inches wide, costing two dollars a piece. The cotton diaper costs from sixty to eighty cents a piece.

Flannel shawls, about thirty inches square, can be bought from seventy-five cents upward. The baby may have three flannel wrappers made on short yokes, which may be embroidered with a little dot or flower. Ready made, they can be found at a dollar and fifty cents upward. The long outdoor cloak can be made of silk, if desired, and interlined with wool; but it is more serviceable if made of cashmere or Bedford cord. Cloaks can be bought ready made from about five dollars upward. Ready-made socks and bootees cost from twenty cents up to one dollar a pair. Bibs from fifteen cents upward. French nainsook caps from forty cents upward. In winter, a cap of silk or cashmere, interlined with white lambs' wool, will be required. These can be bought for from one dollar and fifty cents upward.

The bassinet for holding the baby's layette may be made of a hamper basket, which can be bought untrimmed for about five dollars, and wadded and lined with silk and muslin to suit the taste of the mother. Some of the prettiest layette baskets, however, that I have ever seen were not made out of the expensive hampers intended for that purpose, but were made of small clothes-baskets, daintily lined with cambric and covered with muslin. Still another even prettier one, which had a cover, was made by an ingenious young mother from a champagne hamper, which she had bought at the grocer's for twenty-five cents. And while we are on the subject of baskets, we may as well tell of the ingenious device of another young mother who made her baby's crib out of a large-sized clothes-basket, softly wadded throughout, and making as dear a little nest for Baby Bunting to sleep in as the most marvellous Lohengrin swan ever made out of white enamel and brass.

Dress for Young Children.

The dress of young children has quite as important hygienic aspects as the dress of babies. It is the first right of the child to be comfortable; whether he looks well or not is a small matter to him. Mrs. Frances Hodgson Burnett was probably the first mother to exploit the decorative possibilities of children in the home. It was the golden curls and velvet doublet of Little Lord Fauntleroy that first gave young women with artistic instincts and pretty little children something to think of; and, other things being equal, picturesqueness in the child's costume is well worth considering and achieving. But health should come first. If the graceful and artistic knickerbockers are worn in cold weather by boys, the lower limbs should be carefully clad in long drawers and protected besides by cloth or leather leggings for out-doors. The little girl's skirts should not be so long as to make running difficult or give the little back too great a weight to carry. The big hat should not be heavy with trimming, neither should it be so warm as to overheat the brain, nor so insufficient as not to protect the head. Above all, the neck and sleeves of gowns should not be sacrificed for any effect, no matter how picturesque, nor should the short English stockings leave the upper half of the leg bare even in warm weather. A principle most important to remember in dressing children is to distribute the covering evenly over the body. The loss of vitality in resisting cold in any exposed part is too great to be unattended with danger. The underwear of children should be of wool the year through, if possible, and should cover the body from neck to ankle. The Jaeger and Jaros underwear are somewhat expensive, but are exquisitely soft and are endured by the most sensitive skin. The shirts for a child of four years cost about two dollars; the union garment about twice as much. For children who have any hereditary tendency to weak lungs this underwear is especially desirable, as it is double-breasted. Other knit underwear, in wool and cotton or silk and wool, is to be recommended, and is to be bought at all shops for prices varying from fifty cents to five dollars. Underwaists for children can be bought for fifty cents apiece; but they are simple to make at home, and two yards of twill at fourteen cents a yard will make four. Plain tucked drawers can be bought for twenty-five cents apiece, the price rising as the decoration is elaborated. A child should have eight or ten pairs at least. Pride of the West is a very serviceable muslin for drawers, and a yard for a pair is a fair estimate. Flannel skirts for winter and for cool summer days are necessary. These may be knitted or made of flannel bought for the purpose, embroidered or plain. Ready made, they can be bought for from seventy-five cents to two dollars. Domestic cambric, at about twelve and one-half cents a yard, is best for children's petticoats, and the heavy laces are more suitable to trim them than embroidery, unless the latter is hand wrought on the fabric of the skirt. Ready-made skirts can be bought for from fifty cents upward. It is well, however, in the case of children, and of adults too, for that matter, to consider the advantages of clothing the legs with more warmth and wearing fewer skirts. This plan has several advantages. Drawers are easier to launder than skirts, much more warmth is afforded with less weight, and much greater protection from the sudden changes in temperature is secured. One mother makes drawers, summer and winter, for her little girls, and herself as well, out of that fleecy cotton fabric known as outing flannel. A pair of these is worn in summer with one twilled muslin petticoat. In winter they wear Jaeger underwear, one pair of outing-flannel drawers, and still one petticoat, this time of soft flannel. The soft, loose texture of outing flannel makes it specially grateful during the heat of summer, as it quickly absorbs moisture and never chills the body. Nightgowns made of this also are excellent for children, either in the robe, the princess, or the drawers pattern, both for summer and winter. For restless children the drawers pattern is to be preferred, or the robe nightgown, cut very long, and stitched together at the bottom like a bag, so that there is no danger of the child's becoming uncovered at night. The ordinary muslin nightgown for children can be made of Berkeley muslin at twenty cents a yard; two and one-half yards is enough; ready made, they cost from one dollar upward. Good cotton stockings for children, in black and colors, can be bought for from thirty cents upward; woollen ones usually cost twice as much. Children's shoes cost from one dollar and a half upward, in russet as well as black. In buying shoes for children two points especially should be observed. First, that the shoe is quite long enough, and second, that it fits closely in the heel. The former will promote comfort and the shapeliness of the feet, and the latter, more than anything else, will prevent the undue wearing out of the heels of stockings.

A little girl needs ten or twelve dresses. The materials for these may be of cotton, soft wool, or simple silk for best, varied to suit the season.

Ginghams and percales are the most satisfactory in cotton for ordinary wear in summer, with nainsooks and batiste for occasions. In winter, soft-wool goods, in solid colors, such as the cashmeres and plain diagonal, or in tiny stripes and checks, are most suitable, with India or surah silk for finer wear. In the matter of little girls' dresses it is a great economy to make them at home, as the cost of ready-made dresses is about twice the actual cost. A short double-breasted coat for out-door wear in ordinary weather should be made of French flannel, with one of Bedford cord or serge for best. Dress hats are of leghorn or chip, while the rough straws are prettiest for everyday. Daintiest of all are the shirred hats in lawn, white, of solid color, with shirred brims, and perhaps little falls of lace about the face. Felt hats or velvet or silk bonnets are best for winter. In winter the long coat should be of some cloth as heavy as beaver, or, if of a lighter cloth, it should then be interlined with lambs' wool. A caution here to be observed is against making children's coats too heavy. A little child often carries about in a garment a weight heavy enough to tire it out, and warm enough to make the body especially susceptible to cold. Always resist the temptation to dress a child too finely. Elaboration does not belong to childhood, and no better comment on the lack of taste or judgment in the mother can be set forth than an over-dressed, fussy-looking little child.

DRESSES FOR SCHOOL-GIRLS.

The same caution applies quite as much to the dress of young girls in school, whose clothing should be tasteful and substantial, but simple to the verge of plainness. A little miss busy with her studies will need two dresses for school alone. Fine wool goods for winter and cotton for milder weather are dedicated to such purposes. A piece of wool goods that will turn, and even one that will wash, is most desirable. Serge and the soft-wool diagonal are invaluable for such purposes. Good serges can be bought for from one dollar to two dollars per yard, and diagonals, in plaids and stripes, for about the same. Five to seven yards of yard-wide goods is generally enough. Nothing more elaborate in the way of decoration than fancy braids or velvet or ribbon bands should be permitted on such gowns. Two or three—four at the most—other dresses for Sunday and occasional wear, such as parties, dancing-school, etc., should be made of cashmere, challie, India silk, or some other inexpensive material, trimmed with ribbon or lace, but not too elaborately. For summer wear, crisp, cool ginghams, percales, lawns, and nainsooks are better than anything else. Good percale can usually be bought for a shilling a yard. Ginghams, lawns, and nainsooks for from twenty-five to forty cents. Wash shirt-waists cost from sixty cents upward. The best make of cheviot shirts cost from two to three dollars, but these will outwear any number of lighter ones. Chambray waists cost about half as much. Any of these with serge skirt or jacket will be most serviceable for all kinds of summer wear, and are especially suited for travelling. A winter coat for a young girl can be bought from ten dollars upward, and a lighter wrap for spring for six dollars upward. Hats for misses cost, suitably trimmed, from four and five dollars upward, and no hat costing more than eight or ten dollars is admissible for a young girl.

DRESSES FOR ADULTS.

Mrs. Harrison, in her delightful chapter in this book, has set forth the dicta of the best taste and the best people in regard to special dress for special occasions, and Mrs. McGlasson has discussed the æsthetic principles that should guide one in the selection of this one individual part of one's self. It only remains for this paper to point out such general truths and rules as, sifted down out of the universal experience of woman-kind, have proven themselves particularly serviceable. Any woman, young or old, not an invalid nor a business woman, with an ordinary and sufficient number of duties to perform in a day, needs for her wardrobe the following number of gowns: First, the street dress; second, a house dress, not a wrapper; third, a simple house dress, also not a wrapper, for morning wear during house duties; fourth, a dress for calling, afternoon teas, etc.; fifth, a dress for small dinners, informal evenings, etc.; and last, an evening dress or more, if her taste or surroundings draw her to evening entertainments.

The first of these she will wear on the great majority of occasions that call her into the street, such as shopping, going to matinées, church, travelling, making informal calls. This costume must be of cloth for the winter, simply made and without decorations. If a coat be added, making a complete costume, so much the better. There is no hesitation in saying that for all these purposes a tailor-made suit is the best. The only drawback to a tailor-made suit is its first cost. There is no use trying to make a tailor product by home talent, and there is no compromising with a tailor who furnishes the materials for less than sixty or seventy-five dollars. Many tailors charge double this price for some supposed special excellence in cut or finish. But an excellent costume of three pieces—skirt, waistcoat, and coat—lined throughout with silk, and of exquisite fit and finish, ought to be obtained for seventy-five dollars. There is no doubting the real economy of such a suit as this. It is light, graceful, easily kept fresh, and with occasional repairing at the hands of the maker will last three or even

House Dress Modelled on a Dutch Costume.

four seasons, especially if a second-best tailor suit be kept for marketing, rainy days, and the occasions that are most trying to good clothes.

The house dress should be of cloth or silk, with a little more elaboration than for the street, to be worn afternoons and in the house when one is not entertaining. The morning dress for the house will need to be of simple cloth, such as cashmere, mohair, with cotton for summer. A calling or carriage dress will be of cloth, made with silk or velvet, and trimmed with fur, lace, passementeries, or whatever the present mode suggests. It should include a handsome wrap, and there must be donned with it a becoming bonnet and dainty gloves, for any occasion demanding more than the ordinary silk dress, such as an afternoon tea, ladies' luncheon, and formal calls. The fifth gown should be of silk, not India or surah, dark or light, plain or fancy, made and decorated as the prevailing mode suggests. For a woman of moderate means and social proclivities, or of too slender figure, this gown may be made high in the neck and with elbow sleeves; the bodice should have a garniture of lace, or of something equally dressy, and the skirt should be slightly trained. With this gown gloves and flowers may be worn, and such jewels as best fit the fashion of the garment and the occasion. It is proper to wear this gown at any evening function where full evening dress is not necessary. The evening dress should be more elaborate than any of the others, of light-colored silk or satin, or of some diaphanous material, as chiffon or tulle, if the dress be dark in color. The neck of this gown should be low, or half low, even if it be necessary to drape a somewhat angular outline in soft lace, and the sleeves should not reach below the elbow. This evening dress may be as elaborate as one's taste dictates, or as severe as one's beauty warrants; but it must evidence the most scrupulous thought and care in all its details and its adaptation to the wearer. In small towns, where the entertainings are of a much less formal nature than in the large towns, it is possible to dispense with this evening dress, wearing in its place the silk gown designed for dinner, especially if this be made of light or parti-colored fabrics. For summer wear nothing is so serviceable to take the place of the tailor-made costume for ordinary wear as a good quality of surah or India silk in a dark or neutral tint and simply made. Such a silk as this is inexpensive, cool, easy to keep clean, and will wear well with ordinary care. For travelling and light purposes it is unsurpassed, and when it is outworn as a frock, the remnants of it make good blouse waists and petticoats. With this number of gowns a woman may feel herself smartly and suitably dressed for any occasion, from a club meeting to a christening party, though she may, and probably will, add to its number certain crisp linens or prints for summer wear and dainty silk blouses to wear with the tailor skirt and coat for cooler summer weather, and a wrapper or two, and perhaps a tea-gown. All these things will add to her comfort and her complacency, but, with the exception of the

Tea-Gown

wrapper, are hardly to be counted as necessities.

It now remains to discuss the other gown which is absolutely essential for those women whom necessity calls out of their homes every day, in all weathers, into an office, or a shop, or a place of business—that large and constantly increasing class known as professional or business women. Such a woman needs a business dress, and the requisites of the business dress are comfort, fitness, health, and gentility. Such a dress must be made, whether for summer or winter, of material that will stand dampness and sun and hard usage; that will be suitable for indoor wear and yet suited to the street. The writer knows of no material so good for all the year round as serge. This material comes in many weights, shades, and qualities. There is the storm serge for winter wear, so closely woven that its texture sheds water like a denser substance. Nothing can be better than that for business wear. And now we come to the serious discussion of how the business suit for business women shall be fashioned. That this is a serious matter there can be no dispute, when we remember that columns in the newspapers have been written about it; that business and professional women have been widely and minutely interrogated on the subject; nay, that conventions themselves have been called for the discussion of the weighty matter. Throughout all this agitation one question has refused to down, viz., the length of the skirt, which is really the only point in which the business suit needs to be differentiated from the ordinary tailor suit. There is no disguising the fact that the ordinary skirt reaching to the ground is more difficult for woman to contend against than her political inequality. If she is a dainty woman and sensitive to uncleanliness, it must be her continuous thought to keep it clear from the pavement. If she is a delicate woman, the weight of the garment drags on her back; if she is neither of these, but simply a wideawake and energetic woman, who doesn't mind carrying her own bundles on occasions, she often finds herself in situations where she would be glad to go back to the conditions of her simian ancestors and be endowed with a tail, for the sake of the service it would afford her in relieving her occupied hands from the care of her skirt. It does seem as if, logically, the business woman must find herself committed to the skirt that reaches not quite to the ankles, for any woman knows that a skirt which comes lower than this, and is struck by the boots in walking, gets quite as soiled as one that sweeps the pavement. Therefore it appears that if a due regard to the canons of cleanliness and comfort be observed, the skirts must not be so long as to be touched by the boots in walking. This brings the skirt to a point midway between the knee and ankle. The following illustration, representing the suit in which Mrs. Bertha Morris Smith appeared before a convention of the W. C. T. U., gives an idea of what such a skirt would be. Both illustrations and description are taken from Helen Ecob's book, "The Well-dressed Woman." It is made of navy blue serge, the skirt bell-shaped, with a reversed box-plait in the front to give greater freedom while sitting. The skirt in length covers the garter line, entirely concealing a pair of Turkish trousers of medium width, made of the same material, and gathered below the knee by a rubber band. A pair of long gaiters, buttoned down the entire length of the side, are strapped under the instep. The most desirable effect is produced when these gaiters are also made of the suit material. Those in

A Proposed Business Dress—Front View.

whose length reveals the shapeliness of the leg, is more artistic, hence less objectionable, than that which approaches the boot-tops, bringing the feet into more prominent notice under circumstances not the most favorable.

For summer wear a light but firm wool skirt, which need not be lined, and a coat with blouses of cotton or silk, is to be preferred, with petticoats of washable cotton or pongee silk, or Turkish trousers of the same material as the gown may be worn if desired. In general it is well to observe that being a business woman does by no means release a woman from the obligation of looking well. Nowhere is careful dressing more directly advantageous, from a purely business point of view, than in business. Aside from the very direct and helpful influence the consciousness of being well dressed has upon the mind of any woman, the fact of her being so impresses others in her favor. Good

the illustration are of jersey cloth. An underwaist of drilling or percaline, extending well over the hips, cut low in the neck, and with large arm-holes, can be sufficiently fitted to the form to support the ordinary bust, thus taking the place of the corset. The skirt may be sewed permanently to this waist at the waist line, or it may button on. The vent in the skirt is at the front plait. A second row of buttons on the waist, an inch or more below the waist line, supports the trousers. The vest and jacket are permanently attached to each other. The vest may be made with a silesia back of its own, or small rubber straps an inch or two in length, sewed at intervals along the under arm of the seam, may button or hook the jacket to the vest. Either of these plans readily admits a lighter-weight vest or a cooler waist for summer wear made of silk, linen, or muslin, over which the jacket may be worn when needed. Mrs. Smith, the designer, claims that a short skirt,

Rear View.

clothes give her an air of prosperity which, in a working-woman who supplies her own needs, stands, in the eyes of the world, for good pay, and good pay means capable work. More than that, the habit of wearing good clothes implies a recognition in the wearer of her own dignity and work which others are very quick to see and acknowledge. It ought not to be true, perhaps, but it is true, that there is a quick instinct of consideration in the minds of most men (and business life brings most working-women chiefly into contact with men) toward a well-dressed woman that does not manifest itself toward an ill-dressed forlorn-looking creature, and so the good clothes give her a pleasanter atmosphere of approbation and easier conditions in which to do her work.

"I firmly believe,". said a successful business woman to the writer not long ago, "that my persistence in dressing well, even when I was desperately poor, has been worth a good many dollars a year to me. I learned this lesson on that bitter day when I made my first venture out into the world in search of bread and butter. I went to an editor and asked for work as a fashion writer for his weekly paper, and some worldly-wise instinct led me to put on the best gown I had. A shabbily dressed woman sat talking with him; he offered her fifteen dollars a week to do half the fashion work. She took the offer gratefully and left. Then he turned to me. 'I want to do the other half of that fashion work,' I said. We talked a few minutes about it, and then he offered me what he did the other woman—fifteen dollars a week. 'I can't do it for that,' I answered; 'I couldn't live on fifteen dollars a week.' He looked me over critically, from the top of best hat down to my best French kid boots. 'No,' he said, slowly, after a bit, 'I

Artistic House Gowns.

fancy you couldn't. You look different somehow. I will give you twenty dollars a week.'"

As to the use of rubber mackintoshes in stormy weather for business women, school-girls, or any whom emergency calls out of doors, something adverse is to be said. A well-known physician declares that mackintoshes and pneumonia are twins. "A rubber garment, whether of silk, alpaca, or wool on the outside, is an exceedingly warm garment, as any woman knows who has perspired and prayed for grace inside the folds of one for an hour at a time. The temptation in putting one on, because of this, is to put nothing underneath in the way of a wrap. And here comes the danger, because the majority of the mackintoshes are loose and with only sling sleeves or no sleeves at all. While they serve, therefore, as a perfect protection against the damp, they heat certain parts of the body unduly, leaving the portion about the arms exposed to sharp winds and sudden chill. These are exceedingly sensitive parts of the body, and just the very ones that pneumonia is sure to attack. A long loose cape of wool, or, better still, of storm serge, which is protective but not heating, over the ordinary wrap will afford just as much protection from the damp, with no correspondent danger from chill. An ulster is best of all."

Other wraps for adults vary in number and kinds, according to the necessities of life and means, but no woman can be comfortable without at least four, a light-weight jacket or wrap for spring, a heavy coat or other wrap for winter, a shoulder-wrap for summer nights, an ulster or light, long garment for bad weather, to which number a fifth garment must be added for an evening wrap, if one is in the habit of going to entertainments. For young women, jackets or coats are prettiest, but elderly women look best in wraps. The prices of wraps are more diverse even than the prices of gowns, and nowhere, perhaps, in her entire wardrobe does a woman feel more tempted to extravagance than in the purchase of outer coverings. It is almost useless to attempt to give prices for any of these garments, as they vary so from season to season. A little inquiry at the shops will give a woman a better idea of expense than pages of statements. It may be well to say, however, that a perfectly plain short jacket of light French cloth, suitable for spring and summer wear, can be bought for eight or ten dollars, and a medium long, plain beaver coat for winter wear for fifteen or eighteen dollars. A handsome winter coat costs from sixty to one hundred dollars. For evenings a light wool shawl in white or pale tints is suitable. These can be bought as low as four or five dollars. A Chuddah shawl costs twice as much. The very pretty device of a young girl for a summer evening wrap was as follows: She bought a piece of cream-white nun's veiling three yards long and made a two-inch hem all around it, sides and ends alike; then she bought ten yards of cream-white lace about five inches deep and fulled this slightly around the entire scarf. In wearing she folded it lengthwise, but not exactly through the middle, so that one row of the lace fell just above the head of the other row. There was no effort to shape the scarf, but she threw it carelessly over her shoulders and arms, and knotted the long ends over the bust. It was prettier than any shawl, and no more costly.

An ulster should be of medium-weight cloth, such as rough cheviot or some of the English mixtures, and should have a detachable cape, the ulster itself being a half-fitting coat with sleeves. A loose garment is an added care on a windy day, as well as a deception and a snare in storms in the matter of even warmth.

Women of moderate means, to whom the purchase of a handsome winter wrap is something of an event, usually consult all their women friends, and end by concluding to buy a seal-skin wrap of some shape or other. Such a purchase has obviously several things in its favor. It is rich-looking, warm beyond all question, and, with proper care, will look handsome for several seasons and be wearable for several more. It also has several disadvantages, not so obvious, perhaps, but that each wearer is sure to find out for herself. One is that the sealskin wrap is in reality too warm for any but the coldest weather, and yet the temptation to lay it aside in favor of a more suitable one is hard to resist, when it is the only handsome wrap one possesses. Neither does it always prove wise to lay it aside, even when its weight and warmth are burdensome, because the wearing of so warm a garment in moderate weather is sure to induce over-sensitiveness to cold, and many a woman has discovered that, having once donned her sealskin coat for the winter, she is obliged to wear it continuously and unseasonably in order to keep from catching cold. Another reason why some women should not wear sealskin is that it makes a young face (or, more serious still, one that is "still young," as Julian Hawthorne says, adding ten years with the adjective) look older. Its beautiful, soft, rich pile has an effect on the face similar to that of black velvet, and places it, therefore, in the catalogue of materials best suited to middle age. There is no question of the desirability of a sealskin garment in the wardrobe of a woman who can supplement it with half a dozen others, and who is able to relegate it to its proper use in very cold weather alone. But, as a single stand-by, for all kinds of wear and weather, its suitability is greatly to be questioned.

In buying a sealskin garment, where economy is a consideration, the coat-shape is to be preferred, on the whole, to the half-sleeve garment, not only because the former will be less likely to go out of fashion and is much more easily remodelled if it is out of fashion, but also because the snugger-fitting shape with sleeves is much more healthful than the loose garment, as leaving no part of the figure exposed. It is well not to buy inferior sealskins. The best skins are the London-dyed, and the best, but not the usual, way to buy a sealskin garment is to select the skins and to have the garment made. In that way one is sure not to have inferior pieces in the less conspicuous parts of the garment; and if one wishes a short or medium garment, it is wisest to have the skins made up unstretched, thereby securing a closer, thicker pile in the fur and a stronger texture in the skin. It is not generally known, outside of the trade, that stretching the skins and not piecing them is the device by which the lengths of fur are secured that are made up in the ulsters and long wraps. It is clear that a stretched skin will be both less durable and have thinner fur than an unstretched one; hence the desirability of buying, if possible, the skins themselves and having them made up without stretching.

HATS.

As every woman needs four wraps, so she needs, at the very least, four hats for a season's wear. For winter there should be a dress bonnet for receptions, calls, and theatre wear, and for church, if not too fine. This should be small and of handsome material, such as velvet or jet. There should be another for shopping and street wear and mornings. This is most suitably of felt, and certainly dark in body and decoration. If she finds herself limited for spring and summer wear to two hats, one of these should be of dark straw with moderately wide brim, in a conventional shape, and with simple trimming. The other would best be a fancy straw bonnet with dainty, but serviceable trimming. One of the best investments of bonnet-money in all the world is a black jet bonnet of good quality. This is always fashionable, and equally suited for summer and winter wear. It is practically indestructible, and can, with a difference in the trimming, be entirely made over an unlimited number of times. Besides this it has become quite necessary nowadays that the wardrobe of every woman, without distinction of purse, shall contain a small bonnet for wear at theatres and places of evening entertainment, both out of regard to the growing demand for more elaborate dress at such places, and out of courtesy to those in one's immediate rear, who often, because of the hat of the woman in front of them, become like the heathen, in that "having eyes they see not." For such purposes as this a jet bonnet with bright ornaments is the most economical and becoming that can be added to one's wardrobe.

A witty man recently defined a bonnet as a thing made partly of ribbon and partly of lace, but principally of price, and the definition was true as well as witty. There is nothing so made up of price as the average fashionable hat or bonnet. There is probably no product of manufactured skill in which the price asked is so much in advance of the actual cost of production; and yet, ask any discerning woman whether a French bonnet is worth its price or not and mark her unhesitating answer. She knows that the value of the article lies not in the value of the frame or the ribbon or the flowers, but in that indefinable something called "the style," that stamp of distinction, which makes the bonnet a work of art, as distinct from a mere unrelated mass of flowers, and lace, and ribbon. The technique of the artist who made the bonnet is quite as well worth paying for as the technique of the other artist who makes an immortal landscape out of mere canvas, and pigment, and oil. So it is quite fair, it will be seen, that a bonnet, if it have style, should be principally "price." There is no woman who will not nod assent to this dictum, and who will not gladly exchange the price for the bonnet, if she has the former. But these fortunates are few. The average woman finds it necessary to exercise as much unselfish forbearance in the matter of bonnets alone, as would suffice to carry a man through his entire wardrobe. The average woman has six wants to one bonnet. It is for such women that these hints are offered.

Suppose a woman has several gowns and can afford only one hat, the best thing for her to do is to have black for the foundation. If the hat is of straw or felt, avail yourself of a facing, folds, or jet to finish the edge. For trimming, use ribbon, lace, or velvet, with jet if you wish it. Thus far the hat is all black; now for the color. Any color may be combined with black, but some colors blend better than others. For an olive-green gown get olive-green velvet or ribbon; make two or three small rosettes or butterfly bows and place on the hat where it may be turned up or against the hair, and lo! there is a hat to suit the gown. If red is wanted for another gown, make up the same in red and put on in place of the green. So on with blue, yellow, pink, white, or any color that may be desired. Different flowers also may be used. The hat is identical in every case, yet it harmonizes with the gowns, and a woman does not feel that she has only one hat.

If a hat is wanted to match a gown, take great care in selecting the color. *Colors.* Remember that many colors influence one, and it is very difficult to keep to the original color. Take brown, for instance—red brown, golden brown, olive brown, gray brown; one must not put two of those together, because, if one does, the hat will be a failure. If one wishes to combine other colors with brown, like care must be taken. In order to make a successful combination of pink with brown one should employ a yellow pink, while the brown should show some red and yellow. Green to look well with golden brown must have yellow in it, and the brown must show the tint of the green.

Black and white are always used together, and many people think there is no art in mingling them. This, however, is not true. They should never be used in equal quantities; there should always be more black than white, or vice versa. A cream white and never a blue white should be used with black.

In buying one must remember to choose colors that will harmonize with hair and complexion. Otherwise, though the hat and gown may be both beautiful and stylish, they will not be a success.

Materials. Do not buy cheap material. By this I do not mean to advise the selection of the most recherché and expensive material, but of a given material get the very best quality you can afford. Cheap velvet is its own accuser, and nothing else ever makes a hat look so "shoddy." Moreover, cheap velvet does not wear well. If one cannot pay at least one dollar and a half a yard for velvet it is better to get velveteen, which is cheaper, wider, and looks very well when made up. Two dollars a yard is a fair and safe price to pay. It will look and wear well and probably can be used twice.

It is usually easy to detect the inferior quality of cheap flowers, not so much in the blossoms as in the leaves. Roses and violets, particularly, are made up in such a cheap, flimsy fashion that unless one can afford good flowers they had better not be bought. Mignonette, thistles, forget-me-nots, poppies, chrysanthemums, and apple-blossoms are always safe to purchase. The flowers, as a rule, are well made and can be used more than once.

Feathers and lace can be used season after season until they become shabby; therefore it is wise never to buy any but the best.

Renovating materials. Old material may be renovated easily if not too much worn or faded. Velvet and ribbon must be well brushed before steaming. If you have not a patent renovator, use a hot flat-iron or stove-lid. Lay two thicknesses of wet muslin over the iron and draw the wrong side of the material over it several times, or until it is freshened. Lace may be dampened and laid between blankets, then pressed with a hot iron. This will not flatten the threads. To stiffen the lace steam it over the tea-kettle and wind it tightly around a bottle or cylinder. It can also be steamed after it is wound on the bottle.

Children's hats. Special care should be taken that hats for children under twelve years of age be not overtrimmed. Neither should they be bent very much, as a simple, flat hat is more becoming to a child's head. Leghorns are always popular and in good taste; trimmed with lace, flowers, or feathers, and *narrow* ribbon one will make a suitable hat to be worn with either silk or gingham dresses. White mull hats are pretty, and are made with casings through which wire or cord is run. A simple trimming of flowers or loops of the mull is all that is required. These hats may also be made of gingham and used for common wear. They may be washed or cleaned, so that they are very serviceable.

Country hats for children of more than twelve years of age may be made of mull, thin silk, muslin, or Brussels net. They are made in the same way, except that the back is narrower than the front; wire is always used, and the

Gowns for Stout Women.

color from the face. A young girl in the first flush of youth, with her face full of curves and color, can wear black and look the better for it; but the elderly woman looks older and paler and sharper. The single advantage that black possesses over colors is that it reduces the apparent size of the figure, as everybody knows, and thereby becomes specially suited for the use of stout women; but elderly ladies, who do not need to regard this point, should wear soft pale tints—fawns and browns and amethyst and lavender and silver gray and cream white. Deep reds are not unbecoming and rich purple. These will give color and richness to a very wan presence.

The elderly woman should also possess herself of the dignity that lies in long lines. If she be very stout she will find that the sweeping lines of the princess, with loose outlines—not close ones—reduce the avoirdupois and add height and stateliness to the figure. If she be slender, she will find the tendency to angularity best hidden by loose draperies. It is especially the privilege

trimming is more elaborate. But it is not well to make the trimming too heavy for a shirred hat.

Small hats or bonnets should always be worn for dressy occasions. They *Hats and* may be made elaborate or simple. *bonnets.* A crownless bonnet for street wear is neither hygienic nor in good taste. See section on "Millinery at Home."

Dress for Elderly Ladies.

Among the mistaken ideas bequeathed to us by our grandmothers that we have been brave enough to put aside at their true value, and they were many, is the belief that black is the most becoming and suitable fabric for elderly ladies. In point of fact, black is exactly what they ought not to wear. Its presence close to the face throws dark shadows upward, which increase any tendency to thinness, and subtract all

of the elderly lady to wear heavy silks, rich brocades, velvets, and old lace, all of which lose greatly in effect if cut into short lines and small bits at the dictates of fashion. With some regard to the prevailing mode, it is best that an elderly woman should be her own authority in matters of dress.

It is to be regretted that the small white lace cap known as the "dress cap" should be so little worn by women past middle life. It is so dainty, so fresh, and so universally becoming and softening to the face that its absence is an artistic loss. A suitable and becoming pattern once provided, there is no reason why these should not be easily made at home, though they are always to be found in shops at prices ranging from two dollars and a half upward indefinitely, according to the value of the materials used. For ordinary wear the valenciennes and some of the imitation French laces are very suitable. Any of these are to be bought for less than a dollar a yard in exquisitely fine patterns.

UNDERWEAR.

A good axiom to start out with, in shopping for underwear, is: The more trimming the less value. That is to say, the wily manufacturer appears to find it necessary, in placing his cheaper goods upon the market, to present with them yards of cheap Hamburg edging and imitation lace, in order to tempt the victim to her unhappy extravagance. The really fine underwear to be found in the shops—fine, that is, in both ways, in fabric and taste—is little decorated; its value consists in the exquisite quality of the material, the beautiful fit, and the hand-work. It is quite as economical to buy one's underwear to-day at a good shop as to have it made; and if one knows what to buy and how to buy it, the result may be even better. The prices of underwear made to order at most of the fashionable places are fabulous, and quite as good results are obtained in the French hand-made underwear that may be found at the leading shops; these range from very moderate prices to those that are greatly extravagant. Percale and nainsook are the materials used in the French underwear, cut in the newest and prettiest shapes, and daintily trimmed with fine lace or embroideries, hand-wrought upon the fabric itself. Bridal sets, which consist of a nightgown, chemise, and pair of drawers, made of nainsook and trimmed to match, can be bought for from twenty dollars a set upward. Nightgowns alone, made of fine percale, with wide collar and cuffs, hand-wrought, and with finely tucked bosom, powdered with tiny sprays of blossoms, may be bought for about four dollars. The value of these nightgowns may be extended upward almost indefinitely, but very delightful ones may be bought for six and seven dollars. Very simple nightgowns may be found in the same French underwear, costing from one dollar and a half upward. These are made of fine percale and hand embroidered on the gown itself. They wash and wear beautifully, and though perhaps not so becoming as those trimmed with ruffles of lace, are a sensible purchase for common wear. Chemises are still worn by very many women, and the reason is not far to discern. This garment is pretty, becoming, and essentially feminine. The hand-embroidered nainsook chemises cost two dollars and upward. Hand-embroidered drawers, made of percale, range in price from one dollar and a half to four dollars a pair, the price varying with the amount of work upon them. Nainsook drawers, prettily trimmed, range from two dollars and a half up to ten and fifteen dollars. The French underwear is usually hand made.

A new pattern in corset-waists is made low-necked with a row of fine tucks across the back and the front, and with a drawing string around the waist regulating the size. They are specially designed for slight people, and may be bought, prettily trimmed, for three dollars and upward. Those made of percale with a simple embroidered scallop are very inexpensive, though the more elaborate ones may be made to cost almost any price. White skirts with simply scalloped ruffles cost from two dollars upward. The nainsook hand-embroidered skirts cost nine and ten dollars, while those made of the same material with ruffles of Hamburg edging cost from three dollars upward. Short flannel skirts cost from one dollar and a quarter to ten dollars, white flannel, embroidered slightly in silk, costs two dollars and upward. Hand-wrought flannel costs a trifle more. Flannel under-petticoats trimmed with embroidery and lace are especially pretty and cost from four dollars to ten. French flannel skirts with a fine colored stripe and trimmed with a single ruffle can be bought for three dollars, and those of outing flannel from one dollar upward. For summer wear no skirt is so good as pongee silk, which may be washed like a piece of cotton and is delightfully cool and fresh. These may be bought in prices varying from three dollars to twelve. Mohair skirts are exceedingly good for winter. They may be bought for two dollars and a half to five dollars. Moreen is also an excellent material for winter skirts, as it is warm and durable and can be washed without danger of shrinking. Any woman equipped with two pongee skirts and three white skirts for summer, one moreen or mohair and one silk petticoat for winter, has a sufficient supply. A good black silk skirt may be bought for about twelve dollars, those made of taffeta silk with pinked ruffles for four dollars and upward. The cheaper grades of these are not to be recommended. Colored wash skirts in seersucker, gingham, and other fabrics cost from seventy-five cents up to three and four dollars.

Divided Skirt Designed by Jenness Miller.

Corsets. There is a prejudice among many women, and one that the shopkeepers are very careful to encourage, in favor of expensive corsets. While it is undoubtedly true that a corset which costs ten dollars is better in many ways than one which costs two dollars and a half, it is also true that for very many persons the two dollar and a half corset is serviceable and comfortable. A very well-made plain white coutil corset can be bought from two dollars and a half to five dollars, the prices varying according to the size, the length of the waist, the number of the bones, etc. A good black corset can be bought for five dollars. Net corsets for summer wear cost from two dollars and a half to ten dollars. A specially comfortable summer corset is made of linen and is sold for seven dollars. Silk and satin corsets for special occasions may be bought from ten dollars up to thirty and forty. It is a fact that very stout women are compelled to pay high prices for their corsets because of the extra boning and the added strength of the material required for them, but there is no reason why a woman of ordinary size and proportions should not obtain a good ready-made corset for from two to five dollars.

The domestic underwear costs considerably less than the French. It is machine made, of heavier material, and usually more elaborately trimmed. It is very serviceable, however, and is bought by many who do not wish to pay the price of the French wear. Nightgowns trimmed with Hamburg edging can be bought from one dollar up to five dollars, chemises from eighty cents upward, drawers from fifty cents upward, corset-waists from twenty-five cents to ten times as much, and white skirts from one dollar to five dollars. For those who prefer to have the work done at home the Berkeley cambrics at twenty cents a yard, and the nainsooks, which range from twenty-five to fifty cents a yard, are the best materials to use. The decorations will be entirely a matter of taste, and well-fitting patterns for all these garments can be obtained of the houses publishing them.

Undervests. Undervests for summer wear are to be found in many different materials— in cotton, lisle thread, gauze, wool, silk and wool, silk and cotton, and silk. The silk-ribbed garments are worn by most women and are durable and dainty. The prices of these range from one dollar to ten. Those at one dollar are of spun silk or of silk and cotton, and perfectly plain. Better qualities of the same kind may be bought, costing two and three dollars. The pure silk or twisted silk cost three and four times as much as the silk mixtures. They are much warmer, but wear a great deal longer. Many women find them all they require for winter wear. A new decoration for low-necked silk vests is a deep ruffle of lace around the neck. Such garments as these cost from four dollars upward; any woman, however, will be able to add the ruffles for herself. Very pretty vests also have silk crochet work set in bands and points about the neck. These vary in price according to the amount of work, costing from two dollars upward. A very long silk garment, called a chemise-skirt, is made especially for very stout women. It is woven so as to fit well down over the hips and prevent any danger of pulling up as ordinary vests do. They cost from three to five dollars. Union suits in all these materials can be found in summer weights. These cost usually about twice as much as the vest of corresponding texture. A lisle-thread union suit can be bought for about two dollars, thin cotton and wool from two dollars and a half upward and silk and wool from four dollars upward. The hygienic underwear is also made in the most exquisite all-wool gauzes suitable for summer wear for delicate persons and those who prefer to wear wool the year round. Not only are these materials found in the made-up garments, but the most beautiful woollen fabrics suitable for skirts, drawers, and night-dresses are to be found at their special shops, in weights varying with almost every month in the year. For winter wear, either pure silk, silk and wool, or all wool are to be recommended, with high necks and long sleeves or not, as the taste and bodily constitution of the wearer dictate. Good silk and wool mixtures cost about as much as either pure silk or pure wool, and the prices of all of these differ very little. The Jaeger flannels of pure wool alone can be bought in high-neck and long-sleeve garments, double-breasted, for about six dollars. The silk and wool will cost just as much, but will shrink less in washing. The pure silk will cost a trifle more and will not shrink, but will not be so warm as the wool, nor is it so healthful for delicate people. Despite all the claim of manufacturers, there has not yet been discovered any kind of wool underwear that will not shrink with washing, though care in the treatment of these garments will diminish the risk very greatly.

A few women cling to the use of India and China silk for nightgowns, chemises, and drawers. The taste of this choice is to be questioned. Silk cannot be properly laundered as cotton is, and to people of refined tastes it seems by no means sufficient to submit such intimate garments as these to a laundering process that does not include the old-fashioned and cleanly method of boiling. Pongee silk can be treated exactly as cotton cloth is, and is, therefore, the only silk that seems specially desirable for underwear next the skin. Charming négligé gowns and wrappers for bedroom use are made in nun's veiling, wool crépon, and thin silk. These are made up plain or elaborately trimmed and vary in price accordingly, ten and twelve dollars being the price in the shops for the simplest ones, while dainty gowns made of striped and sprigged wash materials, such as percale, batiste, and nainsook, can be bought for from five dollars and upward. Short flannel dressing-sacques are to be bought in all colors for about five dollars, the price increasing as the decoration does, and lawn and linen jackets are to be found at a dollar and upward.

Stockings. Black stockings have held the first place in favor for so long as to be rightfully considered the standard, in place of the old-fashioned white and unbleached. However, unless these black hose are warranted stainless and stamped to that effect on each pair it is best not to buy them, as the results of the staining are sometimes as injurious as blood-poisoning. Cotton stockings in black and in colors can be bought for from twenty-five cents to a dollar a pair. A very good stocking can be bought for about sixty cents. There are few colors used, except those of russet and tan, which are bought to wear with the light leather shoes, and which cost from fifty cents to a dollar a pair. Lisle-thread stockings cost a trifle more than cotton ones, but are especially delightful for summer. Very good ones can be had for seventy-five cents a pair. Very few women understand the difference between the three kinds of silk hose offered for sale, viz., the plated silk, spun silk, and pure silk. Of these three, the plated silk is the only one that is not all silk. This is a mixture of silk and lisle thread or cotton so skilfully woven that the outer covering of the thread is of silk, the inner part is of the other material, and the outside of the stocking looks like the spun silk, but on turning the stocking it will be seen that the underside shows the lisle or cotton threads. A plated-silk hose can be bought for a very little more than lisle thread, and is in no way better. Spun-silk stockings are made from pure silk thread of inferior quality and short length, spun together, but not twisted. The stockings made of this, therefore, are thinner and do not wear so well as those made of the twisted silk thread, which cost considerably more, but will wear three times as long. Spun silk stockings cost from seventy-five cents to three dollars a pair, twisted-silk from one dollar and a half to five dollars a pair.

Shoes. Cheap shoes are like cheap gloves, alluring but delusive. By cheap shoes is meant a high kid boot that sells for less than five dollars. Those sold for less than this are not only apt to be made of poor or unequal leather, but are also shaped on a last that has little conformity to the shape of the foot. It is a great pity to put upon these much-used and important as well as beautiful members of the body the affront of compelling them to do efficient work under the most impossible conditions. No wonder the rebellion comes in the shape of corns and blisters and bunions and ingrowing nails. It ought to be logically clear that the shoe should be made for the foot and not the foot for the shoe; and yet let any interested person take the ordinary priced shoe, put it on a piece of paper, draw a line around it, and then draw over it the outline of the undressed foot bearing the weight of the body, and note the difference. It is a fact, better known to physicians than to the sufferers themselves, that diseases of the feet resulting from badly fitting shoes are a source of spinal sensitiveness and irritation, often resulting in nervous prostration. A really well-fitting shoe should be quite as broad in the sole as the foot is when it bears the weight of the body; a trifle longer than the foot; should be straight in the inner line and not incurved toward the toe, as most shoes are; should fit snugly at the heel and ankle, and have moderately low heels. It is clear from this that the best boot in which to clothe the foot is one made for the foot itself; for feet are as individual as the owners of the feet. It may not be so clear, except to one who has tried it, that this is also the most economical thing. One pair of custom-made shoes will outlast two pairs of ready-made ones. The writer has proven this many times in her own experience. The best bootmakers charge nine dollars for a pair of ordinary lace or button kid shoes of the best quality, and six or seven dollars for low shoes. In buying ready-made shoes the most expensive ones are of soft French kid, hand-turned. These cost from six to ten dollars. For heavier wear dongola kid in bright or dull finish is admirable, as it is soft, smooth, and wears exceedingly well. Such boots as these cost from five to nine dollars. Street boots may be either square-toed or pointed, the former being more becoming to broad feet and easier on sensitive ones. If a pointed toe is chosen the boot should be half an inch longer than the foot. Patent leather is not a good choice for street boots, as it is warm in summer and cracks in winter. House shoes and dress shoes may be of kid or patent leather with moderately high heels. Very dainty shoes of this kind cost from four dollars upward. Slippers in kid, bronzed or black, and in suède in various colors, may be bought from two dollars upward. Those with French heels for dancing cost somewhat more. Satin slippers cost almost twice as much as the kid ones, and are usually chosen to match the dress. A woman with a large foot should never wear a white or very light shoe or slipper, as the apparent size of the foot is greatly increased thereby. Russet shoes are cool, soft, serviceable, and especially pretty when worn with summer gowns. They are made of many different kinds of leather, the cheaper varieties of which are not to be recommended. A good russet shoe will cost four dollars, and the best one seven. A few russet boots are made, but are much less in favor than the low shoes. Tennis shoes with rubber soles cost from two dollars and a half up. There is nothing so good for those who go in for athletics and who walk or climb as fine French calfskin shoes, hand-made, with extension soles. These will cost about the same as kid boots and are best made to order. There are people who say, and who sincerely believe, that they cannot wear the common-sense shoe. This is because the shoe does not fit, usually in the heel, and allows the foot to slip, inevitably causing callous spots and corns. A correctly fitting common-sense shoe is always tolerable.

Furs.

Since furs are expensive things to buy, whenever one buys them, it is best for people of limited means to make these occasions as few and as far between as possible. This is to be done in either of two ways—going without furs, or buying thoroughly good furs when one does buy. Among good furs the following are to be named: Sealskin, Russian sable, otter, beaver, mink, astrakan, chinchilla, ermine, Alaska sable, brown marten, and blue fox. There are others known to the trade as "fancy furs," which are fairly good and fairly durable, but the only value of which is that of the caprice of the passing moment. Since the fashionable life of these is always short lived, they are not to be recommended as economical purchases. The purchase of a sealskin cloak has been treated in another part of this article. The prices of this garment vary from year to year, with a steady upward tendency. It is safe to say that probably never again will it be possible to buy a thoroughly good sealskin cloak in half length for less than three hundred dollars. Muffs cost from twenty-five to fifty dollars; capes from seventy-five to three hundred; small collars from sixty-five to one hundred and twenty-five; and one-inch bands of seal cost from one dollar and a half to three and a half a yard; doubling the width doubles the price. Russian sable, which is not so black as its name would indicate, is the most costly of furs. Muffs in this fur cost from one hundred to five hundred dollars, and the collars from five hundred up to a thousand; a single little tippet, just large enough to clasp the throat, may be bought from one hundred to three hundred dollars. Bands of fur two inches wide cost sixty dollars, and can be bought as high as four hundred dollars a yard. There are two kinds of chinchilla—the Eureka chinchilla, which is very expensive, and the Bolivian chinchilla, which is much less costly. Muffs and collars of the former cost from one hundred dollars each up to three times that, and the bands for trimming cost twelve dollars a yard and upward. Muffs of the latter can be had for twenty-five dollars and collars for one hundred, the bands costing half the price of the other variety. Ermine bands cost three dollars a yard if they are one inch wide; doubling the width doubles the price exactly. Ermine muffs can be bought from twenty-five dollars upward, and large collars from forty to one hundred dollars. Astrakan also comes in two varieties—Astrakan and Persian lamb. The finest skins of the Persian lamb are those of the still-born lamb; that is, the lamb taken from the mother before birth; these are naturally exquisitely fine and soft, but not durable. Astrakan in narrow bands costs from one dollar to two dollars a yard, and the muffs from five to ten dollars; the capes costing twenty-five dollars upward, according to size. Persian lamb bands cost a trifle more than the astrakan; the muffs costing from six to thirty dollars, the collars corresponding. Narrow bands of the short, thick, dark-brown fur of the mink, which is excellent to wear and very becoming to brown-haired women, can be bought for from two to six dollars a yard. Mink muffs cost from twenty-five to forty dollars, and capes from thirty to two hundred, according to quality and size. Alaskan sable costs from two to ten dollars a yard, and the muffs from ten to twenty dollars.

Mourning.

It is fortunate that the regulations regarding the wearing of mourning are not so strictly observed of late years. To people of taste the extravagant observance of the period of sorrow, especially as manifested in the outer garb, has always been questionable. Simplicity in mourning is, above all things, to be considered. The period of mourning prescribed for widows is two years of deep mourning, in which the only wear is woollen stuffs and crape. After that, mourning silks, grenadines, and other dull-finished cloths may replace the wool, and a nun's veiling veil may replace the crape. The widow may wear the white cap and the muslin collars and cuffs as she chooses, though the white ruche in the bonnet is well-nigh obligatory. During these first two years the only decoration permitted on her woollen dress is crape, and this is apt to be put on in greater quantities than is necessary or essential, since crape is both costly and very easily ruined by dampness or dust.

Black and white is much in use at present for second mourning, and grays, purples, and lilacs are worn just before colors are resumed at the end of the third year.

Children wear deep mourning for their parents one year; the crape can be left off the second year, and if black is worn the third year it can be considerably lightened by black and gray. The length of time for a mother to wear black for her children varies somewhat according to the age of the child; if the children are grown up it will be from two to three years; if younger, a shorter period of time. Children generally wear mourning for their grandparents for one year.

Black Henrietta cloth is worn for first mourning, and costs from one dollar and twenty-five cents a yard to four and five dollars. Black nun's veiling comes from one dollar a yard upward; all-silk grenadines from one dollar and a quarter upward, and mourning silks for the same. English crape in the proper width for veils comes from three dollars and a half to ten dollars a yard.

The soft veils of nun's veiling cost from three dollars and fifty cents, and silk grenadine veils from seven dollars upward. The crape veils, although heavy to wear, are usually chosen by widows and mothers for the first period of mourning. The nun's veiling veils are lighter in weight, more healthful, and more graceful. When the veil is thrown back a face veil of plain net or tulle is worn, sometimes with a narrow crape border. A small crape or nun's veiling bonnet is worn under the veil. Black felt and straw hats are first trimmed with crape, and later with dull-finished ribbons, to which can be added any appropriate decoration in the way of black feathers, flowers, and dull jet. The black flowers are designed especially for trimming summer hats. They should always be of good quality, and can be bought from seventy-five cents a bunch upward. Four-buttoned black kid gloves can be had from one dollar and a half upward. In black gloves it is a great mistake not to buy the good quality, as the cheaper ones are affected by the dye and do not wear well. Undressed kid gloves cost from one dollar and fifty cents to two dollars and a half. They are soft and pleasant to wear, but are not so durable as the dressed kid. All black kid gloves are liable to crack in summer, and black silk gloves are often substituted for this reason. They cost from seventy-five cents a pair upward. It is in better taste in selecting black-bordered handkerchiefs not to choose those with too deep borders. Half an inch is as wide as the border need ever be, and the narrower edge is quite as suitable, even for the first months of mourning.

ACCESSORIES.

When it comes to certain accessories of the toilet, notably handkerchiefs, every American woman has cause to regret that she was not born in Paris. The French handkerchiefs are so superior in texture, in ornamentation, and so maddeningly cheap in comparison. In Paris, exquisitely fine linen cambric, with an initial or finely wrought sprays of flowers, are to be had for four or five francs, a trifle more than the plain linen handkerchiefs cost here. These latter are to be bought, as most women know, in the shops in all our towns for from twenty-five to fifty cents. Sheer linen hem-stitched handkerchiefs come from thirty-five cents to a dollar and a half each. There is a slight reduction when handkerchiefs are bought by the dozen. The French hand-embroidered linen handkerchiefs cost from two dollars apiece up to twelve dollars. This is in New York, be it understood, and not in Paris. Machine embroidered handkerchiefs come from twenty-five cents to a dollar apiece. Colored bordered and mourning handkerchiefs come from twenty-five cents to two dollars each; but these, except in the latter case, are happily no longer in fashion. Perhaps it may be well to say something here about the well-known "bargain counter" handkerchiefs, which appear at intervals in many of our shops to lure women away from their good taste and sound convictions by a sudden temptation. The bargain counter handkerchief is seldom of linen, and then only of the coarsest quality. It is usually of a flimsy cotton muslin with enough dressing in it to give it a linen finish, which disappears in its first washing. It is also usually heavily decorated with the cheapest and coarsest kind of machine embroidery, which one or two launderings show to be innately depraved with all kinds of ravelled-out attachments.

These are seldom to be bought for less than two dollars a dozen, and when one considers that they are neither in good taste nor durable in wear, it is well to ask oneself if it is not better to buy instead half a dozen medium, plain, hem-stitched handkerchiefs for the same price, which are certain to give one durable wear for a year at least. The so-called fancy handkerchiefs, made of chiffon in colors or white, and embroidered with much silk, are also not to be recommended. A handkerchief is for use primarily, and certainly unobtrusive use, and its adoption as an ornament for the toilet is not to be sanctioned by the canons of good dressing or good taste. The more delicate it is in fabric and color, the less suitable it is for the purpose for which it was intended.

Twilled silk umbrellas of fair quality are to be bought for two dollars. These are usually of the Gloria silk, which has a mixture of cotton with the silk, but which wears the better on that account, although it is not so convenient to handle as the pure silk, which is lighter and less bulky. A very good pure silk umbrella may be bought for from three to six dollars; where the price is higher than this the value is usually to be found in the handle, and not in the quality of the silk. Twilled silk wears better than the taffeta, although the latter, because they wrap more closely, are considered more desirable. The finest umbrellas, both in taffeta and twilled, have the selvedge edge instead of the hem, and many of them have the steel rod in place of the wooden stick. Parasols vary in price as much as hats do, and there is as great art in choosing a becoming parasol as in choosing a becoming hat. Silk parasols in dark or light colors may be found at two dollars and a half, and from this up to as much as one wishes to pay. A good parasol of heavy gros-grain silk may be bought for five dollars; fancy silks in good quality, sometimes with borders of lace or insertion, may be had for about the same price. When one comes to the lace-covered and chiffon parasols, there is no limit to the price one may pay. The cheap lace parasol is a purchase sure to be regretted; one that is not cheap may easily cost a fortune. A caution just here against the improper use of fancy parasols may be of service. Fancy parasols of lace or chiffon, or those decorated with anything elaborate, have no place in the city except in a carriage, and only the most occasional and ceremonious use anywhere else. If a woman can afford to buy but one parasol a year, let her never choose any of these dainty confections. Parasols of white and écru silk are pretty and cool for country use, but are not so restful to the eye as one of darker silk. A lined parasol is much more becoming to the face, especially if the lining be of red or pink, than a plain parasol. Judiciously managed, the parasol may be made one of the most helpful adjuncts to a becoming toilet, and may set off the face to greater advantage even than the hat.

Contrary to the advice of physicians and oculists, contrary perhaps to their own convictions of what is well for them, women continue to wear the veil as an essential part of the toilet. The reasons for this are two— and sufficient. A veil is becoming and keeps the hair in order. It is to be hoped, therefore, fashion will allow their use for many years to come. Within the last few years the Russian net has appeared in the market in large quantities. This is a very fine silk thread woven in a large variety of open work patterns. It comes in every color and many prices, ranging from twenty-five cents to a dollar and a half a yard. Many of these patterns have small or large dots scattered at intervals over the surface. They are to be found in double and single widths. Of the single width it takes one yard to go comfortably around a hat, and three-eighths to five-eighths for a bonnet. Plain tulles and net come in all colors and are always pleasant to wear, and better for the eyes than the coarser meshes. These cost twenty-five cents a yard and are three-quarters of a yard wide, so that one yard cut in two lengthwise will make two veils. A heavier silk veiling is to be found for travelling, or as a protection to the skin from wind or sun; this costs about fifty cents a yard. There are always lace veils to be found ready-made and with designs specially suited to their shape. These cost from one dollar upward, and often wear better than the veilings which come in the piece. The attempts to revive the veil of Brussels net, hand-wrought in sprigged designs, so much worn by our grandmothers, has happily been a failure. It was entirely unbecoming and inartistic. Quite as much care is to be bestowed upon the selection of a veil as upon any other part of the costume. Women who have dark hair and eyes and a bright color, can wear veils with the dots larger and nearer together. Dark women who have clear skins, also look well in white veils, while a woman who has not so much color and has fair hair and light eyes, generally looks better in a black veil with a fine mesh and small dots far apart. White veils tend to make the skin look fairer. A combination that is pretty and usually specially becoming, is a fine white veil with small black dots not too near together. A brown blonde is very apt to look especially well in a brown veil a little lighter than the color of her hair. A dark-blue veil makes the skin look clear and fair. A gray veil, except

Dress from a Practical Standpoint.

where a woman has much color, makes the wearer look wan and ghastly. A red veil makes anybody but a very pale woman look like a boiled lobster. four-button suède gloves (by which is meant the undressed kid), the prices range from one dollar and a half to two dollars. Twenty-button length

Modern Russian Fan.

Gloves. Most of the gloves sold in the United States are imported from France and England, although there are some manufactured in America that are quite as good, and which cost as much as the imported ones. Many gloves are not kid at all, but are made of goat, lamb, chamois, or even dog- mousquetaire, in suède, are to be bought for about four dollars. Four-button glacé, or dressed kid gloves, in all shades, cost from one dollar and a quarter to one dollar and a half. The latter will outlast two pairs of a cheaper quality. There are inexpensive gloves, however, that are fairly good and often

A Decorative Fancy.

skin. These are not so fine as kid, but are often well made and very useful. The prices of the best gloves are high, but they wear proportionally well, and are worth the money asked. For wear well. Dog-skin gloves are very serviceable for winter wear, and cost from one dollar to two and a quarter a pair. Those for a dollar and a quarter are very serviceable. The Biarritz glove, which is a mousquetaire glove, in six-button lengths, without the opening at the wrist, may be bought for eighty-five cents. These are strong and loose fitting, and are especially comfortable to wear in travelling, shopping, and warm weather. Occasionally very good gloves can be bought at bargain sales for less than the regular price; but in the mass of cases the gloves are inferior in quality and irregular in make.

It is more economical to pay a high price for pearl and white and very pale-tinted gloves than for the medium shades, which soil just as quickly and which show every attempt at cleaning them. A light evening glove, if cleaned carefully, can be renewed half a dozen times, although each time it will soil more quickly than the time before. It is really better to buy for such a purpose a well-made glove that will keep its shape and not break, and clean it frequently, than to buy a fresh pair of cheap gloves every time one has occasion to wear evening gloves. From ten to twenty cents a pair is asked for cleaning gloves at a good scourer's.

Carved Ivory Guards.

This may be done at home by using naphtha and washing the glove carefully, stretching it out afterward and rubbing it with a soft flannel. Many of the large shops mend gloves. A braided skein of assorted colors of fine cotton (which is much better than silk for mending gloves) can be had at most of the shops.

The fan has been the intimate and

Modern Lace Fan.

Fans. confidante of woman ever since women and fans began. To it has she whispered her hopes; behind it she has shielded her blushes; it has been her sceptre of royalty and the interpreter of her mood. No wonder that many a woman collects fans as a hobby and loves them as she does her next of kin, or that the average woman shopper allows her eyes to fall longingly, even enviously, on the exquisite fans in the shops! If a woman, however, may not look upon fans with the eye of the collector or the favor of a lover, but only with a view to finding what will best supply her various needs at the least possible outlay, she will find that all fans, unlike all Gaul, may be divided into two kinds—the fan for day usage and the evening fan. Now, it is clear that the fan designed for day use is preeminently the useful fan, and not designed as an adjunct to the toilet. The fan with the single purpose of use must be substantially made. Its framework should, therefore, be of bamboo or some other light wood. The covering of this frame may be of parchment or of cloth, decorated or not, but the charming Japanese decorations add greatly to the interest and the beauty.

Fans of this kind may cost five cents or they may cost two dollars, at which price are to be found the quaintest and most artistic designs, making the fan almost dainty enough for evening

Fan Painted in the Manner of Watteau.

wear, and much more satisfactory than many that are bought for that purpose. Parchment fans are really to be preferred to cloth ones, as being lighter and more susceptible of appropriate decoration, as well as less expensive. Such fans as these are useful for house or street, for travelling, church, and the theatre, unless one is in evening toilet.

Now, as to evening fans: These may be of the simplest or the most elaborate and expensive kinds. To the latter kind belong those in mother-of-pearl and enamel, and gold and silver, and ivory and tortoise, enriched often with jewels and covered with lace that might have fallen across the wrists of Titania, or of royal plumes, or painted by masterly hands. Such treasures as these are the single purchases of a lifetime, or the rare inheritance from a more fortunate ancestor, and are not to be found in the ordinary shops. What one may find there, however, is an evening fan that is delightful in quality and only moderately expensive.

Such an one is an ostrich feather fan. A cheap feather fan is not a judicious purchase. By this is meant fans of inferior or imitation ostrich tips, of quills painted or plain, of marabout, or of any of the fancy combinations costing from one to five dollars. These are fragile and do not bear service or cleaning. Moreover, they look cheap, which is not in their favor. A really good ostrich feather fan costs from fifteen to fifty dollars, and even more, if it be mounted in some specially expensive way. Such a fan as this is a good investment, as it is always handsome and will last a lifetime. Rather than buy a cheap feather fan for evening, buy a gauze one, or one of silk or satin in light color and decorated with a spray of flowers. In choosing the decoration, remember that what is spoken of so reverently in the shops as "hand-painting," may be desperately bad as well as fairly good. An unambitious bit, as a spray of flowers painted silk in Empire form, with inlaid violet-wood sticks, can be bought for two dollars, and much the same fan, with spangles instead of painting, may be had for half that sum. Lace fans may be bought either in black or white, in a lace that looks like Chantilly, for from five dollars upward. Point lace and duchesse lace fans cost from thirty dollars upward. Such a fan as this should only be carried by a married woman. Light fans are specially the perquisites of girls and young women. Elderly women find dark fans, especially those of ostrich feathers in black or natural colors, most suitable.

There is a tradition among women that no gentlewoman will wear cheap or imitation jewelry. That *Jewelry.* did very well for the days prior to the wonderful art of the goldsmith and artificer in metals and enamels, resulting in a wealth of exquisite and artistic reproductions, as well as in original designs in cheaper

Modern Black Lace Fan.

well done, is better than a whole court scene, painted a great way after Watteau and Vernis Martin. An artistic and serviceable fan need not be expensive. A charming one in hand- mediums, which leave nothing to be desired except cost. This statement is not to be taken as under-estimating the real value of beautiful gems and rare confections in precious metals,

Escurial.

or as countenancing in any way the tawdry and inartistic. It is to be taken only as directed against the mistaken prejudice which condemns a piece of jewelry simply because it is cheap, or because it is an imitation. Many of the imitations to-day have a distinct artistic value of their own. Many of the floral designs in French enamel, imitating the real enamel closely, and costing one-tenth as much, are quite worthy to be accepted on their own account, so charming and natural are the designs. Even more true is this of many of the semi-precious stones found to-day in such abundance in the high-class jewellers, and bearing the stamp of their thorough approval. There are amethysts in all their variety of color — not purple alone, but pale green, yellow, light pink, and blue; a collar necklace of such stones as these, running all the gamut of color, costs about eighty dollars. What woman, with a proper standard of values, would cavil at this because it did not cost a hundred times as much, which it easily would if it were made of precious stones? Then there are the topazes, pink and yellow, and beryl, brown; the aquamarines, still pools of deep-green seawater; the olivine-like emeralds, shot with yellow sunlight; the opalescent moonstones; the star sapphires, chrysoberyl, and the golden carnelian; all

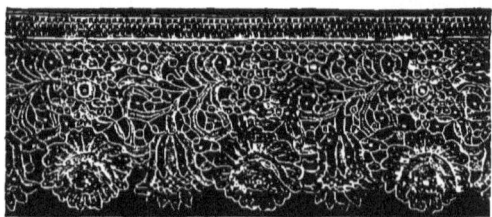

Rose Point Lace.

these and many others are to be found to-day at a price that makes possession of them an easy joy. So, too, is it with the reproductions in silver, in Russian enamel, and even in wrought-iron, of antiques in buckles and clasps, and chains and armlets, many of which

Duchesse Lace.

are as genuine works of art as the originals. All these are cheap, and in many cases are justly to be called imi-

Valenciennes.

tations, yet their artistic value is high. Such articles as these are peculiarly within the province of young girls, to whom the value of real gems at once makes them prohibited, and whose most appropriate ornaments are such as are simple and dainty, and artistic and inexpensive. And further, as to those

Point de Gênes.

gems that are not even genuine of their own kind, as are the semi-precious stones, but are distinctly imitations—even these are not to be despised. If the shimmering translucence of a natural pearl be valued at thousands of dollars, shall we argue for no value whatever in the shimmering translucence of an artificial pearl, which none but the most skilful expert is able to discriminate from the real one? It is well known that many of the magnificent jewels of the nobility and of royalty never see the sunlight, but are locked away in the family safes, and are replaced by imitations so skilful that even their owners cannot detect the difference.

It is evident that imitation jewelry and cheap jewelry may and do have a distinct value and usefulness, and that a gentlewoman may not infrequently wear both without reproach. The artistic value, and not the money one, is the first thought of the discriminating mind. Let us agree to amend the maxim to-day, so that it will read: "No gentlewoman will wear cheap imitation jewelry." A cheap imitation must necessarily be a vulgar one, and vulgarity, we can all agree, is decrying.

Perhaps it is hardly necessary to say that the wearing of jewelry on the street, other than the necessary adjuncts to one's toilet, is wholly inadmissible. A well-dressed woman wears a brooch or fancy pin to fasten the neck of her dress, a watch, and an appropriate clasp or chain, but no bracelets, no ear-rings, no dangling things of any kind. For full dress, she may wear jewels on her throat, arms, bosom, and hair, if she likes, but only then. It is a good thing to have these possessions, but meantime the silver and enamel ornaments

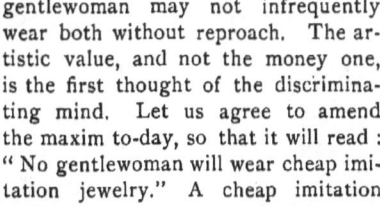

Point de Gênes.

and the semi-precious stones are not to be despised.

What has been said elsewhere of the value of imitation and cheap jewelry, applies as well to laces. There is no denying the value of real lace, but let us, in all candor, also admit the value of certain imitations. The laces most commonly found in the

Laces.

Cream Chantilly.

shops, both in real and in imitation, are point lace, point appliqué, rose point, duchesse, thread lace, valenciennes, guipure, and chantilly. All these are successfully imitated, and the imitations are to be found also. Naturally, the prices of these laces vary greatly, even in the same kinds, with regard to the intricacy of the pattern, the fineness of the net, the width of the piece, and many other considerations.

Point lace in very narrow widths, suitable only for edgings, can be bought for four or five dollars. A five-inch width of medium quality costs twenty-five or thirty dollars; rose point about the same width costs eighteen to twenty dollars. In this, the rose in the pattern has exquisite raised leaves. Point appliqué can be bought much cheaper, a width suitable for use on bodices costing about seven dollars. Duchesse lace about five inches wide costs six or seven dollars; duchesse and point combined costs about double the price of duchesse alone. Thread laces cost from two to one hundred dollars a yard, either in black or white. Valenciennes is a beautiful pillow lace, especially suited for the decoration of fine linen. It comes in a great many different prices, costing from twenty-five cents a yard upward. A good piece three inches wide can be bought for two dollars. The imitations of valenciennes often called platte valenciennes, are most successful and inexpensive, costing from five cents a yard for the narrowest widths up to one dollar. The modern guipure is a heavy black silk lace, especially suited to the decoration of silks, satins, and velvets. It ranges in price from one dollar upward; a medium width of good quality costing about five dollars a yard. Chantilly lace is a silk blond lace of great delicacy and beauty. It can be bought both in black and white. The cost of the real chantilly lace is approximate to that of the point. It is imitated successfully, usually in cotton, and costs in imitation from twenty-five cents to five

Torchon.

dollars a yard. Other good and inexpensive laces to be found in all the shops are torchon, a coarse linen lace, and Medici, a finer variety. Both are used principally for trimming underwear and prints. Venetian point and point de gênes, imitations of an exquisite old lace in white and écru, are useful for many purposes, from trimming frocks to edging table-cloths. Besides these there are to be found point de Paris, an imitation of Brussels lace; the oriental laces and the bourdonne, a black heavy silk lace used greatly for black silk dresses. All these cost but little, and are artistic and decorative. In buying laces, it is well to remember the fact that, while white and écru laces made of cotton thread are very serviceable, black cotton lace is sure to fade and grow rusty with wearing. The greater part of the fine lace that has made permanent the work of the great lace-makers has been done in white lace for this reason. It is real economy, therefore, when buying black lace, to pay a higher price and buy a piece made of silk thread.

Trousseau. The glamour of romance which surrounds the entire preparation for the new life often induces, in the mind of even the most practical woman, a certain aberration of judgment which leads her to choose her trousseau with reference to her taste rather than to her actual needs. Two facts she must keep constantly in mind in selecting her wardrobe—the place in which her new life is to be, and the conditions in which it is to be passed. If she is to live in a large city

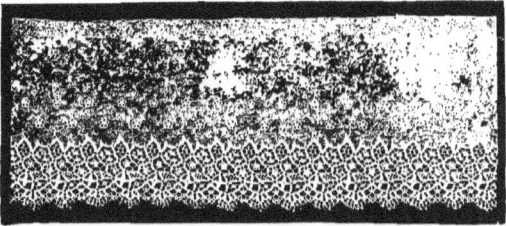

Point de Gênes—Net Top.

she will need a very different wardrobe from that necessary in a small town; so, too, will the size of her visiting list in her new life determine many of her purchases. Still more will her husband's financial condition, and their choice of a place in which to live, weigh in her selection. Suppose they decide to live in that intermediary purgatory known as a "boarding-house," in a hotel, or in lodgings, taking their meals out. She must then reluctantly give up all thought of the many light-tinted and softly-draped négligé gowns, so becoming to a woman in the privacy

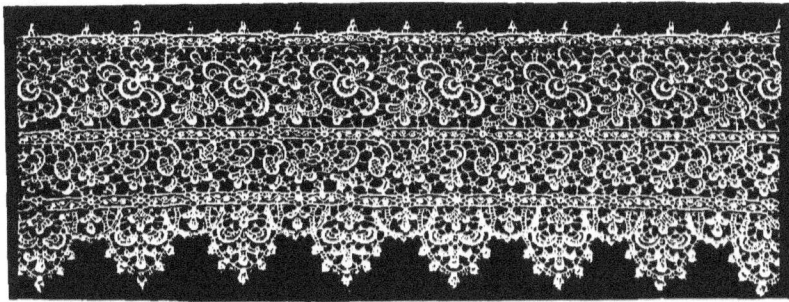

Venetian Point.

of her own home, and so wholly unsuited to hotel or boarding-house wear. Or, if her husband has a circle of friends, but not an income which permits that greatest of luxuries in a large city—a carriage, her gowns must of necessity be chosen with some reference to the possibility of wearing them in public conveyances, and her evening cloak will be long and dark, covering her from head to foot. There is also a multitude of toilet accessories perfectly in place for outdoor wear in small towns, that are utterly inappropriate to the crowded city's thoroughfare. Such, for example, are the pretty chiffon or elaborately decorated parasols often seen on the streets in small towns, but only carried in New York by those in carriages.

The following trousseau has been arranged as appropriate for a young woman in moderate circumstances who is to live after marriage in a city, and among a circle of friends neither large nor small. The articles named are well-nigh indispensable, and the prices given represent only medium qualities. The list may be indefinitely extended, and a little judicious pruning may be able to cut it down somewhat.

The prices given for gowns include estimates for making, of from fifteen dollars to twenty dollars a gown, with silk linings in some cases and good cotton linings in others:

Gown for Bridesmaid.

Wedding gown, cream white satin,	$100
Tulle veil,	10
One tailor gown and jacket,	75
One handsome visiting gown of cloth and silk,	50
One reception gown, high neck and long sleeves,	50
One dinner gown, low neck and half sleeves,	50
One ball gown, chiffon and silk,	50
One house gown, Empire, if becoming	20
One négligé,	12
One bath robe,	5
Two fancy silk waists,	20
Two dressing sacques, one silk and one flannel,	10
Eight sets of underwear, including one bridal set,	120
One silk skirt,	15
One skirt,	6
Two skirts (white),	8
Two skirts (white),	5
Four pairs of silk stockings,	8
1½ doz. handkerchiefs,	15
Six pairs of cotton stockings,	4
One pair of kid boots,	7
One pair of heavy kid boots,	6
One pair of evening slippers,	5
One pair of house shoes,	5
Six pairs of gloves,	12
One handsome hat,	15
One evening bonnet,	12
One plain hat,	10
One long plain coat,	25
One handsome wrap,	50
One short jacket,	20
One evening wrap.	35
	$835

THE CARE OF CLOTHES.

If half the secret of being well dressed is in knowing what to wear, the other half consists in keeping one's clothes in that exquisite daintiness which is better and more winning than style. The best time to take care of one's clothes is on taking them off, if possible. Cloth dress skirts should be brushed before they are hung away, by an open window and with a whisk broom, which is better for this purpose than a softer brush. Silks and satins are best cleaned by wiping them with a soft flannel. All spots should be removed as soon as possible, with a suitable detergent. Grease or dust on wool fabrics that do not spot are best removed with alcohol or naphtha. The former does well for wool, but naphtha is best for silk and delicate mixtures of silk and wool. Fuller's earth or French chalk is also effective in removing grease, if it is first mixed with water enough to make a thick paste, spread on the grease spot, and left for several days. If the first application does not remove the spot, the second usually will. Stains of any kind are more difficult to remove. Sometimes tepid water and ivory soap will suffice, but experiments, especially with ammonia and other strong cleansing agents, are usually dangerous. The safest way is to send the garment to a professional cleanser. In removing spots from delicate fabrics, if the color be affected, sponging with chloroform will often restore it. If the spot is made by an acid, touch it delicately with ammonia, which will neutralize the acid. If an alkali, such as ammonia, soda, or potash, be the spotting agent, reverse the former process and touch the spots with weak acid, such as lemon juice and water, or vinegar and water, with a soft cloth. Black silk is best cleaned and renovated by being first rubbed with a flannel, then saturated with a mixture of strong tea and vinegar, and ironed while still wet with a very hot iron.

Dresses carefully folded and laid away in large boxes or drawers, probably keep fresh longer than those hung in a closet. This, however, is not always possible in the case of one's every-day frocks. These, if hung away carefully, the skirt by tapes, and the waists on the shoulder-frames which are made for that purpose, will surely not suffer thereby. A clever woman once made a substitute for these curved shoulder-frames by winding barrel-hoops cut in half with strips of soft cheese-cloth. Coats are better hung by loops from the upper (not under) armholes, than folded in boxes, as their own weight is

Gown for Bride.

likely to crease them. If bags, fastened at the top with a draw-string, be used to encase these garments, they are almost hermetically sealed against dust, and there is little added danger from crushing. Hats and bonnets should always be brushed with a soft brush upon being taken off (a paint brush is excellent), subjected to that dainty digital manipulation which will restore any disarrangement of the trimming, and then kept in a hat-box. If they are laid on a shelf instead, a cone made of tissue paper should be slipped like a sheet over them.

Gloves should never be rolled in a ball when taken off the hands, nor should they be laid away if there is the least suspicion of moisture about them. Stretch the fingers out carefully, smooth the body of the glove, straighten the wrists, and then lay the glove, full length if possible, in a box or case. To clean gloves, nothing is so good as naphtha, with a few teaspoonfuls of ether added to a quart. Wash the glove in the fluid, just as you would a pocket-handkerchief, then lay it smoothly on a cloth, and with a soft cloth rub the especially soiled spots until clean. Then give the entire glove a second washing in clean naphtha and stretching out again, rub everywhere until perfectly dry. This last will prevent spotting. If this method be followed exactly, the results will be as satisfactory as the work of professionals. Shoes, to be kept in good condition, should have a little glycerine or sweet-oil rubbed into them occasionally, especially after being wet. Care in the selection of a shoe-dressing is very necessary. One that contains glycerine and no ammonia is warranted not to crack the kid. For the earlier stages of shabbiness before a shoe-dressing needs to be applied, nothing is so surprisingly renovating as the white of an egg, applied with a soft cloth to the leather, after this has first been wiped free of dust. If you don't believe this, try it. Russet leather should never be treated with anything except the dressing that is to be found for that purpose in the reliable shops. Kid and satin slippers may be cleaned with naphtha, like gloves. So may the suède shoes, fashionable not long ago. Patent leather should also be treated only with the varnish sold for the purpose: water causes it to lose its gloss and damp cracks it. The writer has found the most convenient and desirable way of keeping shoes to be in a small open book-case, in the bedroom, where each pair can be carefully placed on its shelf, and a cretonne curtain keeps dust out.

Wraps need special care only in the matter of packing them secure from moths when not in use. The secret of packing garments and furs away from moths lies, first, in exterminating any signs of eggs from the garment, and second, in effectually preventing the entrance of moths to the place where they are packed. The most valuable aid to the destruction of eggs is gasoline or naphtha. First brush the garment or whip the furs well, then, with a tiny sprinkling-pot filled with naphtha, or a sponge, saturate the garment with the fluid. It will not hurt it in any way and will effectually prevent the hatching of any eggs that have been laid therein. If then the garment is packed in a box or trunk which is or can be made proof against the entrance of the moth-fly, your concern for coats, furs, blankets—anything treated and packed thus—may be at end. This may be effectually secured by pasting cloth or paper over all cracks in the box and even over the lock and the joining of lid and box.

If fine laces are kept in a box of powdered magnesia, which can be bought very cheaply at the drug-shops, they will keep clean much longer than if they are kept in a box. When, however, it becomes necessary to clean them, it is best to send them to a professional cleanser's. If this cannot be done, then the following is the best way of doing the work at home: Baste each piece on a bottle covered smoothly with linen. Beginning at the bottom, wind the lace around the bottle, basting it fast at both edges to the linen. Soap it well with ivory soap, rinse well by plunging up and down in a pot of cold water, and then put it into a pot of hot water and boil until it is white. Set in the sun to dry, and if it has been carefully basted it will need no ironing.

Black lace may be renewed by passing it three or four times through a liquid made by dissolving a teaspoonful of spirits of wine and a teaspoonful of borax in half a teacupful of very soft water, then rinsing in a cup of hot water in which a black kid glove has been boiled. Pull out the edges of the lace until nearly dry and place in a heavy book for two days to press.

Jewelry should be washed in hot water in which has been dissolved some white soap and ammonia, using a moderately soft small brush. Then lay in a box of sawdust to dry, and the result will be satisfactory. Stones in their settings may be cleaned by using the soft and moistened end of a wooden toothpick in the interstices. Alcohol is also effective in dissolving dirt.

II.—MILLINERY AT HOME.

By BESSIE ANNIN LOSEY.

THIS section is prepared for such women as feel that they cannot afford to pay a milliner her price, yet do not know how to produce the desired results themselves. By carefully following the directions given below, any woman should be able to make a satisfactory hat; whether she can trim it well or not depends upon her own taste and nimble fingers.

Let me begin with the wiring. Many people think that the wire counts for little, but if it is not put on properly a hat is often ruined. The wire should not be tighter than the hat, because if it is it will cause the hat to roll under, so as completely to spoil the shape. Never use wire a second time. As it is very inexpensive, it never pays to use wire that is at all "kinky," as old wire is apt to be. In sewing it on a straw hat, a long stitch sewed through the wire and hat is used; a small stitch is imbedded in the straw on the right side of the hat.

Wiring.

For buckram the wire should be buttonholed close to the edge, with stitches about one half an inch apart. The wire should always be lapped three inches where it is joined. Silk wire, when used for a finish, is put on with a blind stitch.

Plain folds are always in vogue, and look well on any shape in felt or straw. They vary in width according to the taste of the wearer, but are never wider than three-quarters of an inch; when anything wider is desired a pattern is cut. The prettiest width is one-half inch. The material is cut on the bias one inch wide. It should be cut a little shorter than the hat and joined in a circle. Draw the two edges together by catching first under one side, then under the other, but do not let them lap. It is then stretched carefully and pinned on the hat over the wire, which is about a quarter of an inch from the edge. Blind-stitch it neatly with the long

Folds.

stitch in the fold. If more than one fold is desired, it is better to cut the folds narrower.

For a round fold one requires wire or cable cord. Measure the cord or wire around and cut the fold twice the width. Make the same as for plain fold, then overhand the edges together over the cord or wire. It is sewed on with a blindstitch, and the hat is not wired.

A milliner's or French fold is cut on the bias two inches wide and made as plain fold. Turn up the lower edge on the wrong side about two-thirds of the width and blindstitch.

Making Milliner's Fold.

In buying for folds always get the material on the bias. One-eighth of a yard will make two plain folds for a hat of medium size.

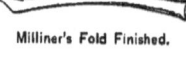
Milliner's Fold Finished.

Wire the hat about one-half inch from the edge on the upper brim. Cut the material on the bias two and one-half inches wide. Sew close to the wire with a long stitch and short backstitch, stretching the material slightly and making a bias join in the back. Draw it over the edge of the hat, turn under the edge of the material and blindstitch it.

Binding felt hats.

Buy the material on the straight. Lay a corner of it across the front of the hat. Smooth and stretch it on until it fits firmly. Turn under the outer edge about one-quarter of an inch and blindstitch it over the wire, which is usually placed near the edge of the hat. Slash the headline and sew in with a long stitch inside the hat and a short one outside

Plain facing.

Half Facing—Plain.

Half facings may be made by covering a certain portion of the brim, either from the edge or from the headline.

Cut the material on the bias three and one-half inches wide and use one and five-eighths of the length of the hat for fulness. Wire the hat one-half inch from the edge on the upper side of the brim. Pin the puff on, arranging the fulness evenly, and sew with a long stitch and backstitch close to the wire, turn over, keeping the fulness even with that on top and blindstitch one-half inch from edge. This will extend the puff one inch beyond the edge of the hat, and the fulness can then be arranged with a pretty, soft effect. A puff can be made with a heading, and, in that case, when cutting, an extra allowance should be made. Three-eighths of a yard on the bias will make a puff for a medium-sized hat.

Puff bindings.

Puff Binding.

These can be made of any pretty, soft material, but the fulness is varied according to the weight of the material. *Crêpe de chine* requires twice the fulness; chiffon twice and a half; Brussels net three to four times, according to the size of the hat; silk once and three-quarters. They can be made with simply a heading; in that case cut them as many inches as desired wider than the broadest part of the brim. If tucks are preferred, make an extra allowance for those from one-half to one inch for each tuck. The heading may extend beyond the edge if desired. Arrange your fulness evenly, plait it into the head-line, turning the plaits toward the centre of the front, unless it be on a perfectly round hat.

Shirred facings.

Shirred Facing.

Always bind the edge of the frame

with a narrow strip of crinoline, cut on the bias; this prevents the velvet from rubbing on the edge. Cut a paper pattern for your under brim, fitting it perfectly; if necessary, a few plaits may be put in the paper and securely pinned. Cut a notch for the centre of the front (placing a pin to correspond in the hat) and put a pencil-mark on it to designate the right side. When reversed this pattern may be used for the upper brim. Then cut a pattern for the side crown, joining it where it will show the least and marking and notching it the same as the brim pattern.

Covering hats.

Shirred Hat.

The material, if used only for covering, should be bought on the straight, as it cuts to better advantage. One yard will be sufficient for that, but if the same is desired for trimming, buy the material on the bias and allow from one-quarter to one-half a yard extra.

Cut for the upper brim first, laying the right side of the pattern to the right side of the goods, the centre of the front across the corner of the material, allowing a margin. Cut the material one-half inch larger than the pattern. If the material is bias, place the centre of the pattern across it.

For the lower brim place the wrong side of the pattern to the right side of the material. In cutting, allow one-half inch outside and three-quarters of an inch at the head-line.

Lay the side-crown pattern in the same way as under the brim with the centre of the front across the bias, and in cutting allow one-half inch more than the pattern on both sides and at each end.

Use a corner of the material for covering the tip of the crown. Place the point at the front, bringing the bias across the crown. Sew one-quarter inch below the top with a long stitch and short backstitch, stretching the material as you sew. Trim it off close to the sewing, as it is best not to have any more material than is necessary under the side crown.

Adjust your upper brim, slashing it slightly around the head-line. Draw it on smoothly, allowing at least one-quarter of an inch to extend beyond the hat. Trim this off evenly and turn over the edge, sewing it with an over-and-over stitch to the buckram, not allowing the stitches to come through to the upper side. Sew around the head-line with a long stitch and backstitch.

The lower brim is drawn on very firmly, pushing all fulness to the least conspicuous part of the brim, usually the back, where a neat blindstitched "join" is made. Turn under the outer edge one-quarter of an inch and blindstitch it to the edge of the hat. This is an important piece of work and great care should be taken that the stitches do not show or that it does not slip below the edge. Slash the head-line and sew with a long stitch.

The side crown is adjusted last. Draw it on snugly, turning under the lower edge about one-half inch. Turn the upper edge under one-quarter of an inch by running a bodkin around it, then blindstitch where joined.

Very few rules can be given for covering a bonnet, as the styles change each year. There are always fancy square-crowned bonnets, which can be covered the same as the hats, but without finishing the edges. Use a quarter of a yard on the bias for a pretty draped edge. Hem both edges of your velvet and shirr them for about four or five inches in the centre. This makes a fulness for the face and the sides can be drawn back loosely or

Covering bonnets.

plaited, according to the taste of the wearer; milliners' folds or ribbon for the ties and some pretty trimming for the front. Bonnets, as a rule, require very little trimming. Too much trimming produces a top-heavy effect.

For soft crowns use material on the bias and allow three-eighths to one-half yard. One yard on the bias will make a bonnet, including the ties, and usually allows a little to be used in the trimming. Jet may enter largely into the making of a bonnet. A good piece of jet can be used many times.

It is often impossible to buy a felt bonnet that will match a gown exactly. In that case procure a pretty round-crowned bonnet and cover with ladies' cloth or light-weight felt. Place the corner of the material under the back of the frame and draw all fulness toward the front. Do not be afraid to stretch the material and the fulness will gradually disappear. Any remaining fulness may be laid in plaits where they will be covered with the trimming. The edge can be bound with velvet and a pretty braid or jet band added for a finish, or a full edge can be used if preferred.

Lining. Lining, like wiring, is often considered to be an unimportant matter; yet this is not the case. Always line a hat or bonnet. There is a saying that a milliner never lines her own hat; let it prove false in the case of those who make use of these directions.

Buy marcelline silk for lining. Three-quarters of a yard will make four linings and tips. Use the material on the straight; a bias lining will stretch. Cut it one and a half inch longer than the head-line and one inch wider than the deepest part of the side crown. Sew through the hat, if of straw or felt, with a long stitch holding the lining in place. If of velvet, sew with an over-and-over stitch.

Seam it up the back and make a quarter-of-an-inch hem in the edge. Run a narrow piece of ribbon through the casing thus formed and tie in a very small bow. The tip can be sewed to the hat at each corner, or mucilage can be used very lightly.

In cutting bonnet linings use the same measurements as for a hat. Sew with an over-and-over stitch, and blindstitch the ends to the back of the bonnet. Also blindstitch the tip across the back, tacking the sides in place.

Bows and rosettes. Someone has said that to make a pretty, stylish bow a person must be a born milliner. That is not always the case. We shall grant that there should be taste for the work, but a great deal comes with practice. Use wire with discrimination. The loops that stand upright, and occasionally the ends, are all that require the wire, unless the ribbon is very flimsy. In that case the ribbon may be wired throughout the whole length. Use ribbon wire, the full width, if the ribbon is wide; if narrow, separate and use one of the small wires of which the ribbon wire is composed. Sew the wire through the centre of the ribbon with buttonhole stitches about one inch apart, taking care that the stitches do not show on the right side. The ends should be wired near the edge, with the stitches close together. In making up your ribbon do not tie it, as it requires more, and the bow is apt to appear stiff, which is the very thing one wishes to avoid. Wind your loops with thread or fine wire, fastening it securely and

Bow for Front of Hat.

Pretty Striped Bow.

Small Bow for Bonnet.

How to Make Bows and Rosettes.

For Side of Hat.

For Back of Hat.

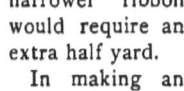
Stylish Bow for Front of Hat.

Alsatian Bow.

Butterfly Bow.

Butterfly Bow.

Shirring for Rosette.

Making Rosette.

Rosette Finished.

winding each loop close to the others. Turn over the edges of the ribbon as it is being wound and the bow will have a softer and prettier line. In placing the bow upon the hat arrange the high loops so that the side of the loop is against the side of the hat. Never allow high loops to stand across the hat or with the width, as they will surely proclaim the much-dreaded fact that the hat is home-made. Two yards of four-inch ribbon is sufficient to make a large bow; narrower ribbon would require an extra half yard.

In making an Alsatian bow (see illustration) always have an even number of loops of even length each side of the knot. Make a long loop, two shorter loops, then another the length of the first, placing the knot between the two smaller loops and drawing it very tightly. The "waist" of the bow should always be small and snug.

Butterfly bows are made with an end, two loops of even length and another end, the knot being between the loops. They are arranged as the illustrations show, either the ends standing together or opposite each other.

If one intends having ends to a bow, it is better to start with an end. Unless ends are used do not cut the ribbon any more than is necessary; if it is in short lengths it is of very little service a second time.

Rosettes of velvet, cloth, or silk are cut on the bias. Other materials, such as *crêpe de chine*, Brussels net, etc., are used on the straight. Of the latter material, if the rosette is to be three inches wide, use one yard in the length; if two and one-half inches wide, thirty-one inches in length; if two inches wide, twenty-seven inches long. Turn the ends in one-half inch, bringing the two edges together; shirr into a space of five inches and sew this length on a tiny circle of crinoline, making the centre irregular. A rosette when made round and round is very precise looking and does not add to the style of a hat.

Heavier material does not require as much length or the rosettes will be too full. Shirr the material up tightly and arrange it in shape without placing the rosette on a foundation.

Baby-ribbon rosettes are made by sewing four or five loops at one time on a strip of wire, continuing the groups and keeping them close together until the end of the ribbon is reached. Roll the wire around, securely fastening it on the back. Ten yards are usually needed for one rosette.

Mourning. Mourning hats and bonnets should always be made simply, but of the best material. Good taste requires that fashion should not enter too largely in this work. Feathers should never be used on crape nor jet on black silk, unless it be dull jet, and then not in large quantities. Cheap crape soon grows rusty. Light silk and nuns' veiling are frequently used instead of crape veils. They are more comfortable and hygienic.

It is not well for a novice to undertake to work with crape. But in case one must, a few hints may be given. Never stretch crape; it is always placed on loosely so that the whales do not separate. The lines of the crape (or whales as they are properly called), must be straight when used, as that brings the goods on the bias. Folds are always used on crape with a very simple trimming.

Black silk is more easily handled. It is used very much in the same way as velvet, allowing a little extra for seams and fulness, as it is inclined to stretch more. In making it up care should be taken that the grain runs all one way, and when seaming, to sew *in* the grain and not across it.

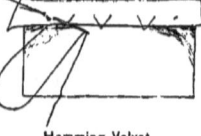
Hemming Velvet.

Always buy the material on the bias, unless for a plain facing or covering, and *always use* it on the bias. Use thread for sewing; never use sewing-silk unless for shirring.

General hints. Black pins with round glass heads should always be used for pinning work, as they will not mark the material like the common brass pin.

If the fingers press the velvet wrap a small piece of the goods around the thumb, which will relieve the pressure.

To make a perfect bias, fold the material so that the cut edge is even with the selvage, and there will be a perfect triangle.

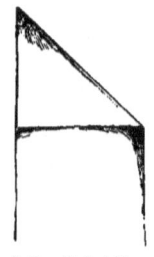
Folding Perfect Bias.

III.—DRESSING ON FIXED SUMS.

By FRANCES BACON PAINE.

Estimate for Dressing on $500 a Year.

Boots, Shoes, Etc.

1 pair boots, ...	$8.00
1 pair boots, ...	6.00
1 pair russet low shoes, . . .	3.50
1 pair patent low shoes, . . .	4.50
1 pair slippers, ...	2.00
1 pair slippers, ...	3.50
1 pair rubbers, ...	.50
1 pair arctics, ...	1.50
	—— $29.50

Underwear.

6 pairs cotton stockings (winter weight) at 50 cents, ...	$3.00
6 pairs lisle-thread stockings at 50 cents, ...	$3.00
2 pairs black silk stockings at $1.50, ...	3.00
4 winter underskirts at $1.25, .	5.00
5 summer-silk vests at 90 cents, .	3.60
1 pair corsets, ...	2.50
1 pair corsets, ...	5.00
3 winter underdrawers at 75 cents, ...	2.25
6 white drawers at 68 cents, . .	4.08
4 nightgowns at $1.50, . . .	6.00
3 flannel petticoats at $1.25, . .	3.75
4 underwaists at 75 cents, . .	3.00
2 underwaists at $1.25, . . .	2.50

Dressing on $250 or $500 a Year.

4 white skirts at $1.25,	$5.00
2 white skirts at $1.98,	3.96
	—— $55.14

Winter Dresses.

8 yards material at $1.50 (for winter street dress),	$12.00
Making and linings for same,	17.00
5 yards fancy silk for waist at $1.00,	5.00
Making and lining for same,	7.00
8 yards material for house dress at $1.00,	8.00
Making of same by sewing-woman (3 days at $2.00),	6.00
Linings, etc.,	2.00
12 yards dark silk at $1.50,	18.00
Trimming, linings, etc.,	5.00
Making of same,	16.00
12 yards light evening silk at $1.50,	18.00
Making,	16.00
Trimmings, etc.,	8.00
	—— $138.00

Summer Dresses.

2 shirt-waists at $1.50,	$3.00
5 yards wash silk for shirt-waist at 60 cents,	3.00
Making of same,	2.50
8 yards material for spring costume at $1.50,	12.00
Making and linings for same,	18.00
3 1-2 yards material for plain skirt at $1.00,	3.50
Making at home,	2.00
Lining,	1.00
10 yards percale at 25 cents,	2.50
Embroidery for same,	1.50
Making for same (2 days at home)	4.00
10 yards gingham at 30 cents,	3.00
Embroidery or ribbon for same,	2.00
Making (2 days at home),	4.00
10 yards muslin at 50 cents,	5.00
Lace and ribbon for same,	6.00
Making for same (2 days at home),	4.00
10 yards foulard or fancy silk at $1.25,	12.50
Making and linings for same,	18.00
10 yards light fancy material for evening wear at $1.00,	10.00
Making and linings for same,	18.00
Trimming,	6.00
10 yards Scotch flannel at 40 cents,	4.00
Making same (3 days at home),	6.00
	—— $151.50

Coats, Etc.

1 winter coat,	$16.00
1 summer coat,	12.00
1 evening wrap,	20.00
1 water-proof cloak,	6.00
	—— $54.00

Hats and Bonnets.

1 best winter hat,	$10.00
1 winter hat (made at home),	4.00
1 bonnet (made at home),	4.00
1 best summer hat,	8.00
1 summer hat (made at home),	5.00
1 summer bonnet (made at home),	4.00
	—— $35.00

Sundries.

1 umbrella,	$5.00
1 parasol,	3.50
12 hemstitched handkerchiefs at 25 cents,	3.00
6 handkerchiefs at 50 cents,	3.00
Veiling,	4.00
1 best fan,	2.50
1 paper fan,	.75
2 pairs long evening gloves at $1.75,	3.50
3 pairs walking gloves at $1.50,	4.50
3 pairs suède gloves at $1.50,	4.50
6 pairs summer gloves,	8.00
	—— $42.25
	$505.39

Estimate for Dressing on $250 a Year.

2 pairs boots at $5.00,	$10.00
1 pair patent-leather low shoes,	4.00
1 pair slippers,	2.00
1 pair rubbers,	.50
	—— $16.50
6 pairs cotton stockings,	$2.00
6 pairs lisle-thread stockings at 35 cents,	2.10
3 winter undershirts at $1.00,	3.00
4 summer shirts at 50 cents,	2.00
1 pair corsets,	2.50
1 pair corsets,	1.75
3 winter underdrawers at 50 cents,	1.50
4 pairs drawers at 50 cents,	2.00
2 flannel skirts at $1.00,	2.00
4 underwaists at 50 cents,	2.00
4 white skirts at 98 cents,	3.92
4 nightgowns at $1.25,	5.00
	—— 29.77
8 yards material at $1.50 (for winter dress),	$12.00
Making of same (at home, 3 days at $2.00),	6.00

Lining, etc.,	$2.00	10 yards silk at 75 cents,	$7.50
8 yards material for house dress at 75 cents,	6.00	Trimming and lining,	4.00
		Making (2 days at home),	4.00
Making of same (2 days at $2.00),	4.00		$58.77
Linings, etc.,	1.50	1 winter coat,	$16.00
12 yards silk at $1.50,	18.00	1 summer coat,	10.00
Trimmings and linings,	4.00	1 evening wrap (made at home),	12.00
Making of same (3 days at home),	6.00		38.00
For making over evening dress on hand,	10.00	1 winter hat,	$8.00
	$69.50	1 winter hat (made at home),	3.00
		1 bonnet (made at home),	3.00
2 shirt-waists at $1.50,	$3.00	1 summer hat,	6.00
8 yards material (spring costume) at $1.50,	12.00	1 summer hat (made at home),	5.00
		1 bonnet (made at home),	3.00
Linings,	2.00		26.00
Making of same (3 days at home),	6.00		
3 1-2 yards material at 75 cents (for plain skirt),	2.62	1 umbrella,	$4.00
		1 parasol,	2.00
Lining,	1.00	12 handkerchiefs at 25 cents,	3.00
10 yards percale at 12 1-2 cents,	1.25	2 handkerchiefs at 50 cents,	1.00
Embroidery,	1.00	Veiling,	2.00
Making (1 day at home),	2.00	1 fan,	1.50
10 yards gingham at 19 cents,	1.90	1 pair gloves,	1.50
Embroidery,	1.50	2 pairs walking gloves,	2.50
Making (1 day at home),	2.00	3 pairs summer gloves,	3.00
10 yards muslin at 30 cents,	3.00		20.50
Lace for trimming,	2.00		
Making (1 day at home),	2.00		$259.04

IV.—DRESSMAKING AT HOME.

By S. T. ALLEN.

THE object of this section is to make clear various troublesome points not usually mentioned in works on dressmaking; to make the rules, in fact, so direct and comprehensive that no good needlewoman need hesitate to cut and make an ordinary dress without previous experience.

It is well to begin with the skirt, as the basque or waist should be fitted over the *finished* dress skirt; otherwise it is apt to be too tight around the hips. In most cases the "riding up" of basques, and their tendency to wrinkle, is caused merely by their having been fitted without the finished skirt underneath.

Skirts.

The hang and finish of a skirt is a much weightier matter than it is ordinarily considered, as a well-made, evenly hanging skirt gives an air of grace to the whole garment, and to the wearer as well; while the slovenly made, unevenly hanging skirt—the skirt that dips in one place and is too short in another—makes even a graceful woman appear awkward, and is an indication of an incompetent dressmaker.

For a person of medium height, a dress made with a full, plain skirt would require thirteen yards of twenty-two inch goods; eleven yards of twenty-seven inch goods; seven yards of thirty-six inch goods; five yards of forty-eight inch goods; four and a half yards of fifty-four inch goods. For the foundation skirt, when used, four yards of yard-wide material would be sufficient; of lining-silk, six or seven yards; and of soft-finish cambric, six yards.

In cutting the foundation skirt, a pattern is not necessary. It is far better to cut by measurement and learn to allow for differences in proportion than to be limited to skirt patterns. First, take the skirt length by measuring from the belt downward, beginning with the front breadth. The length must, of course, vary according to the height of the person. For a skirt of medium length, or thirty-nine inches when finished, the front and side breadths should be cut forty-one inches in length, two inches extra always being allowed for the making. The back usually should be of the same length, but for people who are short-waisted *in the back*, the back breadths should be cut two inches longer than the front and sides. After cutting the number of lengths necessary, take one of the forty-one-inch lengths and fold it lengthwise

Graduating Gowns.

through the centre, measure five and a half inches from the centre and notch it through both thicknesses of the goods. This is the top of the front width; the bottom should be treated in the same way, measuring thirteen inches from the folded centre. Crease through both sides of this folded breadth, from the notches at the top to the notches at the bottom, and remove the extra material by following the creased folds in cutting. For the top of the side breadths, measure from the selvage edge, six inches *across* the goods, and notch it; for the bottom of the breadth measure, in the same way, sixteen inches, and notch at the measurement. Graduate the breadth by folding it lengthwise between the notch at the top and the notch at the bottom, cutting it on the fold. Place this measured width on the other side breadth, and cut it to the same size. The back breadth, or breadths, for a full-gathered, or pleated back, should be of the same width throughout, and measure from two to two and a half yards. These measurements are for the lining to a plain skirt, where the outside, or dress material is cut to the same size, or for the foundation skirt of a draped skirt. From one to two inches must be added to, or taken from, the width of each breadth when the skirt is four or more inches longer or shorter than the medium size above mentioned, excepting where the person requiring a long skirt is very slight, or one requiring a short skirt is exceedingly stout, in which case it should be graduated accordingly.

To finish the foundation skirt and prepare it for the overdress or drapery, cut from the dress goods strips wide enough to extend well under the drapery. Place these on the outside of the skirt-lining, and baste firmly across at the bottom; turn in the upper edge on the lining, and baste for stitching. Then stitch the upper edge of each—the edge that is turned in—on the lining. After these are all stitched, take the front breadth and one side breadth, and, beginning at the *top*, sew the front to the straight edge of the side breadth; proceed in the same manner with the other side. Sew the back, beginning at the top, to the bias edges of the side breadths; when all are thus joined, pin the skirt evenly together down the corresponding seams, lay it on a cutting-table or some solid surface, and trim it evenly around at the bottom. Next cut a facing—for the inside—of linen canvas, hair-cloth, or cross-bar crinoline, about six inches deep, and sew together a sufficient number of widths to reach around the skirt. Take velveteen skirt-binding and baste evenly to the edge of one side of this stiff facing; then cut from silk or other plain material—of the same color as the dress—a sufficient number of strips, about five inches deep, to cover the length of the facing. Turn in one edge of the silk or other goods very slightly, and baste the turned-in edge one quarter of an inch over the upper edge of the velveteen binding which has been already basted, to the edge of one side of the stiff facing, and stitch it in place. Baste this *prepared* facing very smoothly to the edge of the skirt, holding the facing uppermost and on the right side of the skirt, with the silk covering against the right side of the skirt. When firmly basted in place, stitch the edges together in a small seam; turn the prepared facing over to the wrong side of the skirt, so that the crinoline lies next the wrong side of the skirt, and baste again, being careful to draw up the facing sufficiently to leave only enough of the velveteen visible to make it appear like a fine cording. Turn in the silk or other facing on the wrong side of the dress, over the stiff inside facing at the top, and hem to the lining of the skirt, being careful not to let the print of the stitches show on the outside material of the skirt.

About three and a half inches from the middle of the skirt front, at the top, make pleats one half inch deep on each side; open and press. Gather the skirt from the centre of each side breadth to the middle of the back breadth, and draw nearly all the fulness to the back, leaving almost none in the side breadths. Open the back breadth down the middle for about fifteen inches, hem one side—the overlapping side—and sew to the other side a piece of the dress-goods four inches wide, making it long enough to fasten to the skirt lining two inches below the opening. Bind this at the top with ribbon, and let it extend beyond the *end* of the belt, to which the bound top should be attached. From the lining material cut a belt of the required length, allowing a little for turning in at the ends and the edges. Sew the skirt to the back or under edge of the belt in the same manner as in making muslin underskirts, leaving the front edge of the belt free, to be sewed down *after* the drapery is attached, or the full-round skirt is added. Should the skirt "hoop" or bind across the lap, or ride up when the wearer is *sitting*—and it should always be tested in that way before the belt is permanently fastened—rip the front and the sides from the belt, and place the pleats on each side of the front breadths, about an inch nearer the centre. If the skirt still continues to bind, move the pleats a little further forward, and also draw a little fulness from the back breadths and add to the sides. Skirts are very apt to have this fault where the wearer has large hips and a high stomach; and in such cases the better way is to fit the skirt to the wearer until it hangs correctly, independently of any rules.

The directions just given are for skirts with only one side gore, a style of skirt which is nearly always in fashion. Other skirts, however, with two or more side gores, may easily be cut by following the same general directions. One style of umbrella skirt is cut three and a half inches wide at the top, and eight and a half at the bottom, from the centre of the front breadth—folded as in the skirt already described. The gore next to the front is five inches wide at the top and fourteen at the bottom. The second gore, which joins the back breadths, measures four inches at the top and fourteen at the bottom. The back breadth, or breadths, which are joined to the bias edge of these gores, are also slightly sloped on the sides which are sewed to the gores, and must measure across, for the *entire back* of the skirt, forty-one inches at the top and fifty-six at the bottom.

Mountain and tennis skirts are frequently made up without lining, or foundation skirt, having four straight breadths gathered to a belt and the skirt hemmed by hand or stitched twice at the top of the hem, which may be from four to six inches deep. From three and a half to four yards is the ordinary width for a *full round* skirt, and it is of the same length when finished as the foundation skirt, over which it hangs. Other skirts are four, and sometimes even five, yards wide. The latter is particularly elegant when made of heavy silk, and worn with a slightly pointed or a straight round waist and handsome belt. No drapery at all is used with these full skirts, the breadths being pleated or gathered all round, rather scantily in front and at the sides and very full in the back.

As the clinging, straight skirt is not becoming to all figures, it is often desirable to vary it by drapery, particularly for thin materials. Draping is not so difficult a matter as it may appear to the uninitiated. A little practice and perseverance soon give facility. The use of a skirt form is a necessity in learning to drape well, and these are now so reasonable in price as to be within the reach of everybody. A regular "dressmaker's form," combining both waist and skirt, is the best.

The attempt to give directions for draping may be considered novel, as it is generally asserted that the ability to drape well is a natural gift—something which cannot be acquired. A few general hints, however, may be of use to those who have the latent talent, undeveloped because untried. Almost anyone may acquire a little knowledge of the art and succeed nearly as well as some dressmakers—at least in the matter of slight drapery, if they never get to the more elaborate styles.

To drape from a fashion-plate, put the foundation skirt on the form, and beginning at the front, pin the dress goods to the top of the foundation skirt, as nearly as possible in the manner shown in the illustration. If possible ascertain whether the drapery is straight or bias at the top of the front width, as it makes a difference in the hang of the drapery and its likeness to the copy whether it is cut in the same way. This can usually be determined by trying the effect both straight and bias; that which approaches more nearly to the appearance of the model being, naturally, the correct way. Above all, do not be discouraged if the first attempt does not give the desired result. It is well first to experiment with some old material or the cheapest cheese-cloth. Try a few times with either of these, and the facility which may be attained by a little practice will surprise you. Several trials in copying illustrations will soon give a proficiency that will make it an easy matter to drape without a copy, following the prevailing modes, of course, but giving to it your own individuality.

A small cutting-table, or a good lap-board, is necessary in cutting and basting. It would take too much time and space to give here the complete rules for cutting from measurement. Doubtless few amateurs would care to take the time required to master fully the rules. It is advisable that they should get a trustworthy pattern, a plain round basque pattern, agreeing as nearly as possible to the bust measure. Such patterns may be purchased at any pattern store, and may be had with or without allowance for seams. To ascertain the required size, pass a tape-measure around the body close under the arms, just above the fullest part of the bust, and draw it slightly snug. The number of inches thus ascertained will be the correct size and should be mentioned when ordering the pattern. As only half of the pattern is given, but one side can be fitted. First pin the pattern piece for the back down its straight edge to the dress waist at the centre of the back, being careful to keep it smooth. Then pin on the front piece, following this with the curved piece for the back, and last the under-arm piece. If the edges of these pieces just meet, with the back and front edges of the pattern exactly in the centre of the waist, it will be safe to cut from the pattern without alteration. Where seams are *allowed* on the pattern, each seam-line should be placed directly over the corresponding seam-line in the next piece. If seams are to be allowed it will be so stated on the pattern. When the pattern is too large in any part, cut away until the edges meet evenly, as above described. Should a pattern be too tight across the hips, over the stomach or the bust, pin in pieces of paper or muslin until the desired fulness is obtained, then divide the added portion equally between the two adjoining pieces. If too short on the shoulder, too low in the neck, or too narrow across the back, pin on extra pieces and cut to a correct fit. Remove the pattern and pin it smoothly to the lining intended for the waist, keeping the added parts attached to the pattern until the cutting is completed. Place the lining on the cutting-table and have it doubled so that from each part of the pattern two corresponding pieces may be cut at the same time.

Waists.

Cutting and Basting Waists.

With a tracing-wheel or sharp-pointed instrument follow the pattern *closely*, as the slightest variation on the edges, so little as a pencil-mark, will make the waist too large or too small. This traced line should be indented in both thicknesses of the lining, as it is intended to show where the seams are to be sewed, and, therefore, should be carefully followed in basting. A half inch outside of this line should be allowed for seams. Nothing need be allowed for seams at armholes or the neck, though it is well to allow a little at these places for alterations. *Do not cut out the darts until the waist is satisfactorily fitted.*

In cutting the fronts, place the pattern lengthwise on the doubled lining, straight with the selvage from the neck to the centre of the front, thus throwing the lower part back at the under-arm seam and making that edge bias, as in the accompanying cut (Fig. 1), the dotted lines showing the selvage of the goods and the other lines the pattern. Some patterns are not much curved in front, and for slight figures the curve is scarcely necessary. For stout figures the curved front and bias under-arm seam are a great help in fitting, as this bias portion gives more readily to the contour of the figure, making the waist less liable to wrinkle at that point.

The back, side-back, and under-arm pieces should be cut straight with the grain of the goods of both the lining and outside, the threads of each running the same way.

It is of the utmost importance to emphasize the fact that *careful basting* is the essential feature in perfect fitting. For brevity, however, the most necessary rules only will be given here. If strictly followed they will prove to be all that are really requisite for the work.

Place the lining on the dress goods

Fig. 1.—Outline of Dress-front.

and cut and baste each piece separately. Begin with the front, at the top of the shoulder, and baste an inch from the edge around the neck and down the front to the bottom, not across it, then down the shoulder and around the armhole, thence down the edge under the arm. Full the lining a little at the waist-line from an inch above to an inch below; that is, the lining should be basted one-half inch fuller than the outside on each part of the waist at the waist-line and just above and below it. The reason is obvious—the dress goods being on the inner or shorter curve, and the lining on the longer or outer curve, and, therefore, needing additional length. The front should next be basted from the highest point of the shoulder down through the centre of the first dart to the bottom, then through the other dart in like manner. The spaces between the darts should next be basted and fulled a little, as already suggested for the other parts. Baste the back and side pieces in the same way, beginning at the top. Then baste each piece with short stitches across the bottom before the seams are sewed, allowing the lining to be shorter than the outside, to keep the fulness at the waist-line. Before basting the seams should be pinned together, the pins being placed a few inches apart and removed as the basting proceeds. All the seams must be basted from the top downward—*never* from the bottom up. The centre seam at the back may be joined first, and in basting the parts together the stitches should not be over a quarter of an inch in length. The side-backs come next, and the curved part should be *stretched* one-third of an inch on the back over a length of four inches, starting an inch from the armholes; that is, hold the curved side-form tighter than the back for the distance given, sufficiently to make the back one-third of an inch fuller, this fulness to be divided equally over the four inches of length. To do this correctly notch the back and the curved side-back each one inch from the armhole; then notch the side-back four inches from this notch and the back four and one-third inches; the side-back is then stretched until the notches meet. This is to make the proper curve over the shoulder-blade and avoid the wrinkles so apt to appear in the back side-form. Baste to these the under-arm pieces. The darts in the fronts may next be basted up and the fronts joined to the side-forms; the fronts should be stretched half an inch on the latter, partly above and partly below the waist-line, in the way described above for joining the curved side-forms to the back. The shoulder-seams may now be basted, and here the fronts should be cut three-quarters of an inch shorter than the backs and stretched to fit them. Most of the stretching should be done close to the neck. After basting, the back portions will have a puckered appearance, but when stitched and pressed this will all disappear.

To fit the basted waist to the person put it on wrong side out and pin the front edges together as you would sew a seam, not overlapping as when buttoned. If it appears baggy over the bust, pull it up at the shoulder-seams and pin tightly there; then let the wearer sit naturally and pin up again if any bagginess remains. The latter trial is an excellent plan for persons large in the bust, whose waists often stretch and soon grow too loose in that place. The back may next be fitted, then the side-backs, and lastly, the under-arm seams. These last should not be stitched until the other seams have all been stitched, pressed, and the waist again tried on, as any final alterations can generally be made at these seams. Do not pin too tight at any one seam, but pin in a little at a time, until all are snug and smooth; examine them all carefully, to see that no seam is pinned tighter than the corresponding seam on the other side, in order to have the waist even, as much of the ugly twisting of waists is due to the unevenness of these corresponding portions. If the person fitted is inclined to be round-shouldered, set the shoulder-seam as far back as possible. This may be done by ripping open the seam, taking more from the back part and lessening the width of the seam at the front.

Now trim the fronts on the edge, if

necessary; then run a strong thread close to the edge over the most curved part of the fronts, nearly to the waist-line; draw it slightly tight and fasten the thread. This will prevent stretching and generally obviates cutting out a V-shaped piece, as is sometimes done for full busts and sloping shoulders. Instead of hemming, these fronts should be interlined with stiff crinoline or canvas and then faced, which is the better way to treat them when curved. The facing should be cut to fit the fronts, and the same way of the goods; *not* perfectly straight, and *not* bias

Remove the waist and baste the alterations; try on again, the right side out, and, if satisfactory, it may be stitched and pressed. Before pressing trim away all extra material at the seams—allowing about a quarter of an inch to remain—notch each seam at the waist-line and above and below it. All the seams, with the exception of the shoulders and the curved side-backs, should be opened in pressing. For this purpose a black-walnut board without any covering is the best, and should be planed and rubbed perfectly smooth with sand-paper; not oiled or varnished, but left in its natural condition. Such a board may be rounded at the edges and made small enough to fit the sleeves. (See Fig. 2.)

The seams require *no moistening* with such a board, as the heat of the iron draws sufficient dampness from the wood, and, strangely enough, this moisture will not discolor the most delicate fabrics, as we have tried white and all light shades of wool goods, also silk and satin, both white and colored. Any carpenter can make a board of this sort from the description and measurements here given. The seams pressed over such a board will not look shiny, and do not need much pressure.

In overcasting the seams leave the stitches a little loose or easy, excepting in the curved seam of the back, which should be drawn a little tight just over

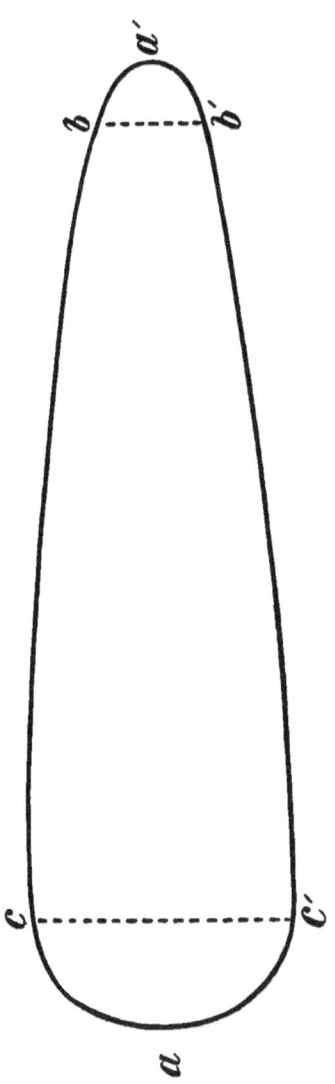

Fig. 2.—Sleeve-board.

the curve, when the two edges are overcast together, and it is only necessary to open them when thick fabrics, such as cloth and velvet, are employed. The shoulder-seams are likewise overcast together, except when using the heavy fabrics mentioned.

Whalebones may be used, if desired, in all the seams, except the curved seams in the back, where they should never be placed, though some dressmakers put them in every seam. If a dress is properly fitted, and worn over a well-fitting corset, whalebones are not really needed in any seam. When required, however, fasten them at the upper end to the desired height; then, holding the dress seam as tight as possible, baste the whalebone in place.

The seams of the waist may be merely overcast or bound with taffeta ribbon, which comes for that purpose. The bottom of the basque may be finished with two rows of stitching, bound with ribbon or braid, corded or merely faced and pressed smoothly.

The first step in making a sleeve is to prepare a perfectly fitting pattern.

Sleeves. A great aid in the work will be, first, to procure a good paper pattern two inches larger around than the arm, and from this make a permanent, perfectly fitting muslin sleeve pattern. Cut a sleeve by the paper pattern from cheap white muslin, making allowance for seams. Beginning at the top, baste the upper and under parts of this muslin sleeve together, the outside seam first, with the stitches half an inch from the edge and close together; then place the inside edge of the upper and under sleeve part together; slip them back and forth until the fold near the outside seam, formed by thus holding it, hangs perfectly even. Baste up the inside seam without regard as to whether the upper and under parts of the sleeve are even at the top or the bottom. They can be trimmed in fitting. In cutting it is always advisable to add an extra inch at the top and bottom to allow for this unevenness. This applies to the *muslin* which is advised for the trial sleeve, and not for the lining proper.

To fit this sleeve put on the waist—the seams of which should be already stitched and pressed, the buttons on, and button-holes made—and pin the sleeve over the top of the armhole from seam to seam; raise the arm to a level with the bust and bend it forward. If it draws or wrinkles, repin, and try again until it fits smoothly. When the sleeve wrinkles across the top, it is either not high enough over the rounding part or not set right in the armhole. In the first case draw up the sleeve sufficiently to make the top as round and full as desired, cutting away the corresponding length under the arm until it fits correctly there. Then if the curve for the elbow comes too high on the arm, cut off the sleeve midway between the shoulder and the elbow, and lengthen it by pinning in a strip of muslin sufficiently deep to bring the curve directly on the tip of the elbow. If the curve comes too low on the arm, cut apart in the same place and shorten by means of pins until the curve for the elbow is rightly adjusted. Where the sleeve is too loose, pin in the *outside* seam until the desired snugness is obtained. Should the sleeve twist so that the inside seam turns up over the arm, rip it open and add to the upper portion a piece of muslin, taking an equal amount from the lower portion, until the seam comes in the proper place. In fitting the muslin pattern mark distinctly on both the waist and the sleeve where the two are to be sewed together when the sleeve proper is finished. This pattern, after being perfectly fitted, should be trimmed close to the pins around the top and along the seams. The sleeve *lining* is then cut from this pattern, the edges followed by a tracing-wheel as directed for waists, allowance of half an inch being made for seams. Baste each piece of the sleeve lining separately on the dress goods before cutting, and have the grain or threads of both lining which should be first notched to make it lie open more readily. In pressing turn the sleeve wrong side out and place the pressboard inside the sleeve and run a hot iron over the open seams;

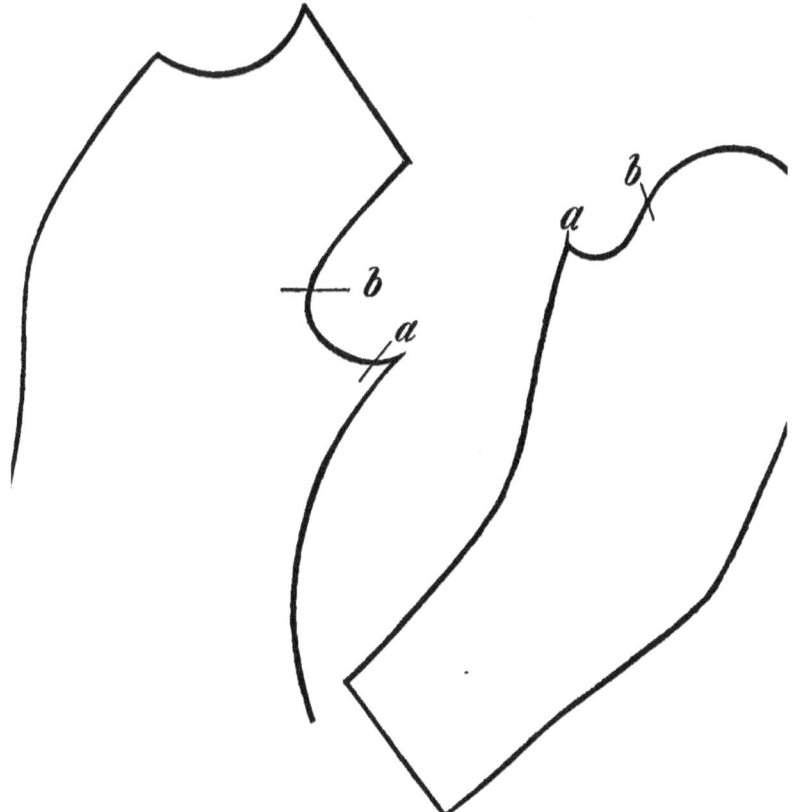

Fig. 3.—Diagram Showing How to Fit Sleeve to Armhole.

and outside run exactly the same way. Follow the lines of the tracing-wheel in basting the seams, keeping the corresponding tracings exactly opposite. Baste the sleeve temporarily to the armhole for trial. If satisfactory, remove, stitch up the seams, and press them. When made of silk, cashmere, or heavier fabrics, they should be pressed open, particularly the inside seam, the moisture from the black-walnut board will dampen them sufficiently. The back seam in heavy fabrics should be opened and pressed; when this is not done, as in thin fabrics, the seam should be turned toward the under-arm part and fastened to the lining.

Much of the trouble in fitting the sleeve is caused by its not being cut out enough at the upper part where it fits into the waist, just opposite and slightly above the bust. Here the sleeve should be hollowed out to fit the curve in the armhole (see Fig. 3), and generally needs a little cutting away on the under part of the sleeve in the final fitting to the armhole. To fit the sleeve to the armhole, cut the curve in the sleeve to fit the curve in the waist, and baste the curved parts evenly together. The inside seam in the sleeve is generally placed about an inch and a half in front of the seam which joins the front and side form of the waist, and the back seam of the sleeve at, or very near—a trifle above or below—the curved seam which joins the back and back side-form. If there is any extra fulness in the under-part of the sleeve between these places, sew it in by making a little pleat turning toward the front.

The sleeve may be stitched in satisfactorily by machine if the sleeve is held down on the feed and the waist uppermost next to the needle. Done in this manner the seam is just as even as when sewed in by hand, and is much stronger. After the sleeve is stitched in trim away all unevenness at the armhole and overcast the edges together. Take the stitches slanting, and draw the thread rather tightly over the top of the shoulder. This keeps the armhole seam inside the sleeve, and throws the fulness up over the waist on the top of the shoulder.

Fashion is so lavish in the variety of styles permissible for finishing the necks of dresses that it would take too much space even to enumerate them. Among these, however, and a fashion which always holds its own, is the straight standing collar. This collar is usually cut bias of the material, whether of silk, velvet, or dress goods. When finished it should be of the same length as the neck of the dress, and may be from one to two inches deep.

Collars.

Line the collar with two thicknesses of linen canvas or stiff crinoline. For the inside a facing of silk or satin is generally preferred to the dress goods. The neck is sometimes bound before the collar is sewed on, in which case the collar is first finished on the lower edge, then blind-stitched to the dress, otherwise the right side of the collar is sewed to the neck on the outside of the dress waist, and the other side of the collar hemmed down to the inside of the dress.

A turned-over or rolling collar is often cut straight with the goods, and folded so that the fold will form the outside edge of the collar. The cut edges should be hollowed in the middle, gradually sloping toward the end, where nothing should be cut away. It may be from three to four inches wide when finished. Line and finish according to directions given for standing collar. Other collars are merely pieces of embroidery or lace sewed in the neck and turned over. Pleatings of lisse, mull, India silk, and lace are also used in the same way.

To prepare a pattern for a princess dress—which should be cut with skirt and waist combined in one—pin sheets of paper to the lower edge of the plain round basque pattern already described, the pattern having first been pinned to the dress waist of the person being fitted. The paper should be long enough to touch the floor all round. Cut the skirt pattern from the paper thus pinned on, plain and smooth for the front and side-breadths. At the back the paper should be in two breadths, each from thirty to forty inches wide, according to the length of the skirt. Pin the centre of these breadths to each back of the basque pattern, an inch or two below the waistline. Then pleat the extra fulness between the basque backs in a double box-pleat, to come underneath when the

Princess Dress.

seams are sewed. Trim the pattern evenly all round the bottom, allowing a little more than two inches in length for making and finishing off the bottom of the skirt. From this combined pattern cut the lining for the princess dress.

A skirt with a train may be cut by the pattern for the foundation skirt, by adding at the back from three to five full breadths, according to the width of the material, and may be cut as short or as long as the wearer chooses. Trains are usually cut round or oval at the bottom, and just touch the floor at the sides. At the top these breadths may be thickly pleated or gathered. The back-breadths, when of silk or similar fabrics, are lined separately. Before the seams are sewed, each breadth, to make the train hang full and soft, should be covered the entire length with thin sheets of wadding, held in place by coarse tarlatan. The bottom of the skirt should be faced with alpaca or silk the color of the dress. The dress material is turned over nearly an inch on the under side and covers the lower edge of the facing. The bottom is then completed by a balayeuse or pleating of silk or lace, set so far up on the facing that the edge is scarcely visible below the dress. The train is held back and made to fall in graceful folds by tapes sewed to the seams and middle of each breadth underneath, and placed at intervals between the belt and the bottom of the skirt. The backs of trained dresses are often cut in one piece with the waist, princess style, and the top of the skirt pleated underneath the bodice, the front and sides of which are cut in short basque shape.

Trained Skirt.

Pratt Institute, in Brooklyn, gives a very thorough course in sewing, dressmaking, and millinery. The classes in sewing, which number two a week for three months, cost five dollars for the first, second, and third grades, each. The evening classes cost two dollars each. In dressmaking, for the same number of lessons, the first grade is ten dollars, the second, third, and fourth grades, fifteen dollars each, to take about three weeks. The pupils are first taught how to cut dresses and garments of every shape. The system is one of accurate measurement. When the principle is once understood, any shape can be cut. They are also taught how to baste the lining on the material, how to put a waist together, how to match striped and figured material, how to whalebone, how to press, and how to try a garment on.

The evening classes are less expensive. The first grade is five dollars, and the others ten dollars each. In millinery, the three grades cost ten dollars each, a term, and five dollars for the evening classes.

Everything in the line of sewing and dressmaking, from the first principles to the most complicated problems, is comprised in these different grades. Nothing could be more thorough than this arrangement of study. It is not at all impossible to do sewing, to a less elaborate extent than is taught by these courses, at home, and without mastering any special system. Paper patterns can be bought of every kind of wearing apparel, in every size. This simplifies matters very much, for a good pattern is most essential. Complete instructions, how to use the pattern, are printed on each one. Dress forms are a great help, and come in different prices, up to the most improved ones, which can be arranged for any sized figure desired.

Other manual training schools in different parts of the country provide some or all of the same facilities. In New York and Brooklyn the Young Woman's Christian Association has excellent classes in dressmaking and millinery, and information about such schools can often be obtained by applying to the local branch. In Chicago the Armour Institute offers most excellent opportunities.

VII.
HYGIENE IN THE HOME.

VII.

I.—HYGIENE IN THE HOME.

By J. WEST ROOSEVELT, M.D.

Cleanliness.	Exercise.
Heat.	The Nursery.
Light.	Education in Hygiene.
Ventilation.	Physicians.
Plumbing.	Trained Nurses.
The Water Supply.	The Sick-room.
Bathing.	The Patient.
Clothing.	Medical and Surgical Notes.

HYGIENE is the department of medical science that treats of the preservation of health, and it embraces all subjects directly or indirectly connected with that object. It applies to all the surroundings of the healthy, and, if a person is sick, to any general measures, other than the direct use of medicines, which tend to improve his condition. The care of the room; the heat, light, and ventilation; the care of the patient's bedding, the disposal of the excrementitious matters—all, in short, except the direct medical treatment, are called hygienic measures.

For the purposes of this article I shall make three main divisions of the subject. The first is hygiene as applied to the dwelling-house and grounds; the second, hygiene as applied to individuals; and the third, the application of hygienic principles in cases of illness. Before going into details I wish to call attention to certain general principles which bear upon health, and to state them very distinctly.

There is one protection against disease which exceeds in importance all *Importance of* others possible, and it will *cleanliness.* be noticed that throughout this entire article we finally go back to *cleanliness* as the great aim of all hygienic measures. It has been said, many years ago, that "if cleanliness is next to Godliness, cleanliness comes first;" and those who would preserve their health and continue their lives in this world, as well as those who would make the most use of their lives with an idea of preparing for the next, alike should observe this maxim. Now, what is meant by cleanliness? Cleanliness, as used in this article, means absolute freedom from any noxious dirt; *Dirt and its* it makes no difference *dangers.* whether the dirt is simply unpleasant but harmless, or whether it is dangerous from the fact that it is poisonous in a chemical way, or that its danger lies in the fact that it contains the living germs of disease. There is a great deal of dirt which is harmless, as far as any tangible injury to health is concerned. An immense amount of dust may be inhaled, provided the dust contains no poisonous substances, and apparently do very little harm. At the same time, in most cases where there is visible dust and dirt, there is also actively dangerous dirt; that is, dirt which is sometimes not visible, but which contains active poisons. Therefore, all visible dirt becomes objectionable. I use the word "visible" in connection with dirt to distinguish it from that which the eye frequently cannot see and which nothing but the microscope can demonstrate, yet which is the most dangerous of all of the enemies with which the human race has to fight. It is possible for countless millions of bacteria which produce infectious disease to exist in a room or on a small surface and be absolutely invisible. Now, in speaking of the necessity of cleanliness, I wish it to be understood that it includes not only the absence of visible dirt, but equally the absence of invisible dirt, and I repeat that statement because of its immense importance. The

What constitutes real cleanliness.

spreads were on them, but when these were taken off there was something suspicious about the careless way in which the blankets and sheets were tucked in, and also something suspicious about the appearance of the blankets themselves. They did not look dirty, but they also did not look so clean as blankets bought at the same time and kept in other wards. This started an investigation, and we found that every available dark corner of the various small cupboards around the room had been made a receptacle for all sorts of objectionable things. The ends of bandages, in some cases lit-

 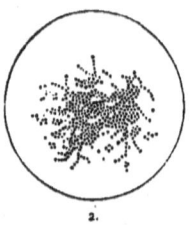 

Fig. 1.—Bacteria highly magnified. 1 and 2 are found in infected suppurating wounds. 3. Another form of disease-producing bacterium containing spores. The body of the bacillus is black, the spores are white in the cut.

general notion of cleanliness possessed by the larger number of otherwise excellent housekeepers is something very surprisingly small. Most women, and most men, mistake neatness for cleanliness; and what is more common than to see a room which looks very neat until you begin to examine it closely, when you find that really the neatness is due largely to the fact that it has no dirt in any large collection in any one place? I once knew a nurse in charge of a ward in a hospital whose ward had the most extraordinarily neat appearance, and who for a year or so was regarded as a rather remarkable example of a thoroughly competent hygienic cleaner. After a while I noticed that the beds in that ward all looked beautiful so long as the white tle-used dressings, dust, etc., were found. The fire-escape, in one of its corners, was a veritable curiosity-shop. In this fire-escape, which was a brick tower with a spiral staircase, there were discovered remnants of almost everything in the way of waste that a ward could furnish. They were all carefully swept into the angles of the stairs and into the corners of the tower, and in one corner the pile was concealed by means of a box inverted over it. Now this story has a moral, for the nurse in question had not the least idea, when these matters were called to her attention, that anyone would seriously object to them. She said that the ward was clean, and that these things did not do any harm. Now, there was a case of a room which looked clean, but was not.

Dust is the greatest source of danger with which the housekeeper has to contend. The danger is twofold: first, because it so frequently carries in its particles the germs of infection, and secondly, because it is so very easy to scatter dust around a room and to make the latter look clean when it is not. The process of sweeping a room, as generally performed with a dry broom and with or without open windows, is a most pernicious one. It is true that a large amount of the dirt that lies upon the floor or carpet is thus swept together and carried out, but if you look at the trail of a sweeper who uses a broom dry you will see that there is a cloud of dust which for a while hangs in the air, and, after a longer or a shorter time, if the air is still, deposits itself evenly but invisibly on the floor, and deposits itself in such a way that the lightest touch thereafter is apt to throw it up into the air again. If any housekeeper doubts this statement, it would be worth her while to make the experiment. When the time comes for cleaning any room, wipe off the surface of a wooden table with a damp rag until it is perfectly clean, put that table in the room and sweep, and after you have finished sweeping look at the top of the table. In fifteen minutes you will probably be able to write your name with ease in the dust that has fallen upon it. Dry sweeping is bad enough, but the most pernicious of all household ceremonies is that which is called dusting. It would be a great thing for mankind had the feather-duster never been invented, and it would still be a great blessing if all those implements could be destroyed and never made again. The duster has this difference from the broom. When a housewife wishes to have a room cleaned with a broom, there goes with the broom usually a dust-pan, or at least the idea is that with the sweeping a quantity of dirt shall be gathered together and carried away finally. When the feather-duster is used for cleaning, no such pretence as that is made. The feather-duster does just what, if you come to think of it, it is meant to do. It scatters dust far and wide through the air of a room so as to spread it over a larger surface. To take a feather-duster and go around dusting things is very much like trying to clean a wash-tub which has in its bottom a little dirty water, by turning the wash-tub about and tilting it over so as to spread that water over the entire inner surface. No one would dream of doing that; no one would dream of cleaning a saucepan, for example, by simply taking a cloth and with it carefully smearing what dirt there happened to be in the saucepan all over its interior. If one wished to clean either the tub or saucepan, one would go to work with water in quantity, and water which would be thrown away, and before either vessel would be considered clean the last drops even of the water thus used would be carefully wiped out. Your feather-duster cleans the room no better than the tub or saucepan would be cleaned by the smearing process mentioned. It leaves just as much dirt as there was before, only scattered more widely about. Now, the proper way to clean a room is, first having gotten *How to clean a room properly* firmly in mind the fact that what you wish to do is to get the dirt out of that room, you proceed to use, as much as you can, a damp cloth to take the place of the feather-duster, and you should use something to prevent the rise of dust from the floor when sweeping. The old-fashioned moist tea-leaves are as satisfactory as anything can be for this purpose when the floor swept is carpeted. If the floor is covered with rugs, these, of course, should be carried outside and into the open air, where the dust which rises from them will do no harm. They can be swept or beaten while dry. On a wood or other uncarpeted floor, if the broom be wrapped around with a piece of moist cheesecloth, it will be found the dust does not rise from it, and you practically gather the dirt together in one place and carry it off in your dust-pan.

To get an idea of what would constitute as nearly perfect cleanliness as human power can obtain, I will describe briefly the method in which an infected room is cleaned by the best scientifically directed disinfecting corps. The first thing done is to carry into the room cloths, which are usually tarpaulin or rubber, and everything that can be removed from that room is carefully wrapped up, the tarpaulin being tied tightly around the various articles, and after everything has been thus fastened up, the outside of each tarpaulin-wrapped package is washed with a solution of corrosive sublimate sufficiently strong to be fatal to any living organism which might have fallen upon the tarpaulin. The room being stripped, all carpets, furniture, hangings, and everything movable wrapped up in the way I have described, the cleaners now divide it up systematically among certain gangs of men. Beginning at the corners farthest from the door, if the room is painted, every square inch of the wood-work, ceiling, and walls is washed down first with a disinfecting solution, and then with soap and water applied by means of a mop or of a hand-cloth. If the room is papered, in order to get it as clean as possible without destroying the paper, the cleaner begins close to the ceiling with a handful of somewhat stale bread crumbs, and systematically rubs the paper down with it, and the

Cleaning an infected room.

crumbs, which gather up the dirt, when they reach the floor are allowed to stay there until the final washing of the floor itself. After the walls are thoroughly cleaned, beginning in each case in the corners, the floor is thoroughly scrubbed with a disinfectant and then with scalding water, and care is taken that all of the dirt removed in this way is pushed nearer and nearer the door; the cleaners, we may say, wash themselves and the dirt out of the room together. When the ceiling and walls have been treated in the manner described, and when the floor has been once washed in this way, and subsequently, as an extra precaution, again washed with hot soap-suds, that room is as nearly absolutely clean as is possible. Practically, it is more clean than we need for the maintenance of health. The ordinary cleaning of a room would, of course, not necessitate the removal of all the furniture, or the covering up with tarpaulins, or the use of any disinfectant; but what it does necessitate is system, and everyone should be taught to work in the same way in the case of each room, always starting in the corners and always pushing the dirt toward the door, so that it is sure to be entirely removed.

HEAT, LIGHT, AND VENTILATION.

There are many matters, in regard to which authorities on hygiene differ, but upon these subjects there is a singular unanimity of opinion. To begin with light, about which all that needs to be said can be said in a very few words, the most important hygienic fact to be remembered is that you rarely can have too much of it. A dark room, that is to say, a room into which light can not be admitted freely, is always a more or less unhealthful room, and the more sunlight can be allowed to enter into any chamber, the

Light.

better. Of course, I do not mean that one should live the entire time in a blaze of sunlight, but I do mean that, as far as possible, one should be able to admit the direct sunlight in large quantities into any room in which people live. You may have curtains or blinds if you will, you may and ought to have shades, but the sun should not be excluded all the time by any of these contrivances. For as many hours as possible, no matter whether the carpet fades or your curtains or your furniture covering grow pale, the sunlight should be admitted, at least once a day when the sun shines, for one or two hours. The admission of sunlight is more important for bedrooms than for sitting-rooms or dining-rooms, but most important of all is it for the nursery. Of all hygienic factors for children's preservation, sunlight is the most important. Use for your nursery or for a children's playroom the sunniest room in the house, and remember that children are far more sensitive to the absence of light than are adults. Having plenty of sun in a nursery will often make the difference between a healthy, vigorous, strong baby, and a pale, sickly one. It has been demonstrated of late years, that the direct sunlight is capable of destroying effectively the germs of many of the most virulent disorders, and of doing so in a very short time.

Importance of direct sunlight.

In regard to artificial light there is little to be said except that it is extremely necessary to have it sufficiently bright to make easy whatever we may have to do with its aid. It is worse than folly to attempt to read, or to use the eyes in any way, without having abundant illumination.

It is only necessary to speak in a general way of methods of heating. The fact that an open fireplace, although by far the most expensive and troublesome form of heater, is the very best, is well known. I must, however, protest somewhat against the immense amount of abuse which is heaped upon the stove. In the United States, in many places, with the terribly severe winters, to heat a house by means of open fireplaces would be practically impossible, unless the fireplaces occupied almost as much space as do the rooms, and unless the fuel burned were about fifteen or twenty times as abundant as it is. Stoves we have got to use in many places. Now, a stove certainly gives an extremely unpleasant heat if the stove is not properly constructed and properly tended. It is a mistake to say that a stove does not ventilate a room. It does. If it did not, the fire would not burn. That the oxygen is consumed by the coal-fire in the stove is a direct indication that a quantity of air is being removed from the room. It evidently does not ventilate so well as does an open fire, because with the open fireplace a very much larger amount of heat and a very much larger amount of air are carried up the chimney. If a stove is rationally looked after, there is no need of producing such an unpleasant kind of heat as is so often done by careless people. In the first place, a stove should have a large surface of metal in order that it may give out heat in the most satisfactory way. Red-hot iron always makes a very disagreeable heat, because it allows the passage through it of a great many of the harmful gases which are generated when coal is burned. It also has a property of directly affecting the oxygen in the air, so as to make that unpleasant. And probably it removes and decomposes a good deal of the moisture from the air. If a stove has a large enough surface of metal, so that the heat is distributed over the iron pretty evenly, without having any part heated to red-

Stoves.

Heat.

ness, the most objectionable quality will be done away with. In addition to having a large metal surface, the stove should also have a large receptacle for water, because, without that, it furnishes such a very dry air as to be disagreeable and more or less injurious. It would be a good thing for the community, and especially for those who dwell in apartment houses, to realize that the ordinary steam or hot water radiator, which is seen in so many parts of the country, gives absolutely no ventilation whatever, and is for that reason far more objectionable than a good stove, well cared for. A furnace gives far more fresh air than do these radiators, unless the latter are so arranged that the outside air is admitted and passes continually over their pipes and enters the room in that way. In regard to furnace heat, there is no doubt that the hot-water or the steam-coil furnaces give a pleasanter heat than the ordinary hot-air furnaces.

Radiators.

Furnaces.

At the same time, any good old-fashioned hot-air furnace, if the fire is properly tended, if the water-pan is kept continually full, and if the cold-air box opens directly on the fresh air and draws its supply from out of doors, can be made to give just as pleasant a stream of warm air as do the more elaborate and more expensive modern inventions. For the purposes of hygiene, the most important thing to impress upon the minds of most of our countrymen is that heat ought not to be excessive. We are apt to have rooms of all kinds entirely too hot in this country. Not only is it wasteful to overheat a room, it is absolutely injurious. For the winter time a temperature between 60° and 70° F. is warm enough for any room in which healthy people are living, including the nursery. The nurseries and children's bedrooms are almost always excessively overheated, just as they are almost always very badly ventilated. People do not take cold, as we are afraid they will, in rooms which are moderately cool, and people who live in such rooms will take cold far less frequently than those who go from a very hot house suddenly into the cold outer air.

Everyone must have noticed that there is a great deal of difference in the quality of heat, whether artificial or natural. We speak of the heat of a summer day sometimes as being "oppressive,"

Dry and moist air.

Fig. II.—Arrangement of steam-pipes for heating. Fresh cold-air is admitted through a pipe shown at the right.

or perhaps say that the air is "heavy" or "lifeless." Again, we notice that while the thermometer registers the same degree of temperature, there is something in the quality of the heat which makes it less enervating. In respect to artificial heat, we occasionally say that the air is "dry" or "parched" by the heating apparatus, or that the room is "oppressively" hot, when the recorded temperature is not higher than that of another room which we find perfectly comfortable. The main cause of this difference in the quality of the heat, and in the resulting pleasant or unpleasant sensations, is the amount of vapor of water which the atmosphere contains. This statement needs perhaps explanation, since some of my readers may not remember their physics very clearly.

Atmospheric air is composed mainly of oxygen and nitrogen when pure. There are small quantities of other gases in it, notably carbonic acid, which is exhaled in the breath of animals, but the principal constituents are the two first mentioned. In addition to the true gaseous substances, however, there is a certain amount of *water* in the form of vapor, and while the relative proportions of the former (except in closed rooms in which living animals or human beings are rapidly removing the oxygen and giving out carbonic acid in breathing) remain practically unchanged, the amount of vapor of water in a given volume of air varies greatly. There is always a larger or smaller amount of vapor in air, unless artificial means have been used to remove it. Its presence is demonstrated by the formation of clouds and mist, and of dew and rain or snow. Vapor differs from what we call steam in some important respects; for steam is produced only when water is heated to a certain degree, and, provided the water is made sufficiently hot, steam can be produced until all the fluid has disappeared. It is true that steam is only vapor of water given off in large quantities when the boiling-point is reached, but the vapor I allude to is given off at all temperatures until the air becomes "saturated" as it is called—*i.e.*, can take up no more.* The amount taken up before saturation is complete increases as the temperature rises; the hotter the air the greater the amount of moisture it can absorb. When saturated air is cooled, more and more of the vapor is converted into water as the temperature falls.† If the air is warmed and the quantity of vapor remains the same, absolutely, as it was when the temperature was lower, the relative amount is lessened, and the heated air feels dryer.

Very important physical phenomena result from the relative dryness or moisture of the atmosphere. Upon the human body the effects vary greatly in different individuals—some doing best in very dry, others in moderately moist, and still others in very damp air—but it is safe to say that few people are comfortable in air which is near the saturation point of water-vapor, whether the tempera-

---

*The fact that water in contact with air which is not confined evaporates and disappears is well known. It is not so well known that *ice* also evaporates, even in very cold weather—and evaporates, moreover, *without melting* yet such is the fact. Ice disappears in the form of vapor just as does water.

† The amount of aqueous vapor in the atmosphere is indicated in the weather reports of the Signal Service of our army in what are called "degrees of humidity." The "humidity" (dampness) of the air is expressed by the amount of aqueous vapor at the time of observation compared with the amount which would saturate it at the same temperature. Total saturation is called one hundred per cent., absolute dryness is 0 per cent. A scale divided into one hundred parts is used. Thus the term "humidity twenty-five per cent." means that the atmosphere is one-fourth saturated. Fifty per cent. means one-half saturated; ten per cent. one-tenth, etc.

ture be high or low, and that very dry, super-heated air also causes discomfort, while very dry, cold air does not. Saturated or nearly saturated air makes hot weather oppressive, and in cold weather gives the penetrating chill which is called "raw" or "piercing." It is necessary that a certain amount of moisture be present, in order to satisfy the requirements of comfort, but if there be too much or too little, we are apt to suffer. In cold weather, when we use a stove, furnace, or radiator for heating purposes, we deal with air of a very low temperature containing comparatively little moisture. When we heat it, we must add to the moisture, if we do not wish to make it practically dry; for the saturation point is reached in the case of hotter air only after much more vapor has been absorbed than the colder can carry. Therefore a vessel of water must be heated in such a way as to make up the deficiency. This is done in well-managed houses by placing a tank in the furnace-chamber, if furnace there be, or on the stove or radiator.

Importance of adding to the moisture of heated air.

When an open fire is in use the air is not dried to any extent, and a water-pan is not needed. The open fire not only ventilates a room far better than any other heater, but also gives out radiant heat to a greater extent. Heat thus thrown out does not warm the air through which it passes so much as it warms solid bodies, therefore it does not alter the degree of humidity very perceptibly.*

* Radiant heat is the heat which we can stop by means of a screen placed between us and a hot body. It behaves much as does light. The rays of light may be partially shut off by an opaque body; so can heat rays. Light rays can be reflected almost completely by certain bodies, and absorbed more or less completely by others; heat rays are similarly reflected or absorbed, though not by the same substances in all cases. Light rays may be deflected from their course when they pass through certain bodies; thus is it also

If a radiator is used to heat a room there should be some provision similar to that shown in sketch to provide for the entrance of fresh air.

As generally arranged and tended, I think it is safe to say that the sanitary advantages of the various means commonly used for heating rank as follows: first, the open fire; second, the stove; third, the furnace; fourth, the radiator. It is proper to add

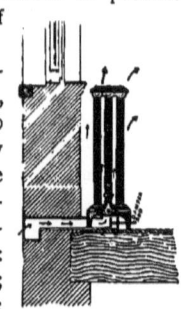

Fig. III.—Radiator with a pipe communicating with the outer air in order to secure ventilation.

that the last is very much behind the other three, and that some authors would place the furnace before either open fire or stove.

Ventilation.

Ventilation is the problem of changing the air in a room with sufficient rapidity without at the same time creating draughts. In spite of the years of careful study which many skilful men have devoted to the subject, ventilation cannot yet be said to have been effected in a satisfactory way, save in a very few instances, even in large public buildings like hospitals, schools, and theatres. As for the majority of dwelling-houses, they are built without the least pretence of providing for any change of air in the rooms, except such as results from accidental leaks in doors, windows, or walls. Indeed, many a house seems to have been designed with the idea of preventing, as far as possible,

with heat. The common "burning-glass" demonstrates the similarity between light and heat rays; it concentrates both, so that it is easy to set fire to inflammable materials by holding the lens so that a sunbeam passes through it, and allowing this to fall upon the substance which it is desired to set on fire. The fact that heat passes through the glass without heating it is also shown, since it does not become uncomfortably warm, while enough goes through to kindle a fire.

any change of air within it. But for the fact that no building materials and no doors nor windows are absolutely airtight the air in some of our modern dwellings would become unfit to sustain life.

The problems of ventilation as presented in a large room where many people are accustomed to gather together (as in a theatre, school, or lecture-room, and those presented in a hospital ward, where a number of sick persons are grouped together) differ greatly from the problems which occur in a private dwelling, where the number of persons who consume the air is relatively small in comparison with the total amount of oxygen contained in any one room.

In the former case many difficulties present themselves which do not obtain in the latter. It is needless to mention these in detail; it is sufficient to say that in a large room it is impossible to get sufficient ventilation by means of the windows and doors, by the direct action of heat upon the air, while in smaller rooms there is no need of elaborate and complicated apparatus for this purpose, since, with proper arrangements as to heating, it is possible easily to get rid of foul air and to substitute fresh air for it. In a large building power of some sort, other than that required in small ones, must be used. Thus to ventilate properly a large hospital ward fresh air must be forced in by a steam-engine, and the foul air drawn out in some way. In a smaller house it is necessary only to make use of the direct action of heat upon the air itself, and to provide sufficient means for its entrance and egress, in order to fulfil sanitary requirements. We are concerned only with dwelling-houses and ordinary rooms.

I do not intend to attempt to state in figures the quantity of air breathed by each occupant of a room per hour. I do not think that anything like exact figures can be given, and, if they could, it is unimportant. We are able to judge the state of the air in a room sufficiently accurately for all practical purposes by the use of our unaided senses. If there is a stuffy, unpleasant odor noticeable in a room when we enter it fresh from the outer air, that room is not ventilated and is not healthful. If a room feels hot and "close," its ventilation is defective. We may safely assume that ventilation is good so long as the air of an apartment seems to us neither foul-smelling nor close *when we enter it immediately after leaving the fresh outer air.* We cannot judge of its condition after having been in it for some time, for the nose and body soon get accustomed to a great many unpleasant sensations and no longer notice them.

The object of all plans for ventilation is, of course, to substitute fresh for foul air. It is desirable to do this without causing draughts, yet with sufficient rapidity to prevent the accumulation of the products of respiration in quantity sufficient to do harm, and also to supply oxygen to replace that which is absorbed by the lungs with every inspiration. Let us consider the more important facts concerning the behavior of both fresh and foul air which bear upon our subject. If these facts be borne in mind, and if their relations be understood, the ventilation of ordinary rooms, under ordinary conditions of occupancy (*i.e.*, when not overcrowded), becomes a comparatively simple matter.

It is well known that warm air rises when surrounded by air which is cold. *Behavior of fresh and foul air.* We take advantage of this fact both in heating by means of a furnace or similar apparatus and in ventilating. There is one error which is frequently made in regard to the tendency of heated air to rise which has caused more or less trouble. This is the idea that the air rises simply because it is hot—that it has the power of rising of itself. This is not so; it rises only because it is lighter than the cold air around it. It does so for the same reason that a cork rises to the surface of water and floats, or that air itself rises through water and floats. Now the reason that hot air is lighter is that when heated it expands, so that the same quantity of it occupies more room than it did before it was warmed. Since in its expanded condition it tends to displace the cold air, the latter presses with

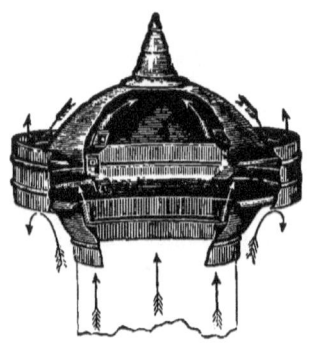

Fig. IV.—A practical ventilator.

more force against it, and, being heavier, glides under it and drives it upward. Unless some arrangement is made so that the cooler air can do this, the warmer does not rise at all. It is, therefore, necessary to have a cold-air box connected with a furnace in such a manner that the cold air outside of the house can pass through it, and drive that which is heated upward through the house. If such an arrangement is not made, no amount of fuel will do much to warm the rooms with which the furnace communicates. At first it may seem strange that in order to warm a house it is necessary to let more cold air into its furnace, but a little thought will make the reason plain. We frequently arrange to ventilate a room by means of a flue, opening into it either near the ceiling or near the floor, and communicating with the outer air at some point higher than the top of the room. The flue is warmed either by utilizing the waste heat of some neighboring chimney or by means of a gas-jet within it. The relatively cool air of the room displaces the warmer in this flue, and that which has entered it being in turn warmed is also driven upward. Thus a continuous current is produced. The air drawn up the flue must be replaced by some which finds its way in through the doors, windows, or walls, or through some aperture constructed to permit its entrance. Two things must be remembered when considering the use of a warmed flue for a ventilator : one is that the stronger the draught the greater is the difference of temperature between the atmosphere of the room and that of the flue; the other, that the column of heated air does not exert sufficient force to overcome the effects of a wind which may happen to blow in such a way as to drive it down again. An enormous number of devices have been invented with the object of stopping such back-draughts. None of those which I have seen do so completely at all times ; the best, so far as I know, is called the "Globe Ventilator," which is exceedingly ingenious yet simple.

It is impossible to ventilate all parts of a room equally. The air in the corners, for example, usually either remains almost stationary, or tends to form eddies in the way shown in Fig. V. The warmer air also tends to accumulate in the upper part of a room, and it does not change so quickly as that nearer the floor, unless some special device is adopted to displace it. The simplest way to get rid of this air rapidly is by means of a ventilating shaft which is built close to the chimney, so that it is

Impossible to ventilate equally.

Laws of the Diffusion of Gases.

heated by the waste heat in the latter. This shaft has one or more openings either near the ceiling or near the floor,

Fig. V.—Diagram showing direction of air-currents when drawn out by a heated chimney through an open fireplace elevation.

or sometimes both in the upper and lower parts of the room. Suitable valves are provided which regulate the size of the openings, and permit them to be completely closed when necessary.

There is a prevalent idea that, since carbonic-acid gas is heavier than air, *Foul air does not always sink.* and since a considerable quantity of this gas is exhaled by the body, the air in the lower parts of a room becomes charged with it sooner and to a greater extent than that in the upper parts. It is a very rare thing for such a condition to obtain ; for the quantity of the gas given off is relatively very small (probably not more than from three-fourths to four-fifths of a cubic foot per hour by an adult and far less by a child), and it is thoroughly mixed with the air of the entire room very soon after it is exhaled, and is thus evenly distributed. Even if such an admixture did not take place so quickly as in fact it does, in a large proportion of cases the compound would rise, not fall. There is not much difference in weight between the atmosphere and carbonic-acid gas diluted with air to the extent it is as it comes from the lungs when the tem-

peratures of breath and atmosphere are equal. If, as is usually the case except in hot weather, during which open windows make other ventilation needless, the breath is warmer than the atmosphere, all of the expired substances (carbonic acid, water-vapor, nitrogen, oxygen, and the unknown compounds which give the peculiar odor to the breath) tend to rise, and continue to do so until they either reach a level at which an equal temperature is reached, or are stopped by the ceiling ; but in any case they are soon distributed more or less evenly through all of the air confined in the room, following the laws of the diffusion of gases.* So far as danger of breathing too much carbonic acid is

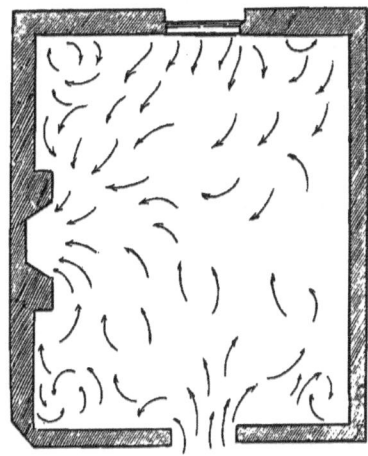

Fig. VI.—Ground plan of same room. It will be seen that the air in the corners tends to form eddies as shown by the arrows.

concerned, there is usually less in most modern rooms near the floor than near

* When two or more gases are put in contact with one another, no matter what be the comparative weights or volumes, they immediately begin to mix. "The mixture takes place rapidly and is homogeneous—that is, each portion of the mixture contains the gases in the same proportion" (Ganot). This is what we call the "diffusion of gases." It takes place whether the lighter or heavier gas be originally in the upper or lower part of the chamber in which they are confined.

the ceiling. It will be understood that I speak of ordinary living or sleeping rooms which are not overcrowded ; of course in crowded rooms the lower air is more charged with the products of respiration than the upper, simply because the total quantity exhaled per hour by a large number of people is, proportionately to the total air-space, very great, and diffusion does not occur sufficiently rapidly to dispose of it.

There is in dwellings a very close connection between the methods adopted for heating and those intended for ventilation. Practically, as I have already said, we depend upon the behavior of warm air in the midst of colder to ventilate dwellings. That is to say, we make use of the fact that the latter is heavier than the former, in order to secure the necessary removal of foul and admission of pure air. The most common blunder made by those who try to build houses with the idea of arranging for ventilation is their failure to remember *that provision must be made both for the removal and admission*, and that air will not rise simply because it is warmed, nor flow through a ventilating flue either upward or downward, unless forced in some way so to do. It is useless to put a ventilating shaft anywhere in a house, and assume that the hot air will straightway begin to stream up it, because hot air *rises*, as it is said. As I have pointed out, hot air does not "rise," unless some force compels it to rise—it is not endowed with some peculiar qualities which annul the operation of the law of gravitation. If you want hot air to rise, you must employ colder to push it up. If you expect your shaft to pour hot air out of its top, you must have cooler near its base. This can be accomplished either by heating the shaft itself directly or indirectly, or by constructing it in such a way that it acts as a mere passage-way for air already heated and forced upward by cold air below. A good example of the first plan is the tall chimney so often used to secure a strong draught for large furnaces in factories requiring very hot fires for their business. These tall chimneys increase the draught in two ways ; first, they become themselves heated, and give up their heat whenever the gases within them become cooler than they should from any cause ; and, second, they make the momentum of the moving column of air within them useful, for air, like all moving bodies, when once set in motion is hard to stop. So the ascending column helps to increase the draught by creating a partial vacuum in case the supply from below is diminished from any cause.

A ventilating shaft in a house may be made to work in a similar manner if its walls be warmed, or if the air within it be heated by means of a gas-flame or radiator or stove. The ordinary furnace, with its distributing pipes for hot air and its cold-air box communicating with the colder air without, is an example of the principle applied in ventilation, when the shaft is so constructed that the movement of air within it depends upon the power of heavier cold to force out the lighter warm gases. In a furnace the heat of the fire causes the air within it to expand and become lighter than before. As it expands it exerts an increased pressure in all directions. It is unable to push the brick sides of the hot-air chamber away, and it therefore expends its force upon the pipes which open into that chamber. It meets with greater resistance at the mouth of the cold-air box than at the mouths of the pipes which open into rooms in the house, for the outer temperature is lower than that within, and the outer air, therefore, heavier. Naturally it overcomes the least resistance, and some of it begins to flow through the pipes leading to the rooms of the house. Soon it becomes sufficiently expanded to move rapidly through these pipes. It acquires momentum enough to continue to flow after it has expanded as much as its increased temperature demands; it produces a partial vacuum, and the cold outer air rushes in to fill it. This in its turn is heated and follows the same course as that which preceded it. Again and again is the process repeated and a steady movement of hot air is produced through the house. It is possible in a similar way to force hot and impure air through a ventilating-shaft if the latter is constructed so as to resemble the hot-air pipes of a furnace, and if the room from the top of which it rises has something similar to the cold-air box of that form of heating apparatus.

In practice, however, it is hard to use any device which closely resembles the furnace; for it is desirable to avoid the direct admission of enough cold air at any part of a room to expel the hot sufficiently quickly. "Draughts" are of no importance in the former; they must be avoided in the latter. Beside this, it is not easy to warm a room equably into which a stream of cold air is constantly pouring—particularly when it is necessary to heat that air enough to make it flow out of a shaft which opens above, not into a room, as does the furnace-pipe, but into the open. In dwelling-houses it is better to secure the out-flow of foul air by means of an open fire or a stove, or through a shaft which is heated in some way, than it is to rely upon heating it enough in a room to compel it to travel through an unwarmed shaft. If a sufficiently powerful outflow is insured, the inflow, in most houses will take care of itself—or at least it can be regulated by means of windows and doors. An apartment ventilated in a theoretically perfect way is a rare thing to find in this world—indeed it is almost beyond belief that perfect ventilation can be obtained; but there is no reason why many of the dwellings in this country should not be made far more healthful than they are to-day, and far more comfortable, if greater pains were taken to get rid of the foul air by means of hot chimneys or heated ventilating-shafts than is at present the custom.

It is often impossible to admit enough fresh air to a room without opening the window. In such cases it is better to lower the upper sash, when possible, rather than to raise the lower. This admits the cold air to the upper parts of the chamber, and causes a change of the air more rapidly than would be the case were it admitted lower, while it also lessens the sensible draught. It is a good plan to have one or more screens in a room which requires the opening of a window for such a purpose while it is occupied. Screens are too little valued from a practical standpoint; they are of the greatest use, both for shutting off the excessive radiant heat of an open fire or stove, and for checking injurious air-currents. In the nursery and in the sick-room they are invaluable, and, in our northern climate they are useful in almost any room.

There is far too much difference of opinion among those who have *Plumbing.* made special study of sanitary plumbing, concerning so many important practical details of construction and design, for me to think of attempting to do more than call attention to a few of the most evident dictates of common sense respecting this branch of hygiene.

I confess that the first suggestion which occurs to my mind after reading a few of the controversial discourses of sanitary experts in questions of plumbing, reminds one of a celebrated suggestion made by "Punch." The advice given by that astute philosopher to "young men about to marry" was "Don't!" It really seems well to say to those who are about to introduce plumbing into their homes: "Don't!" If we are to believe all who denounce various details of its arrangements as being dangerous, we are forced to conclude that there is no safety attainable by human ingenuity, if a single sink or water-closet is constructed in connection with a single drain! So in the matter of drainage, after studying the opinions of experts upon such questions, one is constrained to think enviously of the happiness of the Welsh landlady set forth in the same journal. When the traveller complains of a bad smell in an inn, and asks if the drainage may not be defective, the hostess explains with great satisfaction that she is sure it can't be the drains, "for there ain't none"!

Whatever dispute there may be about plumbing, one thing is clear, namely; the less there is of it the better. If possible, place all fixtures as nearly as may be in a direct line one above the other. The accompanying diagram will serve to illustrate my meaning. In it one soil-pipe runs straight to the roof, and two sets of fixtures are provided upon each floor.

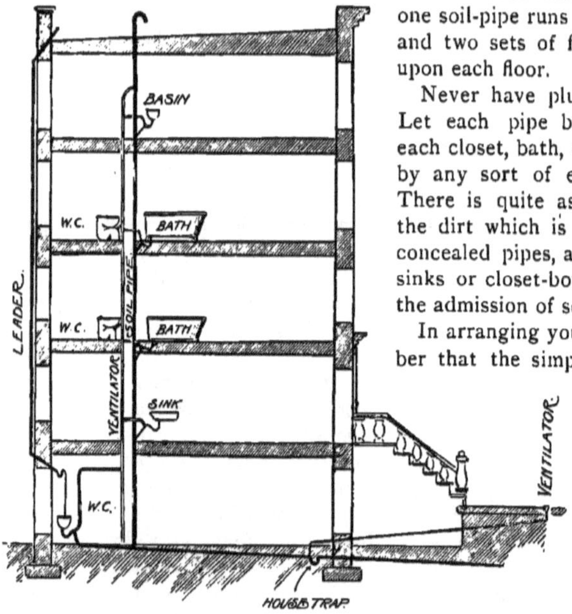

Never have plumbing out of sight. Let each pipe be in full view, and each closet, bath, or basin be unhidden by any sort of enclosing woodwork. There is quite as much danger from the dirt which is apt to gather round concealed pipes, and beneath enclosed sinks or closet-bowls, as there is from the admission of sewer-gas.

In arranging your plumbing, remember that the simplest way to prevent the accumulation of dirt is to make it easier to be clean than to be dirty. Therefore put your sinks where there is plenty of light, and make them of such a shape that there is little chance for water to splatter when poured into them.

Fig. VII.—Diagram of plumbing with soil-pipe and ventilator running straight to the roof.

Make everything as simple as possible, and also try to place the various fixtures so that they can be reached with the least possible trouble.

Pure water is most important for the preservation of health. This fact is *The water* beginning to be appreciated by the public; but its extreme importance is not yet fully understood. Most of us have some share of a strange mental quality which causes us to understand fully that certain facts exist, to see the exact bearings of these facts—and calmly to act as though they were *not* facts. This is the reason why so many people who know that contaminated water is dangerous to health, not only continue recklessly to drink such water, but also hardly take the trouble to do anything to prevent its contamination. One would think that the knowledge that, if a cesspool is built in certain kinds of soil and of certain materials, it will age is harmless after filtration through so much earth, and continue to drink diluted sewage as had been their custom. Personally I have a strong objection to swallowing the stuff which is poured out of a cesspool, no matter how dilute it may be. Perhaps it will be said that I am too fastidious—I do not think so myself.

The accompanying diagram is no exaggeration of the way in which not a

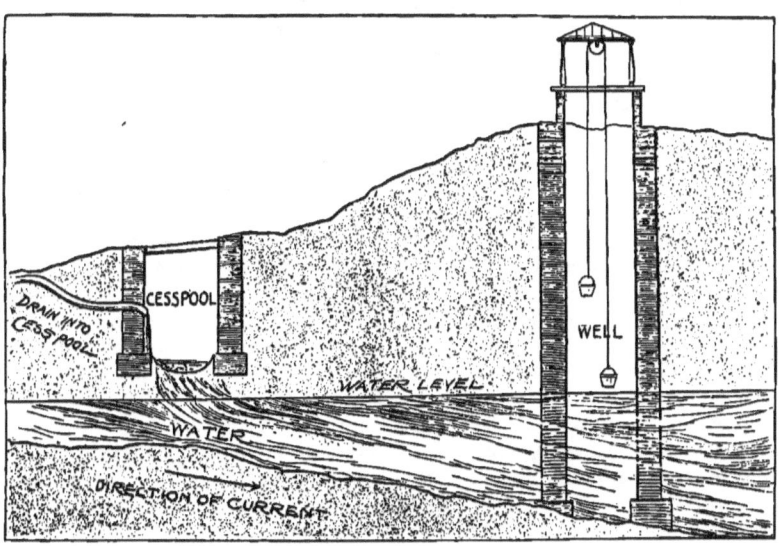

Fig. VIII.—Diagram showing contamination of well-water by cesspool.

sooner or later begin to allow its contents to leak into the surrounding earth; and that the filth will penetrate the soil to a great depth, and that it will thus inevitably find its way into the water of a well, would lead any man to choose some other site for his cesspool, or at least to refrain from drinking the water into which such filth might be pouring. Yet many do nothing of the sort. They calmly construct the cesspool on the dangerous spot, and drink the water without hesitation. Sometimes, when the danger is pointed out to them, they inform us that the sewfew of our fellow-citizens arrange their wells and privy-vaults or cesspools.

In the diagram the vault is shown with its leaky floor and sides dug down to within a few feet of the water from which the well is supplied. The filth is shown to flow into the underground stream and thus to find its way into the neighboring well. The figure also shows the folly of the custom that exists in some parts of the country of digging the well on a hill with the idea of protecting its water. It would have been far safer to have reversed the relative situations, and built the privy on the hill while digging a well in the valley; for the chances are that a much longer time would elapse before the vault contents would have reached the water than would be the case if less earth separated them from the water.

There is no doubt that certain diseases are directly due to living germs, and there is no doubt that many of these germs live for a long time in water. It is not proven that all of the germs are killed by passing through soil, and it is neither pleasant nor safe to run the risk of their so being. Therefore do not put a privy near a well, or construct it so that it can leak into the earth at all.

In case there is reason to fear that drinking water has become infected, it can be rendered harmless by boiling it for three quarters of an hour. The unpleasant flat taste of boiled water is largely removed, if, after boiling, the water be allowed to stand exposed to the sunlight for some time. In order to prevent the entrance of dust while the water is so exposed, it is well to pour it while still hot into a bottle (which has been thoroughly cleaned, and also heated so that it does not break from the heat of the water), and having closed the bottle by means of a plug of loose cotton, stand it in some sunny place for several hours. If two bottles are used and the supply for the next day is boiled and put into one of them while that already in the other is used, it is easy to let each day's supply stand exposed for twenty-four hours.

There is much which is not yet clear in respect to the best way to dispose of *Sewage disposal.* sewage. In the light of present knowledge and in view of existing conditions, it seems to me that the only practical method to adopt is to get rid of excrementitious substances by spreading them in a thin layer over the surface of the earth. That is to say, to use them as manure. Although it is by no means demonstrated that this procedure insures the destruction of all dangerous bacteria or chemical compounds which may exist in excrementa, it is proven that a very great number of species of bacteria are killed when exposed under like conditions to the action of sun and air. Whether perfectly safe or not, this plan certainly reduces the risk to a minimum, puts waste substances to a good use, and is the only one known to me that may be put into practice, save in the rare instances where a large stream can be used to drain away the sewage —in which case, be it remembered, dwellers upon the banks of the stream below us may be poisoned by our arrangements for getting rid of a troublesome question—or when a body of salt water subject to tidal currents makes it possible for us to carry a drain-pipe out well beyond low-water mark, and feel sure that we have done our whole duty to our neighbors and secured ourselves from quite a little anxiety as well as some risk.

There is no excuse, however, for making use of a privy vault or privy. Such dirty and dangerous plans are utterly without justification; for their use increases the risk of infecting the well-water very greatly, and fills the air with foul odors. Some form of earth closet can always be used instead of them, and that too without additional expense. All that is needed is a water-tight pail or similar vessel under the seat, and a barrel of dry earth with a small shovel or scoop within easy reach. After using the closet the earth is thrown over the excreta. When necessary, the pail is emptied upon a compost heap or elsewhere. If thoroughly mixed in, earth destroys the odors of sewage very completely and very rapidly. At the proper time the mixture can be used as manure. Although the disinfection of sewage is not absolutely certain, this plan is the best practicable.

HYGIENE OF THE INDIVIDUAL.

As it is with the dwelling so is it with the person, the most important sanitary precaution is cleanliness. Curiously enough many people have no more idea of what real personal cleanliness is than they have of real household cleanliness. Superficial neatness is compatible with considerable personal uncleanliness. Clean clothes do not make a clean skin, although dirty inner garments do make a clean body impossible. All this is self-evident, and anyone who is dirty because he does not try to be clean sins deliberately. It is perhaps a rather startling assertion to make, but it is true when I say that a frequent cause of want of cleanliness is the habit of taking a daily cold bath!

Let not the reader suppose for a moment that I know any objection to the daily "tub," so dear to the well-bred Briton and quite as dear to the American of the same class of society, although the latter does not, as does his kinsman from over seas, become so infatuated with this part of his toilet as to devote a considerable share of his daily conversation, no matter what company he is in, to detailed descriptions of his matutinal experience with cold water. On the contrary, I think it a most excellent habit for persons who are strong enough to bear it; but it should be regarded as a stimulating luxury more than as a method of cleansing the body. It removes some of the dirt, of course, and when taken just after exercising, while sweat is still exuding from the pores, a cold sponge bath followed by brisk rubbing cleanses pretty efficiently. But to succeed in getting really clean, soap is absolutely, and hot water almost, indispensable. It is not necessary to take a warm bath daily in addition to the cold sponge; but warm baths should be taken frequently, even though the others be daily.

The rule for determining whether cold or warm baths are best suited to any particular individual is very simple: If a bath, either hot or cold, is followed by a sense of comfort, that bath is beneficial. If a hot bath is followed by a sense of weakness or faintness, or a cold one by shivering and cold extremities, the bath is harmful, and not beneficial. It is useless to try to lay down a hard-and-fast rule in such matters which shall be applicable to all cases; some people are invigorated by cold bathing and some are weakened, and the same is true in regard to hot bathing. The immediate results indicate the proper course in every case. A rough comparison between the actual temperature of a bath and its temperature as appreciated by the body may be given as follows: Water at a temperature of less than 40° F. feels very cold, and when it is less than 36° F. it is absolutely painful when the body is first submerged. Between 40° and 50° F. the water feels decidedly cold. As the temperature rises one feels less and less sensation of chill in the water, and when the thermometer registers from 85° to 95° F. it becomes tepid or warm. Between 100° and 102° F. the bath feels decidedly hot, and when a temperature of 110° to 112° F. is approached the heat is scarcely bearable to one who is not used to it.

Temperature of baths.

The subject of clothing is treated in detail elsewhere in this book. What I have to say about it is so commonplace that, were it not that so few people actually carry into

Clothing.

effect the very simple rules, which must be known to everyone who has thought for a few minutes about the matter and has considered the plain dictates of common sense, I should not make the following suggestions.

Starting with the proposition that, hygienically considered, clothing is worn for the purpose of protecting the body and increasing comfort, it is obvious that the material and thickness of the garments should be determined by the temperatures to which the wearer is exposed, and by his personal sensations. Lighter clothing for warmer and heavier for colder weather is, of course, worn by those who are able to make the change.

In the Northern States it is the rule that people in general dress too warmly. In summer, in the city of New York, the costume which reason prompts one to adopt would on many hot days consist of a suit of modified pajamas. Custom requires men to wear clothes rather more than twice as thick as is compatible with comfort. The spectacle of a man dressed on a very hot day in a cloth suit, put on over a starched shirt and a set of underclothing, is neither elevating nor pleasant. Neither dignity nor suavity is often able to withstand the wilting of the shirt, and the discomfort of its wearer. There are signs of more reasonable summer clothing, but it is useless to fly in the face of fashion, and it is more with winter dressing than with summer that I wish to deal; for in respect to this more can be accomplished without shocking the conventionalities in the least.

The mistakes made in winter are: first, that our rooms are usually far too hot to permit wearing with safety clothing which is comfortable in the house when we go out into the cold of winter. If our garments are thick enough to withstand the outer cold they are too thick to wear with comfort in the inner heat. If rooms were habitually kept at a reasonable temperature much risk to health would be avoided, for we should not be compelled to face such a sharp change as we now do when we leave the house in an overheated state during cold weather. Second, it would be far better did people habitually wear light clothing in the house and use heavier wraps when leaving it. It is unwise to pay so little attention to the actual state of the weather as most of us do, and in order to keep warm and comfortable when the thermometer is low make ourselves hot and uncomfortable when it is high.

Any peace-loving man must approach the corset question with some dread. *Corsets.* All that need be said about it is, first, there is no *necessity* for the use of corsets, at least unless they have been worn so long that the wearer has lost the power to do without the support which they afford.

Second, corsets are injurious to a certain extent to all women. The restriction of free movement of the chest and of all the muscles of the trunk is a very objectionable thing; but we cannot prove that the injury is so severe as to produce serious consequences to health or length of life, except when the wearer has laced tightly, or unless they are worn by girls who are not sufficiently developed to stand their restraint.

Third, corsets are decidedly dangerous if worn at too early an age.

There is no truth in the assertion that the breasts need the support of the corset. When the breasts begin to need support, which they never do when they first develop, there are other ways of supporting them which do not involve the use of any stiff, unyielding garments at all. It would be a blessing could the corset vanish from the earth at an early day, for so it must sooner or later.

The amount to be taken and kind of exercise to be selected differ in individuals. A certain amount of training in certain forms is invaluable, especially for growing girls and boys, and is useful for adults. To secure erect carriage and graceful movements the very best are some of those called by army men "setting-up exercises." (See *Appendix*.)

Exercise.

The Delsarte method is good; but better still in many ways is that to be had by the systematic practice of precisely the same movements as are used by women who are practising to become public dancers. This form of exercise is peculiarly fitted for children, and is one of the most satisfactory means which can be used for the purpose of developing the muscles of the entire body, and giving a remarkable suppleness and grace. It has the advantage, which is important, of interesting and amusing at the same time that it improves the physical condition of a child. Such training can only be conducted under the instruction of a competent teacher. It may be begun as early as the seventh or eighth year of age.

It is a fortunate thing that the young girls of to-day are encouraged to engage in out-door sports, and to look upon exercise as a necessary part of their education. We are under a great obligation to those who introduced the game of lawn tennis to the world ; it has done much for the health of both sexes, and has been the means of improving the physical condition of young girls to a degree which is most satisfactory. Like all good things, it has been overdone by some people, and has been injurious to them. The bicycle promises to be a valuable promoter of good health for both sexes. It is a fascinating form of exercise, and has the merit of being comparatively cheap, after the first expense for the machine. It is needless to enumerate the various forms of out-door sport which are healthful; they are well known.

In the desire to improve the physical condition of young girls we must never forget that they *are girls*, and neither young sexless animals nor boys! Inasmuch as they are developing *human females* their sex imposes certain physical limitations upon them which cannot be disregarded without serious risk to health of body; and inasmuch as they are also developing *women* their sex demands that the beauty, and purity, and tenderness conferred upon woman by virtue of her potential motherhood should not be sacrificed in the slightest degree for the sake of some slight addition to her physical strength as a mere machine. It is in no case either right or necessary to regard a young girl as anything but what she is, whether physical or mental education be considered ; indeed, if the physical laws are infringed nature inexorably punishes the transgression. When I speak of the education of girls, and maintain that its methods must adapt themselves to the fact that they are *girls*, I do not mean to say that the education of women should not be carried to the highest point, nor do I mean that the subjects studied by them should necessarily differ from those studied by the other sex. I simply mean that the physical facts make it absolutely impossible to teach the two sexes in precisely the same *way*. The subject of the hygiene of education will be considered more fully in the chapter on the nursery, where also attention will be called to one of the most neglected, yet most important branches of education, namely, instruction in the art of WORKING EFFICIENTLY BUT NOT WASTEFULLY, and it may be added also of RESTING in the same way. Want of instruction in these two matters has been the cause of incalculable harm to the world.

II.—HYGIENE IN INFANCY AND CHILDHOOD.

<small>Care of the new-born child.</small> THE care of the babe during the first few weeks of its life is a more serious matter, from one standpoint, than is generally appreciated. People seldom realize that upon the management of the child depend what may be called the *morals of the body* — its habits of sleeping and nursing, etc.—and that the subsequent health and happiness of the little one are, to a large extent, determined by the influences of these early days of life. Nor is this all; for the comfort of all who have to do with the child is greatly increased, if the proper course is adopted in its early training. Dr. Keating, in his excellent little book, "Maternity, Infancy, Childhood," says: "It is not necessary to dwell at length on the fact that the child at this age is a noted creature of habit; indeed, as we come to consider infants as they grow, and we study the many causes for that most distressing state of affairs, sleeplessness, we can trace it back, I can almost say in one half of the cases, to the unfortunate indiscretion in humoring the child when it is not more than a few weeks old." Many more ills than sleeplessness have their origin in the same "indiscretion;" the digestion and assimilation of food, the growth of the little one, its strength and its comfort, are all interfered with unless regular habits are formed within a very few weeks after birth. Moreover, the health of the mother requires such regularity; she cannot stand the strain of nursing unless she gets sufficient sleep at regular intervals; and she cannot get such sleep unless the baby is taught to wake and nurse at the proper hours. If a mother is not well her baby suffers from poor or indigestible milk; this tends to make the child both feeble and cross. It seems to the young mother cruel to allow a little baby to cry for a long time, as little babies often do, when she can stop its wailing by nursing it. She is sure it is hungry—regardless of the fact that she has nursed it within the hour. She declares that *this* baby has such a nervous temperament that it cannot be treated so harshly; it is dangerous to allow it to become so excited. All this is natural—but it is wrong. Unless a baby is extremely feeble, and most babies are not, it can, within a few days or weeks, be taught to nurse and sleep so regularly, that it varies but a few minutes from the hours as marked by the clock. Those who have not tried to train an infant to habits of regularity, will be surprised to find how easy the process is, after the first week or two. Begin with the day of its birth. Do not hold the little thing in your arms to put it to sleep, but lay it on its pillow, of course seeing to it that the room is warm enough and the little body protected from draughts. As soon as the milk has come in quantity to permit it, arrange a regular time-table—and keep to it! Usually the intervals between nursings should be two hours during the daytime, and from three to four hours at night. Do not allow the small tyrant to elect to reverse the custom of the rest of the world, and choose the night for frequent nursing, while devoting much of the day to sleep. Why babies should so often try to do this I know not; but many of them certainly do so, and must be taught the evil of their arrangements. There is nothing worse for child or mother than to allow the formation of a habit of falling asleep while nursing, or of nursing at very

short intervals. The baby ought to take a sufficient amount of food at a time to fill its stomach, and then to wait long enough for that organ to become empty; this permits time enough for digestion and for subsequent resting-time for the child, while it also gives the mother enough repose to produce the best milk in sufficient quantity.

I have dwelt upon the necessity of regularity, partly because so few seem to appreciate it, and partly because it is one of the most important of hygienic rules. Do not think that I intend to say that there is any fixed rule about the time which should intervene between nursings; I have suggested two-hour intervals as usually proper. Babies are not all cast in the same mould, and some do better if the interval is longer or shorter. I mean only to say *that some regular interval should elapse,* and some time-table should be selected. Regularity is, next to cleanliness, the greatest protection to the health of children.

It is not within the province of this article to treat of all details of nursery hygiene. I shall deal only with general principles.

When preparing the paper I asked a friend who is the mother of several children, and who has in them irrefutable evidence (if evidence were needed) that she knows whereof she speaks, to write for me a description of the methods which she thought best to adopt in the physical care of infants and little children. Upon reading her response to this request, I saw that the best way to cover much of the ground which belongs to this article would be to publish her views in her own words. She consented to allow me to do this, and I give it in full, feeling sure that nothing that I could write would give such clear, succinct, and complete directions.

The nursery. " I take it for granted that the nursery is the brightest, sunniest room in the house. Let it be also pretty and gay and not like a ward in a hospital. Even a very young baby is sensitive to its surroundings and enjoys the gay pictures on the walls and pretty ornaments on bureau and mantel-piece.

" A hard wood floor, or, if this is impossible, a painted floor, is more desirable than an all-over carpet, but I prefer to rugs a square of carpet well lined and nailed down so as to leave a margin of wood floor all around the room. This square of carpet is much warmer than rugs and, in case of sudden illness, may be taken up at a few moments' notice. A bare floor—always hygienic—is indispensable in cases of contagious disease.

Fresh air and sunlight. " Do not be afraid of plenty of fresh air and sunlight. Let carpet and pretty muslin curtains fade, but let the sunlight stream into the room. Whether the day be warm or not open the windows, and do not fear to open the windows really wide. You will have less draught than by opening a slit. Many doctors will forbid a little infant to be taken out in winter. This is undoubtedly a safe precaution in a severe climate, but a little baby longs for fresh air quite as much as an adult. Let him have it by throwing wide open your sunny nursery window, dress him as though for going out and put your bassinet or cradle, or, for lack of anything better, a clothes-basket with pillows in it, close to the window in the sun, and cover him warmly. You will be surprised to find what a restful sleep and what rosy cheeks the little creature will have after its sun bath.

" Give up almost any luxury rather than an open fireplace in the nursery.

" Keep your nursery cool—68° F. is warm enough even for bathing an infant, and 66° quite warm enough for children old enough to romp and play. Remember that they take an immense amount of exercise, from the little six months' old who strains every nerve to lift a very small toy, to the four or five year old who plays horse for hours together. I have seen children in profuse perspiration while the mother sat quietly reading or sewing and asking for a shawl. [*See reference to "Franklin Stove" in* APPENDIX.]

Temperature of the nursery.

"Every trained nurse has her own ideas about bathing an infant, just as every mother has, so it is hard to make any fixed rules. Air the room thoroughly, first, and wait until it is warm again before beginning. Have everything ready, the little clothes all prepared and warm, and laid where they are reached easily. A large flannel apron and a large soft bath-towel are necessary. Take off the baby's night-clothes quickly and firmly. He will not mind it half so much as if you apologize to him between each garment for the liberties you are taking. When you reach the band, before taking that off, let him have a short air-bath with plenty of exercise, and you will be surprised to see how much exercise the little arms and legs can take. Wash the face and head thoroughly before putting him in, then dip him gently into the water, as sometimes even an older baby will suddenly get violently alarmed. Hold him with the left hand, rub all over with the right—either with or without soap, according to the needs of the baby; take a good-sized sponge (don't confine yourself to what is commonly called a 'baby sponge,' they are wretched little things except for a new-born infant) and sponge him thoroughly. Lift him into your soft bath-towel, fold this and your flannel apron around him and rub gently but thoroughly keeping him covered all the time. As to the temperature of the bath—it must be determined by the physical condition of the child and the family doctor, but it can and ought to be gradually cooled until it is what is commonly called tepid. The greatest care should be taken in washing the mouth. Fifty cent's worth of absorbent cotton will more than last through babyhood. Always use fresh cold water and never use the same piece of cotton twice. The colder the water the better a baby seems to like it, though by this I do not mean ice-water! Don't be afraid to let him suck the water from the cotton. In this way he will get a drink, which an infant needs and ought to have daily. As he grows older, give him at least twice a day a little cold water, for milk does not always quench thirst.

How to bathe an infant.

"About the dressing of an infant, opinions vary, but the following suggestions apply to children living in a climate such as that of New York and in a house kept reasonably warm, *i.e.*, having a nursery temperature of 66° to 68° F. and the temperature of the rest of the house more or less in that neighborhood.

How to dress an infant.

"For a new-born baby you will probably have to yield to the superior judgment of your trained nurse whether you approve of it or not. We shall therefore consider first a six weeks' old baby. Use only the lightest and finest of flannel for bands, barrow-coats, and night-gowns; as a rule, a gauze undershirt is the only one needed. We will begin, then, with the flannel band, a light gauze undershirt, a barrow-coat or flannel petticoat, preferably mounted on a flannel band or waist, a short thin nainsook petticoat, and what is known as a slip instead of a dress. Avoid most carefully long, heavy, clumsy white dresses. They only add weight and no warmth.

"My rule is no shoes or socks. This is so great a heresy that I feel I must give my reason for it. A young baby wearing socks will invariably do one of two things—though he generally does both! He will either wet the sock or kick it off. Then the little foot, accustomed as it is to the warmth of the sock, feels the chill and the mother is surprised to find that the baby has cold feet. On the other hand, the little bare feet are constantly rubbing against the flannel petticoat and, even if wet, are dried in a few moments by the friction.

"At night, let the dress be just the same—only exchanging for the white petticoat and dress a long, loose, flannel night-dress. This, with a soft, warm, knit blanket wrapped tightly around the baby just under the arm-pits will keep the little body warm and comfortable all night. Don't be afraid to leave the head uncovered. A baby likes air quite as much as you do. If you fear draughts, draw a screen or a curtain around the little bed.

"Use only the lightest of knit or light woollen blankets, and have them of small size, as the weight of a large blanket is uncomfortable and unhealthful.

"The proper age for putting a baby into short clothes depends, of course, *Short* upon the season of the year, *clothes.* the child's health, and the necessities of the case. Except under unusual circumstances, I should give six months as the limit for keeping infants in long clothes. By that time the desire for exercise and freedom becomes very marked. With great care and discretion the change can be made as easily in winter as in summer, provided the child is ordinarily healthy. First, put on the short white slip instead of the long one, leaving the other two long petticoats on. In a day or so take off the long white petticoat, though the baby will look rather odd with a long flannel petticoat hanging far below the others. After two or three days, make the final change of the long flannel skirt for the short one, putting on at the same time little socks or stockings and very light soft shoes or slippers.

"In regard to foot-covering, the child's temperament must be considered carefully. If he is a full-blooded, sturdy, active baby, the little socks that I know mothers are so fond of can do no harm, especially if the napkins are frequently changed so that the upper part of the leg is kept warm.

"Don't be alarmed if the baby's skin on arms or legs feels cool to the touch. It is only when hands or feet are very cold that extra clothing is needed.

"The clothing at night should remain the same, though lightened in summer by taking off the flannel petticoat and even the skirt, but never the band or light woollen night-gown.

"It would be impossible to follow the changes needed all through babyhood. I shall therefore take next the clothing of a child of from three to four years. Keep to the knit or flannel band. It *Lightness,* is one of the greatest safe-*warmth,* guards against cold. Over *and free-* *dom in* this a light, all-wool shirt. I *clothing.* strongly advise woollen drawers of the same quality as the shirt. Thus you have a warm, light foundation of clothing. The outer garments need not be specially warm and must not be heavy. Remember again the great activity of a child of that age and the amount of exercise he takes. I have seen so often a languid, flushed little face the result only of heavy warm clothing. It is as great a mistake to overdress as to underdress a child. When he goes out, however, dress him according to the weather of the day, not according to the weather of the season. In an uncertain climate, two winter coats are almost a necessity.

One should be made lighter in weight and less warm than the other. The lighter coat will be found invaluable on cold spring days as well as on warm winter days, and is, therefore, not the extravagance it seems to be. The headgear depends on the amount of hair a child has, but in this respect also do not err on the side of too great warmth. Remember that in after years the child is destined, whether man or woman, to wear very little head covering, and, if it has much hair falling about the neck and ears, the constant friction of the hair will keep them quite warm enough. When a little girl is old enough to walk, and even when she is growing to be a big girl, do not allow yourself to be tempted to add a muff to the winter outfit. Put on the warmest possible mittens and let her have absolute freedom of her arms. This will help toward giving her the fine, free, swinging walk we so rarely see among our city-bred women.

"My advice for the summer clothing of children, when the weather is very warm, is brief. Put on as few clothes as are decent.

"The question of a time for changing a boy's skirts to trousers is another

"Putting on trousers." difficult matter to decide. The mother's instinct of the fitness of things must come into play, and, as it is not an important matter of health, I need not lay down rules in regard to it. As a child grows older the dress should change according to its needs and its physical condition.

"Common sense is a better guide than all the rules ever written. Health de-

Common sense. pends on common sense quite as much as on doctors' advice. For example, many mothers are as much afraid of rain as of diphtheria. I think that warm summer rains are as healthful for children as for plants, and are not to be avoided and dreaded. To sum up, do not be afraid of cold or heat, rain or sun—except in their extremes. What should we think of the mother fish who decided that her young needed more air and less water? And yet how often the human parent makes just such decisions."

Surely no more need be said upon this branch of nursery hygiene. The sound common sense that characterizes my friend's advice must be the foundation of *all* practical hygiene. It is not such a very complex subject, this hygiene, after all. More accurately speaking, it is not very complicated in most of its details of a practical sort. People who are not compelled to solve problems of the kind which present themselves to professional sanitarians need not burden their minds with a vast mass of details; the questions presented to them have few difficulties. In the nursery, hygienic rules are the rules of common sense, and so are they always. It is impossible to treat all children in precisely the same manner; it is equally impossible to do so with adults. Common sense must be the guide in all cases.

Perhaps some readers will be surprised to find in an article on hygiene

Education and hygiene. any reference to certain matters which are discussed in this paper. Education, for example, is not usually regarded as a *hygienic measure*, though the *hygiene of education* is often considered. Yet I intend to speak of education more in relation to its powers as a means of preserving health, than in relation to the power of health to make possible the highest education. The latter is often mentioned, the former is more important. Children can be *taught to be healthy*—and healthy children can be taught other things. Education is a powerful hygienic force. In order to explain what I mean, I must first state that my idea of education is that it implies such instruction as shall fit the individual for life in this world of ours. It is instruction which begins before the alphabet is learned, and continues long after leaving school or college. There is a difference between hygiene in education, and education in hygiene.

Education in hygiene begins during the first days of life; it is then directed toward the formation of good and regular habits of body. As the child grows older and its intelligence develops, habits of mind begin to be acquired which may be profoundly influenced by training. How few of us appreciate the fact that a very great deal of physical suffering in after life comes from bad mental training in childhood! I do not mean suffering of an imaginary kind; I mean disease which may entirely ruin a life which might have been of use to the world, and which surely would have been happier but for the lost health. Many a chronic invalid might have preserved his health had he been taught to use his brain properly when a child.

Never forget in educating a young child that in the nature of things the chances are that illness will come sooner or later. The illness may be slight or severe; but whether the one or the other, it is of the greatest importance that the physician be able to make a proper examination of the little patient in order to prescribe effectively. A child can be taught to do many things of medical importance as a matter of course, provided the instruction is begun when he is in good health, whereas, without teaching, all efforts to make him do them when ill, result only in bitter protests and angry struggles.

Teach a child to submit to an examination of its throat. Accustom it to open the mouth, put out the tongue, and not to fear the introduction of a spoon or other tongue depressor. *Beyond everything, avoid arousing in his mind fear or distrust of the doctor.* No words can express the wickedness and folly of threatening the poor child with a visit from the doctor and a dose of medicine as a punishment for misconduct. Never lie to a child about doctors or medicine or anything else; but if you feel, as some people seem to feel, that life without lying is an impossibility, at least don't lie about the amount of pain likely to result from a surgical procedure, or about the taste of some medicine. If you know that something to be done will hurt, say so; if a mixture to be swallowed is unpleasant, say so. If you deceive a child once in such matters, do not imagine that it will trust you again. You do not deserve trust, and you will not get it!

We Americans are frequently said to be the greatest sufferers from certain *Learning how to think.* forms of serious nervous diseases in the world. This seems actually to be the case; we seem to suffer from nervous exhaustion, with its consequent physical weakness, to a greater degree than do other nations. Doubtless this is due, in part, to the heavy strain imposed upon us by the hurry and worry of our ways of living; but hurry and worry are by no means the only causes of nervous exhaustion. Indeed, there is great reason to think that *hurry* has little or nothing to do with it, except in so far as it produces *worry*. There are thousands of men and women living in towns, villages, or farmhouses in various parts of this country, who rarely know what it is to be hurried—who may have many long and weary hours of daily work to do, or whose daily task may be very short —yet whose health is lost by reason of nervous exhaustion. They have ground their nervous machinery to pieces, not by undue haste in working or living, but by undue waste of nerve-force. They have never been taught *how* to think or work—they have no idea of the preservation of brain and muscle power—they waste their strength in thousands of ways—and they break down! Let no one think that nervous exhaustion is the name of an imaginary disorder which is fashionably used by doctors to hide the selfishness or laziness of a patient. This is not so. While it is true that certain people cloak their indolent self-indulgence under a pretence of illness, it is equally true that among the sufferers from nervous exhaustion may be found some of the most unselfish and hardest working men and women in the world. It is a very real disease—and a cause of terrible suffering.

Worry is the real cause of almost all cases. Work by itself rarely, if ever, produces it. If one works without mental distress, one may be tired out, but sleep will relieve the fatigue. When worry is added to work, or when it exists independently of work, sleep itself either fails to restore strength or does not come to the weary body and brain save in an unsatisfactory way. If worry be avoided, the amount of work which can be accomplished year in and year out is surprisingly great. Have you ever thought what worry really is? It is simply wasted mental force. It is thought expended needlessly, so far as any good result is concerned. Let us suppose that we have some work to accomplish which it is important to do well, or which it is important to finish within a given time. Is that work improved in quality, or finished the sooner, if besides devoting strength and thought to its accomplishment, we devote additional strength and thought to the consideration of the results of failure? The useless expenditure of energy is what we call worry. Have you ever heard a steam-engine make a clicking sound every time the piston-rod changed the direction of its motion? Engines do so when their working parts are not properly fitted, so that some of the power of the steam is expended in moving pieces of metal to and fro without useful effect. When this happens, the engine is weakened to the extent of the power wasted, and, moreover, the jar of the waste motion racks the machine, and may shake it to pieces. Waste motion is to an engine what worry is to a human being.

Do you exclaim, "All this is very true; but what has it to do with hygiene? Hygiene cannot stop worry." I reply that a most important part of the education in hygiene is precisely for the purpose of making it possible to do away with a great deal of worry. And it *can* do so! If a child is made to think in a systematic way, and is taught to estimate the relative importance of things, one-half of the causes of worry are removed. The engineer in charge of a ten-ton steam hammer—a machine which was one of the great admirations of my childhood—became so skilful in the management of the huge apparatus that he could break an egg which had been put into a wine-glass and set upon the anvil without breaking the glass; yet the whole immense power of the hammer was employed when the egg-shell was struck. A force of hundreds of tons was let loose and checked, and the result was a broken egg, and an unbroken wine-glass! This performance resembles closely the methods of many a human being in respect to the amount of energy expended compared to the results obtained. Too many of us are in the habit of using the power of a steam hammer to break an egg! In our own case we happen to be obliged to furnish the wasted energy out of our own individual store; we do not get it from a steam boiler! The simile would be more accurate were I to say that these people habitually use a sledge-hammer to break their eggs. Not only would they save their strength, but also would they break the shell so as to make better use of its contents, did they select some easier method. It is not wise "to do things too hard."

It is then very important as a hygienic measure to teach children to work hard, but not to spend part of their energy in useful work and waste part of it in useless worry. The way to accomplish this is by teaching them concentration of mind upon whatever is to be done. The kindergarten system, *if really adopted in its true spirit*, does much to attain this desirable end. The real aim of this system is to teach children to *think* and to *know*, rather than to memorize and to recite. It also teaches systematic thinking and systematic observation; and those who learn to think and observe systematically do not waste thought. Moreover, this method exercises the faculty of becoming interested in what is before one and hence is a great safeguard against worry.

Formal education is not the only preserver from mental waste for the child. The way in which it is taught to regard father and mother makes a great difference in its whole life. If its relations with its parents are what such relations should be, affectionate — and *friendly* (there is a difference between affection and friendship)—the little one will be spared much worry, for all perplexing questions will be referred to the two best and wisest friends known to the childish heart. If father and mother have a sense of the wickedness of lying to a child, and speak lovingly and honestly in reply to the sweet confiding little inquirer, they will teach two things which will prevent much worry. In the first place, they will teach confidence, and in the second, they will show that there are many questions to which our only answer can be "I do not know." One of the greatest safeguards against the shattering of ideals is the demonstration to the childish mind that its parents command respect and excite love, and yet may be ignorant of many things.

Not only should children be taught to work without waste of strength: they should also be taught to rest completely. Until the little one is four or five years old there should be a fixed time during the day which is spent in bed. Whether it sleeps or not, insist that it shall stay on the bed. When the age for systematic lessons has arrived, never let the time of rest be interfered with by thoughts of study. Let there be times for work and times for play, and let the play be pursued as earnestly as the work. Too few adults know how to rest or play.

In the matter of instruction the number of hours of study must be considered. It is impossible to lay down any fixed rule for all children. Individuals differ so much that each case must be decided upon its own merits. On the whole, there is a tendency to arrange for too long hours of instruction for very young children. It seems to me that it would be better did we have shorter hours of daily work and shorter periods of complete rest. This I believe is true of almost all our schools.

I now come to the last and in many respects the most important part of the subject of education in hygiene. If I can impress upon the readers of this article anything like a realizing sense of the necessity of understanding the practical importance of instruction *The age of puberty.* in certain physiological facts which force themselves upon the attention of girls at the age of puberty for the first time, I

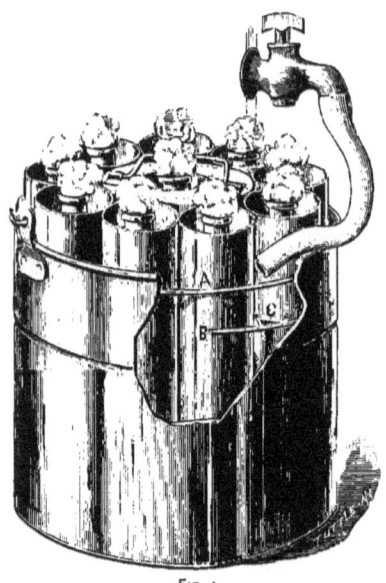

Fig. 1.

feel that the many shortcomings of the paper may be to a certain extent excused, for it will have done some good in the world.

The fact that physiological phenomena impose certain limitations upon the physical and mental training of girls has been mentioned elsewhere. I wish most earnestly to repeat that statement and to protest against the reckless disregard of these limitations which is so common. The world has reached a stage of development in which no excuse exists for the conduct of many mothers in regard to the sort of information which they give to their daughters when the menstrual function is beginning to be established. There is still less excuse for the common habit of permitting the young girl to remain in ignorance for so long as is now usual of the simpler facts concerning the meaning of menstruation and the necessity of great care during the period, especially when it first occurs. Whether a rational explanation of the facts are given or not, it is simply wicked to allow a young girl to continue to study or play when unwell as when well. The whole of her future happiness may be determined by her care at this time. Let the sacrifice be what it may, her education, her amusements, and her exercise must all be directed by the time-table which nature has adopted for her. Never forget that any other schedule of time may result in ruined health.

NOTE ON THE STERILIZATION AND PASTEURIZATION OF MILK.

There is no question that some of the most fatal diseases of childhood result from the use of contaminated milk for food. There is also no doubt that it is easy completely to remove danger from this source by "sterilizing" the milk with the aid of the Arnold Steam Sterilizer or of a similar device.

Fig. 2.

There is a grave objection to sterilization by this method, however, on account of the alteration in the chemical constitution of the milk which it induces. Not only is there a disagreeable taste to milk thus treated, but it is not so easily digested thereafter by certain children.

The method known as Pasteurization, conducted in the manner suggested by Dr. Rowland G. Freeman, of New York City, is far preferable since it does not change the milk materially.

It depends upon the fact that by heating milk to 75° Centigrade (167° Fahrenheit) and maintaining that temperature for a sufficient length of time, complete sterilization results.

Dr. Freeman has invented a very simple apparatus for doing this, which is cheap and easy to use. I give herewith cuts showing the Pasteurizer and its working, together with the directions for its use.

Pasteurization of milk consists in heating it rapidly to about 75° C. retaining at that temperature a short time, and then cooling it rapidly to 20° C. The apparatus is designed to accomplish this purpose.

The apparatus consists of a pail for water and a receptacle for the bottles of milk.

The *pail* is a simple pail with a cover. Extending around the pail is a groove for indicating the level to which the pail is to be filled with water. Inside the pail are three supports (c) for holding the receptacle.

The *receptacle* for the bottles of milk consists of a number of hollow cylinders fastened together. Surrounding and binding together the group of cylinders is a wire (A). It is this wire (A) which rests on the support (c) when the milk is being heated (Fig. 1). Below the wire (A) are three short wires (B). These wires (B) rest on the support (c) when the receptacle is raised for cooling (Fig. 2).

1. Fill the pail to the level of the groove with water, cover it and put it on the stove to boil, the receptacle for the bottles having been left out.

2. Fill the body of each bottle with milk, or milk and water in proper proportion for feeding; stopper with a wad of cotton batting and put in a refrigerator. If all the bottles which the receptacle holds are not needed, fill the remaining cylinders with cold water. Each space in the receptacle must be filled.

3. When the water in the pail on the stove boils thoroughly, take the bottles of milk from the refrigerator and put them in the spaces for them in the receptacle.

4. Pour cold water into each of these spaces so as to surround the body of the bottle.

5. Take the pail of boiling water from the stove and put it on a table or mat. Do not put it on metal or stone.

6. Set the receptacle containing the bottles of milk into the pail of boiling water, so that the wire (A) will rest on the support (c), cover the pail quickly and let it stand half an hour. During this period the pail must not be on the stove and the cover must not be removed.

7. Now uncover the pail and lift the receptacle and turn it so that the wire (B) will rest on the support (c), thus elevating the top of the receptacle above that of the pail. Put the pail containing the receptacle elevated in this manner in a basin under a faucet to which a rubber pipe may be attached connecting it with the pail (Fig. 2). The water will overflow from the pail into the basin.

The above-described method of cooling is the best. When, however, it is not possible to cool the milk in this way, the cooling may be accomplished by placing the receptacle containing the bottles of milk in iced water, or by simply standing the bottles on wood in a refrigerator.

8. To warm the milk for use put the bottle containing it in a vessel of cold water on the stove and leave it until it is warm.

Use a fresh bottle for each feeding.

9. Wash the bottles thoroughly after using, and once a day put all the empty bottles in a kettle of cold water on the stove and let this water boil for an hour. The bottles should then be taken out and stood bottom up until used.

Milk sterilized by this apparatus may be used for food during the following twenty-four hours.

III.—HYGIENE OF THE SICK-ROOM—A FEW WORDS ABOUT DOCTORS AND NURSES.

ALTHOUGH it is hardly within the province of an article upon Hygiene to consider the relations of the family and the doctor or sick-nurse, so much depends upon a correct appreciation of these relations that I feel justified in pointing out certain oft-forgotten facts.

It is regrettable that many people seem to accept their medical attendant much as they do their political beliefs—as a result of the opinions of friends or relatives. Very seldom is much care used in the choice. Naturally more or less mutual misunderstanding follows which might easily have been avoided. When selecting a physician, above all things try to get one in whom you have confidence. If possible, choose one whose personality is attractive to you; for the feeling of esteem and respect for a doctor are almost as important aids in treatment as are drugs. If you do not trust a doctor, get another, if possible, whom you do trust. If you dislike your doctor, it is usually well to try to replace him with one whom you find more congenial; dislike shakes confidence and handicaps the medical man in all his efforts to cure you. It is so often necessary to talk to a medical adviser about subjects of the most private nature connected with yourself or your family, and to rely so much upon his honor and secrecy, that the advantage of dealing with one whom you like and esteem is self-evident.

The choice of a physician.

In these days of "specialists" the wisdom of employing *one* trustworthy general practitioner to take charge of the family as a whole—to be the "family doctor"—is too often forgotten. One would suppose from the multitude of doctors consulted by many a family that we men and women were all constructed of a heterogeneous collection of unrelated organs, instead of each of us having a body in which every part is closely connected with all the others. Nowadays, the advance of medical knowledge has made it impossible for any single man to attain the technical skill requisite for the accurate diagnosis or best treatment of many of the diseases which affect certain regions of the body, *but the best medical adviser for any family is not the specialist, whose view is always narrowed by the attention which he pays to the disorders of a single organ or limited group of organs; what a family needs is the doctor who knows enough to advise intelligently as to the proper course to be pursued in all cases, including among other things the employment of specialists.* Get some good general practitioner to take charge of you and your family; do not have four or five specialists, unless he advises it.

Specialists.

Having selected a physician whom you can trust, follow his advice in case of illness as nearly as circumstances will allow. If it is necessary to disobey his orders, do so; but tell him what you have done, and why, as soon as you can. Do not deceive a doctor upon any account; if he is worth consulting he is worth treating fairly. I do not mean that you should confide to him, as so many people do, any private affairs which are not connected with medical matters; there is no need of doing so. I mean that you should be absolutely frank with him in regard to everything of medical interest, whether it appears to you important or not.

It is a misfortune that the term "medical etiquette" should have come into general use. It has misled very many of the laity and not a few medical men. It has given rise to the idea that for some unknown reason doctors have a peculiar standard which determines their conduct in life. They are supposed to behave like fools in consequence. While I admit that some of them do precisely that thing, there is no reason to lay the blame upon "etiquette." It inheres in the man. There is no more use in attempting to drive the foolishness out of the fool of to-day by means of rules than there was in Solomon's time when that wise king proclaimed the inefficiency to that end of harsher measures: "Though thou bray a fool in a mortar among wheat with a pestle, yet will not his foolishness depart from him." There is absolutely no difference between the principles of the "etiquette" of medical men and of the "etiquette" which should determine the conduct in respect to one another of all human beings. Its rules are the rules of courtesy, and its foundation is upon the "golden rule." The reluctance of a physician to prescribe for a patient who is under the care of another physician is the result of the perfectly natural desire which all really considerate people must have, to avoid interfering with the business of others. If circumstances demand immediate action, "etiquette" requires that such action be taken at once. All of the rules of "etiquette" may be summarized as follows: "Be courteous to and considerate of other doctors. Be courteous to and considerate of your fellow-men, medical or lay. Be guided by common-sense and the interests of humanity. Don't be a fool!"

Concerning "medical etiquette."

The position of a sick-nurse is a difficult one. The difficulties are often increased by avoidable blunders, due to misconception of her duties and of the true relations to the members of the household in which she happens to be at work. The fault is sometimes her own and sometimes her employer's.

Concerning nurses, "trained" or untrained.

Perhaps the most fruitful source of trouble between nurses and their employers is the unfortunate fact that each party usually regards the other with more or less suspicion. The family and the servants in the house alike are accustomed to think that a nurse is a person who will probably "make trouble" sooner or later (which, I grieve to say, she frequently does). The nurse, perhaps from bitter experience with other families, cannot altogether help looking for some unpleasant behavior on the part of some of the household (and her expectations are only too often realized). Thus, since there is no more certain way to cause trouble and misunderstanding than to look for it continually, trouble is pretty sure to occur.

When engaging a nurse, of course one should try to get one who is personally agreeable. Also when engaging one it must be remembered that the transaction is a matter of business; try to settle the business details as soon as possible, leaving no room for subsequent dispute about payment, etc. There is one fact which the employers of nurses seem often to forget, namely: that the nurse does not covenant to render any services save those of a *nurse;* neither does she agree to remain on duty for a longer time than flesh and blood can endure. One of the most common faults of employers is a tendency to keep the nurse on duty too many hours daily at a stretch, and then to wake her up for trifling reasons when she has been allowed a few hours for much-needed sleep. The nurse ought to have ample time for rest and exercise, and ought to be provided with good food at regular hours, unless some emergency makes it necessary for everyone who has to help care for the patient to strain every nerve to avert imminent peril. Then, of course, the nurse, if she is worthy of the name, willingly stands to her work, at no matter what cost, until she can do no more.

I have said that the nurse agrees to perform the duties of a nurse and nothing more. These duties must vary with every case within wide limits; work which in some instances a nurse should do as a matter of course, because no one else can do it so well under existing circumstances, in other instances is no part of her duty. One thing she must never forget, whatever befall: her profession imposes upon her one duty which never varies—that of doing all in her power to alleviate suffering, not alone that directly affecting her patient and resulting from illness, but also which sickness indirectly causes to anxious friends of the invalid. Another invariable duty of a nurse is to care for the room in which the patient lies.

There are unquestionably many graduates of training-schools who are utterly unfit to be nurses, and the majority of untrained nurses are perhaps more unfit; but unquestionably, also, very many employers treat nurses shamefully. It would be better were there more fairness and trust displayed on both sides.

When caring for a sick person, it should be our aim to preserve the patient from all avoidable worry and annoyance. This statement is so evidently true that it would be rather absurd to repeat it were it not for the fact that many people *Personal care of the sick.* act as though they did not know it. Much of the discomfort of a sick person can be relieved by skilful nursing, and almost as much more by the exercise of tact and intelligence on the part of all who may have to come into the sick-room.

The most important element making for comfort for the invalid is perfect quiet and the consequent freedom from worry and nervousness. When I say "quiet," I do not necessarily mean silence, but that sort of restful state which follows the sense that every detail of the various matters connected with the case has been considered and provided for. A patient ought never to be asked any questions, and should never be called upon to consider any of the details of daily life, save in the few instances when important reasons justify inflicting upon him the strain which the resulting mental attention produces. It is very hard for a sick person to make up his mind about any subject. Do not ask whether he is hungry or not (of course I am speaking of patients who are too sick to care for food); bring him the proper food at the proper times and give it to him. If you ask whether he wants anything to eat, and then ask what he would like, he is apt to think that he wants nothing and to refuse to eat what you finally set before him. On the other hand, if you quietly set the food before him as a matter of course, he frequently eats it without offering any objection. Be careful not to put too much in the plate; he is more likely to eat if a small amount is given him at a time. If he wants more, you can bring it when the first is exhausted. *Importance of quiet.*

One of the worst blunders which it is possible to make is whispering in the presence of a sick person. It excites curiosity and suspicion; the same is true of the low- *Whispering in the sick room.*

toned talk which is apt to be carried on just outside the door of the sick-room. If you have to talk, speak sufficiently loud for the sufferer to hear easily what you say. If something must be said which it is not well for the patient to hear, go out of the room, and go sufficiently far from it to be impossible that the tones of your voice reach his ears. The senses of many of the sick are very acute. They are apt to be much worried by little things, particularly by discussion of their own case, which they suppose to be unfavorable in character since they are not permitted to hear it.

This brings to mind the question of the morality and wisdom of deceiving *Deception of patients.* a sick person. In time of sickness as in health a certain amount of deception is absolutely unavoidable. We have no more right to show, by word, manner, or expression, any anxiety which we may feel about an invalid than we have to be discourteous to people in good health. There is no similarity in the reasons for which we control our emotions in these two cases, but in both alike we deliberately deceive others to a certain extent. We are accustomed to carry our deceit further when we deal with well people, for we frequently take great pains to soften the harsher details of life at the expense of the truth. It seems to me that the same general principles apply in our intercourse with one another in sickness and in health. There is a kind of deception (which means nothing more nor less than a kind of lying) which is both honorable and wise; and there is a kind of deception which is incompatible with honor or wisdom. It is both wrong and unwise deliberately to lie in answering a direct question asked by an invalid; it is sometimes better to evade the question instead of answering it. Possibly conditions may exist when deliberate deception (including direct lying) may be justifiable, and may be wise; but, except when dealing with a delirious or insane person, it is hard to imagine what such conditions can be. Looked at as a pure matter of policy, the risk of discovery and the disastrous results which would follow it—the shock and distrust—more than counterbalance the immediately apparent good. Patients, moreover, are rarely injured by facts if told in a tactful way. Of course, I do not mean to advise that the patient should be informed of every unpleasant occurrence in the house, or be needlessly told that his condition is very serious and is rapidly becoming more so, or that the sort of frankness which is akin to brutality be adopted in the sick-room. I wish merely to warn against the policy so often adopted by well-meaning friends of systematic deception; it is a bad plan to add to the troubles which are the unavoidable consequences of sickness in a house, the strain which all efforts to lie consistently and for a considerable time entail. It is far easier to behave naturally and to speak truthfully, and it is better for the patient in almost all cases.

It is the duty of one who has to care for a sick person to exercise as much *Self-control in the sick-room.* self-control as possible. It is not right to worry the patient by giving way to emotions. Only those who have had experience can know what a severe strain it is to nurse the sick. Body and mind suffer keenly from the constant watchful alertness, the long hours, and the anxiety. The sufferings of some patients, the selfish querulousness of others, the horrible vagaries of the delirious, the physical labor—all are exhausting to the nurse. It is hard to keep one's temper in many a case, and still harder to hide nervousness under a calm manner. Yet one must do both. Especially is it important never to lose one's head. If possible, do not be frightened or flurried. At least never appear the one or the other. A quiet, firm manner is one of the most necessary qualities of a nurse. Of course, tact is more important—indeed, good nursing is impossible without it—but, unfortunately, few possess it, and it is not to be learned by those who have it not.

Too little stress is laid upon the importance of making a patient as com-
Comfort important to patient. fortable, physically, as circumstances will permit. In reality small causes of discomfort are to a sick person far more serious

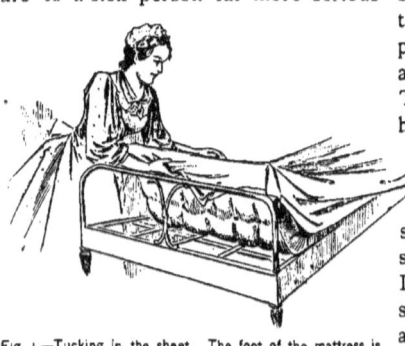

Fig. 1.—Tucking in the sheet. The foot of the mattress is lifted up and the sheet held firmly and the mattress lowered, thus stretching the sheet tightly and smoothly.

matters than one would suppose. A badly made bed may make the difference between fairly quiet sleep and active delirium; and what to one in health would be almost unnoticed, may cause really severe suffering to him during sickness. It should be remembered that discomfort fatigues the mind, and fatigue is a serious matter for a weakened person; it may even result fatally. The greatest care should be taken to avoid it.

The most common causes of discomfort are a badly tended bed, lack of cleanliness, bad or improperly served and administered food, bad ventilation, and a room too hot.

The bed should be placed so that the light does not fall directly in the patient's face. The mattress upon *The bed.* which he lies should not be too soft; one made of hair is the best. Under this it is well to have a spring mattress of woven wire, if such can be obtained, though other springs will do. If the patient is liable to soil the bedding, a rubber sheet should be pinned over the mattress and a blanket put between this and the sheet, and over the sheet a "draw sheet" should be placed. This is a folded sheet which is so arranged that it can be drawn from one side of the bed toward the other under the patient without moving him. When a part of it is soiled it is pulled away and a clean portion is thus substituted. The bed-covering should not be too heavy nor too warm. Sheets should be large enough to fold well under the mattress. It is of the greatest importance to have the sheet upon which the sufferer lies absolutely smooth and free from creases. It must be firmly tucked in both at the sides and ends (Fig. 1). Cotton sheets are better than linen. Both sheets should be frequently changed. It is not difficult to change bed-clothing even when a patient is helpless. The under sheet may be turned back from one side of the bed and the fresh one either folded, as shown in the cut, or laid flat in its place, with its edge slightly overlapping the soiled one. It is best to tuck the clean one under the side of the mattress in the same way one would do were one making up the bed with no one on it. (It is needless to say that during these manœuvres the coverings over the patient have only been turned back, not removed; he has not been exposed at all to cold.) We now have the soiled and fresh sheet close to the side of the invalid; it remains to slip the former out and the latter into its place. There are two ways of doing this. If the patient can be rolled partly over in the direction toward which the sheets are being moved, the latter can be slipped under him so far that by simply rolling him in the opposite direction until he lies partly upon the other side, the edges of both sheets will be cleared by his body and can be at once drawn still further, so that when he is again turned upon his back he will lie entirely upon the fresh one. Another plan may be adopted when it is not advisable to turn the patient upon the side. The soiled sheet is turned back as before and the fresh one laid so as to overlap it in the same way (Fig. 2). Now, having gone to the opposite side fresh over the soiled and then slip the latter out. Be sure that all bedclothes are well tucked in. If a patient is very restless fasten the bedclothes to the

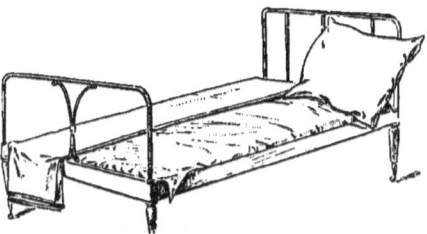

Fig. 2.—Clean sheet folded and overlapping the soiled one.

Fig. 3.—Position of hands in drawing the sheet beneath the patient.

of the bed, the nurse slips both arms under the patient's pillow and slightly raises his head and shoulders. With the hand nearest the head of the bed she draws the upper corners of the sheets toward herself (Fig. 3). By pulling strongly the soiled sheet is made to slide from under the upper part of the body and the clean one to take its place. The same thing is done at the feet (Fig. 4). Next, taking hold of both sheets near the middle, they are easily drawn completely into place.

In changing the upper covering loosen that which is to be removed and tuck that which replaces it in at the foot of the mattress. Next spread the mattress with safety-pins. Be careful to remove bread-crumbs or any other particles of food or dirt which may have found their way into the bed.

It is not difficult to bathe a patient while in bed. All that has to be done *Bathing the sick* is to wash a small part of the body at a time without uncovering the rest. The water should be warm. Especial care should be taken to keep the parts upon which the weight of the body rests most heavily, *i.e.*, the shoulders and buttocks, thoroughly clean, in order to prevent bed-sores. The cleaning of the mouth and teeth is important. A soft rag with warm water containing a little boric acid or listerine is an excellent means of cleaning the mouth and teeth.

It is the business of the physician to prescribe the kind and quantity of food to be given ; but it is the rule that food should be given in small amounts at frequent reg-

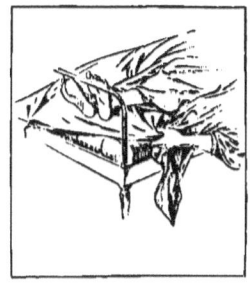

Fig. 4.—Drawing the sheet under the feet.

ular intervals. This regularity is very important. As to drink—well, *water* is the best thing to quench thirst, and it is a pity that so many seem to fear to give it. It rarely does harm and it often does good, especially in fevers. When you give it let the patient have enough at a time to satisfy him, unless his demands are too excessive.

When possible, the sick-room should be large and have windows opening toward the sunny side of the house. It should be where the greatest freedom from noise can be secured. It ought to have an open fireplace, or if this does not exist, some other means of providing at the same time heat and ventilation. The windows should have shades and blinds, so that the light can be regulated. The hinges of the doors should be oiled so that they do not make a noise when the latter are opened or shut. The window-sashes should also be made to move easily and noiselessly. There should be no carpet; rugs may be put where needed.

The sick-room.

It is best to place the bed so that it is easy to get at both sides of it, and the patient should lie with his face away from the window.

A screen made of some cheap material which can be destroyed, if need be, after the sickness is over, is a very useful thing to have. The furniture should not be heavy, and only articles of real use should be in the room. No hangings ought to be permitted, especially in cases of infectious disease. No cooking should be done in the room, and all remnants of food, soiled clothing, slops, etc., should be removed from it as soon as possible. Scrupulous cleanliness must be maintained; but the process of cleaning must be carried on quietly so as not to disturb the patient. In cases of contagious disease, the doors should be protected by hanging over them sheets soaked with some disinfecting solution. In such cases, also, the clothing of all who enter should be prevented from spreading the infection. This may be accomplished by putting a gown made of some wash stuff over the clothing when entering. The disinfection of excreta, etc., is described elsewhere.

SUMMARY OF THE MORE IMPORTANT RULES OF CONDUCT IN THE SICK-ROOM.

1. Avoid worrying the patient. Move quietly when doing anything in the room. Permit no needless bustle or confusion.

2. Do not ask unnecessary questions of the sufferer as to his wants; try to anticipate them and meet them without asking. Do not consult him about food; simply give it to him at the proper times.

3. In handling a patient, be careful to do so gently; but if you have to turn or lift him, or help him to move himself, always let your touch be firm. Do not let him feel that you may let him fall. Be sure also before attempting to help him move or putting your hands upon him for any purpose, that you know exactly what you want to do and how it is to be accomplished; thus you will save much strength and avoid much fatigue both for yourself and your charge.

4. Do your work quietly and quickly, but avoid all *appearance of hurry*.

5. When you have to talk in the sick-room, speak softly yet perfectly distinctly, and speak so that the patient can hear what is said. *Never whisper.*

6. Do not deceive a patient if it can be avoided.

7. Control your emotions and do not appear excited or frightened.

8. Be careful to have the bed comfortable.

9. Give nourishment at regular times.

10. See that the room is well aired and the temperature comfortable.

IV. — MEDICAL AND SURGICAL NOTES ON TREATMENT.

Amateur doctors. IT is safe to assert that the attempts of the majority of those who, without thorough medical training, undertake to treat their sick or injured neighbors or relatives cause far more suffering than they relieve. Certain "household remedies" in common use have been the means of crippling not a few by converting trifling injuries into dangerous, infected wounds. Others have made the sick much sicker than the disease treated with them would have done had the patient been left to nature. Indeed, many deaths must be attributed to the treatment adopted by amateur doctors, male and female, who infest the land, and who, being without other qualifications, are so ready to place the ones which they possess — dense ignorance of every truth of medical science, minimum of common sense and maximum of complacent self-conceit — at the service of anyone ready to submit to their orders.

Let me say that each word of the preceding paragraph has been carefully weighed, and that each sentence is a statement of what I believe to be a fact. In respect to the assertions that slight wounds have been infected and sick persons made sicker by the use of "household remedies," I may say that I have seen such occurrences many times. I have also seen fatal illness directly caused by failure to obtain skilled advice. If the number of lives needlessly sacrificed through the officious interference of women who "have had experience" in cases of confinement could be tabulated, the figures would be appalling. If it were possible to present a statement of the amount of suffering which our race has had to endure as a result of false medical theories, we should be able to appreciate the responsibility assumed by anyone who presumes to treat the sick or wounded. One of the most curious survivals of superstition which still has a strong hold upon mankind is that the worse any form of treatment is, the *better* it is. The more discomfort it causes, the more good it does! For this reason there is a tendency to put salt pork, etc., on wounds, and to give all sorts of bad-tasting mixtures to cure people. There is no subject of which educated people are so ignorant as of the first principles of medicine and surgery; and there are no problems which sensible people consider with so little regard for the dictates of common sense as those presented by disease or injury.

The first aids to the injured. The following directions are intended only to set forth the general course of treatment to be followed in some of the commoner medical and surgical emergencies which may arise when a physician is not at hand. They apply only to the period which must elapse before skilled aid can be obtained. The most important rule to be observed in all cases is this:

SEND FOR A DOCTOR AT ONCE. DO NO MORE THAN WHAT YOU ARE OBLIGED TO DO BY THE NECESSITIES OF THE PATIENT BEFORE SKILLED HELP CAN BE OBTAINED.

It is impossible to give directions which will cover every emergency requiring medical or surgical skill. I have attempted merely to give briefly the general principles of treatment in some common emergencies. The treatment indicated is often not the best, but it is the most practicable known to me, for unskilled hands. Before anything, remember these principles:

If a person is sick and suffering pain, try to give him rest and quiet. If a limb has been injured, so bind it as to prevent its movement. If there is a wound, clean it thoroughly and keep it clean, and do not meddle too much with it; let it heal itself in rest. Do not do too much for anyone who is ill or injured. Nature cures, and she knows how to do it better than we. Be careful, lest in trying to aid her you merely interfere with her. It is often much harder, and needs much more real skill, to let a patient alone than to try to help him to get well (or rather to try to *make* him get well). We are so anxious to relieve suffering—to *do something* for the sufferer—that we too often fail to do the one best thing for many cases of illness, namely, to do nothing except what is necessary to make the patient as comfortable as may be without recourse to drugs. It would be a great blessing if more energy were devoted to the improvement of unfavorable surroundings and the removal of causes of discomfort (including useless and officious would-be comforters of the human species), and less to giving drugs or interfering with wounds.

INFLAMMATION OF WOUNDS DUE TO INFECTION BY BACTERIA.

The "germ theory" of disease is sufficiently widely understood, so far as its fundamental principle is concerned, to make a detailed explanation of the term unnecessary. The theory explains the occurrence of certain diseases as the result of the growth and multiplication of bacteria within the body. Although there is room for doubt as to the application of the theory to some of the disease-phenomena which are thought to be explicable by it, there is no more reason to doubt that certain disorders are directly caused by certain species of bacteria than there is to doubt the theory of gravitation.

In the case of wounds, the multiplication of certain forms of living germs causes inflammation with the formation of pus, or "matter" as it is commonly called. The inflammatory process with pus formation is called "suppuration" or "maturation" or "festering." Sometimes the germs find their way into the blood, and their multiplication in it causes what is called "blood-poisoning." It is possible for blood-poisoning to occur without much suppuration, for there are germs which find their way into the system through wounds without causing much local disturbance, and yet produce severe illness and even death. There is no question, in the minds of any rational people who have studied the subject, that the direct causes of evil in the instances mentioned are bacteria. The idea that matter is necessarily formed in wounds simply because of the injury to the tissues of the body due to the wounds themselves, and without infection, is exploded. Surgeons no longer regard fever and suppuration after operations as a matter of course; they know that *clean* wounds heal without either. The aim of surgical treatment is to insure *cleanliness*. Fever or suppuration means failure in this respect.

Suppuration and blood-poisoning.

Cleanliness.

The common plan of putting a poultice on a wound in order "to draw out the inflammation," or to "draw out" some foreign body, like a splinter, is simply and deliberately to infect the tissues. The same is true in the case of any application which "draws" or makes an injury "come to a head."

Poultices rarely useful and often harmful.

I do not wish to be thought to condemn the use of poultices absolutely and in every case; I simply wish to state most emphatically the result of their use upon wounded surfaces. It may be thought desirable to cause inflammation by infection with bacteria —something which the ordinary poultice is well adapted to accomplish—or it may be that the poultice is employed to hasten the formation of pus, and assist that which is formed in burrowing through the tissues and reaching the surface of the body.

It is most important to realize that the production of inflammation, fever, and blood-poisoning by the multiplication of germs which have been introduced into wounds is not a matter of theory. It is proven beyond all shadow of doubt. A rusty nail, when it penetrates the body, does not make an injury likely to be followed by inflammation because the *rust* on it is poisonous; it does so because the rusty surface is very apt to be a good resting-place for germs, which are by it carried into the wound. The same is true of a pin; it is more or less dangerous, not because it is brass, but because it is apt to be covered with germs.

The aim of all wound treatment should be to prevent the entrance of bacteria. This is attained only by the most thorough cleanliness. Dirt means danger.

First dressings for wounds. Whenever you are called upon to dress a wound, no matter where it is situated or how it has been caused, do not begin your treatment with the idea that inflammation necessarily will follow; try to prevent its occurrence by removing carefully all dirt, and try so to apply the dressing that, in case you have failed to free the wound from all infecting germs, and inflammation *does* set in, the pus formed easily can make its way to the surface without having to burrow through previously uninjured tissues and greatly increase the damage already done by the original cause of the wound. Matter which is not confined does but little harm, but that which is prevented from escaping may form abscesses or even cause death from blood-poisoning. Actual death from the infection of a slight wound is rare; but severe illness is common, and more or less permanent and serious deformity or crippling are frequently observed, which are the direct consequences of dirt that has been either left in a wound because of insufficient washing, etc., or has been introduced by means of a dirty dressing.

How often do we hear that some one had run a rusty nail or a splinter or a thorn into a hand or foot, and that inflammation had followed after a few days, and the matter which had formed had been "drawn" by a poultice to the surface—but the injured person had had a very sore arm or leg! How often do we learn that such a person has been unable to use hand or foot properly since the accident! How often do we inquire whether such a result might have been prevented!

The fact is that very few people reason at all where medical or surgical matters are concerned; *Ignorance of medical and surgical matters.* the majority content themselves with doing whatever they have heard is "good for" any case which happens to fall into their hands. In respect to wounds the belief which was accepted for centuries by medical men, and has only lately been abandoned, is still accepted by a large number of laymen. The idea that pus formation is something rather to be encouraged than avoided, and that pus is a satisfactory surgical operator, capable of doing far better than an intelligent surgeon, dominated medical practice until very recently, and still holds sway over minds ignorant of the marvellous results of antiseptic methods.

THE IMMEDIATE TREATMENT OF WOUNDS. — A PRACTICAL APPLICATION OF THE GERM THEORY.

In practice the importance of the germ theory cannot be overestimated. It is one of the greatest discoveries of modern times that the gravest consequences of wounds, not in themselves fatal, can almost always be averted by preventing the germs from growing in them. In order to explain the principles of modern surgical treatment the following facts respecting bacteria must be stated; they are important:

First. Although bacteria are abundant everywhere around us most of them are harmless to mankind. A few varieties only are capable of infecting wounds, and the virulence of the infectious varieties varies greatly.

The germ theory in practice.

Second. The infectious varieties, although not numerous in comparison with the harmless ones, are widely distributed over the world, and frequently are to be found upon the persons or clothing of healthy people. They do not penetrate the uninjured skin, but seem able to thrive upon its surface and its outer layers. The hands of anyone dressing a wound may be the means of infecting it by reason of this fact. Germs may lodge upon the surface of any material used for a dressing, and be introduced when this is applied. They also can live in water for a long time.

Third. The body is able to destroy even virulent bacteria, provided they are not too numerous, and provided they are brought into contact with living tissue well supplied with freely circulating blood. Thus a cut with smooth surfaces which have accurately been brought together rarely becomes inflamed, even if little care has been taken to exclude the germs; the contact of the latter with the living tissue is so close that, unless an enormous number be present, they are killed. If, however, the surfaces are not closely applied, so that spaces exist which become filled with fluid exuded from the tissues, even a few bacteria may cause serious trouble, for they multiply rapidly in such places, secure from the attacks of the body cells, and soon become sufficiently numerous to overpower the latter. So also when the tissues about a wound have been torn or bruised so that their vitality is impaired, or the circulation in them has been seriously impeded, bacteria finds a good soil to grow in. In such a case a very few germs may multiply without difficulty, and may overpower the body.

Fourth. If bacteria are not shut in by the wound so as to make it impossible for them to be swept away in the discharges, the system is usually able to expel them with the exuded fluids so quickly that little or no suppuration occurs. In such cases, nature does precisely what the surgeon does when he washes a wound and dislodges any bacteria which may be in it by means of a stream of fluid. The skilled surgeon usually can accomplish the desired result with far less disturbance to the comfort of the patient than Nature produces when the task is left to her. It is a true saying that "Nature is a better physician than surgeon;" her methods for the repair of injuries are very crude unless she is aided by human skill.

Let us now consider the bearings of these four facts upon the treatment of wounds; for by so doing we are enabled to understand the principles of modern surgery in such a way as to be able to apply them. When these principles are once understood it is needless to burden the memory with detailed rules for dressing a wound, and what seems at first a very complicated process when described as "antiseptic surgery" is seen to be a perfectly simple and sensible one.

The object of antiseptic surgery. The object of this method is to exclude germs. Although many bacteria are harmless, those which are infectious are so common that their entrance into wounds is very frequent. Since they often cling to the hands, it is of vital importance that the hands of anyone who must dress a wound be thoroughly clean. The first thing to be done is to wash the hands thoroughly in hot water, using plenty of soap. Subsequently, the soap should be completely removed by means of clean water *which has been boiled* and which is used as hot as can be borne. The reason for boiling the water is that the heat kills any bacteria that it might contain. After this some antiseptic solution may be applied. (For the best antiseptics and the strength in which they are used, see under heading "Antiseptics" in the paragraph on "Medical and Surgical Household Supplies," APPENDIX.) Remember that the application of the antiseptic solution is far less important than thorough washing.

It is a strange fact that very few people really know how to wash their hands. *The antiseptic cleansing of the hands.* The best way to get really clean is to use very hot water, and first dip the hands into it. Then rub the soap thoroughly into the entire surface of both hands, using as little water as possible. The thick coat of soap must be rubbed so that it fills the parts above and under the nails. The next step is to dip a nail-brush into the hot water and rub it on the soap until it is fairly loaded with suds. The hands should then be scrubbed with the brush and from time to time dipped into the water in order to remove the dirt which the soap and nail-brush have worked into the lather. Finally, the hands must be rinsed in clear water. The nails may need further cleaning with a knife or a nail-cleaner. If these requirements are fulfilled the skin will be practically clean. An antiseptic solution may be used finally to rinse the hands; BUT IT IS FAR BETTER TO HAVE THE HANDS REALLY CLEAN THAN TO TRY TO SUBSTITUTE DISINFECTANTS FOR PLAIN SOAP AND WATER.

Doubtless dead germs are not particularly harmful, but no disinfectant can be trusted to kill *all* of those upon the skin. Whereas soap and water can practically remove them, and a germ which has no chance to get into a wound is even more certainly harmless than is the dead body of one which once had life. It is far better to prevent the admission of all infectious matter than it is to trust to killing that which may have obtained entrance, and it is far easier to *wash* off such matter from the hands than it is to destroy it by germicides. Besides, soap and boiled water are cheap and easy to obtain.

If we can exclude all bacteria we attempt so to do because of the dangerous qualities of some of them. *The cleansing of wounds.* The dangerous kinds easily may exist upon the skin of the patient or upon his clothing, or upon the hands or clothing of the operator. Having thoroughly cleansed ourselves, we next proceed to clean the wound and its surrounding skin. Again boiled and still warm water is our best disinfecting agent. Soap may be freely used on the surface of the body and up to the very edges of the wound itself; it is irritating when it comes in contact with raw surfaces, and therefore it is better to avoid letting the suds run into the wound. Water, either poured from a height or forced into the wound by a syringe, is almost always sufficiently effective, if used very freely, to sweep away all dirt, including the germs. After cleaning with water some germicide may be used; but thorough washing is the one absolutely essential thing, as it is in the case of the hands.

Finally, with a view to excluding infection, we must cover the wound with *The dressing of wounds.* a dressing which is both free from germs and capable of keeping them out. A dressing should, first, be clean; second, it should be sufficiently thick to insure the perfect exclusion of dirt from its inner layers after it has been applied; third, it should be absorbent; fourth, it should be comfortable. The best material for a dressing is what is sold as absorbent gauze. This is cheese-cloth which has been freed from germs and prepared in such a way that it can absorb a good deal of liquid into its fibres. It can be bought prepared with an antiseptic incorporated in it. It is better to use gauze thus prepared. The kind known as sublimate gauze is perhaps the best. It keeps indefinitely and is very powerfully antiseptic.

The precautions described are evidently suggested by the first two of *Securing close contact of the surfaces of wounds.* the statements enumerated concerning infection. The third fact, that the body can overpower infectious germs which are not too numerous and which are in direct contact with living tissues, is also of great practical importance. Next to thorough cleansing, the most important measure to insure rapid recovery without inflammation is to secure close contact of the surfaces of the wound, provided there has not been so much bruising or laceration that their vitality is greatly impaired, or that so much flesh has been removed by the wound that close contact cannot be secured. If the wounded surfaces can be brought together throughout their whole extent, without leaving spaces in which germs can grow, the chances are very strong that if a few of them have been left after all the efforts to disinfect, they will perish without doing harm.

In cases where there is reason to think that disinfection has failed, or *Cases in which wounds must be kept open.* where close contact of wounded surfaces cannot be safely insured, the fourth peculiarity of the body's power to expel germs, provided free passages exist through which fluid exudation can flow, is made useful. In these cases, after cleaning the wound and its surrounding parts as well as possible, the former is allowed to remain open (or, if need be, kept open by filling its cavity with absorbent gauze, or introducing a tube of suitable material into it) and the dressing so arranged that the discharges are not retained in contact with the raw surface.

The proper treatment of a wound may be summarized as follows: *After bleeding ceases or has been checked, wash your hands thoroughly. Then wash the wound and its neighborhood. When everything is clean, put on a perfectly clean dressing, consisting of eight or ten layers of sublimate gauze (if this is at hand, if not, some other clean absorbent material will answer), fasten the dressing in place with a bandage. After this do not disturb the dressing unless there be fever, severe pain or bad odor, or unless the discharges soak through the coverings.*

Whenever it is necessary to change the dressing be sure to have everything clean before applying another.

SHOCK AND BLEEDING.

There are two immediate dangers in all cases of severe wounds. The first occurs only if the injury be very great, and is called shock. The symptoms of shock are great weakness, pallor, sweating, rapid, weak pulse, and shallow breathing. When such symptoms arise the patient should be given whiskey or brandy in doses of a tablespoonful at a time, diluted with water. Bottles of hot water, wrapped in blankets, so as not to burn the skin, should be applied to the feet and legs and to the sides of the body. The patient must be kept absolutely quiet, on his back.

The second immediate danger is bleeding. The bleeding may be from an artery, in which case the blood is bright red and comes out in repeated spurts with a good deal of force; or it may be from a vein, in which case it is dark in color, and wells up without any spurting from the wound; or there may be simply slow oozing of blood from very small vessels.

In stopping bleeding, the first necessity is presence of mind, and it should *How to stop bleeding temporarily.* always be remembered that no one need bleed to death if the wound be where you can put your hand on it. The bleeding from arteries may be stopped temporarily by tying a hand-

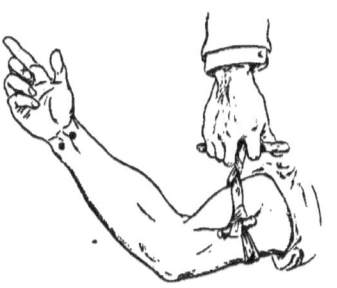

Application of improvised tourniquet to arm.

kerchief or strip of cloth around the wounded limb above the wound. The handkerchief should be tied loosely, a knot being made in it so as to compress the large artery, and then it may be tightened by twisting it with a stick. Remember that such a handkerchief cannot be left on for many hours or mortification will follow. It is only to be used temporarily. The bleeding from a vein rarely continues if the patient is laid on his back and the wounded limb elevated, or if a compress be bound over the wound.

For permanently stopping bleeding, the best method is to tie the cut vessels with a piece of prepared catgut or silk. The artery must be caught with a forceps and the ligature slipped over the end of the vessel and tied

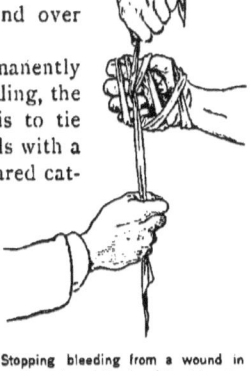

Stopping bleeding from a wound in the palm of the hand by tying the thumb and fingers over a handkerchief crumpled into a ball.

in a square knot. If this cannot be done, a compress of clean absorbent *How to stop bleeding permanently.* cotton, wrapped in gauze, or clean gauze alone, rolled up tightly, may be applied directly over the wound and tightly fastened on with a bandage. Remember that such a compress is not put on to soak up the blood. It is meant to stop the bleeding by direct pressure. There is no use in covering a bleeding vessel with a lot of cloth unless pressure is applied. Soaking up blood does no good, but rather harm, as the cloth, wet with warm blood, makes a poultice which increases the flow. Nature stops bleeding by forming a clot in the ends of the divided vessels. The application of a compress is designed to assist the formation of this clot by closing the vessels. This can be done only by considerable pressure.

In addition to stopping bleeding by pressure or by some of the ways recommended, it is very necessary, whenever much blood is lost, to make the patient lie down flat, with the head low, and to keep him very quiet. This is done for two reasons: First, because the bleeding itself will diminish when a patient is lying down, as the whole of the blood-pressure in the body is lowered. Second, in order to prevent fainting.

If the patient has lost much blood, certain symptoms arise which resemble those of shock. It is important to distinguish them, however, as unless the hemorrhage has been checked, stimulants should not be given.

The symptoms produced by severe loss of blood are faintness, pallor, restlessness, anxious expression of face, clammy sweat, rapid, very weak pulse, cooled extremities, thirst, and often gasping for air or frequent sighing. It will be observed that the patients suffering from loss of blood are restless; those suffering from shock are dazed and quiet.

Mere faintness, where the patient loses consciousness, is not in itself dangerous; but when in addition the symptoms which have been described arise, the patient is in immediate danger. The treatment is absolute quiet; stopping of the flow of blood at all hazards by any possible way; the application of warmth to the surface of the body; and, after the bleeding has been checked for some time, whiskey or brandy may be given in small amounts. If the symptoms continue and the patient becomes very weak, bandage the limbs tightly, beginning at the feet and hands, so as to squeeze the blood from the limbs into the body. Leave the bandages on for some hours.

The amount of blood which may be lost without danger varies a great deal. One thing should be borne in mind: that a very small quantity of blood can cover a very large surface. If one spills a tumblerful of water on the floor or on the table, it is easy to see how much this small amount of liquid will cover. Before deciding how much blood a patient has lost, observe the condition of the patient; do not look at the blood.

Certain forms of bleeding must be spoken of separately.

Bleeding from the nose. Nose-bleeding is occasionally troublesome, and in almost every case a very simple method will check it. If the patient lies on his face, moving as little as possible, with the nostrils plugged with cotton or with the nostrils simply held together by the fingers, and remains in this position for ten or fifteen minutes, the bleeding will almost invariably stop.

Bleeding from the lungs. Bleeding from the lungs, though alarming, is rarely fatal. The quantity of blood which a person may cough out is sometimes very great; but patients, unless they have severe lung trouble, generally recover. For such bleeding the patient should be made to lie down. If the bleeding is very profuse and lasts a long time, an ice-bag should be applied to the chest, over the heart. There is little else to be done.

Bleeding from the stomach. Bleeding from the stomach, with vomiting of blood, is treated on the same plan.

Internal bleeding. Sometimes after injuries, or as the result of disease of the blood-vessels, bleeding may take place internally. In such cases the symptoms of the loss of blood are observed. These cases are most serious, and little can be done for them except what has been recommended for cases of bleeding from the lungs.

Wounds of the head. Wounds of the head are dangerous because of possible injury to the brain. Severe blows upon the head commonly produce unconsciousness. Sometimes the skull is fractured; sometimes vessels within the skull are ruptured, and death is caused by hemorrhage compressing the brain. Sometimes inflammation of the brain or its coverings comes on a few days after the injury. The treatment of fractured skull is outlined under "Fractures." Whenever a blow severe enough to cause unconsciousness has been received, the patient must be put to bed, ice applied to the head, and he must remain quiet for several days until he has no more headache. If this be not done inflammation may follow.

Wounds of the chest may penetrate the heart or great vessels, in which case death soon occurs, or they may penetrate the lungs. In the last case, the best thing to do is to put on a compress of antiseptic material, held in place by a firm bandage, and put the patient to bed. Frequently recovery takes place. *Do not try to wash out a wound which penetrates the lungs;* clean the skin, but don't inject any fluid into the wound. The wound may cause the lung to collapse, but if it has not, any attempt to inject fluid is pretty sure to do so. If the lung be wounded, there is usually more or less blood coughed up.

Wounds of the chest.

Wounds opening into the abdominal cavity are peculiarly dangerous because they are apt to injure the intestines and allow their contents to escape and cause fatal peritonitis, or to injure some other important organ, or to penetrate some large vessel and cause death by internal hemorrhage. The best that can be done, in the absence of a surgeon, is to put the patient on his back, and in case any of the intestines project from the wound carefully to clean them with pure water *which has been boiled* and which is about blood heat, and then return them to the abdomen and wash out the cavity very thoroughly, by means of a tube introduced into it, with boiled water, which has also cooled to blood heat. Then the wound in the walls of the abdomen must be sewn up, and a large dressing put on. If no intestines project, and if the wound is small, it is better to sew it up without attempting to inject any fluid, merely cleaning the wound.

Wounds opening into the abdominal cavity.

Never use an antiseptic solution in wounds of the abdomen, or you may poison your patient. It is better to take the chances of the germ infection, merely trying to wash the germs away, and not to kill them, than to endanger the life of a patient by using fluids which are irritating, and when applied to a large surface like the peritoneum, may be poisonous. After the wound has been dressed, keep the patient quiet. Give morphine enough to relieve pain. If the abdomen becomes swollen and tender, and the temperature rises, the pulse becoming more rapid, peritonitis is to be feared. On the whole, the best thing to do for this form of peritonitis seems to be to give a rather sharp purge, and, introducing a rubber tube deep into the wound, to wash out the peritoneal cavity again with water. The chances are poor of recovery.

Wounds opening into joints are apt to become infected. They should be thoroughly cleansed with an antiseptic solution and then dressed. If the wound is small, and has been made by a clean, sharp instrument, it is better to seal it up with the dressing. If it is large, and has been made with a dirty instrument, it is best, after washing it thoroughly, to put a piece of gauze into it with the forceps, leaving one end hanging out, and then to put on a large, rather loose dressing. This is done because it is probable that there has not been thorough cleansing, and it is better to provide an outlet for any matter which may form. The gauze acts as a drain. It is very important

Wounds opening into joints.

to put the joint at rest by means of a splint (see "Fractures"), and to put it in the best position for future use, in case, as is probable, the joint becomes stiff. The leg should be dressed so that it is straight. The arm should be bent at the elbow. Always put the dressing on with the limb in the position in which you intend it to remain.

Wounds penetrating to broken bones, see "Compound Fractures."

Bullet-wounds. Bullet-wounds are more serious than they seem at first sight. They may open joints or penetrate the chest, abdomen, or skull. They are apt to become infected, not from the bullet usually, but from pieces of dirty clothing carried in with it, and, not infrequently from well-meant but ill-advised efforts to find the ball, by fingers, probes, etc. If there is reason to think that the skull, chest, abdomen, or a joint has been entered, the treatment is the same as that recommended for other wounds in these places. It must be remembered, however, that bullets glance in a peculiar way, and one must not assume that because a wound looks as if it ought to penetrate one of these dangerous spots, therefore it does. If examination of the clothing shows that probably none of it has been carried in, seal up the wound. If, as is often the case, some cloth is carried in, wash the wound with an antiseptic and introduce a gauze drain deeply into it. If there is much bleeding, it may be necessary to enlarge the wound with a knife, find the bleeding vessels and tie them before dressing. If a bullet has splintered a bone, the best that can be done, short of amputation, is to clean everything and introduce a number of drains. Do not try very hard to find the bullet, and never run the risk of infecting a clean wound by introducing dirty fingers or instruments into it in trying to get at the ball.

When matter has formed, it is best, by means of free cuts, to let it out. *Infected wounds.* Its presence is detected by the recurrence of heat, swelling, pain, and redness near it, and by a peculiar, elastic sensation conveyed to the fingers when both hands are pressed gently on the affected spot. If you are sure that matter is present, it is not advisable to wait till it "comes to a head." Better let it out before it burrows too much. Make deep, free openings with a clean knife. In cutting there is but little danger of wounding any important vessels if the cuts be made parallel to the long axis of the limbs, and not directly over the large arteries. After opening, drain; but unless it is impossible to get free drainage, do not wash the cavity out; simply provide free vent for the matter, and do not poultice; if you want to get the effects of a poultice, apply a thick layer of cotton, saturated with hot solution of corrosive sublimate $\frac{1}{1000}$, and cover with thick cloths, wet with the same solution.

Injuries to the eye are very serious; sometimes a cinder or piece of *Injuries to the eye.* dirt penetrates the surface of the eye. Always look very carefully for these, using a strong light, which must fall on the eye *from the side*. If seen, these bodies often may be removed by gently brushing them off with a small piece of cotton, wrapped round the end of a match. Sometimes the piece will be found under one of the lids, when it may be removed in a similar way, the lid having been turned inside out. If severe injury be done to the eye in any way, or if inflammation occurs in it, the patient must stay in the dark and must apply cold water to the eye and head, and must drop into the eye a solution of corrosive sublimate $\frac{1}{5000}$ (never stronger) every half hour, until medical aid can be obtained. No precaution is too great to take when the eyesight is at stake.

Fractures. When a bone is broken and there is no wound communicating from the break to the air, it is called a *simple fracture*. When there is a wound, it is called a *compound fracture*. If a bone is broken in several places or splintered, it is a *comminuted fracture*.

Simple fractures of the long bones of the arm or leg usually give rise to extreme pain, usually most marked directly over the break; inability on the part of the patient to move the limb; a point where, if we bend the limb, we find motion which does not normally exist; and often, on moving the bones a peculiar grating sensation (produced by the rubbing together of the broken ends) is felt.

In a compound fracture there are the same signs; and, in addition, there is a wound leading to the broken bone. Sometimes the bone may protrude.

When treating a fracture, we should endeavor to get the bones in place and hold them steady. The former can often be done by pulling the limb straight down until the bone is felt to slip into place. It must then be retained by splints. These may be made of any thin wood. They are cut to the right shape and size and then padded with cotton held in place by a bandage wrapped round them. Having put them on the limb, a turn or two of rubber plaster round the outside of them will hold them. Over the plaster a bandage is rolled. Never put a bandage or a plaster inside of the splint. If swelling occurs below the splint bandages must be loosened. Usually, in the case of the arm, it is possible to keep it temporarily still by simply bandaging it firmly to the body with handkerchiefs or strips of cloth. As a temporary splint for the leg a cane or broomstick or any piece of wood may answer.

In compound fractures, the main thing is to clean the wound; the splints are not so important. The wound must be treated like a wounded joint.

Fractured skull is a serious thing. If there is found a depression anywhere over the skull after a severe blow with loss of consciousness, the only thing to do is to cut down to it and lift up the depressed bone with the forceps, and then treat it like a compound fracture. Free drainage of the wound must be provided for.

Fractured ribs give rise to intense pain when a deep breath is taken. The pain is generally relieved by putting a broad strip of plaster completely around the body after making the patient breathe out as far as he can, emptying the chest. This restricts the motion of the ribs.

Dislocation. When the bones which compose a joint have been displaced it is called a dislocation. These injuries are difficult to deal with.

It is generally easy enough to replace the bones if we only can appreciate how they were displaced; but to do this it is necessary to have considerable knowledge of anatomy. It is pretty safe to say that any dislocation can be replaced as well at the end of a week as it can when it first occurs. If it is possible to get a physician within this time, wait for his arrival.

In any attempt to reduce a dislocation it must be remembered that too much force must not be used. It is possible to make matters a great deal worse than they originally were by tearing the tissues of the injured joint. It is easy to see that in the case of large bones you have an immense leverage when you attempt by turning them to get them back into their places. So one must be very careful not to do more harm than good.

Sprains. Sprains are the result of injuries which have produced more or less stretching or tearing of the ligaments or tendons.

A sprain apparently does not seem as severe at first as it afterward proves to be.

The treatment is to give the injured parts absolute and immediate rest. If an important joint, like the ankle, has been sprained, it is much better to lie by for a few days rather than to attempt to use it. In the case of the knee-joint, if there has been any sprain, the only safe thing to do is to put the patient to bed as soon as it is possible, and to keep him absolutely quiet until all pain has subsided. It must be remembered that a slight injury of the knee, if neglected, frequently leads to more or less severe crippling which may last for life.

As soon as possible after a sprain has occurred in any joint, apply hot water — as hot as the patient can bear it — for from fifteen to twenty-five minutes; being careful to change the water sufficiently often to prevent its cooling. After the injured limb has been removed from the hot water, dash a little cold water on it; then put on a rather firm bandage and splints so as to keep the joints immovable.

Burns. The best dressing to apply to a burn is a weak ointment of carbolic acid in vaseline (one part of the acid to twenty-five of vaseline). Before applying the dressing, wash the burnt surface thoroughly with a solution of carbolic acid in water (1 to 50 parts). If there are any blisters they should be opened carefully with a clean pair of scissors and then a thick coating of carbolized ointment should be spread over the whole injured surface and kept in place by a lightly applied bandage. Carbolic acid stops the pain wonderfully.

The general principles of dressing a burn are the same as those of dressing a wound. *Keep it clean, and don't interfere with it too much.*

In very severe burns shock is often dangerous and may cause death. Stimulants should be given freely in such cases.

Many people lose consciousness from slight causes — such as disagreeable sights or sounds, or from slight or severe pain.

Loss of consciousness. This form of unconsciousness is called fainting, and is the result of sudden weakness of the heart's action. When arising from the causes mentioned, it is rarely, if ever, of the least importance. If the patient is laid down, clothing loosened, and if left pretty much alone, recovery will take place. It is necessary, though, that the patient should be laid down, and that the head should be kept very low.

Fainting rarely lasts more than a few minutes; but sometimes, even in cases which are not at all dangerous, it may last for half an hour or more.

The symptoms are sudden weakness; usually some disagreeable nervous feelings; often a little sweating; very marked pallor; and then complete unconsciousness.

The treatment is generally good in proportion to the small amount attempted. If the patient remains unconscious for a long time, it is advisable to give stimulants and to apply warmth to the body; but if the attack is only temporary and arises from a slight cause, beyond dashing a little cold water on the face and keeping the patient's head low, nothing is necessary.

Faintness which is the result of severe exertion, or attacks of faintness occurring in people who are known to have heart disease, are very much more grave affairs than the last. In such cases stimulation is extremely necessary; whiskey or brandy, and ammonia, if any is to be had, should be used very freely.

In fainting, the cause of the unconsciousness is, as has been said, failure of the heart. There is another form of unconsciousness in which the heart is not at fault, but which is the result of interference with the action of the brain. Such cases are called coma.

Coma.

Coma may be the result of injuries to the head; falls and blows; of diseases of the brain, as apoplexy; of disease of the kidneys; and of quite a number of poisons, especially alcohol and opium.

The symptoms of coma, the result of some injury to the head, are, in the first place, loss of consciousness; which loss of consciousness is complete, but it is accompanied by a strong, full pulse.

Coma, the result of disease, is generally preceded by headache; this being followed by delirium, then stupor, which gradually deepens into complete coma.

Whatever be the cause of coma, as the patient becomes more and more overcome by it, the breathing generally gets very noisy, and is accompanied by snoring; after the coma has lasted some time the face is often dark in color; and when the patient is dying from coma, the darkness of the complexion is generally much deepened; and as well as the snoring respiration, we hear large, coarse bubbling sounds with the breathing.

In some cases of coma, the result of injuries or of diseases affecting the brain, it may be seen that the muscles on one side of the face and of the body are relaxed and paralyzed. In such cases the eyes will usually be found, if the lids are open, turned away from the paralyzed side.

In coma produced by opium poisoning the pupils are very finely contracted. This is the most important distinguishing symptom of opium-poisoning.

Persons exposed to extreme heat, especially if the exposure is prolonged, and the patient takes alcohol, may suffer from two forms of sunstroke.

Sunstroke.

The more common form is simply marked prostration, usually accompanied by headache, and usually giving the same symptoms as does fainting. There is little or no rise of temperature in this form.

The treatment is quiet, rest, and cold applied to the head, or perhaps to the body, and if the faintness be prolonged, a little whiskey or brandy. Patients often suffer from headache and more or less discomfort for a long time after, and especially if exposed to the sun.

A much more severe form of sunstroke occurs. In this the patient first has a severe headache and he becomes entirely unconscious, and his skin is hot and dry; his face unusually flushed, breathing more rapid than usual, and as he grows worse, snoring in character; pulse rapid; temperature rises very high, 106 to 110 degrees or higher; such a patient is in immediate danger. Cold water must be freely and continuously poured over him until the temperature in the rectum has fallen three or four degrees or more. When the temperature reaches 102 degrees to 103 degrees it is well to stop the water for a while and see if it does not continue to fall. If the patient regains consciousness put ice on the head and keep him quiet, but watch the temperature closely for thirty-six hours. If he becomes very weak give stimulants.

The following is an extract from "First Aid in Illness and Injury," by James E. Pilcher, M.D., U. S. A., p. 214 *et seq.*

SMOTHERING.

"Smothering, suffocation, or asphyxia is a state of unconsciousness due to cutting off the supply of oxygen to the lungs. Smothering may be due to a number of causes. The most common is drowning, where the water prevents

Restoring the breathing by Sylvester's Method—Inspiration.

the access of air to the lungs. Hanging and strangling, where the passage of air through the windpipe is prevented by compression of that tube, are well known. Anything that closes the air-passage will produce smothering; such are bits of food and other articles diverted from their proper channels in the attempt to swallow; a variety of croup, in which the windpipe is stuffed up by secretions, comes into this class. Pressure upon the chest sufficient to prevent its movement in breathing is another cause. The methods of Othello and Richard III., causing smothering by pressing a pillow tightly down upon the face, are classical. Smothering is the cause of death in persons who have been buried under avalanches of snow or sand, grain falls, and the like.

"Another variety of smothering is that produced when the atmosphere is so filled with other gases that the proper amount of oxygen cannot find its way into the blood. Smothering by breathing air filled with illuminating gas is a common accident in cities, where the victims, from carelessness or ignorance, have failed to turn off the gas in extinguishing a light. The gas formed by burning coal and decaying sewage, and the smoke of burning buildings, produce insensibility from the same cause.

"The restoration of the function of breathing is the chief aim in treating cases of smothering—by this means carrying off the waste, poisonous products from the blood and giving new life to the system by an abundant supply of oxygen.

"*Restoring the Breathing.*—The act of breathing is restored by causing the chest-walls to expand and contract in the same manner as in the normal acts of inspiration and expiration. This is called *artificial respiration* and is performed in several ways. One of the most convenient and useful is *Sylvester's method*, which is as follows:

"Lay the smothered person on his back, with a pillow of folded clothing or other articles under his shoulders.

"Take a position at the head of the patient, grasp his arms just below the elbow, and draw them slowly and steadily up over the head, holding them there long enough deliberately to count four.

"Then push the arms down upon the chest, bending the elbows as they come

Restoring the breathing by Sylvester's Method—Expiration.

down, and press them strongly, but gently, against the chest long enough again to count four.

"Repeat these movements until the patient begins to breathe naturally, or until it is evident that life is beyond recall.

"The first sign of returning breathing

is a change in the color of the face; if white, it becomes red; and if red, it changes to white. With this a faint fluttering breath may be seen passing the lips.

"Drawing the arms up over the head pulls upon certain muscles which expand the chest, creating a vacuum which the air rushes in to fill. Pushing the arms down upon the chest again compresses it, and forces the air out of the lungs. Air is thus drawn into and forced out of the lungs in the same manner as breathing. The blood is gradually purified by the oxygen brought into contact with it, and the system is again inspired with life."

POISONS.

When poison of any sort has been swallowed, give warm soapsuds freely until vomiting occurs. Do not concern yourself with the question of what is the best antidote. *Produce vomiting and send for skilled assistance.*

1. LOCALLY IRRITATING POISONS.

POISON.	SYMPTOMS.	ANTIDOTE.
ACIDS: Muriatic. Nitric (aqua fortis). Oxalic. Sulphuric (vitriol).	Excessively severe burning pain in the mouth, throat, and stomach. Difficult swallowing. Great depression. Extremities cold and clammy. Convulsions. (Death.)	Alkali (baking soda, saleratus, magnesia, chalk, lime, plaster)—3 or 4 teaspoonfuls in a glass of water. Drink soothing fluids, like oil. Stimulating drinks, if necessary. Opiates to relieve pain.
ACID (CARBOLIC): Creosote.	Vomiting of frothy mucus. Lining membrane of mouth white, hardened, and benumbed. Severe pain in belly. Cold, clammy skin; insensibility. Snoring breathing. Odor of carbolic acid.	White of eggs. Milk, or flour and water. Rest. Opiates.
ALKALIES: Ammonia (hartshorn). Lye. Pearlash. Potash, caustic. Soda, caustic.	Painful burning in mouth, throat, and stomach. Difficult swallowing. Bloody vomiting and purging. Great depression, etc., like acids.	Dilute acids (vinegar or lemon-juice). Soothing fluids, like oil, melted fat, thick cream, etc. Stimulating drinks. Opiates to relieve pain.
SILVER: Nitrate (lunar caustic).	Same as above.	Copious draughts of salt and water. Soothing drinks. Opiates.

2. GENERAL POISONS, CAUSING LOCAL IRRITATION.

MERCURY: Corrosive sublimate. Calomel. Vermilion.	Burning pain in throat, stomach, and bowels. Metallic taste. Vomiting and purging — frequently bloody. Increase of saliva. Sleepiness. Convulsions. Stupor.	Raw eggs, milk, or flour and water. Castor-oil. Stimulating drinks.
ARSENIC: Fowler's solution. Green coloring matter. Paris green. Rough on Rats. Scheele's green.	Burning pain in stomach and bowels. Tenderness of belly on pressure. Retching. Vomiting. Dryness of throat. Clammy sweat. Convulsions.	Give hydrated oxide of iron made by adding 8 parts of ammonia water to 10 parts of solution of tersulphate of iron. Then castor-oil. Rest, and stimulating drinks if needed.
COPPER: Verdigris. Blue vitriol. Food cooked in copper vessels.	Similar to those of arsenic. Coppery taste in mouth. Tongue dry. Colic. Bloody stools.	White of eggs, if obtainable,—if not, flour and water. Ice. Opiates to relieve pain and excitement.

2. General Poisons, causing Local Irritation.—*Continued.*

POISON.	SYMPTOMS.	ANTIDOTE.
IRON: Copperas. Green vitriol.	Burning pain in throat, stomach, and bowels. Colic. Vomiting. Purging. Cold skin. Weak pulse.	Baking-soda in water. Then raw eggs and milk. Opiates for pain. Stimulating drinks for depression.

3. Sleep-producing or Narcotic Poisons.

POISON.	SYMPTOMS.	ANTIDOTE.
CHLORAL: A white, crystalline substance, with an acrid taste.	Profound sleep. Breathing slow and shallow. Pulse weak, rapid, and irregular. Remains of poison near by.	Stimulating drinks. Heat. Motion.
OPIUM: Laudanum. Morphine. Paregoric. Sleeping mixtures in general.	Giddiness. Heaviness of the head. Sleepiness. Stupor. Pupils of eyes contracted to fine point. Signs of the poison near by.	Stimulating drinks—strong coffee. Keep up breathing. Warmth. Keep patient awake by whipping, if necessary. Motion.

4. General Poisons.

POISON.	SYMPTOMS.	ANTIDOTE.
ACONITE: Wolfsbane. Monkshood.	Great depression. Extreme weakness. Cold sweat. Numbness of extremities. Weak and slow pulse.	Stimulating drinks.
BELLADONNA: Atropia. Deadly nightshade.	Eyes very bright, and pupils enlarged. Dryness of throat. Paralysis of excretory organs. Delirium. Convulsions.	Opiates to relieve nervous excitement. Rest.
LEAD: Red lead. Sugar of lead. White lead.	Metallic taste in mouth. Cramps. Paralysis. Vomiting. Increase of saliva. Giddiness. Convulsions. Stupor.	Large doses of Epsom or Glauber's salts. Stimulating drinks.
PHOSPHORUS: Matches.	Pain in stomach and bowels. Vomiting. Purging. Signs of poison near by.	Magnesia in water. Soap-suds. Rest. Warmth.
PRUSSIC ACID: Cyanide of potash. Oil of bitter almonds. Laurel-water.	Death may occur instantly in ordinary doses. In very small doses, giddiness, blindness, convulsions, fainting. Death may occur from smelling the odor only.	Stimulating drinks (strong) without delay.
STRYCHNINE: Nux vomica.	Slight shuddering. Feeling of constriction of throat. Startings. Paleness. Intermittent jerkings. Convulsions. Ghastly grin	*Cause vomiting* once or twice. Rest. Opiates. Chloral. Tannin.
VEGETABLE POISONS: Berries (Bitter-sweet, Deadly night-shade, Mountain ash, Poke, Potato). Hellebore, Hemlock, Horse chestnut, Indian tobacco, Jamestown weed, Wild lettuce, Wild parsley, Rhubarb leaves, Toadstools, Tobacco plant.	Nausea. Depression. Intoxication, stupor, etc., varying somewhat with the poison.	Stimulating drinks. Rest.

[*For further specific information see section on* HYGIENE IN THE HOME *in the* APPENDIX—SUPPLEMENTARY INFORMATION.]

VIII.

THE TRAINING OF CHILDREN.

VIII.

THE TRAINING OF CHILDREN.

By KATE DOUGLAS WIGGIN.

Early Training.
Habits.
The Parental Office.
Froebel.
Evolution in Education.
The Kindergarten.
Rights.
Duties.

Literature for Children.
The Art of Story-telling.
Clothes.
Amusements.
Toys.
Country Life.
Simplicity.
The Relation of Books to Nature.

"Perhaps the most touching passage in all literature is that in which the hero of Troy prays for a son more heroic than himself. Gladly will Hector die in battle with the Greeks if the gods grant that his son may rule nobly in Ilium. The glory of living is to transmit a higher life. The dying flame burns on in the brighter flame which it has kindled."—*Susan E. Blow.*

IF only one could create an atmosphere at will, so that the spirit in which one longs to be read might steal gently in upon the reader, inspiring him to break down the barrier of clumsy word and bungling phrase, and set free the message that lies prisoned in them. One sent the message warm and vital from a full heart, but the pen has been a non-conductor, and the reader has to do for himself what the writer would fain have done for him. Mutual sympathy and comprehension are more necessary here perhaps than elsewhere, for there is no subject in the discussion of which one is so likely to encounter misunderstanding, choler, and resentment, torrid argument and freezing satire, rivers of contumely and oceans of abuse, as in this well-worn one of the training of children.

One can tell a woman many things with impunity ; how to cook a lobster, how to build a portico, how to take spots out of linen, crochet a bedquilt, give a dinner-party, win a lover, hang a *portière*, keep a bank account, manage a husband ; but beware of advising her in the matter of bringing up her children. She will first ask you how many you have yourself, their sizes, ages, and dispositions. If your premises do not agree at all points with her premises, you may be sure she will have none of your conclusions, but will assert triumphantly that your so-called knowledge, convictions, opinions, views, or what-not are absolutely worthless ; and that you, who have never been the mother of her John and her Jane have had no proper opportunity of testing the brittleness of theory. As to books, she finally remarks with considerable heat, who should know best about children, the person who has brought six of them into the world—four of them addicted to croup in the night and no doctor within three miles — or those purveyors of idle theories, the unappropriated spinsters, childless matrons, and more - wise - than - nice bachelors who write the essays on child culture ? If this is not logic it has all the effect of logic, giving the hapless theorist a healthy feeling of self-distrust, and a determination to walk less confidently on other people's grass-plots.

Knowing full well the dangers that beset my path, and understanding beforehand that no woman will agree with me save the one who already believes precisely as I do, I shall try to feel that this chapter is a quiet corner frequented by young (and somewhat docile) mothers—a quiet corner in which there will be no dogmatic assertion, no interference with vested authority, no scornful gibes at maternal incompetency, nothing but a cosey sitting down and reasoning together, a discussion of ways and means, of causes and effects, a keen glance at the true meaning of our woman's round of little cares with little people, and, most of all, a fresh look into the face of that imperishable ideal that lives in the heart of each one of us. We shall have little exact knowledge to offer each other, very few hard-and-fast rules of procedure, almost nothing to make a note of and try next day, as we tried the last new recipes for waffles and wine-jelly. We may even go out from our chat feeling that the method that made little Hildegarde an angel will never cause the sprouting of a feather on Hannah's wings, and that each child is a fresh revelation, needing a special interpreter and a revised text-book.

During the early part of a young child's life, when we are occupied chiefly with his physical well-being, mothers in Israel may give definite instructions about sterilized milk and safety-pins that the haughtiest parent can accept with self-respect and follow with blind meekness; but the moment Master Baby loses his unbleached and wrinkled visage, gains a better modelled nose, evinces some consciousness of Ego—in a word becomes an individual, crowned with his mother's virtues and stamped with his father's foibles—that moment it becomes difficult to offer advice and still more difficult to take it.

This is the moment when we must nip in the bud that most foolish of human fallacies, the idea that we need not begin the serious work of training and educating this small human being for two or three years yet. Think not, pretty mother of a new baby, that you can have a dozen or two months of blessed inaction before you begin to cultivate your human flower! The ploughing and sowing, watering and fertilizing, must be done in the earliest spring or there will be no summer bloom, no bountiful autumn harvest. Well for everybody concerned (and in the largest sense there is no one who isn't) that you learned some of your life lessons while you were girl and woman and before you became a mother; better still if your ancestors, too, had some vision of their duty to posterity, for then the new heir will bring a goodly heritage into the world with him and your task is easier.

You discover speedily that in all the more difficult problems that confront maternity the understanding of one baby does not help you in the least to the comprehension of another. It teaches you to hold and bathe and dress them with more facility—little else. Babies have a capacity for being different from each other that must perplex the people who regard them, up to the time they enter upon the age of reason, merely as young animals. Number one (named Joshua, for his doting grandfather) was large-eyed, broad-browed, bald, solemn, judicial. He showed no astonishment, pain, delight, or emotion of any kind when a rattle was moved before his eyes, and you felt that he would have preserved the same impassibility had you made a supreme effort and waved a Bengal tiger in his face. There were no surprises in the universe for baby Joshua.

Number two is Jack; an adorable, radiant, spontaneous, gregarious baby. He is never yours, even at home; he belongs to the world. When you are travelling he carries all before him. His wraps taken off, he begins his conquests. He has the nice little girls and the maternal ladies smiling at once ; then, by easy stages, the sour misogynists and even the college boys succumb to his charm. In the horse-car he smiles, and waves his hand benignantly at the gruff old gentlemen and the callous conductor. In company he sits confidingly in everybody's lap, and everybody in whose lap he is not sitting looks on jealously; predestinate spinsters crooking knotty forefingers and cooing, as if matrimony, after all, might have its compensations.

In matters of discipline you could appeal to Joshua's judgment and reason (or you felt as if you could) when he was two years of age ; Jack's reasoning power seems to be less, but his heart melts at a touch. Helen cannot endure spanking ; Harriet likes it better than scolding. Rufus keeps the nursery in continual disorder. Paul kept all his playthings in their right places from the days of the rubber doll up to the rocking-horse period.

Woman's instinct of itself will never teach her to develop truly and guide rightly these differing individualities intrusted to her care. Instinct must be lifted into the realm of clear consciousness, must become conscious procedure. "Doubtless there are women who have a genius for motherhood," says Miss Blow, in " Symbolic Education." "These are the artist mothers, but, like other genuine artists, they are few in number, and the great majority of women cannot claim to be more than mechanics of the mind." Shall we be artist or artisan mothers ? The training necessary for any art demands toil, self-sacrifice, patience, enthusiasm ; but the creation of the thing of beauty is compensation for all the travail of the soul. If this be so of sculptured marble or painted canvas, of poem or book, how much more true is it of the immortal child, born of passion purified and spiritualized ; wrought upon with conscious purpose, loved, not coddled ; led, not driven ; respected as an individual, not tolerated as a chance ; guided to walk freely in directed paths ; to slay caprice and to liberate will ; to kill selfishness and to conquer self ; helped by the shining of your steady light to a vision of the relationship between the world of nature and the world of spirit ; kindled by your torch into sympathy with all truth, all beauty, and all goodness, until the meaning of life unwinds itself from the mysterious coil, its sombre threads shot through with rainbow tints.

This is no easy task, but there is no other in the world so far-reaching in its effects, so well worth while, so satisfying, so glorious. These are no sentimental phrases. You often breathe more glowing ones to your own heart, in those golden moments when you sit before your fire, the " heavenly downy necklace " of your child's arms about your neck.

Mothers are " going out," so the pessimists say. I doubt it, and I hope, too, that fathers are " coming in." I meet many parents like those of Browning's Pompilia :

" Two poor ignoble hearts who did their best,
Part God's way, part the other way than God's,
To somehow make a shift and scramble through
The world's mud, careless if it splashed and spoiled,
Provided they might so hold high, keep clean
Their child's soul, one soul white enough for three."

Do not fear that the absorbing cares of maternity will make you petty, stupid, or commonplace. Conscious motherhood never does this. The mother who has no conception of the parental office, save that it means endless feeding and clothing, unlimited kissing, and occasional spanking, who is entirely engrossed in her children's bodies and frocks—this woman is incorrigibly dull when she steps out of her nursery.

That ill-behaved fish, the father stickleback, no sooner sees his offspring safely hatched from the eggs and launched into a watery world than he eats up the mother stickleback, whose fostering care has made the little sticklebacks an accomplished fact. It is true his friends and supporters say that he makes a meal of his finny spouse simply that she may be diverted from her own intention of devouring the aforesaid little sticklebacks. I only hope he can prove the purity of his motives; but I have known certain mothers of large families who became so narrow, so dull, so lifeless, so hopelessly uninteresting in the discharge of their maternal duties, that the fathers of those families might be pardoned if they coveted Papa Stickleback's appetite and envied him his digestion.

On the other hand, if one's intercourse with children is carried on from the higher level, it is a matter of intellectual as well as spiritual profit. If one has never had an opportunity to study children, that has been his or her profound loss. The child, a child, any child I had almost said, is the Columbus of an undiscovered world in you; in your heart that goes without saying, but in your mind as well. Dress up your half-digested knowledge, your disconnected facts, your shallow evasions, in a few rags of conventionality and offer them to a child. See the unsatisfied soul look out of his questioning eyes. It makes one think; a child's "Why?" always brings one back to first principles.

> "Oh, dearest, dearest boy, my heart
> For better lore would seldom yearn,
> Could I but teach the hundredth part
> Of what from thee I learn."

But we teach nothing, and, worse still, we learn nothing, if we trust to blind instinct, to chance, to caprice, to the casual impulse of the hour. No one of these things gives us a clear view of the road we have travelled or throws any light on the path we have to tread, and thus the great principle of continuity is lacking and our education of the child becomes a farce, or still worse, a tragic failure.

"Now, I mean by education that training which is given by suitable habits to the first instinct of virtue in children; when pleasure, and friendship, and pain, and hatred are rightly implanted in souls not yet capable of understanding the nature of them, and who find them, after they have attained reason, to be in harmony with her. This harmony of the soul, when perfected, is virtue; but the particular training in respect of pleasure and pain, which leads you always to hate what you ought to hate and love what you ought to love, from the beginning to the end, may be separated off; and in my view will be rightly called education." *

At the very word education the page bristles with theories. There is the highly moral method, like that practised in the school presided over by Bradley Headstone and Charley Hexam, where "young women studied the adventures of little Margery who resided in the cottage by the mill; severely reproved the miller when she was five and he fifty; divided her porridge with the singing birds; denied herself a new nankeen bonnet on the ground that the turnips did not wear bonnets, neither did the singing birds," etc., etc.

Then there is the Mrs. Pipchin theory as unfolded to Mr. Dombey. "There is a great deal of nonsense, and worse, talked about young people not being pressed too hard at first and being

* (Plato's Laws, Book II.)

tempted on and all the rest of it, sir. It never was thought of in my time, and it has no business to be thought of now. My opinion is, keep 'em at it!"

There are the Pumblechooks who bother Pip with arithmetic while he is eating his breakfast; there are the Murdstones who torment their poor little Copperfields to the verge of insanity, and the Gradgrinds with their relentless pursuit of facts. Finally there is the alluring practicality of the Squeers's system.

"We go on the practical mode of teaching, Nickleby; c-l-e-a-n, clean, verb active, to scour. W-i-n, win, d-e-r, winder, a casement. When the boy knows this out of a book he goes and does it. When he has learned that botany is a knowledge of plants he goes and knows 'em. That's our system, Nickleby."

As to specific advice regarding the teaching of the young idea I shall be as dumb as the sphinx. The relative merits of public and private schools, the age at which a child shall be taught to read and write, the primer he shall use, the manner in which he shall approach geography and grammar, these subjects are always labelled "dangerous" in my mind, and I never touch one of them without expecting it to explode and wound somebody. Any ideas I may possess as to the general training of children come from my study of and experience with Froebel's educational philosophy. The kindergarten itself I shall not dwell upon, nor, save in the briefest way, its working apparatus of blocks and sticks, clay and paper, plays and stories. These have no transforming power in them so that by touching them the child is made whole. The power is in the philosophy that underlies them, and the genius of the kindergartner who rightly interprets and uses them.

You can accept the blocks and sticks and mats, or you can decline them, dear mothers, but I cannot maintain this tone of courteous indifference when it comes to the man himself, "the guide, philosopher, and friend" who labored with more than woman's patience in the making of these toys. If Froebel does not help you in the nurture of your children, if he does not thrill you anew with the importance of your sacred office, inspire you with courage and ambition, baptize you with consecrated zeal; if he does not broaden your mental and spiritual horizon, fire your imagination, give you a magic sword with which to slay your nursery lions, then I know not where to lead you for inspiration.

I am not speaking of technicalities, of courses of study, of methods of reading or writing and arithmetic; get these when and where and from whom you will; but for insight into child nature, for a vision of the ideal relationships your child should sustain toward all created things, for help in transforming your mother-love into mother-wisdom, for a clew to that great problem, the teaching of your child how to live, go to Froebel.*

The kindergarten is only one part of his system, and its modest attempt is to fit the education to the child instead of fitting the child to the education.

"The child," writes Froebel, "develops like every other essential being in accordance with laws as simple as they are imperative. Of these laws the most important and the simplest

---

* Will you not buy and read these five books, in the order named, and if they chance to be new to you, thank the good fortune that led you to them?
"Symbolic Education," by Susan E. Blow.
"Froebel and Education by Self-Activity," by Courthope Bowen.
"Reminiscences of Froebel," translated by Mary Mann.
Froebel's "Mother Songs and Plays," translated by Frances and Emily Lord.
"The Education of Man," by Friedrich Froebel.

is that force, existing, must exert itself; exerting itself, it grows strong; strengthening, it unfolds; unfolding, it represents and creates; representing and creating, it rises into consciousness and culminates in insight."

Will you bear with me through a few pages while I endeavor to set some of Froebel's educational ideas before you? Because, if you are not familiar with them, or if you have gained a distorted view of them through the medium of some unfortunate concrete example, you will be glad of a simple practical statement. I cannot give you a clearer one than by dipping here and there into Mr. Courthope Bowen's admirable book on "Froebel and Education by Self-Activity."

To begin with, Froebel's great claim to distinction will always rest on the fact that he was the first to apply the theory of evolution soundly and completely to education and having so applied it, to translate it into practice. His is the only system of education in which the details of actual practice are the real outcome of sound psychological principles, and in their application are continuously governed by those principles.

"We say," writes Mr. Bowen, "that a thing is fully developed when its internal organization is perfect in every detail, and when it can perform all its natural actions or functions perfectly. . . . The next thing to consider is, how this development is to be produced. How can we aid in promoting this change from the partially developed to the more highly developed thing? The answer comes from every part of creation with ever-increasing clearness and emphasis—development is produced by exercise of function, use of faculty. If we wish to develop the hand, we must exercise the hand; if we wish to develop the body, we must exercise the body; if we wish to develop the mind, we must exercise the mind; if we wish to develop the whole human being, we must exercise the whole human being." . . .

"But will any exercise suffice? Again the answer is clear. Only that exercise which is given at the right time, which is always in harmony with the nature of the thing, and which is always proportioned to the strength of the thing, produces true development. To produce development most truly and effectively, the exercise must rise from and be sustained by the thing's own activity. If, for instance, we decide to further the development of a plant, what we have to do is to induce the plant (and the whole of it) to become active in its own natural way and to help to sustain that activity. We may abridge the time, we may modify the result, but we must act through and by the plant's own activity. . . ."

That is simple enough and sensible enough, is it not? We then come to the principle of continuity in education.

"As that which is exercised grows constantly capable of higher and more varied activity, so must the exercise given grow continuously higher and more varied in character, every stage growing naturally out of that which precedes it. Facts in isolation and unrelated to each other do not form knowledge. Froebel wishes that education should be one connected whole, and that it should advance with a growth as orderly, continuous, and natural as that of a plant." Wordsworth gives us a poet's corroboration in the lines, "If we view objects in disconnection, dead and spiritless, we wage an impious warfare with the very life of our own souls."

Now, as to the character of the self-activity which Mr. Bowen mentions. With Froebel, observation and discovery are not enough, though he would agree to Artemus Ward's homely saying, "One thought you have born and raised on your own premises is worth a whole orphan asylum of other people's thoughts." He wishes the child to "work up" his knowledge, so to speak, into his very self, and to use it as a means of higher and more complete life. This *doing* will call into activity more and yet more *thinking* power.

"The making of new forms and combinations, the giving of definite expression to ideas and mental images, the making of the inward outward, is the great Froebel doctrine of creative activity, and together with the doctrines of continuity and connectedness forms the true heart of his system, for it gives the very life-blood to all the songs and plays, and it is the living principle in all the occupations."

The dignity and educational power of all necessary human labor, not only as a means of bread-getting, but as a means of spiritual development, is a striking thought in Froebel's philosophy. He would say with Carlyle, "Labor is life." "Properly thou hast no other knowledge but what thou hast got by working." The concluding words in Carlyle's chapter on the everlasting "Yea" might be Froebel's own. "Produce! Produce! Were it but the pitifulest infinitesimal fraction of a product, produce it, in God's name! 'Tis the utmost thou hast in thee, out with it then!"

As to his use of children's play and of their love of stories—many others recognized the value of play in early childhood—Plato, Quintilian, Luther, Fénélon, Locke, Richter—"but to Froebel alone belongs the credit of having seen its true evolutionary meaning, and the part it should take in education."

Then there is much stress laid upon nature-study and the educational value of art. "Here the knowledge of external fact is not the only thing nor the chief thing which Froebel seeks. . . . Besides exercising faculty, he desires that the child should gradually and continuously come to feel and to see that laws underlie all organic formation, and that conformity with those laws is the fundamental, unvarying condition of all true every-sided development toward perfection—in other things first and then in himself." . . .

"When using art as an instrument of his system he does not undertake to form artists, but seeks to awaken the ideal side of human nature and produce in the child a feeling and perception that, in all beauty there is a perfection of the thing *after its own kind*, another experience of the beneficent results of law and harmony."

Thus I have enumerated some of the principles upon which Froebel based his plan of education. The theory of natural, orderly development, or evolution, strict continuity or connectedness of procedure, self-expression by means of creative activity, the appeal to the child's love of beauty, the sympathetic study of nature, productive occupation, organized play, a unique use of stories, a unique system of object lessons to arouse the senses (which are always to be treated as the organs of mind and never as the organs of mere sensuous pleasure), and the insistence at every point that the child shall be regarded and trained as the child of nature, the child of man, and the child of God, a being capable, at least, of devout feeling, high thinking, noble doing. "'Tis not a soul," says Montaigne, "'tis not a body that we are training up, but a man, and we ought not to divide him."

All this seems formal, stilted, dead, in comparison with the living reality. If mothers could only work out these ideas under fairly advantageous conditions, they would not wish to content themselves with phrases. They would see the children themselves develop, both as individual and social beings; see them grow in clearness of observation and discrimination, in vision of duty, in sweet reasonableness of conduct, in recognition of the rights of others, in self-reliance, in self-government, in cheerful productive activity, in joyful self-expression; above all, find in them a clear, and ever clearer, comprehension of the diversity yet interdependence of all life.

It is the broad humanity of this educational process that makes it seem like a deep breath of fresh air. If Froebel had been a prophet, he could not have foreseen more clearly the needs of to-day's civilization, its evils, its cares, its responsibilities, its problems. If his principles could be applied from nursery to university, I believe we should all be better, wiser, simpler, truer.

I would rather my child had this sweet and simple wisdom, this balance of the faculties, this accuracy of mind and hand, this ability to see clearly, this moral health, this control of the ordinary human powers, this quiet sensible recognition of human rights and privileges, this intelligent submission to the true conditions of life, than all the wealth of the Indies.

I have not been giving you these dry bones of theory for the purpose of persuading you to begin your children's education by sending them to a kindergarten. If you have an intelligent kindergartner in your vicinity, I certainly think she is your best ally, your most sympathetic co-worker; but if she be never so wise and helpful she can only share your responsibility; you and you alone are the commanding influence in your child's life during the early years of which we are speaking. I am pleading for some earnest study of educational philosophy, for some adequate knowledge of the laws that govern the child's physical, mental, and spiritual development, because this study and this knowledge will illuminate the thousand seeming trifles of your daily discipline, lifting it from a commonplace round of meaningless and disconnected duties into a thing of dignity and importance, fine in its conscious purpose, splendid in its serene order and continuity. Mr. Oscar Chrisman, of Clark University, makes a plea for the new science of child-study. He believes that a systematic course of inquiry into the life, the growth, the ideas, the very being of the child, as the science of botany lays bare a plant, or mineralogy a mineral, would be of incalculable benefit to the race. Such a scientific study of the child in all his phases would afford "material for a scientific application of its results to pedagogy, to medicine, to theology, to the home training and care of the child, and the like."

He ventures the prediction that ten years hence, in all the leading colleges in the land, the child will be a topic of study, and that we shall live to see the day when the science of the child will have taught the world more about the child in fifty years than the world has learned during the preceding five thousand years.

If young mothers and fathers could only be brought to look upon parenthood as a science, an art, a profession, a vocation, a sacred office, as something at least beyond an accident or a social custom, so that they would give a tenth of the time to a preparation for it that they give to medicine, law, theology, millinery, or type-writing! All systematic education is a preparation, it is true, and all the accomplishments, the graces of mind and body and soul that can embellish womanhood, are of as great import and as practical use to the mother as they have been to the woman and wife; but over and above all this, there is a crying need for some specific knowledge of educational processes, some training which will preclude the making of tragic blunders in the nursery.

Excuses may be made for women in the light of the fact that the bringing up of a family is the most varied, difficult, complicated, momentous task that confronts the human being. It requires more brains, wisdom, culture, patience, energy, self-control, firmness, steadfastness, tact, insight, imagination than anything else in the world; or if we had a clear vision of the fatal consequences of wrong policy, or had any means of measuring the extent and results of failure, we should say the wise bringing up of her children is not only the most difficult task that confronts a woman, but the one involving the heaviest penalties for failure. I have known women who ordered their households with economy and discretion, managed their servants wisely, discussed their husband's business affairs intelligently, fulfilled their social duties pleasantly (all this proving the possession of a clear head and good judgment), who would make mistakes such as these in the government of their families: Paying children small sums of money to be good: making and breaking promises impetuously; talking gossip and scandal before children (I am not going to advise the proper time and place for this diversion); sending untruthful messages by them to neighbors or callers; threatening them with policemen and various other ogres; administering severe correction for small sins, no correction at all for graver ones; that is, no attempt to make "the punishment fit the crime"—the apparent method being to punish faithfully when there is plenty of time and let it go when too busy; taking children habitually to places of amusement; criticising nurses, governesses, and teachers in their presence. I pause for want of breath, not for lack of matter.

These things could not often happen were mothers better instructed in the profession of motherhood; they are follies born of ignorance and thoughtlessness.

Is it any wonder, when the moral atmosphere surrounding the child is so hazy, when his vision of right and wrong is so hopelessly confused, when, look which way he may, he cannot see any clear connection between causes and effects—is it any wonder that he grows up morally cross-eyed? The habit of looking askew at physical objects often has this effect on weak vision. Nor is this strabismus confined to the domain of ethics; it is intellectual as well as moral, so that the child sees nothing truly because he has always looked at the universe from a false angle.

Schlegel, the great German dramatic critic, sneered at the Grimm brothers for their patient browsing among long-forgotten nursery tales, myths, and legends, scornfully terming their painstaking research a "meditation on the insignificant." The verdict of modern scholars has been very different, however, for that meditation on the insignificant forms the basis of our folklore, and has been of inestimable value to students.

Your first impression on reading Froebel may be that he, too, meditates on the insignificant, because of the stress he lays upon little things; the gravity with which he treats baby rhymes and jingles, bed-time stories, rattles and balls and play-materials in general, dolls, pet animals, plants, and mud-pies. This will strike you very forcibly when you first open his "Mother Plays and Songs" (*Mutter und Kose-Lieder*), with their mottoes and commentaries for the mother, their rhymes for the baby, and their pictures for both. But the attempt to label things great and little is very unsafe. I have an idea that the mind and heart of God never makes these arbitrary distinctions. Christ's teachings were certainly an exaltation of the little things. The sorrow of the widow for the lost sixpence, the search for the one ewe-lamb when the ninety and nine lay safely in the fold, the five loaves and the two fishes, the gathering of the fragments, the parable of the mustard seed, the numbering of the hairs of our head, the noting of the sparrow's fall —all this tells the same story. There are no little things, unless we make them so. Everything is great if we have the grace and the wisdom to lift it into greatness.

If you find upon further reading that the book still appears to you incongrous or silly, you should begin to be anxious about yourself (I speak in all seriousness !). I can hear you say modestly, with a puzzled wrinkling of your eyebrows, "It is very curious. It seems, if Froebel writes of this book 'He who knows what I mean by it has learned my inmost secret;' it seems, if psychologists say that, judged by the true tests, it is one of the world's great books, one that stands absolutely alone, a whole class by itself; it seems that there must be something wrong with me."

You are quite right; there *is* something wrong ; you lack spiritual insight, and you should go into treatment for the defect, just as you would if you were maimed in some other direction.

"Can one *learn* spiritual insight ? " you ask ; " I thought one had to be born with it."

Certainly it can be developed, and from a very small germ too. Why not? Simply withdraw your mind a little from its accustomed channels and dwell more upon the things of the spirit. Live a little closer to nature, put off the strait-jacket of conventionality ; take a tuck in your common sense (oh, heresy !) and let out your imagination ; give your soul an inch of breathing and stretching room, and it will spread its wings and fly ; when it flies—you will understand Froebel's " Mother Play."

Let us talk a little about play and playthings, for they are most important factors in nursery education.

" The first self-revelation of the child is through play. He learns by it what he can do ; what he can do easily at first trial, and what he can do by perseverance and contrivance. Thus he learns through play to recognize the potency of those "lords of life " (as Emerson calls them) that weave the tissue of human experience, volition, making and unmaking, obstinacy of material, the magic of contrivance, the lordly might of perseverance that can reinforce the moment by the hours (and time by eternity). The child in his games represents to himself his kinship to the human race—his identity, as little self, with the social whole as his greater self."[*]

You can learn more of your child's nature, his strength, his weakness, his disposition, his general tendencies, through watching his plays and noting his selection and use of playthings than you can by hours of questioning.

Behold the child among his new-born blisses,
A six-years' darling of a pygmy size !
See where mid work of his own hand he lies,
Fretted by sallies of his mother's kisses,
With light upon him from his father's eyes ;
See at his feet some little plan or chart,
Some fragment from his dream of human life,
Shaped by himself with newly learned art !
A wedding or a festival
A mourning or a funeral,

[*] Dr. William T. Harris.

---

[*] Froebel's wife said of the book—*Mutter und Köse-Lieder* (" Mother Plays and Songs ") :
' A superficial mind does not grasp it,
A gentle mind does not hate it,
A coarse mind makes fun of it,
A thoughtful mind alone tries to get at its meaning."

> And this hath now his heart,
> And unto this he frames his song:
> Then will he fit his tongue
> To dialogues of business, love, or strife;
> But it will not be long
> Ere this be thrown aside,
> And with new joy and pride
> The little actor cons another part,
> Filling from time to time his "humorous stage"
> With all the persons, down to palsied age,
> That life brings with her in her equipage,
> As if his whole vocation
> Were endless imitation.
> —WORDSWORTH.

One little friend of mine forsakes all her old dolls when a new one appears; another plays with headless dolls for weeks together, mourning, like Rachel, for her children, and refusing to be comforted because they are not. One likes nothing but quiet games and evidently thinks thoughts and lives a life of her own when she sits like a mouse among her blocks and puzzles and toy animals. Another cannot conceive of play without noise. Two chairs make a sufficient paraphernalia so long as there is a hullabaloo. Engines that hoot, bears and lions that growl and roar, steam-cars that puff violently, bulls that bellow, brass bands that toot. "Only two chairs needed for properties, ladies and gentlemen," Rufus might say; "only two chairs and my magnificent lungs supply all deficiencies."

Another small boy is a source of great interest to me; I watch him, over the edge of my book, for an hour at a time. His plays always circle about some great calamity. There is a general crescendo, an onward march in the direction of chaos, then, when the crisis has been reached, he stalks upon the scene with order in his hand. I should write the pronoun He with a capital H, for it is undoubtedly with a capital H that He stalks upon the scene. He is a guardian angel, a defender of the defenceless, a promoter of peace, an avenger of the injured; anything, so long as he can be It, and so long as the affair is no tempest in a tea-pot, but a truly awful catastrophe demanding the greatest nerve and the most invincible heroism. Paul in the next room is playing ferry-boat, industriously loading and unloading freight, taking on passengers; but this is too tame for Rufus. His ships always break their propellers, are upset by a whale, founder at sea. Then he saves the passengers, kills the whale, and makes a new propeller out of something he happens to have in his pocket. (The great man is always lucky!) The family psychologists are in doubt about Rufus. His mother thinks he is destined to be the savior of his country in some hour of peril; his father that he will be a policeman. I wonder how grown people can watch children and fail to generalize from the particulars given them in this way. They are always sending out important telegrams to us, but we are often too stupid and indolent to read them.

The simplest playthings are the best. There is no need of buying expensive mechanical toys. The more imagination and cleverness and genius the inventor has put into the toy, the less room there is for the child's imagination and cleverness and genius. The more you give to the child the less chance he has to develop his own resources. "The too perfect toy chills the imagination, and hence the child turns from it to objects which, by remotely suggesting an ideal, heighten the activity of fantasy. The true plaything is only 'a distaff of flax from which the soul spins a many-colored coat. It must be indefinite, capable of many transformations, and able to act many parts. Only thus can it fulfil its twofold mission—to stimulate creative activity and satisfy the hunger of the soul for the ideal."[*] The electric dolls, the elaborate *papier mâché* contriv-

---

[*] Susan E. Blow, in Symbolic Education.

ances, the mechanical animals whose internal organs get so frightfully out of order, the ballet-dancers that can never be persuaded to dance after the first day, what are these compared with the useful sofa-arm, the spirited rocking-chair, the highly acceptable cane, the towel-rack, and the boot-jack? These stimulate the imagination: the others furnish only a languid amusement to the mind and never appeal to the heart, as do the rag doll, the woolly lamb, the string of spools, or some battered thing that the child has grown up with and learned to love. You realize the child's devotion to certain favorite playthings when you find that your youngest, who has been put to bed at five o'clock for some misdemeanor, has gone to sleep with the tears of repentance glittering on his lashes and a canton-flannel kitten locked to his bosom. That happy kitten was probably the recipient of his pent-up woes and the healer of his sorrows. Do you remember Coventry Patmore's little poem that gives such a touching picture of the child's relation to his playthings, and their office as comforters in times of infant tribulation?

> "My little son, who looked from thoughtful eyes,
> And moved and spoke in quiet, grown-up wise,
>   Having my law the seventh time disobeyed,
>   I struck him, and dismissed
>   With hard words, and unkissed,
>   (His mother, who was patient, being dead);
> Then, fearing lest his grief should hinder sleep,
>   I visited his bed,
> But found him slumbering deep,
>   With darkened eyelids, and their lashes yet
>   From his late sobbing wet.
>   And I, with moan,
> Kissing away his tears, left others of my own;
>   For, on a table drawn beside his head,
> He had put within his reach
> A box of counters and a red-veined stone,
> A piece of glass abraded by the beach,
>   And six or seven shells,
>   A bottle with bluebells,
> And two French copper coins, ranged there with careful art,
>   To comfort his sad heart."

I give you a list of sensible and useful playthings made out by the members of the mothers' class in the Chicago Kindergarten College, because I believe it will be of real service.

TOYS FOR CHILDREN FROM ONE TO TWO YEARS OF AGE.

Linen picture-books.
Rubber animals.
Canton-flannel animals.
Rubber rings.
Worsted balls.
String of spools.
Knit dolls.
Rag dolls.
Rubber dolls.
Wooden animals (unpainted).
New silver dollar.

TOYS FOR CHILDREN FROM TWO TO FOUR YEARS OF AGE.

Blocks.
Dolls.
Balls (uncolored; also six of red, yellow, blue, green, orange, purple).
Woolly lamb.
Cradle.
Chair.
Picture-book of families of birds, cats, dogs, cows, etc.
Anchor-stone.
Blocks.
Furniture for dolls' houses.
Express cart (iron or steel).
Spade, rake, or hoe.
Biscuit-board and rolling-pin, a churn, a wooden case with a six-inch rule and pencil in it.
A box of non-poisonous paints, water-color, pair of blunt scissors.
Paper windmill.

TOYS FOR CHILDREN FROM THREE TO FIVE YEARS OF AGE.

Blackboard and crayon.
Building-blocks.
Balls.
Train of cars.

Doll and cradle.
Wooden beads to string.
Small glass beads to string.
Rocking-chair.
Doll's carriage.
Books with pictures of trade life, flowers, vegetables, etc.
Tracing-cards and paper dolls.
Toy poultry yard with fences, trees, a woman, and a dozen ducks and chickens.

TOYS FOR CHILDREN FROM FIVE TO SIX YEARS OF AGE.

Kitchen, laundry, and baking sets.
Balls, building-blocks, picture-puzzles, dissecting maps.
Historical story-books.
Outline picture-books to color with paint or crayon.
Trumpet, music-box, desk, blackboard, wagon, whip, sled, kite.
Pipe for soap-bubbles, train of cars, carpenter's tools.
Jackstraws, hobby-horses, substantial cook-stove, sand-table.
Skates, rubber boots, broom, Richter's stone blocks, shovel.
Spade, rake, and hoe.
Marbles, tops, swing, and see-saw.
Strong milk-wagon equipped with cylinder cans, substantial churn.
A few bottles filled with water, spices, coffee, sugar, etc., for a drug-store.

Another of the fine points leading to fine issues is the reading to your children and the telling of stories. Story-telling has gone out of fashion as an art, but it still survives by the fireside, for the very good reason that so long as the child is born into the world with the power of speech, so long will he continue to cry of his own volition. "Tell me a story." This time-worn phrase, being interpreted, means simply "Read me the riddle of life. Tell me of deeds in which I can gain the clew to my own impulses. Show me types in which I can behold myself. Give me ideals in which I can know myself and forget myself!"

> "Oh! give us once again the wishing-cap
> Of Fortunatus and the invisible coat
> Of Jack the Giant Killer, Robin Hood,
> And Sabra in the forest with St. George!
> The child whose love is here at least doth reap
> One precious gain, that he forgets himself."

There is some little difficulty in making a choice of stories, but it ought to be an impertinence for an outsider to choose for the mother. She needs no catalogue of the best books, she needs only a catalogue of principles to guide her choice. Froebel's couplet, printed at the head of one of his mother-plays, gives us a text for the ethical side of the question.

> "Yet therein dear to you should be
> The child's young spirit's purity."

It is obvious that no mother would consciously disobey this injunction, yet I fear that some stories told to children by ignorant and superstitious nursery maids, and others read in an absent-minded fashion without any clear idea of their influence or example, might well disturb the young spirit's purity. There are fairy stories, for instance, in which the moral is sweet and healthy, and there are others essentially coarse in grain. Better than the last, and still not good, are the flotsam and jetsam of the holiday publications: aimless, worthless, gaudy, silly books, that seem to have been written as well as printed by machinery. There is in them no style and no matter. Children educated on this sort of diet will never have a growing appetite for the masters of English, that is very certain. You must not always expect diversion for yourself when you are reading to young children. The story that gives you something to think about is not likely to be suitable for the little person at your knee. The book you think the very thing is not sure to be the one the child locks to his gingham bosom and refuses to be parted from for an instant; for some so-called children's authors apparently write what amuses them at the child's expense.

You in the "sweet safe corner of your household fire" hardly realize perhaps what a fountain of instruction and amusement and inspiration the story hour is to your children. It is always a touching scene in the free kindergartens when the small army of babies gathers about the feet of the kindergartner, for if she be of the true motherly sort, she somehow gives the impression that the children are all gathered, mother-fashion, at her knee; that her lap is boundless in its capacity, and that there is swimming room in her heart for the whole ragged flock. They generally know how to choose, and how to tell stories, these kindergartners, and one of the sweet and helpful things they are doing in their mothers' clubs and classes is the teaching of stories to these hard-working, overburdened, dispirited women.

Seldom enough have they had time for the poetry of life, but this gives them a vision of its possibility. Having the story to tell gives them the idea of telling it, and out of that first telling, that new intimacy, may spring a hitherto unknown union between mother and child. I shall never forget one of those sacred moments, born like many another beautiful thing, in that same free kindergarten. It was Mothers' Day. There were two hundred children present (three schools gathered in one) and perhaps seventy-five mothers, fresh from wash-tubs and ironing-tables, fruit and flower-shops and sewing-machines. For the most part they had no keen sense of the real meaning of the occasion; but there had been a preconcerted plan to kindle the mother-spirit whenever and wherever it could be kindled. At a certain juncture the children who were grouped on the circle, burst into this little song:

"Hundreds of stars in the lovely sky,
  Hundreds of shells on the shore together,
  Hundreds of birds that go singing by,
  Hundreds of birds in the sunny weather.

" Hundreds of butterflies on the lawn,
  Hundreds of bees in the purple clover,
  Hundreds of dewdrops to greet the dawn,
  But only one mother the wide world over!"

The children had been born three or four years before, but there were some new-born mothers in that moment. As the last simple line was sung with childlike feeling and smiling emphasis to mark the sentiment, a wave of emotion swept over those dull, tired, prosaic women, and the impress left upon their face was something not to be described.

In your story-telling you will find the serial form wonderfully useful, for you need only give the slightest hint that there is a little more to tell about Hetty, or something else to impart about Hilda, and the small audience flocks to your side. You never have to give a synopsis of the last chapter. Each child remembers the number of hairs in Hetty's eyebrow and can recite a list of her deeds without missing. If you do not wish to meet a battery of reproachful eyes (how lovely, how clear, how innocent they are when they trip you up, those eyes!) then do not, in a momentary aberration, link any of Hilda's performances on to Hetty's story, or confuse the dramatic incidents of Dorothy's career with those of the fair Dulcibella's. These are liberties that no group of young listeners will accept from an absent-minded historian. This serial form is a great assistance to the mother who lacks invention and who is not a natural story-teller. It obviates the need of creating a new hero or heroine at every sitting, an operation rather difficult for an average parent who has not been born with a genius for making literature. It also precludes the necessity for continual description and analysis of character and motives, for Hetty and Hilda, once created and set in motion, live up to themselves of their own accord. They may even do rather commonplace things sometimes, yet retain their aureoles undisputed. It is astonishing, too, how Hetty and Hilda, or Donald and Daniel, have in the serial story of their lives committed some of the very peccadilloes and displayed some of the self-same virtues exemplified in the nursery careers of your listeners, and that, too, within the memory of the youngest inhabitant. Another useful hint to the poor distracted story-teller who has no invention and less expression : when completely out of matter, begin your intended chronicle with the six magic words : "When I was a little girl." After this any stupidity will be pardoned. If, when you were a little girl (but not otherwise), you went across the road, climbed over a fence and plucked a strawberry leaf, this event is clothed at once with fictitious solemnity. If Hilda did it, it is open to criticism ; your hearers perceive at once that she should not have climbed the fence for fear of tearing her frock, and whether she did it or not it was not a thrilling thing to do. If you, however, did it when you were a little girl, every step across the road, every rail of the fence, every vein of the strawberry leaf is a point of vital interest.

Your stories will grow in interest and helpfulness as you gain confidence and experience. If you live in the country many charming and useful texts will be suggested by your rambles and excursions. If you are not an observant woman you will learn to be so in your children's company, and the birds and bees, the trees and flowers, the sunrise and the sunset will make a poet of you almost without your knowledge.

If it is not possible for you to give your children a few months of country life each year, try and bring the country to them. Of course, it will be a makeshift, but it will be better than nothing. There is never a day but I "thank Heaven fasting" that my childhood was passed in the country. Nature's playthings are the best for the soul. The child learns to see "by wholes," feels a dawning sense of his relationships, a premonition of the divine scheme of education, when his preludes to the printed book are the green earth, the mystery of its sleep and its awakening, a friendly intercourse with animals, the music of the forest trees, the singing of birds, the humming of insects.

It seems to me, as I look back, that a childhood in which the sermons are found in the stones and the books in the running brooks, gives one an abiding sense of peace and completeness found in no other way. It is so difficult to give the town-bred child simplicity nowadays. There is no simplicity to be had either for love or money. The social atmosphere is charged with problems. It is easily possible that your nurse is a Christian Scientist, your governess an Altruist, your cook a Nihilist, your butler a single-tax man. Then if you are a Suffragist and your husband a Mugwump, the children are certainly in a fair way to have the fullest advantage in the matter of modern ideas. In the midst of all this activity, some of which is growth and more of which is fermentation, the child may miss his childhood. Now that I am surrounded by infants who discuss microbes and know that they are bacteria, and who inquire for paper dolls dressed in the fashion of

1830, I feel a positive sense of exhilaration that nobody can rob me of my innocent, my unsophisticated past; my linsey woolsey frock, my knit hood, my round comb, and copper-toed boots; my tea-sets of broken china; my chickens and dogs and calves and colts; the singing fir-tree outside my bedroom window, and the little river that lulled me to sleep at night. With the memory of these to sweeten and strengthen life, I am able to cope with microbes and endure the 1830 styles; but how about the young people who are struggling against the questions of the hour with no such reinforcement? Let us give our children their childhood if we have to deny them many other things. Accustom them to humble pleasures, simple playthings, frugal feasts, small expenditures. It will not be a sober life; we may crowd it full of joy, full to the brim and running over, but let us remember that joy ought not to consist wholly in dancing-school, promenades with nurse, five minutes of dessert at dinner-parties, drives in a close carriage, matinées, and children's parties. None of these leaves as sweet and helpful an impression as a game of hide-and-seek behind the haycocks in the mown field, a ride on the load to the barn, a search through tangled alder-bushes for the source of the brook, a hunt for hens' eggs, the daily sight of the ploughing or harrowing or sowing, of the cider-press, the threshing-machine, the corn-husking, the gathering of leaves and nuts and shells —all this goes to make up a life in which the child can share, and in the sharing of which he is moved to a sense of his own responsibilities.

Froebel's mother-plays and pictures will help you to see this very clearly and enable you to interpret rightly that first feeling of kinship with all created things, that awe and wonder, that faint stirring of the spirit which is the mind's presentiment of its ideal nature and destiny. Froebel believes that by a process we cannot trace, the mind moves on from its perception and love of Nature's symbols to a realization of the truth symbolized. When you were a child did you ever push away the thick leaves in some wilderness of shrubs and, peering into the darkness, discover a mother bird covering her little ones? Do you remember her eyes looking into yours from out that dim, green chamber? I recall such a moment and know that the tender thrill that stirred my young heart led me on to a clearer comprehension of the human relations between mother and child.

These are blessed experiences, but they cannot be bought at the shops; so, if you cannot take the babies to the country be of good cheer, nevertheless, and bring the country into the town: a bit of garden in which the children can work, or, failing even that, some plants in pots; a sand pile in the back yard (material there for geography and history, poetry and romance), a bird, a kitten, a puppy, or a rabbit, not so much because they are pets as because they are responsibilities.

Everything becomes simple when we realize what are the truly helpful influences with which we wish to surround these growing bodies, minds and souls. The difficulties spring mostly from the lack of definite plans and clear ideals. I have said that small responsibilities are very necessary to the development of the child's character. Froebel does not say "Come, let us live *for* our children," but "Come, let us live *with* our children." You can only supply the right conditions for growth; the moment you attempt to do the growing you make a fatal mistake. The child is born into a world of duty; it is never too soon for him to learn this truth, and as a matter of fact I believe there was play the development of the race as well as of the individual, he relives history and catches glimpses of eternal verities.

The stories, too—you need to see how they form the text for the day's doings, or serve as the culmination, the knitting together and binding into a connected whole of the activities that have preceded them. They are worked into the games, the play-lessons, the building, the clay, the pictures, the wet sand.

As to discipline, there are no punishments in the usual sense, but there are righteous penalties. Each child may have all the liberty he can use wisely, the only limitation being that he shall not interfere with the liberty of someone else. If he cannot abide by the laws that govern the circle games, he must stay outside the circle. If he does not do his own work faithfully, of course he cannot be trusted to help his neighbor.

The marvel is that very few of these things occur. In the large public kindergartens you watch fifty or sixty little creatures at work and play together, acting for the most part up to the most ideal standard of conduct, and that without compulsion, until you begin to wonder whether there has not been some mistake about the total depravity theory. Good behavior, generosity, helpfulness, industry, cheerfulness—all these are taken very much as a matter of course. At the insubordination of some new-comer the kindergartner says serenely, "We don't do that here." "O—h!" is the mental attitude of the little rebel, and he stops doing it; why, I never quite understand, but he does. It is the power of that editorial "we," the force of that well-behaved majority that makes him feel an alien.

The kindergarten teaching is all positive: it preaches the loveliness of right-doing rather than the hatefulness of evil; its gospel is stimulating, not deterrent—*do*, not *don't*. Its morality is unconscious; it does not "remember to be good, it forgets to be naughty;" it does not tangle children up prematurely in mental processes; it gives them material with which to work out their mental images. If a child has instruction given him right end first he can assimilate it, it becomes fruitful ,knowledge. If the process is reversed he is helpless; his powers are paralyzed instead of fertilized.

Do you know that charming verse about the centipede? It contains a highly useful educational truth which exactly illustrates this point:

"The centipede was happy quite
   Till the toad one day in fun
Said, ' Pray *which leg goes after which?*'
   This wrought his mind to such a pitch
He lay distracted in a ditch
   Considering how to run!"

It is quite useless for anyone to say that he or she does not "approve of" or "believe in" the kindergarten when it is a fair expression of Froebel's educational ideal. One might as well say one does not believe in electricity or gravitation. It is not an exact science, a finished or perfected institution, but it is the most rational basis of education, the most logical beginning we know anything about at present, and we should realize its possibilities before we take the next step.

I do not exaggerate when I say that it has proved, and is proving, a school of life to the mothers and fathers who practise it, the children who are taught by it, the kindergartners who teach them, the men who marry the kindergartners, the matrons who scrub the floors of the kindergartens, and the janitors who build the fires. I suppose nine out of ten of my readers will think this a bit of facetious nonsense, whereas it is a plain truth, to which the matrons and janitors themselves would cheerfully subscribe. I believe with all my heart that the working out and perfecting of the kindergarten means as much to the adult half of the community as it means to children. One has only to see its power over those who come in contact with it; one has only to note its efficacy with group after group, neighborhood after neighborhood, representing different conditions of prosperity and adversity, wealth and poverty, different ages, sizes, colors, and nationalities, to come to the conclusion that the idea has some transforming power in its veins.

IX.

THE EDUCATION OF WOMEN.

IX.

THE EDUCATION OF WOMEN.

By LYMAN ABBOTT.

Elementary Education.
The Atmosphere of the Home.
The Kindergarten.
Governesses.
Boarding Schools.
Day Schools.
Public Schools.
Private Schools.

The Higher Education.
Colleges and Universities.
Post-graduate Work.
Advantages of Foreign Study.
Advantages of Study in America.
Study at Home.
Scholarship.
Social Culture.

A TEACHER at Hampton Institute, Va., was one day reading the Parable of the Virgins to a class of Indians, one of their number acting as interpreter. Observing a smile stealing over the faces of her saturnine pupils, she stopped to inquire what caused their amusement, and discovered that the Indian tongue had but one word for maid and virgin, and but one for bridegroom and husband, so that the story which reached their ears through the interpreter was, that ten maids lighted their lanterns and went out to look for a husband.

This was formerly a very common conception of woman's education; she went to school that she might light her lantern and better look for a husband. And the consequent education took on two forms: it was either practical or ornamental. Woman was taught cooking, sewing, and the housekeeping arts generally, or she was taught a little French, music, and drawing, and just enough of literature and history to preserve her conversation from being wholly unilluminated. She was trained either to be an upper servant or a parlor ornament. And her subsequent life as a wife was fashioned on this general plan. She was not supposed to know or care anything about business, or public affairs, or the great world generally. If she saw that her husband had a clean house, a comfortable bed, good meals, and a tasteful drawing-room, at economical charges, she was an exemplary wife; and if, in addition, she could shine in society, she was a supremely excellent one. In short, according to the male interpretation, the second of the two accounts of the Creation in the Book of Genesis was accepted, and interpreted to this effect: that God made man the lord of the earth; that he brought the animals to man and found in none of them an adequate companion; and so, as an after-thought, made a woman to be a help-meet for him.

I repudiate both the interpretation and the doctrine built upon it. "God created man in his own image; in the image of God created he him; male and female created he them;" and to these twain, made to be one flesh, he gave dominion over the earth. Woman is to be educated to be a wife and mother; but not more than man is to be educated to be a husband and father. And this is not the primary end of education in either case. The absolute precedes the relative; the general precedes the special. First, as the end of education, comes manhood and womanhood, for its own sake; then fitness for the more common duties of life—those of the household; then for the more specific duties of citizenship; last of all, for the technical and professional ends—fitness to teach, to preach, to administer justice, to carry on a particular trade or profession.

The first thing to be said, then, respecting woman's education, is that in its primary and most fundamental elements it differs in nowise from man's education. Both live in the same world, mix in the same society, are subject to the same natural, social, and moral laws. There is no more one moral law for the boy and another for the girl, than there is one science of numbers for the boy and another for the girl. Both must learn the nature of the world and of its laws; the organization of the human body and the conditions of its well-being; the history of the past, which has conducted mankind to its present state; the thoughts of the greatest thinkers, that is, the best literature; the laws of social order and organization; and the principles which will lead forward to a better and nobler future. We are all embarked in the same ship, on the same ocean; and we must all learn the same laws of navigation.

It is not material for my purpose, in this chapter, to inquire whether woman is likely to exercise more *power* in the future than she has in the past. She is certain to exercise all the *influence* which she possesses, and as it is her duty to exercise that influence in the wisest way and to the noblest ends, so she has a right to whatever education will both increase that influence and give it a beneficent direction.

Nor is there any ground either for supposing that she is unable to receive as thorough an education as her more rugged brother, or that a more shallow and imperfect education will serve her sufficiently. Her right to an education is the right of every creature God has made, to all that is necessary to its best development. It is quite needless to cite statistics here to show that woman is capable of the best work in the most difficult departments. If she were not, it would make no difference. She is to have the opportunity, that she may herself prove what she can, and what she cannot, do. It is impossible to decide what a man or a class may become, by considering merely their past history. Christendom excluded Jews from all but the mere money-making vocations, and then scoffed at them for being money-makers. America shut up the negro to menial employments, and then patronizingly pitied him for being by nature a menial. We forbade the Indian to come off from his hunting grounds, and then contemptuously dismissed him from the category of civilized men, as a hopeless barbarian. Similarly society has, in the past, forbidden women anything but the most superficial culture, and then concluded that she was capable of nothing else. " I know," says George William Curtis, " of no subject upon which so much intolerable nonsense has been talked and written and sung, and above all preached, as the question of the true sphere of woman, and of what is feminine and what is not; as if men necessarily knew all about it."* With that sentiment I heartily agree. Men have for ages been trying to determine by *a priori* considerations what is woman's sphere, and to keep her in it; and they have not achieved such success as to justify a continuance of the endeavor. It is quite time that women were left to find their own sphere, and it is quite safe to leave them to make their own voyage of discovery.

It is very probable that some will be injured in the process, and that in the reaction against the commingled servi-

---
* Quoted in the Forum, vol. vii., p. 44.

tude and coddling of women in the past, society may swing for a time too far in the opposite direction—of this more presently—but nature may be trusted to assert itself; and if society leaves women free to follow the guidance of their own moral instincts, those instincts will eventually prove a better safeguard than restrictions devised by men. Woman is not a caged canary, who will fly to her own destruction if the cage door is open and the windows up. There may be—personally I think there is—in the present reaction, some danger of forcing her into positions to which she is not inclined, and for which she is not fitted; but if that force be removed, and she be left free, there is but little danger that she will injure herself. It is true that there are vocations which are unwomanly, as there are others which are unmanly. The sexes are not duplicate, but supplement each other. Marriage is necessary to the perpetuation of the race; therefore marriage is one of the conditions in the future life of both young man and maiden, to be kept constantly in view in determining their education. In general, the man is to provide for the house by his industry, and protect it by his strength; the woman is to administer the home and nurture the children. And this natural division of labor in the house indicates a broader division in society. The natural activities of every man are paternal, of every woman maternal; and this whether they are married or no. But while it is necessary to bear this truth in mind in devising schemes of education for the two, it is not necessary to enforce this law of nature by either legal or social restrictions on liberty of development. Adam ought to get enough out of the wilderness by the sweat of his brow to support Eve and her daughters; and if he will attend to his own business, and do his work well, he need not fear that they will rush into the field and take the hoe out of his hand for the mere pleasure of wielding it.

My strong affirmation of these two principles must be borne in mind by the reader, if he wishes to understand what follows in this essay. First, woman is entitled, in her own right, to the highest and best education which can be given her—education not shaped to fit her to be a conventional type of wife and mother, determined beforehand for her by man, but shaped to make her the noblest and truest woman. The best way to make a true wife and mother is to make a true woman. And second, the formal and conventional restrictions on womanly liberty are to be removed—as to a large extent they have been—and she is to be free to find for herself her sphere, and to determine by her own unhindered and even aided experiments, what is the education which she needs for the perfect development of her own nature. The law of liberty is woman's best safeguard.

But while all this is truth, and fundamental truth, the title of this chapter assumes that there are to be differences in the education of the sexes. Indeed, the very title of the book assumes a difference both of nature and of functions. And this is often ignored in current discussions. What is meant by the phrase "equality of the sexes?" For that matter, what is meant by the term equality as applied to persons? The phrase is constantly used, as such phrases often are, without any clear apprehension of any meaning. Is the poet equal to the man of action? or the statesman to the soldier? or the preacher to the merchant? or the farmer to the lawyer? It is like asking, Is oxygen equal to hydrogen in the air? In the one case each is equally necessary to the constitution of the air; in the other each is equally necessary to the constitution of society. But neither is able to take the place or fulfil the functions of the other. Is the eye equal to the ear? Not when you are listening to an orchestra. For you close the eyes that you may hear the better. Are the husband and the wife equal? In nursing the infant he is not equal to her; in fighting the savage she is not equal to him; and which is the more important service depends upon circumstances. The phrase "equality of the sexes" has two intelligible meanings, and only two. It may mean that men and women are equally entitled to liberty and the best conceivable development. That equality, I affirm. It may mean that their respective services in society are equally essential to its well-being, and equally divine. That equality I affirm. But it cannot mean that their services are, or their development is, to be the same. That is not to affirm equality of character, but identity of function and education, and that is a totally different affirmation. Life is often, and fitly, compared to a battle-field. Men and women are engaged in a campaign. If it were an actual campaign, with a visible foe in the field, the men would learn the manual of arms and go to the front to do the fighting, and the women would take lessons of the doctors and do the nursing in the hospitals. Some men might nurse better than some women, and some women might fight better than some men. And if it became necessary for the latter to handle a musket, no one would deny them the right; on the contrary, everyone would admire their heroism. But on the whole, Joan of Arc is not the type of womanhood. The world would not be bettered by turning General Grant into a hospital nurse, or Clara Barton into a major-general.

With these general principles in mind, I shall endeavor to unfold some of the more special principles which ought to be applied by society in its organized efforts, and by the mother in the individual care of her daughters, to the education of women.

The reader must, however, remember that it is not possible to lay down any general laws according to which all women should be educated. For every individual is different from every other individual, and every life is different from every other life; therefore every education must be different from every other education. All that is here attempted is some hints, to be applied by the individual in solving for herself or for her daughter this complicated and ever-varying problem.

The baby lies in the cradle—What shall we do with her?

Far more important than the education is the training, and more important than the training is the atmosphere into which she is received. Some households receive her as a toy. "A home," says Shelley, "is never perfectly furnished for enjoyment unless there is a child in it rising three years old, and a kitten rising three weeks." So some parents, especially fathers, receive the babe—as a kitten; they frolic with her for ten minutes in the morning or ten minutes at night, and then toss the burden off upon the mother. A new toy! and we soon weary of our toys; and generally grown people weary sooner than children. Some households receive the baby as a new calamity. The child is looked upon as born in sin and to sorrow. Perhaps this notion is wrought into the religious faith of the household: the babe sinned in Adam and must suffer the penalty of its unconscious transgression; or the babe is a reincarnation, and comes into the world bringing with it the poison of its past experience; it is not a little child, but a little old man, and comes laden with past sins and wailing in unconscious reminiscence of shame and guilt in a pre-existent state. So theosophy portrays it. Some households receive it as an added burden: one more mouth to feed, one more body to clothe, one more soul to train, one more helpless creature to care for. This mother carries her child upon an always anxious heart, ever foreboding, ever dreading the worst in the unknown life that lies before the potential woman. To some households the babe comes as an unwelcome guest. The parents had the heart, but not the wretched courage, of a Pharaoh or a Herod, and would have slain the unborn child had they dared; nay! perhaps have dared, and tried, and failed. For this form of infanticide is not uncommon in America, and Rachel weeps, not because her child is not, but because it is; she would fain have escaped God's gift of love in the little child. When the babe is received as a toy, or as a child of divine wrath, or as a burden added to a life already overburdened, or as an unwelcome guest, no methods of education will be of much avail. Atmosphere is more than formal education; spirit is more than method.

I believe that the babe is innocent, without any touch or stain of guilt; a child of God in its birth, belonging to its heavenly Father; with infinite possibilities of good, but not therefore virtuous; with infinite possibilities of evil, but not therefore sinful. The babe is God's best gift to the home, the gift of his gracious love, and the witness of his strange confiding; for he apparently trusts the future of this child of his to the mother-love and the father-love. In this babe in the cradle there may be a heroine or a coward, a voice that shall be eloquent with new revelations of God's truth, or a life that shall be one long living lie; a fresh flower from the eternal gardens, or a new weed poisoning everyone who touches it. And what it is to be, depends upon what life shall make of it; and that again depends more upon the early influence of the home than upon all other influences combined. Life is a march from innocence to virtue, through temptation. Virtue can be won only by battle, and battle cannot be fought without possibility of defeat. If sin were not possible, virtue would be impossible. In this babe is innocence, but not virtue; no courage yet, nor truth, nor piety, nor faith, nor hope, nor love; but in her the possibility of all, and therefore in her and for her father, mother, brother, sister, friend, a great opportunity. And education means seizing this opportunity, and making out of this bundle of possibilities the largest and noblest soul development.

"Education," says Professor Huxley, "is the instruction of the intellect in the laws of Nature, under which name I include not merely things and their forces, but men and their ways; and the fashioning of the affections and of the will into an earnest and loving desire to move in harmony with those laws. For me, education means neither more nor less than this. Anything which professes to call itself education must be tried by this standard, and if it fails to stand the test, I will not call it education, whatever may be the force of authority, or of numbers, upon the other side."* This education begins at the cradle, and the first and most potent factor in it is the unconscious influence of the life of the home into which the babe comes at birth.

The wise father will leave the early education of the child in the hands of the mother. He will simply content himself with enforcing her authority. He will pay his wife scrupulous respect,

---

* *Science and Education.* Essay IV., p. 83.

and so teach the children to pay respect to their mother. Only the grossest injustice will justify him in interfering; for the children will suffer less from occasional blunders in their queen than from a divided rule. And the wise mother will early perceive the difference of sex asserting itself; and will neither be anxious to develop it on the one hand, nor allow herself to disregard it on the other. The girl will take to dolls, the boy to stage-driving with chairs for a team. The boy will be storekeeper, the girl will be customer. But if it should be otherwise, the mother need not be troubled. If the girl wants to try her hand at ball, or climbs the trees, dress her appropriately and let her have her way. This inclination does not indicate masculinity to be repressed, but a vigor of physical constitution to be encouraged. It may be needful to guard her against hoydenish ways as she grows older; but if her mother's example be safe to follow there will be little need to enforce it with anxious precept. The example of those she reveres and her own womanly intuitions will suffice to protect her from the danger of mannishness.

If there be a good kindergarten in the neighborhood, by all means send her to it. If there be none—or whether there be one or not—the wise mother will study enough of Froebel's system to understand its essential principles and their simple applications, that she may make a kindergarten, that is, a Child-Garden, out of her nursery. If the child be slow to learn, if she be taciturn, talks little, is laggard in learning to read, do not be troubled. Slow growths are often the best; precocious girls do not always become great women; and growths that are forced are never healthful. Do not be in haste to send her to school. There are plenty of lessons to be taught at home, which the school cannot teach. It is generally time enough to send a child to school when she begins to show some anxiety to learn. It is better to sit down late to the table with a good appetite, than to come early with a distaste for the food. When she begins to go to school, do not let her studies absorb all her energies. She has for many years much to learn from her mother; and no scholarship will compensate for the sacrifice of a mother's companionship.

Most fathers cannot be the companions of their boys, for business carries the man away from home early and suffers him to return only late. But the wise mother is a home-stayer, and her daughter will receive from the mother a love for the home for the lack of which no tuitions of the schoolroom can compensate. Encourage the daughter to be with the mother in the household tasks; to sew, to iron, to cook, to dust, to make beds, to do that miscellaneous work dubbed in New England homes "putting to rights." It is to be hoped that she will have a home of her own one day; and it is better that she should practise home duties as a child, under her mother's guidance, than practise them as a bride under no guidance at all.

No age can be fixed for sending her to school; one girl is older at eight than another at ten, and in one home a mother can do for her daughter what in another home an equally conscientious and consecrated mother cannot do. But school instruction is as indispensable to the best development of the girl as of the boy. England has given the method of education by governesses at home a very thorough trial, and the testimony to the failure of that method is substantially unanimous. The wretched experience of the governess in the English family has been the theme of many a satirist and novelist; and under God's beneficent laws no system is good for one person if it robs or wrongs another. Improvement in female education in England began with the institution of schools for girls, which are increasingly taking the place of instruction by governesses at home. Indeed, woman's education had sunk so low under the governess system that it could not go much lower. Its condition under the Georges is thus described by a recent English writer:

"Probably at no time in our history was the education of woman generally at a lower point than in the time of George IV., whether as regent or king. Dancing, the merest smattering of drawing, French, and music were generally all that was taught a girl. As for more solid accomplishments they were, generally speaking, utterly neglected. An album fifty or sixty years old is of all dreary things the dreariest. Trumpery verses, puny little copies of a drawing-master's stock-in-trade of flowers, fruit, and impossible cottages make them up."[*]

Education is afforded not by books or lectures or even catechetical instruction. It is afforded by the attrition of mind on mind. In the school the girl brushes against her companion, is spurred on by competition, learns, on the one hand, not to be vain of her achievements, for she discovers that many are abreast of her and some in front of her; and, on the other hand, not to be disheartened or self-distrustful, for she discovers that she can keep ahead of many and in advance of some. In other words, she learns that most girls can do what she can do, and also that she can do what most girls can do, and so, by the same lesson, is disabused of her conceit, on the one hand, and of her self-distrust, on the other. The girl who is taught wholly at home naturally becomes narrow in her views, and what is worse, in her sympathies, and is liable to become self-centred in her thoughts, if not selfish in her life.

The question between public school and private school is perplexing and one to which no definite and universal answer can be given. Each has its typical faults. The private school—I speak here of the primary and grammar grades—is not apt to be as exact in its work as the public school; it is subject to cliques among the scholars and to favoritism in the teachers; wealth and family count for too much and mere personal worth for too little; the teacher not unfrequently imagines, and not always incorrectly, that to retain her pupils she must please the parents, and to please the parents she must please the children. Thus the work is too often superficial, the discipline lax, and the social spirit violated by false social standards, the standard of a debased aristocracy. On the other hand, in the public school the classes are too large; the teachers too professional; the methods too mechanical; the moral and spiritual development too much neglected; the social fellowship often morally dangerous, and the social standard that of a false democracy. With proper guardianship at home the boy may rub up against rough companions and not be injured, may even be benefited; for it will be his duty in after life to meet with all sorts and conditions of men, and the lesson is one he may well begin to learn early in life. But it is not so easy to guard the girl against a permanent vitiation of the imagination, if not of the manners and the character, from too close an intimacy in early life with coarse and vulgar natures. The wise parent will consider the school question in selecting his home, and will determine it, not by any general distinc-

[*] Thomas Markly, the Contemporary, vol. i., p. 401.

tion between public and private school, but by the actual merits of the schools immediately available for his own daughter. This involves considerable painstaking inquiry; but this chapter is not written for careless or indifferent parents. The only practical counsel for such parents is "Cease to do evil and learn to do well."

There does not seem to me to be the same difficulty in choosing between the day-school and the boarding-school. The boarding-school affords some very distinct advantages to the boy. He must live the larger part of his life outside his home—whether the first home of his parents or the later one of his own founding; for one-half to two-thirds of the waking hours of almost every active man are spent outside the walls of his own dwelling. They are spent in the struggle of life, in conflict with other men. An important lesson, therefore, which a boy has to learn, is how to get along with other boys—with friends in co-operation, with competitors in conflict, or with enemies in battle. And he can learn this lesson in the boarding-school far better than in the day-school. He is not buoyed up by the sympathy of his parents. He has not father and mother to take his part; or if they do by correspondence, they cannot help him much. He is thrown on his own resources, and must fight his own battles. The girl, on the other hand, will probably spend the major part of her life in the home. The same reason which makes the boarding-school better than the day-school for the boy—that he may learn to live the life that is outside the home—makes the day-school better than the boarding-school for the girl; for in the day-school she still retains the home-life, and it is in the home she is to spend the chief portion of her life, and for the home she is to consecrate the wealth of her nature and her endowments.

I assume this; but since this is just now a matter somewhat under debate, perhaps it will be wise to both interpret and qualify the declaration, even at the hazard of seeming, on the one hand, to repeat, or, on the other, to contradict, what I have already written.

Formerly women were educated only for the home. They were trained in the house in domestic industries—to cook, to sew, to dust, to sweep, to make a bed. They were taught, though not in the earlier stages of woman's education, to read and write and cipher, and, in the so-called higher circles of society, there were added some "accomplishments." At eighteen the education was finished. Then the accomplished maiden was "brought out." In some circles this "bringing out" was a formal act; in others it was informal; but in all it was essentially the same. The girl was ready for society because she was ready for a husband; and she was brought out into the matrimonial market that a husband might find her. If there were need, the mother became a matchmaker and scanned the market for an available husband.

It was inevitable that in the reaction against this conception and method of education, thoughtful people should have gone to the other extreme. All phases of education are, in one form or another, open to women. Nearly all vocations are open to her. Marriage is seldom mentioned as a probable destiny to the maiden. It is the fashion to educate her for a life of independence. Her honorable ambition to be equal to her brother finds its expression in an endeavor to secure the same education as he, and this leads on to the idea that she is to be educated to do the same work. A limited observation among young men and young women in their respective colleges, leads me to believe that as many women as men will be found in the senior class to have selected a profession and to be looking forward to it; while a larger proportion of young men than of young women in such colleges will be looking forward with hope to a married life. For the son is taught to expect to be married, while the daughter is taught that if marriage comes to her at all, it must come as a surprise, if not as an accident.

Independence is a very popular word in America; but independence is of no value. God has not made us to be independent of one another. The employer is dependent on the employee and the employee on the employer; the mistress on the servant and the servant on the mistress; the husband on the wife and the wife on the husband. And the more highly life is organized the more intricate and elaborate is the system of interdependence. The Robinson Crusoe state of society is the lowest and least desirable. We should not train our children to independence, but to interdependence; to bear one another's burdens; to exchange one another's services; to share one another's lives. We do so train them in everything except as regards the home. The merchant is not trained as a carpenter or a farmer, but depends on others for mechanical and agricultural products. The wise man never mixes his own home-made drugs, but calls a doctor. The layman who attempts to act on the motto "every man for his own lawyer," has a fool for a client. The congregation does not trust for religious instruction to any pious mechanic who thinks he has a message, but employs an educated preacher. God, who has set men in society, thus to exchange their services, has set them in families also. That man is best prepared for home life who is trained to be dependent on his wife for wifely counsel, cheer, and services; and that woman is best prepared for home life who is trained to be dependent on her husband for support and protection. It may be very well for the boy to learn how to sew on a button or cook a steak in case of need; but this is not his work; he is appointed to be the bread-winner of the family. It is important that the girl should have practical knowledge of affairs in general, and also some specific qualifications which she can put to useful service in bread-winning, in case of need; but under ordinary circumstances to be the bread-winner of the family is not her appointed task, and if she sacrifices training for the other, and, in most cases, really higher service, that she may acquire a money-making profession, she has made one of those unfair exchanges which is a robbery. The history of heredity makes it tolerably clear that great fathers have not often had great sons, while great sons have almost always had great mothers. "Women," says Dr. Wither Moore, "are made and meant to be, not men but mothers of men."* If this be true their education should keep probable maternity always in view. If that education is so conducted as to destroy a good mother and produce a distinguished collegian, it has been a very sorry education.

For the mother is the home-builder, and the home is the basis of civilization. The girl should be taught to look forward to marriage as her probable and natural destiny, as the boy also should be. She should be taught to regard wifehood and motherhood as the highest and most sacred of all callings. She should be habituated to think of the one as leading to the other. She should be accustomed to regard man, not as her natural foe, not as her remorseless competitor, but as her God-given pro-

* Quoted in Fortnightly, vol. xlvi., p. 503.

tector, supporter, defender, companion and friend. Much, and not too much, has been said of the duty of training men to reverence woman. But women should also be trained to reverence man; for the divine image is in both men and women, and in both alike to be revered. The too-current scoffing at the virtue of men in certain modern novels is not healthful reading for any girl; as such pictures of women as are furnished in Becky Sharp are not healthful reading for any boy. The devil is a cynic, and cynicism is of the devil. A cynical man is bad enough, but his cynicism may evaporate in the market-place and do no great damage. But the cynical woman at the head of the household poisons life at its fountain. The father and mother should so cultivate mutual respect and give expression to it, that the children shall learn respect for humanity, by the unconscious parental influence. One other lesson the daughter must learn at home, which no school can teach her—the mystery of her own womanhood. No girl should be allowed by her mother to grow up in ignorance of this sacred mystery; or be left to pick it up in fragments from her companions; or from literature, whether imaginative or scientific. From the mother the daughter should learn what marriage and what maternity mean. The instinctive shrinking of the mother from this duty is itself her preparation and ordination for its fulfilment.

The girl is now a girl no more; she is sixteen or eighteen years of age, and is just entering upon womanhood. She has gone through the kindergarten, or its home equivalent; she has gone through the primary or secondary schools, public or private; she has acquired some practical domestic skill at home; she has reached an age and has obtained acquirements which make it possible for her to enter college. Shall she go to college? and if so, to what kind of college shall she go?

The first of these questions must necessarily be answered in the negative in a vast majority of instances, for the girl as it is for the boy. Only the minority of either sex can go to college; nor is this a fact wholly to be regretted. It is an open question whether a college education is an advantage or a disadvantage to a business man. It might, without disrespect to woman, be equally regarded as an open question whether such an education affords an advantage, commensurate with the expenditure of time and money, for the woman who is not fitting herself for a profession. Without concealing my own opinion that the largest education is desirable for everyone, man or woman, who proves a capacity to receive it, it must nevertheless be conceded that there are *pros* and *cons* upon this question, that for the girl there are advantages in a college education and other advantages in a home education, and that in determining the question, Shall I send my daughter to college, these relative advantages must be compared. There are some educational advantages which can be secured only in an institution of learning, where the pupil will have the use of a large library, good scientific apparatus, highly trained teachers, experts in their several departments, and, perhaps most important of all, competition with other students. Only training in such an institution, except in the case of rare geniuses, who are independent of circumstances, will give exactness of knowledge, and the kind of intellectual power which grasps a great theme, and thinks it out to its logical conclusions—conclusions which, once obtained, can be held against all cross-questioning and all adverse arguments. But this training, unless supplemented by inherited culture, previous home training, and the habit of society, may, and probably will, leave the college graduate deficient in grace, refinement of taste, broad sympathies, social readiness, and quick capacity to use in social converse all her resources and womanly tact.

Most popular prejudices have some basis and the popular prejudice against the blue-stocking is not an exception to the rule. It indicates the dangers of an exclusively scholastic training. On the other hand, if home training develops tact and skill in the ready use of small resources, it also tends to superficiality of knowledge, inaccuracy of apprehension, and therefore of statement, and unsteadiness of purpose resulting from a well-grounded lack of self-confidence in one's imperfectly trained powers. A few exceptional women, such as Mary Somerville, have worked out for themselves scholarship despite their lack of institutional education, and a great many more women have attained social ease, elegance, and culture, although they were scholars; but in general, social culture is the result of family tradition, home training, and refined social life; scholarship is the result of institutional training; and the best womanly character combines both the social culture and the scholarship. A cultivated girl, coming from a cultivated home, need not lose and may gain in culture during her college course, and a girl who has not had early social advantages may gain something from intercourse with the various members of the faculty, the directors of the college, and those of her fellow-students who have enjoyed in early life greater social advantages. The college and university do not undertake to supply intellect or social tact and resource; they undertake only to develop them. Failing in this respect, they fail to fulfil their mission.

Let me suppose, then, that our girl of sixteen or eighteen has decided not to go to college. How can she pursue her studies at home? In offering some hints in answer to this question let me conceive myself no longer as addressing the mother but the daughter herself; for it is certain that she will get no education at home unless she is inspired by very resolute ambition to obtain it.

1. Set yourself to some systematic course or courses of reading, and convert these systematic courses of reading into courses of study. Concentrate your attention on this reading, and examine yourself afterward on it. Get enjoyment out of your reading, but do not read merely for enjoyment. "I read *hard* or not at all," says F. W. Robertson; "never skimming, never turning aside to merely interesting books." "Reading without purpose," says Bulwer Lytton, "is sauntering, not taking exercise. . . . A cottage flower gives honey to the bee, a king's garden none to the butterfly." "Read," says Lord Bacon, "not to contradict and confute, nor to believe and take for granted, nor to find talk and discourse, but to *weigh and consider.*" It is by weighing and considering that we fasten in the mind. If we do not fasten the stitch when the work is done, it is liable to ravel out. This is the value, and the only value, of that most dangerous pastime, journal keeping; it helps to cultivate the habit of concentration of attention. It is a dangerous pastime, because we are apt in it to concentrate our attention on the very things we ought to forget. How you feel Monday morning when you get up is a matter of not the slightest consequence to yourself or anyone else; what resolutions of last week you kept and what you broke, is a matter equally unimportant. A broken resolution is like a broken looking-glass; you cannot mend it, and it is a waste

of time to mourn over the pieces. Throw them away and get a new one. Write in your journal what you have seen, heard, or read ; thus compel yourself to give to yourself an account of your own acquisitions through the day or the week. Then you may burn your journal ; writing it in the page has also, you will find, written it in your memory. The mere act of formulating knowledge gives it clearness. The pen precipitates knowledge which before was held in solution. "Reading," says Lord Bacon, "maketh a full man ; conference a ready man ; and writing an exact man ; and therefore if a man writeth little, he need have a great memory." The corollary is evident ; if he have a poor memory, he needs to write much.

2. America gives a library to almost every home, in the periodical publications — the daily journal, the weekly paper, and the monthly magazine. Either the daily or the weekly newspaper furnishes in quantity abundant material for study and material in quality well worth study. The modern newspaper gives a history of human life. In it you may read the record of God's work in our own age ; and in no age has His work been grander or human progress more rapid. In France, an empire transformed into a republic, and religious liberty, which had been exiled two hundred years ago, summoned back to the home of the Huguenots ; in Spain, the Bourbon queen driven from her disgraced throne and a constitutional government borrowed from England for the land of Philip II., a noble revenge for the Spanish Armada of the sixteenth century ; Italy, which has given law to Christendom, once more clad with law ; and Rome, mother of republics, once more made republican in all but name ; Germany, united in a great empire out of heterogeneous materials and welded into a nation in the furnace of war :— these are some of the events that have taken place within the last cycle. Of these books will not tell you. For them you must go to the newspaper. What in interest and importance to us are the Gallic Campaigns of Cæsar, or the strifes between Plebeian and Aristocrat in Rome compared with this history, in which we live, and of which we form a part ? Study the newspaper ; if possible, study it with encyclopædia, with atlas, with gazetteer— but study it. No literature is worthier your study. Waste no time on the shameful scandals, the bitter political controversies, the ecclesiastical broadsword exercises, and the idle paragraph gossip. A war of words is no more dignified in a journal than on the street ; gossip is no worthier your attention because printed by *The Daily Tatler*, than when whispered by *a* daily tattler. Who was married and what she wore can be safely dismissed in a casual reading, perhaps better with none at all. But how God is working a new continent out of Africa, by the labor of a Livingstone and a Stanley, by what processes he is preparing England for a dynasty of democracy, how he is redeeming France from the curse she brought upon herself by the cruelties first of a religion without humanity, and then of a humanitarianism without religion — these are themes worthy of study, and the newspaper is the library in which to study them. There is no more fascinating intellectual occupation than watching the course of contemporaneous history. The *dénouements* of Wilkie Collins and Charles Reade are nothing to those of life's actual drama. The romance of fiction is inane by the side of the romance of facts.

3. In this study the monthly periodical will aid you. The American magazine is rightly named. "A magazine," says

Webster, "is a storehouse, a granary, a cellar, a warehouse in which anything is stored or deposited." The world has never known such storehouses of well-selected mental food as our American monthly magazines. The ablest writers of America are laid under contribution, the ablest artists are called on to add both the attractions and illuminations of the pencil, the highest prices are paid to both. The magazine skims the cream from current literature and gives it to its readers.

4. But to the journal—weekly or daily—and the magazines add some study of books. It does not require a great deal of money to gather a valuable library. The great classics are now issued in half-dollar editions, or still cheaper. Begin with what is congenial. Choose not what you *ought* to know, but what you *want* to know. Therefore let no one else choose for you. It is a rare mind that can keep itself to a course of distasteful study. It is not safe for anyone to assume, without proof, that he has a rare mind. Do not lay out for history Hume, Macaulay, and Miss Martineau, with the idea that when you have finished these fifteen volumes you will be well versed in English history. It is very true that you would be; but you will never finish them. Read Jacob Abbott's Life of Charles I. or II., or Macaulay's Pitt, or Lord Chatham, or Thomas Hughes's Alfred the Great. One thing at a time; and that thing short and simple. Putting the word *done* opposite a purpose is a wonderful incentive to a larger achievement in the next attempt. Buy a dictionary, an atlas, and if possible an encyclopædia. If you have not the money, make over an old bonnet. No harm will be done if it cultivate the habit of making over old bonnets. If this does not supply the increasing demand for increasing facilities, try some other economies. Equipped with dictionary and atlas, never pass a word the meaning of which you do not know; the name of a place the location of which you have not fixed, or a reference to an event which you do not comprehend. In invading a new territory never leave an unconquered garrison behind you.

5. Theme and tools selected, it still remains to secure time. For the best advantage this should be regular, systematic, uninterrupted. The early hours are the best, when the brain is fresh and the mind alert. To the mind and body rightly trained, half an hour before breakfast is worth an hour and a half after supper. But this requires an opportunity to shut out intrusion, which perhaps the housekeeper cannot secure; and ability to shut out the more subtle intrusion of thick, on-coming cares. Some cannot lock the door of the library; others cannot lock the door of the mind. But if time cannot be taken from one hour, take it from another; if it cannot be taken with regularity, take it when chance offers. The blacksmith's forge is not a convenient desk, but it was at the blacksmith's forge, holding his book in one hand and blowing the bellows with the other, that Elihu Burritt learned his first languages. The nursery is not the place one would choose for astronomical calculations, but it was in the nursery, beset by her children, whom she never neglected, and interrupted by callers whom she rarely refused, that Mary Somerville wrought out her "Mechanism of the Heavens," which caused her to be elected an honorary member of the Royal Astronomical Society, and put her in the first rank of the scientists of her day. A cue at the post-office is not the ideal place for study; but it was as an errand-boy at Amsterdam, standing in the long line of boys at the post-office,

often in the rain, book in hand, that Dr. Schliemann laid the foundation of his future career as the great Greek explorer of the century. Where there is a will there is a way. She who can find no time for study has little real heart for it.

6. In this study you may get material help from organizations formed for the very purpose of aiding in such work. The best known of these are probably the C. L. S. C.—Chautauqua Literary and Scientific Circle — and the Society for Promoting Studies at Home. Neither of these societies will take the place of an institution of learning. Neither will make the correspondent a scholar. But either of them will furnish her with courses of reading, put her in communication with others like-minded with herself, give her facilities in getting the best books at reasonable prices, and aid her in special difficulties by correspondence from experienced guides.

7. Finally, going from your study into the home circle, carry your newly acquired intelligence with you. Your reading of the newspaper will enable you to talk of the events of the day; and your reading of history will enable you to comprehend those events and talk intelligently of them. It is not necessary to choose between being ashamed of these resources and displaying them. It is possible simply to use them. The cultured and intelligent lady is a more interesting member of society than the ignorant one. The less she has to do with the society in which that is not true the better, unless she goes into it as a missionary.

But studies at home cannot confer the best education. That can be gained only at a collegiate institution. And if the girl has an aptitude for study, and her parents have the means, she has a right, I repeat as I have intimated above, to what the college can give her, whether she eventually chooses a professional or a married life. For the best education is not too good for a wife and mother. The more complete is this education, the better companion will she be to her husband—the companion of his higher life, and an inspiration to him to live that higher life; the better companion to her children, and the wiser guide in all their life development. It is pitiful to see a boy growing away from his mother, or a husband unconsciously separating from his wife; not because they choose to do so, nor because she chooses that they shall; but because her education has been so narrow and so superficial that she cannot share their life with them. God intended her for a home-maker; and she has become merely a housekeeper. It is rarely wise to send either boy or girl to college who has no aptitude for learning; but it is infinitely pathetic to refuse the highest education to one who longs for it. There are sadder cases of starvation than ever are reported in the newspapers.

In New York State, about 1820, Mrs. Emma Willard petitioned the Legislature for aid in establishing a school for the advanced and thorough education of women. When she filed this petition she also published her protest against the absurdity of sending ladies to college, an absurdity which she said "would strike everyone."* In 1888, out of 389 colleges in this country empowered to grant degrees, 237, or nearly two-thirds, were co-educational, and there were 207 institutions for the superior education of women exclusively, with 25,000 women students.† Oberlin College was the first of American colleges to open its doors to women, in 1833; Mount Holyoke, organized by

---

* Kate Stevens: Forum, vol. vii., p. 43.
† Mrs. A. F. Palmer: The Forum, vol. xii., p. 29, etc.

Mary Lyon avowedly to do for girls what Harvard did for boys, was, I believe, the first institution for women exclusively organized with so high an educational aim; it was founded in 1836. Out of these two movements, that of Oberlin in 1833 and that at Mount Holyoke in 1836, have grown the two forms of woman's higher education, the co-educational and the exclusive. Which shall the parent choose for his daughter?*

To this question I am not prepared to give a dogmatic reply. It has been much debated; and the two experiments are going on upon a large scale in this country, side by side.

The argument for co-education is twofold. It is contended that to-day the highest learning can be secured by women only in co-educational institutions. No woman's college possesses an endowment which compares with that of Harvard, Yale, Princeton, Columbia, and Cornell. It is not possible in half a century to secure either the money, the equipment in apparatus and library, or the personnel in the faculty; or, what is perhaps most important of all, the traditions and the atmosphere obtainable in institutions founded in colonial days. It is contended, too, that God has intended men and women to live together, or that he would not have put them together in families and in society, and that to separate them for the six or eight educational years of their lives is dangerous to their morals and inconsistent with their best and most normal development; that the exclusive school is, in brief, a remnant of the monastic institutions of a past age.

It is contended, on the other hand,

* To these a third system should, for completeness, be added—that of Radcliffe College, Barnard College, and Evelyn College, in which education is given to women separately, but by the faculties of Harvard, Columbia, and Princeton Colleges, respectively.

that in all co-educational institutions the girls are in a minority; that to separate a girl of sixteen or eighteen from her home and put her into the world, in competition with young men of all sorts of culture and character, is to submit her to abnormal conditions unparalleled in the natural life of the home; that such a life threatens to impair the delicacy of her womanhood; that it subjects her to a great moral peril, which, however small, is a peril of an awful disaster; and finally, that her physical conditions are such that intellectual competition with men is fatal to her best physical development; that the years from sixteen to twenty, or eighteen to twenty-two, are the very years when she ought to be laying up a store of nervous energy for the future life of motherhood, and that this she cannot do under the strain of life in a co-educational institution. Medical authorities as weighty as Sir Henry Maudsley, in England, and Dr. Weir Mitchell, in this country, protest against co-education on the express ground that it does thus tend to undermine the constitution of all but the most exceptional women.* Experience of such institutions as Oberlin, Cornell, and Michigan University have proved groundless the fear of danger to the moral life from co-education, but I am not equally clear that they have disproved the physical dangers; personally I should hesitate to put my own daughter under a strain which medical authorities so eminent pronounce hazardous to health. And although it is true that the best colleges for women still necessarily lack some elements of value which can be found in our greatest universities, the American colleges for women have fully kept pace with the secondary schools for women. With the choice

* See, for a full discussion of this subject, Dr. Clarke's monograph, Sex in Education.

afforded by such institutions as Bryn Mawr, Vassar, Smith, Mount Holyoke, and Wellesley, no girl need lack the highest education for want of institutional advantages in the exclusive colleges, except, possibly, in a few branches directly valuable only to a limited number of experts. It is to be added that the Annexes — Radcliffe, Evelyn, and Barnard Colleges—in which the young women do not mingle with the men in college life, offer to a great extent the facilities for special research enjoyed by the young men at Harvard, Princeton, and Columbia Colleges respectively.

As to the question of study in America or Europe, it may be dismissed in a few words. A foreign language can always be best attained in the country where it is the vernacular. And there are certain special branches of postgraduate work which can be better pursued abroad—especially in Germany — than in the United States. Thus Stuttgart offers unrivalled facilities for the study of music; Paris, Munich, and Dresden for painting; and Paris and Rome for sculpture. But, in general, the best place for either a man or a woman to prepare for American life is in America. And this is especially true of the woman, not only because she thus becomes habituated to the life which she is to lead here and acquires the knowledge which she will most need to use; but also because there are no collegiate institutions abroad which are comparable for general educational development with the best institutions in America.

From some personal study of both classes of institutions, on the ground, and with special facilities for such study, I do not hesitate to say that neither Cambridge, Oxford, Glasgow, nor Edinburgh afford better facilities for general education than Princeton, Columbia, Yale, and Harvard—I speak here only of institutions which I personally know—and Girton and Newnham do not equal in advantages for general education the best American colleges for women, from Mount Holyoke, the earliest and perhaps the most general in its work, to Bryn Mawr, the latest and perhaps the most special.

Let me, then, in a paragraph, sum up the results of this chapter.

Woman is not to be educated to be a housekeeper or a social ornament; she is not to be educated to be an appendage to man. She is to be educated to be a child of God, and the best and highest education is not too good nor too high for her. Nevertheless, the distinction of sex is to be recognized in education, and because she is to have intellectual advantages equal with those of her brother, it does not follow that the curriculum is to be identical. What is the best education for men is a question on which we have been experimenting for centuries, and the experiments are still continuing; it is not therefore strange that, after only a trifle over half a century of experiment, we are still somewhat in the dark as to the best education for women. This question I have not assumed to discuss; it must be left to be solved by the divers experiments now being conducted in England and in this country. I have confined myself to the simpler and more immediately practical question, What shall the father do for the education of his daughter, with the facilities which are available? The answer is, in brief, that he does not need to send her abroad, that the facilities are greater in the United States than in any other country; that the education should begin in the kindergarten or in kindergarten methods in the home; that under ordinary circumstances the day school with home culture added is better than the boarding-school without home culture; and either school is better than the governess; that the question between public and private schools must be determined by the character of the individual schools available; that after the daughter has reached the age of sixteen or eighteen, home studies may be made to yield culture, but not the best scholarship; that for the best scholarship the college is as essential to the girl as it is to the boy; that in choosing between a woman's college and a co-educational college, the moral hazards supposed to be involved in the latter may be disregarded, for experience does not confirm the prophecies of danger; but that the physical hazards are considerable and must be carefully guarded against; and finally, that while the woman is not to be educated merely to be a good wife and mother, but to be a noble woman, nevertheless wifehood and motherhood are to be kept constantly in mind by the parent, and by the instructor, as the probable and normal destiny of woman, exactly as in the education of the young man it is to be kept in mind that he will naturally and normally become a husband and father — the bread-winner and defender of his wife and children. For the woman is the maker of the home, and the man its supporter and protector.

X.
BOOKS AND READING.

X.

BOOKS AND READING.

By THOMAS WENTWORTH HIGGINSON.

American Culture.
Women's Clubs.
Public Libraries.
Systematic Reading.
Greece and Rome.
History.
Biography.
Essays.

Poetry.
Fiction.
Realism.
Romanticism.
The Modern Novel.
Journalism.
Magazine Work.
Personal Equation in Literature.

CHARLES DUDLEY WARNER suggested, some time since, that there was danger lest American women might come to have the monopoly of American culture. The remark did not, however, originate with him. Miss Elizabeth Peabody, who virtually introduced the kindergarten into the United States, and who lately died in her ninetieth year, says that her mother called her attention in girlhood to an article in Dennie's *Portfolio*, published in Philadelphia about 1800. This essay took the ground that women were destined to be the custodians of literature and art in America, because men would be, for a century or more, too much absorbed in material pursuits.

The vast spread of women's clubs now often recalls this prediction. Nothing makes an author so feel his responsibilities as when he receives a circular from some little town in Wyoming or Oregon—perhaps some settlement of which he never before heard and which his cyclopedia is not recent enough to include—where there is a club of women who devote an afternoon a week to the study of living authors, and desire to have a few facts as to his particular education and opinions; suggesting also, if possible, the contribution of a photograph. He knows, with an approach to certainty, that there will already have been formed, in that remote frontier post, a Shakespeare Club, a Dante Club, and a Browning Club; and that it is only through an inexhaustible feminine energy that, having thus provided for the great writers, they are now coming round to the small ones.

The rapid spread of public libraries has increased enormously the opportunity of obtaining books; and they have also been cheapened—that is, the books no longer copyrighted—almost beyond belief. A compensation, however, attends all this advantage, and the individual volume is naturally less prized than when harder to gain. It is to be observed, too, that cultivated people tend more and more to congregate in cities, and there to find many entertainments more seductive than reading. The most systematic reading ever done in this country, perhaps, was done by educated families in country towns, fifty years ago, when the evening's books afforded the recognized reward after the day's cares were over.

My mother and elder sisters, living in such a town, chose invariably a fixed subject at the beginning of winter. One year it would be British India, perhaps; another year the Kansas question, then pending; and again, Arctic or African exploration. It gave them an activity of mind and a solid fund of information, such as I rarely found in those days among the men I met in the cities. Such men were and are too busy to read anything thoroughly. Of whom do we traditionally expect mental training, if not of the legal profession? Yet President Walker, of Harvard University, once said to me, in his weighty way, "Put it down as a rule that no eminent lawyer ever reads a book."

It is in these ways that women have or had the advantage; I ought rather to say "had," because the vastly increased openings for women in professional or executive affairs, have greatly diminished the proportion of those who can give time to real reading. Then the great increase of travel and of art-knowledge draw off into other branches of cultivation those who once used books only. Margaret Fuller's reading, during her retirement at Groton in youth, "was at a rate like Gibbon's," Emerson says.

I still find that, in the public library of which I am a trustee, the greater part of valuable suggestions as to the purchase of books come from women, though probably in directions more discursive and less concentrated than the reading of the older and sedater generation. English literature has come more into prominence than formerly as a study in school and college; but it is still apt to be pursued in a technical and unenthusiastic way.

An accomplished Englishwoman in a New England village, whose children had all been educated at home by tutors and governesses, told me that she once had a curiosity, during a Teachers' Institute, to entertain several of the teachers as guests. They were a perpetual surprise to her, she said, for they knew so many things of which she and her daughters were utterly ignorant, and were ignorant of so many things which she supposed everybody to know. This was especially true of literature; there were authors whom she had thought universally familiar, yet of whom these maidens had never heard. At last one of them would perhaps say, "Oh, yes, I think there was something of his in the Fifth Reader." All literature, this good lady thought, was to them not a familiar world, but a remote region from which samples had been brought, to be displayed, as in a museum, in some part of the series of " Readers."

This thrust tells, I think, against all our recent modes of literary instruction. The technical training at Harvard College gives a very good drill in point of style; but as for any enthusiasm in regard to authors or literature, it might as well have been looked for in an ice-chest, until last year a young Scotchman came along, who had been reared at Edinburgh by Professor David Masson, and to the amazement of everybody his lectures were thronged. We must always remember that there is a vast difference between good technical training in style and an ardent love of literature.

Miss Elizabeth Peabody has also left it on record that in her mother's school, where she was taught—as were also her gifted sisters, Mrs. Horace Mann and Mrs. Nathaniel Hawthorne — young girls were systematically trained in English literature and literary analysis. Girls of ten or twelve studied Kaimes's " Elements of Criticism " and Blair's " Rhetoric." Mrs. Peabody read to them from Homer, Tasso, Addison, and the *Edinburgh Review*, and translated passages from Chaucer and Spenser into modern English. They read also the lives of learned women, like Madame Dacier, Elizabeth Carter, and Mary Somerville. To these she would doubtless have added, were she now teaching, those of Madame Roland,

Living Room.

From a Water Color by Francis Howard.

Harriet Martineau, Elizabeth Fox, Margaret Fuller Ossoli, Anna Jameson, Harriet Beecher Stowe, Madame d'Arblay, and Mrs. Piozzi. After all, the most natural and congenial diet for growing minds is the record of other minds; and if this be autobiographical, so much the better.

Madame Roland was trained by "Plutarch's Lives," a book which still remains, as Emerson said, "in the highest degree medicinal and invigorating." I think with pleasure on a certain young girl known to me in New Hampshire, dwelling in a farm-house on a mountain-side, miles away from any other house, alone with her widowed father, and bitterly disappointed at losing the winter's schooling she had expected, who has found sunshine for the winter in reading and re-reading "Plutarch's Lives." All summer she wanders fearlessly for miles and miles in the woods and on the mountain, bringing to summer visitors the largest berries, the finest trout, and the rarest orchids; and all winter she dwells in Greece and Rome with Plutarch. Is it not a liberal education? Except for the human intercourse it would give, the "academy" for which she pines could do no more, and it is probable that it would not do as much.

It is not a popular mistake which puts history and biography at the foundation of all reading; and it is only through our literary inadequacy that these studies are ever found dull. No Dutch novel can ever be so absorbing as Motley's "Dutch Republic," and Parkman gets far more out of the French and Indian period of Canada and the Northwest, than Mrs. Catherwood puts into her attractive fictions on the same themes. Nothing ever made the early revolutionary history a reality to me until I read Mrs. Hannah Winthrop's account of "the horrors of that midnight cry," as she calls it, when the women of Cambridge fled before the march of the redcoats going out of Boston to Concord, and made their way to Andover the next day, walking over the unburied bodies of the men at Lexington. It is now nearly thirty years after our great Civil War, and not a work of fiction worthy the name has yet been founded on it, while of General Grant's autobiography six hundred thousand copies have been sold. If we only knew how to write history and biography, they would be far more absorbing to us than any fiction, for nothing is naturally so interesting to us as the affairs of our fellow-men. The trouble is that this department of literature has usually been the refuge of the driest of men, who have enabled all their readers to fulfil Sidney Smith's dream of happiness in summer—to take off one's flesh and sit in one's bones.

The usual medium of introduction of women to literature, whether as readers or writers, is apt to be the daily press —a most perilous beginning. Work on the newspapers has certain great advantages; it puts one in close contact with affairs, teaches promptness and clearness of head, and shortens one's sword in action. But the avenue by which women begin is almost always that of the "personal" department, and this involves so much of petty gossip, puts such a premium on inquisitiveness and audacity, and so dulls the sense of delicacy and dignity, that it is a thing to be deprecated, in nine cases out of ten.

The young girls who stand all the long day behind the counter, unrolling goods for customers who never buy, are to me far less objects of pity than those other young girls who haunt drawing-rooms or door-steps, pencil in hand, for the least atom of gossip— harmless it may be, but if perilous, worth so much more to them—begging for lists of names, for costumes, and meeting all resistance with tears and with the assurance "but my very means of subsistence depend upon it." Worse yet, because more demoralizing, are the tales they can all tell of persons who profess to desire seclusion, and yet covertly press a five-dollar bill into the hand of the reporter who has puffed them; and it is not strange if they end in believing that there is no such thing in the universe as a sincere preference for privacy. They learn some things by the experience; they learn to open their eyes and sharpen their pens, but in all that relates to true mental training or real literary work, they are farther from success at the end of a year of this work than at the beginning. And the same drawbacks that attach to writing for newspapers, attach to making them one's main intellectual food.

With the multiplication of college-bred girls, there is the possibility of beginning higher up than formerly; but the essential drawback remains, on the intellectual side, that you are doing in journalism work which is essentially ephemeral and which, at the best, will be forgotten to-morrow. There is an old motto that what is written is permanent, *litera scripta manet;* but this is not even physically true of the newspaper, for librarians say that the very paper of which it is made is now so flimsy that it is doubtful whether it will last bodily for a hundred years.

Magazine work is, of course, more permanent, and it looks, more and more, as if the libraries of the future were to consist of vast accumulations of bound magazines in "long sets," relieved at intervals by new combinations of Poole's Indexes. Magazine work still means, for the vast majority of women, only poetry and fiction; and this can hardly surprise us when we see how well they handle this department, and how much the rising generation of men is disposed to accept the same definition.

Yet it is worth while to look back over history and see what are the books that really endure. The author of "Festus" nobly says:

"Trifles like these fill up the present time; The Iliad and the Pyramids, the past."

But there are works of mingled thought and knowledge—"Plato's Dialogues," "Plutarch's Lives," "Gibbon's Roman Empire," which remain as monumental and as little capable of displacement as a pyramid or an epic; and of work, I will not say of this kind, but in this direction, women have done as yet an insufficient share, and American women are doing relatively little. New writers of short stories appear among them, and these of marvellous fertility and skill. Our women's colleges are beginning to produce monographs, historical and scientific, which do the utmost honor to their authors. Miss Alice Fletcher has placed herself absolutely at the head of authorities in regard to the myths and observances of American Indians. Mrs. Fanny D. Bergen, for years a prisoner in a sick-room, has made some branches of folk-lore peculiarly her own. Miss Harriet W. Preston has written fresh and original studies of Roman life and literature. Mrs. Van Rensselaer has done great service as an art critic, and Mrs. Olive Thorne Miller as a writer on birds. Of course these do not exhaust the list. That there is a demand for genuine literary work on the part of women, aside from fiction, is shown by the ready welcome accorded to the writings of Miss Repplier, though these never go far below the surface, and are always strongly suggestive of paste-pot and scissors. But I do not know a woman in America who is writing anything which is, in a purely literary way, so strong and well adjusted as Margaret Fuller Ossoli's essays, of fifty years ago, upon Goethe or Sir James Mackintosh; or so rich in thought and knowledge as Miss Elizabeth Peabody's essay on Athenian and Spartan life, called "The Dorian Measure," in the volume edited by her, and named "Æsthetic Papers."

It was one source of value in the old classical training, that it gave as a basis of all knowledge the history of the two nations which gave the background of our language, our history, and our art. In the solidity and clearness of Greek literature, and in the extraordinary vigor and vastness of the national character of Rome, we find a source of interest so inexhaustible, that we must still turn to these studies, after they have grown trite through many centuries and have been dulled by much pedantry. I have never encountered so fine and terse an analysis of these salient points of the Greek and Roman types, as that found in a sketch by Margaret Fuller Ossoli, in a fragment of autobiography contained in her "Memoirs" by Emerson.

It still remains difficult for persons not trained in Greek, to know what the name of Homer, for instance, has signified to the world. Fortunately we have now a prose translation of the "Odyssey," by Professor Palmer, of Harvard University, so fresh and delightful that Homer, the narrator, seems like a man telling events which took place yesterday. But Homer's "Iliad" still remains practically untranslated, and all versions show one record of successive failure, from the sonorous lines and craggy epithets of Chapman to the tameness of Pope and Bryant. A student can really learn more of the peculiar character and scope of the "Iliad" by reading Matthew Arnold's essay on translating Homer (in his "Essays in Criticism") than by any possible study of translations.

So of Plato. No single translation of him is to be compared to that of Jowett; which is, after all, largely a paraphrase, but so admirable as to be almost better for the general reader than the original. Next to these comes the version of a few of the most important dialogues by Miss Ellen Mason, of Boston, under the title, "Socrates."

No translation from the Greek dramatists is, on the whole, so fine as that of Fitzgerald, from the "Agamemnon" of Æschylus; and as this stands at the head of Greek plays, Fitzgerald should be read, though he adds a good deal of his own, as Chapman did to Homer. Church's "Stories from Homer," and "Stories from the Greek Dramatists," and "Stories from Herodotus," are valuable, in the same way in which Lamb's "Tales from Shakespeare" is valuable, as showing how fine the legends are even when reduced to prose. For Aristophanes there is Mitchell; and for Theocritus there is Lang, who, however, belittles his author, as he does everything else, by a certain cockneyish and Leigh-Huntish flavor.

Mrs. Perry gives a charming glimpse of the domestic life of the Greeks in her "Garden of Hellas," a series of translations from the Greek "Anthology." This work is to Greek heroic literature what the Tanagra figurines are to the heroic sculpture; and even the prose versions from the "Anthology" in Bohn's series are full of charm.

To frame a course of reading is by no means my object; but I would strongly urge upon those of my readers who wish a more intimate knowledge of Greek life, to read St. John's "History of the Manners and Customs of Ancient Greece;" a book unequalled by any similar work since its day, so far as I know, in popularizing a profusion of information in regard to its theme. It is especially valuable for women, since he takes a far more favorable view of the position of women in Greece than is taken by other writers, as, for instance, by Becker in his "Charicles," which is the next best book.

I have thus dwelt upon Greek literature as the foundation and must leave further details, except to urge some divergence into the newly opened stores of the farther East; Omar Khayyám, for instance, who has suddenly leaped into the position of a new classic out of the elder world. In Max Müller's wonderful series of "Sacred Books of the East," there is an endless store of noble and elevated thought on which to ponder; and in a little book lately published, called "The Imitation of Buddha" (London: Methuen), there is a perfect casket of gems of thought and beauty, each supplied with accurate reference to the precise quarry whence it came, and of infinite value both for Christian and non-Christian minds. When we come back to the point where we can trace the European intellect down through books, we find so vast a range that we must cease to specify. But it must be remembered that the influence of what is called "the personal equation" is very large in literature, and each judgment is much influenced by the early atmosphere of the reader.

It is a characteristic thing that the only serious attempt to select the "Hundred Best Books" has come, not from a literary man, but from a man of science, Sir John Lubbock; who would not think for an instant of trusting a literary man to select for him his hundred best scientists. Lowell, who had a right to select, only chose the five leading names; that is, Homer, Dante, Cervantes, Shakespeare, and Goethe; keeping within the limits of *belles-lettres*, and omitting a figure so conspicuous as Plato. When Howells tells us of the early influence upon him of the "Vicar of Wakefield," it is impossible not to see that the influence was partly accidental; he might have hit upon some other book, with equal results.

No author, except Emerson, ever did so much to mould me as the German Jean Paul Richter, whose memoirs and translated books were attracting attention when I was eighteen; yet I now find him hard reading, except perhaps his "Levana," and he is fast falling into a very secondary place, though feebly reflected again in a book spoiled for me by the imitation, the "Chevalier di Pensieri Vani."

These instances show how very difficult it is to eliminate the personal element from the process of selection. There is a gradual "consent of the competent" in literary selection, and true indeed is the saying of old Felltham, that "there never yet was a good tongue that lacked ears to hear it;" but the ultimate decision is very slow and full of fluctuation. Think, for instance, of the changed position of Lord Bacon in the world of thought—the only chance for whom seems now to lie in the wild effort to prove that he was also Shakespeare.

A large part of the reading of modern women is necessarily in the line of fiction; indeed, the most pious of our grandmothers used to read Bunyan's "Pilgrim's Progress," and Mrs. Hannah More's "Cœlebs in Search of a Wife." The only passage now really readable in the latter book is a scene where the youthful Cœlebs, still in quest of a helpmeet, finds himself dining at the house of two ladies whose table is so very poorly furnished that he concludes his young hostesses to be proficient in Latin, at least, and very probably in Greek. He therefore resolves to look only for mental enjoyment, and asks the elder sister if she does not think Virgil the finest poet in the world. She blushes, and he decides that her modesty is equal to her condition. The question being repeated, she frankly says that she never heard of any such person. On being asked what writer she prefers, she admits that her favorite books are "Tears of Sensibility," and "Rosa Matilda," and the "Sorrows of Werter." "Yes," adds the younger sister, eagerly, "and we have read 'Perfidy Punished,' and 'Jemmy and Jenny Jessamy,' and the 'Fortunate Footman,' and the 'Illustrious Chambermaid.'" Cœlebs soon finds that he has lost as much in their opinion by his ignorance of their literary favorites, as they in his for never having heard of Virgil ; and he says, "I rose from the table with a full conviction that it is very possible for a woman to be totally ignorant of the ordinary duties of life, without knowing one word of Latin; and that her being a bad companion is no proof of her being a good economist."

More than half the obstacles to the higher education of women would have been avoided, if this invaluable passage could have been placarded in every girls' school ; and we can fairly wish for it that immortality which Mrs. More's admirer predicted for her when he wrote on the sea-sands :

> "Along the shore
> Walked Hannah More.
> Waves, let this record last!
> Sooner shall ye,
> Proud earth and sea,
> Than what she writes, be past."

As for novels, the modern novel is to this generation what the drama was to the Elizabethan age ; we must simply accept it as the now recognized mould, into which the brightest contemporary intellect is cast. It is something for woman to remember, that the distinctly modern phase of this art—though a phase perhaps already passing by—had its origin in a woman. We still turn to Jane Austen as the one person who has brought to perfection, in English, that charm which lies in what she herself defined as a little painting on ivory, two inches square. Scott himself meekly subordinated what he called his big bow-wow style to her, and she is the one woman of her age whose fame is still steadily growing.

The surpassing genius of Hawthorne kept us in America away from this type, for a time, and gave us one even higher. The so-called provincial life of America, fifty years ago, gave us masterpieces from Hawthorne such as the accumulated talent of London and Paris has striven in vain to equal, in its kind ; but, nevertheless, the pendulum has swung the other way.

It is most fortunate that we have had Howells to take the lead in the realistic direction ; but it has perhaps been unfortunate that he has identified himself, in his criticism, with a too exclusive assertion of his own department. Coleridge wrote, long since, that we should take every man's opinion of the value of what he knows, but should distrust his opinion as to the valuelessness of that which he does not know ; and all Howells's criticism of the romanticists should be taken with this allowance. On his own ground, as a writer of fiction, he is unquestionably the best result which our country has yet produced ; and it is interesting to see how he has grown by holding to his own soil, while Bret Harte and James have been impeded and dwarfed by transplantation—the latter having grown insufferably prolix, and the former having simply repeated over and over again, with increased feebleness, his early types.

Of all the English contemporary novelists, Hardy is the only one, as it seems to me, who is to be set above Howells ; since Meredith loses us in a swamp of words and personages, while

Black always paints the same group and catches the same salmon. On leaving English soil we encounter larger figures; the fancy for Maertens and Maetterlink will pass, as that for Ibsen is already passing; but there is no doubt that the strong Russian tribe will hold its own for a long time; and such novelists as Emilia Pardo Bazan in Spanish, and Matilde Serao in Italian, show the extraordinary international vigor that came in with realism, and may pass away with it.

France still remains the headquarters of delicate (and indelicate) perfection, and the marvellous skill of de Maupassant—as shown even in the translation of "The Odd Volume"—has had a distinct effect in setting a standard for all our younger American story-tellers, even if they never read a word of him. It is now impossible to have Scott's preliminary chapters of genealogies or his careful dismissal of every character at the end; we must strike at once into the story and leave it when finished; even the moral must be implied, not stated. It is curious to find a writer who is so vigorous, even to the extent of crudeness and brutality, as Hamlin Garland, and who yet begins and ends each chapter of his "Main-travelled Ways" as strongly as if he had taken de Maupassant as a model. Mary Wilkins, Sarah Orne Jewett, Julien Gordon, Viola Roseboro, Grace King, Eva Wilder McGlasson, all show the same tendency to concentration. Jean Paul thought that women could never command armies, because each would need a long paragraph into which to expand the word "Halt!" But many women now say "Forward! March!" at the beginning of a story and "Halt!" at the end of it, with a precision which shows that they can manœuvre their imaginary battalions without obstacles.

In reading poetry, our young people have curiously come back to English, after the profuse Italian and German of half a century ago. Those who now travel, speak these languages, but those who then stayed at home, used to read them. After all, however, the English is the best for us, at least; and the immense and constant study of Shakespeare, and in a minor degree of Browning, and Emerson, and Tennyson, takes us in a direction where we ought to go. It is a surprising thing that a single century has brought us to these last masters from the period when Miss Anna Seward wrote in her letters that the Scotch peasant Burns was never successful when he grew sentimental, but that an age which had produced Mason and Hayley could never want the fire of genius; or when the *Gentleman's Magazine* gravely declared "that it is trifling praise for Mrs. (Charlotte) Smith's sonnets to pronounce them superior to Shakespeare's and Milton's."

In this country a period less than a century has introduced into poetry not merely new touches of genius, but a new world of tradition and allusion. From a time when American poets duly celebrated the lark and the nightingale, which they had never heard, and when it was regarded as "a foolish affectation of the familiar" for Emerson to write of the bumblebee and Lowell of the bobolink, there is a great change to the time when, whether our poetry be good or bad, it is at least indigenous and not exotic.

It must be remembered that literature, unlike painting and sculpture, is not limited in its training to the centres of cultivation; its material is everywhere and its masterpieces can at any time be put up in a hand-bag and carried to any sod-house in Oklahoma. "After that," said Emily Dickinson to me, describing her early reading, "I made acquaintance with Shakespeare; then, of course, I needed no other book." But

I lately bought a new set of Shakespeare in thirteen little volumes (Routledge's edition), perfectly readable and portable, for the sum of two dollars and ninety-eight cents. Nay, the masterpieces travel even more cheaply than this ; and the poorest daily paper will constantly find room, amid the prize-fights and the murders, for some golden fragment of verse which purifies its polluted air. Of all gifts of genius, that of song is most universally available and transportable, and in its appreciation women have the merit of taking the lead. In the list of members lying open before me, of an influential Browning society, there appear the names of two hundred and twenty-six women and twenty-three men.

If the question be raised why it is that, with all this appreciation of poetry, women have not taken the leadership more conspicuously as poets, the question lies too deep for discussion. The essential answer is that women have still lived, up to this time, under what may be called the shadow of the harem ; that we are not yet long past the period when Monsieur de Scudéry used to lock his sister into her room to write interminable romances for him, and then put his own name on the title-page, and when the Mendelssohn family were willing that their Fanny should publish " Songs without Words " in her brother's name, but not in her own.

We must wait for a few centuries of equal education and encouragement before we begin to draw comparisons. But this is to be noted as to poetry : that this is not an age of epics, but of brief masterpieces. It is something that Elizabeth Barrett Browning wrote " Aurora Leigh," and that the English dramatist of the day, who is admitted to have most of the Elizabethan quality, Michael Field, turns out to be a woman, or, more strictly, two women.

But it is more important to consider how many of the imperishable gems of modern English poetry are by that sex also. Think of that extraordinary series of detached Scotch songstresses : Mrs. Blamire's " And Ye Shall Walk in Silk Attire ; " Lady Nairne's " Land o' the Leal ; " the twin ballads of " The Flowers of the Forest," by Mrs. Cockburn and Miss Elliot ; Jean Adams's " There's Nae Luck About the House ; " Lady Grisell Baillie's " Werena my Heart Licht," and Isa Craig Knox's " Brides of Quair."

Then, in England itself, recall the two immortal hymns, both written by heretics and sung by saints, Helen Maria Williams's " While Thee I Seek, Protecting Power," and Sarah Flower Adams's " Nearer to Thee ; " and that wonderful agnostic poem, almost a hymn, " O, May I Join the Choir Invisible," by George Eliot. Add also Jean Ingelow's " Divided," Dinah Craik's " Philip, my King," Menilla Smedley's " Little Fair Soul," and Graham R. Tomson's " Le Mauvais Larron."

It would be hard to find in modern England or Scotland an equal number of men, each of whom has written his separate masterpiece to equal these. In this country we have Julia Ward Howe's " Battle Hymn of the Republic ; " Helen Jackson's " Spinning ; " Lucy Larcom's " Hannah ; " the Jewish war-cries of Emma Lazarus, and the amazing fragments of Emily Dickinson. Tried by the test of the short poem, which is the test of to-day, it is evident that women have already proved their credentials and won their spurs.

But our American fame in pure literature must after all stand or fall, not with any woman, but with Emerson. He is our bid for long-range genius ; the one man since Goethe, as we maintain, who is entitled to a world-influence. If this position is not sustained, we are lost; and the dapper little Londoners, with their two-foot rules, can have their way with us. Happily, it is still good form to admire him; he may be classed, as Matthew Arnold classes him, with Marcus Antoninus rather than with Bacon or Shakespeare, and may still hold his own—for is not Marcus Antoninus secure? But did that philosophic prince ever take a snow-storm and subdue it forever to verse? As I write, the "blizzard" howls round the window,

"The sled and traveller stopped, the housemates sit
In a tumultuous privacy of storm."

For myself, I would rather have produced that one phrase "tumultuous privacy" and put it where it belongs, than have written every word that Matthew Arnold ever produced. For greatness and consummate expression of detached thought, I know no writer since Shakespeare who surpasses Emerson; perhaps Joubert comes the nearest to him; and Emerson might say, even more than Joubert, that if any man ever lived who made it his aim to put a whole book into a page, a whole page into a phrase, and a whole phrase into a word, he is that man. (*S'il est un homme tourmenté par la maudite ambition de mettre tout un livre dans une page, toute une page dans une phrase, et cette phrase dans un mot, c'est moi.**)

You may say that this is, after all, intellectual pemmican rather than a well-ordered meal; no matter, it is on pemmican that starving or banished men live the longest. Plato left no system; he lives by his detached thoughts, his sentences. The successive system-makers die and are forgotten; Herbert Spencer is rapidly following in the path of the once autocratic Bacon and Coleridge and Schelling and Hegel and Cousin and Buckle; but the man who lodges in the memory of man a phrase which is the summary of a thought, has accomplished something as indestructible as the pyramids. Of these too it might be said that they are detached from one another and lead nowhere. The man or woman who has read Emerson has received a liberal education.

* Pensées de J. Joubert, p. 8.

[*For list of books see section on* BOOKS AND READING *in the* APPENDIX—SUPPLEMENTARY INFORMATION.]

XI.

THE ART OF TRAVEL.

XI.

THE ART OF TRAVEL.

By ELIZABETH BISLAND.

The Matter of Packing.
Modern Trunks and Dressing-cases.
Clothing and Preparations.
Comfort on the Train.
Seasickness and its Treatment.
Travelling in the Tropics.

Safety in Travelling Alone.
Guides, Money, and Tickets.
Custom Officials and their Treatment.
Living in Lodgings Abroad.
Economical Travelling.
The Value of Coolness.

THERE is a right way and a wrong way of doing everything, and the difference between the right way and the wrong way in travel is the whole space which lies between pleasure and disappointment. The proper method of travel is an art which may be learned perhaps only by personal experience, and some one else's personal experience is, on the whole, the cheaper sort. One personal experience can be summed up in a pair of phrases, which, rightly used, have the value of those magic amulets benignant witches presented to young heroes when starting out to see the world, and which, applied to all difficulties, at once solved or removed them.

The first of these potential phrases is, "When in doubt use commonsense." The second grows naturally out of it : "Do in Rome as do the Romans." In these two sayings lies the whole art of agreeable travelling.

We will suppose that the woman who travels does so for pleasure. It is sometimes, of course, of necessity ; but there is, because of that, no need that this necessity should be made more unpleasant than it must be.

This chapter is primarily written for the use of the woman of moderate means who travels for the pleasure to be derived from novel sights and experiences, and to gratify that "intelligent curiosity" which Dr. Johnson believed was the very root of wisdom and culture. Those to whom economy is of no importance need little instruction. In every country there is a method of attaining a reasonable degree of comfort, and even something resembling luxury, at very moderate cost, if only a little pains is expended in the search for it, and a few words of suggestion—the personal experience of another in short—may make that search briefer and surer of attaining its end.

So much of the pleasure of travel depends upon the physical condition of the traveller that such a paper as this had best begin with a few suggestions under the head of "Preparations." It is a difficult prescription to follow, but a good one, that one should begin a journey fresh and unfatigued. Packing should be well in hand twenty-four hours previous to setting out, and, under ordinary circumstances, a little forethought will obviate that furious hurry and scurry at the last moment which leaves the nerves tingling with excitement.

The question of luggage is to be governed, of course, by such considerations as the length of absence, the season, and one's destination. My own opinion and experience is that a woman can travel comfortably to any distance, and to any climate, with one trunk, a dressing-bag, and a shawl-strap. Very recently a great advance has been made in the matter of trunks, and already one begins to look back on one's contentment with the bungling old boxes full of trays as a piece of quite phenomenal ignorance. This of weightless celluloid, made in an excellent imitation of tortoise-shell or amber, replacing the heavy glass and silver which made a dressing-case a burden to be avoided at any cost. Now that the objection of weight is removed, the dressing-bag, with its compact toilet appliances, is quite indispensable to comfort in travel. It

A Bureau Trunk.

new box has a hinged top, which, being lifted, exposes a series of drawers both large and small, so that instead of struggling with refractory trays and breaking one's back in search of some object that has, in a spirit of pure wantonness, descended into the depths at the instant when most needed, one whips out the shallow drawers and in a twinkling can pounce upon the most elusive and wily of one's possessions. The newest dressing-bag also is a great improvement over any previous efforts in this line; the fittings being wrought should contain hair-brush and comb, clothes-brush, nail-brush, and tooth-brush, soap-case, cologne-bottle, hair-pin case, scissors, button-hook, pen-knife, portfolio, and travelling ink-stand. To these should be added one of the small morocco sewing-cases to be found at the dry goods shops, with thimble, needles, glove and shoe buttons, sewing-silk, thread, and tapes, as well as a few hooks and eyes. A pin-cushion filled with safety-pins, hat-pins, and dressing-pins, black and white, added to a sponge-bag, com-

The Question of Luggage.

plete the list and prepare one to meet any emergency with calmness. These dressing-cases are somewhat more costly than the ordinary bag, but they are usually of good material and therefore wear well, and the saving in time, and the comfort of knowing one's belongings are tidy and ready to hand, is worth the extra cost ten times over. Heretofore, because of being obliged to carry all one's own hand-luggage in this country, the dressing-case has not been popular with us; but this difficulty of weight removed, no wise or skilled traveller will be without so great an addition to her convenience.

A medium-sized bag, convenient for a woman's handling, will have space as well for a night-dress, a pair of soft, heelless dressing-slippers, and a light dressing-gown—China silk in summer time, or soft wool for winter. A gray Chudda shawl of large size can be cut into such a dressing-gown, and is so soft and compressible that it occupies but little space.

The shawl-strap should contain an ulster, travelling-rug, overshoes, and umbrella. Another matter to be considered in preparing for comfort in travel is the possession of a definite place for everything, so that everything may be found in its place the instant it is wanted. Therefore cases for handkerchiefs, gloves, and veils, bags for shoes and for soiled linen, should all be provided, and every article being carefully laid away in its proper receptacle after using, not only insures against losses that cannot be repaired at critical moments, and frantic searches for strayed belongings, but keeps one's boxes and clothes dainty and fresh.

By natural sequence the next point to be considered is that of toilets. There is no need, in addressing American women, to inveigh against frowsy unkemptness in travelling—their tendency as a rule is toward "over-smartness;" but where a question of the quantity and weight of luggage is to be dealt with, it may be worth while to plan how an immaculate appearance and comfort are to be maintained out of trunks of small compass.

A man who had circled the globe half a dozen times, and travelled to the obscurest corners of it, declared his experience persuaded him that the pleasantest way was to carry everything he might by any remote possibility desire, and that wherever transportation grew difficult, he established a sort of *dépôt* of supply from which the needs of special expenditures were extracted, and the main army of trunks lay there until a *détour* was made to recover them or the ubiquitous telegram went back and fetched them round by another route. It was this same man of whom his travelling companions related that he was invariably discovered at moments of the most violent turmoil calmly—like Charlotte of frugal memory—cutting sandwiches, which later always fitted into some perfectly unforeseen exigency of appetite, and caused his fellow-travellers to rise up and bless him. There is much to be said for his point of view, but, after all, it has a tendency, as have most agreeable luxuries, to become expensive. Therefore, to return to the limited luggage question, the economist must consider space.

The many women who wear silk or wool tricot undergarments find them easily carried in small compass. Those who do not like this form of dress will discover that for long journeys there is nothing so satisfactory for underwear as silk. The original cost is rather large, but it proves an economy in the end, as clothes of the soft India (not China) silk are so easily laundered—requiring no starch—shed, instead of gathering, dust; do not conduct changes of temperature; and, keeping the body at an even temperature, are the greatest safeguards against colds. Nothing can be a greater luxury, in sea-sickness, or after a hot day in the cars, than to slip for the night into a silky garment which neither heats nor chills the skin, nor retains the dust and wrinkles of a previous wearing, as would cambric or linen.

this convenience, if intended for hard usage, is a bengaline silk, which does not crumple, and, like Mrs. Primrose's wedding-gown, has stamina enough to carry it over into another generation. With a *pièce de résistance* of this sort, a few of the pretty accessories of ribbon, velvet, and lace that the shops furnish

An English Sleeping-Car.

The ideal travelling gown is undoubtedly a very plain tailor skirt and coat of some neutral-tinted serge or tweed, with a silk bodice, as it can stand the stress of weather, of sea-damps, and railway dust, is easy of fit, and can be adapted to the tropics by removing the coat, or adjusted to the arctic zone by the addition of furs. A simple and satisfactory adjunct is a black silk dress with two bodices—one adapted for evening. The best form of ready-made, will supply all the variety of costume needed in travel.

Most of the travelling done within our borders is, of necessity, on the railway, and despite our persistent self-glorification in this very matter, we have—in many things—much to learn from Europe. The Continental *wagonslits*, and the English sleeping-cars are in several respects improvements upon our own. For one thing they avoid that promiscuity which so greatly shocks the foreigner travelling in America. In Germany one may secure a first-class carriage for one's self at an expense no greater than that of a whole section in a sleeping-car, and attached to this is a private dressing-room with all conveniences. Here one is as secluded as in one's own bedroom, and instead of futile wrestlings in the curtained pigeon-hole provided in American cars, one dresses and undresses at one's ease, with plenty of space and no possibility of intrusion. All the through-trains leaving Paris for Constantinople, Vienna, Berlin, Rome, and Nice are provided with *wagons-lits*, cars which have a narrow passage-way upon one side, upon which opens a series of small bedrooms, securing the privacy for many that American cars only offer to the one party rich enough or lucky enough to secure the single " state-room " at the end of the sleeper.

While few of the Continental trains have a dining-car attached, those without one are provided with a small kitchen at the end of the *wagon-lit*, where the guard concocts pleasant little meals, largely made of fruit, salads, cheese, and good crusty loaves, and serves them in each room upon movable tables.

The *trains de luxe* between Calais and Paris, between London and Dover, and London and Edinburgh, have beautiful dining arrangements, and the saloon carriages are spacious and luxurious beyond any comparison with the best we have to offer. Another point deserving mention in the European trains is the studied simplicity of the decorations. Smooth, handsome blue broadcloth takes the place of stuffy plush, and the tempest of gilded ornamentations is conspicuous by its delightful absence.

In making long trips in England or on the Continent it is as well that the woman travelling alone should go to the expense of taking first-class tickets to secure the advantages of the added luxury and privacy ; but for all journeys of moderate length—and very few are as long as twelve hours—second class is quite good enough and a great deal cheaper. For journeys of an hour or two many English people go third class, since the carriages in this class are perfectly clean and fairly comfortable, and one is not likely to suffer any inconvenience from the manners of one's fellow-travellers, which are almost without exception quiet and decent. On the Continent a woman unaccompanied had better content herself with the economy of second class, as her experiences might not be agreeable in the third.

Wherever one may be fated to spend any length of time in land travel it is best to follow certain rules. One of these is to be sure of plenty of fresh air. In our own country this is sometimes made difficult by the over-heating of cars, the double windows, and the lack of proper ventilation ; while in Europe the loosely fitting sashes and lack of artificial warmth gives one at times too much of even that good thing. An excellent practice is to get out wherever a stop of more than a few minutes is made and walk briskly, filling the lungs and stirring the blood. In almost all cases where a traveller finds herself unable to sleep in the cars the difficulty may be corrected by a supply of fresh air.

A good plan is to undress entirely, as at

home, slipping over the night-gown the loose silk or wool dressing-gown, thus protecting one's self against danger of colds, and being prepared in case of accident. Have the berth made up with the pillow at the end toward the front of the car, and no matter how cold the weather, open the window next the feet a little to the outer air—a pencil or a folded newspaper will admit enough—covering the body, and particularly the feet, very warmly. In this way the air enters at the lower end of the bed only and circulates freely without making a draught. The result of all which is that one's body being quite free from compression of clothes, and the lungs fed with adequate oxygen, one wakes in the morning fresh and vigorous after healthful sleep, and is prepared for the new day's trials or pleasures. A woman who makes a five days' journey in a sleeping-car without fatigue or discomfort thus describes her plan for her toilet. She says: "One of the causes of so much wretchedness in travel is lack of a morning bath, and that, too, when one particularly needs it—all dusty and stuffy from railway grime! My method is this: Before going to bed I look around the car. If there are only a few women, I lie in bed late and let them quite finish with the dressing-

A Sleeper on a Vestibuled Train.

room so that when I do get up I may have it to myself. If there are many, I get up a full hour earlier than any of them are likely to rise — even five o'clock is better than an uncomfortable or hurried toilet, which sets me wrong for the whole day. I slip my skirt and coat over my dressing-gown, knot a lace scarf I always carry over my unbrushed head, make a neat parcel of my other clothes, and with these and my bag I seek the toilet-room. Here I lock myself in, give my hair a good brushing to rid it of cinders, fill the basin and add some cologne to the water, and by means of hanging every thing out of the way, a towel spread on the floor, and a sponge, manage to achieve a bath from head to foot. Then I dress quietly and completely to the last pin, and am so refreshed and comforted that I am ready for anything that may happen. I can do it all in half an hour, too, by dint of having everything to my hand, and putting each thing where it belongs the moment I have finished using it, so that there has to be no general packing up at the end. But I won't be hurried, and it throws me into spasms of nervous rage if impatient women come and bang on the door while I am within — which is why I either rise early or lie late, in order to combine a toilet and peace of mind."

There are now but few parts of this country in which every convenience is not supplied by the public conveyances. Some of the remoter parts of Florida, where journeys must be made by boat, drive one to good-humor and philosophy as one's only resource; and to Mexico one must go provided with many of the comforts ordinarily supplied in the United States. One of these comforts is a portable bath-tub, since hotels in the obscurer parts do not afford toilet appliances.

Of late years the travel to Alaska has grown to such an extent that the tourist may look for perfect comfort by train and steamer, since wherever the demand for convenience is great, the supply meets it.

American Dining-Car.

To take, for instance, what is called "The Square Tour"—which unfortunately is less frequently made by Americans than by visiting foreigners—will prove the universal comfort of travel in this country, and the possibility of being absent for months with the limited luggage specified. Leaving New York on the Florida train the first of March, it is possible to see—with a stop-over ticket—all the towns of importance along the Southern Atlantic coast within a week, and in all will be found good hotels, and the climate will vary so little that the removal or addition of a coat will be all that is required. Florida is dotted with admirable hostelries within easy journeys of one another, and every point of interest is reached by fairly comfortable means. Here one will be obliged to add the coat mornings and evenings while near the sea-coast, but will permanently abandon it while inland or by the waters of the Gulf.

New Orleans may be reached by rail, but a charming route is across the Gulf by steamer, and up through the mouth of the Mississippi. Here one takes the Southern Pacific to California, seeing Texas *en passant*, and slowly climbs the Western coast by local lines, seeing the beautiful fruit ranches of the South, Los Angeles, Sacramento, San Francisco, Puget Sound, and finally takes the steamer to Alaska, reaching there about June 1st. Returning, a landing is made at Victoria, and thence by Canadian Pacific through the wildest and most beautiful railway route in the world to Montreal. From there more railroading brings one to the Lakes, to Chicago, to Buffalo, Niagara Falls, and New York by July 1st. By this process there has been no exposure either to extreme heat or cold, nor any rough methods of travel in a journey of four months, that gives one a most comprehensive knowledge of the North American continent.

The green spectre of sea-sickness looms up for most women at the very mention of "the oceans of say" to be faced when they venture off of their own continent, and the whole art of travelling by water is, for eight out of

The Deck Steward.

ten, simply a question of evading or assuaging those insufferable pangs. Long and severe experience has proved to most sufferers that the advice to struggle against those painful and surging emotions is but the brutal egoism and lack of sympathy of those who know not such sufferings because of their own internal arrangements

One important precaution is to see that the system is clear, and the liver active, at least a week before sailing. Then, if it be possible, a voyage should not be begun in a state of nervous fatigue. Perhaps the most important advice is to go to bed at once, before the "jobbling of the ocean" awakes a single qualm. Arrange all one's be-

More Comfortable on Deck.

being set on an even keel. There is on earth perhaps no anguish so bitter, and none which meets with so little true tenderness and comprehension as sea-sickness. To escape without ribald mockery is more than most can hope.

It is useless to suggest a remedy, for the cure of one is the doubled agony of another, and only precautions and palliations are worth suggesting, since the cure for sea-sickness is like salvation, each must find it for himself.

longings snugly and handily. Undress completely and get into bed, with a book near by in case of *ennui*, and some clean, faint-flavored toilet-water ready for use. It is better not to read, but to go to sleep at once, generally an easy task after the fatigues of preparation and farewell. With no compression of garments, stretched at full length, with the body warm and as much fresh air as is attainable, it is just possible one may escape the tendency to nausea, which once set up is so hard to conquer. For the first twenty-four hours all soups and hot drinks, wines, lemonades, and the like, should be avoided ; the diet being confined to cold, dry meats, and dry biscuits. By strict observance of these rules I myself, who have descended all the seven rounds of the hell of seasickness, am enabled to make a voyage with only moderate discomfort, and even to enjoy life by the third or fourth day. Should the sorrows of the sea overtake one in spite of all precautions, cracked ice and bromides are the most simple and effective palliatives. A cold salt-bath is an excellent aid to recovery when the worst of the nausea has passed and the interval of excessive languor and depression supervenes. It requires courage to undertake it, but the result is worth the effort—the best way being to step into a warm bath, and sponge freely with cold water as it runs from the cock. This shortens by many hours that period of reaction which is almost as painful as the more active illness.

A Novel Method of Landing Passengers at Natal, South Africa.

These remedies are necessary only upon such wicked seas as are to be found in the North Atlantic and Pacific, or in the stormy channels surrounding England. The beautiful tropic waters about the West and East Indies are— in the winter at least, when travellers for pleasure make their acquaintance— smooth lakes without even the long heave and pulse of our calmest summer seas. The Peninsular and Oriental steamships, from the moment they enter the Suez Canal until they finish their voyage at Hong Kong, a whole month later, might carry a glass full of water without even spilling a drop. Consequently, for one of the Eastern journeys, which are every day becoming more popular, the preparations are quite dissimilar from those undertaken for a trip to Europe. As there is no steerage travel to the East, the whole large, comfortable bed-chambers, with iron bedsteads, and a long divan on the sea side, where a great section of the ship opens outward, forming an awning from the sun but letting in all the coolness of the sea. The bathrooms are spacious, and the great marble tubs, filled with cold salt water, offer the most irresistible temptation in that hot atmosphere.

Promenade Deck of an Orient Liner.

vessel is given up to the comfort of the first-cabin passengers. Decks are wide and steady enough for very agreeable moonlit dances and strolls. Little afternoon tea-tables make their appearance among the clusters of Bombay lounging-chairs, where young women in muslins and straw hats pour tea for young men in white duck, with silk sashes replacing their waistcoats. The saloons are adorned with growing palms, and occasionally a blooming orchid plant or two hang among the canaries' cages. The state-rooms are

At half-past six in the morning a white-capped maid comes with tea or coffee, a biscuit and fruit. It may be against all one's good American habits to eat at that hour and in bed, but a little further knowledge will prove here, as elsewhere, it is best to follow the example of those who have had long knowledge of the needs of a climate. If one refuses to adapt one's self to this custom, and insists upon doing in Rome as the Americans do, the result will be a feeling of great exhaustion after dressing that robs one of appetite for breakfast and spoils the day. In the tropics less nourishment is needed than in temperate zones, but it must be taken at much more frequent intervals; and after the heavy relaxed sleep of those moist, warm nights, the body requires the stimulus of food before undertaking any exertion. The same advice applies to the afternoon siesta. One may have had a most vigorous scorn of the indolence implied by sleep in the daytime, yet between three and four o'clock an almost irresistible drowsiness will overtake one, and the wise voyager succumbs to Nature's hint of her needs.

It cannot be too much urged upon the traveller by land or by water, in temperate or tropic zone, that there should be no chance for exercise neglected. The change of air induces, as a rule, a more vigorous appetite, and the enforced sluggishness of long days on board vessel and car makes it difficult for the digestion to cope with its added task, the result being disorders which are apt to rob one of all pleasure and predispose one to colds and infection.

These suggestions apply to the case of the woman journeying under the escort of what is known as her natural protector, and treat principally of her physical comfort and well-being; but for the woman who sets forth into the world alone there are many matters still to be considered.

To the indolent, the timid, and the inexperienced among women there is something extremely terrifying in the thought of lonely wanderings, unaccompanied by some man to save trouble and bear the blame of mishaps; but there is, in reality, nothing to prevent a woman from seeing every civilized, and even semi-civilized, country in the world without other protection than her own modesty and good sense. There is a vast amount of chivalry and tenderness distributed in the hearts of men, and while the woman who goes guarded may be quite unaware of it, because nothing in her case calls it forth, the chivalry is there, and ready for almost unlimited draughts upon its patience, devotion, and sympathy. In all accidents by land or water the first thought of those in authority is the safety of the women, and while all yet goes smoothly the very defencelessness of a lonely woman appears to put every man upon his honor, and make him feel, in a certain sense, responsible for her comfort and enjoyment. That women travelling alone have at times painful experiences cannot be denied, but I boldly assert that in nine cases out of ten it is due wholly and solely to their own fault. A few have been so warned against the wiles of a wicked world that they are unable to discriminate between an honest desire to be of use and mere vulgar effrontery, and reward courteous attentions with suspicious rudeness. A still greater number look upon their own needs and discomforts as matters of cosmical importance, before which the affairs of the universe—notably the affairs of the masculine half—should give way; and their petulance, peevishness, and aggressive assumptions drive even the meekest of their fellow-travellers into open revolt. Still another cause of difficulty is an embarrassed timidity in cases where instant repression is needed; and a lack of courageous dignity in the face of insolence.

The woman who is cool-headed, courteous, and self-reliant, can travel around the world in every direction and find no word or look to daunt or distress her. Indeed if her manners be sweetly gracious and dignified she will find all lands full of brave cavaliers who will spring to gratify her smallest request, who will see and meet her needs before they are put into words, and who cheerfully will imperil and even yield up their lives in her defence and to insure her safety.

The garment of modest purity is as magic a defence to-day as when Una wore it, and the sight of a good woman who needs their aid wakens in even bad men some part of the spirit of a Bayard. The woman who knows how to accept a favor frankly and without tiresome protest, and is at the same time gratefully aware that the service is a favor and not a duty, makes every travelling man her faithful servitor.

A cool and nimble wit is generally the best defence against vulgar aggression, and achieves its end more neatly than would angry protest.

A very young girl was once making a long railway journey alone, and to amuse her solitude dabbled a little in an attempt at literature. She was aware that a man in the opposite section of the sleeping-car was endeavoring to attract her attention, but she kept her head bent over her manuscript and gave no sign of being aware of his existence. Finally, all his efforts failing, he crossed the aisle between them and laid his visiting card on the adjustable table before her.

"That's my name, miss," he said, and

The Ladies' Saloon of a Hamburg Steamer.

added, with insinuating familiarity, "I guess we're two of a kind."

The girl regarded the card distantly, and raising her eyes to his face, coolly contemplated it during several minutes of silence.

"Really!" she replied at last, "you flatter me. In what respect may I hope to resemble you?"

"Oh," stammered the small cad, getting red and embarrassed beneath her calm gaze, "you seem to be a writer, and I am one myself; I'm a reporter.

"Guess we're a pair of Bohemians, ain't we?"

"You mean *that?*" she answered politely, glancing at the thirty or forty pages of manuscript she had covered. "I fear it has misled you. That is a letter to my husband. Good-morning!" And she quietly dotted an i, and went on with her work. The car heard her and understood, and the car smiled satirically at the unmatched Bohemian, who sneaked away to the smoker and was seen no more by daylight in his seat.

Impertinence is not the only matter with which the solitary woman must deal; she must be alert, accurate, and quick-witted, and while she is sure to find assistance she must act as if she did not count upon it, and take all possible precautions for herself.

It is well to secure one's seats, sleeping-berth, or state-room well in advance, and trust nothing to luck. Beginning early and having, therefore, the power of choice, select, if possible, for a day's journey, seats in the centre of the car, or if for the night, a berth near the ladies' toilet-room. Take an outside state-room; the air to be had through the port-hole, whenever the sea is calm enough to admit of opening it, is worth much in moments of fatigue or nausea.

Take enough hand-luggage to be quite comfortable. Some one can always be found to carry it for a very small tip. Do not sit down and wait to be told when things happen and where all conveniences are situated. A few judicious inquiries will ascertain the hours of meals, the locality of the bath-room, what rules and regulations must be observed, and what privileges are to be had. Be ready to take prompt advantage of any opportunity for amusement, and be profoundly versed in the gentle science of Baedeker and Murray.

Perhaps this is a point at which the whole question of tips might be appropriately dealt with. All through Europe they are expected, but a regular tariff is fixed, and it is not necessary to give more than is the custom. Some few independent souls refuse to recognize the demand at all, but they are always badly served. In very many cases those who serve them are not liberally paid by their employers because of the extra fund supposed to be contributed by the traveller, and she who refuses to tip is in reality receiving services gratuitously from the poor employee. On long sea-voyages it is customary to give one's own stewardess five dollars when special services are asked, or two and a half dollars when no particular demands are made on her time. About the same is given the table steward, and one dollar to the deck steward—but this proportion may alter according to the amount of service rendered. It is a wise precaution and insures more care and consideration if the tipper gives the stewardess a small instalment of the whole fee during the first day out, intimating that more is to follow on reaching port.

In England the cabmen expect a gratuity of two pence, in France two big sous. Six pence are ample for the transportation of luggage or any small services from the guard on railway trains in England; half a franc in France. In the expensive restaurants a shilling in London and a franc in Paris is sufficiently munificent, while in such places as the Maison Duval, or the A. B. C. restaurants, two sous, or two pence, are quite enough.

There are, for the solitary woman traveller, a number of tourists' agencies —such as Cook's, Gaze's, and Low's,— whose branches reach to over beyond Jordan, and are established among even the dwellers in Mesopotamia. These for a very small percentage will buy tickets, check and transfer luggage,

In the Grand Saloon of an Ocean Steamer.

furnish all useful and useless information, and do one's banking, besides supplying valuable aid in finding satisfactory lodgings.

It is at the offices of these agencies that one may change bank-notes most conveniently and secure fresh currency of the different countries in which one is sojourning. In carrying large sums it is better to rely upon the letter of credit on some prominent and trustworthy bank; but where the sum to be used in travelling is moderate, as convenient a way as any is to carry a few Bank of England notes, and deposit these as an account at one of the tourist agencies, or at a bank, and draw checks against it. Say that one means to go abroad for two months or three, and means to limit one's expenses to a few modest hundreds; then the simplest and least troublesome fashion of arranging the matter is to procure Bank of England notes for that sum. Get a letter from a trustworthy tourist agency to its office in London or Paris containing an introduction. On arriving one has only to present the letter and the money, deposit the latter, and get a sheaf of checks in return, and a needed supply of foreign gold and silver. In moving from one large city to another, it is necessary only to carry a letter from the agency to its bureau in the new capital, and there, the office having been privately notified of the original deposit, the checks are again honored. For short tours from the base of supply a small amount of gold is the most convenient form of provision.

It is well that the woman travelling alone should always deposit her valuables in the safe of the hotel, being sure to take a receipt for them. In the daytime, and while on the cars at night, a soft silk bag about the neck is the best receptacle for large sums. It is now so easy to change one's money, and so many conveniences are provided for travellers in this respect that it requires but little effort to obtain the current coin of the realm where one may happen to be, and in all countries English gold and bank-notes are honored, as they evidently stand high in the estimation of the whole world.

The Gang-plank—just before sailing.

There is much diversity of opinion and experience in the matter of guides and couriers, but a good rule seems to be that in countries where one understands the language they are unnecessary, while in localities where the language is absolutely unknown, one is apt to miss many pleasures for lack of an interpreter. In England, France, Germany, Italy, and Spain, the routes are so well known and so constantly travelled, that an energetic, enterprising traveller can see all that is to be seen without aid ; but in Norway and Sweden, Russia, Holland, and Turkey, in Egypt, and in Japan, where the languages are so difficult that even the few phrases needed by the traveller are more troublesome to acquire than the result is worth, a guide and interpreter are quite necessary. In India English is so generally spoken that an American woman does not find herself at a disadvantage.

It is the gentleman who sits at the receipt of custom who fills with vague alarm many a gentle female soul, but experience usually robs him of all terrors. Strangely enough, England, which is supposed to be entirely free from

The End of the Voyage.

An English Guard.

any protective measures, is a most troublesome port to enter. Brandy, cologne, silver plate, tobacco, and the Tauchnitz novels are not permitted to enter the tight little island, and it is generally some well-behaved, eminently conventional matron who is most sharply questioned as to the presence of tobacco and brandy in her trunks, and has her stockings, underlinen, and bonnets tossed madly about in the search for contraband means of dissipation. On the Continent more discrimination is shown, and for the most part the officers of the *douane* discern at a glance whether one is likely to have diamonds concealed in one's boot-heels, or owes the rich contours of one's figure to tightly rolled consignments of lace. The slightest reluctance to have one's belongings searched, however, at once arouses suspicion, and only the cheerful and prompt handing over of keys achieves the much-to-be-desired mere lifting and closing of the lid. My own experience leads me to believe that the most courteous and kindly of customs officials are those in the port of New York—and that even under the McKinley tariff regulations; but memory preserves in the amber of gratitude one gentle-hearted Gaul, who, looking into the weary eyes of a lonely woman newly arrived in Paris at eight o'clock in the evening, was moved to real compassion and chalked with his mystic sign four large boxes without word or question.

Here we have the lonely female well on her journey's way at last. She having read, marked, learned, and inwardly digested the luminous wisdom, and didactic advice of the foregoing lines, has travelled by land and sea in great comfort, luxury, and safety, and now—triumphantly vindicating the innocence of her luggage from accusations of brandy and chewing tobacco—stands inside the customs barrier of a foreign land. For the sake of extreme probability we shall call this port Liverpool.

It is explained to her at the railway station how a merciful English company has attached, for the convenience of desperately homesick Yankees, a Pullman car to the train, and that, finding themselves only recovered from *mal de mer* to fall victims to *mal du pays* —passing from naupathia to nostalgia —these expatriated Americans welcome this token of home with tears of joy. She may have a place there—if she wishes.

No, indeed! Had she been so irresistibly enamoured of things at home she would have stayed there. She has come away for change, and means to see life entirely from a foreign point of view. She will go first-class in one of the little English carriages, though she knows that "only dukes, fools, and Americans go first-class." This is a small single luxury she is treating herself to.

rying about on the windy docks since breakfast. She removes her hat, recoifs her hair, and sponges her face with cologne. Doubling up the arms that divide the long divan into chairs, she heaps her rugs into a semblance of sofa cushions by the window and reclines at length, with her book, the

An English Dining-Car.

"Here's half-a-crown, guard, and I hope I shan't be disturbed. And please wire to Lincoln that I want a hot luncheon, with wine."

"Yes, mem. Thanky, mem. It shall be attended to." He locks the door, and the wily woman is alone in a large, clean, blue boudoir, with perfect privacy and plenty of space. No one can enter and no one see the bit of a toilet she sets about making. The steamer arrived early, and she has been wor-

lovely English scenery, and an occasional nap to help her through the hours. Here is Lincoln. A man comes to the carriage-window and hands in a little luncheon hamper, for which he is paid another half-crown. The train slides out of the station and the traveller leisurely prepares for her meal. The little hamper contains a half-pint of table claret with the cork half-drawn, a hot English chop with two potatoes and some green vegetables, a salad, a piece of cheese, bread and fruit, besides a knife, fork, glass, napkin, pepper, and salt. She eats at her ease, and when done closes all the remains into the basket and slips it under the seat. It is no further concern of hers. The company has its agents to attend to the matter of returned empties.

"It may be soothing to one's homesickness to come to London in a Pullman," she says to herself, "but it certainly is not so comfortable nor so novel."

Arrived at Charing Cross she waits to see her trunks come out of the luggage-van. All the heavier pieces are left in the luggage office to be called for, and the things very necessary for the moment are heaped on the roof of a hansom. She is too wise to go to one of the great caravansaries affected by the average travelling American. The huge hotels are costly everywhere, and she drives to Trafalgar Square to see the tourists' agent, bank her letter of credit, and get the address of some of the smaller hotels. They can recommend some dignified hostelries of the simpler sort near to Piccadilly, or if she wishes to be very economical there are pleasant small hotels on the Embankment, close to Charing Cross, where she may have bed, breakfast, and bath for six shillings and can make her other meals cost what she chooses.

She decides upon the latter, since she means only to spend the night there, and finds it clean, simple, and very comfortable. Once installed she immediately sets off for Bond Street, to shop, to put herself in touch with all the delicious novelty of a foreign world, and to drink a cup of tea in one of the small tea-shops. To-morrow, armed with a list of advertisements cut from *The Times*, she sets out early to look for lodgings, and wanders South Kensingtonwards in her search. In a tiny street opening upon a garden square full of trees and flowers she

An English Railway Carriage, Midland Road. First and Third Class and Luggage Compartments.

comes upon the very thing she needs—a bright, fresh, little drawing-room, hung and upholstered in chintz, an equally pleasant small dining-room, a bedroom fitted with brass bedstead and every appointment for comfort, and a tidy, well-arranged bath. This is to be had at four pounds a week, including lights and all attendance. She could have found cheaper accommodations if she had been content with merely sitting-room and bedroom, but meaning to present letters of introduction she wishes to have agreeable quarters in which to receive. She is careful to make an exact bargain with her shrewd landlady, who would add in, if she were not checked, all the endless "extras" over which the Briton so loves to potter and over which the American grows so impatient.

"There's the light over the hall-door, a shilling a week; and the kitchen fire, half-a-crown; and there's six shillings for coals, and three for lights, and ten shillings for attendance, and six pence for the use of the cruets, and tuppence for——" "I'll give you four pounds a week for *everything* included," interposes the lodger, having made a rapid calculation and deducted a small amount from the total. There is a little more haggling and then the bargain is struck. The lodging-house keeper's husband is a retired butler, who will serve the lodger in the same capacity; she will be cook, and her trig little niece act as housemaid. So the lodger finds herself mistress of a pretty little house, with butler, cook, and housemaid, all for the sum of twenty dollars a week. Her meals she orders every morning, and with a little care and simple living they should come to not much more than another ten dollars.

Behold her installed and her letters presented. She is a wise woman, this traveller. She realizes that people in a great capital are always very much occupied and not particularly anxious to add more acquaintances to their list; that they are likely to think it a bore to have to hunt her up, and she does not expect too much. A hasty card is dropped at the door, a line is scribbled perhaps asking her to come in to afternoon tea. The traveller goes meekly, and makes herself agreeable. Will not the Englishwoman fix a day to come and have tea with her?

London Underground Railway Station.

Meantime this wise woman has, for what seems to her an infinitesimal sum, had boxes affixed to her windows overflowing with lovely blossoms, and has palms and ferns and blooming plants scattered about the apartment. All her small belongings and pretty purchases are gracefully disposed, and a warm welcome awaits the visitor. She is careful to avoid complaining of any inconveniences she may suffer, and when she cannot warmly praise English things and methods has the discretion to keep silence. Without intrusion or apparent intention she offers small pleasures and courtesies herself, without waiting to have them come first to her. One person whom she has obliged takes her to drive in the Park. Another asks her to luncheon; she repays each civility promptly by some equal courtesy, and before many weeks are passed she is full of charming engagements and is booked for some country-house visiting later—which is the reward of common-sense and good-nature.

In almost every part of the British isles she finds this lodging-house system the best and cheapest method of living, and she has discretion enough in each country to find out the most characteristic feature of the life there and adopt it, and to do in Rome as Romans do—up to a certain point.

Should the traveller in England be desirous of still further economy—as many are—it is extremely easy to achieve it. Those who have gone abroad for study, and many who merely go for relaxation, must, to achieve their purpose, count rigidly every penny. For these there are in London, Paris, Berlin, Rome—all the great capitals—furnished chambers for rent at sums varying from two dollars to ten dollars a week, according to accommodations, and meals may be had at most reasonable rates in these foreign towns if one knows where to look for them. London is full of such aids to the light purse. The pastry-cooks' shops are the refuge of the economical; the A. B. C. (under which abbreviation the restaurants of the Aërated Bread Company are known), the British Tea-Table, the Alliance, the Express, Pearce's, Lockhart's, all furnish food at the most moderate rates, and are clean and comfortable. The woman who is a frequenter of the British Museum—that infinite treasure-house of knowledge—will also be familiar with the well-known restaurant provided for the army of daily students there, and will know how to feed herself comfortably at small cost while pursuing her studies. She can reckon her living by pennies rather than by quarters. If she is content with a European breakfast, a cup of coffee, an egg, and buttered rolls will cost her at any one of these places about eight pence—or sixteen cents. A luncheon of bouillon, a meat patty, bread and butter, and jam will cost her eight pence again, and she can dine comfortably for a shilling—her whole day's nourishment not costing her more than sixty cents a day, or in round terms about four dollars and a half a week. In the country towns of England, such as Oxford, Leamington, and the like, one can find, with a little effort, good clean lodgings with board for a little over two pounds a week. These things are not attainable by the mere bird of passage. The rolling stone not only does not gather moss, but loses it in its swift career; but in small European countries it is far wiser to study the map and pick out a town lying centrally to many places of interest, take up one's lodging there, and circle about in pursuit of sight-seeing. It is far cheaper and more comfortable, more satisfactory in every way; though not until it has been tried, does the American realize how close

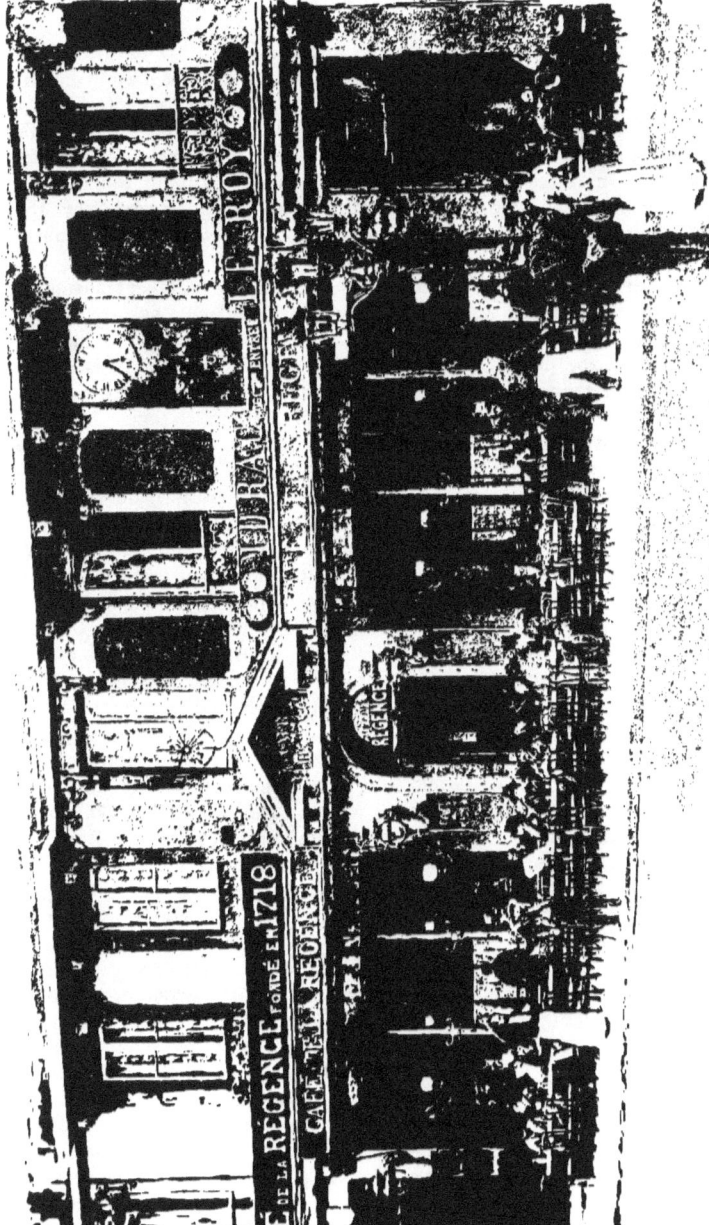

Café de la Regence, rue St. Honoré, opposite the Palais Royal.

all the visitable places lie together in those small kingdoms. In this way, too, an interesting district can be fully studied, and no guide-book can ever reveal all the points of real attraction as will personal investigation. Take Oxford as an example. Within an hour of that town there are—outside of its own inexhaustible attractions—a sufficient number of artistic and historic pilgrimages to occupy many weeks of steady sight-seeing. No more perfect illustration of the point I wish to make can be found than in a conversation overheard in an Oxford hotel. "Why, girls!" said an American traveller looking up from her guide-book, "just listen at this book!—it says you couldn't see all there is to see in this town if you was to stay a month—well, I guess there ain't no use of our staying, then. We'll take that 2.40 train to Warwick—" and she did.

In England an American woman is permitted a thousand liberties that are denied to the natives. "That's American, you know," covers a multitude of infringements of the code, and almost the same feeling exists in France and Germany. They are not very clear as to just what is "American, you know," and what is not, but they are convinced that it allows the transatlantic visitor a vast deal of liberty, and they rather resent than not too much conventionality and propriety of demeanor. One kindly hostess offered cigars to an American woman lunching with her.

"Oh, but do take one!" she cried. "Of course we are all very liberal about such things, and though we don't smoke ourselves we know you are from the South, and that all South American ladies do. We should really enjoy seeing you smoke it"—and was rather hurt than otherwise at her guest's continued refusal.

Another hostess took an American woman aside just before dinner and said, apologetically: "There is claret, and sherry, and champagne for dinner. I hope you like some one of them; I asked the butler, but he said he didn't in the least know how to make a 'mixed drink.'" And to this day she does not quite understand why the guest was so convulsed with amusement.

Now imagine the traveller transferred to the Continent. She has struck her lodging-tent in London, and has set up her gods in a hotel in Paris. For France is not familiar with the lodgings system of accommodation. The *pension* flourishes in its stead, almost as rankly as does its prototype, the boarding-house in America. But, except in the need of extreme economy, it is not to be sought after, for it is usually filled with Britons and Americans, and one gets none of the flavor of the French life, which one is there to see; and the French folk who inhabit pensions are, as a rule, not the sort one wishes to meet, and are rather to be avoided. There are hundreds of pleasant, gay, clean apartment hotels where accommodation can be had most reasonably. The traveller picks out a quiet dwelling-place near the Rue Rivoli, and but a stone's throw from the Place Vendôme and the Avenue de l'Opéra. Here she climbs quite up to the top, but since there is an *ascenseur*, what matter of that. She gets a tiny bedroom and sitting-room which looks into a court, where there is a fountain and flowers, and an elderly parrot, once the property of an opera singer, who practises his piercing and raucous scales every forenoon with a fidelity learned from his lately deceased master, and spends the rest of the time administering profane, spiteful rebukes to a noisy small dog, his companion.

Still faithful to the fashions of the country she may happen to inhabit for the moment, the traveller has brought to her bedside, at eight o'clock, a pot of steaming tea or coffee, a plate of crusty rolls, and a pat of butter. After *café complet* she rises, has her bath (a source of unending surprise to the French servants, who cannot understand the meaning of daily ablutions, and attribute it to a sort of American madness), and lingers reading and writing until twelve, when she goes to breakfast. If it be early spring, with some east still in the wind, the traveller will doubtless seek the nearest *Maison Duval*, of which there are fully a score distributed about the city. These restaurants are perfectly clean, well served, and cheap, and they are one of the institutions of the city. Unlucky is the economical visitor to Paris who misses them.

. . . A little marble table; a neat woman in a black gown and crisp linen Normandy cap. She spreads a napkin, brings a little basket full of rolls, and a pat of butter. Here is the list to choose from: All sorts of omelettes and cheap dishes, perhaps the most expensive is *Chateaubriand*, a tiny filet of beefsteak, which costs a whole franc, and is very good. This traveller is economical and chooses an *omelette au jambon*, full of chopped ham, and served deliciously hot. Next comes a cream cheese, cool and sweet, and served with a spoonful of jellied white currants. A cup of *café noir*, and now the bill. Omelette, ten cents; cream cheese, ten cents; napkin, two cents; bread, two cents; butter, two cents; two cents for the "cover," and a tip of two cents —two big sous—is all that is expected by the smiling friendly woman in the Normandy bonnet. Thirty cents for a breakfast well-cooked, pleasantly served, and eaten at one's leisure near a window looking out on all the inimitable, inexhaustible charm of a Parisian street!

After breakfast is over behold this well content female pacing placidly toward the Tuileries garden, to sit in the sun and watch the fountains play, and the funny French school-children in black baize aprons disport themselves among the statues—to read her newspaper or book; perhaps to scribble a letter upon a writing pad on her knee. All the treasures of the Louvre are at her left hand, all the charms of the *Bois* at her right, to vie in offering pleasures for her afternoon!

It is plain to see what a sensible woman this is—so she lingers till all the horse-chestnuts in the *Champs-Élysées* are in bloom, like glorified Christmas-trees full of pink and white candles—till the grass is green, the flowers out, and all the French world comes, after its pleasant fashion, out-of-doors for its meals and amusements.

Ignoring the *Maisons Duval* now, she goes to a *Champs-Élysées* café and sits on the gravel path under an awning, and eats. The green grass and blossoming trees are about her; so are the scarlet geraniums and pinks. A big fountain splashes near by. Here she ends her meal with a bowl of wild strawberries over which is emptied a pot of Norman clotted cream—and all this in the very heart of a great city, too.

Here as in London she inquires as to possible excursions, and finds she can go every day for a month to some new place of interest and be back by night. If she is tired with an afternoon's hard work in the picture galleries or museums, she goes to Columbin's, in the Rue Cambon, and has tea, and is amused to see the smart French folk come in to do the same thing, and to meet unexpected American friends. She dines in her own sitting-room at her hotel.

Twice a week she goes to the *Marché aux Fleurs*, on the steps of the church of the Madeleine, and strolls

Before the Café Riche.

along a lane of flowers. Here are valley-lilies, forget-me-nots, and cornflowers which she has bought at home at great expense from the florist, gathered by children from the fields and sold in big bunches for a few cents. Here are plants of every description in pots, a tall rose covered with unfolding buds for one franc fifty centimes; a blooming hydrangea for two francs. She plunges into furious extravagance and goes all the length of a dollar, and for the rest of the week her little sitting-room is a bower of perfume. . . .

At the end of the week she sits down to reckon up her spendings. Her rooms, lights, attendance, baths, dinners, and morning coffee and rolls have cost her ninety francs—that is to say eighteen dollars. Then she has spent one dollar upon flowers; her *déjeuners* (breakfasts) have cost on an average two francs a day—two dollars and eighty cents for the week. Total twenty-three dollars and eighty cents. Her list of pleasures and self-indulgences may be as light or heavy as she chooses to make them.

Should more space be needed, or should she desire to entertain, the traveller will find a wide choice of *appartements meublés* (furnished apartments). These "flats," as we should term them, are often deliciously pretty and convenient—the homes of Parisians who wish for some reason to sublet for a time. These can be had in good neighborhoods most cheaply—that is to say, for prices ranging from forty dollars to one hundred dollars. One servant in a small family will be quite sufficient, provided the occupant of the flat will conform herself to French ways—take her quickly prepared tray of coffee before rising, and make rather a practice of lunching at the restaurants. This French servant will be quite content with ostensible wages of twelve dollars a month—ostensible, because she recoups herself after another fashion. Many Americans come home and rail violently at the dishonesty and knavishness of the French servant, but after all the matter is financially as broad as it is long. Here one would have to pay a neat clever creature who could get one up delightful little dinners, brush one's frocks, mend, clean, act as lady's maid, and housemaid, and butler — all with equal competence — three times the wages the Parisian asks, and would look upon her as a rare blessing sent straight from heaven. She would probably be quite honest, and would not exact tradesmen's commissions, but neither would she rise at daylight, tramp half a mile, perhaps, to market, and carry her heavy basket of purchases up half a dozen flights on her return. It is the custom of French servants to ask small wages for a great deal of cheerful, competent service, and then make up part of the difference by a little juggling with the market books. Then why not accept the French way when one is in France? It certainly avoids much friction and wear and tear. The experienced traveller will, however, by a little experiment in the markets herself, get a general idea of the prices of things, and thereby be enabled to check any attempt at really gross overcharging. The French woman will respect her the more, for she, with all her race, dearly loves a bargain, and admires the shrewd bargainer — when she is not pushed too close.

In travel through France this same system of bargaining is always to be observed. The whole country is dotted with little inns of excellent quality, where one had best put up during mere transient excursions of a few days or a week; but it is a wise precaution to ascertain all about prices at once, and

The Gateway between the East and the West—Entrance to the Suez Canal at Port Said.

have a clear understanding what they are to be.

Very much the same advice given as to France, serves in Italy and Spain—only that in the last two mentioned countries they are even sharper bargainers, and must be dealt with firmly. There are *pensions*, but the same rule holds good here as in France. A sitting-room, bed-room, and dressing-room cost, roundly, about a hundred francs a month. Service and meals, lights and fires, are all extra, and are more or less according to one's needs. The *trattoria* system is in vogue in Venice and Rome, and one Italian servant—of which there are many good ones—is quite sufficient here, for as a rule she serves only as house-maid, and makes the morning coffee; it being so widely the fashion to lunch and dine at the restaurants. Another way is to take part of an Italian house, which is even cheaper than an apartment—since there are so many people of good birth and education living upon extremely narrow means in Italy, and with more space in their homes than they need. They furnish all service except the furnishing of meals—which they would be quite willing to add if the American lodger can reconcile herself to grease and garlic.

In Rome, Madrid, and in Paris, of course, there are excellent dressmakers to be had at most reasonable rates. They will come to one's house and do all the fitting at such hours as are most convenient, and in Paris some of them will dress their tiny mannikins in models of such gowns as may be desired, to give the purchaser a chance to see how the combination of colors and materials she has chosen will look when finished. In all the Latin countries the shop-keepers are such keen traders that it is considered no trouble to bring goods of any sort to one's house to choose from.

In London the dressmakers—with the exception of a few famous and expensive *couturières*—are generally incompetent and unsatisfactory. Their prices are high, they will not use the customer's own goods, and their cut and finish are quite "*impossible.*" Here the better way to shop is in the great haberdasheries, where excellent ready-made and partly-made things are to be found at most reasonable rates. Very many Americans borrow an English friend's ticket to the enormous Army and Navy Stores, and make there admirable bargains.

London is the best place to shop for old silver-ware, and for Sheffield plate, which make such beautiful souvenirs of travel. Paris is the place for old lace, the dainty and inexpensive jewelry of the moment's fashion, and all toilet articles; but this is a subject too profound and expansive to be lightly touched in a single paper. All travellers will soon discover for themselves the characteristic souvenir.

A similar story is true of every country, and every capital thereof. A little ingenuity and patience, a little study and forethought, achieve for the traveller all delights, and smooth all her paths. In Berlin she lives in a *pension*, for that is the best mode of life there. In St. Petersburg she takes a furnished apartment. In India or Japan she rents a whole house, furnishes it, and hires a corps of servants. If only passing through on a flying trip, she goes to the hotels and finds life fairly comfortable in all of them. But wherever she goes she carries her talisman; she frankly and pleasantly accepts the ways of the country she is in and adapts herself to them, and is amiable, grateful for courtesies, self-reliant, and thoughtful in making plans for the future, as well as quick to grasp the demands of any situation.

All directions and suggestions to

travellers must of necessity be vague and general; each voyage, like each life, is individual and unique; but common sense and cheerful good temper are the two safest guides and most agreeable travelling companions.

A House near Tokio occupied by an English Traveller.

[*For further specific information see section on* THE ART OF TRAVEL *in the chapter of* SUPPLEMENTARY INFORMATION.]

www.ingramcontent.com/pod-product-compliance
Lightning Source LLC
Chambersburg PA
CBHW030553300426
44111CB00009B/959